SCRIPTURE AND HERMENEUTICS SERIES

VOLUME 7

CANON AND BIBLICAL INTERPRETATION

The Scripture and Hermeneutics Series

Series Editors
Craig Bartholomew
Anthony Thiselton

Consultant Editors
Ann Holt
Karl Möller

Editorial Advisory Board
James Catford
Fred Hughes
Tremper Longman III
Francis Martin
Gordon McConville
Christopher Seitz
Janet Martin Soskice
Nick Wolterstorff

SCRIPTURE AND HERMENEUTICS SERIES

VOLUME 7

CANON AND BIBLICAL INTERPRETATION

editors

CRAIG G. BARTHOLOMEW • SCOTT HAHN
• ROBIN PARRY • CHRISTOPHER SEITZ • AL WOLTERS

series editors

CRAIG G. BARTHOLOMEW
• ANTHONY C. THISELTON

First published 2006 jointly
in the UK by Paternoster Press, an imprint of Authentic Media,
9 Holdom Avenue, Bletchley, Milton Keynes, MK1 1QR, UK
And 129 Mobilization Drive, Waynesboro, GA 30830-4575, USA
www.authenticmedia.co.uk/paternoster
Authentic Media is a division of Send The Light Ltd,
a company limited by guarantee (registered charity no. 270162).

and in the United States of America by
Zondervan
5300 Patterson Ave SE, Grand Rapids, Michigan 49530

10 09 08 07 06   7 6 5 4 3 2 1

British Library Cataloguing in Publication Data
A catalogue record for this book is available from the British Library
ISBN 1-84227-071-0

Library of Congress Cataloging-in-Publication Data
Canon and biblical interpretation / editors,
Craig G. Bartholomew [et al.].
        p. cm. — (The scripture and hermeneutics series; v. 7)
Includes bibliographical references and indexes.
ISBN-13: 978-0-310-23417-3
ISBN-10: 0-310-23417-4
1. Bible—Theology. 2. Bible—Criticism, interpretation, etc.
I. Bartholomew, Craig G., 1961- II. Title. III. Series.
    BS543.C26 2006
    220.1'2—dc22
2006011942

Cover Design by Jeremy Bye
Typeset by WestKey Ltd, Falmouth, Cornwall
Printed in the United States of America
Printed on acid-free paper

Contents

Part 2
Reading the Old Testament Canonically

Torah

Prophets

Writings

Preface

From its inception the Scripture and Hermeneutics Seminar has been deeply concerned with how we read the Bible so as to hear God's address today. In this respect the Seminar shares the concerns of the minority revival in what is being called 'theological interpretation', as evidenced, for example, in Baker Academic's recently published *Dictionary for Theological Interpretation of the Bible* (2005). This meant that a topic the Seminar would have to engage sooner or later is canonical interpretation of the Bible, particularly associated with Brevard Childs. And this we did in an exhilarating consultation at the Pontifical Biblical Institute in Rome in June 2005. Catholic participation in the Seminar has grown over the years and holding the consultation in Rome reflected the creative, ecumenical dimension of the Seminar.

The Pontifical was a wonderful context in which to meet – one was constantly aware of the global church as the context in which and for which we read the Bible. As is evident from the contents of this volume we tried to reflect on the major parts of the canon, but without in any way intending to be exhaustive. A lacuna was a focus on Paul and I am delighted that Anthony Thiselton has addressed this in his introduction. A particular highlight of the consultation was the gracious presence of Jean Vanier, and I am delighted that he has written up his material with a commentary by Frances Young for inclusion in this volume. Through Jean Vanier's participation we sought to bring interpretation of the Bible as canon into dialogue with *lectio divina* type approaches. Jean has recently published a superb devotional reading of John's Gospel in his book *Drawn into the Mystery of Jesus through the Gospel of John* (Darton, Longman and Todd, 2004) and we sought to encourage reflection on how this type of 'eating of the Word' relates to more academic styles of theological interpretation.

Al Wolters, my colleague at Redeemer University College, has been very helpful in overseeing the editing of this volume, and I am indebted to him for undertaking this task. Anthony Thiselton has kindly taken on the task of writing an introduction, for which I am most grateful – as I am to Rosemary Hales who has continued to administer the project with thoroughness and attention to detail. Without her support and the financial support of the British and Foreign Bible Society the project would have been impossible. In organizing the consultation in Rome, Rosemary was much helped by Sister Nuria Calduch-Benages, Professor of Wisdom Literature and Biblical Anthropology at the Pontifical Gregorian University in Rome, and it is this kind of communal help that gives the Seminar its richness and vitality. Canon has often been a highly divisive topic as regards Catholic-Protestant dialogue but our intention with the consultation and this volume is not to divide but to explore together how approaching the Bible as canon helps in discerning God's address. And our hope is that the publication of this volume will stimulate scholars to focus their energies on readings of Scripture that will lead us again and again to Christ.

Craig Bartholomew
Cape Town,
South Africa,
February 2006

Contributors

Craig Bartholomew is the H. Evan Runner Professor of Philosophy, and Professor of Theology and Religion at Redeemer University College, Ancaster (Canada) as well as Visiting Professor in Biblical Hermeneutics at the University of Chester. He is the author of *Reading Ecclesiastes* and co-author of *The Drama of Scripture*. Craig heads up the Scripture and Hermeneutics Seminar.

Stephen Chapman is Assistant Professor of Old Testament at Duke Divinity School, where he also serves on the Board of Directors for the Baptist House of Studies. He is the author of *The Law and the Prophets: A Study in Old Testament Canon Formation* and co-editor of *Biblischer Text und theologische Theoriebildung*. An ordained minister in the American Baptist Churches, he is an active participant in the Baptist World Alliance.

Brevard Childs 'retired' in January 2000 after teaching for forty-one years at Yale University where he served in the Divinity School, Department of Religious Studies, and the Department of Ancient Near Eastern Languages and Literatures. He is the author of several books, including *Biblical Theology in Crisis*, *Introduction to the Old Testament as Scripture*, *The New Testament as Canon*, *Old Testament Theology in a Canonical Context*, *Biblical Theology of the Old and New Testaments*, and commentaries on Exodus and Isaiah. His latest book, published in 2004, is *The Struggle to Understand Isaiah as Christian Scripture*.

Stephen Dempster is the Stuart E. Murray Professor of Christian Studies at Atlantic Baptist University in Moncton, New Brunswick (Canada). His research interests are Biblical Theology, Wisdom Literature, the Old Testament Canon and Hebrew Linguistics. He has published in these areas and has recently written *Dominion and Dynasty: A Theology of the Hebrew Bible*.

C. Stephen Evans is University Professor of Philosophy and Humanities at Baylor University. He also taught philosophy at Calvin College, St. Olaf College and Wheaton College. His published works include fifteen books, among which are *Kierkegaard's Ethic of Love: Divine Commands and Moral Obligations* and *Why Believe?*

Denis Farkasfalvy is a research scholar and Adjunct Professor of Theology at the University of Dallas and a teacher of mathematics at the Cistercian Preparatory School. His Hungarian publications include commentaries on Romans and the Gospel of John, an Introduction to the New Testament, a translation of the Psalms and a Theological Introduction to Biblical Studies. He is also the co-author of *The Formation of the New Testament Canon*.

Scott Hahn is Professor of Theology and Scripture at the Franciscan University of Steubenville. He also holds the Pope Benedict XVI Chair of Biblical Theology and Liturgical Proclamation at St Vincent Seminary, USA. He is Founder and President of the St. Paul Center for Biblical Theology and Director of the Institute of Applied Biblical Studies. He is the General Editor of the Ignatius Catholic Study Bible and author of over a dozen books, including *The Lamb's Supper*, *Lord Have Mercy*, *Swear to God*, *Understanding the Scriptures* and *Letter and Spirit*.

Eugene Lemcio is Professor of New Testament at Seattle Pacific University. He is the author of *The Past of Jesus in the Gospels*. He also co-authored *The New Testament as Canon: A Reader in Canonical Criticism*.

Tremper Longman III is the Robert H. Gundry Professor of Biblical Studies at Westmont College in Santa Barbara, California. He is the author of numerous books including commentaries on Ecclesiastes, Song of Songs and Proverbs.

Gordon McConville is Professor of Old Testament Theology at the University of Gloucestershire. His books include *Law and Theology in Deuteronomy*, a commentary on Deuteronomy and *God and Earthly Power*, a study of Old Testament political theology. He has also published a number of other books and articles on topics in Old Testament theology and interpretation.

Ryan O'Dowd is Assistant Professor of Old Testament at Briercrest College and Seminary, Canada. His PhD thesis 'The Wisdom of Torah: Epistemology in Deuteronomy and the Wisdom Literature' was completed in 2005 at the University of Liverpool.

Robin Parry is Commissioning Editor for Paternoster. His books include *Old Testament Story and Christian Ethics: The Rape of Dinah as a Case Study* and *Worshipping Trinity: Coming Back to the Heart of Worship*. He has also co-edited *Universal Salvation? The Current Debate*, *The Futures of Evangelicalism* and *Out of Egypt: Biblical Theology and Biblical Interpretation*.

Christopher Seitz is Professor of Old Testament and Theological Studies, University of St Andrews. An Episcopal Priest (USA), he is the author of commentaries on Isaiah, *Word without End* and *Figured Out*. He is President of The Anglican Communion Institute (ACI).

Anthony Thiselton is Emeritus Professor of Christian Theology at the University of Nottingham and Research Professor of Christian Theology at the University of Chester. He is also Canon Theologian of Leicester Cathedral and of Southwell Minster. His books include *The Two Horizons*, *New Horizons in Hermeneutics*, *Interpreting God and the Postmodern Self*, *The Promise of Hermeneutics* (co-author), *The First Epistle to the Corinthians: A Commentary on the Greek Text*, and *Thiselton on Hermeneutics: Collected Works*. He holds three doctorates and is a past president of the Society for the Study of Theology.

Jean Vanier is co-founder of l'Arche, France, and co-founder of the 'Faith and Light' communities. In 1997 he received the 'Paul VI International Prize for Peace and Development' from John Paul II. He has authored over twenty books including *Becoming Human*, *Community and Growth*, *Drawn into the Mystery of Jesus through the Gospel of John* and *To Welcome the Stranger*.

Gordon Wenham recently retired from the University of Gloucestershire where he was for many years Professor of Old Testament. Among his numerous writings on Old Testament topics are his two-volume commentary on Genesis, commentaries on Leviticus and Numbers, and several works on ethics including his recent *Story as Torah: Reading the Old Testament Ethically*. He is now a part-time lecturer at Trinity College, Bristol, and is working on a book on the ethics of the Psalms.

Al Wolters is Professor of Religion and Theology/Classical Languages at Redeemer University College, Canada. His publications include *Plotinus 'On Eros': A Detailed Exegetical Commentary on Enneads III, 5*; *Creation Regained: Biblical Basics of a Reformational Worldview* and *The Song of the Valiant Woman: Studies in the Interpretation of Proverbs 31:10-31*.

Christopher Wright is the International Ministries Director of Langham Partnership International. Prior to that, he taught Old Testament in India from 1983–88 before returning to the faculty of All Nations Christian College, where he was Principal from 1993–2001. He has written several books, including commentaries on Deuteronomy and Ezekiel, and *Old Testament Ethics for the People of God*.

Frances Young taught in the University of Birmingham from 1971 and held the Edward Cadbury Chair of Theology from 1986 to 2005. Her main interests have been New Testament and Patristic studies, the two coming together in her study *Biblical Exegesis and the Formation of Christian Culture*. For some years she has assisted l'Arche in articulating theological reflection on its experience of community with those who have mental disabilities.

Abbreviations

AB	Anchor Bible
AUSS	*Andrews University Seminary Studies*
BBR	*Bulletin for Biblical Research*
BCOTWP	Baker Commentary on the Old Testament Wisdom and Psalms
BIS	Biblical Interpretation Series
BibInt	*Biblical Interpretation*
BJRL	*Bulletin of the John Rylands University Library of Manchester*
BR	*Biblical Research*
BRev	*Bible Review*
BZNW	Beihefte zur Zeitschrift für die neutestamentliche Wissenschaft
CBQ	*Catholic Biblical Quarterly*
CBR	*Currents in Biblical Research*
CTJ	*Calvin Theological Journal*
EvQ	*Evangelical Quarterly*
EvTh	*Evangelische Theologie*
FAT	Forschungen zum Alten Testament
HBT	*Horizons in Biblical Theology*
HCOT	Historical Commentary on the Old Testament
HS	*Hebrew Studies*
HTR	*Harvard Theological Review*
HUCA	*Hebrew Union College Annual*
HvTSt	*Hervormde teologiese studies*
IJST	*International Journal of Systematic Theology*
Int	*Interpretation*
JBL	*Journal of Biblical Literature*
JBR	*Journal of Bible and Religion*
JBTh	*Jahrbuch für Biblische Theologie*
JETS	*Journal of the Evangelical Theological Society*
JR	*Journal of Religion*
JSNT	*Journal for the Study of the New Testament*
JSOT	*Journal for the Study of the Old Testament*
JSNTSup	Journal for the Study of the New Testament: Supplement Series

JSOTSup	Journal for the Study of the Old Testament: Supplement Series
JTS	*Journal of Theological Studies*
MT	Masoretic Text
Neot	*Neotestamentica*
NIB	*The New Interpreter's Bible*
NICOT	New International Commentary on the Old Testament
NIGTC	New International Greek Testament Commentary
NIVAC	The NIV Application Commentary
NTS	*New Testament Studies*
OTL	Old Testament Library
ProEccl	*Pro Ecclesia*
QD	Questiones disputatae
RBL	*Review of Biblical Literature*
RevExp	*Review and Expositor*
SBLMS	Society of Biblical Literature Monograph Series
SHS	Scripture and Hermeneutics Series
SJT	*Scottish Journal of Theology*
SNTSMS	Society for New Testament Studies Monograph Series
SubBi	Subsidia Biblica
ThTo	*Theology Today*
TLOT	*Theological Lexicon of the Old Testament* (3 vols.; ed. E. Jenni, assisted by C. Westermann; trans. M.E. Biddle; Peabody, MA: Hendrickson, 1997)
TRev	*Theologische Revue*
TynBul	*Tyndale Bulletin*
VT	*Vetus Testamentum*
WBC	Word Biblical Commentary
WMANT	Wissenschaftliche Monographien zum Alten und Neuen Testament
WUNT	Wissenschaftliche Untersuchungen zum Neuen Testament
ZAW	*Zeitschrift für die alttestamentliche Wissenschaft*

Canon, Community and Theological Construction

Introduction

Anthony C. Thiselton

The Controversial Status of a 'Canonical' Approach

Arguably the disintegration of an emphasis upon the unity of the biblical writings, initially witnessed by widespread disenchantment with the so-called biblical theology movement, gathered momentum first by the concurrent rise of redaction criticism and then more recently from the impact of a postmodern cast of mind and an emphasis upon diversity among communities of faith and within academia.[1] Fragmentation and suspicion of 'grand narrative' are hallmarks of postmodern thought.[2]

At one level theological interpretation and theological construction become impossible without some notion of biblical canon as serving 'to mark out the circumference of acceptable diversity'.[3] In the early centuries of the Christian church Irenaeus argued that if the church were to accept Marcion's expulsion of the Old Testament from the Christian Scriptures, the church would lose the frame of reference within which the New Testament was to be interpreted, and the coherence of the biblical witness to Christ would be disrupted.[4] Paul the Apostle likewise sees the Scriptures of the Old Testament as

---

[1] This point has been made well by Robert H. Gundry, 'Hermeneutic Liberty', in Gundry, *The Old is Better*, 15–16.
[2] Cf. Lyotard, *The Postmodern Condition*; Harvey, *Postmodernity*.
[3] Dunn, *Unity and Diversity*, 376.
[4] Irenaeus, *Against Heresies*, I:27:2; II:28:4, and elsewhere.

the frame of reference within which the death and resurrection of Jesus Christ are to be understood in accordance with the pre-Pauline tradition that he cites (1 Cor. 15:1–3). According to Luke, Jesus also affirms a two-way hermeneutical interaction in which the Old Testament interprets his work, and his work provides an understanding of the Old Testament (Lk. 24:27 and 43). Ulrich Luz rightly observes, 'For Paul, the Old Testament is not in the first place something to understand, but itself creates understanding.'[5]

All the same, those who bring to the issue more pluralist, phenomenological, or postmodernist perspectives, as well as some more traditional biblical specialists may well respond to our quotation above from James Dunn with the question: *to whom* is the boundary of diversity that marked out the canon 'acceptable'? Is not this supposed boundary an artificial construct imposed by the Christian church (or its dominant theologians) of the third or fourth century? Does not the insistence of Irenaeus, for example, on working with the four Gospels as a canonical unity reduce and flatten down the distinctive witness and tradition of each evangelist as representative of a particular tradition into a monochrome 'harmony' of the Gospels?

Suspicions concerning the validity of a 'canonical' approach to the biblical writings have been expressed on both phenomenological and theological (or anti-theological) grounds. Thus, in terms of the first point, James Barr declares, 'In biblical times the books [of the Bible] were separate individual scrolls. A 'Bible' was not a volume one could hold in the hand, but a cupboard … with a lot of individual scrolls. The boundary [of] … what was Scripture … was thus more difficult to indicate.'[6]

In relation to the second area of contention, some will remain unmoved by the implicit arguments of Irenaeus and Tertullian that theological construction necessitates reference to the whole potential 'canon' of Scripture rather than only to selected biblical texts. Robert Gundry's essay of 2005 is among the most recent to argue that theological construction *does* necessitate recourse to the variety and diversity of the canon. He argues, for example, that a Christology based on Mark alone would be of a different shape from one based only on the Fourth Gospel or only on Paul.[7] By contrast Heikki Räisänen insists that 'recognition by biblical scholarship of the wide diversity of beliefs within the New Testament itself' renders ways of using the Bible for theological construction or synthesis 'unviable'.[8] 'The New Testament has turned out to be filled with theological contradictions.'[9] Räisänen goes further and writes in a

---

[5] Luz, *Das Geschichtsverständnis*, 134.
[6] Barr, *Holy Scripture*, 57.
[7] Gundry, *The Old is Better*, 4–15.
[8] Räisänen, *Challenges*, 227–28.
[9] Räisänen, *Challenges*, 229.

dismissive tone: 'Conservative theologians have stressed the alleged theological unity of the two Testaments and striven towards a canonical, pan-biblical, theology (Childs 1992: Stuhlmacher 1992).'[10] Pressing professional courtesy to the limits he states that this 'runs counter to the rules of sound scholarship'.[11] This amounts to a declaration of war upon the canonical approach, and invites critical scrutiny of this allusion to 'rules' of sound scholarship.

In the history of modern discussions of canon, Brevard Childs notes in his chapter below that in his essay of 1950 to the World Council of Churches Ernst Käsemann asserted that the canon served not as a source of unity, but as a source of disunity.[12] Childs also alludes to an increasing tendency to follow Harnack, Sundberg, and Gamble on seeing the formation of the New Testament canon as the product of contingent historical factors deriving from outside the church in the second and third centuries, as against the view of Westcott, Metzger, and others that the canon constituted a recognition of the impact and nature of Scripture through internal processes and judgements within the Christian church.[13]

While most biblical and hermeneutical specialists will endorse the importance of the subject-areas of the first six volumes of this Scripture and Hermeneutics series, this seventh volume carries a title that provokes controversy, even hostility, in some circles. Renewing biblical interpretation (volume 1), exploring hermeneutics and language (volume 2), engaging with ethical aspects of the biblical writings (volume 3), hermeneutics and history (volume 4), and the formative impact of Lukan texts (volume 6) are universally accepted parts of the agenda of biblical hermeneutics. The subject-matter of volume 5, hermeneutics and biblical theology, may raise a suspicious eyebrow in some circles, but none of these areas remains more open *prima facie* to controversy than the subject area of the present volume.

However, if some claim that theological construction cannot be undertaken without reference to larger stretches of the biblical writings than individual traditions or textual units, and some even try to insist that a canonical approach allegedly violates 'the rules of sound scholarship', we must either grasp the nettle of canonical approaches or give up the enterprise of seeking to build Christian theology upon biblical foundations.

Nevertheless, on further investigation Räisänen's language appears not only inflated beyond that expected of a fair-minded scholar, but also reflects some widespread mythologies and illusions about precisely what a canonical approach necessarily involves.

---

[10] Räisänen, *Challenges*, 231.
[11] Räisänen, *Challenges*, loc. cit.
[12] Brevard S. Childs, 'The Canon in Recent Biblical Studies', below.

Towards a Clarification of what Canonical Approaches Involve

There is no more a single, uniform, canonical approach than there is a single, uniform, 'historical-critical method'. In my judgment the term '*the* historical-critical method' should be banned from all textbooks and from students' essays. There may well be overlap or resemblances between the kind of biblical criticism practised by Westcott, Lightfoot, F.F. Bruce, George Caird and N.T. Wright on one side and by Räisänen or Philip Davies on the other. But it achieves nothing for Räisänen to imperialize and restrict 'the rules of sound scholarship' to a virtually non-theistic or supposedly value-free approach. As Francis Watson has argued elsewhere, the isolation of 'biblical exegesis' and 'biblical interpretation' from theology is itself arbitrary, reductive, and overshadowed by illusory notions of value-free enquiry. Non-theism or positivism is no more value-free than theism.[14] Similarly within 'canonical approaches' there are strong family resemblances between the canonical perspectives of Brevard S. Childs, James A. Sanders, Rolf Rendtorff, Gerald T. Sheppard, and Christopher Seitz. But differences of emphasis between them suggest the impropriety of offering careless generalizations about 'canonical criticism'.

Canon criticism in James A. Sanders

The terms *canon criticism* or *canonical criticism* were coined by James A. Sanders (b. 1927) in his first major work on the subject, *Torah and Canon*.[15] Twelve years later he gave the sub-title *A Guide to Canonical Criticism* in his book *Canon and Community*.[16] Another volume of essays, *From Sacred Story to Sacred Text* carried the sub-title *Canon as Paradigm*.[17] Contrary to what might be inferred from Räisänen's polemic, Sanders urges that canon criticism does not reject the methods of modern biblical criticism. Tradition history, form criticism, source criticism, and the clear identification of theological diversity within Scripture, remain part of the agenda. However, what is probably more objectionable to Räisänen (although it can be done at the reductive level of phenomenology of religion) is that Sanders wishes to place the Bible 'where it belongs in the believing communities of today'.[18] Mythology about restricting attention solely to 'the final form of the text' cannot be attributed to Sanders. He sees

---

[14] Watson, *Text, Church and World*, 1–14, and *Text and Truth*. Cf. Thiselton, *Thiselton on Hermeneutics*, 685–700.
[15] Sanders, *Text and Canon*.
[16] Sanders, *Canon and Community*.
[17] Sanders, *From Sacred Story*.

canon as a dynamic process that operates within and behind the text, shaping traditions and books *en route* to canonization.

Sanders emphasizes the dynamic and dialectical relationships between texts, traditions, and communities of faith. The Exodus theme, for example, finds fresh shape and a fresh hermeneutic in Isaiah 40 – 55. Deuteronomy becomes reduced or re-shaped if it is separated from the rest of the Deuteronomic history from Joshua through to 2 Kings. Continuities within the biblical writings do not exclude diversity, but they witness to monotheism rather than polytheism. To focus piecemeal only on atomistic textual units and books without considering their role in the process of contributing to a broader whole is to miss the transcendent dimension of the whole. Intertextual resonances form part of the hermeneutic of the biblical traditions themselves. Sanders completed his Ph.D. dissertation under S. Sandmel on 'Suffering as Divine Discipline in the Old Testament and Judaism', and it is difficult to imagine how any thinker could embark upon this without considering the tension and dialectic between the deuteronomic traditions and Wisdom traditions of Job.

The canonical approach of Brevard S. Childs

Brevard S. Childs (b. 1923), who is more widely regarded as the founder and pioneer of a canonical approach, is widely said to have shared initially the use of Sanders' term *canon criticism* in the early 1970s, although he soon discarded this term in favour of the term *canonical approach*. In a recent interview with John Knox/Westminster Press, however, Childs is on record as insisting, 'I have always objected to the term "canon(ical) criticism" as a suitable description of my approach'.[19] This objection stems partly from the fact that Childs is not proposing 'a new critical methodology analogous to literary, form, or redactional criticism', but an exploration and evaluation of 'the nature of the biblical text being studied'. This includes an understanding of the Bible not simply as 'a literary deposit', but as 'the sacred Scriptures of the church', and as a 'living and active text addressing each new generation'.[20] In an era when Old Testament scholarship often or typically explored relatively small units of texts or tradition, Childs turned to the larger shape of more extensive textual expanses. In contrast to the mistaken mythologies about a canonical approach in his early work, Childs strongly criticized the tendency of the biblical theology movement to betray 'lack of rigor', or to use material as 'homiletical topping', and to pay insufficient attention to distinctive 'context'.[21]

---

[19] Childs, 'An Interview with Brevard S. Childs', www.philosophy-religion.org/bible/childs-interview.htm.
[20] Childs, 'Interview', loc. cit.
[21] Childs, *Biblical Theology*, 93 and 97.

In the case of his critique of 'biblical theology', however, a new emphasis upon canon began to emerge. First, it is a mistake to suggest that any ecclesiastical body 'can ever "*make* a book canonical"'. Rather, the concept of canon was an attempt to *acknowledge* the divine authority of its writings and collections.'[22] 'Canonicity as the "rule of faith" was a confession of the divine origin of the gospel that had called the church into being … Scripture served not as "interesting sources" of historical information … but as testimony that the salvation and faith of the old covenant was one with that revealed in Jesus Christ.'[23] The concluding chapter of *Biblical Theology in Crisis* affirms the unity of the two Testaments in relation to 'the God of Israel and the Church', stressing 'the identity of the Christian God with the God of the Old Testament'.[24]

It would be a mistake, however, to see this as merely an assertion of dogmatic theology. Childs tests the scope of the method and 'the claim of continuity' in terms of the biblical writings themselves.[25] Moreover, it becomes clear that (in common with Sanders) Childs recognizes the correlation between *canon* and *community*. In spite of Räisänen's dismissive comment about 'the rules of sound scholarship' it is axiomatic for serious hermeneutical endeavour that author-centred and text-centred hermeneutics do not offer all dimensions of hermeneutics or communicative action unless at least some attention has been given to the stance of *communities of readers*. Of necessity the 'reception' of earlier texts and traditions will, in turn, serve to re-shape the development of texts and traditions in an ongoing dialectic.[26] Value-free scholarship (if such were to exist) would not be served by insulating text from 'reception'. The *biblical writings* become '*Scripture*' for those communities of faith for whom they are divine revelation and *formative*.[27]

In 1972 Childs urged an understanding of closer interconnections between the books of the Pentateuch.[28] Two years later he published his magisterial commentary on Exodus. This volume serves to dispel any false mythology about a lack of 'the rules of sound scholarship' with convincing effect. Each unit of the text of Exodus first receives careful scrutiny at the textual level with a new translation of the Hebrew text. This includes 'restoring the best text' but also 'seeking to understand how the text was heard and interpreted by later communities'.[29] One can scarcely imagine serious textual criticism in action

---

[22] Childs, *Biblical Theology*, 105; first italics mine; second italics Childs'.

[23] Childs, loc. cit.

[24] Childs, *Biblical Theology*, 203.

[25] Childs, *Biblical Theology*, 211–19.

[26] In addition to other writers, cf. Jauss, *Toward an Aesthetic of Reception*, 3–45.

[27] On the hermeneutics of *formation* see Bartholomew et al., *Reading Luke*, especially 3–78, 125–56, 229–65 and 440–49.

[28] Childs, 'The Old Testament as the Scripture of the Church', 709–22.

[29] Childs, *Exodus*, xiv.

without a correlative study of the theological traditions of later copyists. Next, *pace* many of his uninformed critics, Childs examines 'the historical development which lay behind the final form of the biblical text ... in considerable detail with regard to both oral and literary levels'.[30] This section includes form-critical and traditio-historical analyses, and careful source analysis. *Only after this* does the 'final form of the text' become the focus of critical reflection.

Childs moves on, in the third place, to what he calls the heart of the commentary. This explores the text in its final form, 'which is its canonical shape, while at the same time recognizing and profiting by the variety of historical forces which were at work in producing it'.[31] Without this, the text becomes fragmented and leaves the reader 'with bits and pieces'.[32] But still more important, Childs adds, is the theological dimension. This is the shape which engages the synagogue and the church. A study of the pre-history of the text is useful only if it serves this larger goal.

Three more sections remain. Childs includes the New Testament's reading of the Old Testament material; a section on the history of exegesis (its post-history or reception-history); and finally 'a theological reflection on the text within the context of the Christian canon'.[33] This anticipates both the current interest in reception history, initiated especially in theoretical hermeneutics by H.R. Jauss, and Childs's later work. One immediate effect is to broaden an understanding of the *sensus literalis,* in ways close to those explored more recently by Walter Moberly.[34] The literal sense is not merely the semantic or linguistic level of meaning alone, but an *actualisation* of the text for each successive generation of the community of faith based on the linguistic meaning in its canonical context. Moberly argues:

> To read the Old Testament in the light of Christ is not to introduce into the text something that is not really there (references to Jesus or a suffering Messiah), but rather to read the text in a particular kind of way, with reference to the construal of the significance of the text by the New Testament witness to Christ.[35]

This comes close to 'the "literal sense"' since it takes with full seriousness 'the integrity of the biblical text'.[36]

The canonical approach of Childs reaches its full flower in his *Introduction to the Old Testament as Scripture* (1979) and *The New Testament as Canon* (1984).

---

[30] Childs, loc. cit.
[31] Childs, loc. cit.
[32] Childs, *Exodus,* xiv–xv.
[33] Childs, *Exodus,* xvi.
[34] Childs, 'The Sensus Literalis', 80–93.
[35] Moberly, *Bible,* 226; cf. 25–42.
[36] Moberly, *Bible,* 232.

Again we should note that each section of his 1979 work includes discussions of the history of the discipline of 'Old Testament Introduction', the problem of canon and, in the case of each individual book of the Old Testament, 'Historical Critical Problems', before moving on to its canonical shape and theological and hermeneutical implications. Childs is well aware of the claims of Johann Semler (in 1771–76) about the purely 'historical' or contingent status of the Hebrew canon.[37] Semler's critique that the status of the canon rested upon a 'misconception', however, ignored the axiom that 'the literature formed the identity of the religious community which in turn shaped the literature.'[38] In most historical-critical approaches since Semler and Eichhorn this dialectic of the canonical process is lost. Thereby an unhealthy polarization emerges of 'liberal versus conservative, scientific versus ecclesiastical, objective versus confessional … [which] poses a false dichotomy'.[39]

It was not merely 'contrived' for Irenaeus and Tertullian to set individual portions of Scripture in the larger context of the sum of Christian tradition. Childs in fact rejects Sanders' understanding of the growth of the canon as a contingent 'search for identity in times of crises'.[40] Similarly, to overstress the role of 'a dogmatic decision' in defining the canon 'is to overestimate one feature within the process'.[41] Contrary to the claims of many critics 'the whole point of emphasizing the canon is to stress the *historical* nature of the biblical witness' (my italics) in relation to the communal experience of Israel and subsequently the church.[42] 'It treats literature in its own integrity.'[43] Childs appeals to the hermeneutics of Paul Ricoeur in relation to 'what lies 'ahead' (*devant*) of the text, not 'behind'.[44]

We cannot trace the impact of Childs's approach here on more than two or three biblical books as examples. In the canonical shape of Samuel the theme from Hannah's song (1 Sam. 2:1–10) resonates throughout the corpus, namely that of 'the God who "brings low and also exalts", who "judges the end of the earth", who "will give strength to his king".'[45] Chapter 2 offers an interpretative key. As the narratives unfold 'the people think they are solving an immediate problem with the demand for a king, but the dominant note is the prophetic warning … against the dangers of their being "like other nations".'[46] The over-

---

[37] Childs, *Introduction*, 35.
[38] Childs, *Introduction*, 41.
[39] Childs, loc. cit.
[40] Childs, *Introduction*, 57.
[41] Childs, *Introduction*, 58.
[42] Childs, *Introduction*, 71.
[43] Childs, *Introduction*, 73.
[44] Childs, *Introduction*, 77.
[45] Childs, *Introduction*, 273.

reaching themes do not 'harmonize' tensions between two or more traditions within Samuel, but place them in a new light and larger horizon.

Childs enumerates difficulties left by previous approaches to Jeremiah. Within the framework of Deuteronomic traditions, however, Jeremiah's commission both 'to destroy and overthrow' and 'to build and to plant' constitutes a dual theme echoed throughout the book.[47] Indeed, the presentation of Jeremiah within the tradition of preachers of the law reconciles 'an alleged conflict between the law and the prophets'.[48] Hosea provides an example of a bold adaptation of older language to a new situation: 'Yahweh, not Baal, was the Lord of the land, who was Israel's faithful lover and forgotten provider of bounty.'[49] Hosea's language on the triumph of love goes beyond his situation. It is 'extended' to become 'transformed into a symbolic language which continued to offer judgment and hope to future generations far beyond the temporal confines of Hosea himself'.[50] This is different from timeless allegorizing or psychologizing, because this 'extension' depends upon subsequent *actualisations* of the text in the *historical life* of the ongoing community of faith.

Pressures of space also prevent our discussing in any detail Childs's more recent works *Old Testament Theology in a Canonical Context* (1985), *Biblical Theology of the Old and New Testaments* (1992), and *The Struggle to Understand Isaiah as Christian Scripture* (2004). In his two works on biblical theology Childs seeks to re-define this subject after its virtual collapse in the demise of the biblical theology movement in the early 1960s. He is rightly more cautious than his Yale colleague Hans Frei of speaking of intra-linguistic, non-referential, 'history-like' narratives. 'The biblical text continually bears witness to events and reactions in the life of Israel ... The literature cannot be isolated from its ostensive reference.'[51]

More than enough has been said to indicate that any suggestion to the effect that a 'canonical' approach is harmonizing or ahistorical rests upon a mistaken mythology generated by critics who have never properly engaged with it. Childs, like Sanders, fully appreciates *biblical history, particularity, diversity and situational contingency*. In his recent book on Isaiah in Christian interpretation Childs equally stresses the historicality, or historical conditionedness, of communities of interpreters.[52] But this is far from the whole story. It may not be unfair, therefore, to speak of some approaches that ignore this canonical dimension as 'reductionist'.

---

[47] Childs, *Introduction*, 351.
[48] Childs, *Introduction*, 353.
[49] Childs, *Introduction*, 378.
[50] Childs, *Introduction*, 383.
[51] Childs, *Old Testament Theology*, 6.
[52] Childs, *The Struggle*.

Canon and Interpretation in the Essays (mainly in Part 1) of this Volume

The essays below fall into three broad categories. First, those by Brevard Childs, Christopher Seitz, Stephen Evans, and to a large extent Denis Farkasfalvy, address issues that concern either a canonical approach as such (Brevard Childs and Christopher Seitz) or canonicity and apostolicity in the context of a rule of faith (Stephen Evans and Denis Farkasfalvy). These make up Part 1, although I discuss within the third group of essays that by Eugene Lemcio, as a case study of the role of the Gospels within the canon. (Regrettably, the essay by Stephen Chapman had not come into my possession when the publisher's deadline for the submission of this present essay overtook me. I understand that it was commissioned late on, and certainly after the Rome Consultation.)

Second, although still within Part 1 as arranged by the Editors, in a different vein Scott Hahn places canonical reading of the two Testaments within a *liturgical* context, and Jean Vanier and Frances Young explore the *formative and transformative* impact of biblical reading, in continuity with volume 6 in this series, *Reading Luke*.

Third, the remaining essays offer illuminating case-studies of the canonical shape and canonical context of specific biblical books or theological traditions. Thus Gordon McConville explores the interrelation between the Book of the Covenant, the Deuteronomic Code, and the Holiness Code within the Pentateuch and its canonical context; Gordon Wenham explores factors that relate to a canonical reading of the Psalms; Tremper Longman and Ryan O'Dowd consider canonical criticism and the wisdom literature; Robin Parry considers Lamentations in a broader canonical context; and Eugene Lemcio examines the contours of the four Gospels within the New Testament canon. (Once again, regrettably neither an essay by Christopher Wright in response to Gordon McConville nor an essay on the prophets by Stephen Dempster has yet reached me by the date of the publisher's deadline for this essay. I understand that Craig Bartholomew commissioned these after the Consultation, so that in common with Eugene Lemcio's these have received no discussion from participants.)

The debate about the canon in recent thought: Brevard S. Childs

The essay in this volume by Brevard S. Childs covers substantially different ground from my brief discussion of his earlier work above. He traces an increasing tendency to view the formation of the canon, especially the canon of the New Testament, in historically contingent and phenomenological terms, often in ways akin to a history-of-religions perspective. In particular Harnack,

Sundberg, Albertz, and Davies promote this trend. Moreover, Käsemann and Räisänen insist that the problem of theological diversity resists any coherent theological construction on the basis of the canon, as we have noted.

While he urges respect for the work of James A. Sanders, Childs expresses understandable reservations about his emphasis upon the *fluidity* of canonical traditions, as if these were decisively shaped by the varying religious needs of communities of faith in particular times or places. This is a different view from the more traditional and more theological notion of a rule of faith to be guarded and preserved as a common apostolic witness to Christ. We might well ask whether this pragmatic understanding of the grounding of 'truth' in quasi-local or contingent communities has roots in the distinctively American tradition of pragmatic hermeneutics, which has most recently assumed a radically postmodern neo-pragmatic form in the philosophy of Richard Rorty.[53] This would risk making socio-ecclesial need the basis of canon and truth.

In broader terms these trends, especially in North America, come closer than is appropriate or perhaps wise to the use of history-of-religions categories. This approach cannot be said to have an unblemished record of wise judgments about biblical or theological material, especially in the earlier years of the twentieth century. The German debate over canon, by contrast, may be said to embody some more constructive theological aspects. The polarizations formulated by Sundberg and Albertz have received relatively little support in Germany, Childs argues, while such writers as Rolf Rendtorff, C. Dohmen and M. Oeming have explored more constructive understandings of the unifying force of the canon through exegetical re-interpretation and a new interest in reception history. We have already urged the importance of this dialectic of *reception* with particular reference to H.R. Jauss. Yet Childs acknowledges some misgivings about the possible influence of liberal Protestantism in some Catholic circles of biblical scholarship, and urges the importance of the apocalyptic dimension of Pauline theology including 'the cross as divine rectification of the ungodly, gospel versus law, God's eschatological victory over evil'. There still lurks the ghost 'of fragmenting the theological issues crucial to the canon into historical minutiae'.[54]

This is a succinct progress-report of the more recent debate, and it also formulates a number of issues that are close to the heart of most of the essays in this volume.

---

[53] See Corrington, *Community of Interpreters*; Rorty, *Truth and Progress*, especially 1–42 and 290–326; and Thiselton, 'Two Types of Postmodernity', in *Thiselton on Hermeneutics*, 581–607 and Part IV, 'Philosophy, Language, Theology and Postmodernity', 537–683.

[54] Childs, 'The Canon in Recent Biblical Studies', below.

Canonicity and apostolicity: Stephen Evans and Denis Farkasfalvy

We noted Childs's comment that no ecclesiastical body can ever '*make* a book canonical'. Rather the concept of canon was an attempt to *acknowledge* the divine authority of its writings.'[55] Stephen Evans puts forward a parallel argument in his essay on canonicity, apostolicity and biblical authority. Paul the Apostle derives his authority from his status as a member of the foundational apostolate of the Christian church, not from his personality or his theological genius.[56] Likewise the later church does not stand 'over' the Bible to 'decide' what counts as revelation. Rather, the church became 'the means whereby that revelation *is recognized and transmitted*' (my italics).[57] F.F. Bruce goes still further than this, beyond the valid term *recognition*. He writes, 'We are not dealing so much with the recognition of the Biblical oracles as authoritative … as with the formation of these writings which had *already* the stamp of authority upon them.'[58]

Abbot Denis Farkasfalvy takes up the connection between canonicity and apostolicity in his essay 'The "Apostolic Gospels" in the Early Church'. First, he reminds us, the earliest pre-Pauline *paradosis* expressed the kerygmatic heart of the gospel as 'according to the Scriptures' (1 Cor. 15:3–4), that is to say, drawing on the Scriptures of the Old Testament as a frame of reference for its understanding.[59] Earlier in this essay we cited the reciprocal relation of interpretation and understanding to which Luke 24:27 and 44–45 bear witness. Abbot Farkasfalvy speaks of this as the 'two way road' linking the understanding of Christ and that of the Scriptures.[60] 'The prophets and apostles' become foundational for notions of Scripture and canon, and a stable tradition emerges on this basis that gives a privileged place to the four canonical Gospels. These four Gospels do not suppress diversity, but hold a degree of diversity together in a way that is 'limited and controlled'.[61]

Some may retain reservations about one or two of the arguments of these two essays. However, it is worth comparing the respected comments of Hans von Campenhausen:

---

[55] Cited above from *Biblical Theology in Crisis*, 105 (first italics mine; second italics are Childs').

[56] Evans, 'Canonicity, Apostolicity and Biblical Authority', below.

[57] Evans, 'Canonicity, Apostolicity and Biblical Authority', below.

[58] Bruce, *The Books and the Parchments*, 95. Cf. Bruce, 'The Canon of the New Testament', in Bruce, *The New Documents: Are They Reliable?*

[59] Farkasfalvy, 'The Apostolic Gospels in the Early Church', below.

[60] Farkasfalvy, 'The Apostolic Gospels in the Early Church', below. Palmer takes up the same point in his *Hermeneutics*, 23–26.

[61] Farkasfalvy, 'The Apostolic Gospels in the Early Church', below.

> The apostles ... are not simply ... teachers, but also founders of Christian communities ... With this testimony therefore, they are in truth earlier than the Church, which is based on that testimony and must continually renew its relationship with it ... Directly implicit in this once-for-all character of their function is the fact that the rank and authority of the apostolate ... can be neither continued nor renewed once this (i.e. the apostolic age) has come to an end.[62]

Research on collaborative leadership in the New Testament suggests a broader understanding of apostleship in the first century, even in the 'foundational' sense of *apostle*. Evans rightly disengages the *shared office* of apostle from notions about the *person* of apostles. This coheres with the argument of J.A. Crafton, who has rightly distinguished between person-based apostolic *agents* and witness-based apostolic *agency*.[63] This argument may be less controversial than Evans' claim that *all* writings named as 'apostolic' (for example, 2 Peter) may be 'apostolic' in the most literal or personal sense of the term. This issue may appear less critical in the light of arguments from Paul Holmberg and other New Testament specialists that *networks* of *apostolic* authority spread *beyond individual persons and local churches* to ensure a recognizable 'rule of faith' and a recognizable identity of theological traditions and doctrine.[64] Anders Eriksson has demonstrated the importance of *common apostolic tradition as shared premises* on the basis of which further interpretation and theological argument may be based.[65] A modicum of sober, sane, theological judgment will appreciate the 'apostolic' status of the epistle to the Hebrews, in spite of late acceptance into a formalized canon as 'the epistle that would not be denied' in comparison with, say, the Epistle of Barnabas.

As our earlier comments about the canon and our citing of Brevard Childs's observations indicated, the church did not '*make*' the canon, but through its life and identity *recognized* the formative impact of divine revelation through the call of the 'prophets and apostles' as a whole. Indeed, the more that we appreciate the *occasional* character of specific Gospels, epistles, or other books, as addressing specific situations, the more it becomes a matter of sober common sense to move beyond these particularities of the constraint of a single historically conditioned writing to heed other voices also within a broader canonical context. As we have argued, and shall argue further below (under 'polyphonic voices'), this need not reduce or flatten the distinctive witness of an individual

---

[62] See von Campenhausen, *Ecclesiastical Authority*, 22–23.

[63] Crafton, *Agency*, throughout; cf. Best, 'Paul's Apostolic Authority'; and Schültz, *Paul*.

[64] Holmberg, *Paul and Power*, especially 58–69; Olrog, *Paulus*; Banks, *Paul's Idea of Community*, 49–63 and 149–58; Chow, *Patronage and Power*, 183–212; Ellis, 'Co-Workers'; and Harrington, 'Collaborative Ministry'.

[65] Eriksson, *Traditions as Rhetorical Proof*.

'voice' or text. As Abbot Denis Farkasfalvy writes: 'The oneness of the gospel is not defined by the very sameness of the way in which it is formulated or the identity of the behavioural expectations connected with it.'[66]

Even *within* the New Testament Paul rejects the desire of many in the church in Corinth to construct their own 'local' theology, to choose their own leaders (1 Cor. 1:10–12), to formulate their own ethics (1 Cor. 6:12 – 11:1), to forget the rest of the church (1 Cor. 1:2; 12:14–26). Against this he affirms the nature of the church as one, holy, catholic and apostolic (1 Cor. 1:2; 3:11–17; 6:19–20; 10:14–17; 11:23–25; 12:4–11; 15:3–5).[67] His allusions to the pre-Pauline tradition that he received and transmitted merge into a theology in accordance with which the church does not 'make' its doctrine through social construction, but 'guards' what it has received, often (although not exclusively) through the faithful witness of its bishops and elders (Titus 1:9). Apostolicity is linked with unity and catholicity as well as with collaborative apostolic leadership across the whole church.

A defence and clarification of a canonical approach: Christopher Seitz

Alongside Childs, Sanders, Rendtorff, and Gerald Sheppard, Christopher Seitz has become a well-known exponent of a canonical approach.[68] In contrast to either fundamentalism or 'the advance of Biblical criticism' as it is often practised, in *Figured Out* (2001) Seitz stands alongside the Church Fathers and Reformers in reading 'the final form of the text of Christian Scripture as canon, the parts informing the whole, the whole informing the parts, according to the rule of faith'.[69] Seitz makes some trenchant comments on the frequent *de facto* separation of the Old and New Testaments in too much specialist literature: 'In the early Church the problem was not how to square faith in Christ with an Old Testament regarded as outmoded, but the reverse. How, in the light of a Scripture everywhere regarded as authoritative … could it be said that Jesus was … one with the Father who sent him?'[70] In Part III of his book (91–193) he promotes the canonical status of the four Gospels; the canonical shaping of Revelation 22 and its warning against adding to, or subtracting from, the prophecy; Jesus and the Old Testament, including Isaiah; Scripture as the rule of faith (including its bearing on sexual ethics); and the Old Testament as Christian Scripture. In several essays Seitz prefers the term 'figural' reading to

---

[66] Farkasfalvy, 'The Apostolic Gospels in the Early Church', below.
[67] Thiselton, 'Significance of Recent Research'.
[68] Seitz, *Figured Out*, 3–47, 91–129 and 177–97. Cf further Rendtorff, *Old Testament;* Sheppard, 'Canonization', 21–33.
[69] Seitz, *Figured Out*, 81.
[70] Seitz, *Figured Out*, 65.

'canonical' reading.[71] His main target is 'historicism', especially when this is rigidly developmental in outlook.

Seitz refines some of these robust contentions in his essay in this present volume. First, whatever the problems of historicist or 'developmental' approaches that tend to reduce revelation or theology to a mere history of human religion, it *cannot* be said 'that a canonical method subsumes history into intra-textuality, or merely into "the text's own world"'. [The Bible is] not simply the story of a community-creating narrative.'[72] Seitz defends both Childs and Barth against such a charge. David Demson's work, we may observe, corroborates this by insisting that 'apostolicity' grounds Barth's readings in history in a way that is not the case for Frei.[73]

Second, Seitz seeks to defend the canonical approach against a double criticism from John Barton and others that (a) attention to the final form of the text compromises serious concern for developing traditions within the text; and (b) that attention to the canon smooths over disagreements or differences of perspective in individual books or units of tradition. This point has already been addressed in summary above, although whether Barton sees canon as 'an external force' may perhaps be debated further.[74] The general upshot of Seitz's first dozen or so pages is to call attention to the subtlety and complexity of Child's work, and its resistance to over-easy criticism.

Seitz sums up the issue of the 'final form of the text' in observing: 'The final editors have never ceased hearing the word of God as a word spoken *through history*' (my italics).[75] When he moves to the New Testament, he draws constructively on the tradition of scholarship now increasingly identifiable as a distinctive emphasis found in Richard Hays, N.T. Wright and Francis Watson.[76] These writers perceive Paul as self-consciously participating in the narrative of the Old Testament saying in effect, 'With the coming of Christ we are now up to here in the grand historical narrative of God's dealings with the world.' To abstract 'Pauline Theology' from the Old Testament would be to undermine its very dynamic and indeed its very foundation.

Yet this, Seitz urges, needs to be refined further. To see the Old Testament *only* through the eyes of the New would obscure what Walter Brueggemann calls its 'wild and untamed' theological witness, or its unruly, polyphonic,

---

[71] Seitz, *Figured Out*, 9–10, 28, and 30–32.

[72] Seitz, 'The Canonical Approach and Theological Interpretation', below; cf. also Seitz, *Figured Out*, 13–23, 82–88; 109–10; and elsewhere.

[73] On the key difference between Barth and Frei see Demson, *Hans Frei*, especially 69–110.

[74] Seitz, 'The Canonical Approach and Theological Interpretation', below.

[75] Seitz, 'The Canonical Approach and Theological Interpretation', below.

[76] Cf. Watson, *Hermeneutics of Faith*.

witness. Rolf Rendtorff echoes this criticism. He sees Brevard Childs as standing somewhere 'between' Brueggemann and Watson in this search for a valid
exposition of the 'canonical' relation between the two Testaments.[77] John
Barton has asked whether Childs too readily sees the biblical text in the 'Lutheran' perspectives as speaking 'with rough edges, set over against us ... as
adversarius noster.'[78] But Seitz perceives neither Childs nor the canonical
approach in quite this way. It is precisely *theological* interpretation, rather than a
'developing religion' approach, that allows the biblical writings to retain their
cutting edge and transforming effect.

Canonical readings as liturgical and transformative: Jean Vanier, Frances Young and Scott Hahn

Jean Vanier and Frances Young, and Scott Hahn address precisely this last issue
of how biblical reading has a formative effect. We discussed this in Volume 6
of this series, *Reading Luke*, with which their essay stands in continuity, but
with reference to John. We cannot exclude a theistic, Jewish, or Christian
dimension of the biblical text. As Paul Ricoeur notes, alongside modes of prophetic, narrative, prescriptive, and wisdom discourse, 'hymnic discourse'
embodies praise, supplication, thanksgiving and other norms of address *to
God*, and this takes no less a place than other modes of discourse within the
biblical writings.[79] Such discourse witnesses to the *I–Thou relation*, concerning
which Ricoeur alludes to Martin Buber and Gabriel Marcel. *This I-Thou
relationality receives strong emphasis from Jean Vanier*, although also from Frances
Young and Scott Hahn. In relation to our previous paragraphs on canon, it
contradicts the notion that there is anything bland or un-subversive about
canonical readings.

Frances Young observes that as Jean Vanier reads the Fourth Gospel from
the perspective of the l'Arche experience 'it is John's Gospel that he reads',
and 'we expect to *be changed* by what we read'.[80] 'The l'Arche communities

---

[77] Seitz, 'The Canonical Approach and Theological Interpretation', below.

[78] Barton, *Reading the Old Testament* [cited by Seitz, 'The Canonical Approach and
Theological Interpretation', below.]. Barton offers two main criticisms of Childs's
'canonical' approach: first, that different readers and communities define the canon
of the Old Testament in different ways; second, that an alleged tendency to downplay earlier traditions and sources smacks of a 'pre-critical' approach. The foregoing
pages are sufficient to dispel the second criticism; the first seems relatively marginal
unless 'canon' presupposes a 'canon within the canon'. This is an *early* critique of
Barton, which he might not wish fully to endorse nowadays.

[79] Ricoeur, *Essays on Biblical Interpretation*, 88–95; cf also 75–88.

[80] Young, 'Methodological Reflections', in Vanier and Young, 'Towards
Transformational Reading of Scripture', below.

challenge the assumptions of modernity.'[81] Vanier expounds John in terms of a process of growth and 'in relationship with Jesus'.[82] In John 'Jesus meets and transforms people.'[83] This appears when Jesus meets the disciples of John the Baptist, the women of Samaria with her broken relationships, the blind beggar, and Jesus' friends Martha, Mary and Lazarus.[84] It is acknowledged that Vanier's reading is as much a *lectio divina* reading of John as a canonical one.

Language about 'relationship with Jesus' confronts the widespread divorce of biblical studies from theology. We are thereby prompted to reflect on the arbitrariness of such a divorce in many cases. For example, is it not arbitrary that when we mention Schleiermacher in a New Testament lecture some may wish us, and expect us, to set theology aside; while, if as a theologian Schleiermacher is part of our lectures on Christian theology, we not only *may* but also *must* expound his understanding of Christian faith in terms of a personal relationship with the living Christ? Deploying the New Testament in the service of Christian preaching, Schleiermacher urged, is like 'striking up the music' and awakening 'the slumbering spark' so that others will catch the fire that set the writers of the New Testament alight and on the move.[85] Like more recent canonical approaches, he encouraged a dialectic between canonical *wholeness* and 'the rootedness of the New Testament authors in their *time and place*'.[86]

Scott Hahn demonstrates the inseparability of liturgy and Scripture for the communities of faith, together with their canonical frameworks. How can praise to God who is the source and goal of all fail to presuppose narratives of creation or images of the End? Creation and covenant become all-pervasive themes that offer continuity and framework to so many textual units.[87] How can the church ascribe 'Glory to the Father and to the Son and to the Holy Spirit' without adding 'as it was in the beginning is now and shall be for ever'? The Psalms echo praise that resonates with God's mighty acts of covenantal deliverance in the saving events of Exodus, the period of deliverance, conquest, and settlement from Deuteronomy and Joshua through to Kings and to the return from exile. The priestly kingship of David and priestly office of Jesus Christ resonate equally with the brief narrative of Melchizedek in Genesis 14:18, with the Melchizedek Psalm (Ps. 110) and much of the epistle to the Hebrews (Heb. 7:1 – 8:7; also 4:14 – 6:20 and 8:8 – 10:25). Much of the Christian church appropriates and re-actualizes the Venite (Ps. 95) and the Jubilate

---

[81] Young, 'Methodological Reflections'.

[82] Vanier, 'The Gospel of John', in Vanier and Young, 'Towards Transformational Reading of Scripture', below.

[83] Vanier, 'The Gospel of John', below.

[84] Vanier, 'The Gospel of John', below.

[85] Schleiermacher, *On Religion* 119–20; cf. his *Hermeneutics*, 139–40 and 148–51.

[86] Schleiermacher, *Hermeneutics*, 104; cf. 139–40.

[87] Hahn, 'Canon, Cult, and Covenant', below.

(Ps. 100) day by day or Sunday by Sunday. Praise for the saving acts of God stretches from a celebration of Exodus through to the death and resurrection of Christ. In the book of Revelation the paean of praise: 'You are worthy our Lord and God ...' must include 'for you created all things, and by your will they existed and were created' (Rev. 4:11). Christian apocalyptic within the canon (and other material) tells 'a grand narrative' of divine cosmic acts, even if other narratives recount the twists and turns of divine-human relationships in the smaller, more humdrum micro-narratives of daily life. The canon offers a paradigm of dialectic between grand narrative and the little narratives of everyday particularities. As Hahn notes, however, the larger narrative is not the exclusive property of apocalyptic. The hymn that Paul uses in Philippians 2:6–11 'underscores the dramatic reversal of Adam's sin' in cosmic perspective.[88]

Hahn also expounds the *covenant* as a critical indicator of *continuity* through the biblical writings. He might have gone further. For covenant ensures a spelling out of the terms of God's relationship with humankind. A participant in a covenant knows with full assurance *where he or she stands; it speaks of love and faithfulness*. It provides *stability* in contrast to more 'fluid' notions of canonical continuity about which Childs rightly expresses reservations. As Gadamer might have said if he had addressed this particular issue, *biblical and liturgical actualisations* take *various* multiple forms, *but do so* within a stable canonical tradition of continuity and constraint. It is no accident that the visible and sacramental divine eventful word of baptism and the Lord's Supper find liturgical and sacramental actualization in the explicit context of covenant theology and canonical recital.

The Canonical Context of Specific Texts or Books: The Essays of Part 2

Law codes in the Pentateuch: Gordon McConville

Gordon McConville considers the distinctive features of the Book of the Covenant, the Holiness Code, and the Deuteronomic Code mainly within the canonical context of the continuous narrative of the Pentateuch. Like Childs, he notes the relationship between this plurality of law codes and the 'formative events' that shape them in Israel's life. The diversity and particularity of these three codes cannot be lightly dismissed, for they address similar topics at times in quite different ways (e.g. on the tithe in Deut. 14: 22–29 and Num. 20:21–24; or on the position of women in Ex. 21:7–11 and Deut. 15:12,17b).

McConville does not try to sidestep or smooth over this problem of diversity and particularity. He notes John Barton's warning against allowing 'prior

---

[88] Hahn, 'Canon, Cult, and Covenant', below.

religious commitment' that may lead to over-easy strategies. Within their canonical framework a plurality of possible responses or strategies has in fact emerged. One of these that may suggest an advance is Michael Wolter's notion of 'canonical intentionality'. This may be understood as inviting us to explore the phenomenon of intertextuality. This slippery term seems to be used in the sense in which Umberto Eco employs the term, and may be placed within a canonical context. In this way texts that may seem awkward or alien may come to assume a constructive role, even when they address readers from across a wide cultural distance.

This borders on a notion of 'indirect' communication with which literary theorists have made us long familiar. It readily applies to the genre of wisdom literature, parable, narrative, or *mashal*. Whether such 'open' texts function in this way within *legal* or *prescriptive* discourse is a more unusual suggestion, and it may merit further reflection.[89] Such an approach will be a contribution to an ongoing enquiry, to which no easy or glib 'solution' is readily available. It serves to corroborate a point consistently made in this volume (and in this present essay) that a canonical approach as such does not deserve to be identified with a tendency to ignore historical particularity or theological diversity. It seeks simply to place this in a larger context. Jonathan Culler defines intertextuality as a prior body of discourse in terms of which a given text becomes intelligible, or as that which the text 'implicitly or explicitly takes up, prolongs, cites, refutes, transposes'.[90] The term need not indicate self-referring or intralinguistic relations between texts, as M. Riffaterre uses it.

Research on the Psalms: Gordon Wenham

Gordon Wenham explores a canonical reading of the Psalms. He traces the developing shape of twentieth-century Psalm study from Gunkel and Mowinckel through to a turning point in the work of Gerald Wilson and a subsequent wave of new Psalm studies after Wilson's work of 1985. This new wave includes contributions from McCann, Murphy, Brueggemann, Mays and especially P.D. Miller (1993). In 1996 Norman Whybray provided a substantial British contribution under the significant title *Reading the Psalms as a Book.*[91] The arrangement of the Psalms within the whole corpus, Whybray argues, brings out the two main themes of obedience to the law and the

---

[89] McConville alludes mainly to Umberto Eco, *The Limits of Interpretation*, especially 'Intentio Lectoris', 44–63, and 'Overinterpreting Texts', 64ff. However, on 'closed' and 'open' texts and intertextuality, see Eco, *Role of the Reader*, 4–33.

[90] Culler, J., *Pursuit of Signs*, 101; cf. 100–18. See further Worton and Still (eds.) *Intertextuality*.

[91] Whybray, *Reading*.

promises to David. The Royal Psalms 2, 72 and 89 are positioned at the seams of the books. Psalm 72 not only looks back to the promises to the Davidic dynasty of 2 Samuel 7, but also looks forward to 'a future saviour-figure'.[92]

After a consideration of the titles of the Psalms Gordon Wenham considers the work of Martin Kleer and of Hossfeld and Zenger. Zenger consciously offers a 'canonical exegesis', and explores subsequent settings of psalms in the section of his commentary on 'context, reception, meaning'. Wenham concludes that these more recent canonical approaches provide 'a deeper and richer theological approach to the reading of the Psalms'.[93] He also distinguishes between the three canonical contexts of the Psalter as a whole, the Hebrew Bible or Jewish canon, and the Christian Bible of the Old and New Testaments.

For hermeneutical theory perhaps the most significant issue arises from arguments for the legitimacy of multiple contexts within which meaning is generated and understood. Can we logically do justice to such an approach if we were to have an equally strong concern to endorse Calvin's notion of a single meaning: '*verum sensum scripturae, qui germanus est et simplex*'?[94] I recall participating in a conference on hermeneutics at Gordon College, Boston, in which James Barr and Richard Swinburne argued against each other with some passion for opposite answers to this question.

Issues regularly debated in the philosophy of language suggest that the impact of changing contexts decisively re-shapes meaning. To reject this may entail retreat to the era before Schleiermacher when 'philologists' restricted 'meaning' to its semantic dimension alone. However, decisions about meaning also rest upon judgment about the genre of texts. A 'closed' text that conveys propositional information at a wholly didactic level may resist contextual reformation more strongly or readily than 'open' or 'productive' texts. Calvin seems to be thinking primarily of texts in relation to doctrinal construction in this context, and of mediaeval abuses of multiple meaning. Most of the Psalms would arguably be understood as 'open' texts of *worship, re-actualization, and rootedness in more than one single situation*; it is more difficult to see them as circumscribed transmissive, didactic, or 'engineering' texts, as Lotman terms them.[95] This appears to confirm the constructive nature of the proposals that are viewed sympathetically in Wenham's essay.

---

[92] Whybray, *Reading*, 92.

[93] Wenham, 'Towards a Canonical Reading of the Psalms', below.

[94] Calvin, *Epistles of Paul*, 85.

[95] Lotman and Eco rightly distinguish between 'engineering' texts where reproduction, replication and precise transmission are necessary to their purpose; and 'literary', symbolic, poetic, or 'productive' texts that include creative engagement with, and on the part of, the reader.

Wisdom literature and canon: Tremper Longman and Ryan O'Dowd

Tremper Longman and Ryan O'Dowd consider Wisdom books within a canonical context. First, both writers take up the distinction between 'open' and 'closed' texts (discussed above), rightly identifying wisdom literature as in general reflecting the genre of open texts. Second, also rightly, both writers perceive Ecclesiastes and Job as offering 'a canonical corrective' to a reading of Proverbs that would draw from this book the over-simple generalizing axiom that 'the righteous always prosper and the wicked always perish'.[96] Any thinking person who has sought to undertake a response to the problem of evil and human suffering with reference to the biblical writings will become aware of the need to address the theological dialectic between Deuteronomy and Proverbs on one side, and Job and Ecclesiastes on the other. Theological construction cannot avoid issues raised by canonical contexts.

Tremper Longman recognizes that Ecclesiastes and Job are minefields of diverse interpretation. All the same, he observes, 'No matter how this [for example, Ecc. 7:15–18] is interpreted, one cannot imagine finding anything like this in Proverbs!'[97] Similarly, 'Job serves as a canonical corrective to an overreading of Proverbs.'[98] Yet the tension, he adds, should not be exaggerated. The 'rewards' outlined in Proverbs are 'not promises'.[99] Moreover, Longman extends his canonical frame to include the culmination of the Wisdom figure in the person of Christ in the New Testament. Paul's allusions to, and understanding of, Christ as God's wisdom (e.g. in 1 Cor. 1:30; Col. 1:15–17; 2:3) associate Christ with Proverbs 8 explicitly. Hence a Christological reading of 'wisdom' is no merely arbitrary or 'external' reading of the wisdom material.

Ryan O'Dowd questions Longman's use of the term *overreading* to denote an understanding of Proverbs in which the righteous are rewarded and always prosper. 'The methods which Longman rightfully critiques are not cases of seeing too much in the text, but rather of seeing too little.'[100] These methods have been distracted by social theories, which are symptoms of '*underreading*'. Interpretation requires *imagination* to test probabilities and postulate solutions. O'Dowd rightly links with biblical reading the classic distinction since Dilthey (and implicit in Schleiermacher) between *Verstehen* and *Erklärung*. The full range of the wisdom genre in its canonical context is not a cluster of

---

[96] Longman, 'Canonical Criticism and the Old Testament Wisdom Books', below; and O'Dowd, 'Wisdom as Canonical Imagination', below.

[97] Longman, 'Canonical Criticism and the Old Testament Wisdom Books', below.

[98] Longman, 'Canonical Criticism and the Old Testament Wisdom Books', below.

[99] Longman, 'Canonical Criticism and the Old Testament Wisdom Books', below.

[100] O'Dowd, 'Wisdom as Canonical Imagination', below.

explanatory components but 'a theological-historical-existential picture *of the whole*', which itself makes possible an understanding of the uniqueness of wisdom's identity *in each era.*[101] The key point about Ecclesiastes in this context is that it explores an *epistemology*. It is concerned less with *what* is known than with the more transcendental philosophical question: *How* is knowledge found? O'Dowd finds the canonical frame of New Testament thought not simply in passages about Christ as God's Wisdom, but in Paul's *creation* Christology. This coheres with our contention throughout this essay that no text or individual book can speak of 'God' without implicitly alluding to God as source of all, i.e. alluding implicitly to the creation narratives.

Robin Parry on Lamentations and Eugene Lemcio on the four Gospels

We have space only to allude briefly to two other essays. Robin Parry explores the canonical context of Lamentations. He sees Lamentations 3 as especially significant for understanding the book as a whole; calls attention to the role of Isaiah 40 – 55 for reading Lamentations as a whole; and suggests that 'the theological connections made in canonical texts between the sufferings of Israel and those of humanity in general, of Christ in particular and even of the Spirit, have the potential to put Lamentations in a quite new light.'[102] Conversely, Lamentation may place the suffering of humanity, Christ, and the church, in a new light. The meanings that the text of Lamentations generates 'will be diverse', even within the constraints imposed by disciplined reading in a canonical context.[103]

Eugene Lemcio addresses the place of the four Gospels in relation to other books within the New Testament canon. In contrast to a number of scholars in Continental Europe, especially in the Lutheran tradition, he reverses the tendency to make the Pauline epistles almost a privileged canon within the canon. He emphasizes the unique and privileged role of the Gospels as narrative as against what he regards as the didactic or more discursive material of the epistles.[104] Among other differences between the four Gospels and Paul or other parts of the New Testament canon, Lemcio identifies Jesus' proclamation of the reign of *God* and of the gospel of *God*, and theological centrality of *God*, in contrast to the pre-Pauline and Pauline kerygma and creed 'that *Christ* died for our sins … *Christ* was buried … and *Christ* was raised' (1 Cor. 15:3–4), and the

---

[101] O'Dowd, 'Wisdom as Canonical Imagination', below.

[102] Parry, 'Prolegomena to Christian Theological Interpretations of Lamentations', below.

[103] Parry, 'Prolegomena to Christian Theological Interpretations of Lamentations', below.

[104] Lemcio, 'The Gospels within the New Testament Canon', especially below.

confession that *Jesus* is Lord (Rom. 10:9–10; 1 Cor. 12:3). Further, in Paul 'Repentance and following are not the means of relating to him.'[105] The proclamation of God's kingly rule must 'be given its due' rather than the 'juridical metaphor' drawn from the courtroom.[106] Certain ways of reading the New Testament witness to the death of Jesus 'impose a standard external to the Gospels themselves [with] perhaps a preference for Paul'.[107] The Fourth Gospel also brings its own distinctive perspective, including the theme of eternal life. The 'theocentricity' of the Gospels prevents Christian faith from becoming 'a cult of Jesus'.[108]

As one who belongs firmly within the Anglican tradition I regularly stand reverentially to hear the Gospels, but sit to hear the epistles. My file of sermons is probably larger on the four Gospels than on Paul and Hebrews. I sympathize with a need to reverse any tendency to allow the epistles to overshadow the Gospels. A genuinely canonical approach promotes a both … and … here, but not an either/or.

In *exegetical and theological* terms, however, I have some considerable difficulty in recognizing the 'Paul' of this essay, or of seeing John as other than at least as Christocentric as any writing in the New Testament. The positive point that the Jesus of the Synoptic Gospels points not to himself but to God is well made. It is standard material in New Testament studies, and is strongly emphasized in modern theology, not least by Paul Tillich. All the same numerous specialist New Testament studies also argue rightly that *Paul is theocentric rather then Christocentric*. As long ago as in 1970 the conservative scholar Leon Morris argued this, and Neil Richardson's major study of 1994 is one among a score of studies to this effect.[109]

Yet if statements in this essay may appear unguarded and perhaps open to question, clearly every part of the New Testament canon, including especially its four Gospels, has an honoured place and an irreducible part to play in the polyphonic chorus of voices that are 'the New Testament'. Against some who would downplay the concern of the Pastoral Epistles with apostolic doctrine and church order in contrast to the 'living fire' of an earlier Paul on grace and the cross, the very contingency and temporal particularity of the New Testament writings should make us think twice before we lightly downgrade

---

[105] Lemcio, 'The Gospels within the New Testament Canon', below.
[106] Lemcio, 'The Gospels within the New Testament Canon', below.
[107] Lemcio, 'The Gospels within the New Testament Canon', below.
[108] Lemcio, 'The Gospels within the New Testament Canon', below.
[109] Morris, 'The Theme of Romans'; cf. more recently Richardson, *Paul's Language about God*, 95–138 and 240–307. See further the literature cited in Thiselton, *First Epistle to the Corinthians*, 59–60, 67–8, 613–16, 630–39, 806–809, 1215–16, and 1229–40.

the so-called Deutero-Pauline literature. Each of the 'voices' within the canon speaks to situations that may appear again even if not in identical form, and together they address readers today as a polyphonic chorus.

A Concluding Comment: Polyphonic Voices, Canon and Theological Construction

If the biblical writings are to address readers beyond an immediate context in the ancient world, and if, further, they provide any foundation for theological construction, a reflection on canonical contexts cannot but arise. The problem of human suffering, as we have noted, cannot be addressed responsibly without placing Proverbs and Deuteronomy alongside Job and Ecclesiastes, together with Psalms of accusation and lament, perhaps Lamentations, and certainly the Passion narratives of the Gospels and a broader framework of understanding divine goodness, sovereignty, providence, and purpose.

Robert Gundry's recent essay on hermeneutical liberty and theological diversity reminds us that attempts to understand the recitals of God's saving acts require us to place divine promise in Joshua 1 – 12 alongside the turmoil and setbacks of life in the book of Judges; or that to construct a broad Christology requires us to explore Mark's account of the Spirit's anointing of Jesus along-side Luke on the Virgin Birth, John on the eternal Word made flesh; Paul on the last Adam and the resurrection, and the Epistle to the Hebrews on the human Jesus as perfect high priest, perfect sacrifice, and definitive divine Word and exact imprint of God.[110] The more we emphasize the 'historical occasionalism' of the biblical writings, Gundry seems to imply, the more we need to respect biblical diversity within a certain limiting frame. The canon provides 'boundaries' beyond which the biblical writings as a whole forbid us to go, even if Gundry observes, 'Maybe systematicians should not even be looking for a unifying center.'

Gundry's approach is different from that of Käsemann or Räisänen. Räisänen describes the polyphonic voices within the canon as 'contradictions' on the basis of which theological construction cannot be undertaken with integrity. He fails to see that even at the non-theological, reductionist, positivist, level of his approach, *literary theorists and hermeneutical specialists* have long since explored the literary phenomenon of polyphonic voices as contributing *depth and self-involving engagement* with texts to a degree and of a kind that a monochrome solo voice could never achieve.

We might have hoped, if not expected, that even the device of *dialectic* and *indirect communication* as practised by Socrates, in the earliest *Dialogues of Plato*, in

---

[110] Gundry, 'Hermeneutic Liberty'.

many (although not in all) of the parables of Jesus, by Kierkegaard, by the later Wittgenstein, and to a lesser degree by Collingwood, would urge a measure of caution against equating a plurality of voices with logical inconsistency. Indeed, the deliberate use of polyphonic voices within the book of Job, then in the nineteenth century by Dostoevsky, and more recently in the early and mid-twentieth century by Bakhtin offers evidence to the contrary.

Mikhail Bakhtin (1895–1975) draws on philosophy, literary theory, theories of communicative action, aesthetics, and even post-Einsteinian physics, to formulate an understanding of communicative action through multiple voices that is more than fruitful for discerning how diversity within the canon nevertheless leaves ample room for legitimate theological construction, albeit of an 'open' and ongoing kind. Bakhtin published his *Problems of Dostoevsky's Art* in 1929, but was later arrested under the Stalinist regime partly because of his religious sympathies, and partly because the notion of plural voices was not congenial to a hardline Marxist regime. Only during the 1960s did students of Dostoevsky 're-discover' him, and he was rehabilitated.

Like Hans-Georg Gadamer he traces *dialectic* discourse to Socrates and the early *Dialogues of Plato*. Like Gadamer and Ricoeur he stresses the vital role of *'the other'* and *alterity* for processes of creative textual communication. In common with mainline hermeneutical tradition from Dilthey to Gadamer, Apel, Betti, and Haberhas, he underlines the *communal* dimension of understanding and communication. This derives in part from the concept of *sobornost*, 'togetherness', in the Russian Orthodox Church. He rejects abstract literary formalism, urging that communication is performed as *an act within a concrete situational context*.

It is not difficult to appreciate how these four concerns or themes shed light on the interactions between the 'voices' that address us from within the biblical canon. Bakhtin finds an admirable model of this kind of polyphonic communication in Dostoyevsky. Thus in Dostoyevsky's *The Brothers Karamazov* no single voice prevails over, or eclipses, others. Albert Camus selects a dominant voice of protest on behalf of anti-theism, just as Berdyaev suggests a dominant voice on behalf of Russian Orthodox theism. But the characters Ivan, Aleshe, Zosima, perhaps the narrator, and even the reader's 'filling up of the gaps' contribute *together in community, without uniformity*, to the process of wrestling with the issues actively and with self-involvement, to generate meaning in *sobornost*, or togetherness.[111] Within this complex framework of *sobornost* even a plurality of voices may lead us in a coherent direction, using, rather than suppressing, the voice of 'the other'. Bakhtin saw in Einstein's physics a parallel paradigm of *differences* that were acknowledged but were also, in turn, *relativized*.

---

[111] On polyphonic discourse in Dostoevsky, see also Thiselton, 'Polyphonic Voices'.

Räisänen may perhaps fail to see this point either because he is unaware of it, or because he construes 'doctrine', or theological construction, in terms that Bakhtin calls *monologic*, and many Christian traditions would not or might not recognize. Monologic discourse denotes a set of propositions *abstracted from life* and placed, as it were, '*there*' to inform or to serve as a 'timeless' reference-book of axioms or general principles that are incapable of development or revision. Monologic discourse is to teach or to inform; but it does not attempt to provoke or entice anyone into active thought through their hearing more than a single voice.

Some New Testament scholars seem to have a poor record of appreciating the finer nuances of open texts and indirect communication. The debate about parable-interpretation may serve to illustrate this with reference to the work of Adolf Jülicher and Joachim Jeremias. Robert Funk complains that Jeremias' treatment of the parables largely as *historical sources* for reconstructing the teaching of Jesus undermines their primary hermeneutical function. This was in many cases to project narrative 'worlds', to entice hearers to enter it, and to transform their horizons or 'world' from within. Funk writes, 'Like Jülicher ... Jeremias derive[s] a set of *ideas* from the parable'; this robs parables of their eventful, formative, life-changing character, and they thus 'foreclose the future'.[112] Admittedly there is a place for a *retrospective* reconstruction of their cognitive content; but neither Jülicher nor Jeremias shows adequate interest in their hermeneutical dynamic. Indeed, in another direction on the basis of Jülicher's assumptions about a 'liberal' Jesus who taught only timeless general truths, and Jeremias's assumptions about the value of his form-critical criteria for authentic Jesus-sayings, they unintentionally perhaps devalue any canonical context. By repeatedly 'stripping away' the interpretations of the evangelists or the framework of the apostolic canon as 'inauthentic' (*uneigentlich*) they arguably get the worst of both worlds: on one side they focus only on a 'flat', informative, didactic content; on the other side they leave the impression that the teaching of Jesus carries first-class status that the canonical context or the evangelists cannot in any sense match. It is as if the apostolic church is inferior, secondary, or even obstructive.

We return to our main point: is *Christian theological construction* to be thought of as *monologic discourse*? Several considerations suggest otherwise. First, doctrine evolves through corporate and communal endeavour.[113] This has been the case since apostolic times. Even Paul did not develop his theology in isolation from his co-workers or fellow-apostles. The church for Paul is one, holy,

---

[112] Funk, *Language*, 149 and 150.

[113] See the Church of England Doctrine Commission Report, *Believing in the Church*, throughout, but especially Thiselton, 45–78; Bowker, 159–89; and Harvey, 286–302.

catholic, and apostolic. Second, Christian doctrine like Christian Scripture is *formative*. It actively shapes a community of faith. Its 'texts' are not merely transmissive, closed, and incapable of creativity and growth, but self-involving, open to the future, and dynamic. Third, especially but not exclusively in Anglican tradition, doctrine is not only rooted in Scripture, but also inter-twined with life, liturgy and practice. Philip Turner writes perceptively that Cranmer saw Anglican doctrine *expressed in 'faithful lives* ... formed and lived through reading, marking, learning, and inwardly digesting the *Holy Scriptures* ... for *"edification"* ... as the practical *"organizer of life"* for ... an ordered com-munity.'[114] This coheres with what Paul called *building up* (cf. *Bildung* as 'forma-tion' in Gadamer), not least since love, not 'knowledge' (*gnosis*) is that which builds or constructs. The dozen or so uses of the Greek verb οἰκοδομέω (*oikodomeō*) and the dozen or so occurrences of its cognate noun in Paul's epis-tles serve to corroborate this.[115] This more than indicates the role of a canonical context or approach for theological construction.

---

[114] Turner, 'Tolerable Diversity', 29 and 31.
[115] On the verb: 1 Cor. 8:1,10; 10:23; 14:4, 17; Gal. 2:18; 1 Thes. 5:11; cf. Rom. 15:20; for example of the noun, 1 Cor. 3:9; 14:3, 5, 12, 26; 2 Cor. 5:1; 10:8; 12:19; 13:10; Eph. 2:11; 4:12, 16, 29.

Bibliography

Banks, R., *Paul's Idea of Community* (2nd edn.; Peabody, MA: Hendrickson, 1994)

Barr, J., *Holy Scripture, Canon, Authority, Criticism* (Oxford: Oxford University Press, 1983)

Bartholomew, C.G., J.B. Green, and A.C. Thiselton (eds.), *Reading Luke: Interpretation, Reflection, Formation* (SHS 6; Grand Rapids: Zondervan and Carlisle: Paternoster, 2005)

Best, E., 'Paul's Apostolic Authority', *JSNT* 27 (1986), 3–25

Bruce, F.F., *The Books and the Parchments* (London: Pickering and Inglis, 1953)

—, 'The Canon of the New Testament', in *The New Documents: Are They Reliable?* (Grand Rapids: Eerdmans, 2003)

Calvin, J., *The Epistles of Paul to the Galatians, Ephesians, Philippians and Colossians* (Edinburgh: Oliver & Boyd, 1965)

von Campenhausen, H., *Ecclesiastical Authority and Spiritual Power in the Church of the First Three Centuries* (London: Black, 1969)

Childs, B.S. *Biblical Theology in Crisis* (Philadelphia: Westminster Press, 1970)

—, 'The Old Testament as the Scripture of the Church', *Concordia Theological Monthly* 43 (1972), 709–22

—, *Exodus: A Commentary* (London: SCM, 1974)

—, 'The Sensus Literalis of Scripture: An Ancient and Modern Problem', in *Beiträge zur alttestamentlichen Theologie: Festschrift für Walter Zimmerli zum 70 Geburtstag* (ed. H. Donner; Göttingen: Vandenhoeck & Ruprecht, 1976), 80–93

—, *Introduction to the Old Testament as Scripture* (Philadelphia: Fortress and London: SCM, 1979)

—, *Old Testament Theology in a Canonical Context* (Philadelphia: Fortress and London: SCM, 1985)

—, *The Struggle to Understand Isaiah as Christian Scripture* (Grand Rapids: Eerdmans, 2004)

Chow, J.K.M., *Patronage and Power: A Study of Social Networks in Corinth* (JSNTSup 75; Sheffield: Sheffield Academic Press, 1992)

Church of England Doctrine Commission Report, *Believing in the Church: The Corporate Nature of Faith* (London: SPCK, 1981)

Corrington, R.S., *The Community of Interpreters: On the Hermeneutics of Nature and Bible in the American Philosophical Tradition* (Macon, GA: Mercer University Press, 1995)

Crafton, J.A., *The Agency of the Apostle* (JSNTSup 51; Sheffield: JSOT Press, 1991)

Culler, J., *The Pursuit of Signs: Semiotics, Literature, Deconstruction* (London: Routledge & Kegan Paul, 1981)

Demson, D.E., *Hans Frei and Karl Barth: Different Ways of Reading Scripture* (Grand Rapids: Eerdmans, 1997)

Dunn, J.D.G., *Unity and Diversity in the New Testament* (London: SCM, 1977)

Eco, U., *The Role of the Reader: Explorations in the Semiotics of Texts* (London: Hutchinson, 1981)

—, *The Limits of Interpretation* (Bloomington: Indiana University Press, 1990)

Ellis, E.E., 'Co-workers, Paul and His', in *Dictionary of Paul and His Letters* (ed. G.F. Hawthorne and R.P. Martin; Leicester: Inter-Varsity Press, 1993)

Eriksson, A., *Traditions as Rhetorical Proof: Pauline Argumentation in 1 Corinthians* (Stockholm: Almqisk & Wiksell, 1988)

Funk, R.W., *Language, Hermeneutic and Word of God* (New York: Harper, 1966)

Gundry, R.H., 'Hermeneutic Liberty, Theological Diversity and Historical Occasionalism', in *The Old is Better: New Testament Essays in Support of Traditional Interpretations* (Tübingen: Mohr Siebeck, 2005), 1–17

Gasque, W.W., and R.P. Martin, (eds.), *Apostolic History and the Gospel: Essays Presented to F.F. Bruce* (Exeter: Paternoster, 1970)

Harrington, D.J., 'Paul and Collaborative Ministry', *NTR* 3 (1990), 62–71

Harvey, D., *The Condition of Postmodernity* (Oxford: Blackwell, 1989)

Holmberg, B., *Paul and Power: The Structure of Authority in the Primitive Church as Reflected in the Pauline Epistles* (Lund: Gleerup, 1978)

Luz, U., *Das Geschichtsverständnis des Paulus* (Munich: Kaiser, 1968)

Lyotard, J.–F., *The Postmodern Condition: A Report on Knowledge* (Manchester: Manchester University Press, 1984)

Morris, L., 'The Theme of Romans', in *Apostolic History and the Gospel: Essays Presented to F.F. Bruce* (ed. W.W. Gasque and R.P.Martin; Exeter: Paternoster, 1960), 240–63

Ollrog, W.–H., *Paulus und seine Mitarbeiter: Untersuchungen zu Theorie und Prakis der paulinischen Mission* (WMANT 50; Neukirchen: Neukirchener Verlag, 1979)

Palmer, R., *Hermeneutics* (Evanston: Northwestern University Press, 1969)

Räisänen, H., 'The New Testament in Theology', in *Challenge to Biblical Interpretation: Collected Essays 1991 – 2001* (Leiden and Boston: Brill, 2001), 227–49

Rendtorff, R., *The Old Testament: An Introduction* (Philadelphia: Fortress, 1986)

Richardson, N., *Paul's Language about God* (JSNTSup 99; Sheffield: Sheffield Academic Press, 1994)

Ricoeur, P., *Essays on Biblical Interpretation* (London: SPCK, 1981)

Rorty, R., *Truth and Progress: Philosophical Papers* (Cambridge: Cambridge University Press, 1998)

Sanders, J.A., *Text and Canon* (Philadelphia: Fortress, 1972)

—, *Canon and Community: A Guide to Canonical Criticism* (Philadelphia: Fortress, 1984)

—, *From Sacred Story to Sacred Text: Canon and Paradigm* (Philadelphia: Fortress 1987)

Schleiermacher, F., *On Religion: Speeches to its Cultured Despisers* (New York: Harper, 1958)

—, *Hermeneutics* (Missoula: Scholars Press, 1977)

Schültz, J.H., *Paul and the Anatomy of Apostolic Authority* (SNTSMS 26; Cambridge: Cambridge University Press, 1975)

Seitz, C., *Figured Out: Typology and Providence in Christian Scripture* (Louisville: Westminster John Knox, 2001)

Sheppard, G.T., 'Canonization: Hearing the Voice of the Same God through Historically Dissimilar Traditions, *Int* 34 (1982), 21–33

Thiselton, A.C., 'Polyphonic Voices in Theological Fiction', in R. Lundin, R. Walhout and A.C. Thiselton, *The Promise of Hermeneutics* (Grand Rapids: Eerdmans and Carlisle: Paternoster, 1999), 172–82

—, *The First Epistle to the Corinthians* (Grand Rapids: Eerdmans and Carlisle: Paternoster, 2000)

—, 'Scholarship and the Church: "Academic Freedom, Religious Tradition, and the Morality of Christian Scholarship"', in *Thiselton on Hermeneutics: Collected Works and New Essays of Anthony Thiselton* (Aldershot: Ashgate and Grand Rapids: Eerdmans, 2006), 581–607

—, 'The Significance of Recent Research on 1 Corinthians for Hermeneutical Appropriation of the Epistle Today', forthcoming in *Neotestamentica* 40 (2006)

Turner, P., 'Tolerable Diversity and Ecclesial Integrity: Communion or Federation?', *The Journal of Anglican Studies* 1.2 (2003), 24–46

Watson, F., *Text, Church and World: Biblical Interpretation in Theological Perspective* (Edinburgh: T&T Clark, 1994)

—, *Text and Truth: Redefining Biblical Theology* (Edinburgh: T&T Clark, 1997)

—, *Paul and the Hermeneutics of Faith* (London: T&T Clark, 2004)

Whybray, R.N., *Reading the Psalms as a Book* (JSOTSup 222; Sheffield: Sheffield Academic Press, 1996)

Worton, M., and J. Still (eds.), *Intertextuality: Theories and Practice* (Manchester: Manchester University Press, 1990)

Part 1
The Concept of Canon,
its Formation and the
Hermeneutical Implication

1

The Canon in Recent Biblical Studies: Reflections on an Era[1]

Brevard S. Childs

Introduction

In spite of the wide range of modern biblical studies, it has been possible in the past at times to characterize a given period by focusing on the dominant methodologies, themes, and goals of the research. For example, in the latter part of the nineteenth and early twentieth centuries, much effort focused on source-critical problems both in the Old and New Testaments. Then beginning in the 1920s attention to oral tradition and form criticism moved to center stage with von Rad and Bultmann emerging as leaders.

It is my thesis in this paper that one can make a case for the period from the late 1960s to the end of the twentieth century to be described as one in which large sections of the biblical discipline focused on issues related either directly or indirectly to the subject of canon. Obviously there are many exceptions to be noted, but I think that it can be illuminating to draw some larger synthetic lines as a way toward providing a larger picture.

I shall also argue that renewed interest in canon achieved its greatest activity in the period from the mid-60s through the 1990s. Then there began to form areas of wide consensus, at least in the English-speaking world. The intensity of the debate began to decline as many of the critical problems appeared resolved, and increasingly summaries were published that reviewed the advances and conclusions reached from the debate, I am thinking of recent articles on canon in various modern dictionaries of the Bible, and of various compendia on the history of biblical interpretation. I shall also seek to show that the history of the engagement with the subject of canon moved along different tracks in the German and English-speaking worlds. A good means of showing this difference is to focus on certain crucial volumes.

---

[1] This essay was previously published in *ProEccl* 14.1 (2005), 26–45. It is reproduced in this volume with the kind permission of the author and the publisher.

In 1970, E. Käsemann[2] published a book on canon by reprinting a dozen important articles written largely in the 1950s and early 1960s. Many of the articles continued the older debate of the late nineteenth century between Zahn and Harnack while offering further refinements. The majority of the essays, which represented a wide spectrum from both the left and right, wrestled with theological problems such as the dogmatic function of a fixed canon, the tension between the narrow canonical corpus of the Reformers and the larger canon of Catholicism, and questions regarding the legitimacy of a 'canon-within-the-canon,' especially within the Lutheran tradition (e.g. H. Küng versus Käsemann).

In one sense, Käsemann's book pointed backward and marked the end of an earlier German debate. Only in one particular case, namely, Käsemann's own essay delivered in 1950 to the World Council, was a highly existential question raised which continued to have a lasting impact. His challenge brought to an end a position represented in the immediate World War II period by the ecumenical movement that Christian unity could be achieved on the basis of the common Scriptures shared by all Christian denominations. Käsemann sought to undermine this conviction in stating: the Bible is not the source of Christian unity, but rather of its disunity!

Equally significant in Käsemann's 1970 volume is what was missing. Indeed, it was those very areas that came to dominate the rebirth of interest in canon within the English-speaking world, namely, the impact of the Dead Sea scrolls, the diversity of Hellenistic Judaism, attention to non-canonical, apocryphal and pseudepigraphical works such as found at Nag Hammadi, and a wider comparative approach from the perspective of history-of-religions. In order to trace this development, I turn first to the English-speaking effort before returning to the German academic scene.

A New Interpretation of Canon Within the English-speaking World

The variety of stimuli

The stimuli for new attention to canon arose from different sources. First, the study of the Qumran material broke open the biblical field in many different directions. It provided new evidence for tracing the historical contexts of the Hebrew and Greek textual traditions and demonstrated the enormous diversity, fluidity, and scope of biblical texts. Second, the sheer complexity of Hellenistic Judaism emerged with great force and that demanded a rethinking of the

---

[2] E. Käsemann, *Das Neue Testament als Kanon* (Göttingen: Vandenhoeck & Ruprecht, 1970).

portrait of 'normative Judaism' portrayed by G.F. Moore in his standard text-book. Third, it became also clear that a new appreciation arose for the impor-tance of apocryphal and pseudepigraphical writings, an interest greatly enhanced by the discovery of the Gnostic papyri. Likewise, much attention turned to text criticism and the role of the Septuagint, targums, and midrashim. Of course, Israeli scholars fell within the larger circle of the English-speaking world along with a contingent from Scandinavia and the Netherlands, who wrote largely in English.

In addition, new historical interests broadened the methodological pers-pectives by refining the older history-of-religions' concerns by a rigorous phenomenological approach which in part was a reaction against the earlier focus on theology. Moreover, a history of interpretation was mounted which included not only attention to the classic sources of Josephus, Marcion, and the Church Fathers, but also sought to extend the interpretive context into a his-tory of the reception of traditions. Finally, in contrast to the older theological concerns, a fresh hermeneutical model emerged which brought a new light on the subject.

These new impulses also arose within a new post-Second World War cul-tural climate for the study of the Bible. Particularly in North America, but also to some degree in Britain, university departments of religion were established often in conscious opposition to the curricula of the traditional divinity schools and theological seminaries. The faculties were now constituted apart from reli-gious confession or affiliation. Thus, the academic net was thrown much wider and took on a secular, non-confessional stance, which was further strengthened by the agenda of the professional journals.

Characteristics of the New Approach to Canon

The problem of terminology

The late nineteenth century had seen the learned debate between Zahn and Harnack end in a frustrating stalemate largely because of the lack of agreement on the terminology respecting canon. Zahn assigned citations used by the New Testament and the early Church Fathers as a sign of canonicity and opted for an early date for a core of the New Testament canon. Conversely, Harnack attrib-uted canonicity to a New Testament citation only when it had attained an authoritative status equal to the Old Testament, namely, from the late second century onward.

It was therefore a highly significant contribution of A.C. Sundberg[3] (first in his Harvard dissertation of 1957, and later published in 1964 as *The Old*

---

[3] A.C. Sundberg, *The Old Testament of the Early Church* (Cambridge, MA: Harvard University Press, 1964).

Testament of the Early Church) to have made a sharp distinction between Scripture and canon. The former designated religious writings perceived as authoritative; the latter referred to a list of official authoritative books resulting from the exclusion of those now deemed non-canonical. Sundberg's distinction became widely accepted (cf. the further refinements of Ulrich[4] and McDonald[5]). The initial effect of this terminological distinction was that Sundberg's book marked the beginning of a new phase in the study of canon within the English-speaking world, and shifted the discussion primarily to the historical problems related to the process that ended in the canonization of the Jewish and Christian Bibles (cf. Barton, *The Spirit and the Letter*[6]).

The historical development of the Jewish and Christian canons

The central problem in studying this development historically is that nowhere in the Jewish and Christian sources is there direct information provided which discusses the process of the canonization of either the Jewish or Christian Bible.[7] The task is rather left to a critical reconstruction of the process from indirect evidence (Ben Sira, Josephus, Church Fathers, Talmud, etc.).

Sundberg had also succeeded in undermining the earlier, widely accepted hypothesis of an Alexandrian canon to explain the striking differences between the narrow Hebrew canon of Jerusalem and the fluid state of the authoritative writings of Jewish Greek Hellenism, including the New Testament. Rather, Sundberg argued that the Jewish canon was not yet significantly fixed at the rise of Christianity, and that its restricted collection of twenty-two (twenty-four) books was a late first-century retrenchment. Not only was the 'Old Testament' still open at the time of Jesus, but the canonical formation of the New Testament was a fluid process extending into the fourth century. The Qumran evidence seemed to confirm the enormous diversity within first-century Judaism. This reconstruction of the canonical process was further supported by Sundberg's redating of the Muratorian canon to the fourth century rather than its previous assignment to the second century.

Of course, in contrast to this growing historical consensus respecting the historical growth of the Jewish and Christian canons, there remained a minority opinion represented among several Jewish scholars (Leiman, Lightstone[8])

---

[4] E. Ulrich, 'The Notion and Definition of Canon', in *The Canon Debate* (eds. L.M. McDonald and J.A. Sanders; Peabody, MA: Hendrickson, 2002), 21–35.

[5] L.M. McDonald, *The Formation of the Christian Canon* (Peabody, MA: Hendrickson, 1995), 13.

[6] J. Barton, *The Spirit and the Letter* (London: SPCK, 1997), 157f.

[7] B.M. Metzger, *The Canon of the New Testament* (Oxford: Clarendon, 1987), 1.

[8] S.Z. Leiman, *The Canonization of the Hebrew Scripture: The Talmudic and Midrashic Evidence* (Hamden, CT: Archon, 1976); J.N. Lightstone, 'The Rabbis' Bible: The

and supported by a few Christians (Lewis, Beckwith[9]) that the Hebrew canon had been virtually closed in the century before the rise of Christianity. These scholars were successful in casting serious doubt on the widespread appeal to the 'Council of Jamnia' (ca. 90 AD) as the historical moment for the closure of the Jewish canon. However, the late dating for the closure was largely continued by the majority supporting Sundberg (cf. Sanders' revised theory[10]).

In respect to the canonical development of the New Testament, the older view of Zahn and Westcott was that the major force at work emerged from internal theological pressures. However, beginning with Harnack, the hypothesis increasingly prevailed that external forces, especially from Marcion, the Gnostics, and other dissidents, were responsible for its gradual development. Although Metzger, Gamble, and Ferguson[11] still allowed for some intrinsic forces, the major emphasis shifted to historical reconstructions of extrinsic forces as decisive. There also emerged a widespread consensus that the traditional theological criteria for determining canonicity (apostolicity, catholicity, orthodoxy) were, at best, late constructs without any solid historical evidence. Thus, Gamble[12] concludes his review of the process as follows: 'The scope of the canon is ... indebted to a wide range of contingent historical factors and from a historical standpoint is largely fortuitous.'

History-of-religions categories

Another characteristic feature of the modern approach to canon within the English-speaking world has been the shift from its primarily theological perspective to the dominance of the history-of-religions categories. From this point of view there are no privileged canonical texts, but all texts are treated equally as potential sources regardless of later canonical or non-canonical status.

The focus of the newer studies was also expanded by aggressive attention to historical, sociological, and cultural patterns representing a wide range of comparative religions. Since it was thought by some that the Jewish sources

---

Canon of the Hebrew Bible and the Early Rabbinic Guild', in *The Canon Debate*, 163–84.

[9] J.P. Lewis, 'What Do We Mean by Jabneh?' *JBR* 32 (1964), 125–32; R.T. Beckwith, *The Old Testament Canon of the New Testament Church* (Grand Rapids: Eerdmans, 1985).

[10] J.A. Sanders, 'The Issue of Closure in the Canonical Process', in *The Canon Debate*, 252–63.

[11] B.M. Metzger, *The Canon of the New Testament*, 1–8; H.Y. Gamble, *The New Testament Canon: Its Making and Meaning* (Philadelphia: Fortress, 1985), 57–59; E. Ferguson, 'Factors Leading to the Selection and Closure of the New Testament Canon', in *The Canon Debate*, 296–309.

[12] Gamble, *The New Testament Canon*, 83.

including Qumran had been mishandled and that many of the earlier debates revealed Christian theological biases, much attention was given in describing the historical development of the canonical process in a neutral, scientific terminology of religious phenomenology. Characteristic of this emphasis were the voices of Albertz[13] and Philip Davies in the Old Testament, and those of Räisänen, Funk, and Pagels in the New Testament.

In 1986, J.J. Collins[14] seemed to speak for a larger group in declaring: 'the decline (of Biblical Theology) is evident in the fact that an increasing number of scholars no longer regard theology as the ultimate focus of biblical studies or even as a necessary dimension of those studies at all.' Similarly, Philip Davies[15] spoke of canon formation as a 'cultural phenomenon' ... 'a natural process' in any literate society. The formation of a canon is an exercise of power by a privileged class, defining class values by controlling the politics of reading. Finally, J. Blenkinsopp[16] described canon as the resolution of ideological conflicts, the imposition of an ideology or orthodoxy by force or compromise.

One can only wonder whether such history-of-religions categories will prove more objective and unbiased than the theological ones being replaced. Can such an approach generate enough empathy for interpreting religious texts where the perspective is often radically alien to the entire Western mentality?

Canon and community

A very common emphasis in the newer approach to canon has been the link between canon and community (e.g. Sanders and Carr[17]). This linkage is, of course, highly reasonable since authoritative Scripture is acknowledged as canon by a group, not just by individuals. It is the response of a community that constitutes a canon. Certainly the idea of a multiplicity of religious communities within Israel, acting as tradents of tradition, was central to the

---

[13] R. Albertz, *A History of Israelite Religion in the Old Testament Period* (2 vols.; Louisville: Westminster John Knox, 1994).

[14] J.J. Collins, 'Is a Critical Biblical Theology Possible?', in *The Hebrew Bible and Its Interpreters* (eds. W.H. Propp et al.; Winona Lake: Eisenbrauns, 1990), 1–17.

[15] P.D. Davies, *Whose Bible Is It Anyway?* (Sheffield: Sheffield Academic Press, 1995), 17–27.

[16] J. Blenkinsopp, 'The Formation of the Hebrew Bible: Isaiah as a Test Case', in *The Canon Debate*, 53–67.

[17] J.A. Sanders, *Canon and Community: A Guide to Canonical Criticism* (Philadelphia: Fortress, 1984); D.M. Carr, 'Canonization in the Context of Community: An Outline of the Formation of the TANAKH and the Christian Bible', in *A Gift of God in Due Season: Essays on Scripture and Community in Honor of James A. Sanders* (eds. R.D. Weis and D.M. Carr; Sheffield: Sheffield Academic Press, 1996), 22–64.

traditio-critical enterprise which emerged in the decades preceding and following World War II.

What then is new in the recent approach to community developed by Sanders and others? Canon functions now as a means of a community by which to create, maintain, and adapt its authoritative Scriptures in such a way as to meet its own evolving needs. Because the community's historical context continues to change, the canon retains its relevance for its ongoing life by adapting its Scriptures to conform to the shifting cultural challenges. Canon thus served to identify the community's self-understanding and to reinforce group consciousness.

However, I would argue that this anthropocentric, sociological interpretation of canon for a community is a modem, oblique history-of-religions reading of its role. In contrast, according to the Old Testament pattern (cf. Deut. 31:9–13) the formation of a written authoritative corpus was theocentric in orientation. It identified the will of God for successive generations so that they might live in accordance with the enduring commands of God expressed in Torah. It is not simply a flexible paradigm without an established content.

Canon and literary development

In what sense can the canonical process which led ultimately to closure in the several centuries following the rise of Christianity be traced by means of critical literary analysis of the Bible? During the end of the nineteenth century, following the hegemony of Wellhausen's source critical analysis, it was widely thought that one could correlate the literary growth of the Old Testament with the canonical process. Four distinct periods were identified for the closure of the Pentateuch (ca. 400 BC), the Prophets (ca. 200 BC), the Writings (ca. 100 BC), and the final completion by 90 AD. For a variety of historical and literary reasons, this scheme has been slowly undermined and replaced by the emphasis on diversity, flexibility, and uncertainty in setting exact historical dates for canonical closure.

Interest in the canonical process turned to focus on those historical forces which led to late closure and which were described in the non-theological terminology of the history-of-religions. Although there were a few notable exceptions, by and large, the canonical process became separated from the exegetical task of biblical interpretation. The shaping of both the Old and New Testaments derived chiefly from non-theological forces and did not contribute to the interpretive task of actual exegesis. The term 'canon consciousness' was occasionally used by a few biblical interpreters, but largely the assumption that it was an active theological force at work in shaping the structure and content of the biblical corpus was denied. The concept that theological redactions of both testaments were involved in some fashion was thought particularly unlikely and rejected (e.g. James Barr[18]). As a result, the standard New Testament introductions such as Luke Johnson's or Raymond Brown's, attributed little or no exegetical significance to canon. The subject was often relegated to the period after the formation of both testaments, and usually assigned to the final chapter of the introduction. Within the field of New Testament, occasionally articles (e.g. O. Cullmann and N.A. Dahl[19]) were concerned with the theological implications of the fourfold-Gospel structure or the tension caused by the extreme particularity of the Pauline letters, but the idea of a canonical intent reflected in the biblical structure was largely disregarded.

The theological and hermeneutical function of canon

As we have seen, Käsemann's understanding of canon given in his famous lecture of 1950 shattered an older theological consensus. Still his own position offered only a highly subjective canon-within-the-canon hypothesis to overcome the conflicting theologies of the Bible.

In contrast to this European debate, James A. Sanders[20] proposed the most original attempt at providing a fresh theological interpretation of the role of canon for the English-speaking academy. It was first adumbrated in his *Torah and Canon* (1972), then developed at length in his essay 'Adaptable for Life' (1976). Since then, he has reworked his essay several times with further refinements. Equally significant is that his position has been picked up and adopted by a large number of colleagues and students.

According to Sanders, the major characteristic of Scripture as canon is its dialectical movement between the poles of stability and adaptability. A canon is basically a community's paradigm for how to continue the dialogue in ever-changing, socio-political contexts. Canon functions to articulate a community's identity. It develops stable moments in the community's life by meeting its existential needs, but because its historical and social contexts fluctuate, the community adapts its canon and opens up the stable forms to accommodate its new needs and challenges. Sanders finds a classic example of this canonical process in the Hellenistic period when the Jewish canon had begun to reach a

---

[18] James Barr, *Holy Scripture: Canon, Authority, Criticism* (Philadelphia: Westminster Press, 1983).

[19] O. Cullmann, 'The Plurality of the Gospels as a Theological Problem in Antiquity', in *The Early Church* (ed. A.J.B. Higgins; Philadelphia: Westminster Press, 1956), 39–54; N.A. Dahl, 'The Particularity of the Pauline Epistles as a Problem in the Ancient Church', in *Neotestamentica et patristica: Freundesgabe O. Cullmann* (Leiden: Brill, 1962), 261–71.

[20] J.A. Sanders, 'Adaptable for Life: The Nature and Function of Canon', in *Magnalia Dei - The Mighty Acts of God: Essays on Bible and Archaeology in Memory of G. E. Wright* (New York: Doubleday, 1976), 531–60.

certain degree of stability. However, the group discovered that its canon and its stabilized form could not meet the new religious crises. Therefore, it developed the techniques of midrash by which to exploit the fluidity of its sacred texts in order to reinterpret them into new forms for regenerating its life.

Although Walter Brueggemann's[21] postmodern hermeneutic has a different agenda overall, it does share with Sanders the emphasis on the fluidity of Israel's confessional traditions. It also has in common the emphasis on the text's 'generative' quality as a means by which to transform older biblical imagery into new forms in order to address the community's changing needs.

In my opinion, the major significance of Sanders' hermeneutical proposal, which is not to be underestimated or denigrated, is his ability to reinterpret the traditional Christian understanding of canon which was viewed as an established apostolic rule-of-faith (*regula fidei*), and to refashion it into a flexible paradigm by which continually to adjust the faith to the changing needs of modernity. In this respect, he shares the deepest theological concerns of nineteenth- and twentieth-century Protestant theological liberalism.

However, in my judgment, the problems associated with this formulation of canon are wide-reaching and serious:

1. Traditionally, canon as a rule-of-faith was the church's response to a divine initiative that set forth the will of God for his redeemed people. Sanders has reversed its function from a response to a divine activity testified to in Scripture to a socio-political attempt by the community of faith at a self-definition of its own identity.

2. The Christian canon is no longer grounded in a christological center revealed in a historic incarnation, but has become a repeatable and fluid paradigm moving between two poles, but without a stable theological content.

3. The role of the Holy Spirit in constantly bringing to fresh light the written Scriptures as a divinely spoken Word has been replaced with the exercise of human imagination and ingenuity. I would further argue that the role of Jewish midrash which is central to Sanders' hermeneutical proposal is incompatible with the New Testament's understanding of the authoritative function of the Old Testament which has been continually transformed by the Spirit into the law of Christ (cf. Childs[22] for details of this argument).

---

[21] W. Brueggemann, *Theology of the Old Testament: Testimony, Dispute, Advocacy* (Minneapolis: Fortress, 1997).

[22] B.S. Childs, 'Critique of Recent Intertextual Canonical Interpretations', *ZAW* 115 (2003), 173–84.

Although I would agree that Sanders' hermeneutical model has become the dominant one, certainly in the American scene and probably also within the larger English-speaking academy, it would be amiss not to mention several recent minority proposals which I would judge to be far more theologically adequate. First, in his essay in *The Canon Debate,* Robert W. Wall[23] stressed the enduring theological interest in the final literary product of the canonical process and that the role of the apostolic witness to Jesus Christ is maintained. Then again, François Bovon wrote in his essay of the early structural linkage within the New Testament between the Gospels and the apostolic witness, that is, between revelation and history. Thus the canonical structure of the New Testament establishes an 'indispensable apostolic mediation.'[24] Finally, Richard Bauckham[25] has broken open an important fresh perspective on the canonical process when arguing that the Gospels were written at the outset for all Christians, for every church they might reach. (I have omitted mentioning Stephen Chapman's[26] important contribution because, although written in English, it arises more out of the German context, cf. below).

A summary of an emerging consensus

I began my reflections on 'the era of the canon' debate within the English-speaking world and argued that one could establish fairly precisely the beginnings of this renewed interest in the 1960s. I then sought to describe the various stimuli that evoked this interest and to characterize its major areas of research. Now I would like to argue that one can designate, to a certain degree, an ending of this period. Of course, I do not mean that suddenly interest in canon ceased, but rather that one can observe an evolving consensus. The putative gains over the last forty years are now being frequently summarized. Some of the initial excitement engendered by Sundberg along with the enthusiasm of the early monographs outlining the impact of the Qumran material has subsided.

Some of the evidence for this phase of the debate is provided by the publication of a number of standard works covering the history of research on the subject of canon. Among these I list the following consensus-oriented summaries:

---

[23] R.W. Wall, 'The Significance of a Canonical Perspective of the Church's Scripture', in *The Canon Debate*, 528–40.

[24] F. Bovon, 'The Canonical Structure of Gospel and Apostle', in *The Canon Debate*, 516–27.

[25] R. Bauckham, *The Gospel for All Christians* (Grand Rapids: Eerdmans, 1998).

[26] S.B. Chapman, *The Law and the Prophets* (Tübingen: Mohr Siebeck, 2000).

1. Articles on canon by J.A. Sanders, H. Gamble, G.T. Sheppard in *The Anchor Bible Dictionary*, Vol. I (ed. D.N. Freedman, New York: Doubleday, 1992).
2. J.J. Collins, 'Before the Canon: Scriptures in Second Temple Judaism', *Old Testament Interpretation Past, Present, and Future: Essays in Honour of G.M. Tucker* (eds. J.L. Mays, D.L. Petersen, K.H. Richards; Edinburgh: T&T Clark, 1995), 225–41.
3. M. Sæbø (ed.), *Hebrew Bible/Old Testament. The History of Interpretation* Vol. I/1 (Göttingen: Vandenhoeck & Ruprecht, 1996).
4. D.M. McDonald and J. A. Sanders (eds.), *The Canon Debate* (Peabody: Hendrickson, 2002).
5. A.J. Hauser, and D.F. Watson (eds.), *A History of Biblical Interpretation* Vol. 1 (Grand Rapids: Eerdmans, 2003).

Also significant in the consensus that developed was the marginalizing of other important voices such as Ackroyd, Freedman, Clements, Ellis, and others.[27]

What I find noteworthy in this consensus is the turn largely to the historical growth of the Jewish and Christian canons, the use of history-of-religions categories, and the emphasis on flexibility and diversity as central to the canonical process. Ironically, this highly critical, largely secular, scientific analysis has frequently embraced in the end the hermeneutical hypothesis of J.A. Sanders ('Stability and Adaptability') as being compatible with the modern study of canon. For my part, I was left with the troubling question: Whatever has happened to traditional, orthodox Christian theology within this embrace of modernity? Are there really no other options? A partial answer came when, upon completing my analysis of the English-speaking world, I turned to examine the critical study of the canon within the modern German-speaking academy.

The German Debate Over Canon

Characteristics of the debate

At the outset, some highly distinctive features of the German debate emerge which often offer many fresh and illuminating re-evaluations of the subject of canon. As I have sought to show in my introductory remarks, German scholarship had dominated the research on canon starting in the nineteenth century, and interest had continued throughout the 1950s, as summarized by Käsemann (especially important were W. Bauer and von Campenhausen). Then there was a period of virtual silence as new approaches began to appear in the

---

[27] Cf. for details Chapman, *The Law and the Prophets*, footnote 25, pp. 20–53.

English-speaking world. By the early 1980s German interest in the newer approaches began to surface, led in part by R. Rendtorff,[28] then followed by C. Dohmen,[29] among others. Next in 1988 in volume 3 of the newly established journal, *Jahrbuch für Biblische Theologie*, an entire issue was devoted to the issues of canon.[30]

It was clear that the Germans felt that they had come somewhat late to the debate, and the article assigned to Patrick Miller[31] of Princeton served as a 'catch-up' on the American debate of the previous two decades of scholarship. However, it was highly significant that this German interest arose in the context of an ongoing discussion on the role of Biblical Theology which by that time had almost died in the English-speaking world. This lively theological context shaped decisively the nature of the succeeding German contributions. In addition, the central questions posed by the Germans were, in an important sense, an extension of the critical questions raised in the previous generation according to the traditio-critical, form-critical, and redactional-critical methodologies developed by Alt, Noth, and von Rad in the Old Testament, and Bultmann and Jeremias in the New Testament. In this regard, it is significant to observe that, while in the American debate, New Testament scholars rarely participated in the canon debate, German New Testament scholars were deeply involved from the start (Stuhlmacher, Hossfeld, Frankemölle, Mussner, Söding, etc.).

Another characteristic that distinguished the German interest in canon was its much stronger sense of Christian dogmatics which was evident whether in the Lutheran, Reformed, or Catholic traditions. This feature became especially evident in the lead shortly taken by German Roman Catholic scholars, a large number of whom served in religious orders. The debate over canon remained, by and large, church-oriented, and explicit attention was also paid to the liturgical and sacramental dimensions of canon. Also among the Catholics the theological role of the Septuagint, the Vulgate, Church Fathers, and the history of interpretation was high on the agenda in the ensuing canonical debate.

Finally, an intense interest in the effect of the Holocaust pervaded many of the recent discussions among the younger second generation of German

---

[28] R. Rendtorff, *Canon and Theology* (Minneapolis: Fortress, 1993).

[29] C. Dohmen and M. Oeming, *Biblischer Kanon – Warum and Wozu?* (Quaestiones Disputae 137; Freiburg: Herder, 1992); C. Dohmen, 'Vom vielfachen Schriftsinn – Möglichkeiten und Grenzen neuerer Zugänge zu biblischen Texten', in *Neue Formen der Schriftauslegung* (Quaestiones Disputae 140; ed. F. Sternberg; Freiburg: Herder, 1992), 13–74. C. Dohmen and T. Söding (eds.), *Eine Bibel – Zwei Testamente* (Paderborn: Schöningh, 1995).

[30] *Zum Problem des biblischen Kanon. Jahrbuch für Biblische Theologie*, 3 (1988).

[31] P.D. Miller, 'Der Kanon in der gegenwärtigen amerikanischen Diskussion', *JBTh* 3 (1988), 217–39.

academics following World War II, and led to an intense and ongoing debate on the relationship of the Old and New Testaments, especially regarding the hermeneutics of the Jewish Bible. Of course, this concern lay deeply within the official Catholic ecclesial pronouncements of Vatican II and the Papal Biblical Commission of 1963, evoking an ongoing dialogue within both Catholic and Protestant circles.[32]

Details of the Debate

The terminology of canon

The sharp distinction of Sundberg between Scripture and canon was not adopted within the German debate. Rather, within the larger traditional category of Sacred Scripture, a distinction was made between the canonical process and the end product of canonization (cf. Riekert's and Chapman's arguments against Sundberg's sharp distinction[33]). As a result, the focus did not fall exclusively on the historical forces at work in the process which dominated the English-speaking debate.

Canon and the hermeneutical problem of exegesis

From the outset the German debate developed within a theological framework. Dohmen's assertion was widely shared: 'The canon in its significance for Biblical Theology can hardly be overestimated.'[34] Moreover, very shortly an older controversy going back to the 1920s between Eissfeldt and Eichrodt was reintroduced, namely, the relation between theology of the Old Testament and *Religionsgeschichte* (history-of-religion). The newer form of this debate had been launched by R. Albertz[35] in 1992, which was supported by the so-called Copenhagen school (N.P. Lemche and T.L.

---

[32] Cf. *Interpretation der Bibel in der Kirche: Das Dokument der Päpstlichen Bibelkommission vom 23.4.1993* (SBS 161; Stuttgart: Katholisches Bibelwerk, 1995); Cf. the most recent document, 'The Jewish People and Their Sacred Scriptures in the Christian Bible', from the Pontifical Biblical Commission, 2001. Its contents are reviewed by R. Rutter, *ProEccl* 13 (2004), 13–24.

[33] S.J.P.K. Riekert, 'Critical Research and the One Christian Canon Comprising Two Testaments', *Neot* 14 (1981), 21–41; and Stephen Chapman, '"Canon" versus "Scripture"', *The Law and the Prophets*, 106–10.

[34] C. Dohmen, 'Probleme und Chancen Biblischer Theologie aus alttestamentlicher Sicht', *Eine Bibel – Zwei Testamente*, 15.

[35] R. Albertz, 'Religionsgeschichte Israels statt Theologie des Alten Testaments! Plädoyer für eine forschungsgeschichtliche Umorientierung', *JBTh* 10 (1995), 3–

Thompson[36]), and the Finnish New Testament scholar, H. Räisänen.[37] However, when the subject was debated in 1995 (*JBTh* 10), it was noticeable how little support it received in this radically secular form. Rather, among the Germans there emerged almost a received consensus that the issue was not an 'either/or,' but instead a 'both/and.' In sum, *Religionsgeschichte* could offer some useful, even necessary insights from the perspective of comparative religions, sociology, and the like, but it was not a substitute for Biblical Theology (cf. Rendtorff, Crüsemann, Lohfink in the *JBTh* 10, and the more recent essay of O. Keel[38] in 2001).

It was also characteristic of the German Catholic debate over biblical hermeneutics that the official church pronouncements, both those in the earlier encyclicals (1895, 1943) and the pontifical biblical commission reports, played an important role in channeling the theological debate. Lohfink[39] pushed the dialogue forward when, in an incisive essay, he contrasted two very different emphases respecting the interpretation of Scripture within the one papal commission document (*Dei Verbum*, article 12, 1963). In its introduction the document affirmed the right of a critical study of Scripture set forth in the 1943 encyclical. Then it focused on the role of critical exegesis in recovering the intent of the original biblical author. However, there then followed an addition. In order to understand what God intended to say for today in the biblical text, the faithful interpreter had to observe the unity of the living tradition from all of Scripture according to the traditions of the whole church and the analogy of faith. Lohfink stressed the seriousness of the hermeneutical problem in failing to establish the relationship between the two statements. Could God intend something different from the biblical text?

Much of the debate, both within the Catholic and Protestant churches, arose in a sense to develop a new exegetical paradigm by which to overcome this kind of impasse. Leaders in the field from the Protestant side were B. Janowski, R. Rendtorff, and M. Oeming; from the Catholic side: N. Lohfink, C. Dohmen, E. Zenger, T. Söding, H. Frankemölle, W. Gross, among many others.

---

[36] N.P. Lemche, 'Warum die Theologie des Alten Testaments einen Irrweg darstellt', *JBTh* 10 (1995), 79–92; T.L. Thompson, 'Das Alte Testament als Theologische Disziplin', *JBTh* 10 (1995), 57–73.

[37] H. Räisänen, *Beyond New Testament Theology* (Philadelphia: Westminster John Knox, 1990).

[38] O. Keel., 'Religionsgeschichte Israels oder Theologie des Alten Testaments?', in *Wieviel Systematik erlaubt die Schrift?* (Questiones Disputae 185; ed. Frank-Lothar Hossfeld; Freiburg: Herder, 2001), 88–109.

[39] N. Lohfink, Der weisse Fleck, in *Dei Verbum, Artikel 12'*, *Trierer Theologische Zeitschrift* 101 (1992), 20–35.

Among the larger concern to develop a canonically oriented form of theology, there emerged widely divergent proposals. Lohfink[40] sought to limit theological reflection to the final form (*Endgestalt*) of the biblical text after its stabilization. He relegated the earlier stages of its growth to a separate discipline of historical theology. Then he argued for a consistent synchronic exegesis that closely pursued the canonical order of the text. However, this approach was sharply criticized by W. Gross[41] who, along with a majority, felt critical *Religionsgeschichte* and Biblical Theology were integrally connected and thus a diachronic dimension was essential to exegesis.

Much more characteristic of the new hermeneutical attempts was the commonly shared attention to the use of the canonical process which lay deeply embedded in the structure of the canon and served to illuminate a literary process commensurate with the polyphony of voices evidenced in both testaments. For example, in the search to understand the canonical unity of the Old Testament, in spite of its enormous diversity in form and content, Dohmen and Oeming[42] were able to show signs of early canonical structuring of the Pentateuch in Deuteronomy 34, the larger literary function of the canonical formula in Deuteronomy 13:1 (ET v. 32), and the expanded sapiential role of the conclusion of the book of Ecclesiastes in encompassing wisdom traditions according to an intertextual relationship.[43] While in one sense, the tools of redaction criticism were used, the force of this analysis was driven by the inner-biblical resonance of the canonical shaping. Another illuminating example of the intertextual link between the Old and New Testaments was provided by Janowski[44] in his analysis of the role of the Psalter in the Marcan passion story.

One of the most impressive attempts to offer a new hermeneutical paradigm was offered by C. Dohmen[45] when he argued that the unifying force of the canon lay in providing an ongoing history of exegetical reinterpretation which linked the diversity of biblical voices into a coherent pattern. Of course, how exactly this occurs remains often contested. Söding objected to Dohmen's formulation of theology as the interpretation of Scripture (*Theologie als Schriftauslegung*) lest Scripture fail to remain a witness to a reality outside of itself.[46] Dohmen was also one of the first to develop the hermeneutical

---

[40] N. Lohfink, 'Alttestamentliche Wissenschaft als Theologie? 44 Thesen', in *Wieviel Systematik erlaubt die Schrift?*, 13–47.

[41] W. Gross, 'Ist biblisch-theologische Auslegung ein integrierender Methodenschritt?', *Wieviel Systematik erlaubt die Schrift?*, 110–49.

[42] C. Dohmen and M. Oeming, *Biblischer Kanon – Warum and Wozu?*, 30–75.

[43] Chapman, *The Law and the Prophets*, 150–234.

[44] B. Janowski, '"Verstehst du auch, was du liest?" Reflexionen auf die Leserichtung der christlichen Bibel', in *Wieviel Systematik erlaubt die Schrift?*, 150–91.

[45] C. Dohmen and M. Oeming, *Biblischer Kanon – Warum and Wozu?*, 91ff.

[46] T. Söding, 'Spannungen und Widersprüche, Kohärenzen und Konvergenzen aus katholischer Perspektive', *TRev* 99 (2003), 6.

implications of reception theory that emphasized the mutual interaction of the biblical text and the reader's intentionality, a position which was to play an increasing role in his proposal for a Jewish–Christian dialogue on the basis of a common Scripture.

Jewish–Christian dialogue

A highly significant development occurred in the second generation of German biblical scholars after the end of World War II. Immediately following the end of the war when the full extent of the Holocaust became known, both Protestant and Catholic churches produced a series of statements confessing the Christian church's failure to show solidarity with Jews and not to have actively resisted the genocidal madness of National Socialism. In spite of books with such titles as *Theology after Auschwitz*, there was little direct impact on biblical interpretation until the early 1980s. Then there was a virtual explosion of interest in Germany, first led by R. Rendtorff, but then greatly expanded by German Catholic Old and New Testament scholars.

During the same period there had been numerous Jewish and Christian dialogues among biblical scholars in North America. Probably one of the best known was a symposium entitled *Hebrew Bible or Old Testament? Study of the Bible in Judaism and Christianity* (1990).[47] Yet even here the difference in approach between the English-speaking and the German scholars was striking. The American discussion arose from within a largely secular academic context, but also shared some of the concerns of liberal Protestant ecumenicity. It questioned the appropriateness of the continuing use of such traditional Christian terminology as 'Old Testament' within a multicultural environment which was well represented by Jews. In contrast, the German discussion arose in part from the interest in Biblical Theology's use of two distinct testaments, but even more importantly, from the theological issues raised for Christian theology from the catastrophic Holocaust which had engulfed Europe. In a word, the debate in Germany was from the start highly theological and sought to move the church in a new direction towards Judaism by rethinking the basic problem of the relationship of the two testaments within the Christian Bible, one of which was inherited by Christians from Judaism.

Rendtorff's articles[48] were initially directed to the practical problems of establishing a dialogue between Jews and Christians concerning their common Scriptures. He argued for Christians to show respect for Jewish biblical interpretation and to acknowledge its continuing value and religious integrity for

---

[47] Cf. footnote 14.

[48] R. Rendtorff, 'Toward a Common Jewish-Christian Reading of the Hebrew Bible', in *Canon and Theology*, 31–45.

Christians. Rendtorff's concerns were picked up by K. Koch[49] in a now familiar formulation: 'The Double Reception of the Old Testament in Judaism and Christianity.' However, Koch's arguments were largely oriented towards a history-of-religions perspective and did not address the theological problems in depth.

The same was not the case among the German Catholic scholars whose initial emphasis fell on the need to recover the whole Christian Bible consisting of the Jewish Scripture and the New Testament. Without serious attention to the former, the church had only the half-truth of its Scriptures.[50] In order then to buttress their arguments, several important monographs[51] appeared that focused in great detail on individual topics considered crucial to the theological dialogue, namely, the one irrevocable covenant, and the role of Torah. The overwhelming emphasis of these volumes fell on the unbroken continuity between the Old and New Testaments.

Moreover, increasingly the theological significance of canon was explored. Wide agreement arose that the Jewish Scripture which had been accepted by the Christian church as authoritative largely in an unredacted state, formed the grounds for all Christian theology. Indeed, Christian theology without the Old Testament was deemed impossible. Zenger[52] further developed his canonical approach in a lengthy *Introduction to the Old Testament*, half of which he himself wrote, but the latter part he shared with his students and colleagues. Not only did he press the importance of speaking of the Old Testament as the 'First Testament,' but he argued that the New Testament was actually to be understood as a commentary on the Jewish Scriptures. Somewhat akin, Lohfink[53] defended the view that the newness of the New Testament was in its 'bringing into light' (*Ins-Licht-Treten*) the message of the Old Testament. Its content was already found in the Old, but its manifestation varied because of Jesus Christ.

Nevertheless, it would be misleading to suggest that Zenger's view formed a Catholic consensus. Far from it. In a highly critical response Rudolf Mosis

---

[49] K. Koch, 'Der doppelte Ausgang des Alten Testaments in Judentum und Christentum', *JBTh* 6 (1991), 215–42.

[50] C. Dohmen and F. Mussner, *Nur die halbe Wahrheit? Für die Einheit der ganzen Bibel* (Freiburg: Herder, 1993).

[51] N. Lohfink, *Der niemals gekündigte Bund. Exegetische Gedanken zum christlich-jüdischen Dialog* (Freiburg: Herder 1985); E. Zenger (ed.), *Die Tora als Kanon für Juden und Christen* (Freiburg: Herder, 1996).

[52] E. Zenger, *Einleitung in das Alte Testament* (3rd edn.; Stuttgart: Kohlhammer, 1998); *Das Erste Testament. Die jüdische Bibel und die Christen* (Düsseldorf: Patmos Verlag, 1991).

[53] N. Lohfink, 'Eine Bibel – Zwei Testamente', in *Eine Bibel – Zwei Testamente*, 75.

(1997)[54] characterized Zenger's interpretation of the Old Testament as substituting a Jewish interpretation for the traditional Catholic understanding. Similarly, the New Testament scholar H. Frankmölle[55] was dissatisfied with Zenger's description of the New Testament as a commentary on the Old. More representative of the newer Catholic position was Dohmen's argument that the theology of the Christian Bible was best understood as a continuing history of interpretation as representing an ongoing dialogue between the two testaments.

Equally important in the hermeneutical debate were the questions raised both regarding the continuing role of the Jewish Scriptures and the religious experience of the Jewish community of faith in the pre- and post-Christian era. Dohmen[56] repeatedly pointed out that Jews were shaped by their Scriptures long before the rise of Christianity. Moreover, Judaism has its own history with the revelation of God in Scripture and this double reception of the Hebrew Bible in its very independence from Christianity forms the basis for a continuing force equal in status with the Christian. The fact of this double reception of a common Scripture calls for a continuing dialogical relation between church and synagogue.

In recent years, Dohmen[57] has moved strongly into the field of reception theory. The biblical text is not to be studied simply as a document of Israel's *Religionsgeschichte* from the past, but its hermeneutical function lies in establishing a communication between author and reader, between the giver and receiver of the message. Accordingly, the phenomenon of canon can only be understood within a community of faith (*Glaubensgemeinschaft*) from which a communicative function arises. The act of reception, whether by its first or subsequent recipient, determines its interactive meaning which Dohmen describes in three types: the author, the text itself, and the reader. Dohmen draws the implication that in the light of the double reception of a common Scripture by two distinct communities, an ongoing dialogue is required between Jews and Christians, carried on as equal partners.

Finally, in a profound and passionate presentation of the need for a pluralistic interpretation of Scripture according to the new insights of reception

---

[54] R. Mosis, 'Canonical Approach und Vielfalt des Kanons – Zu einer neuen Einleitung in das Alte Testament', *Trierer Theologische Zeitschrift* 106 (1997), 39–59.

[55] H. Frankmölle, 'Das Neue Testament als Kommentar? Möglichkeiten und Grenzen einer hermeneutischen These aus der Sicht eines Neutestamentlers', in *Wieviel Systematik erlaubt die Schrift?*, 200–78.

[56] C. Dohmen and G. Stemberger, *Hermeneutik der Jüdischen Bibel und des Alten Testaments* (Stuttgart: Kohlhammer, 1996), 133–213.

[57] Dohmen and Stemberger, *Hermeneutik der Jüdischen Bibel*, 192–213.

theory, Dohmen[58] reaffirms the enduring role of the historical-critical approach to the Bible as addressing a different set of issues from those of the various alternative proposals provided by reception theory. Historical criticism deals with the meaning of a text in its original historical context. It focuses on a text from the perspective of the past, according to its growth and transmission. In spite of these limitations in not being able to address the reader of today's world directly, its contribution is enduring and serves as a critical corrective to the various forms of exegesis arising from reception theory. However, in the end, Dohmen sees the challenge of pluralism somewhat akin to the advocates of postmodernism – *ein relationaler Pluralismus der Auslegungsarten* – as a means of addressing the widest range of theological problems, and of checking any move toward entrenchment by the church in its mission to the world.

To summarize: a survey of the role of canon within the German-speaking academy brought to light a very different focus from that of the English-speaking world. By remaining primarily church-oriented, it was able to wrestle with the modern task of biblical interpretation from a canonical perspective in a far profounder theological manner and to break open many new intellectual frontiers. Yet, ironically, the challenge of modernity has also, in the end, pushed the German debate into some of the same areas which occupied the English-speaking academy from the outset. Accordingly, from my perspective, there remain major theological and hermeneutical issues at stake which I will seek briefly to outline in my concluding reflections.

Retrospective Reflections on the Canon Debate

1. There are many features of the German debate that I fully embrace:

(a)   At the heart of the canon debate lies a series of theological problems whose resolution falls within the field of Biblical Theology. The German debate largely retained this focus.

(b)   The continuing attention by Catholic biblical scholars to the pronouncement of the church, even when often critical in response, kept their scholarship in active conversation with Christian theological tradition.

(c)   The basic hermeneutical problem of the growth of the canon was not posed in the German debate as one between canonical process and final form interpretation, as mistakenly occurred in the English-speaking academy. Rather it turned on the nature of the process and the nature of the final form. Accordingly, how the canon functions both as a *norma*

---

[58]   C. Dohmen, 'Vom vielfachen Schriftsinn – Möglichkeiten und Grenzen neuerer Zugänge zu biblischen Texten', in *Neue Formen der Schriftauslegung*, 13–74.

normans and a *norma normata* is crucial for both a historical and theological understanding.

(d) The German debate correctly understood the critical centrality of the theological relationship between the two testaments and rightly focused on the Jewish–Christian dialogue.

2. Nevertheless, from my perspective, there remain serious theological problems that evoke my strong disagreement with aspects of the German debate:

(a) The first issue focuses on the subject matter of Scripture. The problem emerges directly in the controversy between the role of historical criticism and theological (that is, canonical) interpretation. In modern Catholicism since the encyclical of 1943, the historical critical approach to biblical studies has been fully embraced. I judge this move to have been correct, especially when viewed in the historical context of the Catholic church's earlier dogmatic position.

However, I think that this hermeneutical relationship must be viewed in a far more subtle, indeed dialectical manner, because of the unique character of the biblical subject matter. The Bible in its human, fully time-conditioned form, functions theologically for the church as a witness to God's divine revelation in Jesus Christ. The church confesses that in this human form, the Holy Spirit unlocks its truthful message to its hearers in the mystery of faith. This theological reading cannot be simply fused with a historical-critical reconstruction of the biblical text, neither, conversely, can it be separated. This is to say, the Bible's witness to the creative and salvific activity of God in time and space cannot be encompassed within the categories of historical criticism whose approach filters out this very kerygmatic dimension of God's activity.

In a word, the divine and human dimension remains inseparably intertwined, but in a highly profound, theological manner. Its ontological relation finds its closest analogy in the incarnation of Jesus Christ, truly man and truly God. The present danger of Catholic biblical scholarship is that in its genuine sense of freedom from rigid dogmatic restraints, it has moved into the pitfalls of liberal Protestantism in its embrace of modernity along with all of its critical methodologies.

(b) Second, I judge that the understanding of Christology by many modern biblical scholars has been inadequate when developing the relation between the Old and New Testaments. The church has always confessed that the Old Testament is an integral part of the Christian Bible because of its witness to Jesus Christ. Of course, just how this confession has been understood has varied in the history of the church. Yet the newness of the New Testament in its witness to Jesus Christ is of a different order from that of the Old Testament. The gospel is neither simply an extension of the old covenant, nor is it to be interpreted merely as a commentary on the Jewish Scriptures, but it is an explosion of God's good news. The theological paradox is that the radically new has already been testified to by the Old (cf. Mk. 1:12; Heb. 1:1).[59]

(c) Third, I do not feel that the profoundly apocalyptic nature of Pauline theology – the cross as divine rectification of the ungodly, gospel versus law, God's eschatological victory over evil – has been adequately reflected in the recent canonical debate. Indeed there is a mystery between the church and Israel with which Paul wrestles (Rom. 9 – 11). Yet there remains a dark side of the New Testament's witness. A hardening has come on part of Israel. Jesus was rejected by his own people and the Messiah of God was crucified. To be sure, reconciliation is a divine promise: 'all Israel will be saved' (Rom. 11:26). However, it will not be accomplished by religious pluralism or ecumenical inclusivity, but by a divine eschatological event.

(d) Finally, I fear that increasingly the German debate over canon runs the risk, particularly evident in the English-speaking world, of fragmenting the theological issues crucial to canon into historical minutiae. By assigning the function of canon to one of the many alternative options for interpreting the Bible provided by reception theory, the initial promise afforded to theology from its Scriptures has become increasingly blurred and rendered helpless before the onslaughts of modernity.

Fortunately, in spite of it all, when the church of today confesses its Christian belief with the creed, it does so by affirming its Apostolic faith as one shaped 'in accordance with the Scriptures.'

---

[59] C.R. Seitz, 'Old Testament or Hebrew Bible? Some Theological Considerations', *ProEccl* 5 (1996), 292–303.

Bibliography

Albertz, R., *A History of Israelite Religion in the Old Testament Period* (2 vols.; Louisville: Westminster John Knox, 1994)

—, 'Religionsgeschichte Israels statt Theologie des Alten Testaments!', *JBTh* 10 (1995), 3–24

Barr, J., *Holy Scripture: Canon, Authority, Criticism* (Philadelphia: Westminster Press, 1983)

Barton, J., *The Spirit and the Letter* (London: SPCK, 1997)

Bauckham, R., *The Gospel for All Christians: Rethinking the Gospel Audiences* (Grand Rapids: Eerdmans, 1998)

Beckwith, R.T., *The Old Testament Canon of the New Testament Church* (Grand Rapids: Eerdmans, 1985)

Blenkinsopp, J., 'The Formation of the Hebrew Bible: Isaiah as a Test Case', in *The Canon Debate* (ed. L.M. McDonald and J.A. Sanders; Peabody, MA: Hendrickson, 2002), 53–67

Bovon, F., 'The Canonical Structure of Gospel and Apostle', in *The Canon Debate* (ed. L.M. McDonald and J.A. Sanders; Peabody, MA: Hendrickson, 2002), 516–27

Brueggemann, W., *Theology of the Old Testament: Testimony, Dispute, Advocacy* (Minneapolis: Fortress, 1997)

Carr, D.M., 'Canonization in the Context of Community: An Outline of the Formation of the TANAKH and the Christian Bible', in *A Gift of God in Due Season: Essays on Scripture and Community in Honor of James A. Sanders* (ed. R.D. Weis and D.M. Carr; Sheffield: Sheffield Academic Press, 1996), 22–64

Chapman, S., *The Law and the Prophets: A Study in Old Testament Canon Formation* (Tübingen: Mohr Siebeck, 2000)

Childs, B.S., 'Critique of Recent Intertextual Canonical Interpretations', *ZAW* 115 (2003), 173–84

Collins, J.J., 'Is a Critical Biblical Theology Possible?' in *The Hebrew Bible and Its Interpreters* (ed. W.H. Propp et al.; Winona Lake: Eisenbrauns, 1990), 1–17

Cullmann, O., 'The Plurality of the Gospels as a Theological Problem in Antiquity', in *The Early Church* (ed. A.J.B. Higgins; Philadelphia: Westminster, 1956), 39–54

Dahl, N.A., 'The Particularity of the Pauline Epistles as a Problem in the Ancient Church', in *Neotestamentica et patristica: Eine Freundesgabe, Herrn Prof. Dr. Oscar Cullmann zu seinem 60. Geburtstag überreicht* (Leiden: Brill, 1962), 261–71

Davies, P.D., *Whose Bible Is It Anyway?* (Sheffield: Sheffield Academic Press, 1995)

Dohmen, C., 'Vom vielfachen Schriftsinn – Möglichkeiten und Grenzen neuerer Zugänge zu biblischen Texten', in *Neue Formen der Schriftauslegung* (ed. F. Sternberg; Quaestiones Disputatae 140; Freiburg: Herder, 1992), 13–74

—, and F. Mussner, *Nur die halbe Wahrheit? Für die Einheit der ganzen Bibel* (Freiburg: Herder, 1993)

—, and M. Oeming, *Biblischer Kanon – Warum und Wozu* (Quaestiones Disputae 137; Freiburg: Herder, 1992)

—, and T. Söding (eds.), *Eine Bibel – Zwei Testamente* (Paderborn: Schöningh, 1995)

—, and G. Stemberger, *Hermeneutik der Jüdischen Bibel und des Alten Testaments* (Stuttgart: Kohlhammer, 1996), 133–213

Ferguson, E., 'Factors Leading to the Selection and Closure of the New Testament Canon', in *The Canon Debate* (ed. L.M. McDonald and J.A. Sanders; Peabody, MA: Hendrickson, 2002), 296–309

Frankemölle, H., 'Das Neue Testament als Kommentar? Möglichkeiten und Grenzen einer hermeneutischen These aus der Sicht eines Neutestamentlers', in *Wieviel Systematik erlaubt die Schrift?* (ed. Frank-Lothar Hossfeld; Questiones Disputae 185; Freiburg: Herder, 2001), 200–78

Gamble, H.Y., *The New Testament Canon: Its Making and Meaning* (Philadelphia: Fortress, 1985)

Gross, W., 'Ist biblisch-theologische Auslegung ein integrierender Methodenschritt?', in *Wieviel Systematik erlaubt die Schrift?* (ed. Frank-Lothar Hossfeld; Questiones Disputae 185; Freiburg: Herder, 2001), 110–49

Interpretation der Bibel in der Kirche: Das Dokument der Päpstlichen Bibelkommission vom 23.4.1993 (SBS 161; Stuttgart: Katholisches Bibelwerk, 1995)

Janowski, B., '"Verstehst du auch, was du liest?" Reflexionen auf die Leserichtung der christlichen Bibel', in *Wieviel Systematik erlaubt die Schrift?* (ed. Frank-Lothar Hossfeld; Questiones Disputae 185; Freiburg: Herder, 2001), 150–91

Käsemann, E., *Das Neue Testament als Kanon* (Göttingen: Vandenhoeck & Ruprecht, 1970)

Keel., O., 'Religionsgeschichte Israels oder Theologie des Alten Testaments?', in *Wieviel Systematik erlaubt die Schrift?* (ed. Frank-Lothar Hossfeld; Questiones Disputae 185; Freiburg: Herder, 2001), 88–109

Koch, K., 'Der doppelte Ausgang des Alten Testaments in Judentum und Christentum', *JBTh* 6 (1991), 215–42

Leiman, S.Z., *The Canonization of the Hebrew Scripture: The Talmudic and Midrashic Evidence* (Hamden, CT: Archon, 1976)

Lemche, N.P., 'Warum die Theologie des Alten Testaments einen Irrweg darstellt', *JBTh* 10 (1995), 79–92

Lewis, J.P., 'What Do We Mean by Jabneh?' *JBR* 32 (1964), 125–32

Lightstone, J.N., 'The Rabbis' Bible: The Canon of the Hebrew Bible and the Early Rabbinic Guild', in *The Canon Debate* (ed. L.M. McDonald and J.A. Sanders; Peabody, MA: Hendrickson, 2002), 163–84

Lohfink, N., *Der niemals gekündigte Bund: Exegetische Gedanken zum christlich-jüdischen Dialog* (Freiburg: Herder, 1985)

—, 'Der weisse Fleck, in *Dei Verbum*, Artikel 12', *Trierer Theologische Zeitschrift* 101 (1992), 20–35

—, 'Alttestamentliche Wissenschaft als Theologie? 44 Thesen', in *Wieviel Systematik erlaubt die Schrift?* (ed. Frank-Lothar Hossfeld; Questiones Disputae 185; Freiburg: Herder, 2001), 13–47

McDonald, L.M., *The Formation of the Christian Canon* (2nd edn.; Peabody, MA: Hendrickson, 1995)

Metzger, B.M., *The Canon of the New Testament* (Oxford: Clarendon, 1987)

Miller, P.D., 'Der Kanon in der gegenwärtigen amerikanischen Diskussion', *JBTh* 3 (1988), 217–39

Moore, G.F., *Judaism in the First Centuries of the Christian Era: The Age of the Tannaim* (3 vols.; Cambridge, MA: Harvard University Press, 1927–30)

Mosis, R., 'Canonical Approach und Vielfalt des Kanons – Zu einer neuen Einleitung in das Alte Testament', *Trierer Theologische Zeitschrift* 106 (1997), 39–59

The Pontifical Biblical Commission, *The Jewish People and Their Sacred Scriptures in the Christian Bible* (Vatican Documents; Città del Vaticano: Libreria Editrice Vaticana, 2002)

Räisänen, H., *Beyond New Testament Theology: A Story and a Programme* (Philadelphia: Westminster John Knox, 1990)

Rendtorff, R., *Canon and Theology: Overtures to an Old Testament Theology* (Minneapolis: Fortress, 1993)

Riekert, S.J.P.K., 'Critical Research and the One Christian Canon Comprising Two Testaments', *Neot* 14 (1981), 21–41

Rutter, R., '"The Jewish People and Their Sacred Scriptures in the Christian Bible" From the Pontifical Biblical Commission, 2001. Some Incipient Reflections on The Jewish People and Their Sacred Scriptures in the Christian Bible', *ProEccl* 13 (2004), 13–24

Sanders, J.A., 'Adaptable for Life: The Nature and Function of Canon', in *Magnalia Dei – The Mighty Acts of God: Essays on Bible and Archaeology in Memory of G. E. Wright* (New York: Doubleday, 1976), 531–60

—, *Canon and Community: A Guide to Canonical Criticism* (Philadelphia: Fortress, 1984)

—, 'The Issue of Closure in the Canonical Process', in *The Canon Debate* (ed. L.M. McDonald and J.A. Sanders; Peabody, MA: Hendrickson, 2002), 252–63

Seitz, C.R., 'Old Testament or Hebrew Bible? Some Theological Considerations', *ProEccl* 5 (1996), 292–303

Söding, T., 'Spannungen und Widersprüche, Kohärenzen und Konvergenzen aus katholischer Perspektive', *TRev* 99 (2003), 3–20

Sundberg, A.C., *The Old Testament of the Early Church* (Cambridge, MA: Harvard University Press, 1964)

Thompson, T.L., 'Das Alte Testament als theologische Disziplin', *JBTh* 10 (1995), 57–73

Ulrich, E., 'The Notion and Definition of Canon', in *The Canon Debate* (ed. L.M. McDonald and J.A. Sanders; Peabody, MA: Hendrickson, 2002), 21–35

Wall, R.W., 'The Significance of a Canonical Perspective of the Church's Scripture', in *The Canon Debate* (ed. L.M. McDonald and J.A. Sanders; Peabody, MA: Hendrickson, 2002), 528–40

Zenger, E., *Das Erste Testament: Die jüdische Bibel und die Christen* (Düsseldorf: Patmos Verlag, 1991)

— (ed.), *Die Tora als Kanon für Juden und Christen* (Freiburg: Herder, 1996)

—, *Einleitung in das Alte Testament* (3rd edn.; Stuttgart: Kohlhammer, 1998)

Zum Problem des biblischen Kanon: Jahrbuch für Biblische Theologie 3 (1988)

The Canonical Approach and Theological Interpretation

Christopher R. Seitz

In previous publications I have written extensively, and appreciatively, on the canonical approach and have adopted the approach in my commentaries on Isaiah and in other writings. Much of what I say here will not be new to those familiar with my work.

Nevertheless, this consultation provides an excellent opportunity to review the reactions to the canonical approach and to organize a fresh assessment of its strengths and of the horizons that extend out in front of an important movement in theological interpretation.

Additionally, one can note a raft of new publications promoting an avenue of approach broadly termed 'the theological interpretation of Scripture.' It will be useful therefore to locate the canonical approach within this broader movement by giving attention to its parameters and ongoing concerns, as well as the limits it believes are properly placed on theological reflection in the light of the witness of Old and New Testaments in one canon of Christian Scripture.

Introduction

Uncontroversial is the observation that 'canon' and 'theological interpretation' are terms with wide usage at present. Less clear is what they mean. Where once historical-critical or form- or tradition-critical were the adjectives of special coinage and currency amongst interpreters, now we can observe the limitation, recalibration, or rejection of these objective approaches, or at least a sense that something more must be done. Here the term 'hermeneutics' has pushed its way to the front.

But a lack of precision may mar what the terms canon or theological interpretation convey. Is a canonical approach 'canon criticism' and if not, what is intended by the term and to what degree does a canonical approach build upon the prior phase of critical interpretation in which historical approaches dominated, in their own diverse and sometimes confusing ways?

This essay will provide an overview of the canonical approach, as this has been associated with the work of Brevard Childs. It is a working thesis of this paper that already in 1970 Childs had laid out the basic defining features of the approach.[1] These have been modified only subtly or in extending efforts as he proceeded to publish a series of magisterial works on the Old and New Testaments, Biblical Theology and the History of Interpretation, including significant work in the book of Isaiah.[2] It is true that 'canon criticism' was an approach associated in the 1980s with James Sanders,[3] but that project took the form of hermeneutical suggestions, based upon text-critical and tradition-historical instincts, and it never developed into a full-blown approach with subsequent publications or anything like the breadth of Childs's *oeuvre*. Indeed, it would be unfair to compare the two models or evaluate the merits of the two terms, as though they were valid competitors in a market yet to make up its mind.[4]

Already in his 1970 work, *Biblical Theology in Crisis*, now thirty-five years old, one can see at least five features emerging which would prove durable and of sustained interest for a canonical approach: (1) a critiqued and recalibrated use of the historical-critical method; (2) a unique handling of the final-form of the text which, as we shall see, eschews harmonization and the peril of 'the disappearing redactor' on one side, but which also judges the partial observations of historical criticism much less compelling than the whole represented by the final stabilization of the diverse sources and traditions in a coherent literary form; (3) passing yet pregnant observations on the status of the Hebrew and Greek text-traditions; (4) sensitivity to the so-called premodern history of interpretation, and even what has been pejoratively called dogmatic reading, but with a critical evaluation of this history based upon insights from our own historical-critical season of reading and analyzing texts; and (5) biblical-theological handling of the two Testaments, in which the Old retains its voice as Christian Scripture, and Biblical Theology is more than a sensitive appreciation of how the New handles the Old – a dimension which Childs otherwise handles with aplomb in a series of fresh exegetical illustrations in the final section of that 1970 work.

---

[1] Childs, *Biblical Theology in Crisis*.

[2] *Old Testament as Scripture*; *New Testament as Canon*; *Old Testament Theology in a Canonical Context*; *Biblical Theology*; *Isaiah*; and *Struggle*.

[3] Sanders, *Torah*; *Canon and Community*; and *Sacred Story*.

[4] See, however, the analysis of Childs and Sanders (for whom the term 'canonical criticism' is deemed appropriate) by Wall, 'Reading', 370–93. Cf. also Spina, 'Canonical Criticism', 165–94.

What one sees in the 1970 publication is that a canonical approach is fully a child of its own age (I mean this in the best possible sense; see Neil MacDonald's work on Barth in which a similar point is made).[5] That may be clearer now than at the time, when the critical analysis of the then regnant historical-critical approach threatened (wrongly) to highlight only the discontinuity of the approach with what preceded. In my view, what was radical in the approach was not so much discontinuity, but what was being attempted: nothing less than the re-construction, in a new form to be sure, of the length and breadth of aspects of critical reading which had devolved into various sub-specialties, such that an organic and integrated presentation of the biblical witness might be had once again. History, literary analysis, text-criticism, Old and New Testaments, the earlier history of interpretation – all these facets were brought back onto a single field of play by a figure whose competence was only slightly, if at all, out-matched by his ambition. And history bore out the truth of that, for the next thirty-five years would show Childs making good on detailed and painstaking analysis of each of these several disciplines in a series of major publications.

The 'Canonical Approach' is a modern, historical approach, and it operates in this mode in a self-conscious sense. It does not seek to repristinate past approaches, even as it judges our capacity to learn from them, at times, blink-ered and obscured by thick historicist lenses.[6] It does not deny the historical dimension as crucial to what makes biblical texts something other than modern literature; nor the text's inherent relationship to time and space and what has been called 'ostensive reference,'[7] even as it has a view of history which is far more than this.[8] It does not ignore dimensions of the text that can only be explained by recourse to 'sources' or 'authors,' which account for divergences and tensions in the final form, but it judges the task far from complete when attention to these features fails to ask what effect has been achieved by bringing them together in one historical-theological portrayal in the final form of the text.[9]

One difficulty attending the task of presenting the 'canonical approach' for this volume is the degree to which it is tied to one individual. Almost any defense or criticism can easily become personalized, as, sadly, has been the ten-dency in some quarters.[10] It would be an incomplete or disproportionate account which only took the lead from criticisms. Yet because the project has ranged so widely, and has maintained a centrality for such a long period of time,

---

[5] MacDonald, *Karl Barth*.

[6] Seitz, *Figured Out*.

[7] Frei, *Eclipse*.

[8] Seitz, 'What Lesson Will History Teach?', 443–69.

[9] Seitz, 'Changing Face', 75–82; Rowe, 'Biblical Pressure', 295–312.

[10] Barr, *Concept of Biblical Theology*, 401–38.

it is inevitable that in its wake, specific and sometimes trenchant criticisms have been leveled. It would be artificial to proceed as if these were not a useful, if limited, way to organize a positive assessment. Fortunately, there is a small cottage industry in evaluating the contribution of Brevard Childs and the project of the 'canonical approach' associated with him,[11] and several of these have sought helpfully to referee aspects of critical engagement with him. So that need not be my chief task. It is simply an inevitable aspect of the ambition of the project of Brevard Childs that it would succeed in stirring up such a wide-scale and engaging debate. Childs has never himself majored in spotting deficiencies as a project unto itself, even as he has been a tireless evaluator of the field of biblical and theological studies.

One sadness I experience when reading Childs, especially in his later works,[12] involves the awareness that Childs is one of the last persons actually able to critique the discipline, and, more importantly, *to catalog it and identify it as a discipline in the very first place*. Postmodern attacks on objectivist approaches not only challenge historical-critical readings. They also obscure the actual historical character of the discipline of reading itself, both in its premodern and now in its modern form. Historical-critical approaches to reading once-upon-a-time declared themselves a kind of unique mode of reading, superior to what preceded in the premodern period, because capable of laying hold of a dimension of 'historicality' unknown to previous periods. This threatened to cut away one aspect of history (reception history in its premodern form) in the name of another (the 'real history' of Israel and Jesus to which the biblical texts erratically and imperfectly gave us recourse). Early practitioners could have little anticipated that the same fate would lie in store for them, as in time the need to account for the field as a coherent movement would fall to the side, now in the name of the reader in front of the text, with a tyrannical resistance to seeing him- or herself as historically limited and invariably in need of correction from a long history of reading – including now the more recent phases of historical-critical analysis. But perhaps the real culprit here was the overreaching claims of the historical-critical method, which birthed endless sub-disciplines and specialties, whose number and relationship became evermore difficult to taxonomize. Childs not only gave us a fresh approach. He is one of the last figures to comprehend the discipline he was critiquing, and control it at its maximal length and breadth, even as it was becoming too unwieldy in the wake of its own limiting claims and on the verge of crumbling because it was simply too vast an empire. Vastness is, alas, never the same thing as durable, coherent, compelling, or true.[13]

---

[11] Brett, *Biblical Criticism in Crisis?*; Noble, *Canonical Approach*.
[12] 'Canon in Recent Biblical Studies', 26–45; reprinted in the present volume.
[13] Steinmetz, 'Superiority', 27–38.

It has been argued since its inception that the canonical approach has this or that Achilles heel or minor weakness; is limited or deficient in certain key areas; or is ill-conceived and disqualified as an approach. Rarely is it said that it seeks to do too much and is disqualified by virtue of its ambition. As noted above, it is this *desire for comprehensiveness* which I shall argue is the hallmark of the canonical approach and its legacy for our day, and so the fact that this is not singled out as a fault is worth keeping in mind as we consider the various weaknesses that are said to mar the approach. As we shall see, these 'weaknesses' are often deemed to be such by those holding diametrically opposing views.

Among the several faults detected in the canonical approach, we can list: (1) insufficient attention to 'the facts of history' as constitutive of any serious theological approach; (2) lack of attention to these same facts as crucial for non-theological reasons; (3) the importation of a dogmatic lens which overreaches and is prejudicial to an 'unbiased' account of things; (4) overemphasis on the text as exercising a pressure or coercion on the reader, as an objective material witness;[14] (5) confusion about what is meant by special attention to the final form of the text, in the light of its acknowledged literary prehistory (the 'disappearing redactor' and other problems); (6) wrongful privileging of the text's final form over against earlier phases of its development, and so giving a kind of moral authority to later institutionalizing instincts instead of the 'genius of the original inspiration'; (7) the same criticism made on the grounds of a theory of original inspiration and inerrancy threatened by too many later hands at work (several Isaiahs, etc);[15] (8) wrongful attention to the 'discrete voice' of the Old Testament' as a theological witness, independently of the New;[16] (9) failure to let the God of the Old Testament be a God without reference to the New.[17]

The list could be lengthened indefinitely, but one thing that should be manifest is: many of the criticisms of the canonical approach come from opposite standpoints and point up disagreements which plague the discipline *in any event*. The canonical approach, given its range and ambition, illustrates the deep and abiding disagreements that afflict the field of biblical studies in its modern and postmodern guises. This does not mean that the criticisms simply cancel one another out, but it does mean that the canonical approach requires careful study and attention to nuance. It has been around long enough now to engender discussion on various sides of the theological spectrum, at a time when the

---

[14] Walter Brueggemann is not keen on this. He characterises Childs's appeal to 'canonical restraints' as 'apodictic'; such 'restraints' are personal and not text-immanent. See 'Against the Stream', 279–84.

[15] Seitz, 'Isaiah', 113–29.

[16] Watson, *Text and Truth*, 209–19; Seitz, 'Christological Interpretation', 209–26.

[17] The names of Brueggemann, Rendtorff, and Goldingay are capable of association with concerns of this kind, and their publications are generally well known.

methods of biblical study are in disagreement about key issues, including: the objectivity of the text, what is meant by history, authorial intentionality, inspiration, the pressure of historical-critical findings on interpretation, the relationship between the Testaments, and the character and desirability of Biblical Theology as such. The point of listing challenges to the canonical approach at this juncture, before turning to a brief assessment of several of them, is to underscore that adjusting the approach to meet the demands of one kind of challenge will of necessity reinforce whatever criticism was aimed from the opposing direction. One conclusion to be drawn from this is that the canonical approach cannot be inherently flawed, for if it were, critiques on either side would be left to devour one another, or pass like ships in the night.

The canonical approach, then, occupies a meaningful location in our late-modern environment, where anxiety over truth and meaning is high. The fact that opponents aim their objections from opposing directions could well confirm that the canonical approach offers the most compelling, comprehensive account of biblical interpretation and theology presently on offer. That is the verdict of the present essay.

Canonical Approach: Features and Challenges

Historical reference

Some have argued that a canonical approach does not pay sufficient attention to history. Here is a classic place where criticisms are leveled for different reasons from different sides of the theological spectrum. What might it mean to pay better attention to history, one might ask?

It might mean, trying to show that the Bible's literal sense fairly directly and unimpeachably reports matters of ostensive reference, and that for theological reasons it is invested in this kind of referentiality, and a commitment to it above other things, *evenhandedly across its length and breadth*. This being the case, the interpreter is to show that the Bible straightforwardly lodges historical claims (Isaiah wrote the book of Isaiah; Jonah went into the alimentary canal of a great fish; hills of foreskins could be excavated and shown to line up with accounts about them; the sea parted and dry ground existed on the terms given by the words used to say this; the letters attributed to Paul were all written personally by him in the same basic way letters are written today) and that interpretation ought to move from text to reference at this level of concern, or a defense of it against competing claims, in a sustained way.

Of course, an opposite challenge would be to say that a canonical approach, insofar as it sees historical reference as taken up into a fresh account of what history in fact is, lodged at the level of the literary presentation of the final form,

introduces a kind of history at odds with the concerns of modernity and its definition of history. Here both challenges meet as strange and probably unexpected bedfellows.

It has also been said that a canonical method subsumes history into
intratextuality, or 'the text's own world.' Childs has himself worried about this
aspect of reading more generally attributed to 'the Yale School.'[18] The 'strange
new world of the Bible' to which Barth referred was not simply a story or community-creating narrative, however much it may have functioned this way in
subsequent use. Indeed, it is the fact that the Bible *refers realistically to the world*
that has kept the canonical approach insistent that a difference must be registered between midrash and the way traditional Christian approaches have
thought about the Bible's truth-engendering literary development.[19]

What the canonical approach has done is to use the findings of historical-
critical methods and then ask historical questions about what has in fact been
discovered in the light of the text's final presentation. An example from
Childs's treatment of Exodus 33 – 34 will suffice. A problem exists in the presentation of the tent of meeting in Exodus 33, when one reads the larger
accounts. The canonical approach accepts that a genuine problem is being
encountered, and that the best explanation for this is that different sources lie
behind the final form of the text, with a certain roughness resulting.[20] There is
no attempt to argue that Moses had two different tents, as a matter of ostensive
reference; or that at the level of 'story' some deeper significance is to be seen in
the tension, independently of the fact that a tent did indeed get pitched and
used at some point in time and space in the life of Moses and Israel, and that the
text refers ostensively to this. Still, it is not the primary task of the interpreter to
take the historical-critical observation for the purpose of reasonable literary
explanation, and then go about leaving the literary world and reconstructing
the tent and the history of tent-sanctuaries in the ancient Near East as a piece of
elaborated ostensive reference. This would be wrongly to proportionalize one
dimension of the exegetical discipline and art. The canonical approach returns
to the text, and now asks why an aspect of historical reference which causes
friction has been allowed to stand, in the light of some other theological issue
which is the true concern of the final form of the text. As it happens in this case,
that concern is to do with the theological significance of Moses as intercessor.[21]

---

[18] See Appendix A in Childs's *New Testament as Canon*.

[19] Childs, 'Critique of Recent Intertextual Canonical Interpretations', 173–84. Compare the concerns of Sternberg, *Poetics*.

[20] 'I fully agree with the literary-critical assessment of the passage as reflecting an old tradition
of the tent of meeting which parallels the later Priestly account' (Childs, *Exodus*, 591).

[21] Childs: 'In its present position, without being specifically altered, the section witnesses to the obedient and worshipful behavior over an extended period of time,
thereby providing Moses with a warrant to intercede in vv. 12ff' (*Exodus*, 592).

History of the ostensive reference variety is not unimportant, but the biblical narrative uses this realm of reference to write history of its own kind. Moreover, the development of the text into its final form is also an historical fact, worthy of investigation.[22]

The preoccupation with historical reference (for reasons of apologetic defense of 'facticity' and literal sense; or more complicatedly, in order to focus on original sources and their divergent accounts of the world of ostensive reference, as prolegomena to telling us what really happened; or, negatively, as failing to deal with the text's final presentation as a fact worthy of historical attention of its own kind, that is, in the text's own historical emergence as what it is in the form in which we find it) has had a double fallout from the perspective of a canonical approach. Such an approach does not minimize the historical dimension; neither does it seek to do away with approaches that take it seriously enough to spot problems and tensions in the literary presentation. What is at issue is proper proportion and care to return to the final form of the text as its own piece of historical reality and witness to God's ordering of the world.

Harmonization and 'the disappearing redactor': The final form of the text

It has been argued by John Barton that the canonical approach doubles back on itself when it seeks both to honor the historical dimension (the depth of sources and traditions behind the final form) and at the same time believes the sum (final form) is greater than the parts. If the final redactor is so clever at merging the disparate sources into a tidy portrayal, why was he ever there to begin with?[23]

This kind of criticism would appear to merge nicely with another concern of Barton's, namely that the canonical approach has a tendency to harmonize

---

[22] Ward, *Word and Supplement*, 248–50.

[23] Barton, *Reading the Old Testament*, 56–58. According to Barton, Childs's analysis of Genesis 1 – 2 illustrates the close affiliation between the canonical approach and 're-daction criticism proper' (49). Redaction critical analyses of Genesis 1 – 2, however, fall prey to the following dilemma: 'If, say, Genesis 2 follows on so naturally from Genesis 1, then this is indeed evidence for the skill of the redactor *if we know that Genesis 1 and 2 were originally distinct*; but the only ground we have for thinking that they were is the observation that Genesis 2 does *not* follow on naturally from Genesis 1. Thus, if redaction criticism plays its hand too confidently, we end up with a piece of writing so coherent that no division into sources is warranted any longer; and the sources and the redactor vanish together in a puff of smoke, leaving a single, freely composed narrative with, no doubt, a single author' (*Reading the Old Testament*, 57). Similar concerns with Childs's use of redaction criticism are registered in Ward's survey in *Word and Supplement*, 250–51.

or smooth over disagreement when it handles the biblical material. But in fact, the criticisms are distinct, if inconsistent.

Childs is quite prepared to indicate where the tension remains in the final form of the text, and indeed he has been critical of those who have sought to eliminate this element.[24] He does not in fact seek to be so clever in showing the work of the redactor that he pulls the ground out from under the threshold acknowledgment that sources or different authors in fact exist. A brief look at any of the places where Childs calls attention to the genius of the final form's handling of its prior literary history will demonstrate this. There are two different tent traditions. They cannot be harmonized; there is a problem with the first tent appearing when it has not been constructed yet and stands outside the camp rather than inside it. Or, there are two 'creation accounts.' The fact that a redactional notice seeks to link the two in the way Childs and others have noted, does not eliminate the source critical finding, nor does it amount to disappearance of the redactor. And in the classic area of harmony, the fourfold Gospel record, no one could find in Childs any interest in the typical harmonization. Indeed, he is a rather traditional deployer of the Markan priority theory, and does very little in the way of minimizing the challenge of hearing the one gospel through four discrete witnesses.[25]

What Barton's analysis fails to grasp is something of the organic character of what Childs has referred to, probably imperfectly, as 'canonical consciousness.' For Barton, canon is an external force that seeks to set limits or arrange things, after the fact of their literary stabilization. If one sees signs of efforts to relate things, in the process of a text's coming to be, for Barton that can only be a literary move, and one cannot attribute to it any serious theological intentionality, much less use the term 'canonical consciousness' to distinguish it from a bare literary move.

Yet what Childs is seeking to highlight need not be obscured because of the difficulty of terms used to describe it. When Jeremias shows how the messages of Amos and Hosea are related, he does not describe a move at the level of what Barton would call 'canon' (an external decision somehow to relate the two; something, by the way, Barton would probably question as having occurred even at the level of canon in the case of Amos and Hosea – the books are separated by Joel[26]). Jeremias sees the pupils of the two prophets seeking to edit the

---

[24] See Childs's remarks on Calvin in his treatment of the tent traditions (more on this below). Moberly, *At the Mountain of God*, may also be open to this same criticism. Childs's particular indebtedness to diachronic (historical-critical) findings as crucial for apprehending 'the canonical shape' has also been reaffirmed recently by Levenson, in his very insightful essay, 'Is Brueggemann Really a Pluralist?', 265–94.

[25] Childs, 'One Gospel in Four Witnesses'.

[26] Incidentally, this is precisely why Joel has become the source of such attention and renewed interest in recent work on the Minor Prophets. Joel's placement, and

developing traditions in such a way that the two prophets are then viewed as a comprehensive and related witness.[27] There is no disappearing redactor. One can see easily enough, in Jeremias' analysis, where the older tradition ends and the newer editing begins; and there is no confusion as to what the distinctive features of each respective prophet is; these features remain. But at the earliest level of their text's circulation, long before the books receive final literary stabilization (including deuteronomistic superscriptions), an effort is being manifested, and Jeremias shows this clearly, to bring the message of the two into coordination. This is not for reasons of literary or aesthetic tidiness. It has to do with theological convictions regarding God's one word spoken through two discrete prophets.

A further example of the subtlety of Childs at this point can be seen in Bauckham's work on the Gospel collection, to return to the example above.[28] Bauckham argues that John knows Mark and seeks to relate his Gospel to that witness. The Gospel takes form with attention to both itself and something outside it. The contours of Mark are not thereby blurred; it remains a discrete witness. So, too, John can be read by itself. If Trobisch or others seek to show that a redactor has closed John with a notice that relates his message to the others in a final fourfold collection, this does not happen in such a way that the redactor need disappear, nor John and the other three merge into one.[29]

Below we will return to the question of 'the final form' and the degree to which it can be said to comprehend earlier traditions but also make its own special statement. What is at issue is the way in which what the canonical approach calls 'the final form' requires the diachronic dimension as the lens to grasp its force and specificity, as a theological witness. Related to this is the way in which 'the final form' relates to, but also transcends the delineated pre-history. At stake here are complex understandings of 'intentionality' and also 'coercion' or the pressure exerted by the text. For now, the crucial thing to note is that 'the final form of the text' requires attention to the text's diachronic prehistory (with the proviso that this history will always be difficult to sketch, in specific literary terms, and so is always a kind of heurism). Ironically, perhaps, here it is

---

existence as such, points to 'canonical shaping' at the level of theology and hermeneutics, in the development of the Book of the Twelve. This 'canonical shaping' is literary and theological, and does not sit easy to distinctions Barton would appear to like to draw. Among a great many others, see Van Leeuwen, 'Scribal Wisdom', 31–49; and on Joel as 'literary anchor' see Nogalski, 'Joel as "Literary Anchor"', 91–109.

[27] Jeremias, 'Interrelationship', 171–86.

[28] Bauckham, 'John for Readers of Mark,' in *The Gospels for All Christians*, 147–71.

[29] Trobisch, *First Edition; Paul's Letter Collection*. See also now, Porter, *Pauline Canon*. I also have a brief discussion of this issue in 'Booked Up: Ending John and Ending Jesus', in *Figured Out*, 91–102.

that Childs commits himself clearly to a form of referentiality, in the realm of history. This is not 'ostensive reference' in the form of 'brute facts' requiring specification (how many Hittites were there? When did Amos write the parts of his book we believe he wrote? etc), even as this dimension is the arena in which God's word, promised and then enacted, begins its journey on the road called 'revelation.'[30] The referentiality exhibited by diachronic method entails various levels of authorial intentionality, as realities in history. The 'final form of the text' is the way in which God has so commandeered that history as to speak a word through the vehicle of the text's final form, as a canonical approach seeks to comprehend and appreciate that. In so doing, the prior history is not done away with, nor do editors appear and disappear, even as the prior history is taken up into a stable expression of how God is ordering the world and continuing to speak through the 'final form' of the biblical text.

'Final form' will also require reattachment to 'literal sense' as classically understood. Such a concern, however, moves us into the area of typology and how one text and another are related according to the 'literal sense.' This is not the place to address such a significant issue, but it does remain the task of a canonical approach to show why its concerns have a much higher likelihood of linkage with the prior history of interpretation than historical–critical approaches.[31]

Prejudicial 'dogmatic' predisposition

This charge[32] is best suited to an environment in which 'objectivist' reading was running on all cylinders. As we shall see, Childs has his own concern for the 'objectivity' of the text, and is criticized in other quarters for daring to use the noun 'coercion' to describe it.

So this is one of those areas where the deep disagreements – with fault-lines people struggle to comprehend by recourse to terms like 'modern' and 'postmodern' – pollute the environment in which any reasonable discussion can be entertained in the first instance. How can Childs be characterized as 'subjectively predisposed' toward this or that dogmatic stance, when he himself believes that a canonical approach must assume something like stable and

---

[30] Long ago Barr did rightly note, 'A God who acted in history would be a mysterious and supra-personal fate if the action was not linked with this verbal conversation … In his speech with man, however, God really meets man on his own level and directly' (*Old and New in Interpretation*, 78).

[31] See my final comments in 'What Lesson Will History Teach?', 466.

[32] From Barr: 'As we shall see, in many respects this book [*Biblical Theology of the Old and New Testaments*] is neither a work of biblical theology nor one of canonical theology; it is more like a personal dogmatic statement provided with biblical proofs' (*Concept of Biblical Theology*, 401).

objective meaning, or the quest for that as morally obliged and theologically demanded?[33]

The answer of course is that Barr believes there is some kind of objective dimension to the Bible that Childs has encroached upon with his appeal to 'canonical reading,' and the culprit must be a force outside the text, in this case, 'Calvinism' or 'Barthianism' or 'Lutheranism' – all parts of a Reformation heritage Childs honors and which Barr feels he has not understood. This makes for an odd indebtedness and misrepresentation rolled into one.

Recently Barr has revealed that the extent of his concern at this level also reaches rather urgently to the newer reader-response methods, on the one hand (these do not believe in 'objective' intentions and such like in texts; meaning resides in those doing the reading), and newer historical approaches on the other (which eliminate any early depth in texts, as an historical fact, arguing instead that Israel's account of history and itself is a very late importation).[34] So Barr appears consistent in his urgency, though the target is a moving one so far as he is concerned.

It would of course be very useful indeed to know just what kind of objectivity Barr believes Childs is encroaching upon, since by its own statement, a canonical approach seeks to pay attention to the literal sense of the text, and there is nothing if not a certain objectivist concern lurking about that sentiment. For Barr, the 'literal sense' cannot do the objective work Childs seeks to make it do; when Childs does attempt this in each of his publications, he demonstrates thereby that a canonical approach is simply the expression of personal theological proclivities (or prejudices), and one can use whatever label one wants to attach to them ('Barthianism,' 'Calvinism,' 'Reformed dogma,' whatever).[35] That is, Barr has never sought to show that these various labels point to distinctive features, which surely they must, and then that these can be seen

---

[33] He quotes Sternberg to this effect in *Biblical Theology*, 20.

[34] Barr, 'The History of Israel'. This appears to be his effort to improve on criticisms leveled by Iain Provan against the excesses of Lemche, Whitelam, and Davies, among others.

[35] Barr: 'No one who knows modern theology will doubt that this entire work is a manifestation of one particular offshoot of Barthian theology. There are indeed three heroes of the work: Luther, Calvin and Barth, in ascending order. The opinion that most of modern scholarship is in a poor state, which might have some truth in it, is coupled with the converse notion that the Reformation had the right answers all along, a pious delusion which even Childs does not seek to demonstrate. Anyway, the three heroes are pretty well always in the right, or would be, except when they differ amongst themselves. Then there is a definite pecking order. When Luther differs from Calvin, it is Calvin who is right. Sometimes Calvin is superior to Barth. Barth's exegesis can be poor in comparison with Calvin's ... which would make it look as if Calvin was the top hero' (*Concept of Biblical Theology*, 401). On it goes. This

point by point in the canonical approach. 'Calvinism' is less a coherent system than a kind of insistence by Barr that when Childs puts his finger on an objectivity in the text, and it is not the one Barr himself likes, then it cannot qualify as objective and so must come from somewhere else – call it whatever you will.

It would be far more reasonable if Barr simply left himself to the observation that he believes the Bible does a certain kind of objective work (in the history-of-religion) and not in the area of 'literal sense,' without then adding to his problems by associating Childs with a species of reading he has not bothered to describe or justify as applicable in Childs's particular case. Instead what we find is a kind of disparate rant, void of objective analysis – described by one reviewer as 'academic terrorism.'[36] If Barr wants to say, 'Karl Barth has these five tendencies in his small print exegesis (see Job) and Childs does the same thing,' fine. But the question would be no further answered, is this a genuinely disqualifying matter, and if so, why? And not satisfied with this kind of tirade against Childs, he will then turn the tables and say that Barth or Calvin or Luther believed X or Y and Childs does not believe that anyway. Part of the confusion is that Barth or Calvin or Luther do not appear in careful treatments, dealing with them as exegetes or theologians, but only in impressionistic and idiosyncratic ways.

Of course, Childs is fully on record about the kinds of limitations he spots in 'dogmatic' reading (to choose one of Barr's labels). To return to the example of Exodus 33, Childs shows how Calvin 'was certainly on the right track'[37] but was nevertheless hedged in by a specific view of the text's relationship to reality, which forced him to adopt a midrashic instinct whereby Moses moved the

---

simply cannot be credited as objective analysis, but instead is a kind of mockery of Childs, or of himself. As we shall see, Childs has a canonical approach with certain objective contours, and it is on this basis that he renders judgments about the success of the exegesis of Calvin, Luther, or Barth. But from Barr's analysis, it sounds as though this is just a personality disorder in Childs, who he claims gives no reasons for his judgments. This is one of the more embarrassing chapters in modern biblical studies for its devolution into highly personal, *ad hominem* evaluation.

[36] A very judicious and fair review can be found in Brueggemann, 'James Barr on Old Testament Theology'. This is a sensitive and careful analysis, which also registers deep concern at the tone adopted by Barr and the substance of his account of Childs. He characterizes Barr's treatment as 'polemic' (68), 'an embarrassing *ad hominem* attack' (68), 'dismissive and contemptuous of all those who differ' (68), 'emotionalism that contributes nothing to the discussion' (68), and then at the close tries even to provide a kind of psychological explanation for the invective ('sense of wound from authoritarianism,' 72). When the emotion runs as high as it does in Barr's account, it is difficult to refrain from psychological speculation in an effort to reestablish a kind of equilibrium.

[37] Childs, *Exodus*, 592.

tent outside the camp 'because the people had just proved themselves unfit for God to dwell in their midst.' Childs is sympathetic with Calvin's move and sees it as an improvement over other options, but it remains the case that Childs is operating with an entirely different range of options when it comes to his assessment of the issue. The Exodus commentary is replete with examples where Childs assesses the 'objective' solutions (for that is what they claim to be, at a different period of interpretation) offered in premodern reading, and points out the difference between his approach and these earlier efforts – sometimes with sympathy when he spots a 'family resemblance' (his term from the 2004 *Struggle to Understand Isaiah as Christian Scripture*) he can appreciate, and at others points critically.[38] Childs refuses to countenance moves which ask that evidence be provided from something other than the plain sense of what the witness delivers, and his concern in our age with history-of-religion is precisely at the same level: that is, it has reproportionalized what the text literally delivers, and so produces evidence and explanations which, however interesting or compelling in their own realms of concern, are to the side, literally. What Barr likely sees as 'objective' in history-of-religion, Childs sees as objective but external to the proper task of exegesis.

It is also possible to turn to sections of the early Childs for essential objections to 'dogmatic reading' as obscuring what the canonical approach is about. Indeed, Childs likens the obscuring potential of modern systematic theological reflection to the use by biblical scholars of theories of history (Barr's history-of-religion would be an example).[39] Both lead us away from the plain sense. Dogmatic readings in the premodern period do this less by recourse to philosophical categories and more by direct utilization of doctrinal claims. Childs sees Luther's use of Psalm 8 to describe the two natures of Christ as obliterating the voice of the Old Testament, on the false understanding that what makes the Old a Christian voice must be the hearing of it through the categories of the New.[40] More on this below, as it gets at the crucial issue of what is at stake in hearing the Old Testament's own voice, yet as Christian Scripture.

Calvin's approach is different because he does try to hear the voice of the Old Testament through recourse to a kind of doctrinal symmetry across the testaments, due to their shared commitment to the theological world of covenant.

---

[38] Childs: 'All these theories remain unsupported from any evidence within the biblical text itself' (*Exodus*, 590).

[39] Childs: 'For systematic theologians the overarching categories are frequently philosophical. The same is often the case for biblical scholars even when cloaked under the guise of a theory of history' (*Biblical Theology in Crisis*, 158).

[40] Luther does not always have this kind of instinct, and that should be duly noted (see Helmer's excellent treatment of this issue, footnote 108 below). As is well known, Luther changes direction rather famously, in part because of his prolific style (this is particularly true in his many works on the Psalms, for example).

Calvin therefore tries to hear the psalm as speaking of an ideal state in the Garden of Eden from which man has fallen. This honors the Old's capacity to speak theologically, yet it imports a dubious context from the Old Testament's own doctrinal storehouse that is extraneous to the Psalm in order to secure this reading. Childs sees Calvin as useful in his emphasis on the Old Testament as a witness to the One God and his Christ, in its own idiom. But when an external dogmatic overlay secures that voice, it substitutes for the displacing voice of the New the displacing voice of doctrine and destroys the context (canonical shape) of the witness being interpreted. Childs seeks instead to hear the doctrinal voice emerging from the plain sense of Psalm 8, as a distinctive voice, in reciprocity with the New. At the end this will amount to a return to Psalm 8 and its strong doctrine of creation as the Old Testament's Christian and doctrinal corrective of (or potential mishearing by) the Letter to the Hebrews, drawing upon the Old Testament's own plain sense. Here we get a clear sense of how Childs regards the Old Testament in relationship with the New which allows both voices to register, and not with the second voice being the way to assure that the first has a Christian word to say at all.[41] In this, he allows the concerns of early doctrinal readings to demonstrate possible options, but in the end he rejects them both as an insufficient interpretation measured against a canonical approach.

In sum, it is more accurate to say that Childs has sympathy for the doctrinal instincts of the earlier history of reading, to a degree that sets him apart from the vast array of modern biblical scholars. But it is equally true that Childs feels inadequacies can be spotted, and he does this by careful attention to the concerns of the canonical approach, as a distinctive mode of theological interpretation.[42] Childs is no more a 'Calvinist' or 'Lutheran' or 'Catholic' reader than he is a canonical reader; and, frequently there is sympathetic overlap. At times, we can see in the earlier history of interpretation aspects of a broader two-testament concern for interpretation that resonate and show us interpretative moves that modern reading has shut off, to its detriment. But the analysis is not a one-way street, and a canonical approach is not inoculated from registering criticisms of the past, any more than it is inoculated from self-criticism or the kinds of limitations that are bound to afflict any, even comprehensive, approach. We shall see this below where we look briefly at the adjustments the canonical approach has made within its own brief life-span in order to take account of limitations spotted by others or by Childs himself.[43]

---

[41] See Hays' essay 'Can the Gospels Teach Us How to Read the Old Testament?', 402–18; or, by sharp contrast, Brueggemann's emphasis on the Old as a non-Christian but yet theological voice in his *Theology of the Old Testament*.

[42] See Childs, *Struggle*.

[43] It is an incidental reference and so will not be pursued in detail, but an example of mishearing Childs when he adjusts an earlier view can be seen in Lincoln's essay

The 'superiority' of the final form: In what does this consist?

This topic is allied to the one discussed above, but it situates itself more narrowly on what kind of claim it is to attend to the final form of the text, as over against earlier levels of tradition. In this sense, it is a topic that deals with the relationship between modern reconstructions of 'tradition-history' and the fact of there being an end point in that history, in the more or less stable (given text-critical realities) final literary form, arrangement and presentation.

In a recent textbook account,[44] John Collins writes of the relationship between 'original or earliest prophetic speech' and the later shaping and presentation of that into a corpus or canon. He is quoted at length as a fair and representative voice, in that his own work has clearly taken issue with Childs and the canonical approach.

> Much of the history of scholarship over the last two hundred years has been concerned primarily with the original words of the prophets. In recent years the pendulum has swung toward a focus on the final form of the prophetic books, in their canonical context. Both interests are clearly legitimate, and even necessary, but it is important to recognize the tension between them. The historical prophets whose oracles are preserved in these books were often highly critical of the political and religious establishments of their day. The scribes who edited their books, however, were part of the establishment of later generations. Consequently, they often try to place older oracles in the context of an authoritative tradition. In some cases, this has a moderating effect on oracles that may seem extreme outside (or even in) their historical context. In other cases, the editorial process may seem to take the edge off powerful prophetic oracles and dull their effect. The preference of an interpreter for the original prophets or for the canonical editors often reflects his or her trust or distrust of political and religious institutions in general.[45]

Probably four things are being said here which demand fuller explication. Is the final psychological hunch a good guide to anything, perhaps except to Collins'

'Hebrews and Biblical Theology', 316, n. 10. In 1970 Childs wanted to be sure the New's use of the Old was taken seriously as a theological achievement, and not dismissed as exotic exegesis. So he focused on the biblical theological insights to be gained from such an analysis. When later he realized the danger latent in this – perhaps he has observed it in New Testament scholarship in the meantime – he pointed out the limitations of using the New as a lens on the Old for the purpose of biblical theology. Lincoln not only wrongly speculates on the reasons for this; he also pushes forward to argue that the great freedom of the New in respect of the Old (a new version of the 'exotic') ought to be a license for our treating the New in precisely the same way.

[44] Collins, *Introduction*.
[45] Childs, *Introduction*, 286.

own instincts or personal worries? What does the term 'establishment' actually mean in the history-of-religion? Did these scribes, if they existed, think they were linking something to an 'authoritative tradition'? Does the movement from early to later track according to Collins' hunches? All these are questions that could be pursued in the history-of-religion of Israel or the modern sociology-of-religion (M. Weber, et al.). But it is a fair observation that a pendulum has swung, to use Collins' language, and he is to be commended for acknowledging that.

Looked at from the standpoint not of the sociology of religion, but of canonical method, is Collins' brief account the only way to describe what it means to give attention to the final form? Collins' points can nevertheless be used to tease out what might be meant by attention to the final form, in relationship to earlier levels of tradition (however we, in fact, lay our hands on 'the original words of the prophets').

Is there really a 'tension' between original prophet and later editorial shaping in the narrow sense implied by this quote? Another way to view the process of development in prophetic books is to withhold judgment until one actually tracks what is happening, which may also look different from book to book. Not every prophet is highly critical of religious institutions; some have mixed attitudes (Hosea); some focus on the nations (Obadiah); some require belief in a remnant or a superior plan of God for the king and people (Isaiah); some preach forgiveness and undeserved grace (Deutero-Isaiah). So the starting point may not be the same at all.

Second, Jeremias and others have shown the complex ways in which prophetic books acquire additions. In Hosea, the southern kingdom may be contrasted with the fate of Israel. But Judah can also be editorially supplemented into the same book in order to emphasize that she falls under the same word of judgment as her northern neighbor.[46] Frequently we see a movement from local to global that heightens and does not relax the sharpness of the original word. This is particularly true in the case of the Day of the Lord, for example, in the Book of the Twelve. Where Hosea may be shifted to first position to emphasize the grace of God in dealing with a wayward people (thus shifting what we mean by 'original' in the strict historical sense; cf. Amos), the latest canonical book actually raises the stakes in what one might believe to be the remnant of God as the Day of the Lord approaches. The canonical shaping reconstrues the beginning points as well as the later ones, and the presentations do not follow simple, straightforward patterns.

In sum, it may well be that notions such as those entertained by Collins are actually the result of historical-critical investigatory instinct, and not the

---

[46] Childs focused on this dimension in his *Introduction* account on Hosea, and Jeremias pursues a similar interest in his work on Hosea and Amos (see footnote 27 above).

neutral findings of that method when it has done its allegedly objective developmental work. The canonical arrangement of the twelve is but one place where, far from moving from sharp word to domesticated institutionalization, we find the Word of God gathering a kind of steam that resists any such characterization at all.

It is also possible to take issue with valorizing the final form of the text on the grounds, not of obvious sociological or theological bias, but simply because it is selective. Is there some good reason why later levels of traditions ought to be given priority over earlier ones, regardless of how one characterizes the movement itself?

Frequently it sounds like this is a matter of examining a series of integers, all laid out in a row, and choosing the last ones over the first ones.[47] But a canonical approach disagrees precisely with this understanding of the growth of tradition, and at this juncture it offers an alternative understanding of tradition-history. The book of Isaiah is not what the purported last levels of tradition say about it. Later levels of tradition seek to gain a hearing alongside and not above what precedes. If 'Trito-Isaiah' says nothing about David, that cannot say anything decisive about what the book of Isaiah, in its final form, says on this matter.[48] A canonical approach does not value the later over the earlier because the final form of the text does not follow this kind of developmental logic: earlier levels of tradition may even be highlighted by secondary and tertiary accumulations of tradition. Joel may well bring into sharper focus the call for repentance issued at the end of Hosea, as it provides a concrete liturgical enactment of this call as its central burden.[49] Later intrusions of penitential voices in Jeremiah's opening chapters do not lessen the prophetic denunciations in Jeremiah's day; rather, they call attention to these and underscore how imperative it was to heed them, the failure to do so leading to such an awesome and dark tragedy of judgment. Later editors feel the need to say 'let us lie down in our shame' and not 'glad that did not happen to me, here in my institutional redoubt.'[50]

In the context of a different discussion of this issue, Ward has also issued a challenge that might catch the allegedly 'historical' purveyors of interpretation

---

[47] See Childs's discussion of this issue in *Struggle*, 320–21. He mentions his disagreement with Nicholson over the characterization of his work – a confusion he sees as traceable to Barr (*Holy Scripture*, 1983), picked up by Barton (*Reading*, 1984), and now continuing in the work of Barrera (*The Jewish Bible and the Christian Bible*) and others. Nicholson quotes with favor the work of von Rad in Genesis on levels in the text (*Pentateuch*). I have discussed this same appeal by von Rad and conclude that he is a far more likely candidate for seeing the genius of the final form of the text than is traditionally held (see 'Prophecy and Tradition-History', 30–51).

[48] Seitz, 'Royal Promises', 150–67.

[49] Seitz, 'On Letting a Text', 151–72.

[50] Seitz, 'Place of the Reader in Jeremiah', 67–75.

off guard. A canonical method, he suggests, does not value the later hands because of some moral superiority – or lack of it, on Collins' view – they possess. Rather, the later hands have a greater historical perspective, due to the sheer range of their awareness of the past, which is still unfolding at the time of early tradition-levels.[51] History lies out in front of 'the original words of the prophets' because of what God is doing with them, under his providential guidance. It is a legacy of romantic theories of 'inspiration' and 'origins' which has set much historical-critical work off on the wrong foot, and it cannot be emphasized enough that this wrong footing has caught conservative interpreters and their putative opposites both out.[52] This results in maximalist or minimalist accounts of what can be secured for the 'original, inspired author/prophet/source/tradition,' starting from the same quest for an authoritative base independent of the canon's own final form presentation.

The final editors do not have any moral superiority and it is not for this reason that a canonical approach values the final form of the text. The final form of the text is a canonical-historical portrayal, and the final editors have never ceased hearing the Word of God as a word spoken through history. Their very non-appearance, moreover, is testimony to the degree to which they have sought to let the past have its own say and in the case of Isaiah, have deferred to God's inspired word as its presses ahead in all its accomplishing work. No morally superior, or balefully institutional, second or third Isaiahs get the final word. That would be far too thin an understanding of what a canonical approach has sought to comprehend when hearing the present sixty-six chapter book in its final form.

Biblical Theology and a canonical approach: Vetus Testamentum in Novo receptum?

The state of Biblical Theology as a coherent movement, method, or discipline is under discussion at present, with James Barr providing a sustained and argumentative account in his 1999 publication (based apparently upon lectures delivered in 1968).[53] His book is subtitled, *An Old Testament Perspective*. Whilst there may be a decline in Biblical Theology, and the reasons for this the subject of a good deal of profitable reflection, one development has not been chronicled, so far as I am aware. That is the renewed interest by New Testament scholars in the Old Testament. Much of this turns on developments internal to New Testament scholarship. The so-called 'new perspective on Paul' has turned its attention to Paul in his Jewish environment, with attendant, fresh

---

[51] Ward, *Word and Supplement*, 249.
[52] See the discussion in Seitz, 'On Letting a Text'.
[53] Barr, *Concept of Biblical Theology*.

interest in the way in which the Old Testament functions for him and his theological formulations. Several specialist accounts have been given over to describing Paul's use of the Old Testament, with appreciation of the subtle and artful way in which the Scriptures of Israel work within his logic and arguments.[54] Richard Hays, N.T. Wright, and now Francis Watson are among the better-known names within the New Testament guild, who have sought, respectively, to appreciate more comprehensively the way the 'narrative world,'[55] the literary potentiality,[56] or the final form of the Old Testament functions in the New Testament,[57] for Paul and for the basic character of Jesus's own self-understanding and mission.[58]

Whether or not it is consciously intended (this is not always stated), one could see this concern with the theological use of the Old in the New as a species of Biblical Theology. So one kind of decline in Biblical Theology may be matched by a new interest in a different guise: Biblical Theology as an appreciation of the theological use made by the New of the Old. Hans Hübner is one interpreter who has expressly declared this to be 'Biblical Theology.'[59]

There have been dissenters to this view of Biblical Theology, though the reaction is not typically directed at specialist work of the kind mentioned above. Instead, it comes to the fore in the recent concern to let the Old Testament have its own say, over against various kinds of efforts to constrain its voice. For Walter Brueggemann,[60] the stifling efforts are due to what he terms 'reductionisms' and within the discipline of Old Testament scholarship itself, these may headed up by what he calls 'historicism.' The Old Testament is hindered in making its voice heard by demands that it speak up chiefly or only through historical reconstruction of various kinds. But Brueggemann also

---

[54] For the theological minefield that this has always been seen to be, consult the historical account of Frei in *Eclipse*.

[55] See my analysis of Wright's use of the Old Testament in 'Reconciliation', 25–42.

[56] Hays, *Echoes of Scripture*. Hays has a considerably more interesting/fruitful account of the twofold witness in his essay, 'Can the Gospels Teach Us How to Read the Old Testament?'. The title, however, indicates a kind of prioritizing of direction which may prove telling. More needs to be said about this essay than can be tackled here.

[57] Watson, *Hermeneutics of Faith*. Watson moves in a different direction in this volume in respect of Childs and a canonical approach than what he espoused in his earlier work *Text and Truth*. One finds a robust and strategic use of 'canonical method' in the Old Testament, whilst earlier the method of Childs was seen as misguided, measured against von Rad and others. See also the discussion on pages 82–83 below.

[58] See also Wagner, *Heralds of the Good News*.

[59] Hübner, *Biblische Theologie des Neuen Testaments*. Also Stuhlmacher, *Biblische Theologie des Neuen Testaments*. The titles are revealing. See the discussion of Dunn on terminology in 'Problem', 172–83.

[60] Brueggemann, *Theology of the Old Testament*.

argues there is a kind of back-draft from the New Testament, or from Christian theological reflection ('established church faith') or dogmatics more specifically, that blows over the Old and obscures its 'wild and untamed' theological witness.[61] The unruly character of the witness – its polyphony, etc; Brueggemann has lots of terms for this – ought to be left alone, and this is the ingredient most to be encroached upon, he argues, when one comes at the Old Testament with theological lenses provided by the New or by Christian theology. Jon Levenson has remarked on the problematical character of this approach, so far as Judaism is concerned.[62] In less sustained ways, and for different reasons, John Goldingay (in his recently published first volume of Old Testament Theology)[63] and Rolf Rendtorff[64] have voiced similar concerns to let the Old Testament retain its own theological voice.

I believe it is fair to say that Childs occupies considerable space between the two trends just described. For Childs, Biblical Theology should certainly attend to the way the New hears the Old, just as it needs to hear the New as such. When in the final section of his book on Paul's use of the Old Testament,[65] Hays holds Paul up as a hermeneutical lesson for our imitation or edificatory modeling, to the degree to which this is meant to count for Biblical Theology, Childs finds the approach faulty if not eccentric.[66] It is not possible to adopt the pneumatological stance of Paul, even if one thought this a good idea. Paul's stance on the Old Testament is one in which there has yet to be formed a two-testament canon, and Christian theological reflection entails this material (canonical) reality, a reality that for Childs is foundational. Another problem involves the *New Testament as canon*. To stand with Paul would be to isolate his voice over against the other voices of the New Testament witness (it would also likely entail accepting the historical critical canons of what with confidence we can attribute to Paul to begin with) and so wrongly to construct a category of Biblical Theology called 'Pauline theology' (on an articulated historical grid). And then there is as well the problem of whether identification with Paul's pneumatological freedom is to misunderstand what the task of Biblical Theology outside the apostolic circle genuinely looks like.[67]

---

[61] Brueggemann, *Theology of the Old Testament*, 107.

[62] Levenson, 'Is Brueggemann Really a Pluralist?'.

[63] Goldingay, *Old Testament Theology*. See also my brief review in *IJST* 7 (2005), 211–13.

[64] Rendtorff, 'Toward a Common Jewish-Christian Reading of the Hebrew Bible', 31–45.

[65] Hays, *Echoes of Scripture in the Letters of Paul*.

[66] *Biblical Theology*, 84–85.

[67] Much fuller reflection needs to be undertaken on this issue. There is often a readiness in Christian circles to collapse the church into the New Testament without further ado, and then to think of the Old Testament in clear contrast to this (the difference at

Now to spot the problems with this particular understanding of Biblical Theology is not the same thing as saying just how the Old Testament's theological witness is to sound forth, both for its own sake and in the light of a subsequent witness (the New Testament) in which its voice has been taken up (*Vetus Testamentum in Novo receptum*). Here Childs has referred to the 'discrete voice' of the Old Testament. He was earlier criticized by Francis Watson for, among other things, describing a dimension of the witness of the Old Testament in ways that are indebted to historical-critical investigation.[68] Presumably, the innocent and proper worry here would be that such an (historically retrieved) account of what the Old Testament has to say could then never be attached to the New's reception of it, because this latter phenomenon goes on without recourse to historical-critical categories or assumptions.[69] The live question, however, is whether this is what the discrete voice of the Old Testament actually *is for Childs*, and here we are back again to the topic assessed above: how do historical-critical methods function in a canonical approach? It has been argued above that a 'canonical approach' as adopted by Childs gives priority to the final form of the text, and this final form is what Childs means by the 'discrete voice;' this approach by no means holds the final form hostage to historical-critical reconstruction, even as such methods might help us grasp it. To say this is to address the worry that a category is being invented ('the discrete voice') which cannot attach itself to the New's hearing of it.

The problem with Watson's earlier approach has now shifted to the opposite front: by issuing a warning against hearing the discrete voice of the Old Testament, it may end up that the voice of the Old Testament is only what moves uncomplicatedly into the New's version of its own witness. That kind of 'anti-discrete' move would mean a silencing of much that is in the Old Testament, on the one side; and it would also threaten to misunderstand the way in

---

this point with Aquinas' commentary on the Psalms, for example, where Christ prays for his church, is instructive). A canonical understanding of the role of the Scriptures sees the church, for different reasons and to different degrees, in a less direct relationship to both Testaments and certainly not in one which amounts to conflation or simple contrast. More on this at the conclusion.

[68] See his discussion in *Text and Truth* and in an exchange with myself in *Scottish Journal of Theology*: Seitz, 'Christological Interpretation of Texts and Trinitarian Claims to Truth', 209–26; Watson, 'The Old Testament as Christian Scripture', 227–32.

[69] This point has been made at another place by N.T. Wright, and it appears congenial for several reasons with a canonical approach. In a volume which included treatments of the suffering servant by Old Testament scholars, Wright posed the question why they did not ask 'how Isaiah might have been read by Jesus' own contemporaries?' (in W.H. Bellinger, W.R. Farmer, eds., *Jesus and the Suffering Servant* [Harrisburg, PA: Trinity Press International, 1998], 282). See my discussion in 'Prophecy and Tradition-History', 38–39.

which what the New has to say *is genuinely new and fresh and provocative*. This is an irony, in some ways, because this latter dimension had been the source of much focused interest and theological shoring-up in Watson's earlier works, and in his understanding of the relationship between the testaments.

The simple point is that the 'discrete voice' (as Childs means it) is not a voice that cannot sound forth in the New due to historical-critical privileging of some wrong sort (a proper worry), but it is a voice which sounds its own notes just the same, in its own registers, and in so doing is fully capable of doing Christian theology.[70] The New Testament can attend to this voice when it takes up the Old, even as it will transform that voice for the purposes of its own 'second testament' witnessing to God in Christ. But this category of reflection is not determinative for biblical theology, in a way that Watson suggests (or a Brueggemann, Rendtorff, or Goldingay might rightly worry about). It is an ingredient in Biblical Theology, but it is not biblical theological reflection, either of the New or of the Old Testaments in the Christian Bible.

This point was established in the 1970 volume, even at places where Childs was later to question the adequacy of his methods there.[71] Childs rightly saw in a later discussion that if one only focused on the places where the New had taken up the Old, and used this for the purposes of Biblical Theology, the selection would be skewed and significant portions of the Old Testament would fall silent in the work of Biblical Theology. An ingredient would become the full meal, to use the language from above. But even given that probable limitation in his method, one can see in the 1970 volume how Biblical Theology according to a canonical approach nevertheless frees the Old Testament to do the theological work proper to its own witnessing role. For example, Childs carefully analyses Psalm 8's discrete voice before turning to the New Testament's reception and adaptation of it. As seen above, he distinguishes the canonical voice in the Old from a limiting doctrinal filtering he spots in the earlier history of interpretation. He then reflects on the New Testament's hearing of the Psalm in its own medium, and according to certain explicit Christological evaluations it is seeking to make. It is important to note that this movement, from Old to New, *then reverses direction*. The Psalm's high doctrine of creation is allowed to sound forth in the context of Christological focus, and this assures that the incarnation and exaltation of Christ do not become isolated theological ideas, but are tied to God's ways with creation, Israel, and the world. The Old's voice does not somehow 'correct' the New, or

---

[70] See my forthcoming discussion of this, a trial run of which was presented at the Society of Biblical Literature meeting in Philadelphia (2005), entitled 'Theological Use of the Old Testament: Recent New Testament Scholarship and the Psalms as Christian Scripture'.

[71] See his *Biblical Theology of the Old and New Testaments*, 76.

highlight its deficiencies – though if one read the New without this earlier witness continuing to have its proper theological effect, correction would indeed be in order. A canonical approach rather assures that the New's emphases remain rooted in the soil from which they have sprung. The danger is that in the enthusiasm to describe what the New is saying, modern readers simply leave unstated and unfelt what were most certainly the keen pressures and context supplied by the Old in the first evangelical efforts to account for God's work in Christ. For this, we do not have to ask what was in the mind of the authors of the New, because the Old Testament exists as a canonical witness, showing us the horizons set forth from that witness in their own stable deliverance of them, reaching to the authors of the New and beyond to us.

Another analogy may be useful here, from text criticism. If one watched what the New Testament said of the Old Testament in its own Greek language idiom, and sought to contrast this with the Old's own sentences in a different language, what would one be discovering? Sometimes the sense is conveyed that between two conscious choices, one is being adopted and another ruled out by the New Testament, so as to make this or that fresh and determinative theological point. Priority is given both to the language of translation and to the use made of it in the New, in a two-for-one deal. But in a great many places no such conscious decision is being made at all. The New simply operates freely in its own idiom and is unaware it is making a choice of this 'canon' over 'that one' – and certainly not a kind of preferencing choice that later academic analysis might yield, self-consciously aware of text-critical issues in the scientific sense.[72]

It is for this reason that the 'discrete voice' of the Old Testament is not to be identified with what the New makes of it, *simpliciter*. This would be giving to the New's use a kind of conscious replacing or displacing function, when there is little evidence to suggest that the New Testament writers actually meant to be heard as functioning in this way, over against the authoritative Scriptures they are themselves commenting on. So, can we say with any confidence that Paul intended his use of the Scriptures of Israel to determine the direction of Biblical Theological reflection; that is, reflection on a twofold canon of Scripture in which his own statements would be taken up into a canonical witness involving a wide variety of different genre (Gospels, Epistles of very different kinds, Acts, Revelation)? Paul is obviously unaware that a second witness would in time appear in a now *twofold* scriptural canon, formed on analogy with the one he himself has drawn upon in the narrower sense, but now with the same authority and claim to speak as did the prophets of old. I suspect we

---

[72] And sometimes, in the Letter to the Hebrews, the author uses Greek sentences of Scripture that appear in neither an Old Testament (Hebrew) *Vorlage* nor in any Greek recensions either. See the intriguing discussion of this and other matters in Jobes and Silva, *Invitation to the Septuagint*.

should be expected to believe in much recent New Testament work that he did so assume, or that we are nevertheless right to be following his lead as consistent with this view. And yet the formation of the canon points in a direction away from simple or complex imitation of Paul as the starting point for Biblical Theology. Paul's use of the Old Testament now takes place within a larger canonical witness (the New Testament), which is itself given a status on analogy with the first witness. A properly *Biblical* Theology would need to account for the two witnesses in this analogous, but also different, relationship and form.

Childs's biblical theological reflections in his 1970 work formed the ground floor in what would become a series of comprehensive investigations into the relationship between Old and New Testaments, Theology, and Biblical Theology. In a recent work on Paul and the Old Testament, Watson has made a clear-cut decision to inquire into how the final form of the Old Testament might have pressured a reading in Paul – that is, a reading often otherwise credited to Christological or pneumatological insights provided from outside that witness.[73] Here there appears to be some considerable movement on his part toward understanding what the proper relationship is between the 'final form' laid bare by a canonical hermeneutic, and the apprehension of this in the New.

The irony is that there persists a concern to demonstrate this dimension only within the narrower realm of what one might call 'Pauline theology,' and that on at least two fronts. First, there is no attempt to register the limitations of asking about a 'Pauline theology' over against New Testament or Biblical Theology; this seems somewhat strange in a work which will not tolerate any such 'historicising' moves as decisive for understanding the *Old's* final form witness. So, for example, 'Habakkuk' cannot be understand apart from the canonical form in which it appears (The Twelve and the Prophets), yet an 'undisputed' Pauline corpus, determined by historical critical judgments, is the point of departure in the New Testament for investigating the Old's canonical shape. Why this discontinuity, treating the Old canonically and not (more narrowly) historically, but then reversing direction in the New? For the second problem we return to the issue mentioned above, but now from the opposite side, that is, how does the Old Testament sound forth its theological witness? Watson wants to maximize the continuity between the Old's voice and the New's (Paul's) hearing of it, on the grounds that this is historically the case (and he can – or indeed must – demonstrate this by comparisons with literatures contemporaneous with Paul and accessible to him, as he theorizes their existence and

---

[73] Watson has a fine running discussion of the problems of Martyn's approach, in this case chiefly to be found in the recently published, magisterial commentary, *Galatians*, dedicated unsurprisingly to Ernst Käsemann. Much more could be said on this topic but it falls outside the scope of the present survey.

effect on him). That is, the historical Paul read the witness available to him at his moment in history, and he argued for this or that Christological foundationalism on the basis of the Old Testament and as an accurate hearing of it, over against rival attempts to do the same (or arguably in many cases, to do something different).

What happens is complex, it could be concluded, especially in the case of the law. In an effort to secure the special hearing of Paul as coming out of the Old's canonical form, and not as the special effects supplied by the Gospel (Martyn, Käsemann), it will need to be shown by Watson that things like the law's 'fading glory' are deeply imbedded in the law's own plain sense presentation of itself. In some ways what happens is that the two voices (Old Testament and New Testament) are simply fused. The excesses of saying the New hears what it hears because of the overtones supplied by Christian confession, and so 'reads into' the Old Testament something that is not there,[74] are thereby constrained; so too the sense that the New Testament is arguing the Old is a closed or wrong-headed book and cannot yield up such deep mysteries anyway. But the result is a single conflated agreement across the testaments, at the cost of digging less deeply into the paradoxical way in which Paul is seeking to negotiate two distinct realities: the Old's plain sense and the work of Christ. The anguish that task causes him is even expressed by Paul, and rather clearly, in Romans 9 – 11, for example.

But even if this description does not completely capture the burden of Watson's model, what is clear is that the Old's theological witness comes alive for him only in respect of Paul's successful (as Watson has it) hearing of it.[75] At times this hearing works with a concept of intentionality one might call 'canonical.' At other points this is less clear.[76] One can conclude that Watson has thought deeply about the challenge of doing a species of biblical theology, and has outdistanced some weaker formulations, but that there is something eccentric or quixotic in what he attempts. There will always remain space between the New's hearing of the Old and the Old's plain sense. What is at issue is not the elimination of that space, but the careful appreciation of its character.

---

[74] A problem Watson sees in Barton's understanding of Habakkuk's influence on Paul. According to Watson's (insightful) analysis, Barton depends upon a theory of Habakkuk's 'intention' which Watson calls 'historically naïve and hermeneutically perverse' (*Galatians*, 158).

[75] In this sense, in Watson's hands, 'canonical intentionality' appears to detach itself from Israel's lived life: the text refers not so much to events in its day, as to a reception-history yet to be known by it.

[76] Watson has not entirely sorted the problem out, that is, of distinguishing Enlightenment 'intentionality' from the intentionality of the final form. More cannot be said here, as it would require a greater attention to inconsistencies in Watson's otherwise ambitious discussion of 'intention' than is warranted in this context.

Biblical Theology will function properly when it deals with the material reality of there being two different witnesses, and accepts that fact as foundational for interpretation. It is hard to see how the Old Testament can contribute to Biblical Theology in the manner of Childs's handling of Psalm 8, as an example of the canonical approach, if Psalm 8 and Hebrews' use of it are maximally coordinated, for whatever reason. (Just here one sees how difficult it would be to extend Watson's project across the length and breadth of the New Testament canon.) Rather, both Old and New Testament witnesses function in a complementary way for the purpose of Christian Biblical Theological reflection.

Coercion, **adversarius noster,** *'untamed and wild': The character of the final form of the text*

Twenty years ago John Barton wrote:

> It is not surprising that Childs has little following in Germany. One misses in his proposals the sense so dear to the heirs of the Reformation (including many in his own Calvinist tradition) that the biblical text is something with rough edges, set over against us, not necessarily speaking with one voice, coming to us from a great distance and needing to be weighed and tested even as *it* tests and challenges us: *adversarius noster,* in Luther's phrase.[77]

Sweeping statements like this have a way of coming back to haunt one. It was only a year before this, at a public lecture at Yale, when Rolf Rendtorff spoke of his reaction upon reading Childs's 1979 *Introduction*: 'it was as though scales fell from my eyes.' It is hard to say whether any non-German biblical scholar has ever been so thoroughly read and reacted to in German-speaking circles as Brevard Childs. Indeed, when Barton's colleague James Barr speaks of his own training in biblical studies, what seems immediately apparent is the distinguishing fact that Childs was trained in German language scholarship at Basel and Barr in another context.[78] It would be worth a monograph of its own to

---

[77] Barton, *Reading the Old Testament*, 95.

[78] Barr speaks of never having divided a verse, dated a text, etc. and generally describes an Anglo-saxon training devoid of sharp critical instincts and basking in the hey-day of the Biblical Theology Movement. ('I was myself never much of a historical-critical scholar. I do not know that I ever detected a gloss, identified a source, proposed an emendation or assigned a date … On the contrary, scholars who thought that these matters were the essence of exegesis … were laughed at and looked upon as fossils from some earlier age. The cutting edge of Old Testament study, and its impact upon theology, seemed to lie in the concepts of biblical theology,' *Holy Scripture*, 130). Here is another place where Barr's predictions about the field have not proven quite accurate; it is as though historical-criticism is now passé, in Barr's

investigate whether the chief differences between them turn, in Barr's case, on a very different climate of training and ecclesial life. Barr and Barton look in on the continental Reformation as if it is a kind of distant phenomenon, which to some extent it is for them; and so it is strange to see their often partial and intriguing use of the Reformers. This is particularly true in Barton's citation of Luther here.

What Barton appears to have done in this citation is translate the observations of Luther about the content of Scripture (its *Sache* or referent) into the realm of materiality: the Bible is a kind of literary crazy-quilt, a tangle or puzzle demanding the proper critical tools to sort it out. Even when Luther uses this kind of rhetoric ('the prophets have a queer way of talking') it cannot be said that this is what he means when he says the Bible is 'our adversary.' Rather, he means more what Barth means when in a later day he refers to the 'strange world' of Scripture. The Bible confronts us, squares up to us, with the content of its word and its address as such. It does not confront us because it has a strange, confusing, or paradoxical *literality* (awaiting historical-critical sorting). Barton refers to the 'rough edges' of Scripture in a book on hermeneutics in the context of his concerns to keep historical-critical investigation at full employment, as a kind of necessity, given the project to which it must put its hand. Rarely, if ever, does one see the heirs of the Reformation seek to justify historical-critical work along these lines. In another context I have criticized Käsemann and Stuhlmacher for claiming the Reformation instinct demands historical-critical quests for the 'proximate.'[79] But even that was not an appeal to the 'rough edges' of the witness, but rather to the need to overcome what is presumed to be a theological or hermeneutical problem of access to the subject matter, due to *historical distance*. This kind of a problem, it can be argued, is different again from what worried either the Reformation, on the one side, or Barton in his examination of canonical hermeneutics and the literary 'rough edges' of the material form of the witness, on the other.

In a long series of published works, Walter Brueggemann has sought to keep the Old Testament at some considerable distance for the purpose of explicitly Christian theological reflection, using the language of polyphony and other kindred terms, and this bears some similarity to the 'rough edges' that

---

judgment. Yet someone like Nicholson is a good example of the persistence of classical historical-critical interests and concerns, and he is quite representative in many ways of British Old Testament scholarship (cf. G. Davies, Williamson, Barton – all proud deployers of pretty traditional historical-critical methods; for someone interested in biblical theology, I suspect one would turn to the lone Walter Moberly – not a candidate for the 'James Barr prize' for things mainstream, one might have thought).

[79] Seitz, 'Two Testaments and the Failure of One Tradition-History', in *Figured Out*, 35–47.

Barton speaks about. But they are coming from very different places and end up in very different ones as well. Brueggemann worries about 'christianizing' the voice of the Old Testament, or, if a distinction can be made, mishearing or occluding the word of the Old because of the interpretive lens of the New being given precedence over it. The literary reality of the Old Testament lines up for Brueggemann with a theological reality, making this a clear (and for his purposes, a desired) departure from traditional appraisals. The text is at odds with itself, because the God to which it refers only exists in the speech about 'him' and this speech comes at us in testimony and counter-testimony. There is nothing about the 'final form' of the text that points to a settling down of the '*hin und her*' highlighted by Brueggemann. Just because this is so, it follows naturally that the reader must seek some understanding of the text's address, must read it out of the 'wild and untamed' literary witness before us, and the idea that Brueggemann is *choosing freely* to hear what he hears and see what he sees is an idea on his terms without genuine alternative. I suspect the most that could be said in a methodological sense is, the text *can* be read this way and so this is the way Brueggemann chooses to read it. Such would be all that could be required, one assumes, on this kind of postmodern playing field (though why *any* reading is not possible, and also impossible to adjudicate as good or bad, remains somewhat unclear).[80]

It is Childs's notion of a final form, a stable witness, a 'discrete voice' that runs in a direction Brueggemann finds unacceptable. Historical criticism gave us a sense that the texts go through various phases of development. This is fine. The danger for Brueggemann is taking this fact and then constructing something behind the text, in a history-of-religion. This is a domestication or a reductionism, on his terms. The various phases of development point instead to a point-counterpoint and there is nothing in the text itself which gives indication of that '*hin und her*' reaching anything like a coherent final statement (even one with dialectical aspects to it).[81]

Childs has himself tried to assess this particular challenge (and widely disseminated alternative) to his approach, and has done so most recently in a work that may be his final large-scale project.[82] It is striking in some ways that Childs has chosen to give the work a title that also bespeaks our 'postmodern' situation: 'The Struggle to Understand Isaiah as Christian Scripture.' The struggle, however, is not to do with an inherent restlessness of the literature itself, as an indispensable characteristic of it; it is rather to do with what it means to seek to hear the subject matter of sacred Scripture through the medium of two

---

[80] Levenson, 'Is Brueggemann Really a Pluralist?'. Levenson helpfully points out how complex a version of postmodernity Brueggemann actually is.

[81] Seitz, 'Scripture Becomes Religion(s)', 26–27.

[82] Predictions like this are perilous.

discrete, if juxtaposed, witnesses. Precisely because Brueggemann disagrees with the pressure of, the necessity of, hearing both testaments as bearing witness to one another and to Christian foundational claims, as crucial to the task of interpretation, one cannot use the term 'struggle' as Childs means it to describe what he is doing.[83]

On the surface, the idea that the first witness has a stable and more-or-less objective final form (even given text-critical realities we shall discuss next) probably ought to complicate the idea that we must also hear it in relationship to a second witness with the same characteristic final canonical form (comprised of various separate forms of discourse). And of course it does indeed. The 'final form' is neither a single narrative line (plot) nor a series of kindred genres, all lined up in a tidy way.[84] And the fact that the first witness makes final Christian sense in relationship with a second one, means there is always an act of correlation to be achieved, and for that the only proper description is 'struggle.'

It is crucial to keep this aspect of canonical reading clear in one's mind. At one level, Brueggemann's unruly witness is not at all unlike what Childs means when he refers to struggle; indeed, by insisting that we read the Old Testament on its own, Brueggemann has made interior to its witness a kind of inherent 'struggling' that otherwise takes place, for very different reasons, when one seeks to do Christian theological reflection on a single canon comprising two discrete (and merely juxtaposed) sections – with the latter one taking up within itself portions of the explicit semantic level of the first, and also making the delivery of its claims operative primarily at the level of 'accordance' with that same first witness.[85]

This will mean that Childs has no trouble, on the one hand, speaking of the 'pressure' (or 'coercion') of the canonical Old Testament text, in its final form,

---

[83] Williamson notes in a review that Childs has a (more or less) comprehensive coverage of the history of interpretation, with the exception of some more recent commentators. That is because, he conjectures, these newer readers of Isaiah have stopped having to account for the relationship between Old and New Testaments as part of the actual 'struggle' of Christian interpretation ('Review of B.S. Childs, *The Struggle to Understand Isaiah as Christian Scripture*,' *RBL* 4 (2005), available online at www.bookreviews.org/bookdetail.asp?TitleId=4494&CodePage=4494. See www.sbl-site.org/SearchResults.aspx). Brueggemann, however, makes an explicit case for the necessity of having to stop, and so he is treated in more detail by Childs.

[84] See my review of John Goldingay, *Old Testament Theology: Israel's Gospel*, who seeks to isolate kindred genres and collate these for the purpose of three volumes of Introduction. The rhetorical challenge of pulling this off without tedium is enormous and may signal why the final form of the Old Testament – among many other reasons to be sure – has resisted this.

[85] Seitz, 'In Accordance With the Scriptures,' in *Word Without End*, 51–60.

as a discrete and stable voice; and yet, on the other hand, of the *sensus literalis* being a sense with extension beyond itself because of the challenge of rendering the subject matter, which now entails a second accorded witness (this 'extensive' character belongs to the property of the literal sense and is not merely imposed upon it). A 'rule of faith' is required to help us understand another, allied, theological pressure, at the heart of the act of Christian interpretation: the two testaments are related on analogy with the basic Christian confession that the Creator God is the Father of Jesus Christ and his son shares the eternal glory and life of the Father who sent him (Phil. 2:9–11). Yahweh is this triune God and we know it from the first witness itself, when its literal sense yields this up in the light of the second witness.

The best recent effort to describe what Childs means by the pressure of the literal sense, with sensitivity to the challenge of hearing two testaments, is the essay by C. Kavin Rowe, the title of which gives indication of what is being sought in Childs's canonical reading: 'Biblical Pressure and Trinitarian Hermeneutics.'[86] In a piece of historical close reading, Christine Helmer has investigated 'Luther's Trinitarian Hermeneutic and the Old Testament'[87] and she demonstrates on the basis of Luther's understanding of Hebrew semantics how he was able to see the Trinity adumbrated, if not more fully manifested, in the Old Testament quite apart from the traditional proof-texting. In some ways, then, we come full circle and confront again Luther's famous 'our adversary.' 'Our adversary' is neither an unruly literality (Barton) nor a God resistant to creedal claims (Brueggemann) – indeed, on this latter point, Luther uses mature Christian confession precisely to lodge his point in contradistinction to churchly claims and pious enthusiasms both. 'Our adversary' is the *Sache* of the Scriptures' plain sense address.

When Childs speaks of 'coercion' or the pressure of the literal sense, he stands far closer to what Luther meant by 'our adversary' than Barton realized. The Old Testament confronts us: as law and, in Luther's more mature formulation, as Gospel as well. It exposes, as in the famous deployment by Luther of the 'theological use' of the law. It also orders our world, by telling us of God and his Christ and of the Holy Spirit, both in the Old (through its use of Hebrew and in its understanding of the Word of God) and in the New, where the literal sense of Scripture shows us more clearly the Christological or spiritual referent both testaments are fundamentally about. It is 'our adversary,' not in presenting us with a material form which is chaotic or whose parameters cannot be determined except by means of external aids (allegory; or the ironic counterpart of this in history-of-religion or modern critical methods). It is 'our adversary' in

---

[86] In *Pro Ecclesia* 11.3 (2000). See also his 'Romans 10:13: What is the Name of the Lord?'.
[87] In *Modern Theology* 18 (2002).

that it seeks to overcome our world and reorder it. It does this not just by catching us up for a while in imaginative construals. Nor does it do this chiefly by pointing to a world of ostensive reference that we need to reassemble or make more proximate by use of historical tools. It does this by means of the final form of the text, whose words point to a fleshly and a spiritual realm both, in Luther's complex understanding. Because its subject matter is Christ, and this sometimes quite clear and forceful, and other times oblique (as, with Luther, Israel gazes on something it cannot have or cannot yet grasp), it disrupts and reorders our place in the world, and the world itself. This is what Childs means when he speaks of the Bible's address primarily with the language of 'witness.'

It belongs to our specific providential place in time that we must struggle with how the Bible makes its two-testament word heard. But this has always been the case. When Childs speaks of the text's coercion or pressure, at our specific moment in time, it will be against a backdrop of challenges that did not obtain in the same form for Origen, or Chrysostom, or Theodoret, or Luther, or Calvin. Those challenges in our day have had to do with new understandings of historical reference, which make the task of hearing the 'literal sense' sharpened and more finely governed by our sense of the pastness of the past. But that is simply a challenge, and it is akin to what it has meant to struggle to hear the Word of God through the medium of the historical witness of prophets and apostles in every age. A canonical method does not seek to diminish the challenge or change the subject, but it does insist that the 'literal sense' can make its force felt all the same, even under the shadow of our awareness of the complex historical development of the text before us.

Still, this challenge has also come with its benefits and fresh insights. Who could read the historical back-filling supplied by a George Adam Smith and not sense that the minor prophets were somehow coming alive again and making themselves heard in fresh ways, precisely because to his age had been bequeathed the legacy of newer historical methods?[88] He spoke of 'fixing the indemnity' brought about by these methods, and that phrase is fraught with meaning, beyond what he might have seen as the shadows cast by historical approaches which were only beginning to lengthen.[89] The canonical approach has not turned its back on this challenge, nor on the 'indemnification' that would be required for our age. What has emerged in the canonical approach is a text undomesticated and able to speak a word – even 'our adversary' – witnessing to the work of the triune God who occasioned the speech about himself, and equipping us, by the Holy Spirit, to hear the divine word afresh in our generation.

---

[88] Seitz, 'On Letting a Text', 151–72.
[89] Campbell, *Fixing the Indemnity*.

Hebrew and Greek canons: What is at stake here?

Naturally enough, a canonical approach will be required to comment on the more traditional, material, low-flying questions of canon: which canon of the Old and New Testaments has authority for Christian interpretation and witness? But the question is immediately raised, just what is meant by a very specific set of historical and theological/ecclesial parameters pertaining to canonicity? To speak of a canonical approach giving wrongful priority to a Hebrew versus a Greek canon (and then describing these as attaching to distinctive ecclesial bodies) is hopelessly to simplify matters. Under the rubric 'Which Canon?' in *Reading the Old Testament*, John Barton's brief treatment of this issue – about which he has written at length in other publications – gives a nice series of misleading impressions. But chief among them is the statement:

> It is hard not to be swayed by the purely historical arguments of scholars such as A.C. Sundberg – writing before Childs had developed his theories – to the effect that before the Reformation there had never been a time when the Christian Church acknowledged any canon but that of the Greek Bible; so that the attempt by the Reformers to 'restore' the Old Testament canon to its original limits was hopelessly anachronistic.[90]

In this summary one would be forgiven for being unaware that Jerome and Augustine had a series of important exchanges over just this issue, and that the latter was forced to develop something like a theory of inspiration which could cover both 'canons' – a discussion that the canonical approach has itself taken pains to point out.[91] Jerome, of course, rather famously revised the Old Latin and Greek translations available to him by recourse to the Hebrew text. This instinct was followed, of course, in a different day and toward a different end, by 'the Reformers' (by which Barton means Luther and Calvin et al.), but this also included fresh translations by Bellarmine and others on the other side of the 'Reformation.' This instinct carefully to preserve the role of the Hebrew language version of the Old Testament, and to correct extant translations on the basis of it, more than anything accounts for the concern of the canonical approach for not cutting loose the distinctive role of the Hebrew canon – alongside other matters of historical and theological argument, as we shall see.

Barton then goes on to speak of 'Childs's argument that we must take the MT as our norm' and here chiefly on ecumenical grounds, as he sees it.[92] As we shall see, in the context of canonical text (including scope, language, and order)

---

[90] Barton, *Reading the Old Testament*, 91–92.
[91] See most recently, Childs, *Struggle*.
[92] Barton, *Reading the Old Testament*, 92.

Childs has himself spoken about the 'church's ongoing *search* for the Christian Bible.'[93] While a canonical approach will call for significant attention to the Masoretic tradition, it does this on a combination of grounds and not for 'ecumenical' reasons only. These reasons include (1) historical/recensional, (2) theological, (3) the history of Old Testament's reception, and (4) on conceptual grounds. In this latter area, Childs has argued against the sharp division of Sundberg and Barton and others between what they wish to call canonical (scope and institutional fixation) and scriptural (some more open claim to a hearing prior to this) authority.[94]

Still, to say even this is not to valorize a kind of pristine 'Masoretic Text.' It needs to be made clear up front what Childs does *not* mean by calling Christian interpretation to attend to the Masoretic tradition of the Old Testament canon. First, the MT does not have some sort of sacrosanct order to be identified over against the (emerging) different order/s of LXX texts;[95] a canon which ends with Chronicles does not sound some sort of clear and distinctive notes over against one which ends with Malachi. There are a variety of different orders.[96] Internal order and arrangement can well be important indices in a canonical approach, but one must approach the matter with discretion and care.[97] Second, Childs's appeal to the MT is registered in no small part because of an opposite tendency, namely, the effort to prioritize a distinctive LXX text over against the Hebrew canon, in the manner suggested by Barton's quote above. It is as if the Christian Bible ought properly to be regarded as a 'Greek Bible,' which can in turn somehow detach itself from the MT, either because of the

---

[93] Childs, *Biblical Theology*, 67.

[94] See now also Chapman, '"Canon" versus "Scripture"', in *The Law and the Prophets*, 106–10.

[95] Against Sweeney we cannot claim to know for sure why LXX translations adopt a four-fold internal division (where they do) – is it for theological reasons (LXX leans toward the New?) or for lower-flying reasons of confusion and a desire to taxonomize (make the 'Former Prophets' into a category of historical books and then take those from the *ketubim* which are kindred). See his either-or approach in Sweeney, 'Tanak versus Old Testament', 353–72.

[96] On the variety of orders of the Christian Bible, see Ellis, *Old Testament in Early Christianity*.

[97] In a work concerned primarily with reestablishing the coherence and proper 'coercion' of the final form of books in the canon of the Old Testament (Childs, *Introduction*), the prophetic books were treated in their MT order but with little reflection on the shape of the XII as one structured collection (this latter is now an area of considerable and fruitful investigation). Presumably there was enough to do on the first front. Still, Childs will in fact comment on the final form of the Pentateuch, for example, as against a Hexateuch or a Deuteronomistic History beginning with Deuteronomy. I have written extensively on this issue in my own publications.

history of the church which did not 'acknowledge any canon but that of the Greek Bible' (a simplistic and misleading statement) or because this allows the material reality of the New Testament's Greek-language form to say something theologically determinative about the canon of the Old Testament.[98] For a canonical approach, this is a category error. We have mentioned the confusion introduced by an approach that reads the Old Testament's theological witness as *in Novo receptum*. There is a text-critical/canonical aspect to this confusion as well.

We can list several issues that this prioritizing of 'the Greek canon' raises for a canonical approach.

When the term 'the Septuagint' is used, what is meant by this? Because of its character as a translation, Greek-language versions derived from an earlier Hebrew text did not simply fall into a single type; with a fixed length; or a standard internal ordering.[99]

This is also true in the history of the reception of the Old Testament in the church. The wide variety of known Greek language versions of the Old Testament may be a source of excitement or exuberant shows of erudition for a John Chrysostom.[100] For others it is a problem to be overcome or an irritation or an occasion to prefer what appears to be a far more settled Hebrew textual tradition – whatever additionally might be claimed for the priority of the Hebrew on theological grounds.[101]

When appeal is made to 'the Septuagint' what exactly is being said? The New Testament does not quote from a single LXX text; it can also quote from

---

[98] Any amateur reading the history of interpretation (say, on a text like Habakkuk 3) will immediately realize that the church's alleged appeal to a single, clear, contrastable, settled 'Greek canon' is illusory.

[99] The Hexapla of Origen addresses this and other realities and seeks to organize the problem, if not also (it is not clear) to offer a way forward for resolution.

[100] Hill writes: 'Chrysostom's purpose in offering such an array (of Greek translations in his Psalm commentary) to a congregation whom he faults for lack of basic biblical knowledge escapes us, unless it is to impress them with his erudition' (*St. John Chrysostom*, 7). On the problem of sorting out the manifold Greek versions, we are not helped by Chrysostom's own missteps: 'His quotation of Job 31.13–15 (in commenting on Psalm 4.1) in a form markedly different from both the Hebrew and a modern composite text of the Septuagint like Rahlfs' reminds us of the diversity of forms of the LXX current at the time' (ibid., 6). 'Reading to his listeners in one hit the four verses of 7–10 of Psalm 10 plus all the variants leaves us with a picture of a preacher with a mass of material to hand' (ibid., 7).

[101] Here it is clear that the claim that the church preferred a 'Greek Bible' is manifestly in error. In the actual practice of working with a book like Psalms, the history of Christian interpretation in every age sees the natural problems introduced by a translation (Greek or Latin).

a (pre-)MT; and it can provide translations in Greek of the Old Testament that are simply not known in any extant Greek translation.[102] Also, it rarely – probably never – quotes from a so-called apocryphal book as if this were on par with other Greek language versions of the more restricted Hebrew canon.[103]

What does it mean to speak of the Greek (or Hebrew) language 'canons' of the Old Testament as pointing to an open canon not fixed until the Christian era? If the implication is that the Old Testament does not function as canonical Scripture until the church or synagogue later fixes its limits, this is to misunderstand the role of the church or synagogue in respect of how it handles its sacred inheritance (on this see below). The distinction maintained by Sundberg and others between theological and literary determinations in respect of canon cannot be sustained; his is simply a piece of historical speculation simplifying an enormously complex textual and canonical phenomenon, and one with roots in the very inception of the biblical books.[104]

It derives from this that a misunderstanding about the role of the Old Testament in the New is frequently introduced. One cannot move from a notion of relative fixity or 'openness' (in terms of scope or internal orders), much less the simple expedient/necessity of maintaining the same Greek language throughout the New Testament (the Old Testament is not quoted in Hebrew in the Greek language New Testament), to a notion of secondary and subsequent canonical authority, imposed outside of the New Testament's own plain sense depiction of the authority of the Old Testament ('the law and the prophets').

This final point is a crucial one to observe. I have pointed out in another context how confusing the argument about the alleged priority of the New Testament's assertions vis-à-vis the Old can be. Christ does not give the Old Testament its authority, but acknowledges it and distinguishes it from the 'authoritative' statements made by men about it.[105] Neither does the church declare the limits of the Old Testament canon for the first time, as if before then it existed 'only as Scripture,' and so required stabilization and a statement about its authority (now as 'canon') for its first-time appearance in a broader canon of Christian Scripture. The New Testament declares the authority of the Old, and the apostolic witness to Christ is authoritative precisely because it is 'in

---

[102] See Bauckham, *Book of Acts*; see also Attridge on Hebrews' use of Psalm 40 in *Hebrews*; Jobes and Silva, *Invitation to the Septuagint*.

[103] See the discussion in Bauckham, *Jude*, and my essay 'Two Testaments and the Failure of One Tradition-History,' in *Figured Out*, 40–42.

[104] See Jeremias' analysis of the literary and theological factors – these cannot be separated – which lie at the base of Amos's and Hosea's compositional history.

[105] A paraphrase from Matthew might be: 'listen to teachers when they speak as Moses, but do not follow what they teach nor act as they act'; on 'you have heard that it was said,' see my essay 'Two Testaments' in *Figured Out*, 45. Compare the more technical work of Bockmuehl, *Jewish Law*, 1–82.

accordance with the Scriptures.' The authority of both the New Testament and the Christian Scripture as a twofold witness is derived from the claims of the Old Testament – claims presupposed in the New Testament and asserting themselves in the milieu from which its own composition, as 'the apostles' half of 'prophets and apostles', is coming about.

In a rather surprising quote given the source, Adolph von Harnack chided Lessing about the latter's mistaken assumptions regarding the authority of the second testament, the New Testament, as being derived from the church (which also rendered the New Testament problematical for Lessing; Lessing thought something like 'unmediated' witness was or ought to be available and that would be for him 'truth' if one could but get their hands on it). Harnack wanted to emphasize the independent way the New Testament made its force felt.[106] He might have approached the matter as did Luther, who appealed dogmatically to the creedal confession concerning the testimony of the Holy Spirit, as that testimony which gave the New Testament its *'entirely independent and unconditioned authority'*[107] – an appeal which also grounded the Old Testament's authority, both for the New Testament's confession as well as for the church ('who spake by the prophets').[108] Harnack defended the 'entirely independent and unconditioned authority' as derived from the Old Testament's own specific and peculiar status. He states: 'This was indeed only possible because the book at once took its place alongside the Old Testament, which occupied a position of absolute and unquestioned independence because it was more ancient than the Church.'[109]

In part, then, Childs's appeal to the MT is not based upon an overweening concern for one Hebrew text with fixed boundaries and special internal order and a historically monolithic transmission prior to the New. Aspects of this description may well be true, but they require considerable nuance.[110] Rather, what is at stake is the canonical authority of the Hebrew Scriptures as foundational and antecedent to Christian claims, claims that have to do with accordance and fulfillment and not with first-time establishment. The Christological grounding of this perspective is given in the New Testament, as Christ opens the Scriptures and shows them to be everywhere about himself (Luke 24 and others).

Once this perspective is secured, it helps to account for the various rationales that then guided the church as it sought to make kindred claims for the New.

---

[106] Von Harnack, *Bible Reading in the Early Church*. See also my discussion of this in respect of N.T. Wright's work, in *Redemption*, 25–42.

[107] Von Harnack, *Bible Reading in the Early Church*, 145, emphasis in text.

[108] See Helmer's insightful discussion 'Luther's Trinitarian Hermeneutic'.

[109] Von Harnack, *Bible Reading in the Early Church*, 145.

[110] See my own discussion in 'Two Testaments', in *Figured Out*, 35–47.

Too often, however, this antecedent authority, its Christological confirmation and clarification, and the character of them both as influencing the church's claims about the authority of the New are forgotten. This leads to an error of enormous irony, if not perversity: that the Scriptures of Israel become Christian Scripture only by action of the church or by claim of the New Testament by transmitting them in the material form of their Greek language expression.

Brief postscript

Mention should be made in closing about the larger canon of the 'Greek Bible' and the fact that this rubric often serves as an assertion that the MT lacks the additional books which would establish its authority for Christian purposes. Much is made of the circulation of additional books in the larger canon of the LXX, though usually the statements made lack a clear proportionality for argument's sake, and this is so at a number of key points.[111]

It is frequently stated that the New Testament's reference to 'the law and the prophets' indicates that only two-thirds of the Hebrew Scriptures (Tanak) are 'closed' in New Testament times.[112] Second, it is claimed that in the 'open part' would be those books that circulate in the larger canon; and that one can see clear evidence of these books being cited in the New Testament, on par with other books. Finally, it is said that the use of these books in the Christian church means that they are important books, widely read, seen as theologically decisive, and a critical sign that the 'Christian Canon' is not the MT.[113] From this the conclusion also follows that the canon of the Old Testament is not closed until the church estimates this to be necessary, and this happens late (following the development of a second testament, whose authority and status are then translated to Israel's Scriptures). The result is, in the language of this argument, a 'Greek Bible' for Christians.

We have chosen to look behind these details to interrogate what three such assertions *may actually assume about the status of the Old Testament as an antecedent and independent authority*. At the end of the day, arguments mounted along the lines above are not just learned assertions (which lack proper proportionality); they are the means by which one may call into question the stability of the Old Testament – whether in Greek or Hebrew language – as an authority for Christian purposes, prior to the development of the apostolic writings and toward which the authority of the New Testament seeks accordance.

It should be uncontestable that the density of citation of books from the Hebrew canon in the New Testament vastly overshadows even alleged citations

---

[111]　See now Barr in *Concept*, 563–80.

[112]　Barton et al..

[113]　Barr in *Concept*, 576–80.

of non-Hebrew books, by a factor of enormous proportion. Arguing for an allusion here or background noise there, measured against the phenomenon of
direct citation ('proof text'), ought in reality to warn against any effort to compare at all. Appeal to 'law and prophets' for the purpose of showing that only
two-thirds of the Tanak are 'closed' has been quite clearly shown to be a speculation at best, and without secure warrant.[114] And we have seen that the tendency of the history of reception is to be conservative in respect of the Hebrew
textual legacy. To put it differently, no Christian proponent of the 'Greek Bible'
cautions against appeals to the Hebrew *because the former has more books or because
the New Testament cites it in a form that shows the Hebrew canon was not closed.* At that
point, modern argument and ancient convention part company.

If there were indeed a larger and 'open' canon of the Old Testament, the
paucity of reference in the New Testament to books in it would be staggering
and require explanation. This observation is tantamount to a declaration
that the additional books are somehow secondary and insecure, or poorly
circulating, and so forth – that is, for reasons we can only speculate about.[115]
More economical is a view that the Old Testament canon is relatively stable
and comprises a Genesis to Chronicles order, with exceptions to this picture in
the New Testament very few and proving the rule.[116] Such an observation has
nothing to do with Protestant versus Catholic proclivities, ecumenical hope-
fulness, or whatever. Jerome did not invent a distinction between Hebrew and
Greek books (the latter to be read for edification but not doctrine). At a
number of levels and for several good reasons – not least the plain sense witness
of the New Testament itself – he observed one.

In sum, the church did not bestow authority on the Old Testament. The
church was the place where the confession was registered that the authority of
the Old Testament was from the Holy Spirit 'who spake by the prophets.' Following Augustine, a canonical approach will acknowledge the Holy Spirit's
activity in both Hebrew and Greek canons, which guide and constrain the
church's reflection and confession. What is more properly at issue is the antecedent and independent authority of the Scriptures of Israel, in accordance
with which, in the earliest Easter confession, Christ died and rose again.

Canon as Witness

Speech-act theory may be a way to negotiate (or finesse) problems associated
with divine and human authorship of scripture, whose last uncomplicated

---

[114] Most recently by Chapman, *Law and the Prophets*. See the earlier work by Swanson,
       Closing.
[115] See Bauckham's careful discussion in *Jude*.
[116] Beckwith, *Old Testament Canon*.

expression may have been that of Calvin.[117] Modern biblical interpretation 'complexified' the matter considerably, not just because it may have found itself allergic to claims of 'divine authorship' in the wake of Kant. With the rise of modernity, the more compelling region of complexity was *human authorship itself*, as the various biblical books 'gave up the ghost' of the human authors said to be authorizing them (Moses, Isaiah, Jonah, Daniel, Paul's Letter to the Ephesians, Colossians, etc.) and breathed their last.

A canonical approach, it has been argued, has detached itself from a view of human or authorial intentionality.[118] The situation has, however, been seen to be far more complex than that.[119] One can indeed speak of 'canonical intentionality' and find oneself back in the domain of the final form of a biblical book, with an 'authorial intention' — to use the language of the debate at hand. Isaiah 'authored' the book associated with him, or, as we shall prefer to say, the Holy Spirit 'inspired' through Isaiah an intended word. Intentionality persists even as the older views of authorship have had to be adjusted to account for the unique character of biblical books, authors, and authorizing.

The problem of speech-act theory at this point is its level of abstraction, by virtue of introducing a philosophical construct to handle the theological problem of divine-human discourse.[120] The problem is also deeply historical, to put it in more concrete terms. It may be possible to say that God commandeers human language toward a specific intended end, but say practically nothing at all about the constitutive, historically real, indeed 'elected and providentially chosen' manner of speaking through Moses and the prophets and Israel as such. Does the commandeering *depend upon prior, genuine, historical inspiration and human electing and acting*? What role does this dimension play? It would be an odd (if rather exalted) form of inspiration (speaking dogmatically) which insisted on divine intention and discourse, but which reduced the agents of that speaking to Origen's plucked instruments – now on the other side of the

---

[117] See Childs's discussion in *Struggle*, 209–13; cf. Puckett, *Calvin's Exegesis*.

[118] Lindbeck in the Childs 1998 Festschrift writes: 'Even biblical scholars such as Childs and Hays assume that the canonical sense of Scripture is to be determined as much as possible without reference to what was intended by either God or its human authors' ('Postcritical Canonical Interpretation', 48). I confess never to have heard this statement made in Childs, and certainly not with the kind of transparency this quote suggests. Lindbeck continues, 'Fear of the intentional fallacy, it seems, prevents them from recognizing that their exegetical practice is (fortunately) full of appeals to authorial intention.' Perhaps Hays runs afoul of intentional fallacy concerns, but it has not been a feature of Childs's discussion in any obvious sense I am aware of.

[119] Seitz, 'Changing Face', 80–82; Brett, *Biblical Criticism*; Noble, *Canonical Approach*; Barton, *Reading the Old Testament*.

[120] Wolterstorff, *Divine Discourse*.

Enlightenment and with the aid of a philosophical insight about language and communication.

The canonical approach has not released itself from the historical dimension of inspiration. It has broadened this considerably to include the entire process and especially the consolidation of that process consisting in the 'final form of the text.'[121]

There is an inspired and coherent Word of God to Israel and to the world, that in turn uses the historical speech of Amos and Hosea, in the canonical form of the Twelve, but which takes that speech to be about a 'history' they saw only partially (and which God over time was revealing in his history). The canonical approach seeks to describe that process, and 'success' is less in getting every diachronic detail right (that would be a wrong tack and would end in an 'eclipse of biblical narrative' – to use Frei's language) and more in accounting for the present structure and presentation of the Book of the Twelve, to choose but one example, as it now sits before us (or in front of us). The historical dimension of God's real speech with real men and women is not eliminated. Amos preached a message to the Northern Kingdom and to Amaziah the priest at Bethel, and he likely did this before Hosea and most certainly before Joel. A canonical approach wishes to understand this inspired speech in all its historical and human particularity. Those who shape the books associated with them and the collection of books within which they now reside did not treat them like 'plucked instruments' or like the girl (was it a girl?) on the swing whose sweet (but fortuitous) singing converted an Augustine. At the same time, they did seek to hear in their words the abiding and accomplishing Word of God, and so human authorship was always tied up with divine authorship, and with the providentiality of the Holy Spirit's knowledge and work.

Calvin may have been able to move easily between these two realms, but for him the task was far easier in the nature of the thing (however we judge his success at it). The biblical books and their human authors had yet to come apart (though Calvin is beginning to sense that there is a problem). It is difficult to say whether the ease of movement seen in him, between the realms of divine and human inspiration, turned on such an economical and as yet uncomplicated

---

[121] Lindbeck's criticism is at this point over the clarity of what Childs is achieving. If he were clearer, would this meet with Lindbeck's approval? He writes of Childs, 'his primary vocation is to interpret Scripture for the canonical shaping of its content. To lump this highly diverse content together with the rubric "witness," however, does not add clarity to his task' ('Postcritical Canonical Interpretation', 34 n. 7). My response would be to question whether a 'highly diverse content' is as Lindbeck characterizes it; others have viewed the canonical shaping identified by Childs as *too* tidy. Canonical intentionality can more easily connect to a view of 'witness' than Lindbeck seems to suggest. See below.

view of biblical authorship. What is easier to say is that, with the rise of critical methods, and with a severe complication into this tidy picture introduced, the organic character of inspiration came undone, and with a vengeance.

Speech–act theory may feel it can enter this realm of confusion and tidy it all up.[122] Whether it was intended for this kind of operation is another question altogether; I rather doubt it. The biblical witness is carrying too much historicality in its bosom, and it is difficult to see how this dimension will not get short-changed by philosophical constructions being deployed, even if for good reasons and with a prudential concern to guard against something going wrong. A canonical approach retains a specific concern with historicality, and it judges the season of critical inquiry we have been in one that both cannot be avoided and that also brought with it a set of concerns which shed light as well as shade, or indeed pitch-darkness.

Providentiality covers the seasons of interpretation as well as the seasons of original, historical inspiration. The season we are in has raised acute question of historicality and is sensitive to the sheer temporal distance of the events the Holy Spirit occasioned in prophets and apostles both. New is newer than Old, but the relative character of that cries out for resolution. Käsemann spoke of 'proximity to reality' as guaranteed by historical methods. A canonical approach insists the inspired witness is building a bridge to us which is sure and which has our seasons in mind. We are not prophets or apostles, but the canon appreciates this reality with all its witnessing majesty, as we are brought fully into the range of the Holy Spirit's work by virtue of the canon's shape and character as witness.[123]

Childs has used the general rubric 'witness' to organize in an underdetermined way the genre of scriptural testimony. 'Divine discourse' has been viewed as a hopeful improvement on this genre by Lindbeck.[124] Lindbeck likewise contrasts 'witness' in the canonical hermeneutics with a

---

[122] See the discussion of Childs, 'Speech-Act Theory'. He concludes, 'Wolterstorff's application of speech-act theory to biblical interpretation is deeply flawed' (391). He then continues, 'I would also hope that it has become apparent just how high are the theological stakes in this debate. Many of us can recall, often with much pain, that generations of Reformed theologians, especially in North America, were led astray in the late nineteenth and early twentieth centuries when Charles Hodge and B.B. Warfield sought to defend Christian orthodoxy within the framework of Baconian philosophy. It would be sad indeed if a new generation of evangelicals would once again commit themselves uncritically to a new and untested philosophical model, allegedly designed for the twenty-first century' (391–92).

[123] The phrase 'we are not prophets or apostles' is Childs's. See my discussion in *Word Without End*, 102–109.

[124] See his essay 'Postcritical Canonical Interpretation'. He calls this 'interpreting for authorial discourse'.

third 'classic' approach (his language), which he associates with Richard Hays and others ('reading for narrative world').[125] It is not the place here to comment on the taxonomy or the way in which both Childs and Barth fare in such a description.[126]

Witness has to its credit the possibility, as a 'classic approach,' of attaching to older dogmatic insights. Chief among these is the work of the Holy Spirit. The Holy Spirit 'witnesses' to the Father and the Son, and so gives a truthful Trinitarian account whose purpose is to order our lives in his Body. As Luther argued in another context, the Old Testament has an authority grounded in the succinct creedal claim, that the Holy Spirit spake by the prophets. For Luther, this meant that David could actually see into the divine mystery and by the Holy Spirit could describe the relations between Father and Son in the inner Trinitarian life – this all accomplished by the semantics of Hebrew idiom. What was at stake in this elaborate account was the authority of the Old Testament deeply precedent to the church's recognition and confession of it, crucial though that would be, because grounded in the reality of God himself.[127]

For our age, less controversial than Luther's exegesis ought to be his claim to understand how the Old Scriptures do their work. Historical agents are inspired to speak of things – to Israel, in Israel, from Israel – that both pertain to their day and also pertain to things the Holy Spirit alone can see and bear witness to, as an extension of what is vouchsafed to them.

One problem of appeal to 'narrative world' is in the end, 'just whose world?' Typically, for normative purposes, this world will end up in the hands of someone like Richard Hays, 'the narrative world of Paul,' who is then taken to be a normative model for Christian exegesis and faith and life. Who could dispute the sincerity and commendable character of this?

The problem is that, in the realm of a Biblical Theology of the Christian Scriptures as a two-fold witness, the Old Testament is swallowed up into Paul's confessions and construals about it (or in an imaginative reconstruction of a narrative world said to be influencing him, by deduction). Apart from the problem of reifying such a 'narrative world,' it is also not clear whether Paul

---

[125] The phrase he uses is more ambitious, if not more problematical, 'Interpretation for Narrationally Structured Symbolic Worlds' ('Postcritical Canonical Interpretation', 33). Hays finds himself rubbing elbows with Wayne Meeks and others here, and not just the Karl Barth he hoped to meet in his 'strange new world.'

[126] Lindbeck says, for example, of Barth, 'It should be observed that the Bible on the verbal level is for Barth chiefly "God's word in written form" rather than "witness." That this verbalization is not in accord with the content of Barth's position is, however strongly argued by Wolterstorff"' ('Postcritical Canonical Interpretation', 34, n. 7) – and it would appear that with this view Lindbeck is in agreement.

[127] Helmer, 'Luther's Trinitarian Hermeneutic'. See now also Assel, 'Der Name Gottes bei Martin Luther'.

would accept the laurels bestowed on him by Hays; why should his 'narrative world' (as reconstructed by Hays) speak over the manifold witness of the Old Testament said to be generating it? What for Hays is a narrative world exposed by his careful analysis of Paul or the Gospels,[128] is a reduction of what can be said about the witnessing work of the Holy Spirit 'who spake by the prophets' in the Old Testament scriptural attestation. The Old Testament generates its own Christological and Trinitarian doctrine, using its own specific idiom. Paul taps into this potentiality. He does not exhaust it, nor is his example at this local point the warrant for a wider choosing of the New Testament's use of the Old Testament, thus restricting the church's tapping into the literal sense of the Old Testament at its maximal length and breadth, on the terms of its own delivery, as Christian Scripture.

Conclusions

In this essay I have sought to give an account of the canonical approach which does justice to its extraordinary range. Much more could be said, of course. Childs is unique, to my mind, because he has worked at a sophisticated and creative level in areas which are usually the domain of one scholar only, and he has done so with an amazingly integrative touch. New Testament, Old Testament, Church History, Reception History, text-criticism, Theology, and the practice of Christian ministry are but a sample of what he has sought to control and integrate. The canonical approach entails very specific concerns regarding interpretation, but these concerns have been at the service of Christian Theology at the most basic and the most comprehensive levels. A canonical approach is an effort to read texts in a fresh way, to engage in questions of historical, theological, practical, and conceptual significance, and to keep the lines of communication between the testaments, between the Bible and theology, and between them both and the church, open and responsive.

I have not dwelt in great detail on matters of historicity or the final form of the text, even as I have given a brief analysis in the overview above. The explanation for this is that I have written a good deal on these topics in other places, and feel the resources for discussing these topics intelligently are widely available. I also tentatively conclude that in a good many ways, Childs's proposals on final form and on matters of historical reference have actually met with consent (or curiosity and respect) and are presently bearing fruit in commentary treatments and in other areas. I suspect forty years ago no one would have imagined that treatments of Isaiah that did not deal with the challenge of the

---

[128] Hays, 'Can the Gospels Teach Us How to Read the Old Testament?'.

book as a totality would be peripheral and minority accounts. Even Childs himself did not push a detailed canonical approach in areas like the Book of the Twelve, though at present scholars as diverse as Jeremias, Nogalski, Sweeney, House, Schart and Steck would be dumfounded if this approach were not pursued with diligence, and that the delicate matters of historical reference were not front and center, and requiring a careful assessment. Work in the Psalter is similar and one could go on indefinitely at this point. Even in New Testament studies, where the resistance has been manifest (by design or by omitting to notice), canonical approaches and concern with the effect of arrangements and final literary presentation are making inroads. New Testament studies are often content to stay with specific fixed and well-known issues, and to cover them again and again, perhaps aided by some new data recently available, and there is a kind of innate conservatism in the field that is hard to account for. The sociology of knowledge and its relationship to New Testament studies is a topic of enormous interest, to my mind, but it cannot be pursued here.

With a greater appreciation of the effect and sophistication of the final form – a sophistication made even clearer on the other side of our seasons of historical reading – we are now in a position to dismantle the single most decisive claim made by historical-critical reading. And as much as some have sought to describe the historical-critical method as ingredient in the Reformation, and its indispensable genius, gift and fruit, this conclusion is far from clear. For the disentangling of general Renaissance and Enlightenment cultural developments from appeals to things like *sola Scriptura* is exceedingly fraught and requires multi-volume treatments in the history of ideas with deep learning and enormous sensitivity to the challenge to hand. As time passes, and one comes to terms with the exegesis of men like Luther and Calvin, it seems clearer that they inhabit a universe quite distinct, if not unbridgeable, from the one that historical-critical methods bequeathed us in their heyday. Indeed, what would 'the Reformers' *really* make of projects like dating the Yahwist, or the Q phenomenon, or even anodyne accounts of the history of Israel or the Greco-Roman milieu – areas in which we know more than the prophets or apostles themselves, for what that may be worth.

The decisive claim of historical-critical methods, to be able to provide an appreciation of the historical dimension of the Bible never before available, also meant a promethean intuition that what had gone before was blinkered or just old-fashioned and unable to tackle the tasks at hand. The canonical approach has not turned its back on the findings of historical-critical inquiry, but it has put these under a hot light and asked what is really being said that sheds light on the plain or literal sense of the text. Given the season in which canonical approaches work, it must be no surprise that a canonical appreciation of the final form is not the same thing as what a Thomas Aquinas described as 'the literal sense' in Psalm 21 [22]. But the point is: a canonical approach can detect something like a kindred set of concerns linking the reading of Aquinas and its own sense of what is crucial in interpretation, and *it is persuaded this capacity is crucial to its own success as a method for our day, because of and not in spite of historical-critical questions.*

It is for this reason that in the above I have chosen to look in greater detail at matters of (1) the relationship between the Testaments, including text-critical considerations, (2) the possibility of 'doctrinal lenses' (or, the obverse, the impossibility of theologically neutral reading), and (3) Biblical Theology. In my judgment, because of the concerns of dealing with a two-testament scriptural witness, a canonical approach has had to make sensitive forays into the area of text-criticism. It has not done this because it seeks to give some overstated priority to the Hebrew (Masoretic) Text, but because a proper understanding of the relationship between the testaments, as a piece of Christian theology, demands assuring that the choices are not made too stark. Of course, the Christian Bible has circulated with fuller and narrower reckonings of books ('the Apocrypha' et al.). What is at issue is not a (relatively interesting) piece of church history, but instead treating the relationship between the two testaments of Scripture, for the purposes of Christian theological reflection, in a flexible and non-monolithic fashion. Efforts to reify a 'Septuagint' often come in the name of seeking to prioritize the New Testament's hearing of the Old – where said 'Septuagint' is alleged to be crucial – over a sensitive account of how the Old Testament actually does Christian theology from its own plain sense. That is why the issue is crucial from the standpoint of canonical approach: because of the need to account for the Old Testament as Christian Scripture, where its own Trinitarian doctrinal potential is not constrained by a new trend in historical-theological New Testament studies. What one sees in the history of interpretation is a genuine sensitivity to the 'plus' the Old Testament offers in the realm of basic doctrinal reflection, and a canonical approach wants to be sure that the truth of that basic intuition is not lost in the name of a Biblical Theology generated chiefly on the back of historical-critical developments of the past two centuries.

As for the second topic, doctrinal predisposition, what Levenson has shown in his discussion of Brueggemann, and in his own way, in Brueggemann's analysis of James Barr, indicates that it is simply impossible to defer in any honest way the very necessary movement, back and forth, between plain sense reading and a larger theological account of God and his relationship to the dual witness of Christian Scripture. In my judgment, canonical approaches have foregrounded this concern, and rightly, precisely because Christian interpretation will confess that one cannot read the testaments apart from one another, and that because of this, first-order doctrinal claims will and must surface. Here Brueggemann, Levenson and Childs actually all agree, even as they go their own ways, or start with different concerns and contexts. In the case of canonical approaches, the coincidence with postmodern and reader-response instincts is largely just that. All this means that the long and diverse history of interpretation of the Bible is no longer annexed in the name of theology-free reading, or due to the enthusiasms, now waning, of an objective historical approach.

The canonical approach, with its capacity to listen to, appreciate and pene-trate to the abiding theological concerns of a long history of interpretation, now has a long horizon stretching out in front of itself. Because it has not made promethean claims on the order of older historical analysis, in respect of the history of biblical interpretation; and because it has been prepared to make adjustments and acknowledge blind-spots and attenuations,[129] the canonical approach will always have as its chief task the theological interpretation of the plain sense witness of two testaments, and that task is unending. It is hard to imagine what the next season will throw up, under God, as its main challenge. History has been the ingredient most calling out for attention in our past season, and a canonical approach has, to my mind, handled that challenge with proportion and great insight.

The area calling out for greatest clarity, at least in the guild of biblical schol-arship, is just what is meant by the turn to *theological interpretation*. I have chosen in this essay to focus on what several popular New Testament scholars are pres-ently interested in, which is accounting for the role of the Old Testament (Hebrew Bible) in generating New Testament thought, exegesis, and even ecclesiology. All of this is quite hopeful and it arguably benefits from the inroads made by a canonical approach to Scripture – *but only or chiefly on the Old Testament side of the canon*. This deficit must be corrected, for the result could be serious: the Old Testament could function in its final form, for theological pur-poses, but what Childs has meant by 'canonical shape' could become nothing more than a piece of reception-history, seen from the standpoint of a New Testament utilization, theorized by recourse to a standard kit of historical-critical tools now put to a new purpose by New Testament scholarship.

More crucially of concern, and we have dwelt on this above, is the threat posed by using the second witness's theological exegesis of the Scriptures of

---

[129] Having finished writing a commentary on Isaiah, Childs writes in the preface of his next published work: 'I have recently finished a technical, modern commentary on the book of Isaiah. The task of treating the entire book of sixty-six chapters was enormous, but in addition, the commentary had necessitated restricting the scope of the exposition. That entailed omitting the history of interpretation and relegat-ing many important hermeneutical problems to the periphery of the exegesis. *After the commentary had been completed, I was painfully aware that many of the central theological and hermeneutical questions in which I was most interested had not been adequately addressed*' (*Struggle*, ix).

Israel, or an historical reconstruction of the narrative world it is said to be impressing upon key New Testament figures, as a normative category of Christian Theology. The threat is potent because so very subtle. New Testament use of the Old Testament is indeed a species of what might properly be considered Biblical Theology. But it is important to reiterate that Christian theological reflection on the Old Testament has a life proper to itself. That this has fallen out and become largely a species of history-of-religion is a sad fact traceable to developments in the wake of historical-critical inquiry. Correcting this through appeal to a 'canonical shape' is not intended to encourage a reinstatement of the Old Testament, now as a piece of reception-historical utilization seen from the standpoint of a New Testament historical analysis. This improperly delimits the Old Testament from functioning as a major doctrinal source for Christian reflection on God, and obscures or forecloses on the ontological thinking necessary for understanding Christ's work in accordance with an entire scriptural witness. It also releases New Testament scholarship from the obligation to think through what it means to read the second witness *as a canonical witness*, and to reflect theologically on the entire shape of the New Testament, before attempting Biblical Theology in the comprehensive sense.

And here the turn to the prior history of interpretation will serve a welcome purpose, not just for reading the Old Testament theologically, but also for reminding ourselves how the Old Testament and New Testament *together do theology*. Such an examination will not serve to give us role models to imitate step by step for our day: that would be driving with the rear view mirror. What the history of interpretation teaches us is how certain critical interpretative instincts come into play when a variety of factors are demanding constant monitoring and attention, history being but one of these. The vast doctrinal potential of the Old Testament in an earlier history of reflection serves as a warning not to believe the best way to hear the Old is either through historical questions primarily, or by letting the New Testament filter out what is most crucial on this score. On the other side of our great experiment in history acuity, it is time to take stock and be sure that what we are discovering actually aids us in the task of hearing the plain sense, and of relating that sense to the larger figural landscape of God's work in Israel and in Christ, across a dual scriptural witness. History will not evacuate itself in such an endeavor. It will find its proper place as God has intended, by virtue of learning all over again just what the word actually means.

Bibliography

Assel, H., 'Der Name Gottes bei Martin Luther. Trinität und Tetragramm – ausgehend von Luthers Auslegung des fünften Psalms', *EvTh* 64 (2004), 363–78

Attridge, H.W., *A Commentary on the Epistle to the Hebrews* (Hermeneia; Philadelphia: Fortress, 1989)

Barr, J., *Old and New in Interpretation: A Study of the Two Testaments* (New York: Harper & Row, 1966)

—, *The Concept of Biblical Theology: An Old Testament Perspective* (London: SCM, 1999)

—, 'The History of Israel', in *History and Ideology in the Old Testament* (Oxford: Oxford University Press, 2000), 58–101

Barrera, T., *The Jewish Bible and the Christian Bible: An Introduction to the History of the Bible* (trans. W.G.E. Watson; Leiden: Brill; Grand Rapids: Eerdmans, 1998)

Barton, J., *Reading the Old Testament: Method in Biblical Study* (2nd edn.; London: Darton, Longman & Todd, 1996)

Bauckham, R., *Jude and the Relatives of Jesus in the Early Church* (Edinburgh: T&T Clark, 1990)

—, *The Gospels for All Christians: Rethinking the Gospel Audiences* (Grand Rapids: Eerdmans, 1998)

Bauckham, R. (ed.), *The Book of Acts in its Palestinian Setting* (vol. 4 of *The Book of Acts in its First Century Setting*, ed. Bruce W. Winter; Grand Rapids: Eerdmans, 1995)

Beckwith, R.T., *The Old Testament Canon of the New Testament Church* (London: SPCK, 1985)

Bockmuehl, M., *Jewish Law in Gentile Churches* (Edinburgh: T&T Clark, 2000)

Brett, M.G., *Biblical Criticism in Crisis? The Impact of the Canonical Approach on Old Testament Studies* (Cambridge: Cambridge University Press 1991)

Brueggemann, W., 'Against the Stream: Brevard Childs's Biblical Theology', *ThTo* 50 (1993), 279–84

—, *Theology of the Old Testament: Testimony, Dispute, Advocacy* (Minneapolis: Fortress, 1997)

—, 'James Barr on Old Testament Theology: A Review of *The Concept of Biblical Theology: An Old Testament Perspective*', *HBT* 22 (2000), 58–74

Campbell, I.D., *Fixing the Indemnity: The Life and Work of George Adam Smith* (Carlisle: Paternoster, 2004)

Chapman, S., *The Law and the Prophets: A Study in Old Testament Canon Formation* (FAT 27; Tübingen: Mohr Siebeck, 2000)

Childs, B.S., *Biblical Theology in Crisis* (Philadelphia: Westminster, 1970)

—, *Exodus* (OTL; Louisville: Westminsters,1974)

—, *Introduction to the Old Testament as Scripture* (Philadelphia: Fortress, 1979)

—, *The New Testament as Canon: An Introduction* (Philadelphia: Fortress, 1984)

—, *Old Testament Theology in a Canonical Context* (Philadelphia: Fortress, 1985)

—, *Biblical Theology of the Old and New Testaments* (Minneapolis: Fortress, 1994)

—, 'The One Gospel in Four Witnesses', in *The Rule of Faith: Scripture, Canon, and Creed in a Critical Age* (ed. E. Radner and G. Sumner; Harrisburg, PA: Morehouse Publishing, 1998), 51–62

—, *Isaiah* (OTL; Louisville: Westminster, 2001)

—, 'Critique of Recent Intertextual Canonical Interpretations', *ZAW* 115 (2003), 173–84

—, *The Struggle to Understand Isaiah as Christian Scripture* (Grand Rapids: Eerdmans, 2004)

—, 'The Canon in Recent Biblical Studies: Reflections on an Era', *ProEccl* 14 (2005), 26–45; reprinted in the present volume

—, 'Speech–Act Theory and Biblical Interpretation', *SJT* 58 (2005), 375–92

Collins, J., *Introduction to the Hebrew Bible* (Minneapolis, Fortress, 2004)

Dunn, J.D.G., 'The Problem of "Biblical Theology"', in *Out of Egypt: Biblical Theology and Biblical Interpretation* (SHS 5; ed. C. Bartholomew et al.; Carlisle: Paternoster and Grand Rapids: Zondervan, 2004), 172–83

Ellis, E., *The Old Testament in Early Christianity: Canon and Interpretation in Light of Modern Research* (WUNT 54; Tübingen: Mohr Siebeck, 1991)

Frei, H.W., *The Eclipse of Biblical Narrative: A Study in Eighteenth and Nineteenth Century Hermeneutics* (New Haven: Yale University Press, 1974)

Goldingay, J., *Old Testament Theology*, Vol. 1: *Israel's Gospel* (Downers Grove: InterVarsity, 2003)

von Harnack, A., *Bible Reading in the Early Church* (trans. J.R. Wilkinson; London: Williams & Norgate, 1912)

Hays, R., *Echoes of Scripture in the Letters of Paul* (New Haven: Yale Press, 1989)

—, 'Can the Gospels Teach Us How to Read the Old Testament?', *ProEccl* 11 (2002), 402–18

Helmer, C., 'Luther's Trinitarian Hermeneutic and the Old Testament', *Modern Theology* 18 (2002), 49–73

Hill, R.C., *St. John Chrysostom: Commentary on the Psalms*; Vol. 1 (trans. and with an introduction by R.C. Hill; Brookline, MA: Holy Cross Orthodox Press, 1998)

Hübner, H., *Biblische Theologie des Neuen Testaments* (3 vols.; Göttingen: Vandenhoeck & Ruprecht, 1990–95)

Jeremias, J., 'The Interrelationship between Amos and Hosea', in *Forming Prophetic Literature: Essays in Honor of John D.W. Watts* (JSOTSup 235; ed. J.W. Watts and P.R. House; Sheffield: Sheffield Academic Press, 1996), 171–86

Jobes, K.H., and M. Silva, *Invitation to the Septuagint* (Grand Rapids: Baker Academic, 2000)

Levenson, J., 'Is Brueggemann Really a Pluralist?', *HTR* 93 (2000), 265–94

Lincoln, A., 'Hebrews and Biblical Theology', in *Out of Egypt: Biblical Theology and Biblical Interpretation* (SHS 5; ed. C. Bartholomew et al.; Carlisle: Paternoster; Grand Rapids: Zondervan, 2004), 313–38

Lindbeck, G., 'Postcritical Canonical Interpretation: Three Modes of Retrieval', in *Theological Exegesis: Essays in Honor of Brevard S. Childs* (ed. C.R. Seitz and K. Greene-McCreight; Grand Rapids: Eerdmans, 1999), 26–51

MacDonald, N.G., *Karl Barth and the Strange New World within the Bible: Barth, Wittgenstein, and the Metadilemmas of the Enlightenment* (Carlisle: Paternoster, 2000)

Martyn, J.L., *Galatians: A New Translation with Introduction and Commentary* (AB; New York: Doubleday, 1997)

Moberly, R.W.L., *At the Mountain of God: Story and Theology in Exodus 32–34* (JSOTSup 22; Sheffield: JSOT Press, 1983)

Nicholson, E.W., *The Pentateuch in the Twentieth Century: The Legacy of Julius Wellhausen* (Oxford: Oxford University Press, 1998)

Noble, P.R., *The Canonical Approach: A Critical Reconstruction of the Hermeneutics of Brevard S. Childs* (Leiden: Brill, 1995)

Nogalski, J., 'Joel as "Literary Anchor" for the Book of the Twelve', in *Reading and Hearing the Book of the Twelve* (ed. J.D. Nogalski and M.A. Sweeney; Atlanta: Society of Biblical Literature, 2000), 91–109

Porter, S.E., *The Pauline Canon* (Leiden/Boston: Brill, 2004)

Puckett, D.L., *John Calvin's Exegesis of the Old Testament* (Louisville: Westminster John Knox, 1995)

Rendtorff, R., 'Toward a Common Jewish–Christian Reading of the Hebrew Bible', in *Canon and Theology* (Minneapolis: Fortress, 1993), 31–45

Rowe, C.K., 'Romans 10:13: What is the Name of the Lord?,' *HBT* 22 (2000), 135–73

—, 'Biblical Pressure and Trinitarian Hermeneutics', *ProEccl* 11:3 (2002), 295–312

Sanders, J.A., *Torah and Canon* (Philadelphia: Fortress, 1982)

—, *Canon and Community* (Philadelphia: Fortress, 1984)

—, *From Sacred Story to Sacred Text* (Philadelphia: Fortress, 1987)

Seitz, C.R., *Word Without End: The Old Testament as Abiding Theological Witness* (Grand Rapids: Eerdmans, 1998)

—, 'Christological Interpretation of Texts and Trinitarian Claims to Truth', *SJT* 52 (1999), 209–26

—, *Figured Out: Typology and Providence in Christian Scripture* (Louisville, KY: Westminster John Knox, 2001)

—, 'What Lesson Will History Teach? The Book of the Twelve as History', in *'Behind' the Text: History and Biblical Interpretation* (SHS 4; ed. Craig Bartholomew et al.; Carlisle: Paternoster; Grand Rapids: Zondervan, 2003) 443–69

—, 'On Letting a Text "Act Like a Man" – The Book of the Twelve: New Horizons for Canonical Reading, with Hermeneutical Reflections', *Scottish Bulletin of Evangelical Theology* 22 (2004), 151–72

—, 'The Place of the Reader in Jeremiah', in *Reading the Book of Jeremiah: A Search for Coherence* (ed. M. Kessler; Winona Lake, IN: Eisenbrauns, 2004), 67–75

—, 'Prophecy and Tradition-History: The Achievement of Gerhard von Rad and Beyond', in *Prophetie in Israel: Beiträge des Symposiums "Das Alte Testament und die Kultur der Moderne" anlässlich des 100. Geburtstags Gerhard von Rads (1901– 1971) Heidelberg, 18.–21. Oktober 2001* (ed. I. Fischer, K. Schmid and H.G.M. Williamson; Münster: Lit–Verlag, 2003), 30–51

—, 'Reconciliation and the Plain Sense Witness of Scripture', in *The Redemption: An Interdisciplinary Symposium on Christ as Redeemer* (ed. S.T. Davis, D. Kendall and G. O'Collins; Oxford: Oxford University Press, 2004), 25–42

—, review of John Goldingay, *Old Testament Theology*, Vol. 1: *Israel's Gospel*, *IJST* 7.2 (2005), 211–13

Spina, F.A., 'Canonical Criticism: Childs versus Sanders', in *Interpreting God's Word for Today* (ed. W. McCown and J.B. Massey; Indiana: Warner, 1982), 165–94

Steinmetz, D.G., 'The Superiority of Pre-Critical Exegesis', *ThTo* 37 (1980), 27– 38; reprinted in *Ex Auditu* 1 (1985), 74–82, and in *A Guide to Contemporary Hermeneutics: Major Trends in Biblical Interpretation* (ed. Donald K. McKim; Grand Rapids: Eerdmans, 1986), 65–77

Sternberg, M., *The Poetics of Biblical Narrative: Ideological Literature and the Drama of Reading* (Bloomington: Indiana University Press, 1985)

Stuhlmacher, P., *Biblische Theologie des Neuen Testaments* (Göttingen: Vandenhoeck & Ruprecht, 1992)

Swanson, T.N., 'The Closing of the Collection of Holy Scriptures: A Study in the History of the Canonization of the Old Testament' (Ph.D. diss., Vanderbilt University, 1970)

Sweeney, M.A., 'Tanak versus Old Testament: Concerning the Foundation for a Jewish Theology of the Bible', in *Problems in Biblical Theology: Essays in Honor of Rolf Knierim* (ed. H.T.C. Sun et al.; Grand Rapids/Cambridge: Eerdmans, 1997), 353–72

Trobisch, D., *Paul's Letter Collection: Tracing the Origins* (Minneapolis: Fortress, 1994)

—, *The First Edition of the New Testament* (Oxford: Oxford University Press, 2000)

Van Leeuwen, R.C., 'Scribal Wisdom and Theodicy in the Book of the Twelve', in *In Search of Wisdom: Essays in Memory of John G. Gammie* (ed. L.G. Perdue, B. Scott and W. Wiseman; Louisville: Westminster John Knox, 1993), 31–49

Wagner, R., *Heralds of the Good News: Isaiah and Paul 'In Concert' in the Letter to the Romans* (Leiden/Boston: Brill, 2002)

Wall, R., 'Reading the New Testament in Canonical Context', in *Hearing the New Testament* (ed. J.B. Green; Grand Rapids: Eerdmans, 1995), 370–93

Ward, T., *Word and Supplement: Speech Acts, Biblical Texts, and the Sufficiency of Scripture* (Oxford: Oxford University Press, 2002)

Watson, F., *Text and Truth: Redefining Biblical Theology* (Edinburgh: T&T Clark, 1997)

—, 'The Old Testament as Christian Scripture: A Reply to Professor Seitz', *SJT* 52 (1999), 227–32

—, *Paul and the Hermeneutics of Faith* (London: T&T Clark, 2004)

Williamson, H.G.M, review of B.S. Childs, *The Struggle to Understand Isaiah as Christian Scripture*, *RBL* 4 (2005), available online at www.bookreviews.org/bookdetail.asp?TitleId=4494&CodePage=4494

Wolterstorff, N., *Divine Discourse: Philosophical Reflections on the Claim that God Speaks* (Cambridge: Cambridge University Press, 1995)

3

The Apostolic Gospels in the Early Church

The Concept of Canon and the Formation of the Four-Gospel Canon

Denis Farkasfalvy

Preliminaries

The purpose of this chapter is to contribute to the concept of canonical exegesis by reaching back to the earliest phases of the history of the Christian canon. The heart of the matter seems to lie in a fact that characterizes Christian origins. From its inception, Christianity was linked to an exegetical program applied to the Jewish Scriptures.

In describing this fact, I proceed by summarizing my presuppositions in five steps, then turn my attention to the development and the meaning of the fourfold Gospel canon and its impact on the interpretation of the Gospels.

Step One: *From its very beginning, Christianity had an exegetical agenda, which belonged to the core of its program.*

The earliest known form of the kerygma states: 'For I handed over to you as of first importance, what I in turn have received, that Christ died for our sins *in accordance with the Scriptures*, and that he was buried, and that he was raised on the third day *in accordance with the Scriptures*' (1 Cor. 15:3–4). In this statement 'Scriptures' cannot be reduced to a mere selection of scriptural passages[1] and/or to some Christological statements derived from the Old Testament.[2]

---

[1] Mere references to Isa. 53:6 about death and burial and to Hos. 6:2 about the 'third day' give no satisfactory explanation for the repetitive use of the phrase 'according to the scriptures.'

[2] One cannot reduce the early church's interest in the Old Testament to its use of the so-called *Testimonia*, a limited list of Christologically relevant scriptural excerpts detached from their context.

To the contrary, as we will show below, Paul consciously extends this exegetical program so as to include both the whole Christian message and all Scriptures.

Step Two: *The Jewish scriptural texts quoted by the Christian kerygma are involved in a twofold dynamic. On the one hand, the first Christian preaching sought to obtain an understanding of Christ from the Scriptures and, on the other, it sought to understand the Scriptures from words and deeds of Christ.*

Two passages from Luke 24 well illustrate this 'two-way road' linking the understanding of Christ and that of the Scriptures. First, we see the road from the Scriptures to Christ: 'And beginning with Moses and all the prophets, he interpreted to them the things about himself in *all the Scriptures*' (Lk. 24:27).[3] Second, we see the road from Christ to the Scriptures: '"These are my words that I spoke to you while I was still with you – that everything written about me in the law of Moses, the prophets and the psalms[4] must be fulfilled." Then he opened their minds to understand the Scriptures' (Lk. 24:44–45).

Quoted here are Jesus' last utterances in Luke's Gospel to the disciples. They form an inclusion with Jesus' first statement in that same Gospel made in the synagogue of Nazareth: 'And he rolled up the scroll, gave it back to the attendant, and sat down. The eyes of all in the synagogue were fixed on him. Then he began to say to them, "Today this Scripture has been fulfilled in your hearing"' (Lk. 4:20–21).

A 'minimalist' interpretation would not be satisfactory. For Jesus' statement does not refer just to one specific biblical passage of Isaiah. The rolling up of the scroll signifies not only that the whole book of Isaiah is involved, but that now, with the beginning of Jesus' ministry, all prophecy comes to its conclusive stage (cf. Lk. 16:16).

That the Scriptures are now fulfilled means in this context that Jesus himself, filled with the presence of the Spirit, brings them to fullness and, as he speaks and acts in virtue of his fullness of inspiration, the meaning of the Scriptures becomes manifest. The Scriptures are 'fulfilled' in Jesus not because some statements in Isaiah can be applied to him with a high level of predictive accuracy in some or many, even small details, but because, in the person of Jesus, the very ultimate meaning of all prophecy has made its entrance into the world.

---

[3] Unless noted otherwise in this article I use the English translation of NRSV.

[4] This may not be the oldest example for a tripartite description of the Canon (Law – Prophets – Writings), only a two-part scheme (Law and Prophets) with additional emphasis on the Psalms, but, in any case, it means the totality of the sacred writings in Judaism.

Step Three: *For the first Christians the acceptance of the Christian faith was inseparable from 'believing in the Scriptures.' Embracing Christian faith implied taking into possession the Scriptures as 'written for us.' It also meant understanding the apostolic tradition as key to the interpretation of the Scriptures.*

Believing in the Scriptures meant the belief that the Scriptures were inspired by identically the same Spirit who endowed the Old Testament with its prophetic dimension. By the same Spirit who inspired the Scriptures, the apostolic community came to understand Christ as the Son of God, and received its boldness, its παρρησία to announce the gospel.

Of course, the first apostolic preaching addressing the Jews was expected to begin with texts of the Old Testament. But also, when addressing the Gentiles, this preaching had to show its 'scriptural' base, and thus, evidently, the use of the Scriptures was no matter of mere missionary strategy. Since, in order to understand Christ, a church recruited from among Gentiles would need to be instructed about the Scriptures, the delivery of the apostolic kerygma had to be linked to a catechesis about the books of the Old Testament which, in the case of a Gentile audience, had to follow as a second step *after* the proclamation of the gospel.

And so, we repeatedly encounter what we have already seen above in Paul's text: all Christians, regardless of Jewish or Gentile background, would eventually come to treat the Scriptures as their own heritage: 'For *whatever was written* in former days was written *for our instruction*' (Rom. 15:4). We find similar passages in other Pauline texts, including 1 Corinthians which was certainly addressed to Gentiles:

Does he not speak entirely for our sake? It was *written for our sake.*

(1 Cor. 9:10)

Now these things happened to them as a warning, but they were *written down for our instruction*, upon whom the end of the ages has come.

(1 Cor. 10:11)

Step Four: *Therefore, the Christian canon of the Scriptures, including both the Jewish Scriptures and the apostolic writings, reflects complementary dimensions in the church's self-understanding, by which she recognizes both her own apostolic origins and the Scriptures inherited from Judaism.*

In coming to her self-understanding, the church realized that the Spirit who inspired the Jewish Scriptures was identical with the Spirit of Christ who gave the apostles their post-resurrectional faith and the courage (παρρησία) to proclaim and to understand Christ as the meaning of the whole divine salvation plan. This same Spirit animated the apostolic preaching, made the oral message of the apostles take place and find its expression in written records of Gospels and apostolic letters, all guaranteed by the church 'built upon the apostles and the prophets' (cf. Eph. 2:20).[5]

The canonical principle that Christian faith is based on the double pillar of the prophets and the apostles is a theme common to the New Testament and to the early Church Fathers. They give unanimous witness that the unity of the economy of salvation hinges on the one Christ and the sameness of the Spirit and that this unity did not come about *after the canon, as if by hindsight*, but was posited 'a priori' and made the formation of the New Testament canon possible.

Consequently, a canonical reading and understanding of the Scriptures is rooted in the way Christian faith began and the New Testament was formed.

Step Five: *In conclusion, we might state: the canon is based on the principle that the ultimate norm for the content of the Christian faith is the teaching of 'the prophets of old and of the apostles of Christ.'*

The claim found in the early church is that God used chosen spokesmen as tools for mediating his word and that these spokesmen left behind a written record. This claim can be found in several different but equivalent formulas, such as:

- 'the prophets and the apostles' (twofold formula).
- 'Law and prophets, the Lord Jesus and his apostles' (threefold formula).
- the teaching of the prophets, the Gospels and of the apostles (another threefold formula).
- the two Testaments (twofold formula).

Before there is an explicit canon, as a list of books and a definite and closed collection of writings, there is in the church a routine for arguing about the faith by referring to the 'prophets and the apostles.' These references not only make the claim that the witness of the 'prophets and the apostles' is binding on the church, but also that their teachings must be assumed to be harmonious among themselves.

---

[5] Most exegetes see in this sentence, as well as in Eph. 3:5 and 4:11, the linkage of Christian (New Testament) prophets and apostles. Each of these passages is usually referred to 1 Cor. 12:28–29. Because of Lk. 11:49 and its parallel in Mt. 23:34, the issue of interpretation may not be so narrowly defined. In any case, in the second century, 'prophets and apostles' (or in reversed order: 'apostles and prophets') refer to the two testaments, as we can see in several passages of Justin, Irenaeus, and, with a canonical connotation, in the *Muratorian Fragment* (lines 77–78). In a striking sentence, Tertullian makes the terms 'prophets' and 'apostles' both referential to the two Testaments and functionally equivalent: 'Tam enim apostolus Moyses quam apostoli prophetae, aequanda erit auctoritas utriusque officii, ab uno eodemque domino apostolorum et prophetarum.' *Adv. Marcionem* IV, 24, 8–9 (CCL I, 609).

The main passages referring to 'prophets and apostles' are the following: Luke 11:49, Ephesians 2:20, 3:5, 4:11 and 2 Peter 3:2. These are matched by similar formulas in Ignatius of Antioch, Polycarp of Smyrna, the Letter of Barnabas and elsewhere. Beginning with Irenaeus, this 'canonical principle' is abundantly documented throughout the rest of patristic and medieval literature.[6]

Of course, the concept of the unity of the two testaments stems from the 'oneness' (sameness) of the Spirit. About this the most significant passage in the New Testament is found in 1 Peter 1:11–12.

The development and meaning of the fourfold Gospel canon

In this development from canonical principle to canon, probably the most important step is constituted by the formation of the four-Gospel canon, the τεραμόρφου εὐαγγέλιον as it was named by Irenaeus.[7]

We do not know at what historical event and exact date the fourfold Gospel canon was formulated and, afterwards, received by the church. A valid *terminus a quo* is obviously the composition and reception of the Fourth Gospel, but a *terminus ad quem* can be established only with difficulties.

There is little doubt that it preceded Irenaeus' *Adversus haereses* (185 AD). One may also be reasonably confident that it came about prior to the composition of the *Diatessaron* by Tatian (sometime around 160–170 AD). A similar date is suggested by a remark of Celsus quoted by Origen. Celsus accused the Christians of having corrupted the Gospel from its original integrity, to a threefold, even fourfold, or many-fold degree.[8] This would mean that around 160–170 AD an enemy of the Christians had noticed that the εὐαγγέλιον, the basis of the Christian message, although claimed to be unified and one, had been identified with the content of three or four different literary documents that showed variances among themselves.

Probably one can make one more step and go back a couple of decades. It was around 140 AD that Marcion went public – first in Asia Minor, then in Rome – with his program of a single Gospel, that of Luke, of which he, Marcion, provided an interpolated edition.

Hans von Campenhausen conjectured that the fourfold Gospel canon came about in reaction against Marcion by church leaders who then eventually also

---

[6]   See Farkasfalvy, 'Prophets and Apostles'.

[7]   *Adversus haereses* III, 2, 11; II, 47–48.

[8]   'After this he says, that certain of the Christian believers, like persons who in a fit of drunkenness lay violent hands upon themselves, have corrupted the Gospel from its original integrity, to a threefold, and fourfold, and many-fold degree, and have remodeled it, so that they might be able to answer objections.' Origen, *Contra Celsum*, ch. 27.

obtained Marcion's expulsion from the church of Rome.[9] But Marcion's role in the formation of the Gospel canon needs re-evaluation. Marcion's 'one gospel' was linked with his exclusive Paulinism by which he rejected not only all Gospels not connected with Paul, but most importantly, all other *apostles* – Peter and the rest of the Twelve – whom he considered 'Judaizers.' His primary decision was not a selection among the available Gospels and thus a preference for Luke against the others, but the selection of one apostle to the exclusion of the other apostles. He accepted only Paul as 'the apostle of Jesus Christ' and, consequently, he rejected the Gospels according to Matthew, John, and also Mark; the latter decision, incidentally, also confirms that Mark's Gospel had Petrine credentials by the time of Marcion.

Thus Marcion agrees on an important point with the church at large, namely that from among the many Gospels in use in his time only 'an apostolic gospel' should deserve credence. The point of disagreement between Marcion and the great church is about the identity of the authentic apostles of Jesus. While the church accepts both Paul and Peter and the rest of the twelve, Marcion has only one apostle and for that reason only one Gospel. This insight may throw some light on the meaning of the anti-Marcionite position of both Irenaeus and Tertullian: in their argumentation on behalf of the four-Gospel canon, they consistently emphasize the apostolic character of these Gospels as they call Mark and Luke 'apostolic men,' i.e. qualified authors of canonical works because of their connections with Peter and Paul.[10]

How authentic is Marcion's Paulinism and his alleged reliance on Galatians 1:8–9 when he insists on the 'oneness of the gospel?' Is it correct to say that Marcion misinterpreted Galatians just because he misunderstood the word εὐαγγέλιον and replaced its Pauline meaning (= salvific message of Jesus Christ[11]) with a later, second-century meaning (= an account about Jesus' words and deeds)?

First, Paul's position on the 'oneness' of the εὐαγγέλιον is not as unambiguous as it sounds. In Galatians, Paul not only states that there can be only one Gospel (Gal. 1:9), but he also allows for some significant diversity and multiplicity in it. For in 2:7 he distinguishes between the εὐαγγέλιον ἀκροβυστίας and εὐαγγέλιον περιτομῆς, two different presentations of the good news of Jesus Christ, one by himself and the other by Peter. In other words, Paul is

---

[9] Cf. *The Formation of the Christian Bible.*

[10] Cf. Schulz, *Die apostolische Herkunft der Evangelien.*

[11] Fitzmyer writes: 'But in the vast majority of passages εὐαγγέλιον denotes the content of his [Paul's] apostolic message' , *To Advance the Gospel*, 150. Stuhlmacher notes that for Paul, '"the message of Christ" and "the gospel" are the same' ('The Pauline Gospel', 150). Stuhlmacher shows that this interpretation of the Pauline use of the word comes from A. Harnack.

ready to recognize Peter as the leader of the mission to the circumcised as long as he, Paul, is recognized as the leader of the mission to the Gentiles. He calls the message delivered both by himself and Peter the εὐαγγέλιον which, of course, implies the recognition of two versions in the presentation of the gospel. The oneness of the gospel, then, is not defined by the very sameness of the way in which it is formulated or the identity of the behavioural expectations connected with it, but by the sameness of 'the one who worked through Peter for the mission to the circumcised' and of the one 'who worked through me [Paul] also for the Gentiles' (2:8). This means the sameness of Christ and the sameness of the Spirit, not the sameness of a message or a creed.

Second, we must ask if, indeed, the Pauline meaning of the word εὐαγγέλιον radically differs from the meaning of the same word when used in the second century.[12] As is well known, early in the second century the narrative accounts of Jesus' words and deeds received the title ΕΥΑΓΓΕΛΙΟΝ followed by the preposition κατά as in κατὰ Μαθθαῖον, Μᾶρκον, Λουκᾶν and Ἰωάννην. Yet this latter meaning is not as substantially different from its Pauline sense εὐαγγέλιον as many authors might consider it. Our best proof comes from the two parallel versions of the Anointing in Bethany found in the Gospels of Matthew and Mark:

> "Truly I tell you, wherever the good news (εὐαγγέλιον)[13] is proclaimed in the whole world, what she has done will be told in remembrance of her."
> (Mk. 14:9//Mt. 26:13)

What is truly remarkable in this sentence is the way it spells out a number of its presuppositions without which its meaning is lost. First, it supposes that the proclamation of the 'good news' (= the gospel as salvific message) goes together, hand in hand, with 'narrative accounts,' i.e. with the telling of stories like the one to which the sentence belongs, the story of the anointing.[14] Second, the sentence also assumes that whoever is mentioned in these narratives is being memorialized. Third, when Jesus makes the prediction that *this* story of the anointing will be narrated 'wherever the gospel is proclaimed,' he assumes that not all stories are equally narrated everywhere.

Thus we find the assumption that in Galatians the choice of episodes to accompany the proclamation of the εὐαγγέλιον is not considered by Paul to be fully standardized or identical. Some episodes are narrated at one place, and some are narrated at other places. The point made by the Dominical logion is that Jesus guaranteed, or maybe *commanded*, that in connection with any presentation of the gospel message the 'anointing in Bethany' be

---

[12] Cf. Stuhlmacher, 'The Pauline Gospel', 171–72.

[13] The Matthean parallel has 'this good news' or εὐαγγέλιον τοῦτο.

[14] The verb used is λαληθήσεται meaning not just a 'mentioning' but 'narrating.'

narrated everywhere in the world. While such an understanding of the word εὐαγγέλιον certainly does not mean a *book*, and does not necessarily mean the narration of stories as such, it definitely means a proclamation which requires at least *concomitantly* the narration of stories. In this way one can see how and why, in a short time, the word εὐαγγέλιον could have begun to mean in some global way, both the salvific message and the stories about Jesus that accompanied the proclamation of the salvific message about his death and glorification.[15]

The conclusions reached above reveal the connection which existed between the creation of the Gospel titles ('εὐαγγέλιον κατὰ...') and the formation of the four-Gospel canon. The peculiar wording of the titles is not only consistent with but also suggestive of the vision of both Galatians and the pericope of the anointing in Bethany. For these titles assert the oneness of the gospel and promote the concept of its multiplicity in terms of the various presentations, which the gospel receives by different apostolic witnesses. At the same time, the titles bring about a new emphasis that the proclamation of Jesus' good news is necessarily linked to narratives in which a variety of episodes are presented, some selected at random, others by divinely intended necessity. In such a perspective the εὐαγγέλιον as a title for a book containing narratives about Jesus with a disproportionate concentration on his death and resurrection does not appear to be the result of a linguistic accident or a mere shift in meaning, happening randomly in Christian usage, but as the final outcome of a process of theological maturation which accompanied the development of the Gospel tradition through its oral phases and its subsequent literary consolidation.

Therefore I would propose that the formation of the four-Gospel canon was itself a process involving several decades of a rather simple development. It was achieved by Christian churches which came into possession of several compositions with trustworthy claims of apostolic origins and began to use them simultaneously. These compositions quickly replaced the oral narratives that accompanied the proclamation of the apostolic kerygma. Due to the link between those narratives and the kerygma, so obviously present in the story of the anointing in Bethany, the literary works narrating Jesus' words and deeds began to be referred to as εὐαγγέλιον. Yet due to the reception of the Pauline Corpus at the end of the first century, there was enough caution against allowing the word εὐαγγέλιον to be used in the plural and there was enough guidance to consider the various apostolic witnesses to be variant but not discordant witnesses of the apostolic tradition.

---

[15] Such an interpretation opens the road to interpreting the ἀρχὴ τοῦ εὐαγγέλιον (Mk. 1:1) in reference to the whole book of Mark.

Thus the naming of the Gospels with the title εὐαγγέλιον κατὰ … already implies the project of a Gospel canon limited to all and only apostolic Gospels, literary works of Jesus' words and deeds with an apostolic authority, organically connected with the kerygma. The actual decision that from all works circulating in the Christian churches at the time, exactly four, in fact, qualify as such 'apostolic gospels,' could have well been discussed and decided at some formal meetings among heads of the important Christian centers. There is a degree of probability one may attach to William Farmer's reconstruction of the exchange that took place between St. Polycarp and Pope Anicet in Rome in the year of 154 or 155 AD, a meeting intended to resolve the Quartodeciman crisis.[16]

At that time the scandal caused by Marcion in Rome in 144 AD was still of fresh memory. Ultimately, the Quartodeciman dispute itself was about the conflict between various apostolic authorities and traditions: both the church of Rome and the churches of Asia Minor invoked their own understanding of the apostolic tradition.[17] The conflicting reports of the Synoptics and of the Fourth Gospel on the date of the Passover testify that this conflict was, indeed, embedded in the earliest church traditions. One could easily see that when Polycarp and Anicet could not resolve their conflict about the date of Easter, yet remained in communion and celebrated the Eucharist together, they gave testimony about their joint recognition of four apostolic gospels and thus made the four-Gospel canon the cornerstone of both orthodoxy and church unity. Since it is quite probable that at that historic meeting Irenaeus of Lyons was personally present,[18] we discover here also the origins of Irenaeus' ardent and eloquent defense of the four-Gospel canon in his *Adversus Haereses*, to be written about thirty years later.

---

[16] Farmer, 'Development of the New Testament Canon', 71.

[17] Scholars wrestling with the Johannine authenticity of the Fourth Gospel meticulously ponder the fact that in Polycarp's letter to the Philippians no quotation from the Fourth Gospel, and only one allusion to John's First Epistle can be found. But they fail to mention that, according to Eusebius, the *crux* of the Quartodeciman Dispute was a clash between apostolic authorities: Pope Anicet referring to Peter and Paul and Polycarp arguing with the Johannine origin of the tradition of Asia Minor. However, by the middle of the second century, 'Peter and Paul' mean the authorities behind the synoptics (we have Papias' earlier witness about the link of Mark to Peter, and Marcion's testimony about Luke as a disciple of Paul) quoting Johannine tradition in favor of a Quartodeciman practice must be seen as relying on the Fourth Gospel's Passion Narrative. Cf. Culpepper, *John, The Son of Zebedee*, 120.

[18] Irenaeus' familiarity with the situation of the church of Rome is commonly admitted. The trip he made to Rome under Pope Eleutherius concerning the Montanist crisis offers some probability that some twenty years earlier he showed up in Rome at the arrival of St. Polycarp.

Conclusions

The most remarkable feature in the formation of the four-Gospel canon is its ecumenical character and potential. During its relatively short period of formation – less than fifty years in the first half of the second century – the early church was in danger of embarking onto the waves of history without solid structures and provisions for stability: a well defined, written form for the most important portion of its treasure of tradition, the Jesus tradition.

The appearance of several written renderings of Jesus' deeds and words, all with a claim to authentic originality (i.e. apostolic origins), implied the threat that Christianity would branch out into a multiplicity of more or less diverse beliefs and practices. With the onset of the Gnostic movement, the fragmentation of the Christian movement had effectively begun. The churches responded to every novelty by referring to the orally transmitted 'Rule of Faith' and by arguments based on 'prophets and apostles,' the Scriptures of old and the variously transmitted oral and written records of the apostolic teaching.[19]

Such chaotic circumstances are reflected by Papias' fragments, reporting about the confusingly diverse Greek versions of the Gospel of Matthew, all claiming to stem from an originally Semitic apostolic composition, and about Mark whose work Papias tries to defend against charges of lack of order and incompleteness by referring to the apostolic witness of Peter. Such a situation is mirrored by an ancient presbyter's remarks quoted by Clement of Alexandria, with his advice on how to determine which version of a Gospel is earlier and which one is of a later and, possibly, interpolated origin.[20] It is under such circumstances that Papias utters his preference for the 'living voice' of oral tradition, exhibiting an open mistrust of written documents that can be manipulated and pass under fictitious names.[21]

At the same time the church becomes more and more aware of its Pauline heritage, postulating in Galatians one single gospel, and forbidding in 1 Corinthians the use of the various apostolic names for partisan purposes between competing factions.[22] The acceptance of four apostolic Gospels edited as four versions of the one gospel with historically identifiable names, all pointing to the first Christian generation, was a bold, appropriate and efficient measure, but it has also succeeded in rescuing a large variety of ancient traditions and curbing the growth of the Gnostic movements.

---

[19] Farkasfalvy, 'Prophets and Apostles'.
[20] Farkasfalvy, 'The Presbyters' Witness'.
[21] Farkasfalvy, 'The Papias Fragment'.
[22] 1 Cor. 1:12.

From the retrospective point of view of modern Christianity, the four-Gospel canon declared not only the oneness of Jesus Christ but also posited the presupposition of a basic harmony reigning among the various canonical presentations of Jesus, obviously not reachable by any merely human efforts but only when coupled with the postulate of one and the same Spirit, animating the church, validating the sacraments, maintaining the links of faith and charity, and thus enabling the church to discover the same reality presented in a fourfold way. The four-Gospel canon allowed the church to coexist with a limited and controlled dose of diversity and a call to possess unity as a task of holding this diversity together, rather than exchanging it for any brand of reductionism.

A good example may be found in the 2,000-year-old question of the date of the Last Supper. The four-Gospel Canon did not decide the question, but instead demanded that both traditions, that of the Synoptics and that of John be taken seriously, and, at the same time, forbade the disassociation of the Easter mystery of Christ either from the Last Supper and the crucifixion or from the celebration of the Paschal Lamb. By the four-Gospel canon the exegetical task is made immensely more difficult, but the theology of the Christian Passover has become immensely more rich.

Bibliography

von Campenhausen, H., *The Formation of the Christian Bible* (Philadelphia: Fortress, 1972)

Culpepper, R.A., *John, The Son of Zebedee. The Life of a Legend* (Minneapolis: Fortress, 2000)

Farkasfalvy, D., 'Prophets and Apostles: The Conjunction of the Two Terms before Irenaeus', in *Texts and Testament: Critical Essays on the Bible and the Early Church Fathers in Honor of Stuart Dickson Currie* (ed. W. Eugene March; San Antonio: Trinity, 1980), 109–34

—, 'The Presbyters' Witness on the Order of the Gospel as Reported by Clement of Alexandria', *CBQ* 54.2 (April 1992), 260–70

—, 'The Papias Fragment on Mark and Matthew and Their Relationship to Luke's Prologue: An Essay on the Pre-History of the Synoptic Problem', in *The Early Church in Its Context. Essays in Honor of Everett Ferguson* (ed. A.J. Malherbe, F.W. Norris and J.W. Thompson; New York: Brill, 1998), 92–106

Farmer, W.R., 'A Study in the Development of the New Testament Canon', in *The Formation of the New Testament Canon: An Ecumenical Approach* (W.R. Farmer and D.M. Farkasfalvy; New York: Paulist Press, 1983), 7–96

Fitzmyer, J.A., *To Advance the Gospel: New Testament Studies* (Grand Rapids: Eerdmans, 1981)

Schulz, H.-J., *Die apostolische Herkunft der Evangelien* (Quaestiones Disputatae 145; Freiburg: Herder, 1993)

Stuhlmacher, P., *The Gospel and the Gospels* (Grand Rapids, MI: Eerdmans, 1991)

4

The Gospels Within the
New Testament Canon
Eugene E. Lemcio

Introduction

Limitations and thesis

Although ancient and modern authors concerned with the New Testament as Scripture (i.e. as the documents 'which the Church formed in order to form the Church' as my colleague Rob Wall loves to say[1]) have attempted to suggest the means by which the New Testament might be read in the light of the four-fold gospel, they have largely emphasized how the evangelists' message coheres with or amplifies the other witnesses.

However, if one takes with utmost seriousness the diversity of the New Testament as well as its unity, then one is obliged to demonstrate how the diverse witness of the Gospels functions over against the other documents and their theologies in a constructive manner. It is the purpose of this chapter to do so in a way that avoids harmonization, reductionism, and preferential treatment.

In the absence of very much secondary scholarly literature on this subject and in the absence of an ecclesial magisterium, I offer the following study, based upon my own limited experience as a practicing Christian of how the Gospels are (not) used and upon my reading of others' experiences. In proposing my thesis, I am more than ever conscious about the role of the interpreter. Scripture does not interpret itself; nor do the Scriptures teach anything. Only persons can teach and interpret.

So far as the underlying unity and coherence of the New Testament is concerned, I have argued that a formal six-member 'kerygmatic' recital centers the

---

[1] Among several writings where the idea behind this slogan has been developed, see Wall, 'Reading the New Testament', 370–75.

New Testament.[2] This frees me to propose that one can employ a contrapuntal dialectic in constructively exploiting its canonical diversity. For the limited purposes of this chapter, I want to show how thus using the Gospels can contribute to that enterprise.[3]

Caveats

In all of this, I am not assuming anything about the historical character of the Gospels. This is not an historical exercise; it is not even primarily an exegetical one, but a canonical one. And if this term has any meaning at all, it must direct our attention primarily to the received text, not to scholars' often-contested reconstruction of the history behind the text.[4]

As an interpreter who values the canon's diversity and views it as providing the ingredients for constructive 'reproof and correction,' I shall try to assess the community's current or potential situation and then propose a 'mid-course correction' as needed.[5] It then becomes the duty of others within the academy and church to inform, confirm, or challenge my diagnosis and prescription – in other words, to perform their 'canonical function.'

Contemporary usage

If one observes the church's actual usage of the Gospels, it is clear that there are several dynamics at work: ones which will provide a context for the thesis and method of this chapter. Although the Gospels appear first and occupy a prominent position in the New Testament, their usage liturgically is mixed. Even in those churches where the Bible plays a leading role, they are read and proclaimed rather spottily and irregularly. In more sacramentalist confessions,

---

[2] Lemcio, 'Unifying Kerygma'. While one could regard this as an internal criterion, see how the 'rule of faith' might work as an external unifying hermeneutical criterion as developed by Wall, 'The Rule of Faith in Theological Hermeneutics', 88–107. Räisänen, *Beyond New Testament Theology*, 260–61, strangely claims that my proposal does not go beyond Dunn's formula, though it clearly does: 'affirmation of the identity of the man Jesus with the risen Lord' (*Unity and Diversity*, 227–28). Furthermore, Dunn also explicitly denies that which I have tried to show: that there is such a thing as an internal, formal 'kerygmatic' pattern that dominates the New Testament (30–31). For a more extensive and positive estimate, see Segalla, 'La Testimonianza Dei', 311–12, 315.

[3] I attempted a contrapuntal, dialectical approach between the two Gospel traditions in 'Synoptics and John'.

[4] I sought to show the relationship between historical and canonical methods in 'Parables'.

[5] Lemcio, 'Synoptics and John'.

where the lectionary is appropriated, the Gospel is the last of the Scriptures to be read, being given further prominence by certain actions of both priest and congregants. However, the picture is different among hymns and songs: one is hard pressed to find very many whose content deals with the entire course of Jesus' life.

Also diverse is their usage outside of Christian worship. Despite claims of certain 'Bible-believing Christians,' many of whom maintain a view of Scripture's inerrancy, the Gospels are, on the whole, dramatically underrepresented or highly censored. The remainder is confined to a gentle Jesus who welcomed all, loved children, healed the sick, told 'earthly stories with heavenly meaning' only to die a horrible death before rising from the dead.

So far as doctrine is concerned, the focus is on Paul or the Apocalypse – or upon the Gospels read with Pauline or Johannine eyes, wearing Protestant glasses. (The result is either a kind of harmonization or preferential treatment; both moves deny the New Testament's diversity.) As a consequence, the narrative of Jesus' teaching and action is viewed as somehow preliminary, introductory, and preparatory for the Gospel (and therefore optional) rather than as an integral part of it. Among Anabaptists, the opposite is the case. As one colleague from this tradition put it, 'We are passionate followers of the earthly Jesus.'

Procedure

I shall approach the task in two ways. In Part 2, I will attempt to show how the four Gospels collectively could influence the other corpora of the New Testament;[6] and then in Part 3 I shall demonstrate how individual Gospels might affect the subjects of individual authors or corpora. However, in the course of making my case, I shall not be comprehensive, being content to use major categories and themes to illustrate both method and conclusions.

---

[6] So far as I am aware, the first attempt to relate the Synoptic Gospels and the Fourth Gospel theologically in a comprehensive way appears in Lemcio, 'Synoptics and John'. Childs in *New Testament as Canon* reflects upon three traditions shared by both, but he does not address what I regard as the Gospels' most dramatic theological differences. See Wall and Lemcio, *New Testament as Canon*. Marshall, *New Testament Theology*, though devoting several pages to 'The Gospels and New Testament Theology' (51–56) does not suggest a means of relating the two. In treating 'Diversity and Unity in the New Testament' (707–31), the accent falls heavily on the latter. No method of constructively appropriating the variety is suggested. In *New Testament Theology*, 18–26, Caird proposed an 'Apostolic Conference' approach to accommodate the New Testament's diversity; but he has been faulted for both controlling the agenda and not permitting contrary voices to speak.

The Gospel Corpus as a Whole

Genre

I propose that the Gospels' standing first suggests that the most fundamental genre for Christian faith and life is narrative, story. This should prevent the letters from being preferred by the more didactically and discursively minded. It is all too easy to be caught up in confession, to declare who and what is rather than how they and we got there. One might be disposed to favor a writer on aesthetic grounds ('I like the way that James puts things') or conclude on other than textual grounds that, say, Paul's doctrine of justification is at the heart of the New Testament. Recognizing the priority given to such a massive amount of narrative could 'earth' interpretations of apocalyptic literature when visionary experiences lose their moorings, failing to recall how it was that a slain lamb came to share sovereignty with God, the Pantocrator.

Scope

In a related point, the full-blown narrative ought to check efforts to focus the Gospel at the end of Jesus' life – a view sometimes nurtured even by scholars, who uncritically perpetuate the dicta of predecessors. Among these are Martin Kähler's declaration that 'The Gospels are Passion Narratives with an extended introduction.'[7] This assertion seems rather self-evident until one does a basic computation of text devoted to beginnings, middle, and end. Yes, they are extended – by nearly eight times! Fewer than two of Mark's sixteen-and-a-half chapters deal with the actual suffering and death of Jesus. Thus, is the previous material merely 'introduction' or part and parcel of the Gospel itself?

Content

Although this will be treated in more detail below, it is enough to point out two rather dramatic examples. One would never have guessed from the two epistolary corpora that Jesus' main subject of preaching and teaching was the arrival of God's eschatological rule (as it is in the Synoptic Gospels). Moreover, who could have concluded from the letters that Jesus' preferred Christological expression was 'The Son of Man?' It is the only public and narrative title, the

---

[7] Kähler, *The So-called Historical Jesus*, 80 n. 11. In admitted overstatement ('To state the matter somewhat provocatively …'), he complained that something so *theologically* weighty as the Passion Narratives was being minimized by historians. So, he maximized its significance by calling the preceding stories 'introductions', although Kähler had to acknowledge their substantial presence with the word 'extended'.

others being confessional and, so, 'static.' Where else but to the Gospels could one go to discover in any detail what the Son of God, Christ, and Lord had accomplished? Only 'the Son of Man' covers every phase of Jesus' life, both 'historical' and eschatological.

The Gospels and Representative Themes

The gospel

Recently, in a volume devoted to the written gospel, K. Snodgrass claimed that 'The church's gospel is rightly summarized as the proclamation of the death and resurrection of Jesus.'[8] It would surely be more accurate to say that this summarizes the gospel *which Paul received and proclaimed* as good news ['gospeled'] to the Corinthians (1 Cor. 15:1–5). As I hope presently to demonstrate, the synoptic evangelists thought differently. In fairness, Snodgrass attempts to distinguish this from 'The gospel of Jesus;' but his summary here and later indicates the need constantly to recognize that the earliest church thought variously about the subject. In order to illustrate such diversity, it is necessary to delimit the boundaries of this vast topic. Therefore, I shall focus upon representative texts, which contain noun and verb forms of ευαγγελ- and κηρυχ-.

Mark's is the only Gospel that, in its 'headline', refers to 'gospel'. It is also distinct in regarding either the entire document or something in the narrative immediately following[9] as '[the] beginning of the gospel of Jesus Christ [God's Son].'[10] In the end, it does not matter, for in any case the good news cannot be limited to Jesus' death and resurrection. It must include at least his teaching and mighty acts and may incorporate the Baptizer's ministry and the Isaianic good news to prisoners of war in Babylon, who were tempted to doubt that God is King (Isa. 40:9–10; 52:7). Furthermore, Mark, the narrator of the gospel *about* Jesus Christ soon summarizes and then quotes the gospel proclaimed *by* him. 'Jesus came into Galilee preaching [κηρύσσειν] the gospel [τὸ εὐαγγέλιον] of God: "the time [envisioned in Daniel 2:35c and 44?] has been fulfilled, and the Kingdom of God has drawn near. Change your minds [μετανοεῖτε] and believe the Good News"' (1:14–15).[11]

---

[8] Snodgrass, 'Gospel of Jesus', 17 and 43.

[9] Cranfield, *St Mark*, 34–35, summarized 10 possibilities. See France, *Gospel of Mark*, 50–51.

[10] The textual uncertainty regarding 'Son of God' does not affect my case.

[11] For a discussion of the historical issues, see Stanton, *Jesus and Gospel*, 13–20. We disagree about the extent to which Mark makes Jesus to be the exponent of the

Although the evangelist's gospel is about Jesus, Jesus' good news is about God. One is christocentric; the other is theocentric. The latter observation is twice supported by both Mark's summary ('the gospel of God') and the words of Jesus ('the kingdom of God'). Jesus is not himself the subject of his message, whether in his person or with regard to his death and resurrection; nor is belief in him called for. The subject matter is the drawing near of God's eschatological rule; and the response called for is a change of mind, which Jesus attempts to effect by his parabolic teaching. One must think about the kingdom differently: 'the kingdom of God is like …' [this, not (by implication) like the current view] (4:26–32).

A similar orientation prevails in Luke. During the sermon at Nazareth (4:18–19), Jesus cites his Isaianic mission (61:1–2) to be the Spirit-anointed bearer of good news to the poor (εὐαγγελίσασθαι πτωχοῖς; see also 7:22). The content of his proclamation (κηρύξαι, twice) is release to captives and the Year of the Lord's favor. Here, too, Jesus is not the subject of his preaching but its messenger. Nor is the death or resurrection the subject of εὐαγγελίζεσθαι or κηρύσσειν. Although the risen Jesus does cite Scripture's witness to the Christ's suffering and resurrection and that release of sins in his name was to be proclaimed (κηρυχθῆναι) among the nations (24:46–47), such is not the content of κηρύσσειν before then.[12]

How different is the situation in 1 Corinthians 15 and Romans 10. In the former, both noun and verb forms of ευαγγελ- and κηρυχ- occur. At the outset, Paul refers to the gospel that he had proclaimed to them (v. 1): that Christ had died for our sins, been buried, and raised – all according to the Scriptures (vv. 3–4). This was the subject of what witnesses throughout the church currently preached (κηρύσσομεν) and what the Corinthians had believed (v. 11). That the Messiah was raised is the subject of κηρύσσειν, both in its verb and noun forms (v. 14). Earlier (1 Cor. 1:23), Christ crucified had been the subject of Paul's proclamation.

So it is in Romans 10:9–10, a passage dense with the technical terminology of Pauline teaching. The word of faith which they proclaim (κηρύσσομεν) is this: if one confesses with one's lips that Jesus is Lord and believes in one's heart that God has raised him from the dead, one will be saved. The apostle focuses

---

Evangelist's version of the Christian gospel. Stanton does claim that the historically-reconstructed message of Jesus is 'out of kilter with post-Easter tendencies' (p. 17). My claim is that Mark and the others (even John!) preserve his 'out of kilter' Gospel. For the evidence and argument, see Lemcio, *Past of Jesus*, 13–17, 32–33. This calls for a careful reconsideration of the adequacy of Bultmann's famous statement, 'The proclaimer became the proclaimed', in *Theology*, 33–34. See the discussion in Lemcio, *Past of Jesus*, 11–12.

12 Lemcio, *Past of Jesus*, 80–82.

upon the status of Jesus as Lord and the action of God's raising him from the dead. There is nothing about the message of good news which Jesus had announced to the poor or about his proclaiming the eschatological kingdom, and of the mighty deeds that confirmed his preaching. Repentance and following are not the means of relating to him. In attempting to resolve the problem, one cannot say that Paul reflects the post-Easter Christian message, whereas the Synoptic Gospels describe that of the pre-Easter (pre-Christian situation). Mark writes as a post-Easter Christian. Whatever he says about the earthly life of Jesus suits his purposes and meets his hearer's needs.

Having put these differences about the gospel message in such stark terms, how shall the canonical Gospels function in a constructive way? If one has heard the gospel defined exclusively or primarily in Pauline terms (according to 1 Cor. 15 and Rom. 10), then the Gospels will never be regarded as gospel. The teaching and actions of Jesus will be seen as preparatory, secondary, and doctrinally optional.

With the Gospels standing first and occupying an introductory (and determinative?) role to the remainder of the New Testament, is there any justification for the church's proclaiming the gospel about Christ without proclaiming the gospel of the kingdom that Jesus proclaimed? Can one be an evangelist without doing so? Is it possible to be evangelical (whether broadly or narrowly defined) unless one does so?

The kingdom of God

One of the most neglected and least understood categories in the church is that of the kingdom of God. This is despite the fact that, as we saw, it is the central topic of Jesus' preaching and teaching in the Synoptic Gospels. Much of the Old Testament promotes the themes of God as king, both of his people and of the world. One of the primary concerns of eschatological and apocalyptic literature (Isaiah, Daniel and Revelation) is the question: who rules – and how? Although constantly challenged by human alternatives, the Imperium of Yahweh will one day overcome all opposition. Daniel looks forward to the time when the stone uncut by human hands (2:35c, interpreted in v. 44 as the kingdom of God originating in heaven) will destroy all human empires and grow over the entire world. According to the good news proclaimed by Jesus, that time has been fulfilled (Mk. 1:14–15), having been inaugurated by his invasion of Satan's rule (Mt. 12:22–30//Mk. 3:22–27//Lk. 11:15–22).[13]

What might be the effect upon the remainder of the New Testament if Jesus' central proclamation of God's kingly rule (the gospel) were to be given

---

[13] Cullmann, *Christ and Time*, 84; Wright, 'The Kingdom Redefined'; Green, *Kingdom of God*, try to make such scholarship accessible to a non-specialist audience.

its due? The juridical metaphor (prominent in Paul) would not be confined to the courtroom. Rather, it could be viewed as the mechanism for rewarding the allegiance of citizens or condemning them for treason. The cultic (Hebrews) could function as a means of restoring those of the kingdom's citizens who had betrayed their Sovereign. The so-called 'priesthood of all believers' (often viewed in an existential, individualistic, and non-mediatorial sense) needs to be understood as the *royal* priesthood or 'kingdom of priests,' the vocation of mediation and reconciliation to which the entire people of God collectively were called (Ex. 19:6).

The royal understanding of God as Father could help to mitigate the dangers of viewing one's relation to him and other family members in therapeutic, sentimental terms as fed by modern, Western sensibilities. Indeed, Jesus taught his disciples to address God as Father; but the second petition prays for his kingdom to come upon the earth (Mt. 6:9–10//Lk. 11:2).

Following Jesus

All four Gospels present Jesus calling his disciples ('student-learners') to follow him. The Synoptic Gospels universally prefer this language as the way of relating to their Teacher. Never are they called 'believers'; nor are they ever called to believe 'in him'.[14]

Such awareness provides a corrective counterpoint to those who appeal to the Fourth Gospel or Pauline literature to justify relating to Jesus primarily in terms of faith. It could help one to avoid the risk of regarding faith primarily in mental categories, as assent to doctrine or a body of teachings. While there is no denying that maintaining 'the faith' (as in 1 Tim. 3:9; 4:1, 6, 13; 5:17; 6:10, 12, 21) in connection with sound teaching requires no justification, there is a danger that such an understanding might lead to passivity. Not so with following – the daily activity of putting one foot in front of the other in the direction of one's Lord.

This connection with Jesus is costly, requiring the crucifixion of self-aggrandizement, a rejection of the world's values regarding gain and loss (Mt. 16:24–27//Mk. 8:34–38//Lk. 9:23–27) as well as reversing its standards

---

[14] Mt. 18:6 appears to be an exception to the otherwise profound consistency in the Synoptic Gospels. In this lone instance, Jesus warns the disciples in private about offending 'one of these little ones who believe in me'. It is still the case that nowhere in the Synoptic Gospels does he call the public (or even the disciples!) to believe *in him*. Textual support for the Markan parallel in 9:42 is divided over the inclusion of εἰς ἐμέ (supported by B, many Latin mss., both Syriac translations and the Bohairic). The Nestle text favors its absence on the strength of ℵ C D. One can see how a later scribe would tend to make the reading conform to Matthew and John rather than the other way around.

regarding status and role (Mt. 20:25–28//Mk. 10:42–45//Lk. 22:24–27). It will mean coming into contact with the sick and unclean, associating with the downtrodden, challenging religious authorities and institutions, and foregoing a regular resting place and family life.

Likewise, the Gospels' emphasis provides a caution to those whose relation to Jesus is cast exclusively or primarily in Pauline terms. Being 'in Christ' could be construed existentially and emotionally rather than relationally: united in his death and resurrection (Rom. 6:1–10; Eph. 2:1–10; Col. 3:1–4). And even 're-lationship' runs the risk of being understood statically – a matter of being. This is reflected in the well-meaning prayer to God: 'We do not love You for what You do for us, but for who You are.' Perhaps behind this preference for 'is-ness' lies a philosophical dualism that divorces being from behaving. Any normal understanding of relationships involves an entire range of responses: speaking, feeling, thinking, and acting. It is the latter which following Jesus supports.

The Son of Man[15]

Rarely does this 'title' function regularly and significantly in Christian thinking and spirituality. Such a situation is remarkable in the light of two factors. On the one hand, it would not be an overstatement to say that there is no Christol-ogy which occupies scholars more. On the other hand, within certain wings of the church, this un(der)used and misunderstood expression conveys something less than the robust and divine terms 'Son of God,' 'Christ,' and 'Lord.' A majority perceives it as the most human of the titles. Conservatives tend to regard it as the favorite of liberals hanging loose to orthodox convictions.

And yet, 'Bible believers' might be impressed by these astonishing statistics: in all four Gospels, Jesus alone uses the expression. It is never the subject of a confession or address, as are 'Christ,' 'Son of God,' and 'Lord.' Neither Jesus nor anyone else ever says, 'I am' or 'he is the Son of Man.'[16] In the Synoptic Gospels, Jesus avoids the other titles, suppresses them (the so-called 'messianic' or 'Son of God secret'),[17] and substitutes for them 'the Son of Man.' This is the

---

[15] Burkett, *Son of Man Debate*, surveys and summarizes the history of scholarship regarding this highly-contested expression.

[16] There is a partial exception in Jn. 9:35–37. Jesus asks the expelled former blind man, '"Do you believe in the Son of Man?" The man replied and said, "And who is he, Sir, that I might believe in him?" Jesus said to him, "Indeed, you have seen him; and the one speaking to you is the one."'

[17] The classic exposition of this theme was conducted by Wrede, *Messiasgeheimnis*, who failed to read the Gospels as narratives. For him, Mark attempted to resolve two ear-lier, contrary views of Jesus' messiahship. In Wrede's thesis, the second evangelist does not present the reader with a history of Jesus or even a story about him. Rather, Mark reflects a later stage in the history of dogma.

public Christology in the Gospels, especially in the Synoptic Gospels. Further-more, besides being the supremely public Christology in them (and this point is rarely made), it is the narrative Christology *par excellence*, covering every aspect of his earthly ministry and eschatological parousia. All others in the Synoptic Gospels are exclusively confessional; they are non-functional. In the Fourth Gospel, Jesus uses 'the Son' frequently, primarily as an expression of his pro-found obedience and dependence on the Father (rather than as a claim to his divine nature).[18]

It has been said that this Christology, appropriate to the pre-resurrection Jesus, dropped out afterwards – becoming supplanted by others in the earliest church. This is not actually the case. Written in Greek for Greek-reading audi-ences, the Gospels were being read by Gentiles and Hellenized Jews. The point that the Gospels make is that what one thinks about Jesus must be conveyed in narrative terms. Christology must be first and foremost a narrative Christology, grounded in a Jewish context with certain events being vital to be recited. The most appropriate means of making that point is via 'the Son of Man.'

This provides continuity with the Son of God Christology: Jesus concluded his life in the garden as he had begun it in the wilderness: as the Father's obedi-ent son. The account of how that obedience was manifested in public is domi-nated by 'the Son of Man.' It is the category that bridges the gap between the Christ who is and the Jesus who was. Apparently, just as the church cannot preach the gospel about Christ without proclaiming the gospel which Jesus proclaimed about the kingdom of God, so it is that she cannot confess that Jesus is Lord without telling the story about the Son of Man.

To tell that story, the Church must speak as much about Daniel 7 as it does about Isaiah 53. Otherwise, it will miss out on the eschatological politics and the political eschatology that dominate it. The sheer frequency of words for 'kingdom,' 'authority,' and 'rule' in Daniel (and Revelation) drive one to con-clude that the main issue is power. The pertinent questions dominating the texts are, 'Who rules – really – over whom, and how?' The appropriate answers are that God rules human kingdoms and gives them to whomever he wills – even to the most rejected of men (Dan. 4:14). And so it will be at the end of days. A time is coming when the tables will be turned: the Most High God will strip beastly kings of their sovereignty; and the kingdom, glory, authority, and power will be given to one who looked like a frail human (Dan. 7:1–14).[19] Jesus

---

[18] The New Testament's fundamental theo- (or patri-)centricity is being recovered. See Lemcio, 'Father and Son'; Robinson, *Priority*, 350; Das, *Forgotten Father*; and Hoskyns, *Fourth Gospel*, 430: 'Christian faith is not a cult of Jesus'.

[19] Lemcio, '"Son of Man", "Pitiable Man", "Rejected Man"', 67. Twenty years ear-lier, Bowker, 'The Son of Man', had set forth the case that the Aramaic and Hebrew expressions carry the sense of frailty and vulnerability.

is saying, in effect, 'If you want to know what this Son of Man is about, you must refer back to that (Danielic) Son of Man.'[20]

The significance of Jesus' death

I cannot begin to do justice to this vast subject within the confines of a single chapter. So, delimitation is needed. I propose that, just as the Synoptic Gospels broadened the scope of 'gospel', so all four evangelists widen the understanding of what normally comes under the rubrics of redemption, salvation, or atonement. So far as technical terminology is concerned, the Gospel authors do not apply (except for the rare instances discussed below) to the end of Jesus' life the cognates which other New Testament writers associate with his death: εξαγορ-, αιρ-, καταλλασσ-, αφι-, ελευθ-, εξιλασκ-, απολυ-, λυτρ-, σωδ-.

The absence of such terminology has led many scholars to conclude that the Synoptic Gospels (esp. Luke) lack an atonement theology or a theology of the cross – or that what one has is somehow deficient. But this presumes that an evangelist should have an atonement theology or that it ought to be of a certain kind – other than what it is. Why *must* it be so? Surely, this is to impose a standard external to the Gospels themselves – perhaps a preference for Paul, whom we have seen functioning in some academic and ecclesial circles as a sort of canon-within-the-canon. Or perhaps the imperative is driven by certain confessional or dogmatic convictions about what atonement is or should be and how largely the death of Jesus ought to figure in it. I cite one of many instances of an unwarranted defensiveness which leads to harmonization.

> In his survey of Jesus' work and teaching, as well as in his treatment of salvation, Luke says little about the cross. Why is this, especially when Paul makes so much of it?

Or,

> This point is made not to say that Luke is silent about the cross, but that Luke gives it less prominence than it receives elsewhere in the New Testament. An aspect of this difference is likely to be that Luke is aware that the emphasis on the cross is already well known, being grounded in the traditional kerygma, as 1 Cor. 15:1–3 indicates.[21]

Several questions emerge: why does Luke need defense? Why is Paul the base line? How can one assert from silence, and on what basis is it 'likely,' that the

---

[20] Moule, *Essays*, 82–85, and *Origin*, 13, argues that, because the articular form of the expression appears for the first time in the Gospels, the article functions as a mild demonstrative, pointing the listener and reader back to the Danielic vision.

[21] Bock, 'Luke', 360–61, and n. 31. See the nuanced treatment of Luke and other New Testament witnesses in Green and Baker, *Recovering*, 35–51.

cross was emphasized and well known to Luke's audience? In what sense is 1 Corinthians 15:1–3 'the' traditional kerygma rather than one of several? The view just illustrated would deny anything standard about the kerygma that Luke reports Jesus proclaiming in Nazareth (without reference to his death). And it ignores or minimizes the fact that Mark means to include the early career of Jesus as belonging to the gospel about him.

A predilection for the cross as the occasion when sins were forgiven overlooks several obvious, but often ignored or minimized, phenomena. Although this did not occur as often as is assumed, Jesus himself forgave [ἀφιένται: 're-leased'] sins by his word. The first of only two occasions occurred at the paralytic's healing (Mt. 9:2//Mk. 2:5//Lk. 5:20). By a similar pronouncement, he forgave the sinful woman who had kissed and anointed his feet (Lk. 7:47–49). Jesus declared that the penitent tax collector was justified upon the plea that his sin be expiated by God's mercy (ἱλάσθητι μοι, Lk. 18:12–13).[22] The Lord pronounced that salvation had come to Zaccheus' house (Lk. 19:9), leading one to conclude that, for Luke, salvation is where Jesus is, whether that be at Jericho in a chief tax collector's home or on a Roman cross at Golgotha. Strictly speaking, the penitent thief would join Jesus in paradise, not because Jesus would die but because the one, whom the centurion would shortly declare δίκαιος (Lk. 23:47), had said so (vv. 42–43). Such is the case with the textually doubtful prayer to the Father that his executioners be forgiven (v. 34). And, did Jesus not teach his disciples to pray, 'forgive us our sins for we ourselves are forgiving those who are owing us'? (Note the verb aspects and cause-effect relation of the Greek at Lk. 11:4; see Mt. 6:12). None of these salvific, dare we say 'atoning,' acts is directly linked to Jesus or his death per se. And, if there is a Christology here at all, it is that of the authoritative teacher. But they are not the words of a 'mere' teacher. No, the saving word is that of the divinely conceived, Spirit-disclosed, and ultimately obedient Son of God.

But what did the death of Jesus achieve? Before attempting an answer, it is vital to keep certain basics in mind. No one from Adam to Moses offered sacrifices in order to *enter* into relationship with God. None offered sacrifices for sin prior to the Sinai Covenant. God's call preceded the shedding of blood. With Moses, sacrifices for sin (epitomized on the Day of Atonement) were for restoration or *maintenance* of a relationship already established (Lev. 16). Calling preceded atonement. Furthermore, blood sacrifices achieved different things; and the animal victims varied. The Passover lamb was slaughtered, not for forgiveness but for protection from the destroying angel that led to liberation through the Exodus (Ex. 12). The blood of oxen sacrificed by Moses sealed the

---

[22] Most translations have 'mercy'. See Turner, *Christian Words*, 277–79, for the development of this meaning from secular, through Septuagintal, and New Testament Greek.

commitment of Israel (Ex. 24:1–8) to keep the covenant already given (Ex. 20 – 23). Nothing is said about forgiveness. Atonement was to be achieved in two stages using two goats, only one of which was slaughtered. The other remained alive to bear Israel's sins into the desert (Lev. 16).

Perhaps reflecting a certain blending of these discrete occasions during the Second Temple era, Matthew is the only one of the Synoptic Gospels to connect 'the blood of the covenant' with the forgiveness (ἄφεσις) of sins (Mt. 26:28). For the first evangelist, the role of Jesus announced to Joseph was to save his people from their sins (Mt. 1:21). But this concurs with what we saw above: the restoration of those who were *at that moment God's people*, the maintenance of the covenant bond already in place. But what of the Markan and Lukan references to the blood of the covenant? As in the case with Matthew, the reference to 'the covenant' seems to have a particular one in view. And, by implication, this must be a reference back to Exodus 24:1–8, the only covenant connected with blood. We recall from the above that the ceremony occurred after Israel had been called, liberated, and obliged to keep the terms of the covenant established by God through Moses. On this occasion, the people promise to obey. Moses sprinkles the blood of oxen in the direction of the altar and towards the Israelites, thereby sealing the bond between parties, with himself as mediator. What Jesus does is implicitly new: he serves as both priest and victim, displacing Moses and animals; and those joined to God and sealed by Jesus' blood belong to a larger company. Forgiveness is not a benefit. Were the disputed text judged to be authentic, Luke makes the novelty explicit (without mentioning forgiveness), suggesting that Jesus had instituted the new covenant prophesied by Jeremiah (Jer. 31:31–34). But this was to be made with the House of Israel, just as the angel had announced good news to all the people (of Israel, not to all 'people,' as in the Authorised Version; cf. 2:10).

At the only other place in the Synoptic Gospels (besides Mt. 26:28//Mk. 14:24) where Jesus speaks about the significance of his death, it is put in terms of the Son of Man's giving his life as a ransom or means of release (λύτρον) for many (Mt. 20:28//Mk. 10:45). While the ransoming may refer to Jesus' death, it need not. The reference could be to the offering of his entire life. But, assuming the latter for the moment, this is the only time that λύτρον appears in the Gospels. Why should this be so? Is there any continuity with his prior activity? Yes, if one relates those instances where Jesus freed (ἀφιένται) people from their sins [forgave them], from demonic possession, from disease, and from obligation to 'the tradition of the elders' (Mk. 7:8–23, esp. v. 19b, which Mt. 15:17 excludes; Luke omits the entire episode). An observation by G. Caird regarding Jesus' citation of Isaiah 53:12 gets at this continuity: 'He was reckoned with the lawless' [μετὰ ἀνόμων] (Lk. 22:37): 'Why should it be a surprise that Jesus, at the end of his life, was to be found between two evildoers [κακοῦργοι]? He was always in their company.'[23]

So, one could infer that, for the Synoptic Gospels, Jesus' death saved because his life did. It completed what had begun earlier. The Son's obedience during the desert testing (Mt. 4:1–11//Lk. 4:1–13) was perfected during the final testing at Gethsemane (Mt. 26:39//Lk. 22:42). Such a bi-polar understanding of the faithful Son underscores the nature of the sacrifice. Was it the physical death of Jesus that saved? Did the shed corpuscles of a divine being achieve atonement? If so, then this result could have come about at any point in his life – even at infancy during Herod's 'slaughter of the innocents.' Perhaps, then, what was offered up was self-will – but not only at the end. It was not Jesus' death that saved, according to the Synoptic Gospels, but his lifetime of obedience even to the point of death that did. While Paul in Romans 5:19 contrasts consequences brought about by the disobedience of the one man (Adam) with the obedience of another man (Christ), it is not clear whether the Apostle's argument embraces the entire life of Jesus or focuses on the event of his death. Luke ends his genealogy with Adam, the son of God (τοῦ θεοῦ) and immediately launches into the threefold account of Jesus' obedience as the Son of God (Lk. 3:37–4:13).

The situation is both different and similar in the Fourth Gospel. The Baptizer identifies Jesus as 'the Lamb of God which is taking away [ὁ αἴρων] the sin of the world' (Jn. 1:29). The present continuous aspect of the verb is critical. The reference is not to a single act at the end of Jesus' life. Furthermore, in John, the world's sin (not 'sins') is its rejection of the light that is illuminating (again, present continuous) everyone but brilliantly concentrated in the incarnated Word. Sin is refusing to trust Jesus as the Son sent to make known his Father, the only true God – the knowledge of whom is eternal life (see Jn. 1:14, 18 and 17:3). What does the death of Jesus accomplish according to the Fourth Gospel? In addition to providing life through the eating and drinking of the Son of Man's flesh and blood (Jn. 6:51–57), there come protection from attack (10:11), multiplication (12:24), the drawing of all people to himself, the world's judgment, and the expulsion of Satan [from God's court?] (12:31–33).[24] What was finished [τετέλεσται] at the cross, according to John 19:30? One cannot claim that it was atonement via forgiveness in the narrow sense because he died on the day that the Passover lambs were slaughtered. The near

---

[23] I paraphrase a statement that I am unable to attribute, believing it to have been made by G. Caird.

[24] What of 3:14? Neither the lifting up of the Son of Man nor the sending of the Son (v. 16) includes any clear reference to Jesus' death. It is the shock value of the comparison with the brass serpent of Num. 21:6–9 (in the case of the former) that seems to be the (little noticed) point. How could gazing upon an unclean animal (Lev. 11:41–42), responsible for the people's pain and death, and embodied in an unlawful image

context is critical here. At the outset of his prayer (Jn. 17:4), Jesus had said, 'I glorified you on the earth, having finished [τελειώσας] the work which you gave me.' The immediate context supplies the content of that completed assignment: manifesting the Father's name to the disciples (v. 6) and conveying his word(s) to them (vv. 8, 14). This matches the evangelist's early description of the Son's role at 1:18: to make the Father known [ἐξηγήσατο]. Thus, both Gospel traditions counter any view of Jesus' death that excludes his life as determinative for its significance.

This provides a benchmark for evaluating witnesses, including Paul and the author of Hebrews who, at least in some notable instances, appear to come close to including the life of Jesus in their articulation of his significance. The most clear instance of these is the narrative Christology embedded in the 'hymn' of Philippians 2:5–11. Despite the dramatic episodes of self-emptying, taking the form of a slave, appearing in human likeness, and living a life of obedience even to the point of death, no significance *pro nobis* is attached either to Jesus' life or death. All is focused upon the basis for his exaltation and acclamation as 'Lord.' The Apostle narrates the Jesus story in an effort to unify a community rife with self-interest (vv. 1–4). Jesus is to be 'minded,' to be imitated. Christology is employed for ethics, not soteriology. Furthermore, despite his substantial interest in the humanity of Jesus, the author of Hebrews locates the Son's becoming savior at the cross: upon learning to be completely obedient through the things which he suffered (Heb. 5:7–9).

Jesus and Israel

One way or another, whether by narrative, letter, or apocalypse, each contributor to the New Testament connects Jesus to the original people of God. Yet, none does this more explicitly than the Synoptic Gospels. This is clear from the genealogies of Matthew and Luke and from the evangelists' citation and allusion to the Scriptures. However, eclipsing all of these is Jesus' parable of the abusive and murderous farmers (Mt. 21:33–46//Mk. 12:1–12//Lk. 20:9–19).[25] There is no other 'metanarrative' in the New Testament where Jesus'

(Ex. 20:4) be the cause of their salvation? In the same way, can it be that life will come by trusting on one with roots in unpromising Nazareth, on one who seems to be a renegade with regard to Jewish law and tradition, and on one who is to be 'exalted' on a Roman cross?

[25] Snodgrass, *Parable of the Wicked Tenants* and 'Recent Research'. In over-reaction against centuries of allegorical interpretation, many influential twentieth-century critics neglected the diverse range of analogical expression covered by the Hebrew *mashal* and Greek παραβολή. Some scholars uncritically equated the parable genre with a sort of pristine goodness and historical authenticity; allegory signaled ecclesiastical departure from the original message.

story is so closely integrated with that of his people. Furthermore, it is he himself who recounts that 'history' – though by analogy and so, 'slant.'[26]

So far as placement is concerned, all three Synoptic Gospels set the account at the Temple as part of Jesus' final public appearance, shortly before his death. As the longest single narrative in the Synoptic Gospels told in public by him, the parable embraces the story of God's dealing with Israel up to the moment of telling – and beyond. (In the eschatological discourse that follows, Jesus privately informs disciples about the Temple's destruction and the end of the age.) Furthermore, it is the only time that he publicly refers to his place in that story and to his mission as son – albeit indirectly.

The thin veil of the parable hardly obscures who represents whom. This much is standard observation: God establishes the vineyard, an allusion to Israel, as evidenced by the vine imagery of Isaiah 5 and Psalm 80. In the lord's absence, farmers manage the enterprise. That these are the people's leaders is made clear when officials perceive themselves to be the targets of the account. Abused and murdered servants symbolize prophets. Readers recalling the baptism and transfiguration know that 'a beloved son' can be none other than Jesus.

However, rarely developed, and even more important than who's who, is what's what. The mission was neither messianic nor redemptive, as ordinarily understood. The vineyard did not need 'saving' (except perhaps from the farmers). Identical was the point of sending both servants/prophets and beloved son: to receive from the farmers [a portion of] the vineyard's fruit. As heir, the son could have and should have received respect [ἐντραπήσονται] and response (not belief). He was not sent in order to die. Neither his death nor his implied resurrection achieved anything. The twist in the fate of the rejected stone (Ps. 118) indicates reversal and vindication, at most: God's 'yes' to their 'no.'

At one level, the parable poses a conundrum. How is it that the narrative is relatively light Christologically and the death insignificant? Why is there no atonement theology? More historically minded interpreters would see this as evidence of authentic dominical tradition. And it may well be. Or, some redaction critics might speculate that the evangelists, otherwise creative and careful theologians, let this bit of undigested tradition slip through their compositional nets. Others could claim that the Gospel writers' technique is more subtle. I suggest (without denying the significance of their differences) that all three evangelists have either stripped the tradition of heavier theological freight or left it essentially as-is in order to lay bare the main point so that it may broadly control the entire Gospel narrative and here focus on what may be called ecclesiology, and, particularly, the matter of leadership.

---

[26] Snodgrass, 'Allegorizing'.

Because previous generations of leaders had refused both the prophets' and (now) the son's appeal for response, responsibility for the vineyard will be distributed [ἐϰδώσεται] to other farmers, who will return [ἀποδώσουσιν] the fruits in their time (Mt. 21:41). Although Matthew sees this transfer of the kingdom of God to a nation [ἔθνει] producing its fruits (Mt. 21:43), Mark and Luke simply refer to the recipients as 'others.' It must be said that there is no indication that this represents a transfer from Jews to Gentile beneficiaries. If there is an allusion here to the later Christian community, it would have to be identified as a Jewish Christian one.[27] But, so far as leadership and responsibility are concerned, the immediate contextual reference is more likely the disciples as the more responsive farmers/leaders.

What could be the canonical significance of these observations? This parable could counterbalance tendencies towards a radical supercessionism, fueled by a certain reading of Hebrews or even Galatians, Ephesians, and Colossians. An increasing number of scholars is recovering the significance of Jesus' mission to Israel, the original people of God.[28] It is to the insiders, the saved, that he was sent. Rarely did Jesus himself contact Gentiles. Encounters initiated by them were few. Restoring the people of God was the only clear agenda that Jesus set publicly. This is evident from the very start of his ministry: his first reported act in calling disciples to be fishers of men (Mt. 4:18//Mk. 1:17//Lk. 5:10). Read in the light of Jeremiah 16:15–16, where almost identical language is used, Jesus' call is not to worldwide evangelization in the first instance. Their assignment is like that announced by the prophet: to recall and reconstitute all of Israel. A more explicit version of this restricted mission occurs in Matthew 10:5–6, where Jesus forbids the disciples to go among Gentiles and Samaritans. Rather, they are being sent to 'the lost sheep of the house of Israel.'

Faced with what appears to stress radical discontinuity, the eschatological, global, and universal community might be justified in feeling isolated from these historical, local, and Jewish roots. Would it not be better to stress that God made Jew and Gentile one at the cross, obliterating the distinctions, by creating a single new human (Eph. 2:14–15) in righteousness and true [false = Jewish?] holiness (4:24)? Ought not one to prefer the Colossian emphasis that Christians have put on the new humanity, whose continuing renewal is leading to ultimate knowledge (εἰς ἐπίγνωσιν) [no longer conveyed by Torah?] according to the image of the one who created him? In this new condition, there is no longer Jew or Greek (Col. 3:9–11; cf. Gal. 3:27–28).

Without here entering the debate over the authorship of these letters, it could be said that the parable tends to support the approach taken by Luke in

---

[27] Wright, *People of God*, 76: 'The new tenants must be a group of Jews through whom the promise will be fulfilled.'

[28] Newman, *Jesus and the Restoration.*

Acts and Paul in Romans. The third evangelist takes pains to re-Judaize his Gentile readership, whether that be in portraying the original leadership as engaging in Temple worship (Acts 3:1; 5:42), prescribing kosher laws for Gentile converts (Lk. 15:19–21, 28–29), or in reporting Paul as Law observant (Lk. 21:17–26). The Apostle uses the well-known image of Israel as the cultivated olive tree into which wild olive shoots have been grafted (Rom. 11:17–25). No new flora are being created.

The parable supports this conviction about the continuing relevance of Israel: God and the vineyard are the only constants. They remain before, during, and after farmers, servants, and son appear. The people of God are not displaced or surpassed; it is the leaders who change: original farmers are replaced by subsequent ones. The former were to have been God's primary, 'hands-on' agents, mediating between him and them. They had been charged to maintain the enterprise and to give some of the vineyard's produce to the absent lord. Furthermore, neither the lord's intent nor the son's role is to destroy the old vineyard and build a new one. He is the heir of the original effort, not the progenitor of a new one.

By implication, the parable also challenges a view of prophecy that limits its function to an ecstatic, oracular, or textual one. Reading much of the New Testament (including parts of Matthew!), some might conclude that the prophets were mainly talkers or writers, whose purpose was to supply early Christians and their apologists with funds of eschatological and messianic proof-texts. Of course, this is not to deny or to minimize the oracular and written contributions of prophets, major or minor. Nor is it to reduce the significance of prophetic utterance as a gift for the church (Rom. 12:6; 1 Cor. 12 and 14; Eph. 4:11). Rather, it is to challenge the limiting of prophecy to speech and text. The parable aids in that effort by underscoring the costly action, which the servants/prophets undertook as agents on behalf of the absent lord. Their mission to exact from the farmers a portion of the lord's own investment reminds one of such mighty activists as Elijah and Elisha, who had confronted the powers that be, including their own contingent of (false) prophets who gave to their employers unfailing, uncritical support.

The parable casts Jesus in this mode as well. It reinforces and sums up the Gospel tradition's (especially the Lukan) portrayal of his prophetic significance. Such a role might be minimized when one legitimately insists that Jesus was more than a prophet ('greater than Jonah'. See Mt. 12:41//Lk. 11:32). He was (and is) king and priest as well, to use more doctrinal categories. It might also be ignored when Christology inclines towards confession of identity and 'stasis:' 'Jesus *is* Lord;' 'He *is* the Son of God' (as in much of the preaching in Acts and in such soteriological formulae as Rom. 10:9–10). What of task and assignment? Is there any correspondence between what he does now and what he did then?

Because the parable follows the Temple 'cleansing,' where the question of authority comes to the fore,[29] the beloved son and heir epitomizes the prophetic vocation: not only to speak on God's behalf but also to act in his stead. This prophetic calling tends to be obscured when the richly textured text is overlaid and flattened by a royal or messianic Christology, as Croatto has recently argued. He shows how the earthly ministry of Jesus is configured (especially by Luke) in the mold of Elijah and Elisha, who both healed the people of Israel and challenged their syncretistic leaders.[30] This is how the people understood him (Mt. 21:11; Lk. 7:16; Jn. 6:14; 7:40; see Mt. 16:14// Mk. 8:28//Lk. 9:19). What of Jesus himself? Following the parable, he confronts the Jerusalem leadership regarding allegiance to God and Caesar (politics), priorities in their capacities as teachers (doctrine), and their oppression of widows (ethics). In one of the rare (but oblique) public references to his death, Jesus laments the unintended but typical pattern: when prophets go to Jerusalem, they are killed (Lk. 13:33–34; cf. the latter verse paralleled in Mt. 23:37). After the resurrection, some disillusioned disciples had regarded their hoped-for redeemer of Israel as a 'prophet, mighty in word and deed before God and all of the people' (Lk. 24:19). The canonical questions are, 'Did he cease being so? Will the risen Lord visit the new leaders of his people to give a return on his Father's investment? Do the Church's prophets function in this capacity?'

Gospel and Apocalypse

Earlier, we had seen how the Gospels could prevent Pauline thought from becoming the 'canon within the canon.' A similar restraint could be exercised whenever readers are tempted to regard the book of Revelation in this way.[31]

Whereas the Seer (Rev. 12:1) recounts the drama via a great sign (σημειον μέγα), adapting the woman-child-dragon myth shared by cultures in the Eastern Mediterranean,[32] the first evangelist conveys it via a book (Mt. 1:1). The genealogy that follows (vv. 2–17) links the birth narrative to the long history of God's people, from whom the Messiah was born (vv. 18–25). Increasingly, scholars identify the celestial woman with Mother Israel. While John envisions the foundational myth as having cosmic dimensions, Matthew recounts it as taking place in Jerusalem and Bethlehem of Judea. Son, mother, and adoptive father are named, within the story of the awkward circumstances of the child's conception.

---

[29] See van Eck, 'Narratological Analysis', 795.
[30] Croatto, 'Jesus, Prophet Like Elijah', 451–59.
[31] The following is a formal development of a hint by Yancey in 'Cosmic Combat'.
[32] Collins, *Combat Myth*.

Although the great red dragon of Revelation 12 is demonized (or, rather, 'satanized') and begins his career in the heavenly realms, King Herod is the latest historical 'incarnation' of the beast. Earlier, the monster had been embodied by the Egyptian pharaoh (Ezek. 29:1–6), King Nebuchadnezzar (Jer. 51:34, LXX 28:32), and more recently by the Roman general, Pompey (Ps. Sol. 2:25), who had captured Jerusalem in 63 BC.[33]

The δϱάϰων of Revelation 12:3–5 wants to devour the child for the same reason that King Herod wants to destroy it: the exercise of kingly power (ποιμαίνειν). However, the scope differs. The dragon/serpent/satan/devil (v. 9) is envious of the male child's rule over all nations (v. 5). Matthew makes the subjects of that authority local and particular: the coming ruler (ἡγούμενος, 2:6) is to shepherd God's people, Israel (citing Mic. 5:2). The universality is not completely absent from the Gospel account, however. Although the half-Jew dragon-king tries to devour the child who would rule (Mt. 2:13–18), Gentile magi come to worship the new King of the Jews (Mt. 2:1–2). With great irony, the Matthean account makes Egypt to be the safe haven, while Judean territory becomes the arena of oppression and death (vv. 13–15).

The New Testament canon affirms the ecstatic, mythical power of the Apocalypse, whose supernatural protagonists range across cosmic, global, and universal arenas. Nevertheless, the opening chapters of Matthew enable the interpreter to insist that the reality to which the book of Revelation bears witness must be rooted in the 'historical', local, human, earthly, and particular.

---

[33] Wight, 'Psalms of Solomon', 635, n. a.2.

Bibliography

Bock, D., 'Luke', in *The Face of New Testament Studies. A Survey of Recent Research* (ed. S. McKnight and G. Osborne; Grand Rapids: Baker Academic, 2004), 349–72

Bowker, J., 'The Son of Man', *JTS* 28 (1977), 17–48

Bultmann, R., *Theology of the New Testament*, Vol. 1 (2 vols.; New York: Scribner's, 1951)

Burkett, D., *The Son of Man Debate: A History and Evaluation* (SNTSMS 107; Cambridge: Cambridge University Press, 1999)

Caird, G., *New Testament Theology* (compl. & ed. L. Hurst; Oxford: Clarendon, 1994)

Childs, B., *The New Testament as Canon: An Introduction* (Philadelphia: Fortress, 1985)

Collins, A., *The Combat Myth in the Book of Revelation* (Missoula, MT and Cambridge, MA: Scholars Press for *Harvard Theological Review*, 1976; repr. Eugene, OR: Wipf and Stock, 2001)

Cranfield, C., *The Gospel According to St Mark* (Cambridge: Cambridge University Press, 1959)

Croatto, J., 'Jesus, Prophet Like Elijah, and Prophet-Teacher Like Moses in Luke-Acts', *JBL* 124.3 (2005), 451–65

Cullmann, O., *Christ and Time* (Philadelphia: Westminster, 1964)

Das, A., and F. Matera, (eds.), *The Forgotten God: Perspectives in Biblical Theology* (Louisville: Westminster John Knox, 2002)

Dunn, J.D.G., *Unity and Diversity in the New Testament* (Philadelphia: Westminster, 1997)

—, 'The Embarrassment of History: Reflections on the "Anti-Judaism" in the Fourth Gospel', in *Anti-Judaism and the Fourth Gospel* (ed. R. Bieringer et al.; Louisville: Westminster John Knox, 2001), 41–60

van Eck, E., and A. van Aarde, 'A Narratological Analysis of Mark 12:1–12: The Plot of the Gospel of Mark in a Nutshell', *HvTSt* 45.4 (Nov. 1989), 778–800

France, R.T., *The Gospel of Mark* (NIGTC; Grand Rapids: Eerdmans, 2002)

Green, J., *The Kingdom of God: Its Meaning and Mandate* (Wilmore, KY: Bristol Books, 1989)

—, and M. Baker, *Recovering the Scandal of the Cross. Atonement in New Testament and Contemporary Contexts* (Downers Grove: InterVarsity Press, 2000)

Hoskyns, E., *The Fourth Gospel* (ed. F. Davey; London: Faber, 1947)

Kähler, M., *The So-called Historical Jesus and the Historic Biblical Christ* (ed. C. Braaten; Philadelphia: Fortress, 1964)

Lemcio, E., 'The Parables of the Great Supper and the Wedding Feast: History, Redaction, and Canon', *HBT* 8 (1986), 1–26; reprinted in Wall and Lemcio, *The New Testament as Canon*, 48–66

—, 'The Unifying Kerygma of the New Testament', in *The Past of Jesus*, 115–31 and 158–62, combining and expanding earlier articles with the same title in *JSNT* 33 (1988), 3–17 and *JSNT* 38 (1990), 3–11

—, *The Past of Jesus in the Gospels* (SNTSMS 68; Cambridge: Cambridge University Press, 1991)

—, 'Father and Son in the Gospel of John: A Canonical Reading', in *The New Testament as Canon: A Reader in Canonical Criticism* (JSNTSup 76; ed. R. Wall and E.E. Lemcio; Sheffield: Sheffield Academic Press, 1992), 78–108

—, 'The Synoptics and John: The Two So Long Divided. Hearing Canonical Voices for Ecclesial Conversations', *HBT* 26.1 (June 2004), 50–96

—, '"Son of Man", "Pitiable Man", "Rejected Man". Equivalent Terms in the Old Greek of Daniel', *TynBul* 56.1 (2005), 43–60

Marshall, I., *New Testament Theology* (Downers Grove: InterVarsity Press, 2004)

Moule, C., *The Origin of Christology* (Cambridge: Cambridge University Press, 1977)

—, *Essays in New Testament Interpretation* (Cambridge: Cambridge University Press, 1982)

Newman, C. (ed.), *Jesus and the Restoration of Israel: A Critical Assessment of N.T. Wright's Jesus and the Victory of God* (Downers Grove, IL: InterVarsity Press, 1999)

Räisänen, H., *Beyond New Testament Theology* (2nd edn.; London: SCM, 2000)

Robinson, J., *The Priority of John* (ed. J. Coakley; London: SCM, 1985)

Segalla, G., 'La Testimonianza Dei Libri del Nuovo Testamento ad un Unico Kerygama/Evangelo, Buon Annuncio Dell'evento Originario', in *L'interpretazione della bibbia nella chiesa. Atti del Simposio promosso dalla Congregazione per la Dottrina della Fede* (Atti e Documenti 11; Roma: Libreria Editrice Vaticana, 1999), 304–19

Snodgrass, K., *The Parable of the Wicked Tenants* (WUNT 27; Tübingen: Mohr Siebeck, 1983)

—, 'Recent Research on the Parable of the Wicked Tenants: An Assessment', *BR* 8 (1998), 187–216

—, 'From Allegorizing to Allegorizing: A History of the Interpretation of the Parables of Jesus', in *The Challenge of Jesus' Parables* (ed. R. Longenecker; Grand Rapids, MI: Eerdmans, 2000), 3–29

—, 'Modern Approaches to the Parables', in *The Face of New Testament Studies: A Survey of Recent Research* (ed. S. McKnight and G. Osborne; Grand Rapids: Baker Academic, 2004), 177–90

—, 'The Gospel of Jesus', in *The Written Gospel* (ed. M. Bockmuehl and D. Hagner; Cambridge: Cambridge University Press, 2005), 31–44

Stanton, G., *Jesus and Gospel* (Cambridge: Cambridge University Press, 2004)

Turner, N., *Christian Words* (Edinburgh: T&T Clark, 1980)

Wall, R., 'Reading the New Testament in Canonical Context', in *Hearing the New Testament* (ed. J. Green; Grand Rapids: Eerdmans, 1995), 370–93

—, 'The Rule of Faith in Theological Hermeneutics', in *Between Two Horizons: Spanning New Testament Studies and Systematic Theology* (ed. J. Green and M. Turner; Grand Rapids: Eerdmans, 1999), 88–107

—, and E. Lemcio, *The New Testament as Canon: A Reader in Canonical Criticism* (JSNTSup 76; Sheffield: Sheffield Academic Press, 1992)

Wight, R., 'Psalms of Solomon', in *The Old Testament Pseudepigrapha*, Vol. 2 (2 vols.; ed. J. Charlesworth; New York: Doubleday, 1985)

Wrede, W., *Das Messiasgeheimnis in den Evangelien* (Göttingen: Vandenhoeck & Ruprecht, 1901). An English translation appeared seventy years later: *The Messianic Secret* (trans. J. Greig; Cambridge: James Clarke, 1971)

Wright, N.T., *The New Testament and the People of God* (Christian Origins and the Question of God 1; London: SPCK, 1992)

—, 'The Kingdom Redefined: The Announcement', in *Jesus and the Victory of God* (Christian Origins and the Question of God 2; Philadelphia: Fortress, 1996), 226–43

Yancey, P., 'Cosmic Combat', *Christianity Today* (December 12, 1994), 20–23

5

Canonicity, Apostolicity, and Biblical Authority

Some Kierkegaardian Reflections

C. Stephen Evans

In 1843, Adolph Peter Adler, a pastor in the Danish Lutheran church on the island of Bornholm, published *Nogle Prædikener* (*Some Sermons*) in Copenhagen.[1] In the book Adler claimed to have had a special revelation dictated by Christ, and he distinguished in the book between the sermons he had composed on his own and those that had been given to him by the Spirit.[2] He also informed the reader that in his revelation he had been instructed to burn his previous publications, which were of a philosophic nature and had been written under the influence of Hegel. The Danish state church investigated the matter a few months later and eventually removed Adler from his pastorate and offered him a pension.

Søren Kierkegaard was fascinated by the Adler case and soon began work on a book on what he called the 'phenomenon' of Adler.[3] The issues raised seemed immensely important to Kierkegaard, so much so that he returned to the book repeatedly and revised it extensively, leaving among his papers three distinct versions of the work. However, despite all this effort, he never published the book as a whole, partly because of worry that if he did it would have a devastating impact on Adler as a human being, and partly because of a worry

---

[1] I have not read Adler's work myself, but I rely on the account given by Kierkegaard in *The Book on Adler*. Though I cite the Hong translations I have in several cases modified them.

[2] See *The Book on Adler*, 28.

[3] See the Hong 'Introduction' to *The Book on Adler*, xi.

that the specifics of the Adler case might distract readers from the importance of the underlying issues.

The fundamental issue raised by Adler for Kierkegaard was the nature of religious authority, particularly the authority of a revelation. As Kierkegaard saw things, there was a fundamental confusion about the nature of religious authority that could be seen both in the theology and philosophy of his day. The result of this was that the basic and ultimately simple Christian view that the person of faith believes what God reveals because God has revealed it, had become obscured.

It is not difficult to find the grounds of the problem that concerned Kierkegaard. Immanuel Kant's *Religion Within the Limits of Reason Alone* had undertaken the project of seeing what religious truths could be affirmed on the basis of reason independently of faith in any particular historical revelation. What could thus be affirmed on the basis of reason would not have to be believed merely because God had revealed it. Friedrich Schleiermacher had attempted to look at the biblical revelation as the outcome of religious experiences that are in principle available to anyone, and thus had tried to show how experience could undergird acceptance of biblical truths; on such a view a person would not have to believe the contents of the Gospel merely on the authority of the Gospel writers. Lastly, G.W.F. Hegel had attempted to show that the truths of religion in general and Christianity in particular could be vindicated through speculative philosophy. Perhaps ordinary, uneducated people should be content with believing a revelation by faith, but the philosopher could justify the contents of faith by showing that its truths were essentially the same as those of philosophy.

The trouble was not confined to this rarified level, however. Evidently, Kierkegaard found that the preaching in the Copenhagen of his day had fundamentally become confused about the issue as well:

> [F]rom the scholarship the confusion has in turn sneaked into the religious address, so that one not infrequently hears pastors who in all scholarly naiveté … prostitute Christianity. They speak in lofty tones about the Apostle Paul's brilliance, profundity, about his beautiful metaphors etc – sheer esthetics. If Paul is to be regarded as a genius, then it looks bad for him; only pastoral ignorance can hit upon the idea of praising him esthetically, because pastoral ignorance has no criterion but thinks like this: If only one says something good about Paul, then it is all right.[4]

Kierkegaard is clear that Paul is to be believed because Paul is an apostle and as such possesses authority. To make Paul into some kind of genius and to imply

---

[4] Kierkegaard, *Without Authority*, 93. This quotation is from an essay, entitled 'The Difference Between a Genius and an Apostle', that Kierkegaard published as part of *Two Ethical-Religious Essays*, and it is a revision of a section of *The Book on Adler*.

that he should be believed because of his intellectual acumen is actually to undermine Paul's authority as an apostle, an authority which is qualitatively different from the 'authority' of a genius. Kierkegaard makes the point bluntly and with wit:

> As a genius, Paul cannot stand comparison with either Plato or Shakespeare; as an author of beautiful metaphors, he ranks rather low; as a stylist he is a totally unknown name – and as a tapestry maker, well, I must say that I do not know how high he ranks in this regard.[5]

On Kierkegaard's analysis, Adler himself had undermined his case as a bringer of a revelation by not consistently claiming authority. After making his astounding initial claim to have had an experience in which Christ dictated a new revelation, Adler defends himself during the church's investigation by claiming that the content of his revelation is not unorthodox, since one of the things he says Jesus commanded him to do was to 'keep to the Bible.' Here Adler appears to claim that he is simply an ordinary, believing Christian. However, it is not ordinary for a Christian to have Jesus appear to him in the middle of the night and dictate a revelation, and Kierkegaard argues that Adler's 'explanation' confuses the issue. Adler neither recants by acknowledging that his claim to a revelation was an error nor sticks to his guns by clearly asserting that Jesus did in fact appear to him. The issue is not whether the content of Adler's alleged revelation is orthodox or not, but whether he did indeed receive a special revelation. Kierkegaard does not deny that God could give the kind of revelation that Adler claims to have had; nor does he think the church should deny this. After all, the church itself rests on the claim that prophets and apostles have spoken God's word, and at least in the case of Paul, apostolic authority seems to derive from a later vision of the risen Christ rather than from having been a follower of Jesus during his earthly ministry. So if Jesus had really appeared to Adler and dictated a revelation to him, as Adler claimed, Adler would have become what Kierkegaard calls 'the extraordinary,' someone who has authority, not by virtue of genius but by virtue of God having made this individual God's own spokesperson. In principle such revelations are possible, though of course the church may well hold that Adler's alleged revelation is spurious.

Unfortunately, it appears that the confusion over the concept of religious authority that Kierkegaard observed in the early nineteenth century is still with us. I shall cite just two illustrations. Lee McDonald's *The Formation of the Christian Biblical Canon* is widely used in seminaries and undergraduate religion departments, and McDonald is himself the dean of a theological seminary. In the 'Preface to the Second Edition,' McDonald discusses the question of

---

[5] *Without Authority*, 94.

whether the biblical canon should be reopened in light of contemporary historical scholarship: 'There appears to be no doubt, however, that in the future many will question the viability of the current biblical canon.'[6] McDonald himself takes a somewhat cautious approach and does not seem too enthusiastic about any such revision of the canon. However, in his discussion of the issue the question of which authors or books have divine authority seems completely absent. Instead of asking which books possess such authority, he poses some different questions:

> For some of us, however, the matter has to do with whether what is offered as a candidate for future inclusion could in fact improve our current picture of Jesus. Would, for example, the inclusion of the *Gospel of Peter* or the *Gospel of Thomas* in our biblical canons be an advantage or disadvantage? Do they significantly add to our understanding of who Jesus was, what he did, and what he asked from his followers? I can only surmise what the church's response might be from the responses that I have received from women in my classes when they read for the first time (or second or third!) the closing comments of the *Gospel of Thomas*.[7]

McDonald here seems to say that the question of what belongs authoritatively in the canon should be settled by asking what sources might add to our historical knowledge, and that one candidate (*The Gospel of Thomas*) should be rejected because its message would offend women readers. However, from Kierkegaard's perspective, this shows a confusion over the nature of religious authority. A book does not gain canonical status simply because it might provide reliable historical information; nor should a book be disqualified as canonical simply because it might offend contemporary readers.

I certainly agree with McDonald's implied view that including *The Gospel of Thomas* in the biblical canon is a bad idea. However, it seems obvious to me that his reasons for thinking this is the case significantly erode the idea of biblical authority. If we thought that *Thomas* would in fact improve our historical understanding of Jesus should we include it in the canon? Robert Funk has argued that the canon should be reopened in just this way.[8] If contemporary readers find some book in the Bible offensive should we therefore remove it from the canon? Such a 'canon' would clearly have no genuine religious authority.

This kind of confusion is not, sadly, limited to those who write about the canon but also shows itself in contemporary normative theology. Timothy Jackson's recent book, *The Priority of Love: Christian Charity and Social Justice*, often cites New Testament passages in support of his major thesis (a thesis that I

---

[6] McDonald, *The Formation*, xviii.
[7] McDonald, *The Formation*, xviii.
[8] See Funk, 'The Once and Future New Testament'.

believe is fundamentally sound), but does not hesitate to say that Paul is just mistaken where the Scripture seems not to support Jackson's own view.[9] Obviously if I appeal to an authority when it suits my purposes and disregard it when it does not, I do not really respect that authority.

Apostolicity and the Authority of the New Testament

The question of apostolic authority is crucial for Kierkegaard, and it should be for us as well, because it is linked to the question of God's authority. An apostle or prophet should be believed because the apostle or prophet has been authorized by God to speak for God. If this is right, then for those who think of the New Testament as being part of the Word of God, the question as to what belongs in the New Testament is essentially linked to the question as to which writings possess apostolic authority. Apostolic authority is not simply one criterion among many, as many historical treatments of the formation of the canon imply, but is essentially linked to the notion of canon as the central criterion.

To support this claim I must make several qualifications. First, the term 'apostle' is here being used as Kierkegaard uses it, in a somewhat technical sense. An apostle is here understood as someone who has been appointed by God to speak for God. To be more precise an apostle is someone who has been appointed by Christ (who is understood to be God) to speak for God, but the term is not limited to those who knew Jesus during his earthly ministry and were followers of Jesus during that time. One could say that Kierkegaard has a Pauline concept of apostolicity, insofar as Paul views himself as an apostle who is 'born out of season' (Kierkegaard generally uses the broader term 'prophet' for someone who has been appointed by God to speak for God but who has no connection to Christ, but he sometimes uses the term 'apostle' in this broader sense). Given this concept of the apostle, to judge that a book belongs in the New Testament as part of the Word of God about Jesus the Christ is to judge that the book has apostolic authority, rather than to say that the book was written by one of 'the twelve' or by Paul. Of course, 'the twelve' and Paul are for the church paradigm examples of those who possess this kind of authority, but the concept is not limited to these exemplars.

---

[9] See Jackson, *The Priority of Love*, 81–89. In this section Jackson does not hesitate to reject scriptural authority by his rejection of Paul's argument (in 1 Cor. 15:12–34) that the Christian life rests on the hope of resurrection. Jackson rejects this on the grounds that such a view 'risks instrumentalizing the virtue [of love]' (83), and he argues (contra Paul) that 'it is a betrayal of charity to hold that it must eventuate in a postmortem afterlife' (89).

Secondly, the concept of apostolic authority must not be identified with the concept of apostolic authorship. Apostolic authorship certainly is an indicator of apostolic authority, but it is clear that the church, in making decisions about the New Testament canon, did not identify apostolic authority with apostolic authorship. Mark and Luke were accepted as possessing apostolic authority because of a believed connection with Peter and Paul, and Hebrews was accepted as having apostolic authority despite its anonymity (more about Hebrews later). Furthermore, not everything written by someone who is acknowledged as an apostle would necessarily be accepted as authoritative. If Paul wrote a note to remind himself of an appointment he had made, we would not think that note should necessarily be included in the canon, even if it were found. Obviously, there are lots of questions one could raise about which texts of an apostle do possess authority, as well as what kinds of connections need to be present between an apostle and some other writer in order for the product of that other writer to have apostolic authority. I do not here need to settle all such questions, but only want to maintain the somewhat vague thesis that the concepts of canonical authority and apostolicity are closely linked.

Still, one might think that making the concept of apostolic authority central to the canon question is an exaggeration. Did not other criteria, such as catholicity, orthodoxy, antiquity, and inspiration count heavily as well in deciding what books should be accepted? I myself think that these other criteria turn out to be either inessential or else are valued because of a connection with apostolicity.

Let us take catholicity, which I shall define as the degree to which a book was accepted and used by the churches in general, and the most important churches in particular. It is not clear to me that this factor was valued independently of apostolicity; it may rather be thought of as one way of ascertaining which books did indeed have apostolic authority. One would expect genuine apostolic books to be widely accepted by the churches, particularly those churches, such as Rome, which were thought to have preserved authentic apostolic traditions.

Orthodoxy, or the degree to which a book embodied that apostolic content summarized in 'the rule of faith,' is certainly important as a negative test. A book that was judged to contradict apostolic teaching could not be regarded as canonical. However, merely having content that is consistent with apostolic teaching is surely insufficient for genuine authority; many orthodox books did not make it into the canon. Furthermore, even to apply this test, one must already have some way of establishing what is the basic apostolic teaching, either by oral tradition or by having some documents whose apostolic authority is regarded as settled. Harry Gamble notes:

> The criterion of orthodoxy seems never to have been applied to such literature as the letters of Paul or the Synoptic Gospels ... Thus, the criterion of agreement with the faith of the church was used primarily in connection with writings when authorship remained uncertain, and it was applied mainly as a negative standard rather than a positive argument.[10]

Hence this criterion could never by itself be fundamental, but would be most useful in deciding doubtful cases where the main body of the canon is already settled.

It is also worth noting that a book added on the basis of this criterion, if the criterion is strictly applied, could not significantly modify our understanding of apostolic teaching, for if it were too different from that teaching the criterion would exclude it. It appears, however, that the early church did not apply this criterion in a strict way. To see that this is so, think about the fact that many contemporary writers think that the actual New Testament is so diverse as to be full of contradictions. Clearly, neither the early church nor the church through the ages has thought this was so, and I myself believe it is an exaggeration. However, there is clearly a great deal of diversity in the New Testament, and the actual diversity that is present shows that tight coherence with other accepted teachings did not operate *too* powerfully in restricting the acceptance of other documents.

Antiquity by itself is obviously not important at all. A book could be believed old without having apostolic authority. That a book was judged to stem from the first century and was believed to have been used by the early churches were important facts, but the importance again lies in the way these facts point to apostolicity. The *Didache* is a good example: it is a first-century text; indeed some recent scholars such as Alan Garrow have argued that it pre-dates Matthew, a text with which it has some kind of literary links. It is orthodox and catholic, but was not ultimately canonical.[11] A late book could not have come from an apostle and could not even be closely linked to apostolic tradition through those who personally knew the apostles.

As far as inspiration goes, I agree with those who argue that this quality by itself is also insufficient for canonicity. Many writers have claimed a kind of inspiration throughout the history of the church that is not to be equated with apostolic authority. It is true that any book judged to be canonical would also be regarded as inspired, but it does not follow that it is canonical because it is inspired. At least this is so unless one means by 'inspiration' the giving by God of that type of message to someone that has the special authority that constitutes

---

[10] Gamble, *New Testament Canon*, 70.
[11] Garrow, *Matthew's Dependence on the Didache*. This point was suggested by Robin Parry, and I thank him for it.

apostolicity. But in that case inspiration would be the same thing as apostolicity and not a separate criterion.

All of these points of course deserve elaboration and support, but I am confident that this can be done. The judgment that a book belonged in the New Testament, whether that judgment was made in the first four centuries or is made today, is a judgment that a book has divine authority, an authority that derives from someone who has been authorized by Christ to speak God's word.[12]

Canonicity and Pseudonymity

If I am right that apostolicity is the central or key criterion for canonicity, then one might think that contemporary historical scholarship poses a problem for the church's canon. For contemporary historical scholars by and large believe that the judgments of the early church that lay behind the canon were in many cases erroneous. According to Gamble, '[h]istorical criticism has shown that the ancient church was most often mistaken in its claim that the canonical writings were written by apostles.'[13] This skepticism extends over a large range of the New Testament, including even the Synoptic Gospels, but it is especially prevalent with respect to books such as John's Gospel, 1 and 2 Timothy, Titus, Ephesians, and 2 Peter. Gamble concludes that 'the limits of the canon cannot any longer be defended on the basis of the explicit warrants adduced on its behalf by the ancient church.'[14]

Let us suppose for the moment that Gamble's historical claims are correct, though I shall later discuss whether the evidence in favor of those claims is really decisive. If Gamble is right, then many of the books that the church canonized in the belief that they were by such writers as Peter and Paul were actually pseudonymous. Should contemporary Christians then reopen the question of what belongs in the canon, as someone such as Robert Funk urges us to do,

---

[12] Suppose one of Paul's lost letters to the Corinthian church was discovered. Should this letter be accepted as canonical since it was authored by an apostle? This is a complex question. My own view is that it is possible but not certain that it should be accepted. The reason that it might be rejected is that the fact that the letter was lost for such a long period might give one reason to think that God did not intend it to be part of the canon. The argument here parallels one made below that a biblical book that was accepted because it was mistakenly thought to be apostolic might still be properly accepted as authoritative even if we came to believe the book was pseudonymous.

[13] Gamble, *New Testament Canon*, 83.

[14] Gamble, *New Testament Canon*, 83.

or are there still good reasons for holding to the current New Testament canon?[15]

Let me first discuss what I regard as bad reasons for accepting the current canon. If someone argues that a book should continue to be regarded as canonical because the contents of the book can independently be known to be true by philosophical or empirical means, then the authority of the canon has not been supported but undermined. We no longer believe the contents of the revelation because we believe it is revealed and therefore has authority; rather we believe the book is a revelation and has authority because we have certified its truth. But in that case the real authority lies in ourselves.

A somewhat better reason might be to defend the canonicity of a pseudonymous book on the ground that the contents of the book are orthodox, consistent with apostolic teachings or the rule of faith This is better than the first reason, because the apostolic teachings appealed to here still have authority, and that authority, rather than our own judgment, is the basis for accepting the disputed book as authoritative. However, there are significant problems with this proposal. First, if Gamble and the other historical critics are right, and the great majority of New Testament books are pseudonymous, then the amount of apostolic content that is left to be used as the baseline will be significantly reduced.[16] At least this is so if our main access to that apostolic content is through the biblical revelation and not through tradition. To the degree that we have information about apostolic teachings that is independent of the canonical revelation, this will be less of a problem. Still, many Protestants at least would hold that such traditions independent of revelation are insufficient for an accurate knowledge of apostolic teaching, and that our best source of knowledge about the apostles comes from Scripture. If this is right, then if we want to follow this proposal to accept books because they are consistent with apostolic teachings we had better hope that the majority of the texts will not be pseudonymous, or else our knowledge of what counts as apostolic teaching will be greatly reduced. Secondly, as noted above, books that are accepted as canonical on this basis cannot fundamentally modify or enlarge our understanding of the apostolic teaching, and thus books accepted on this basis will to some degree be marginalized. Furthermore, there is the question as to why other books, such as Clement, that are equally orthodox and probably were written during the same period as the pseudonymous books, on the assumption

---

[15] See Funk, 'The Once and Future New Testament'.

[16] Since the titles of the Gospels and Acts do not seem to be original, these books would not be strictly pseudonymous. However, if the traditional authorship of these books is challenged, a problem analogous to the problem of pseudonymity still arises, since we would lack an historical reason to think the books were written by apostles or those with close apostolic connections.

that the skeptical historical critics are right, are not equally worthy of canonicity.

Should we say that Christians should accept the canon because the canon simply is part of what defines the tradition they are committed to? As a matter of fact, the historical tradition we call 'Christianity' has accepted this particular New Testament canon (with some debates between Christian groups about the edges of the canon). Can we infer from this fact that insofar as we are part of this particular historical tradition, we have no choice about the canon? There is something right about such a view; I shall below try to argue that what we accept as the canon is and should be intimately connected to an historical community that is the embodiment of an historical tradition. However, it will not do simply to say 'we just happen to be part of a community that defines itself by these books.' This is so for two reasons. First, there is no necessity about our being part of any such community; if we disagree with the community's view of the canon that may be a reason for leaving the community. Second, there is no reason in principle why this particular historical community could not change its mind about its canon, as it has changed its mind about so many other things. It is not enough to say that we should keep the canon we have because it is the one we happen to have.

How then might the canon be defended if we assume that the ancient church was mistaken in believing that many of the books of the New Testament were written or authorized by apostles? The best reasons surely will be theological and not historical in character. If we assume that God wished to grant to humans an authoritative revelation (and if we do not believe this the question of canonicity becomes moot), then it is highly implausible that God would go to the trouble of seeing that such a revelation is created without also taking care to see that the revelation is recognized and transmitted. There would be little point in God inspiring or authorizing a book if that book vanished without a trace in the first century.

It seems highly plausible, then, that if God is going to see that an authoritative revelation is given, he will also see that this revelation is recognized and transmitted. How might God do this? The most likely way would seem to be to ensure that the community of faith that is to be the beneficiary of the revelation acquires accurate knowledge of its contents. On this view, then, the fact that the church recognized the books of the New Testament as canonical is itself a powerful reason to believe that those books are indeed the revelation God intended humans to have.[17]

---

[17] My suggestion here is of course not original, but has been made by many theologians. For example, Meade proposes that divine inspiration should not be viewed simply on the model of the individual prophet, but rather we should '*put the locus of inspiration in tradition and the community which both creates it and is sustained by it.*'

There are of course various supposed problems with this proposal. First of all, it clearly assumes that a person can have good reasons to believe the theological premises in question, to believe in the truth of the gospel and also to recognize God as working through the church. If one thinks that these theological claims cannot be known, that will certainly be a problem. However, for those who think that the underlying theological claims can be known, this will not be a serious problem, but at most a challenge to produce an account of how such things can be known. I am convinced that this challenge can be met, but that is a subject for another paper.[18]

Some Protestants might worry that such a view subordinates Scripture to the authority of the church. However, this does not necessarily follow. The proposal, as I understand it, is not that the church was endowed by God with authority to *decide* what counts as revelation, so that whatever the church accepted thereby became revelation. That kind of view would undoubtedly subordinate the Bible to the church. Rather, the idea is that the church is an instrument of God's providence; the God who has inspired a revelation has used the church as the means whereby that revelation is recognized and transmitted. So this kind of Protestant worry seems unfounded.

The view I am recommending does not assume that the church is infallible. In fact, just the reverse is the case, since I am assuming, at least for the sake of the argument, that the ancient church made its decisions about the canon on the basis of serious historical errors. The church is certainly capable of error. However, I see no reason why God could not achieve his ends, in this case the recognition of those writings that God authorizes as his word, through human errors.

One might think that such an idea is vulnerable because it depends on the assumption that we can say what constitutes the church. I think that the view does assume we have some knowledge about what counts as the church. For example, the proposal assumes that the ancient Christians who produced the ecumenical creeds are part of the church and that the sects spawned by such figures as Marcion were not part of the true church. However, I do not think the proposal requires any controversial views about whether the true church is constituted by any particular body or group of bodies who are the successors to that ancient church. It is compatible both with the view that some particular body today is the true church and also with the view that the true church is today divided and composed of many diverse bodies. In any case if we have no

---

[Meade's emphasis]. See *Pseudonymity and Canon*, 209. Similar views can be found in Abraham, *Divine Inspiration* and many other authors.

[18] For the kind of account I would myself give, see my *Historical Christ*, particularly chapters 10–12. A similar account is found in Plantinga, *Warranted Christian Belief*, especially chapters 8–10.

idea at all about what constitutes the church I see no reason why we should expect to have any good idea about what constitutes the true Revelation.

Nor is it a powerful objection to this view to note that the church does not completely agree about what constitutes the canon, since various groups of Christians disagree about a few books. As long as the main outline of what books are to be accepted as constituting the revelation is clear, it will not really be disturbing if there are minor disagreements about the outer boundaries of that revelation. It is also not a problem that some genuine apostolic writings, such as some letters of Paul, have doubtless been lost and did not become part of the canon. For we should not assume that everything written by an apostle automatically acquires the status of divine revelation. In much the same way that the church's recognition of certain writings provides reason to think that God authorized those writings, the church's failure to recognize certain writings, for whatever reasons, including reasons that appear to be historically 'accidental,' provides reason to think that God did not desire those writings to be included in the authorized revelation.

My conclusion at this point is then that it is certainly possible to hold that the ancient church erred on historical questions, without thinking that this implies that the question of the canon must be reopened. It is possible that some of the books attributed to apostles or close associates of apostles were not in fact written by those people, but yet that God determined that those particular writings were among the writings that God designated as authoritative revelation. The fact that the author of a particular book was not one of the twelve disciples does not entail that the book is not the work of an 'apostle' in the Kierkegaardian sense in which an apostle is someone authorized to speak on God's behalf. One strong point in favor of such a view is the inclusion of the anonymous Hebrews within the canon. In effect, the church judged Hebrews apostolic without even knowing for sure which 'apostle' wrote the book, and this provides some reason to think that other books may be similarly apostolic even if the authors of those books are unknown or incorrectly identified.[19]

This conclusion is bolstered if scholars such as David Meade are correct in their claims that pseudonymous books do not have to be regarded as inherently fraudulent or deceptive, though I am unsure about whether Meade is right, and I do not think my argument depends upon his being right. Meade argues that in the ancient Jewish world there were different conceptions of what constituted

---

[19] I make no judgment here on the historical question as to why the church ultimately accepted Hebrews. Various factors may have been important, including beliefs, correct or incorrect, about who the author was (Paul, for some), beliefs that the book was accepted as apostolic by important churches, and beliefs that the content of the book is not only consistent with apostolic teachings but helps show the coherence of that teaching.

forgery, rooted in a practice in which members of a tradition attributed their work to what I would term the 'founding father' of the tradition, not with a primary intent to deceive, but rather with a pious intent to credit the founder of the tradition with the insights found in that tradition.[20] Richard Bauckham goes so far as to argue that in 2 Peter we have a 'transparent fiction,' a case where the original audience knew and was intended to know that the book was not by the historical Peter.[21] Rather, the book is an example of an accepted genre of the time, a 'last will and testament' composed by Peter's 'school' of followers which no one would have regarded as a forgery at the time of its composition.

I shall not attempt to say whether Bauckham and Meade are right here; the issues are too complex for my limited competence as an historian. However, if they are right, one difficulty with the acceptance of pseudonymous works as canonical would be eliminated. For it is hard to believe that God would appoint as an 'apostle' to speak for him a person who would intentionally deceive others.

Some Skeptical Reflections about Historical Skepticism

I have argued that if some of the books of the New Testament are pseudonymous, this does not entail that they are not part of God's authoritative revelation. However, must we accept the antecedent in this hypothetical proposition? Specifically, must someone such as myself, not a biblical scholar or an historian, defer to the authority of scholars such as Gamble who claim that the pseudonymity of much of the New Testament has been conclusively historically established?

Why worry about this question if I am right in my argument that the authoritativeness of the canon does not depend on whether the historical judgments of the ancient church were always accurate? I think that there is something at stake here; something valuable may be lost in cases where pseudonymity is affirmed, especially if it is affirmed for a large part of the New Testament. To begin, the paradigm case of apostolic authority is the case where one recognizes a particular individual as an apostle who speaks for God and, as a consequence of this, recognizes what the apostle says or writes as an authoritative revelation. Though it is indeed still possible for an anonymous or pseudonymous book to be accepted as authoritative revelation, the most natural reason for doing so is no longer available.

Secondly, what we might call the first-person authority of the revelatory writing is eroded when we embrace pseudonymity. A classic example of this is

---

[20] See Meade, *Pseudonymity and Canon*, 194–216.

[21] See Bauckham, *Jude, II Peter*, 158–63.

found in 2 Peter 1:16–18, where the author claims that 'we did not follow cleverly invented stories' about Jesus but that 'we were eyewitnesses of his majesty.' If 2 Peter is pseudonymous, even if the author accurately represents Peter's point of view, his own words do not have the authority of an appeal to first-person experience. In addition to this epistemic authority, there is also the moral authority that stems from an author who puts himself forward as a model and asks readers to follow his example. A follower of Martin Luther King, Jr. cannot have the authority King himself has to challenge others to model their behavior on King.[22]

In addition to these worries, I confess that the arguments of scholars such as Meade do not entirely dispel worries about whether pseudonymous books in some cases constitute literary forgery, and if so, whether the work of someone who intended to deceive others, and therefore is not of the highest moral status, could possess apostolic authority.[23] These worries are particularly acute if the writer of the pseudonymous work has only a literary tie to the apostle whose authority is being claimed. It is one thing if a close follower of Peter accurately captures the teaching of Peter to which he has had first-hand access and believes it is more honest and honorable to credit the insights to Peter than to claim authorship himself. It is another thing if someone with no connection to Peter imaginatively creates what he believes Peter would have said.

So it is worth considering how strong the case is that the ancient church was massively mistaken in its historical attributions. And – though I say this with fear and trembling since I am far from being expert in these matters – I am skeptical about some of the skepticism I observe among biblical scholars about the historical authorship of many New Testament books.

So why am I less than convinced? Let me begin with an obvious but still important point that there are people who are competent scholars about such things who also believe that the case for pseudonymity is less than decisive, especially with respect to some of the books of the New Testament that have been questioned. To someone who is not an expert in a field, majority opinion in the field is less than decisive in a case where the majority view is doubted by scholars who seem equally competent and learned as those who hold the dominant view. And that seems to be the case with respect to New Testament studies. Even in the case of 2 Peter, one of the books most often thought to be pseudonymous, there are competent scholars who argue that the book is Petrine.[24] In my own field of philosophy, it carries little weight – and should

---

[22] See Stump's 'Moral Authority and Pseudonymity'.

[23] For an argument that any pseudonymous writings accepted by the early church must have involved deception on the part of the pseudonymous authors, see Wilder, *Pseudonymity, the New Testament, and Deception*.

[24] See, for example, Charles, '2 Peter.' See, too, Kruger, 'The Authenticity of 2 Peter'.

carry little weight – that the majority of contemporary philosophers probably believe some form of utilitarianism in ethics is true, since there are equally competent philosophers who think that utilitarianism can be shown to be false.

However, my grounds for skepticism about the skepticism go deeper than this obvious point. I shall try to explain briefly why some of the reasons commonly given seem to me to be less than decisive. I shall first talk in general terms about the kinds of reasons often given and then move to a quite specific argument. What kinds of reasons are usually given that a particular book was not written by Paul or Peter or John?

One kind of reason has to do with internal literary analysis of the books. If one compares say, Ephesians with 1 Corinthians, or 1 Peter to 2 Peter, an attentive reader notices some significant differences. The differences can be various, ranging from differences in major themes, concepts, and issues discussed on the one hand, through differences in literary style, type of argumentation employed, facility with Greek, on down to differences in favorite types of grammatical constructions employed. The argument is that such differences make it very unlikely that the books being compared are written by the same author. If Paul wrote 1 Corinthians, as most everyone agrees, then he did not write Ephesians, and so on.

Obviously arguments of this type will vary in strength, but in general I find them less than decisive. Let me begin with differences in content. Mere differences in themes discussed, concepts used, etc. do not furnish very powerful evidence for differences in authorship. On this basis I believe I could easily construct an argument that various books I myself have written were by different authors. Differences that amount to actual contradictions would carry more evidential weight, but many of the alleged contradictions between various writings of the New Testament seem to be in the eye of the critic. At the very least one must admit that it is possible to read the various documents in ways that do not see them as contradictory, since many generations of faithful readers have done just that.

What about differences in literary style, grammatical proclivities, and linguistic skill? The problem here is the frequently made point that many of these kinds of differences seem to be the kinds of things that could be explained by the use of an amanuensis, apparently a not-uncommon practice in the ancient world. It is sometimes alleged that some of these differences are too extreme to be explained in this way, but it is hard to see how this could be so, since the practice could be construed very broadly as including something analogous to a modern speechwriter who writes a speech or article for a president. The president looks the speech over, approves it, and it then counts as the president's own words. In this sort of case, grammatical and stylistic features may be wholly derived from the agent of the person we regard as the author, though the author nonetheless gives the writing his stamp of authority by endorsing it.

Another reason for skepticism about this kind of argument can be found by reflection on the writings of Kierkegaard. These writings are extremely diverse from every conceivable point of view. In fact, computerized studies of word usage, grammatical constructions, etc. have been done for the Kierkegaardian corpus that give results that suggest that various books were written by different authors.[25] Yet we know that Kierkegaard wrote them all. If literary arguments to diversity of authorship from diversity of content, style, grammatical usages, etc. are to be really powerful, we need controlled, empirical studies (many of them) in which these literary methods are tested. We could take various groups of books, some within each group by the same authors and some by different authors, and try to see whether the authors could be identified using these literary methods. If such studies have been done, I am not aware of them. I can add that in several cases I have had reviewers or critics infer things about the literary origins or history of some of my own writings based on internal literary analysis and the inferences have been wrong in every case. C.S. Lewis makes a similar observation about the theories critics have developed about the composition of his own works from internal literary analysis, asserting that 'in the whole of my experience not one of these guesses has on any one point been right; that the method shows a record of 100 per cent failure.'[26] Let me move from these general observations to a very specific point. One argument against Petrine authorship of 2 Peter that is regarded by many biblical scholars as very weighty stems from 2 Peter 3:15–16:

> Bear in mind that our Lord's patience means salvation, just as our dear brother Paul also wrote you with the wisdom that God gave him. He writes the same way in all his letters, speaking in them of these matters. His letters contain some things that are hard to understand, which ignorant and unstable people distort, as they do the other Scriptures, to their own destruction.

The problem stems from the author's treatment of Paul's letters as 'Scripture.'[27] Even some quite conservative and traditional scholars have difficulty believing that Peter would have thought of Paul's writings in this way. It seems to me that the assumption that lies behind this difficulty is that it took some time for the church to acquire a belief that the early Christian writings had the status of Scripture and that it is very unlikely that this would have occurred in Peter's lifetime.

---

[25] See McKinnon, *The Kierkegaard Indices* which contains the first fruits of this massive computerized study. For an article describing some of McKinnon's subsequent work, see his 'Mapping the Dimensions of a Literary Corpus', 73–84.

[26] C.S. Lewis, 'Modern Theology and Biblical Criticism', 159–60.

[27] There is another problem some claim stems from this passage, namely that the author's reference to 'all of Paul's letters' shows an awareness of Paul's letters as a collection that dates from the end of the first century. I shall not discuss this issue in this paper, though I do think it can be answered.

Well, perhaps this is right. However, I am doubtful for two reasons that I will try to explain.[28] The first has to do with what I would term apostolic consciousness. I began this paper by looking at Kierkegaard's reflections on the case of Adler, and I think some of Kierkegaard's points are relevant here. The Adler case obviously raises the question of whether there are criteria that might help us to recognize a genuine apostle. One criterion that Kierkegaard advances is that a genuine apostle would have some awareness of his apostolic authority and a willingness to appeal to that authority. After Adler's claims to a revelation were challenged by the church, Adler defended himself by arguing that the content of his revelation was defensible, both on philosophical and biblical grounds, but he notably fails to make any appeal to his own alleged direct experience of Jesus. From Kierkegaard's perspective, the kind of argument Adler made was fatal to his case, because a genuine apostle would appeal to his status as an apostle. Adler lacks a consciousness of apostolicity.

Awareness of being an apostle is qualitatively different from awareness of being very intelligent or very learned or possessing any such quality, just as being an apostle is qualitatively different from being a genius or being a skilled philosopher. One does not become an apostle or even get closer in any way to becoming an apostle when one crosses some threshold of intelligence, say by being certified to have a high enough IQ to join Mensa. An apostle lies in a qualitatively different category.

Now it is notable that Paul passes the test that Adler flunks. Paul shows a clear consciousness of his apostolic status. For example, he begins the letter to the Galatians in this manner: 'Paul, an apostle – sent not from men nor by man, but by Jesus Christ, and God the Father, who raised him from the dead – and all the brothers with me. To the churches in Galatia' (Gal. 1:1–2). So Paul at least possessed the qualitative mark of apostolic consciousness. However, it is a virtual certainty that Paul was not alone in this consciousness, since in affirming his apostolic authority he frequently argues that he possesses the same status that people such as Peter and James enjoy, and Peter and James can be presumed to have had a consciousness of this status as well.

Now how is this relevant to the question of whether Peter may possibly have regarded some of Paul's writings as having scriptural authority? Surely, one might argue, consciousness of apostolic authority is not identical with consciousness of oneself as a writer of Scripture, and thus the possession of the former does not guarantee the latter. I agree that apostolic consciousness and consciousness of oneself as a writer of Scripture are not exactly the same, and that Paul and Peter could have possessed the former without the latter.

---

[28] I must credit Eleonore Stump for a conversation which gave me these ideas and also endowed me with the courage to present them, though I do not claim she would endorse the arguments I give.

However, it is important to see that the two concepts, while not identical, are closely linked. If my earlier claim that apostolicity is the central criterion of canonicity is sound, then the concept of the Scriptures as the Word of God simply is the concept of a body of writings produced by apostles or people who knew and could convey the message of apostles, where an apostle is understood as someone who has special authority to speak for God. To use Kierkegaard's terminology, the concepts of apostolicity and Scripture belong to the same qualitative sphere; both are 'transcendent' in that neither can be understood in terms of such 'immanent' qualities as intelligence or philosophical acumen but are actualized by divine action. Given that Paul and Peter certainly possessed apostolic consciousness, and that each recognized the apostolic status of the other, it does not seem impossible or even highly implausible that one or both could have recognized at least some of their own writings and/or the writings of the other as scriptural. The logical gap between consciousness of the possession of apostolic authority and consciousness of oneself as a writer of Scripture is small indeed in comparison with the logical chasm between any immanent human quality and apostolicity. If it is certain that Peter recognized Paul as an apostle, it cannot be impossible or even highly implausible for him to have recognized some of Paul's writings as having scriptural authority.

The second reason why I am not persuaded that the passage in 2 Peter 3:15–16 rules out Petrine authorship stems from an observation about how writings generally either get accepted or not accepted as scriptural. Let us first take some literature that is regarded, at least by some, as having scriptural authority, such as the *Qur'an*, *The Book of Mormon*, and some writings of the Rev. Moon. It is a striking fact that in such cases the scriptural authority of the books in question was asserted from the very outset; they were presented from the beginning as having special authority. Contrast this with cases of other religious books, which may be exceptionally deep, wise, the result of powerful religious experiences, but which no one has any tendency to regard as scriptural. I would cite here such writers as Kierkegaard himself, Julian of Norwich, Teresa of Avila, etc. Some of these books are arguably religiously deeper and more powerful than some of the books that are regarded as scriptural, even more powerful than some of the books of the New Testament itself. Yet even after hundreds of years there is no tendency whatsoever to elevate these books to scriptural status.

Why should this be so? I think the answer lies simply in the qualitative difference between a book that is wise, learned, and powerful and one that has scriptural authority. By and large it appears that the books that are a candidate for scriptural status are books that are presented from the beginning as candidates, books that from the beginning claim to have this kind of special authority. If this is generally right, then the fact that the books of the New Testament came to be regarded as scriptural itself provides some evidence for the fact that they were regarded as having a special authority from God from the beginning.

I do not wish to claim that this principle is some kind of social scientific law that holds in all cases. It is certainly possible that a book that was not originally claimed to have divine authority might later come to be regarded as having such authority. Perhaps this has in fact happened in the case of some of the books of the Old Testament. My claim is only that a transition from being regarded as a merely human product to being regarded as having scriptural status is difficult to achieve. In a great many cases books that are regarded as scriptural are regarded as having a special status from the very beginning, while the overwhelming majority of books that are not so regarded at the beginning never attain scriptural status, regardless of their religious worth and power.

The principle I am relying on here does not imply that the writers of the New Testament thought of themselves as writing what would later be thought of as the New Testament, a particular collection of books constituting a closed canon. Such a claim would certainly be anachronistic. The claim I am defending is that it is plausible that the writers of what we call the New Testament thought of themselves as apostles who had the authority to speak a word from God, and that this enabled both these writers and others who accepted their apostolic status to understand at least some of their writings as having a scriptural status from the beginning.

I realize of course that there are many other reasons I have not discussed to think that 2 Peter was not written by Peter, and that other books in the New Testament were not by the authors traditionally believed to have written them. Some of those arguments are doubtless such that I lack the expertise properly to appreciate their force. One might think that an article such as this by a philosopher who lacks expertise in biblical studies is an act of hubris. However, it seems to me that when an outsider ventures into neighboring academic territory, he will offer little of value if he is intimidated by the reigning academic fashions and simply reflects back to another field the dominant consensus of that field. Rather, the other field is better served if the outsider, with a due regard for his limitations, is willing to say how things really look to him. And that is what I have tried to do in this paper.

A Final Word About Epistemic Perspectives

It is worth asking what epistemic stance an individual occupies in judging that a particular book of the New Testament is or is not pseudonymous. In making such a judgment, must we take the perspective of the historical scholar? And what perspective is that?

My sense is that many New Testament scholars believe that in making a historical judgment of this sort a responsible person must limit him- or herself to evidence and arguments that would be acceptable to historical scholars generally, regardless of their religious stance. The applicable rules are the ones that would apply in John Meier's imagined 'unpapal conclave' in which individuals of various religious persuasions meet and try to reach agreement.[29] From this perspective, it would be improper to consider such things as my Christian conviction that Peter and Paul were truly filled with the Holy Spirit and that they had a clear consciousness about this and what it implies.

Well, if my goal is to publish an article in the *Journal of Biblical Literature* or construct an argument that might convince a Muslim or atheist friend, such rules make a good deal of sense. However, if my goal is to discover the truth about such matters, and I am convinced that Paul and Peter had such a relationship with the Holy Spirit, then it is not clear to me why the implications of such beliefs should be bracketed when I consider such questions as whether Peter might have written 2 Peter. It seems quite possible that Christian believers might have good reasons to accept certain historical claims which cannot be justified by the rules of historical inquiry as those rules are generally understood.[30] This in turn raises questions about the status of those rules: What exactly are the rules? Are there various sets of rules for various communities? Should those rules be brought up for reconsideration? Such questions range far beyond the topic of this paper but they must not be forgotten in attempting to say what historical truths a Christian can and should affirm.

I conclude that a Christian certainly can accept the possibility that God's word can come through 'apostles' whose names we may not know, and thus that some of the writings of the New Testament may be correctly included in the canon even if not written by apostles or those closely linked to apostles. Christian scholars should honestly investigate issues of authorship. But when they do so they should recognize that some of the evidence may look differently to them than it does to some non-Christians, and that they may have theological reasons for some of their historical convictions.

Above all, in investigating such issues as pseudonymity, Christians must not forget the basic principle that a divine revelation is something that ought to be believed because it has been revealed by God. The existence of such a divine revelation stands or falls with the existence of apostles, people who have been authorized to speak on God's behalf. Christians believe that such men as Peter and Paul were apostles in precisely this sense, and that the New Testament consists at its core in writings by the apostles or by those closely-enough connected to them to embody apostolic teachings. Without a core of apostolic writings in this sense, it is difficult to see how the New Testament could be claimed to be the Word of God.

---

[29] See Meier, *A Marginal Jew*, Vol. I, 5.

[30] For more on the issues hinted at here, see Bartholomew et al. (eds.), *Behind the Text*, especially the essays in the first section, 'Historical Criticism – Critical Assessments'.

Bibliography

Abraham, W.J., *The Divine Inspiration of Holy Scripture* (Oxford: Oxford University Press, 1981)

Bartholomew, C., C.S. Evans, M. Healy, and M. Rae (eds.), *'Behind' the Text: History and Biblical Interpretation* (Carlisle: Paternoster and Grand Rapids: Zondervan, 2003)

Baukham, R., *Jude, 2 Peter* (WBC 50; Waco, TX: Word, 1983)

Charles, J.D., '2 Peter', in *1–2 Peter, Jude* (Scottdale, PA: Herald, 1999)

Funk, R.W., 'The Once and Future New Testament', in *The Canon Debate* (ed. L.M. McDonald and J.A. Sanders; Peabody, MA: Hendrickson, 2002), 541–57

Gamble, H.Y., *The New Testament Canon: Its Making and Meaning* (Eugene, OR: Wipf and Stock, 2002)

Garrow, A.J.P., *The Gospel of Matthew's Dependence on the Didache* (JSNTSup 254; New York/London: Continuum, 2004)

Hong, H.V., and E.H. Hong, 'Historical Introduction' to *The Book on Adler* (trans. and ed. H.V. Hong and E.H. Hong; Princeton: Princeton University Press, 1998), vii–xix

Jackson, T.P., *The Priority of Love: Christian Charity and Social Justice* (Princeton: Princeton University Press, 2002)

Kierkegaard, S., *The Book on Adler* (trans. and ed. H.V. Hong and E.H. Hong; Princeton: Princeton University Press, 1998)

—, *Without Authority* (trans. and ed. H.V. Hong and E.H. Hong; Princeton: Princeton University Press, 1997)

Kruger, M.J., 'The Authenticity of 2 Peter,' *JETS* 42.4 (1999), 645–71

Lewis, C.S., 'Modern Theology and Biblical Criticism', in *Christian Reflections* (Grand Rapids: Eerdmans, 1967), 152–66

McDonald, L., 'Preface to the Second Edition', in *The Formation of the Christian Biblical Canon* (Peabody, MA: Hendrickson, 1995), xv–xxi

McKinnon, A., *Kierkegaardian Indices* (Leiden: E.J. Brill, 1973)

—, 'Mapping the Dimensions of a Literary Corpus', *Literary and Linguistic Computing* 4.2 (1989), 73–84

Meade, D.G., *Pseudonymity and Canon: An Investigation into the Relationship of Authorship and Authority in Jewish and Early Christian Tradition* (Grand Rapids: Eerdmans, 1987)

Meier, J.P., *A Marginal Jew: Rethinking the Historical Jesus*, Vol. I (3 vols.; New York: Anchor, 1991)

Plantinga, A., *Warranted Christian Belief* (Oxford and New York: Oxford University Press, 2000)

Stump, E., 'Moral Authority and Pseudonymity: Comments on the Paper of Wayne E. Meeks', in *Hermes and Athena: Biblical Exegesis and Philosophical Theology* (ed. E. Stump and T.P. Flint; Notre Dame: University of Notre Dame Press, 1993), 59–70

Wilder, T.L., *Pseudonymity, the New Testament, and Deception: An Inquiry into Intention and Reception* (Lanham, MD: University Press of America, 2004)

6

Reclaiming Inspiration for the Bible
Stephen B. Chapman

All scripture is inspired by God and is useful for teaching, for reproof, for correction, and for training in righteousness, so that everyone who belongs to God may be proficient, equipped for every good work.

(2 Tim. 3:16–17 NRSV)

… the claim for the inspiration of Scripture is the claim for the uniqueness of the canonical context of the church through which the Holy Spirit works.

Brevard S. Childs[1]

In the early modern era, it was Johann Salomo Semler who most sharply called attention to the way in which the historical character of biblical canon formation was increasingly difficult to reconcile with traditional theological affirmations about Scripture made by the church.[2] That the historical-critical paradigm in biblical studies arguably thus began, at least in part, with a major critique of canonicity was no accident. The church's concept of a canon lay precisely at the fault line between history and theology. Theologically, the biblical canon was understood to represent God's own words to humankind, but historically the canon was increasingly shown to be a fully human production.

Inspiration, as a cipher for a mysterious process of divine–human co-writing, had traditionally been invoked to safeguard the role of divine agency in the composition of the canon's individual writings.[3] Because of the emphasis on *composition*, however, the phenomenon of inspiration was primarily associated with authorship and could only with difficulty be applied to the lengthy process in which individual writings were subsequently edited, assembled and organized into a canonical collection. This was the difficulty that Semler grasped and used as an analytical wedge, placing his theological opponents at a

---

[1] Childs, *Crisis*, 104.
[2] Semler, *Abhandlung*.
[3] For a useful collection of statements on inspiration from the first three centuries of church history, see Westcott, 'Appendix B'.

serious disadvantage. For how was the challenge to be met? Could the entire process of canon formation be baptized? The theological notions of illumination and providence were routinely employed as loose descriptors of God's agency in the post-compositional aspects of biblical formation and usage. But post-Reformation Protestants were quick to see their particular dilemma: to extend a notion of inspiration to the entire process of biblical formation risked underwriting a Catholic view of tradition and undermining the Reformation heritage of privileging scriptural authority. Anxiety about this risk thus led Protestants to insist all the more strongly on the uniqueness of the compositional process of the Bible.[4]

By contrast, Semler's goal was to use historical argumentation as a means of liberating biblical interpretation from what he considered to be oppressive ecclesiastical control. In pursuing that aim, he persuasively showed the historical formation of the biblical canon to have been gradual, *ad hoc* and subject to significant disagreement, conclusions that have only gained in force and urgency since Semler's day. For anyone unwilling completely to sever biblical scholarship from theological interpretation, Semler's work, more than any other, has therefore continued to represent the methodological 'thrown gauntlet' of modernity: can a theological doctrine of Scripture successfully embrace what history says about how Scripture became Scripture? Is the biblical canon an accident of history or an inspired work of God?

Canon as a Historical Process

At the high tide of historical-critical study of the Bible – the end of the nineteenth century – a particular view of Old Testament canon formation established itself in line with Wellhausen's radical reversal of the history of ancient Israelite religion.[5] Most fully elaborated by H.E. Ryle,[6] this view held that the Old Testament had been canonized in three successive stages, beginning with the canonization of the Pentateuch in Ezra's day (usually dated to the mid-fifth century BC), followed by the closing of the prophetic corpus in approximately 200 BC, and then by the completion of the Writings (and thus the Old Testament canon as a whole) at the end of the first century AD. The brilliance of this model lay in its ability to mediate successfully between, on the one hand, Wellhausen's new critical history of Israel and, on the other hand, a number of historical witnesses to the process of canonization itself (both internal and external to the biblical text). With minimal adjustments and qualifications, this linear three-stage model of Old Testament canon formation remains the

---

[4] Preus, *Inspiration*, 26.
[5] Wellhausen, *Prolegomena*.
[6] Ryle, *Canon*.

majority view today, continues to be upheld by leading scholars and appears in most of the current introductory handbooks and textbooks in the field.[7]

At the same time, there has been sustained skepticism of this model – from the outset – by other scholars whose questions and critiques nevertheless did not ever take the form of an alternative model persuasive enough to displace the majority view.[8] Usually the skepticism of these scholars has been characterized as arising from a simple disagreement about *dating*. Actually, however, the differences go deeper.[9] In contrast to the majority view, in which the canonical process begins relatively late in Israel's history, proceeds in a cleanly unilinear manner and concludes after most of the New Testament already existed in written form, scholars such as Roger Beckwith,[10] Sid Leiman[11] and Brevard Childs[12] have argued (in different ways) not only for an earlier beginning and ending to the process but also for a messier, more multiplex character to canonization as a socio-historical phenomenon. At issue, then, is the nature of the canonical process itself and therefore the *definition* of canon. Rather than defining 'canon' as essentially a matter of delimitation and 'closure' as an official, quasi-legal decision (two basic presuppositions of the majority view), the alternative view understands 'canon' as an issue of authority or communal identity and 'closure' as the consequence of tradition and use.

Although this new canonical perspective emerged first within Old Testament studies, it is now reflected in work on the New Testament canon as well. In addition to Childs's own book on the New Testament,[13] various publications on New Testament canon formation[14] provide grounds (of various sorts) for reopening discussion of the late fourth-century date for the canon's closure that has increasingly become customary (because in part of the stress placed upon the list of biblical books found in Athanasius' Thirty-Ninth Festal Letter of 367 AD).[15] Here, above all, the incisive work of John Barton has

---

[7] Cf. Barton, 'Significance', 68.

[8] For a more detailed history of this minority body of scholarship, see Chapman, *Law and Prophets*, 1–70.

[9] An effort has been made to explore such differences in McDonald and Sanders, *Canon Debate*. Although this volume helpfully reviews much recent scholarly literature and offers rich resources for further study, such as a very full bibliography, its dominant perspective is still regrettably one-sided.

[10] Beckwith, *Old Testament Canon*.

[11] Leiman, *Canonization*.

[12] Childs, *Introduction*, and *Biblical Theology*.

[13] Childs, *New Testament*.

[14] E.g. Trobisch, *First Edition*; Wall, 'Reading'; Wall and Lemcio, *New Testament as Canon*; Metzger, *Canon of the New Testament*; Gamble, *New Testament Canon*; Patzia, *Making*.

[15] McDonald, *Formation*, 222; Bruce, *Canon*, 77–78.

shown with great perceptiveness how prior decisions about the definition of canon lead ineluctably toward earlier or later dates for the establishment of the New Testament canon.[16]

As Barton clearly demonstrates, when the New Testament canon is defined as a fixed list of books, each with a fixed text, then the date given for the existence of the canon will invariably be later than when the canon is defined as an authoritative core of books that could still undergo a degree of editorial change. Indeed, if one presses the idea of uniformity too hard, one is left in the somewhat absurd position of having to argue that it was not until the sixteenth-century that the question of the New Testament canon was actually resolved.[17] Such a conclusion, however, fails to illuminate the distinctive scriptural hermeneutics of early Christianity and strongly suggests that there is a problem with how canon is being defined rather than with the dating itself. In Barton's view, for example, *both* sides in the canon debate, those that stress 'early recognition' and those that advocate 'late formalization', are simultaneously correct.[18] The question remaining is what that seemingly contradictory state of affairs means for how 'canon' was understood in antiquity.

Before exploring further the theological implications of this contemporary discussion for the question of biblical inspiration,[19] it is first important for the purpose of this essay to underscore what both sides in the canon debate appear to share. Whether the canon is dated early or late, and defined as a matter of authority or of closure, all of the current debate's participants have in common the idea that biblical canon formation was a gradual process encompassing considerable editorial activity and documentary organization. To this extent, they are *all* Semler's heirs. Some of the editorial activity involved the reworking of pre-existent sources prior to the completion of a biblical book; some of it entailed significant editorial reworking after a book might have been already extant in some form; some of it consisted of assembling and re-assembling books into larger units and structures.

Yet this basic historical-critical perspective continues to come up hard against the traditional notion of scriptural inspiration as a mysterious divine interaction with an author at the point of a biblical book's composition, a view of inspiration termed the 'prophetic model' by Paul Achtemeier and glossed by him as 'one person writing one inspired scripture'.[20] Semler's challenge

---

[16] Barton, *Holy Writings.*

[17] E.g., McDonald, *Formation*, 225–26.

[18] Barton, *Holy Writings*, 23, 26–27.

[19] For thoughts on implications that go beyond the particular question of biblical inspiration, see also Chapman, *Law and Prophets*, 241–92, and 'Old Testament Canon'.

[20] Achtemeier, *Inspiration*, 102. Achtemeier traces this 'prophetic model' to Orr, *Revelation*, especially 175–96. While Orr's basic framework relies heavily on accounts of prophecy in the Old Testament, he does not, however, restrict revelation to the

therefore still remains acute. In light of the church's traditional model of inspiration, how is the *subsequent* textual work on the biblical books, by persons other than the author, to be construed and evaluated theologically? Merely as conceptual declension and textual decay? Is an edited biblical text necessarily in need of having its meaning restored, only a problem to be fixed? Or is it theologically meaningful in its own right?

One option at this point is to take a stand with the traditional view of inspiration and reject the findings of historical-critical scholarship on principle; this stance continues to be the fundamentalist position.[21] Another option is to follow Semler even further, siding strongly with historical-critical scholarship, and either reject the notion of inspiration altogether or reinterpret it anthropomorphically as something like the striving of the human spirit over time; these moves are characteristic of liberal theology. A third 'evangelical' option also exists; it will need to be explored at length later in this essay. Because evangelicals commendably continue to reflect deeply on the question of inspiration[22] – while many others have prematurely dismissed or simply neglected the topic[23] – their work represents the best discussion partner for the alternative this essay would ultimately like to advance: a fourth, canonically oriented option. By engaging evangelical scholarship this essay's goal is thus to foster dialogue and improved conversation. It is particularly hoped that this essay will demonstrate to an evangelical audience that canonical theology is a friend rather than a foe when it comes to the articulation of a compelling doctrine of Scripture, especially with regard to the inspiration of the Bible.

---

activity of a single individual, as Achtemeier implies; cf. Orr, *Revelation*, 156, for a description of how revelation extends beyond the individual act of composition. For a modern example of the 'prophetic model' applied to the entire process of Old Testament canon formation, see Harris, *Inspiration*. Harris views New Testament canon formation in parallel fashion, using the notion of the 'apostolic.' This notion also entails 'one person writing one inspired Scripture', for, in Harris's view, 'the canonicity of a book of the Bible depends upon its authorship' (284).

[21] My intent here is to use the term 'fundamentalist' descriptively, not dismissively. Fundamentalism typically expresses a desire to take the Bible 'literally', by which is meant that the synchronic presentation of the Bible is to be understood as historically accurate in every case. Of course, characterizing the beliefs of a particular socio-theological group such as this is always difficult, since its membership is in reality fluid and varied rather than monolithic.

[22] For an excellent collection of evangelical essays on this topic, see Bacote, Miguélez and Okholm, *Evangelicals and Scripture*.

[23] E.g. Richardson, 'Rise', 316: 'Most theologians today seem to agree that the non-biblical category of "inspiration" is not adequate to the elucidation of the doctrine of biblical revelation.'

A canonically oriented view of inspiration, one that is suggested and even warranted by the historical study of canon formation, retains room for the transcendent but sees the divine–human encounter as occurring over a lengthier period of time and as including more people than just one author alone. In this view, inspiration would extend throughout the entirety of the process of the Bible's formation and focus as much on the community that transmitted the text as on the role of the text's putative author.[24]

In describing this canonical account of inspiration, it will be argued that the work of Brevard Childs provides the crucial groundwork – that an account of inspiration is in fact implicit throughout his writings, despite recent assertions to the contrary. For example, David Williams charges Childs with only using the term 'inspiration' negatively, as a view to be avoided.[25] Although Williams is correct to perceive Childs's uneasiness with the language of inspiration, the reason for it is Childs's sense that traditional theories of inspiration have arrived at an unfruitful impasse and certainly not that Childs moves 'from a Bible whose meaning is inspired by God to one whose meaning is the result of the canonical process of Israel and the Church.'[26] Childs clearly makes room for the transcendent throughout his description of the canonical process and never pulls the two apart in the manner Williams alleges.

Writing earlier, Paul Noble not only asserted the same deficit in Childs's work, he also argued that the fuller articulation of a doctrine of inspiration was precisely what was needed in order to repair Childs's approach and render it viable.[27] While Noble rightly sees an implicit account of inspiration functioning within Childs's approach, he errs in thinking that this idea of inspiration can be made explicit and even strengthened simply by supplementing Childs's work with a traditional account of inspiration (i.e. one based narrowly upon

---

[24] To this extent, a canonical view of inspiration exhibits similarities with a social construal of revelation. Both positions agree that to ask about *the* author of a biblical book can be a misleading and ultimately invalid question. E.g. Achtemeier: 'Rather, the canon emerged as the result of community reflections on the common traditions in the light of the changing historical situation. It is that model, rather than the prophetic one, which we want to urge as more appropriate …'. Achtemeier's communitarian account of inspiration thus resembles and builds upon a strain of Catholic theology advocating 'social revelation' (*Inspiration*, 108). See, for example, MacKenzie, 'Social Character'; Hoffman, 'Inspiration'. For the historical background to this discussion, see also Burtchaell, *Catholic Theories*. The critical question for such accounts is whether they can do full justice to the Bible's role of standing over the church in judgment when necessary.

[25] Williams, *Receiving the Bible*, 103. The quote from Childs at the beginning of this essay proves that assertion wrong.

[26] Williams, *Receiving the Bible*, 105.

[27] Noble, *Canonical Approach*, 31.

authorial intention).[28] In the end, Noble's suggestions about inspiration and Childs's approach are largely irrelevant because Noble establishes prior ground rules for interpretation (e.g. 'original meaning,' 'authorial intention') without apparently realizing that those ground rules fully undermine Childs's approach and prevent it from obtaining fair and accurate consideration in Noble's treatment.[29] Childs has not simply overlooked the possibilities Noble raises, as Noble seems to believe – Childs has already rejected them in favor of another alternative.

Childs's canonical outlook *does* involve a reappraisal of tradition and ecclesiology from the side of Protestant theology, which has been temperamentally unwilling to find much value in either, except as foils.[30] Of course, there is always the danger in such a reappraisal that something vital to Protestant theology might be eroded or lost. However, it may also be argued that a reappraisal of *tradition* would serve helpful theological purposes in light of the particular situation in which contemporary Protestantism finds itself. Renewed appreciation for tradition would benefit contemporary Protestant churches greatly, given their present historical rootlessness and theological amnesia. Also, heightened attention to *ecclesiology* is arguably more necessary than ever in American Protestantism because of the astonishing accommodation of Christians in the USA to the current cultural religion of capitalistic consumerism and nationalistic fervor. Protestantism does need to retain a robust notion of Scripture in order to provide a normative check on tradition and on the church, but at this specific moment in history Protestantism could find much more value in tradition and the church without endangering in the least Scripture's leading role as *norma normans* (i.e. the norming norm or the norm that norms [other norms]). Present threats to biblical authority arise primarily from cultural accommodation rather than overweening ecclesial tradition.

---

[28] Unlike many of Childs's critics, Noble perceives that Childs makes 'intentionalist' as well as 'anti-intentionalist' claims. But Noble describes these claims as flatly inconsistent and attributes them to arbitrary 'phases' within Childs's work (*Canonical Approach*, 328). What Noble fails to realize is how these claims fit together in a distinctive manner within Childs's hermeneutics – i.e. that for historical reasons both kinds of claims must be made.

[29] See Noble, *Canonical Approach*, 340–50.

[30] Childs, *Introduction*, 80–81. As Childs points out, there has also been an important reassessment of the 'Scripture and tradition' question within Catholicism itself, bringing Catholics and Protestants much closer together on this topic than was previously the case. But some Protestant theologians still ignore Vatican II and the changes in twentieth-century Catholic theology, instead formulating their positions over against the Catholic Church of the sixteenth century. For a very helpful resource in this regard, see Williamson, *Catholic Principles*.

In a recent article, Walter Moberly further describes how the reappraisal of tradition by canonical criticism provides new opportunities for conversation and *rapprochement* between Protestants and Catholics, as well the Orthodox communions.[31] By problematizing the significance of a reconstructed 'original' text and focusing attention on the ways in which the biblical texts accrued a fuller and broader frame of reference within the canonical collection, a canonical hermeneutic reveals how to view Scripture and tradition more as complements than competitors. To the extent such conversation and agreement are possible without sacrificing something essential to a Protestant doctrine of Scripture, it would surely be a good thing.

The Evangelical Tradition and Inspiration

So where does evangelical scholarship place itself in this discussion? Writing in 1990, Carl Henry, the grand old man of American evangelicalism, offered an extended analysis of the work of Brevard Childs and 'canonical theology.' Because of Henry's standing and continued influence within the evangelical community, his views deserve utmost consideration as the expression of a broadly held evangelical perspective.[32]

It may be helpful to relate Henry's ultimate conclusion in advance: 'The weakest link in Childs's canonical proposal lies in its nebulous views of divine revelation and inspiration.'[33] For Henry, Childs's recognition of the biblical canon as a pivotal hermeneutical issue was warmly to be welcomed, as was Childs's privileging of the canonical text and his critique of historical criticism. Yet in Henry's judgment Childs remained too open to the possibility that the biblical books continued to develop and change after their composition:

> In expounding the emergence of Scripture, evangelical scholarship finds less reason for departing from canonically-indicated authors of the component biblical books. It leans more heavily on the factor of divine revelation and prophetic-apostolic inspiration, without on that account minimizing the biblical writers' personality differences and stylistic peculiarities or excluding their use of sources.[34]

In Henry's view the uniqueness of the compositional process (i.e. 'inspiration') lay precisely in its ability faithfully to transmit the content of divine

---

[31] Moberly, 'Canon of the Old Testament', 250.

[32] Henry passed away at the age of ninety in 2003, but many in the evangelical community continue to appeal to his legacy. It is not the intention of this essay to single Henry out for particular criticism but rather to honor him as a significant and fruitful discussion partner for canonical theology.

[33] Henry, 'Canonical Theology', 108.

[34] Henry, 'Canonical Theology', 79.

revelation directly into the propositional subject matter of the original biblical writings.

Once this transmission had occurred, however, it was nonsensical to imagine that any significant changes to the text could have been made, even if they were attributed pseudonymously to the original author:

> ... it seems incredible that believers who received and perpetuated prophetic-apostolic writings imposed as the Word of God would have unprotestingly accepted such misleading attribution and the view that only as redacted by unknown editors could the ancient writings be regarded as normative for future generations of believers (*cf.* 2 Tim 3:14).[35]

In this account, the original biblical compositions had such coherence and such widely recognized authority from the beginning that their collection and organization could have never been anything other than a process of continuity, consensus and conservation. Henry even went so far as to describe 'the evangelical emphasis on an objectively inspired literary deposit *unrevisable* by a process of community interaction'.[36] However, the most crucial feature to note about Henry's argument at this point is that it was primarily theological in nature rather than historical. Henry was concerned to draw a historical line in the sand because of the dangers that he apprehended in 'canonical theology.'

The first danger was that granting a substantial role in the Bible's formation to editors and redactors would compromise the crucial theological significance of authorship:

> Professor Childs speaks of the canon's 'growth' in a way that dissolves interest in verbally inspired autographs ... It avoids the widely held evangelical insistence on a canon constituted essentially of inspired autographs, authoritatively imposed upon the early churches, and received as unrevisable normative statements of Christian revelation.[37]

Without a strong appeal to authorship on the historical level, a hermeneutic based upon authorial intention becomes difficult to maintain – and such a

---

[35] Henry, 'Canonical Theology', 79.

[36] Henry, 'Canonical Theology', 88 (my emphasis).

[37] Henry, 'Canonical Theology', 87. It is a tell-tale indication of the difference between Childs and Henry that here Henry was clearly thinking of the New Testament canon more than the Old Testament canon. As an Old Testament scholar, Childs knows only too well that the kind of historical reconstruction Henry's position implied is simply impossible with respect to the literary formation of the Old Testament books. Similar observations about how attention to the Old Testament shifts the discussion of such hermeneutical questions are also made in Hays, 'Jeremiah', esp. 134, and Grisanti, 'Inspiration'.

hermeneutic was central to Henry's understanding of biblical authority. Without grounding Scripture's meaning in the intent of its authors, Henry feared that Scripture would lose its ability to stand over against the experience of its contemporary human interpreters. For Henry, interpreting Scripture was either a matter of discerning authorial intent or it became a way of evading Scripture's meaning through the substitution of an interpreter's concerns for those of the author. Ironically, this evangelical appeal to authorship is the consequence of a nineteenth-century retreat from what conservatives at that time feared had become an increasingly untenable view of verbal inspiration.[38] By contrast, an author-centered hermeneutic was then thought to allow for a more expansive view of inspiration, with a greater role for human agency.

In reality, however, it was not so much a lack of attention to authorship on Childs's part that Henry found objectionable as it was Childs's refusal to tie authorship exclusively to a notion of 'inspired autographs.' Childs, to the surprise of many of his critics, *has* articulated a place for authorial intent within his method and does *not* uncritically invest the 'final form' of the text with meaning, as some continue falsely to charge.

> The search for the canonical shape of the text begins with a reading which looks for traces either of how the author intended the material to be understood, or of the effect which a particular reading has on the literature. The point is to take seriously a writer's expressed intentionality, but without pulling text and intention apart. At times the canonical text receives a meaning which is derivative of its function within the larger corpus, but which cannot be directly linked to the intention of an original author ...[39]

Authorship thus remains important in Childs's handling of exegetical method, but the text retains hermeneutical priority. Because the text has a history of change and development beyond the stage of composition, not every aspect of the text can be directly attributed to an author's intention.

In addition to seemingly endangering the idea of authorship, however, canonical theology's emphasis on editors and redactors (instead of authors) also threatened to subvert Henry's understanding of inspiration itself:

> When the production of the canon is linked essentially not to inspired prophets and apostles, but is connected instead to fallible supplementers, editors, redactors and interpreters, divine inspiration becomes so insubstantial as to be powerless.[40]

---

[38] Sailhamer, *Introduction*, 65.

[39] Childs, *New Testament*, 49. Granted, this passage may relate more directly to the interpretation of the New Testament than the Old, but many will be surprised to learn it exists at all in Childs's writings. Henry, for example, simply passed it by unmentioned.

[40] Henry, 'Canonical Theology', 103.

Of course, as use of the term 'fallible' suggests, what Henry was rejecting was the investment of theological significance in what was manifestly *not* infallible material. There are plenty of errors, gaps, contradictions, and confusions throughout the wide array of biblical manuscripts available from antiquity; there is no debate about that. In Henry's model, as in many traditional evangelical accounts, the stress therefore shifts to the 'original autographs' of the biblical books (of which there are no extant manuscripts). The interlocking evangelical emphases on authorship, inspiration, and inerrancy all work together to remove any doubts about the veracity of these supposedly 'original autographs' of the biblical books. Indeed, the autographs are placed entirely beyond the realm of question by being turned into an article of faith. The autographs are simply presumed from the outset to be different *in kind* from later manuscripts.

Henry subscribed to a doctrine of providence, naturally, but it seemingly could not bear as much weight as he considered Childs's approach to require. Henry explained his difference with Childs over the question of providence in this way:

> … many evangelicals appeal to special divine providence to explain the compilation and preservation of the canon. If one asks why providential divine sovereignty could not have been equally operative through dialectical canon-formation, the response is that apostolicity is a more compelling principle than dialectical process to account for the reception of the canonical books as authoritative.[41]

But here Henry has quickly substituted 'dialectical process' for 'divine providence.' If the explicit focus on providence is retained, then one might well still ask why it was any less compelling, according to Henry, to believe that providential oversight rather than supernatural composition was responsible for the biblical canon. Henry's answer would most likely be that since God's providential oversight of Scripture had clearly not assured the perfect transmission of biblical manuscripts from antiquity, it was therefore necessary to restrict inspiration to the original autographs.[42]

Thus, there is a striking lack of confidence in providence at the heart of Henry's view of Scripture. The hermeneutical privileging of the 'original autographs' is often viewed, by both evangelicals and non-evangelicals, as an audacious theological claim stubbornly held in the face of modernity. In reality, to restrict revelation to the 'original autographs' represents a defensive action taken mostly for rationalistic reasons, and is therefore more of a concession to modernity than it is modernity's opposition.[43]

---

[41] Henry, 'Canonical Theology', 86.
[42] For further discussion of this point generally, see Beegle, *Inspiration*, 23.
[43] Barr, *Scope*, 70. Cf. Brogan, 'Autograph', 108, who asks plaintively but probingly: 'How do we explain that except for a small handful of people who were permitted to

Of course, to this view of providence as unable (!) to safeguard subsequent copies of the biblical text inerrantly, it may be added that providence did not see fit to preserve any of the original autographs either.[44] So providence would appear to be uniformly weak in Henry's account, even with his retreat to the autographs. Henry's logic also begs a further question: if the original auto-graphs were inerrant, then why would God *not* providentially ensure their (inerrant) preservation? Although Henry neglects to address this question directly, the typical evangelical answer will be that even though only flawed manuscripts of Scripture exist today their flaws are actually quite minor, so that the *concepts or doctrines* that God wished to reveal can still be fully communicated by those manuscripts. Such a response draws upon the principle of 'proposi-tional revelation' to which Henry himself also gave strong approval. Here, again, however, this evangelical move represents a strategic retreat.

Under pressure from modern notions of documentary consistency and tex-tual uniformity (which derive more from the advent of the printing press than from ancient scribal practice), 'propositional revelation' in reality reduces the inspiration of the *text* to the inspiration of the concepts or doctrines that the text is said to contain, which is not at all the same thing. This common evangel-ical position says in effect that the valuable aspect of the Bible lies in its teach-ings but insufficiently reflects upon the form in which those teachings are conveyed. Can contents really be separated from their literary form? Is not the literary form of the Bible in fact part of its meaning? The decisive objection to the idea of propositional revelation is not that the biblical books fail to commu-nicate concepts: it is instead that the biblical literature does *more* than convey concepts.[45] The Bible also influences and forms its readers in a wide variety of more subtle ways, which are just as crucial to its literary impact. The Bible gives its hearers and readers a narrative world to live in. Its phrases and rhythms linger in the mind and its stories often provoke questions more than they provide answers. Furthermore, if only the concepts are to count, and those concepts are viewed as coming entirely from God (i.e. as 'special revelation' in theological terms), then Scripture's human authors cannot be viewed as having contrib-uted anything meaningful to Scripture's content, and a propositional account of revelation becomes problematically 'docetic' in character (i.e. unwilling

---

read possibly *one* of the autographs, everyone has heard and responded to God through reading or hearing "errant" copies of the biblical text, including the transla-tions based on the "scandalously corrupt" Greek text used by most evangelicals today?' (his use of italics).

[44] Cf. Beegle, *Inspiration*, 25–26.

[45] The often vigorous evangelical defense of theological interpretation as necessarily conceptual thus misses the point. The question is not whether interpretation is to a certain extent conceptual, but rather whether the articulation of concepts can account for the entirety of the interpretive task.

to grant true meaningfulness to human agency).[46] The literary features of the Bible cannot simply be peeled away in the search for propositional formulations.[47]

Yet a further problem for Henry with the role of editors and redactors in canonical theology arose at the other end of the trajectory between author and text. If editors and redactors are granted a significant role in Scripture's formation, then tradition must also be granted theological value, in effect re-opening the old debate between Catholics and Protestants about the proper relation between Scripture and tradition. If later tradition could substantively alter, correct, and expand beyond what the biblical authors had written, then it appeared to Henry that later tradition had trumped what God originally intended to serve as Scripture. This situation would in turn provide a warrant for the contemporary church to frame and reframe the meaning of Scripture as it sees fit, so that Scripture would be in danger of losing its crucial ability to correct church tradition.[48]

Henry therefore insisted on the 'prophetic model' of inspiration as a check to precisely such an ecclesially oriented move:

> For if textual normativity is the achievement of a final canonizing community, then the meaning of the biblical text is dissolved into what the early church decided, and the decisive role of the prophets and apostles is effaced.[49]

Henry was correct to see how the authority of the biblical text might be compromised at this point, but he was incorrect to deem that danger a necessary consequence of canonical theology. On the contrary, Brevard Childs has been quite emphatic about the need to honor 'the decisive role of the prophets and apostles.' For Childs, one of the main features of the canon is that it fixes the prophetic–apostolic *witness* necessary for the church to remember its identity.[50] The difference is that for Childs the prophetic–apostolic witness is more than simply what individual prophets and apostles originally said and wrote. Their witness continues to develop and deepen over time, a process reflected in the

---

[46] See Henry's curious argument ('Canonical Theology', 106) that to insist on the human sinfulness of the biblical tradents 'casts baneful implications for divine incarnation.' To the contrary, such insistence can be mindful of the distinction between human beings and Christ, even as it finds meaning in their common humanity.

[47] Sadly, the isolation and extraction of 'principles' from the biblical text is precisely what passes for theological interpretation in much current evangelical teaching and preaching.

[48] For a similar evangelical judgment, see Brueggemann, 'Childs' Canon Criticism'.

[49] Henry, 'Canonical Theology', 83.

[50] Childs has remained remarkably consistent on this point. See, for example, Childs, *Crisis*, 100–101; *Biblical Theology*, 381; *Struggle*, 321; cf. Seitz, 'Not Prophets or Apostles'.

history of the biblical literature itself, until that witness is acknowledged by the community of faith to be complete. Part of the issue here is also Childs's broader understanding of 'revelation', which for him cannot be reduced to a single form of 'special revelation' to individual authors but occurs in and through various communal media of divine apprehension and encounter.[51] For Henry, Childs's formulation may still concede too much to tradition and ecclesiology, but it does accommodate his concern about the importance of the prophets and apostles.

Finally, throughout Henry's treatment of Childs, the problem of historicity is also fundamentally at issue. Privileging authorship and employing the 'prophetic model' of inspiration protects early dates and conservative historical reconstructions. In contrast, Childs's focus on the canonical text was viewed by Henry as relativizing the historical claims found in the biblical books.[52] Henry knew that Childs was aware of the criticism that his canonical approach does not adequately ground itself upon a sufficient historical foundation, yet Henry also considered Childs's defense unsatisfactory.

Childs describes his own position in these terms:

> … it is a basic misunderstanding of the canonical approach to describe it as a non-historical reading of the Bible. Nothing could be further from the truth! Rather, the issue at stake is the nature of the Bible's historicality and the search for a historical approach that is commensurate with it. The whole point of emphasizing the canon is to stress the historical nature of the biblical witness. There is no 'revelation' apart from the experience of historical Israel. However, a general hermeneutic is inadequate to deal with the particular medium through which this experience has been registered.[53]

This framing of the method does not discount history at all; instead it calls into question what 'history' is. What Henry could not see is that Childs is just as theologically committed to history as Henry is, but Childs feels obliged to ask more searching questions about the nature of history and the historical task[54] – questions that Henry, however, has assumed to be settled and obvious. Here again, the issue is not so much historicity *per se* but Henry's uncritical assumption of Enlightenment principles *versus* Childs's post-critical stance with respect to the debates raised by modern historiography. Thus, the crucial question for Childs is finally not whether the Bible is historical, but whether the contemporary understanding of history is biblical.

---

[51] On the various forms of revelation in the Bible, see further Childs, *Old Testament Theology*, especially 20–42.

[52] Cf. the similar verdict in Oswalt, 'Canonical Criticism'.

[53] Childs, *Introduction*, 71.

[54] E.g. Childs, *Struggle*, 321.

From Inspired Author to Inspired Text

Henry is only one evangelical voice, certainly – although a very prominent and influential one. Other conservative scholars have indicated a greater openness to an expanded notion of inspiration, based in large measure upon greater attention to the phenomenon of biblical canon formation, and particularly with regard to the Old Testament. In fact, scholars such as Robert Dick Wilson, E.J. Young, Merrill F. Unger, Bruce Waltke, Ronald Youngblood, Herbert Wolf and Duane Garrett have all sought to resolve the difficulties of an exclusively author-centered hermeneutic by allowing for some degree of inspired 'updating' of the biblical books.[55] At stake, however, is more than a matter of only 'minor adjustments.'[56] Simply seeking to extend an author-centered model of inspiration to a few other 'recognized individuals'[57] only compounds the problem at hand by failing to grapple with the full complexity of the Bible's literary formation.

Recent years have brought renewed interest and debate to the topic of Scripture from within evangelical circles.[58] In this debate, some evangelical scholars have in fact adopted positions on inspiration that move to accommodate the entire history of biblical canon formation. Donald Bloesch, for example, ventures this summary statement:

> I offer this more comprehensive definition of inspiration: the divine election and guidance of the biblical prophets and the ensuring of their writings as a compelling witness to revelation, the opening of the eyes of the people of that time to the truth of these writings, and the providential preservation of these writings as the unique channel of revelation. By the biblical prophets I have in mind all preachers, writers and editors in biblical history who were made the unique instruments of God's self-revealing action.[59]

Bloesch's account effectively redefines the traditional model of revelation in light of canon history. In the process, however, his account not only alters the term 'prophet' so thoroughly that it strains the sensibility of a 'prophetic' model, it also shifts the focus from the composition of the biblical writings to those writings themselves.

---

[55] For further details and citations of their work, see Grisanti, 'Inspiration', 591–93. I would add to this list the name of Daniel Block; see his 'Recovering', 404–405.

[56] *Contra* Grisanti, 'Inspiration', 577.

[57] Thus Grisanti, 'Inspiration', 580.

[58] See the essays in Bacote, Miguélez and Okholm, *Evangelicals and Scripture*.

[59] Bloesch, *Holy Scripture*, 119–20. For a similar formulation, see Brogan, 'Autograph', 109–10.

No one in evangelical scholarship perceived as early or as perceptively as John Sailhamer how increased awareness of the biblical canon might helpfully reorient evangelical hermeneutics, especially in its thinking about history.[60] Sensing a confusion in evangelical scholarship about whether the locus of divine revelation was to be found in the biblical text or in history,[61] Sailhamer strongly argues for a text-centered approach to Old Testament theology:

> The history in which God makes known his will is the history which is recorded in the inspired text of Scripture. When formulated this way, evangelical theology can be seen to be based on a revelation that consists of the meaning of a text with its focus on Scripture as a written document. Even the formula 'revelation in history' is then a question of the meaning of a text.[62]

By putting things this way, Sailhamer does not intend to cast doubt on the historicity of the biblical narratives. On the contrary, he considers them fully accurate and historical. But no historical event is self-interpreting, he maintains, which means that revelation is not to be found in raw events but in the interpretations of those events recorded in Scripture: '[The biblical narratives] certainly are accurate historical accounts of the events, but it is pure naiveté to treat them as the events themselves.'[63] It is no accident that Sailhamer's introduction to Old Testament theology is subtitled 'A Canonical Approach.'

Yet the main trend in recent evangelical scholarship has been to move in a different hermeneutical direction. Rather than expanding a notion of inspiration beyond authorship and toward the canon, most evangelical scholarship has, in effect, retained its traditional focus on authorship by secularizing it. It has been clear for some time that even though many evangelical scholars have largely given up on older, mechanistic models of inspiration, they have also characteristically continued to uphold the significance of authorship for primarily hermeneutical rather than theological reasons.[64] An author-centered hermeneutic has been widely viewed in evangelical circles as the only effective means by which to check the ravages of deconstructionist approaches to the biblical text, in other words, the only way to control interpretive options and choices enough that a normative text remains possible.

---

[60] E.g. Sailhamer, *Introduction*, 57.

[61] Sailhamer, *Introduction*, 67.

[62] Sailhamer, *Introduction*, 56.

[63] Sailhamer, *Introduction*, 67. Cf. Marshall, *Biblical Inspiration*, 14. Kaiser, 'New Dimensions', 38, concedes the validity of Sailhamer's point but then goes on to dismiss it without any real argument.

[64] Longman: 'Evangelicals, for the most part, have also assumed that the meaning of a text resides in the author's intention and the historical background' (*Literary Approaches*, 24). He in turn cites Kaiser, *Exegetical Theology*, 33: 'The *author's* intended meaning is what a text means.' Longman himself, however, advocates a more text-oriented hermeneutic.

The perceived issue is thus the determinacy of the biblical text rather than any theological aspect of a doctrine of Scripture, and a strong view of authorship is commonly viewed in evangelical circles as the only means by which to secure that determinacy.[65] Accordingly, in the widely used evangelical handbook *How to Read the Bible for all its Worth* by Gordon Fee and Douglas Stuart, one reads: 'a text cannot mean what it never could have meant to its author or his readers.'[66] The problem, of course, is that texts *always* mean something they never could have meant to their authors and (first) readers![67] So the position being taken by these evangelicals is one of principle rather than fact, but is it really a principle that evangelicals should want to adopt and defend? Do not evangelicals, of all people, have an interest in defending the idea that God can continue to reveal new and surprising meanings from the biblical texts, even meanings that those texts' authors did not intend themselves?[68]

The deeper danger of this author-centered hermeneutics, however, is that it often serves to provide an opportunity for liberal Protestant theology simply to re-enter evangelical biblical interpretation through the back door in the form of the human experience of the author. Interpretation then becomes an explanation of what 'David' or 'Matthew' or 'Paul' were thinking or attempting to say – rather than an explication of the text itself. At issue here is not only the well-known problem of authorial intention (i.e. how can one really know what is in an author's mind?). Just as problematic from a theological perspective is the substitution of a *reconstructed* authorial viewpoint for the canonical text. Although references to 'David,' 'Matthew,' and 'Paul' may operate successfully as a kind of rhetorical shorthand for what literary scholars call the 'implied author' of the text (i.e. the 'author' perceived on the basis of inferences drawn from the text

---

[65] Thus the prominence of literary scholar E.D. Hirsch in contemporary evangelical hermeneutics; for example, see Blue, 'Hermeneutics'; Porter, 'Hermeneutics', 115; Benson, 'Ignorant'; Dockery, *Christian Scripture*, 155–57; and Longman, *Literary Approaches*, 20–21. Especially in Dockery's treatment, Hirsch, who is neither a biblical scholar nor a theologian, dominates the review of twentieth-century 'biblical interpretation.'

[66] Fee and Stuart, *How to Read the Bible*, 60 (original all in italics).

[67] Above all, see Gadamer, *Truth and Method*.

[68] Dockery thinks so; for a listing of the theological reasons why, see his *Christian Scripture*, 160–61. Cf. Parry: 'Odd as it may seem, the very creation of the canon as a controlling context for the Christian interpretation of any biblical book means that Christian theological interpretation cannot simply be collapsed into the expected reading of a text (i.e. with the implied reader). The human redactor of Leviticus did not have the completed canon of the Christian Bible in mind when he shaped his text, but a theological interpretation of Leviticus would not be Christian if it did not read from a different "location" than that of the implied reader' ('Reader-Response Criticism', 660).

rather than the historical author *per se*), when such language is combined with a polemical insistence on historicity, the effect can be theologically disastrous. An otherwise appropriate commitment to historicity can then erase the text, replacing it with speculations about the decisions and desires of the human authors behind it. Even when those human authors are thought to be prophets and apostles, their wishes and intentions are not canonical, the text is.[69]

At present, author-centered accounts of inspiration seem to be moving in a new direction within evangelical scholarship. There appears to be growing interest in the hermeneutically oriented approach of those like Kevin Vanhoozer, who are attempting to retain a notion of an authorial sense through a sophisticated use of speech-act theory and a double-discourse model of biblical revelation.[70] Driving this attempt is the effort to reformulate an author-centered hermeneutic in a way that can successfully answer the objections to such a hermeneutic from deconstructionists and postmodern literary theorists.[71] As fully elaborated by Nicholas Wolterstorff,[72] this model ultimately tries to explain how God can be said to 'author' Scripture by speaking through its human authors.[73]

---

[69] For an instructive and spirited effort to write a New Testament commentary without shifting the interpretive focus from the text to the author, see Hauerwas's forthcoming volume on Matthew in the new *Brazos Theological Commentary on the Bible* series.

[70] Vanhoozer, *Meaning*; and 'Speech Acts', 1–49.

[71] Fowl, 'Authorial Intention', 72. For a concise but detailed discussion of speech-act theory and its recent appropriation by evangelical scholars, see Porter, 'Hermeneutics', esp. 112–18. Porter also sees Vanhoozer as using speech-act theory in order to retain a commitment to authorship. By replacing a psychological understanding of authorial intent with a notion of the author's 'enacted communicative intention', Vanhoozer hopes to 'rescue current theological interpretation from the slippery slope of postmodernism', according to Porter (114–15). Porter also points out, however, that Vanhoozer still ultimately grounds his account of 'communicative intention' in authorial intent, a stance Vanhoozer refers to as 'critical hermeneutical realism.'

[72] Wolterstorff, *Divine Discourse*. See also the essays in Bartholomew, Greene and Möller, *After Pentecost*, esp. Wolterstorff, 'Promise'. Wolterstorff's work combines a traditional evangelical commitment to authorship with a postmodern conviction that 'there just is no such thing as *the* sense of the text' (82, his emphasis). Since he does not wish to adopt a deconstructionist stance and argue that textual meaning is reader-produced either, however, he is more or less forced to look to authorship for textual meaning because there is nowhere else to go.

[73] For an earlier Catholic effort to ground inspiration in a notion of divine authorship, see Rahner, *Inspiration*. This notion does not prevent Rahner from also arguing that Scripture is 'just as genuinely a self-expression of the faith of the Church' (48) or that the synagogue could not close the Old Testament canon because (in contrast to the

In Vanhoozer's version of the discourse model, the focus of biblical inter-pretation shifts from the author's propositions or 'locutions' to the author's intentional illocutionary acts. Behind this shift is a deeper appreciation for the complexity and slipperiness of human language, the realization that the self-same locutions may be used to perform different illocutions. Interpretation then becomes 'the process of inferring authorial intentions and of ascribing illocutionary acts.'[74] But this move thus still insists that authorial intentions can be adequately known and it restricts the sense of the text to what an individual author hoped to accomplish. Vanhoozer expresses some openness to the idea of a broader kind of 'canonical' intentionality, but only if it can be grounded in a notion of divine authorship.[75]

The result, while impressive in its theoretical weight and subtlety, is finally rather vague about actual exegetical practice and stands in greater tension with the church's traditional doctrine of Scripture than has yet been widely real-ized.[76] As is evident especially in Vanhoozer's work, the theory is also doubly secularized, or at two removes, from a theological account of Scripture. First, the notion of authorship has been abstracted from a doctrine of inspiration and employed hermeneutically rather than theologically. Then a notion of divine 'double' authorship is in turn derived from the more customary understanding of human authorship. This recent direction in scholarship therefore appears to require considerable theoretical justification only to gain a hearing for an idea whose worth is open to theological question.[77] Here a speculative hermeneutical theory about *texts* replaces a doctrine of Scripture.[78]

---

church!) *it* was fallible (46) or that any possible contradiction between the church and Scripture is '*a priori* … eliminated' (72). Each of these three moves domesticates Scripture and diminishes its authority. In Rahner's treatment, 'divine authorship' is thus used to underwrite the authority of the church rather than the authority of Scripture.

[74] Vanhoozer, 'Speech Acts', 25.

[75] Vanhoozer, 'Speech Acts', 37.

[76] Childs, 'Speech-act Theory'. Overlooked in the present discussion, for the most part, is that the language of divine 'authorship' early in church tradition arose as a defense of the unity of the two testaments and was not regularly used to mean that God was somehow responsible for the literary authorship of the Bible. While this latter idea can be found occasionally early on, it was only fully developed and firmly established at the time of Vatican I. Eventually, it was also understood to imply and undergird biblical inerrancy; on this history, see further Vawter, *Biblical Inspiration*, 22–24.

[77] For further evaluation of author-centered interpretation, see Fowl, 'Authorial Intention'.

[78] Interestingly, however, Vanhoozer has also recently argued that the best way to understand providence is by paying attention to the process by which Scripture became Scripture; the structure of his argument broadly parallels the one in this essay. See Vanhoozer, 'Providence', 644.

Out of an awareness of these various dangers, a 'canonical' theology relocates the interpretive focus from an author-centered hermeneutic to a text-centered one. The hermeneutical proposal advanced by Sandra Schneiders is especially congenial for this purpose; she suggests thinking of a text as having an 'ideal meaning' that results from the interaction of three different aspects to a text:

> (a) ... [a] dialectic between sense and reference ... by which the text says something intelligible about something (even if what it says is false); (b) the genre in which the intelligible utterance is expressed and by which it is shaped; (c) the personal style of the author.[79]

By way of example, she interprets the parable of the Good Samaritan as involving:

> a dialectic between what is said (the story) and its referent (what being a neighbor actually means) that intends to say something intelligible about something, namely that the true keeping of the second commandment of the Law consists in actively serving the neighbor in need (whether or not this is true). This truth claim is expressed in the genre of a parable, which allows for its openness and relevance to a wide variety of situations beyond that of a victim of road violence. And it is written in the literary style of the author of Luke. The confluence of these three factors gives the text of the Good Samaritan a dynamic structure that guides interpretation of the passage in a certain direction.[80]

What Schneiders describes as a 'dynamic structure' might be viewed as similar to what Brevard Childs means by the 'shape' of a biblical text.[81] For Schneiders, the move to this hermeneutical position results from aesthetic reflection on what constitutes a work of art.[82] In Childs's case, his stance is the direct

---

[79] Schneiders, *Revelatory Text*, xxxii. The new introduction to this volume provides very helpful (and needed) clarifications to the first edition of Schneider's work.

[80] Schneiders, *Revelatory Text*, xxxii–xxxiii.

[81] E.g. Childs, *Introduction*, 74, and *New Testament*, 38. Although Childs never offers a precise definition of what he means by a biblical text's 'shape', it is clear that the term has more than a merely formal dimension for him; *contra* Barton, *Reading the Old Testament*, 77–103.

[82] Schneiders writes: 'All of the arts corroborate this notion of "ideal meaning." The musical score is a clear example. We listen to Beethoven's "Fifth Symphony" over and over, played by different orchestras, both because it is always the same and because it is always different. Beethoven's "Fifth Symphony" cannot be played any way at all. If the rendition sounds like "Yankee Doodle Dandy" we dismiss it as invalid. On the other hand, if the rendition is a wooden reproduction of some other performance we dismiss it as inadequate. In this sense all renditions should sound

consequence of his reappraisal of the significance of the biblical canon's growth and development.[83]

What sets apart a canonical approach from *both* the typical evangelical and historical-critical approaches to biblical interpretation, however, is its attribution of revelation[84] primarily to the text itself rather than to the history behind it:

> The significance of the final form of the biblical text is that it alone bears witness to the full history of revelation. Within the Old Testament neither the process of the formation of the literature nor the history of its canonization is assigned an independent integrity. This dimension has often been lost or purposely blurred and is therefore dependent on scholarly reconstruction. The fixing of a canon of Scripture implies that the witness to Israel's experience with God lies not in recovering such historical processes, but is testified to in the effect on the biblical text itself. Scripture bears witness to God's activity in history on Israel's behalf, but history *per se* is not a medium of revelation which is commensurate with a canon. It is only in the final form of the biblical text in which the normative history has reached an end that the full effect of this revelatory history can be perceived.[85]

In other words, it is interpreted rather than 'raw' history that is the bearer of God's revelation,[86] and it is the biblical canon that sets the profile and boundaries of that interpreted history.[87]

To say revelation is *in* the canonical text, however, is not to claim the biblical text possesses inspiration as a quality or property. The Bible is no magical talisman.

---

alike, that is, they should each realize the ideal structure inscribed in the score, but every rendition should also be unique and original because of the interpretation by a particular conductor and orchestra' (*Revelatory Text*, xxxiii).

[83] Interestingly, Schneiders also uses the term 'family resemblance' to describe how the interpretation of a biblical text possesses both consistency and innovation (*Revelatory Text*, xxxiv). This is precisely the same term that operates as the central motif of Childs's latest study, a volume on the history of interpretation of the book of Isaiah. See Childs, *Struggle*, xi, 299–300, 322. Childs finally locates the 'family resemblance' of Christian interpretation of Isaiah in the church's rule of faith.

[84] 'Revelation' admittedly continues to be a disputed theological concept. For a volume of essays describing what is problematic about the concept and offering a reformulated 'reaffirmation' of it, see Avis, *Divine Revelation*.

[85] Childs, *Introduction*, 75–76.

[86] For more on this point, see Marshall, *Biblical Inspiration*, 14, 35–36.

[87] The opposite view, that inspiration and revelation properly refer to the historical experience of the believing community behind the text, has been argued forcefully, but to my mind unpersuasively, by Barr; see, for example, his *Scope*, 125. However, he himself provides a more nuanced view earlier in the same volume, and one less starkly opposed to the position being taken here (16).

Neither is it to claim that revelation is found only in the biblical text[88] or that the text is 'verbally infallible and inerrant.'[89] It is rather to say the claim of inspiration is a public confession by members of the Christian community that they are committed to reading and interpreting Scripture as being entirely meaningful; i.e. that *every part* of the canon, under the right conditions (e.g. careful scrutiny, spiritual discernment, faithful proclamation, communal testing), has the ability to express the will of God. Indeed, inspiration exists in this 'canonical' sense even though a biblical author communicates an idea that has admittedly *not* originated in divine revelation (e.g. Paul in 1 Cor. 7:12, 25; 2 Cor. 8:10).

In a canonical account of inspiration, therefore, inspiration *does* ultimately describe a communal practice, yet one adopted and maintained by the church not in the form of a 'free decision' but as a response to, and under the 'pressure' of,[90] the canonical text that it has inherited. David Yeago puts the point this way:

> The church's knowledge is thus not prior to engagement with Scripture in the sense that it proceeds from some pure immediacy of intuition or feeling. Everything the church knows, it knows by attending to testimony, listening to words and performing rites that have been given to it. Nor is the church's knowledge prior to Scripture in any static or absolute way; indeed, every formulation of what the church knows must always be tested and authenticated and corrected through continuous engagement with Scripture.[91]

---

[88] Sundberg notes: 'in forming the canon, the church acknowledged and established the Bible as the measure or standard of inspiration in the church, not as the totality of it' ('Bible Canon', 371).

[89] Cf. Reid, *Authority*, 158. Reid helpfully distinguishes views of inspiration into two categories: those that focus on the words of the biblical text and those that focus on the biblical texts' writers. This essay argues for the first alternative. Reid's own dismissal of that option turns on his assumption that 'inspiration of the words' and 'verbal inerrancy' mean the same thing. While acknowledging that this assumption is frequently made, and not without some justification in light of the history of scholarship, this essay nevertheless also adopts the position that the two are not necessarily the same and may be fruitfully differentiated.

[90] Rowe, 'Biblical Pressure', also points to this feature of a canonical hermeneutic, drawing on Childs's rhetoric. Understanding the dynamic between the biblical text and the community as one of 'pressure' is neither as weird nor coercive as Childs's critics have sometimes alleged. Even Stanley Fish, of all people, apparently thinks texts exert pressure on readers: 'The fact that the objects we have are all objects that appear to us in the context of some practice, of work done by some interpretive community, doesn't mean that they are not objects or that we don't have them or that they exert no pressure on us.' (Fish, *Doing What Comes Naturally*, 153. I owe this reference to Yeago, 'Spirit', 69 n. 26.)

[91] Yeago, 'Spirit', 59. Yeago goes on to add that the theological interpretation of Scripture must also take place on the basis of the church's tradition. Yet even within the

That is why it is important to say, in spite of all possible misunderstanding, that inspiration is in the *text* rather than in the community. Inspiration means that the biblical text, all of it, maintains a necessary 'over against-ness' with respect to its Christian readers.[92] After all, 2 Timothy 3:16 ('all *Scripture* is inspired by God'), as has been frequently noted,[93] locates inspiration in the biblical text itself rather than in the biblical texts' authors![94]

From the perspective of canonical theology, then, historical criticism and evangelicalism do not appear to be strangers to each other at all but unacknowledged bedfellows. Historical criticism is in fact exposed as a secularized version of the evangelical stance toward Scripture, with its privileging of the 'original' or the 'earliest' (why is this any more 'historical' than what happens later?) and its location of meaning in the history 'behind' the text. Similarly, evangelicalism reveals itself to be much more beholden to historical criticism than it realizes or is willing to concede, with its Enlightenment assumptions and empirical anxieties (after defending the miraculous and the supernatural, why turn around and insist on a positivistic account of history?).

---

resulting hermeneutical circle or, better yet, spiral, the testimony of Scripture is decisively *prior* to the church's interpretive engagement with it.

[92] See further Yeago, 'Spirit', 66–70, on 'faithfulness as deference.' A canonical view of inspiration would similarly reject efforts to formulate levels or degrees of inspiration within the biblical literature; for classic examples of such a move, see Sanday, *Inspiration*, 397–98; Orr, *Revelation*, 177–79.

[93] Erickson, *Christian Theology*, 244 n. 14. Abraham, *Divine Inspiration*, 94, adds that most translations (rightly) supply a present tense verb, leading to the conclusion that scriptural inspiration is not being invoked as a previous event of past history but as a present textual reality. Beegle, *Inspiration*, 31, also mentions J.A. Quenstedt's observation that the reference to 'scripture' in this verse hardly means the 'original autographs' but rather the manuscript copies (of the Old Testament!) that circulated in the early church.

[94] The explicit biblical warrant for an inspired process of composition behind the text is usually taken to be 2 Pet. 1:20–21: 'no prophecy of scripture is a matter of one's own interpretation, because no prophecy ever came by human will, but men and women moved by the Holy Spirit spoke from God' (NRSV). But this statement concerns the revealed nature of the prophetic oracles related in Scripture, not the move from oral to written prophecy or the actual process of Scripture's composition. In short, it is inappropriate to use this passage as a warrant for positing some kind of unique and supernatural compositional act; see Abraham, *Inspiration*, 94–95 and Vawter: 'Nowhere in the Hebrew OT … do we find the thought expressed that the written word of prophecy is the work of the Spirit of God' (*Biblical Inspiration*, 11).

Inspiration, Accommodation and Incarnation

Yet if the entire history of canon formation is to be considered 'inspired' then what happens to the idea of inspiration itself? Does it still make sense to speak of 'inspiration' at all? Does the term not become so broad as to be meaningless? At this point a recent work by Peter Enns proves quite helpful.

The great value of Enns's book for the present theme is twofold. First, in the early part of the book he patiently documents with a preponderance of historical evidence how thoroughly the Bible is situated within the ancient world. His careful historical work shows the difficulty of claiming the biblical authors were conduits of special revelation in such a way that they were unaffected by their own historical and cultural situations. Then, secondly, Enns argues courageously that this 'situatedness' should not be viewed as a problem to be overcome but as a spiritual teaching to be taken to heart. By using the analogy of orthodox Chalcedonian Christology, according to which Jesus is considered to be both fully human and fully God, Enns argues that the Bible is both fully mundane and fully divine as well:

> As to the question of the Bible's uniqueness, which is raised by the ancient Near Eastern evidence, it is certainly the case that the Bible is a book like no other, and 'unique' is a very good word to describe it – provided that using this word does not prevent us from recognizing and *embracing* the marks of the ancient settings in which the Bible was written. Its uniqueness is not seen in holding human cultures at arm's length, but in the belief that Scripture is the only book in which God speaks incarnately. As it is with Christ, so it is with the Bible – the 'coming together' of the divine and human sets it apart from all others.[95]

Enns's 'incarnational analogy' allows for a theological re-appraisal of the significance of historical thought forms and ancient literary genres. In elaborating this analogy, Enns also draws upon the theological idea of divine accommodation[96] to suggest that God chose to reveal divine truth incarnationally (i.e. in ways its recipients could understand) by entering fully into the messiness of human culture and society.

The hermeneutical implications of Enns's approach go to the very heart of lived Christian faith:

> … to those who fear the human stamp as somehow dirtying the Bible, marring its perfect divine quality, I say, 'If you wouldn't say that about Jesus (and you shouldn't), don't think that way about the Bible. Both Christ and his word are human through

---

[95] Enns, *Inspiration*, 168 (his use of italics).

[96] For another recent evangelical exploration of divine accommodation, see Sparks, 'Sun'.

and through.' In fact, it is precisely by having the Son become human that God demonstrates his great love. Is it so much of a stretch, then, to say that the human nature of Scripture is likewise a gift rather than a problem? ... It is somewhat ironic, it seems to me, that both liberals and conservatives make the same error. They both assume that something worthy of the title *word of God* would look different from what we actually have.[97]

Enns's 'incarnational analogy' is not new; it has been a prominent idea within church tradition and was given classic formulation for modern evangelicals in Benjamin Warfield's notion of 'concursive action.'[98] Yet Warfield remained too narrowly focused on authorship and composition. Also, as Donald Bloesch points out, the details of Warfield's argument did not actually keep pace with his rhetoric.[99] Warfield persistently tended to slight human agency and action, despite his explicit theoretical formulations.

A more compelling example of a Christological analogy was provided by James Smart, who broadened the idea in order to encompass the entire process of scriptural formation.[100] In this expanded form, the strength of the Christological analogy is clearer: it provides a kind of 'grammar' for the inter-relationship of divine and human forces that went into the making of Scripture. If the divine is stressed too much, an account of inspiration quickly becomes 'docetic'. If the human dimension receives too much weight, the understanding of inspiration becomes 'arian'. Using this analogy as a guide, it is not only possible to speak of 'inspiration' more broadly than in standard evangelical accounts, it is also a grave theological error *not* to because the broader use of the term communicates something so important about what it means to be a human being, about the nature of faith and the mystery of the incarnation.[101]

Yet this Christological analogy breaks down at a certain point, too, even for Warfield:

> But the analogy with Our Lord's Divine–human union may easily be pressed beyond reason. There is no hypostatic union between the Divine and the human in Scripture; we cannot parallel the 'inscripturation' of the Holy Spirit and the incarnation of the Son of God. The Scriptures are merely the product of Divine and human forces working together to produce a product in the production of which the

---

[97] Enns, *Inspiration*, 21 (his use of italics).

[98] E.g. Warfield, *Revelation*.

[99] See this running critique of Warfield in Bloesch, *Holy Scripture*, 88, 118, 128, 327 n. 126.

[100] Smart, *Interpretation*, 160–63.

[101] It is also untrue to the biblical witness, which describes the interaction between human beings and God as one of genuine struggle at times, preserving even some of the human *objections* to God as sacred Scripture; for examples, see Vawter, *Biblical Inspiration*, 13.

human forces work under the initiation and prevalent direction of the Divine: the person of our Lord unites in itself Divine and human natures, each of which retains its distinctness while operating only in relation to the other.[102]

In other words, the analogy remains in the end only an analogy and must not be taken too far.[103]

Telford Work has shown just how deeply the church's attempt to formulate a doctrine of Scripture has relied upon the kind of incarnational analogy that Enns and others have described.[104] Yet Work, too, believes there are theological difficulties with the 'incarnational' model. Drawing upon the criticism of Markus Barth, Work suggests one problem with the incarnational model of Scripture could be that it would inappropriately elevate Scripture to divine status, 'hypostatizing human words.'[105] Similarly, Work notes, James Barr has objected to the use of doctrinal categories in biblical exegesis more sweepingly, contending not only that such doctrinal categories were not originally developed with Scripture in mind but also that they are currently used to insulate conservative theologies from inconvenient facts about the Bible.[106] In Work's own approach, such criticisms finally serve to correct and extend the idea of an incarnational parallel in the direction of a more fully Trinitarian hermeneutic.

A Trinitarian hermeneutic – with its integral relationship to the church's traditional analogy of faith – shows even greater promise for future theological reflection on the nature and function of Scripture.[107] A Trinitarian hermeneutic brings further doctrinal considerations to bear, resulting in a more fully realized theological 'grammar' for interpretation,[108] and also inevitably ties the idea of scriptural inspiration to the work of the Holy Spirit throughout history. In a stimulating treatment along these lines, David Yeago offers a pneumatic

---

[102] Warfield, *Revelation*, 108.

[103] Cf. Marshall, *Biblical Inspiration*, 44–45.

[104] Work, *Living and Active*, esp. 15–27. Work refers to what Enns terms the 'incarnational analogy' as 'the Analogy of the Word.'

[105] Work, *Living and Active*, 27. Work acknowledges this problem but endeavors in his constructive section to overcome it. It is for a similar reason that Enns finally prefers to speak of an incarnational 'parallel' rather than an incarnational 'analogy' (*Inspiration*, 168). The critical remarks of Markus Barth, well worth pondering further, are found in his *Conversation*, esp. 155–70.

[106] Work, *Living and Active*, 28. For yet another difference between Christology and a doctrine of Scripture, see Sparks: 'The Son incarnate is one person, both sinless humanity and infinite divinity. But the Scriptures speak divine revelation through the perspectives of finite and sinful human authors' ('Sun', 130).

[107] Wainwright, 'Trinity', 816.

[108] For examples, see Work, *Living and Active*, 323–24.

account of Scripture based upon the traditional exegetical practice of the church:

> … classical scriptural interpretation proceeded from a rich and complex sense of Scripture's place and role within the economy of salvation; Scripture functions as a quasi-sacramental instrument of the Holy Spirit, through which the Spirit makes known the mystery of Christ in order to form the church as a sign of his messianic dominion. The church's knowledge of Scripture as inspired has therefore interpretive consequences; it calls for a specific art, or perhaps a concatenation of arts, of faithful reading, exposition, and application by which Christ is glorified and the church built up in its distinctive life and mission.[109]

This doctrinal location of Scripture within an account of the Holy Spirit not only tightly links Scripture and church together, it also provides a theological justification for a distinctively Christian 'art' of scriptural interpretation.

Yeago further specifies the doctrinal consequences of his view:

> The scriptures are, most basically, a crucial element within the concrete ecclesial witness of the Spirit by which the witness of faith, hope, and love is formed. Scripture is the standing testimony of the Spirit to the church, for the purpose of forming the church itself as the Spirit's testimony to the nations.[110]

Because Scripture is the testimony of the Spirit *to* the church, the entire process of biblical canon formation is made meaningful even as a qualitative distinction is drawn between the work of the Spirit leading to the formation of the canon and the interpretive work of the Spirit afterwards. This awareness of the integral relationship between the Spirit and the canon is precisely why the theological tradition has traditionally been inclined to distinguish between 'inspiration' as a pneumatic category relating to scriptural formation and 'illumination' as a pneumatic category referring to scriptural interpretation. Both activities involve Scripture and the Spirit, but differently.

From Propositions to Narrative Art

If inspiration extends throughout the entire process of canon formation, then revelation extends to the literary aspects of the canon as well. In other words, the literary dimension of the canon is itself part of what God has revealed. This point was made with great persuasiveness in Luis Alonso Schökel's pioneering

---

[109] See Yeago, 'Spirit', 51. For a similarly pneumatic account of Scripture from a Catholic perspective, see 'An Appendix on the Holy Spirit', in O'Collins and Kendall, *Bible*, 163–69.

[110] Yeago, 'Spirit', 63.

work.[111] Alonso Schökel also grounded his hermeneutic in the incarnation: 'The Word of God in order to be incarnate must assume a concrete, specific language.'[112] The canon's arrangement, form, structure, and literary features are therefore part and parcel of its witness or *kerygma*.[113]

Thus, attention to canon formation leads not away from but back to the idea of an inspired text, yet in a reformulated and expanded sense. The old account of verbal inspiration simply cannot be repristinated.[114] Yet attention to the canon, rather than weakening the notion of inspiration, actually strengthens it by returning to a reformulated version of what still might be termed 'verbal' inspiration – i.e. that the literary features of the text are inspired, too, and not just the concepts. Many evangelicals continue to cling to a 'propositional' hermeneutic and to the primacy of historicity as an interpretive criterion, but few realize that in reality these values actually militate against the attribution of full theological value to the text. Kevin Vanhoozer, one who does realize this, cogently notes, for example, that the search for transcultural propositions is not only subject to the cultural prejudices of the interpreter but also tends to overemphasize didactic portions of Scripture.[115]

Howard Marshall describes how the 'traditional approach' in biblical interpretation seeks to take the commands of the Bible literally – *unless* they are no longer 'universalizable' because an appropriate cultural setting for their literal performance no longer exists.[116] In that case, an effort will usually be made to adapt the biblical command to new contemporary circumstances on the basis of an inferred principle lying behind it. Sometimes, however, the command will simply be considered cancelled. Rarely recognized among evangelical scholars, though, is that this common interpretive strategy is structurally analogous to the method employed by liberal Protestant theology, especially in the nineteenth century. The separation of the 'husk' from the 'kernel' is a goal ultimately inherited from German philosophical idealism – one, however, that was thoroughly discredited in early twentieth-century theology because of its increasingly obvious susceptibility to cultural

---

[111] E.g. Alonso Schökel, *Inspired Word*.

[112] Alonso Schökel, *Inspired Word*, 127.

[113] Cf. Blauw, *Missionary Nature*, 17.

[114] The traditional doctrine of inspiration, with its emphasis on instrumental conceptions of human agency, was likely too beholden to mantic presuppositions and Hellenistic cultural norms from the outset. To the extent that early church theologians described the human role in biblical composition as fundamentally passive, they obscured a truly biblical anthropology and created a false impression of Scripture's character and role within the church. See Law, *Inspiration*, 50–66; Vawter, *Biblical Inspiration*, 14.

[115] Vanhoozer, 'Great "Beyond"', 92.

[116] Marshall, *Beyond the Bible*, 34.

accommodation.[117] As Marshall notes, the 'principles' approach 'tends to focus on specific passages and, while not ignoring the fact that Scripture must be interpreted with Scripture, to pay less attention to the general thrust of scriptural teaching as a whole.'[118]

Similarly, the evangelical emphasis on historicity often focuses exegetical work on the world behind the text rather than the text itself. How sad it is to hear a sermon on a Psalm in which the preacher's main energy goes into proving that David was indeed its author, while the theological riches of the Psalm itself meanwhile go unexplored! Or to encounter a congregation much more familiar with Paul's itinerary than his theology! This is not to say that concepts and historicity are unimportant, of course, only that they are not ends in themselves and can in fact become counter-productive for theological interpretation.

An important question does remain about how far to push the significance of literary context in scriptural interpretation. On the one hand, James Barr asserts that canonical context has never mattered much for Christian theologizing.[119] On the other, there are the new 'formal' treatments of canon that emphasize a high degree of literary organization, structuring, and cross-referencing (e.g. American evangelicals like John Sailhamer and his like-minded colleagues,[120] as well as German Catholic scholars like Erich Zenger[121]). Their redactional schemes raise highly important questions but also risk becoming artificial and forced as they grow increasingly speculative and elaborate.[122] With respect to the matter of inspiration, moreover, its attribution cannot simply be shifted from an 'original' author to a putative final redactor or 'canonicler.'[123] Such a move still privileges

---

[117] The example of the 'supernatural' may elucidate the point. Liberal theology typically rejects supernaturalistic elements of biblical narratives, in effect considering them 'husk.' Evangelical theology customarily argues in contrast that such elements are 'kernel' and may not simply be rejected out of hand. E.g. Marshall, *Beyond the Bible*, 47. But in neither case is the distinction between the natural and the supernatural found in the biblical text itself; in both cases it is a prior cultural assumption of the interpreter. Furthermore, both sides assume that the interpretive goal lies in the separation of the husk from the kernel; they only disagree about which is which.

[118] Marshall, *Beyond the Bible*, 34.

[119] Of course, this point is a debatable one. It depends what is meant by 'canonical context.' For a somewhat more measured critique, see Barton, *Holy Writings*, 161.

[120] See Sailhamer, *Introduction*, 239–52; Dempster, '"Extraordinary Fact"'; several of the essays in Hafemann, *Biblical Theology*, also exhibit this direction.

[121] E.g. Zenger, *Einleitung*, 25–27.

[122] For further evaluation of these approaches, see Chapman, 'Canonical Approach'.

[123] For the term 'canonicler', see Sailhamer, *Introduction*, 240. Despite Sailhamer's strong effort to produce a 'text-centered' Old Testament theology, he still maintains that the Pentateuch has one 'composer' or 'author' (210–12, 242). He also

single-person authorship at the expense of a broader canonical view of inspiration.

In the end, inspiration cannot be adduced as 'proof' of anything. It is not a proof but an inference. In actuality, inspiration has always been properly a characteristic of the text and only derivatively of Scripture's authors – although it has usually been asserted that the relationship between these two things is exactly opposite.[124] Thus, the rhetoric of the argument moves in one way but its logic moves in the reverse direction. So, in an effort to 'prove' the uniqueness of the Bible, many have insisted that the process of composition must have been unique, too. But there is actually no real evidence for this – and much good evidence against it.[125] Evangelicals look at accounts of prophecy from the Old Testament and build their theory of inspiration on them, but in doing so they tend to ignore other biblical traditions (e.g. wisdom, law, post-exilic prophecy, etc.) that offer quite different models of the relationship between revelation and writing.[126] The actual structure of the evangelical argument is revealed by the fact that in the end it offers very little in the way of a concrete account of the *how* of the 'inspiration' it insists upon in theory.[127]

The most explicit effort to meet this specific challenge is that of Millard Erickson.[128] Erickson attempts to describe how the Holy Spirit directed the 'thoughts of the Scripture writer' in such a way that specific words were *prompted*.[129] This formulation is an effort on his part to avoid, on the one hand, the idea of a 'dictation' model, with its many attendant problems, and, on the other, still to affirm 'verbal' inspiration. At points in his account, Erickson seems to suggest that the human writers had a degree of flexibility as to how they would express the inspired 'thoughts' they had received from God. Yet ultimately God ensured that the words came out exactly the way God wanted, so that what Erickson finally offers is essentially only a softer version of dictation theory,[130] and all of the same criticisms of it as entailing the loss of genuine human agency continue to apply.[131]

---

implies that a single individual was responsible for the final arrangement and organization of the Old Testament canon (e.g. 211).

[124] E.g. Henry: 'In the historic evangelical view, divine inspiration is what constitutes Scripture authoritative, and not simply the fact that Scripture comes to us in a comprehensive final canonical form' ('Canonical Theology', 103).

[125] See Enns, *Inspiration*.

[126] See Dunn, 'Biblical Concepts'.

[127] Cf. Marshall, *Biblical Inspiration*, 44.

[128] Erickson, *Christian Theology*, esp. 240–45.

[129] Erickson, *Christian Theology*, 240.

[130] Also the judgment of Abraham, *Divine Inspiration*, 36.

[131] At one point, Erickson describes the process of inspiration as one of 'thought control', *Christian Theology*, 243. Does this accord with Scripture's description of divine–human interaction? In a word, no.

Erickson tries to evade such criticisms by arguing that a major part of how God worked with the biblical writers was through the entirety of their lives, educating them through particular life experiences and relationships, so that when the time came for them to receive the Holy Spirit's promptings to write, they would write with the necessary 'pool of God-intended words.'[132] Erickson goes on to describe the heart of the compositional process as follows:

> Then, at the actual point of writing, God directs the author's thinking. Since God has access to the very thought processes of the human, and, in the case of the believer, in-dwells the individual in the person of the Holy Spirit, this is not difficult, particularly when the individual prays for enlightenment and displays receptivity. The process is not unlike mental telepathy, although more internalized and personalized.[133]

Of course, the problem with Erickson's analogy here is that 'mental telepathy' *does not exist*, and it is quite telling that he should attempt to explain the process of inspiration by reference to a non-existent phenomenon. Thus, authorial 'inspiration' is revealed in his treatment to be an empty cipher, a back-formation from the attribution of inspiration to the text.

Erickson wants inspiration to apply primarily to the writers of Scripture, and only derivatively to the text.[134] He adopts this stance because he also wants inspiration to be a proof of the Bible's authority,[135] but the proper logic of inspiration, as has been shown, is exactly the reverse. The Bible 'proves' its *own* authority and is not in need of supernatural speculation about its origins.[136] The

---

[132] Erickson, *Christian Theology*, 242–43. Interestingly, Erickson is willing to attribute this activity *prior* to the composition of a biblical book to providence. As with Henry, it is only after the composition of the biblical books that Erickson becomes skittish of providence – because empirical evidence (rather than theological doctrine!) makes him reluctant to adopt a position that would otherwise be theologically quite congenial.

[133] Erickson, *Christian Theology*, 243.

[134] Erickson, *Christian Theology*, 244.

[135] Erickson: '*Because* the Bible has been inspired, we can be confident of having divine instruction' (*Christian Theology*, 245, my emphasis). To the contrary, we can be confident of having divine instruction in the Bible because of what the Bible *says* and not because of the process of its composition.

[136] As has been often remarked, even the term 'supernatural' partakes of modernity more than it resists it. The idea that there is a natural realm in which the ordinary laws of science apply, and a supernatural realm in which those ordinary laws do not, is a legacy of the Enlightenment, not the Bible. To be fair, evangelicals have often insisted upon the term because liberals have used criticism of supernaturalism to reject any real role for the transcendent at all. Cf. Orr, *Revelation*, 6–12. However, the Bible consistently describes how God operates *within* the natural world with great freedom, and without positing a metaphysical distinction between the natural and the supernatural.

Bible continues to be the best-selling book of all time; people still become Christians by reading it; the Bible (somehow!) maintains its central role in church life, despite the widespread erosion of its authority throughout modern society. James Orr's famous summary therefore has greater merit as a description of the actual relation between inspiration and biblical authority:

> ... in the last resort, the proof of the inspiration of the Bible – not, indeed, in every particular, but in its essential message – is to be found in the life-giving effects which that message has produced, wherever its word of truth has gone. This is the truth in the argument for inspiration based on the witness of the Holy Sprit. The Bible has the qualities claimed for it as an inspired book ... It leads to God and Christ; it gives light on the deepest problems of life, death, and eternity; it discovers the way of deliverance from sin; it makes men new creatures; it furnishes the man of God completely for every good work. That it possesses these qualities history and experience through all the centuries have attested.[137]

In other words, the Bible is inspired because it continues to inspire – it is a conduit of the Spirit, leading its hearers and readers to God and Christ.

In this way, the presumption of 'canonical' inspiration again leads in the direction of detailed attention *to* the text. 'Inspiration' becomes intelligible as a way of stating theologically that every word of Scripture counts and, thus, as an anticipatory manner of proceeding with the biblical text. That is why the inspiration of the Bible must continue to be affirmed by Christian communities. The best of the exegetical tradition has always exemplified this crucial notion in its practice – what Chrysostom, for example, knew and employed as *akribeia* ('precision' or 'exactitude'). Over and over again he could comment of the details of the biblical text: 'it was not without purpose that ...'.[138] Following his example, as well as the example of countless others, 'inspiration' will mean that Scripture demands, welcomes and does not disappoint the most careful, eager scrutiny.[139]

---

[137] Orr, *Revelation*, 217–18. Orr is right to ground inspiration in the text and to have confidence in the Bible's ability to prove itself, but he neglects here to take the further step of affirming what the logic of his argument demands – the inspiration of the text in *all* of its details and particulars.

[138] E.g. Chrysostom, *Homilies*, 76.

[139] On the tradition of *in scriptura nihil superfluum* ('in Scripture nothing is superfluous'), with additional examples, see Law, *Inspiration*, 68. This potentiality for meaning also has an eschatological dimension: the text may not reveal God's Word *yet* but still may do so at an appointed time in the future. For further reflection, see Sauter, *Eschatological Rationality*, 150–51.

Conclusion

Traditional evangelical scholars like Carl Henry have been correct in viewing a canonical approach to Scripture as a threat to their account of inspiration. However, the best way forward at this point lies not in a misplaced effort to repristinate that shop-worn version of supernatural author-focused inspiration but rather in articulating a version of inspiration able to account for the fullness of what the history of canon formation teaches. Karl Barth saw the fundamental point quite clearly: it was not that God had supernaturally prevented the biblical authors from sinning in their work of composition but that precisely in and through their sin God chose and continues to choose to speak:

> To the bold postulate, that if their word is to be the Word of God they must be inerrant in every word, we oppose the even bolder assertion, that according to the Scriptural witness about man, which applies to them too, they can be at fault in any word, and have been at fault in every word, and yet according to the same Scriptural witness, being justified and sanctified by grace alone, they have still spoken the Word of God in their fallible and erring human word. It is the fact that in the Bible we can take part in this real miracle, the miracle of the grace of God to sinners, and not in the idle miracle of human words which were not really human words at all, which is the foundation of the dignity and authority of the Bible.[140]

This kind of inspiration is not the lesser miracle, as some evangelicals continue to think, but a much greater one.

Yes, there is a danger that 'inspiration' in this broader, canonical sense could become watered-down and anthropomorphized. But the opposite danger is not only that, unless inspiration is construed canonically, it will remain an incoherent and unpersuasive doctrine. The full danger, as Enns and Barth both indicate, is that in reality the now traditional evangelical view of inspiration corrupts crucial knowledge about the Christian faith and life. How so? It communicates that human agency is too flawed for God to use, that God characteristically imposes rather than redeems, and that providence is incurably lame. It also implies by virtue of the traditional Christological analogy between the divine–human relationship in Scripture and the divine–human relationship in Jesus that the humanness of Jesus is a problem to be overcome rather than an honor to be cherished.

---

[140] Barth, *Church Dogmatics* I/2, 529–30. This passage is also partly cited and critiqued in Bloesch, *Holy Scripture*, 101. Bloesch, however, simply refuses to grant the dialectical basis of Barth's argument. He maintains, in effect, that the words of the Bible cannot logically be both errant and inerrant at the same time. Barth, of course, would respond by questioning Bloesch further about the sort of logic he *is* willing to accept and asking Bloesch where his prior commitment to such logic comes from.

James Smart once forcefully expressed the same perspective that this essay has sought to advance, so that his words provide a most suitable conclusion:

> The revelation is *in the text itself,* in the words that confront us there in all their strangeness, and not in a history or a personal biography or an event that we reconstruct by means of the text. The event of revelation is available to us only through the text of Scripture interpreted in the context of the church. It is through these words and no others that God intends to speak to us, and, when he does, we know that there is no other kind of inspiration than verbal inspiration. Far from implying any divinizing of the words of Scripture, verbal inspiration understood in its Biblical sense takes the words of the text with full seriousness as the words of real men, spoken or written in a concrete human situation, and yet at the same time words in which God ever afresh reveals himself to me.[141]

A canonical account of inspiration keeps the theological interpretation of Scripture focused where it should be – on the text.

---

[141] Smart, *Interpretation of Scripture*, 195–96 (his emphasis). Cf. Yeago, 'Spirit', 66. Later, Smart, *Strange Silence*, 148, would emphasize that revelation is 'not just in the book' but in 'the dialectic between the Scriptures and the community of faith.' This essay has sought to show one possible way to affirm Smart's earlier view without neglecting his later qualification.

Bibliography

Abraham, W.J., *The Divine Inspiration of Holy Scripture* (Oxford/New York: Oxford University Press, 1981)

Achtemeier, P.J., *Inspiration and Authority: Nature and Function of Christian Scripture* (rev. edn.; Peabody, MA: Hendrickson, 1999)

Alonso Schökel, L., *The Inspired Word* (trans. F. Martin; New York: Herder and Herder, 1966)

Avis, P. (ed.), *Divine Revelation* (Grand Rapids/Cambridge: Eerdmans, 1997)

Bacote, V., L.C. Miguélez and D.L. Okholm (eds.), *Evangelicals and Scripture: Tradition, Authority and Hermeneutics* (Downers Grove: InterVarsity Press, 2004)

Barr, J., *The Scope and Authority of the Bible* (Philadelphia: Westminster, 1980)

Barth, K., *Church Dogmatics* (2nd edn.; trans. G.W. Bromiley; Edinburgh: T&T Clark, 1975)

Barth, M., *Conversation with the Bible* (New York: Holt, Rinehart and Winston, 1964)

Barton, J., *Reading the Old Testament: Method in Biblical Study* (rev. edn.; Louisville: Westminster John Knox, 1996)

—, 'The Significance of a Fixed Canon of the Hebrew Bible', in *Hebrew Bible/Old Testament, The History of its Interpretation: Vol. 1, From the Beginning to the Middle Ages (Until 1300): Part 1, Antiquity* (ed. Magne Sæbø; Göttingen: Vandenhoeck & Ruprecht, 1996), 67–83

—, *Holy Writings, Sacred Text: The Canon in Early Christianity* (Louisville: Westminster John Knox, 1997)

Beckwith, R.T., *The Old Testament Canon of the New Testament Church and its Background in Early Judaism* (London: SPCK; and Grand Rapids: Eerdmans, 1985)

Beegle, D.M., *The Inspiration of Scripture* (Philadelphia: Westminster, 1963)

Benson, B.E., '"Now I Would Not Have You Ignorant": Derrida, Gadamer, Hirsch and Husserl on Authors' Intentions', in *Evangelicals and Scripture: Tradition, Authority and Hermeneutics* (ed. V. Bacote, L.C. Miguélez and Dennis L. Okholm; Downers Grove: InterVarsity Press, 2004), 173–91

Blauw, J., *The Missionary Nature of the Church: A Survey of the Biblical Theology of Mission* (Grand Rapids: Eerdmans, 1962)

Block, D.I., 'Recovering the Voice of Moses: The Genesis of Deuteronomy', *JETS* 44 (2001), 385–408.

Bloesch, D.G., *Holy Scripture: Revelation, Inspiration and Interpretation* (Downers Grove: InterVarsity Press, 1994)

Blue, S.A., 'The Hermeneutics of E.D. Hirsch, Jr. and its Impact on Expository Preaching: Friend or Foe?', *JETS* 44 (2001), 253–69

Brogan, J.J., 'Can I Have Your Autograph? Uses and Abuses of Textual Criticism in Formulating an Evangelical Doctrine of Scripture', in *Evangelicals and*

Scripture: Tradition, Authority and Hermeneutics (ed. V. Bacote, L.C. Miguélez and D.L. Okholm; Downers Grove: InterVarsity Press, 2004), 93–111

Bruce, F.F., *The Canon of Scripture* (Downers Grove: InterVarsity Press, 1988)

Brueggemann, D.A., 'Brevard Childs' Canon Criticism: An Example of Post-Critical Naiveté', *JETS* 32 (1989), 311–26

Burtchaell, J.T., *Catholic Theories of Inspiration Since 1810: A Review and Critique* (Cambridge: Cambridge University Press, 1969)

Chapman, S.B., *The Law and the Prophets: A Study in Old Testament Canon Formation* (FAT 27; Tübingen: Mohr Siebeck, 2000)

—, 'A Canonical Approach to Old Testament Theology? Deut 34:10–12 and Mal 3:22–24 as Programmatic Conclusions', *HBT* 25 (2003), 121–45

—, 'The Old Testament Canon and its Authority for the Christian Church', *Ex Auditu* 19 (2003), 125–48

Childs, B.S., *Biblical Theology in Crisis* (Philadelphia: Westminster, 1970)

—, *Introduction to the Old Testament as Scripture* (Philadelphia: Fortress, 1979)

—, *The New Testament as Canon: An Introduction* (Philadelphia: Fortress, 1984)

—, *Old Testament Theology in a Canonical Context* (Philadelphia: Fortress, 1985)

—, *Biblical Theology of the Old and New Testaments: Theological Reflection on the Christian Bible* (Minneapolis: Fortress, 1992)

—, *The Struggle to Understand Isaiah as Christian Scripture* (Grand Rapids/Cambridge: Eerdmans, 2004)

—, 'Speech-act Theory and Biblical Interpretation', *SJT* 58 (2005), 375–92

Chrysostom, St. John, *Old Testament Homilies: Vol. 1, Homilies on Hannah, David and Saul* (ed. Robert Charles Hill; Brookline, MA: Holy Cross Orthodox Press, 2003)

Dempster, S., 'An "Extraordinary Fact": *Torah and Temple* and the Contours of the Hebrew Canon', *TynBul* 48 (1997), 23–56, 191–218

Dockery, D.S., *Christian Scripture: An Evangelical Perspective on Inspiration, Authority and Interpretation* (Nashville: Broadman and Holman, 1995)

Dunn, J.D.G., 'Biblical Concepts of Revelation', in *Divine Revelation* (ed. P. Avis; Grand Rapids/Cambridge: Eerdmans, 1997), 1–22

Erickson, M.J., *Christian Theology* (2nd edn.; Grand Rapids: Baker, 1998)

Enns, P., *Inspiration and Incarnation: Evangelicals and the Problem of the Old Testament* (Grand Rapids: Baker Academic, 2005)

Fee, G.E., and D. Stuart, *How to Read the Bible for all its Worth: A Guide to Understanding the Bible* (Grand Rapids: Zondervan, 1982)

Fish, S., *Doing What Comes Naturally: Change, Rhetoric, and the Practice of Theory in Literature and Legal Studies* (Durham, NC: Duke University Press, 1989)

Fowl, S.E., 'The Role of Authorial Intention in the Theological Interpretation of Scripture', in *Between Two Horizons: Spanning New Testament Studies and Systematic Theology* (ed. J.B. Green and M. Turner; Grand Rapids/Cambridge: Eerdmans, 2000), 71–87

Gadamer, H.G., *Truth and Method* (trans. G. Barden and J. Cumming; New York: Seabury Press, 1975)

Gamble, H.Y., *The New Testament Canon: Its Making and Meaning* (Philadelphia: Fortress, 1985)

Grisanti, M.A., 'Inspiration, Inerrancy, and the OT Canon: The Place of Textual Updating in an Inerrant View of Scripture', *JETS* 44 (2001), 577–98

Hafemann, S.J. (ed.), *Biblical Theology: Retrospect and Prospect* (Downers Grove, IL: Inter-Varsity Press; and Leicester: Apollos, 2002)

Hays, J.D., 'Jeremiah, the Septuagint, the Dead Sea Scrolls and Inerrancy: Just What Exactly Do We Mean by the "Original Autographs"?', in *Evangelicals and Scripture* (ed. V. Bacote, L.C. Miguélez and D.L. Okholm; Downers Grove: InterVarsity Press, 2004), 133–49

Henry, C.F.H., 'Canonical Theology: An Evangelical Appraisal', *Scottish Bulletin of Evangelical Theology* (1990), 76–108

Harris, R., *Inspiration and Canonicity of the Bible: An Historical and Exegetical Study* (rev. edn.; Grand Rapids: Zondervan, 1969)

Hoffman, T.A., 'Inspiration, Normativeness, Canonicity, and the Unique Sacred Character of the Bible', *CBQ* 44 (1982), 447–69

Kaiser, W., *Toward an Exegetical Theology* (Grand Rapids: Baker, 1981)

—, 'New Dimensions in Old Testament Theology', in *New Dimensions in Evangelical Thought: Essays in Honor of Millar J. Erickson* (ed. D.S. Dockery; Downers Grove: InterVarsity Press, 1998), 32–45

Law, D.R., *Inspiration* (London/New York: Continuum, 2001)

Leiman, S.Z., *The Canonization of Hebrew Scripture: The Talmudic and Midrashic Evidence* (Hamden, CT: Archon Books, 1976)

Longman, T., III, *Literary Approaches to Biblical Interpretation* (Foundations of Contemporary Interpretation 3; Grand Rapids: Zondervan, 1987)

MacKenzie, J.L., 'The Social Character of Inspiration', *CBQ* 24 (1962), 115–24

Marshall, I.H., *Biblical Inspiration* (Vancouver, B.C.: Regent College Publishing, 1982)

—, *Beyond the Bible: Moving from Scripture to Theology* (Grand Rapids: Baker Academic; and Milton Keynes: Paternoster, 2004)

McDonald, L.M., *The Formation of the Christian Biblical Canon* (rev. edn.; Peabody, MA: Hendrickson, 1995)

—, and J.A. Sanders (eds.), *The Canon Debate* (Peabody, MA: Hendrickson, 2002)

Metzger, B.M., *The Canon of the New Testament: Its Origin, Development, and Significance* (Oxford: Clarendon; and New York/Oxford: Oxford University Press, 1987)

Moberly, R.W., 'The Canon of the Old Testament: Some Historical and Hermeneutical Reflections from the Western Perspective', in *Das Alte Testament als christliche Bibel in orthodoxer und westlicher Sicht* (WUNT 174; ed. I.Z. Dimitrou et al.; Tübingen: Mohr Siebeck, 2004), 239–57

Noble, P.R., *The Canonical Approach: A Critical Reconstruction of the Hermeneutics of Brevard S. Childs* (BIS 16; Leiden/New York: Brill, 1995)

O'Collins, G., and D. Kendall, *The Bible for Theology: Ten Principles for the Theological Use of Scripture* (New York/Mahwah, NJ: Paulist, 1997)

Orr, J., *Revelation and Inspiration* (Grand Rapids: Eerdmans, 1952)

Oswalt, J.N., 'Canonical Criticism: A Review from a Conservative Viewpoint', *JETS* 30 (1987), 317–25

Parry, R., 'Reader-Response Criticism', in *Dictionary for Theological Interpretation of the Bible* (ed. K.J. Vanhoozer et al.; Grand Rapids: Baker Academic; and London: SPCK, 2005), 658–61

Patzia, A.G., *The Making of the New Testament: Origin, Collection, Text and Canon* (Downers Grove: InterVarsity Press, 1995)

Porter, S.E., 'Hermeneutics, Biblical Interpretation, and Theology: Hunch, Holy Spirit, or Hard Work?', in I.H. Marshall, *Beyond the Bible: Moving From Scripture to Theology* (Grand Rapids: Baker Academic; and Milton Keynes: Paternoster, 2004), 97–127

Preus, R., *The Inspiration of Scripture: A Study of the Theology of the Seventeenth Century Lutheran Dogmaticians* (London/Edinburgh: Oliver and Boyd, 1955)

Rahner, K., *Inspiration in the Bible* (QD 1; New York: Herder and Herder, 1961)

Reid, J.K.S., *The Authority of Scripture: A Study of the Reformation and Post-Reformation Understanding of the Bible* (London: Methuen, 1957)

Richardson, A., 'The Rise of Modern Biblical Scholarship and Recent Discussion of the Authority of the Bible', in *The Cambridge History of the Bible: Volume 3, The West from the Reformation to the Present Day* (ed. S.L. Greenslade; Cambridge: Cambridge University Press, 1963), 294–338

Rowe, C.K., 'Biblical Pressure and Trinitarian Hermeneutics', *ProEccl* 11 (2002), 295–312

Ryle, H.E., *The Canon of the Old Testament* (2nd edn.; London: Macmillan, 1895)

Sailhamer, J.H., *Introduction to Old Testament Theology: A Canonical Approach* (Grand Rapids: Zondervan, 1995)

Sanday, W., *Inspiration: Eight Lectures on the Early History and Origin of the Doctrine of Biblical Inspiration* (3rd edn.; London: Longmans, Green, 1914)

Sauter, G., *Eschatological Rationality: Theological Issues in Focus* (Grand Rapids: Baker, 1996)

Schneiders, S.M., *The Revelatory Text: Interpreting the New Testament as Sacred Scripture* (2nd edn.; Collegeville, MN: Liturgical Press/Michael Glazier, 1999)

Seitz, C.R., 'We Are Not Prophets or Apostles: The Impact of Brevard Childs', *Dialog* 33 (1994), 89–93; reprinted as '"We Are Not Prophets or Apostles": The Biblical Theology of B.S. Childs', in *Word Without End: The Old Testament as Abiding Theological Witness* (Grand Rapids/Cambridge: Eerdmans, 1998), 102–109

Semler, J.S., *Abhandlung von freier Untersuchung des Canon* (Texte zur Kirchen- und Theologiegeschichte 5; ed. H. Scheible; Gütersloh: Mohn, 1967; orig. 1771–76)

Smart, J.D., *The Interpretation of Scripture* (Philadelphia: Westminster, 1961)

—, *The Strange Silence of the Bible in the Church: A Study in Hermeneutics* (Philadelphia: Westminster, 1970)

Sparks, K., 'The Sun Also Rises: Accommodation in Inscripturation and Interpretation', in *Evangelicals and Scripture: Tradition, Authority and Hermeneutics* (ed. V. Bacote, L.C. Miguélez and D.L. Okholm; Downers Grove: InterVarsity Press, 2004), 112–32

Sundberg, A.C., Jr., 'The Bible Canon and the Christian Doctrine of Inspiration', *Int* 29 (1975), 352–71

Trobisch, D., *The First Edition of the New Testament* (Oxford/New York: Oxford University Press, 2000)

Vanhoozer, K.J., *Is There a Meaning in This Text? The Bible, the Reader, and the Morality of Literary Knowledge* (Grand Rapids: Zondervan, 1998)

—, 'From Speech Acts to Scripture Acts: The Covenant of Discourse and the Discourse of Covenant', in *After Pentecost: Language and Biblical Interpretation* (SHS 2; ed. C. Bartholomew, C. Greene and K. Möller; Grand Rapids: Zondervan; and Carlisle: Paternoster, 2001), 1–49

—, 'Into the Great "Beyond": A Theologian's Response to the Marshall Plan', in I.H. Marshall, *Beyond the Bible: Moving From Scripture to Theology* (Grand Rapids: Baker Academic; and Milton Keynes: Paternoster, 2004), 81–95

—, 'Providence', in *Dictionary for Theological Interpretation of the Bible* (ed. K.J. Vanhoozer et al.; Grand Rapids: Baker Academic; and London: SPCK, 2005), 641–45

Vawter, B., *Biblical Interpretation* (Theological Resources; Philadelphia: Westminster; and London: Hutchinson, 1972)

Wainwright, G., 'Trinity', in *Dictionary for Theological Interpretation of the Bible* (ed. K.J. Vanhoozer et al.; Grand Rapids: Baker Academic; and London: SPCK, 2005), 815–18

Wall, R.W., 'Reading the New Testament in Canonical Context', in *Hearing the New Testament* (ed. J.B. Green; Grand Rapids: Eerdmans; and Carlisle: Paternoster, 1995), 370–93

—, and E.E. Lemcio (eds.), *The New Testament as Canon: A Reader in Canonical Criticism* (JSNTSup 76; Sheffield: JSOT Press, 1992)

Warfield, B.B., *Revelation and Inspiration* (New York/London: Oxford University Press, 1927)

Wellhausen, J., *Prolegomena to the History of Israel* (trans. J.S. Black and A. Menzies; Edinburgh: A. & C. Black, 1885; repr. Atlanta: Scholars Press, 1994)

Westcott, B.F., 'Appendix B: On the Primitive Doctrine of Inspiration', in *An Introduction to the Study of the Gospels* (8th edn.; London: Macmillan, 1895), 417–56

Williams, D.M., *Receiving the Bible in Faith: Historical and Theological Exegesis* (Washington, DC: Catholic University of America Press, 2004)

Williamson, P., *Catholic Principles for Interpreting Scripture* (SubBi 22; Rome: Pontifical Biblical Institute, 2001)

Work, T., *Living and Active: Scripture in the Economy of Salvation* (Sacra Doctrina; Grand Rapids/Cambridge: Eerdmans, 2002)

Wolterstorff, N., *Divine Discourse: Philosophical Reflections on the Claim that God Speaks* (Cambridge/New York: Cambridge University Press, 1995)

—, 'The Promise of Speech-act Theory for Biblical Interpretation', in *After Pentecost: Language and Biblical Interpretation* (SHS 2; ed. C. Bartholomew, C. Greene and K. Möller; Grand Rapids: Zondervan; and Carlisle: Paternoster, 2001), 73–90

Yeago, D.S., 'The Spirit, the Church, and the Scriptures: Biblical Inspiration and Interpretation Revisited', in *Knowing the Triune God: The Work of the Spirit in the Practices of the Church* (ed. J.J. Buckley and D.S. Yeago; Grand Rapids/Cambridge: Eerdmans, 2001), 49–93

Zenger, E., et al., *Einleitung in das Alte Testament* (3rd edn.; Stuttgart: Kohlhammer, 1998)

7

Canon, Cult and Covenant

The Promise of Liturgical Hermeneutics

Scott W. Hahn

To my mind, one of the most notable achievements of twentieth-century biblical scholarship has been the rediscovery of Scripture's *liturgical sense*. This achievement is rightly associated with the pioneering work of Oscar Cullmann and Jean Daniélou, who demonstrated that the biblical acts of God were intended to be carried on in the church's sacramental liturgy. Their insights were reinforced by Henri de Lubac's study of medieval exegesis, and Yves Congar's historical and theological work on tradition, which focused attention on the liturgy as the original and privileged locus of biblical interpretation.[1]

This movement of recovery, which has continued among both Protestant and Catholic scholars,[2] is usually perceived as being in tension with historical and critical methodologies; but, in fact, these methods have also helped us to see that the church's early cult and worship were decisive in the composition, content, and use of the scriptural texts.[3] As a result of these developments, we

---

[1] See generally, Cullmann, *Early Christian Worship*; Daniélou, *The Bible and the Liturgy* and 'Sacraments'; Congar, *Tradition* and *Meaning of Tradition*. De Lubac comments: 'Let us not forget that Christian exegesis was born, first and foremost, in the office of the liturgy, regarding sacred reading that had to be commented upon. That is where it was developed' (*Medieval Exegesis*, 2:28).

[2] See Van Olst, *The Bible and Liturgy;* Old, *Reading and Preaching*; Vagaggini, *Theological Dimensions*; Ratzinger, *Spirit of the Liturgy*; Corbon, *Wellspring of Worship*.

[3] For instance, source criticism, in moving from hypotheses about original documentary sources, discerns tradition history and liturgical usage underlying biblical texts. Form criticism has also distinguished a variety of liturgical forms such as hymns and prayers, among kerygmatic, catechetical and other forms. Redaction criticism, as well, has focused attention on how the historical situations of the various

now have greater insight into the original purposes of the biblical authors and the ecclesial communities in which these texts were passed on. We can now appreciate that there is always a living and dynamic relationship between *Scripture*, the inspired Word of God in the Old and New Testaments, and *liturgy*, the sacrificial worship and public ritual of God's covenant people.[4]

Recognition of this vital relationship has important implications for the study of Scripture. Indeed, in this paper I will show how the rediscovery of Scripture's liturgical sense points to a new, *liturgical hermeneutic*. Such an interpretive approach leads us to conclude that Scripture is not solely text, and liturgy is not solely ritual, even though the one exists as text and the other exists as ritual. As we can now see, liturgy is where the written text functions as Scripture, as the living Word of God. The liturgy emerges as the proper – though not exclusive – setting for reading and interpreting Scripture, and for actualizing its saving truths.

I begin by showing how study of the *canon* and *covenant* has illuminated both the cultic *content* and *context* of the Bible. This in turn helps us to see what I call the *formal and material unity of Scripture and liturgy* – that Scripture exists *for* liturgy and, in large part, is *about* liturgy. This formal and material unity, I propose, invites us to make a fresh, *liturgical reading* of the integral text of the canonical Scriptures. As I hope to demonstrate, such a reading discloses a *liturgical trajectory* and *liturgical teleology* in the canonical narrative. This liturgical trajectory and teleology in turn suggests three broad principles of theological exegesis – the *divine economy*, *typology*, and *mystagogy*. I propose that these principles, which emerge from an integral reading of the canonical text, help us to lay the foundations for a new, *liturgical hermeneutic*.[5]

---

worshipping communities – the Second Temple, the Johannine Community, and so forth – influenced the final shaping of the texts.

[4] Since 'liturgy' means different things to different readers, depending in large part upon denominational background and worship experience, let me clarify that I am following the understanding of liturgy found in ancient Jewish and Christian sources, primarily the Bible; that is to say, I am considering liturgy as sacrificial worship and public ritual in the context of a divine–human covenant relationship.

[5] These propositions are developed in Hahn, *Letter and Spirit*. For this approach see Ratzinger: 'Since the inner unity of the books of the New Testament, and of the two testaments, can only be seen in light of faith's interpretation, where this is lacking, people are forever separating out new components and discovering contradictions in the sources … *From a purely scientific point of view, the legitimacy of an interpretation depends on its power to explain things.* In other words, the less it needs to interfere with the sources, the more it respects the corpus as given and is able to show it to be intelligible from within, by its own logic, the more apposite such an interpretation is. Conversely, the more it interferes with the sources, the more it feels obliged to excise and throw doubt on things found there, the more alien to the subject it is. To that extent,

The Liturgical Content and Context of Scripture

The formal and material unity of canon and cult

The recovery of Scripture's liturgical sense by Cullmann, Daniélou and others dovetails with two critical findings of modern biblical scholarship: First, the recognition that Scripture's final canonical shape is essential for determining the meaning and purpose of individual passages and books; and secondly, the identification of covenant as Scripture's keynote narrative theme. Together, these findings have helped us to see a unity between Scripture and liturgy that is both formal and material. Their unity is *formal* in that Scripture was canonized for the sake of liturgy, and the canon itself derived from liturgical tradition. Their unity is *material* in that the content of Scripture is heavily liturgical.

Details about the origins of the *canon* as a definitive collection of sacred writings expressing the faith, worship and instruction of the believing community, remain elusive and are still debated.[6] However, there is increasing recognition that the motives for establishing the canon were largely cultic and that cultic use was an important factor in determining which Scriptures were to be included in the canon. Put simply, the canon was drawn up to establish which books would be read when the community gathered for worship, and the books included in the canon were those that were already being read in the church's liturgy.[7]

---

its explanatory power is also its ability to maintain the inner unity of the corpus in question. It involves the ability to unify, to achieve a synthesis, which is the reverse of superficial harmonization. Indeed, only faith's hermeneutic is sufficient to measure up to these criteria' (*Behold the Pierced One*, 44–45; emphasis mine).

[6] See generally, McDonald and Sanders (eds.), *Canon Debate*; Childs, 'Canon in Recent Biblical Studies'.

[7] In considering the contributions of Childs, Sanders has written: 'That which is canon comes to us from ancient communities of faith, not just from individuals … [T]he whole of the Bible, the sum as well as all its parts, comes to us out of the liturgical and instructional life of early believing communities' (*Sacred Story*, 162). Disputing another leading theory concerning the formation of the Hebrew biblical canon, McDonald states: 'Acceptance into a collection of sacred Scriptures did not have so much to do with a notion about the cessation of prophecy as with use in Israel's liturgy, or worship and instruction, over a long period of time' (*Formation*, 53). Bruce, finds similar imperatives behind the formation of the New Testament canon: 'When the canon was "closed" in due course by competent authority, this simply meant that official recognition was given to the situation already obtaining in the practice of the worshipping community' (*Canon of Scripture*, 42). Of the New Testament canon, Ferguson writes: 'Distinctive worship practices also served as

The importance of liturgical use in the origins of the canon is not a new idea.[8] It has long been recognized, for instance, that what became canonical writings originated as oral accounts of God's redemptive interventions in history recited in cultic settings and accompanied by ritual actions. This is true for both the Old and New Testament canons.[9] In each, we have testimony of authoritative scriptural texts being read in the worshipping assembly (Ex. 24:7; Deut. 31:9–13; 1 Tim. 4:13; Rev. 1:3). And textual analysis and form criticism have helped us to also see the profound shaping influence of liturgical use on the composition and final form of individual texts.[10] Broadly speaking, we can say that inasmuch as the exodus was the foundational narrative recalled and celebrated in Israel's liturgy, the 'new exodus' of Christ's death, resurrection and ascension was the 'subject' of the texts heard in the church's eucharistic liturgy.

Covenant and cult

If the cultic worship of the Jewish and Christian communities gave rise to the canon, it is because that worship itself is a response to God's redemptive initiatives. In particular, the worship of Israel and the church is a response to God's covenants. The unity that scholars have perceived between cult and canon is established and constituted by the covenant. Again, this is true for both the Hebrew biblical canon and the Christian Bible.

For both Israel and the church, the Scriptures and the liturgical traditions of worship emerge as a single, inseparable response to God's redemptive initiative expressed in his offering of a covenant to his people. For Israel, the covenant at Sinai is foundational. For the church, the 'new covenant' made in the blood of

---

   preconditions for a canon of Scripture. The Eucharist involved the remembrance of the passion of Christ and particularly the institution narrative. Prayers and confessional statements were grounded in the teachings of Jesus and the proclamation of his apostles. Christian materials were read in the assemblies from quite early (Mk. 13:14; Rev. 1:3). The Church did not have to wait until the end of the second century (and certainly not the fourth century) to know what books to read in church' ('Selection and Closure', 296).

[8] Moule: 'many of the component parts of the New Testament were forged in the flame of corporate worship, and ... this has left its stamp on its whole vocabulary' (*Birth*, 20, cf. 33).

[9] See the early and important work of Östborn, *Cult and Canon*, especially ch. 5: 'The Canon as Cultic Representation'. See also, Weiser: 'The reading aloud of the written word in the cult gave a natural impetus to the collection of the Old Testament as sacred writings. Here is the real setting (*Sitz im Leben*) for the Old Testament as holy Scripture' (*Old Testament*, 334; cf. Leonard, 'Origin of Canonicity').

[10] McGowan, '"Is There a Liturgical Text in This Gospel?"'; Goulder, *Evangelist's Calendar*; Swartley, *Israel's Scripture Traditions*; Daube, 'Earliest Structure'.

Christ (Lk. 22:20) is foundational.[11] Indeed, it is instructive that χανών was not originally the word applied to the list of biblical books. Eusebius, writing in the early fourth century, rather spoke of the Scriptures as 'encovenanted' or 'contained in the covenant' (ἐνδιάθηκος).[12]

It is not surprising that many scholars have recognized the 'covenant' as the recurrent and theologically significant theme in the canonical text. The vast literature on this topic cannot be rehearsed here.[13] Two things are important for our purposes: First, the finding that God's covenants with humanity form the narrative structure and dramatic content of the Bible.[14] Secondly, the conclusion that the biblical covenants are initiated to form kinship or familial bonds between God and his people or family.[15] And thirdly, that covenant-making is a cultic, liturgical act, as much as a legal and ethical one. This last point has not been well-studied. But it is crucial to see the unity of Scripture and liturgy in the establishment, renewal, and maintenance of God's covenant relationship with his people. Again, simply put, for both Christians and Jews, the scriptural texts were originally enacted in the liturgy for the purposes of remembering and ritualizing the divine saving events, and renewing the people's covenant relationship with God.[16]

---

[11] It is perhaps interesting to note that the exegesis of Pope Benedict XVI sees a profound unity between the covenant at Sinai and the new covenant, a unity that reflects the inner continuity of the salvation history told in the canonical text: 'With regard to the issue of the nature of the covenant, it is important to note that the Last Supper sees itself as making a covenant: it is the prolongation of the Sinai covenant, which is not abrogated, but renewed. Here renewal of the covenant, which from earliest times was doubtless an essential element of Israel's liturgy, attains its highest form possible' (Ratzinger, 'New Covenant', 62).

[12] See McDonald and Sanders, *Canon Debate*, 295–320, 432. On these themes, see also, McCarthy, *Institution and Narrative*.

[13] For a review of the relevant themes and literature, see Hahn, 'Kinship by Covenant', and 'Covenant'.

[14] This is a finding that cuts across confessional lines. Congar writes: 'The content and meaning of Scripture was God's covenant plan, finally realized in Jesus Christ (in his *transitus*) and in the Church' (*Tradition and Traditions*, 68–69). See also Segal, *Rebecca's Children*, 4; Wright, *People of God*, 260, 262; Kline, 'Correlation', 265–79.

[15] See for example Ps. 2:7; 2 Sam. 8:14; Lev. 26:12; Deut. 32:6, 8, 18–19; Jer. 30:22; Ezek. 36:28; Hos. 11:1; Gal. 4:5–7; 1 Jn. 3:2. Cross, 'Kinship and Covenant'; Kline, *By Oath Consigned*.

[16] Very few commentators have recognized what Vanhoye has identified as the essential relationship between liturgical cult and covenant in the Bible: 'The value of a covenant depends directly on the act of worship which establishes it. A defective liturgy cannot bring about a valid covenant ... The reason for this is easily understood. The establishment of a covenant between two parties who are distant from each other can only be accomplished by an act of mediation and, when it is a question of mankind and God, the mediation has of necessity to be conducted through the cult'

This helps to explain another seldom-noticed fact: the books of the new and old covenants are heavily liturgical in content. This is what I mean in describing a *material unity* between Scripture and liturgy – the Bible in many ways is *about* liturgy. Much of the Pentateuch is concerned with ritual and sacrificial regulations; significant portions of the wisdom, historical and prophetic books take up questions of ritual and worship. The New Testament, too, is filled with material related to the sacramental liturgy. The Gospel of John, for instance, unfolds as a kind of 'sacramentary' in the context of the Jewish lectionary calendar; the Letter to the Hebrews and the book of Revelation contain sustained meditations on the meaning of the Christian liturgy; and the letters of Paul and Peter are animated by liturgical and cultic concerns. Often it is liturgy, or the culpable neglect of liturgy, that drives the biblical drama. Also, though this topic has not been well-studied, liturgy appears at the most significant junctures of the salvation history recorded in the canonical Scriptures.[17]

Insofar, then, as the canon was established for use in the liturgy, and inasmuch as its content is 'about' liturgy, it follows that we must engage Scripture *liturgically* if we are to interpret these texts according to the authors' original intentions and the life-situation of the believing community in which these texts were handed on. In what follows I want to begin this process of engagement. Through canonical analysis, I want to offer a reading of the 'meta-narrative' of Scripture focusing on liturgy – what it is and how it functions in the Bible's grand 'story.'[18] Such a sketch must necessarily be broad-brush. But by focusing on the central moments in the canonical narrative – creation, the exodus, the Davidic monarchy, and the new covenant – I believe we will see the familiar biblical outlines in a new light.

Reading Scripture Liturgically: The Old Covenant Witness

Homo liturgicus: Scripture's liturgical anthropology

I must begin by anticipating my conclusion: a liturgical reading of the canonical text discloses the Bible's *liturgical trajectory* and *liturgical teleology*. Put another

---

(*Old Testament Priests*, 181–82). Levenson, too, has seen this. 'The renewal of the covenant was a central aspect of Israel's worship in biblical times.' The purpose of liturgy, he adds, is 'to actualize the past so that [each] new generation will become the Israel of the classic covenant relationship' (*Sinai and Zion*, 80–81). See also Haran, 'The *Berît* "Covenant",' 203–19; Faley, *Bonding with God*.

[17] See Hahn, *Letter and Spirit*, especially ch. 3, 'The Unities of Scripture and Liturgy'. See also Brown, 'Johannine Sacramentary'; Pagolu, *Religion of the Patriarchs*.

[18] See generally, Rendtorff, 'Canonical Interpretation'; Bartholomew and Goheen, *Drama of Scripture*; Vanhoozer, *First Theology*.

way: as presented in the canonical narrative, there is a liturgical reason and purpose for the creation of the world and the human person, and there is a liturgical 'destiny' toward which creation and the human person journey in the pages of the canonical text. At each decisive stage in God's covenant relations with humanity, the divine-human relationship is expressed liturgically and sacrificially. The mighty acts of God in Scripture at every point climax in the liturgy, from the sacrificial offering of Noah following the flood to the institution of the Eucharist at the Last Supper. From the first page to the last, the canonical text presents us with a liturgical anthropology – the human person is *homo liturgicus*, created to glorify God through service, expressed as a sacrifice of praise.

This begins in the Bible's very first pages. In the liturgical hymn of Genesis 1, creation unfolds in a series of sevenfold movements, beginning with the first verse which is exactly seven words long in Hebrew, and proceeding with seven clearly defined creative speech acts of God ('Let there be …').[19] Linguistic and thematic parallels between the account of the primordial seven days and the later building of the tabernacle (Ex. 25 – 40)[20] have helped us to see the author's intent: to depict creation as the fashioning of a cosmic temple, which, like the later tabernacle and Temple, would be a meeting place for God and the human person made in his image and likeness.

In the second creation account in Genesis 2 – 3, the Garden of Eden is described in highly symbolic terms as an earthly sanctuary – again with evident literary parallels to later sanctuaries, especially the inner sanctum of the Temple.[21] For our liturgical reading, the most important parallels are those that describe the terms of the relationship between God and man in the garden and in the sanctuary. God is described as 'walking up and down' or 'to and fro' (הלך) in the garden (Gen. 3:8). The same Hebrew verb is used to characterize God's presence in the tabernacle (Lev. 26:12; Deut. 23:15; 2 Sam. 7:6–7). The first man is described as placed in the garden to 'till' or 'serve' (עבד) and to 'keep' or 'guard' (שמר) it. These verbs are only found together again in the Pentateuch to describe the liturgical service of the priests and Levites in the sanctuary (Num. 3:7–8; 8:26; 18:5–6).[22]

These literary clues suggest the biblical authors' intent to describe creation as a royal temple building by a heavenly king. The human person in these pages is intentionally portrayed as a royal firstborn and high-priestly figure, a kind of priest-king set to rule as vice-regent over the temple-kingdom of creation.[23]

---

[19] Genesis 1 describes 'a heavenly liturgy. With a severe and solemn rhythm the same expressions occur again and again throughout the whole chapter like a litany' (Westermann, *Der Schopfungsbericht vom Anfang der Bibel* [Stuttgart, 1960], quoted in Maly, 'Israel – God's Liturgical People', 9.

[20] Levenson, 'Temple'.

[21] Wenham, 'Sanctuary Symbolism'; Stager, 'Jerusalem'.

[22] Wenham, 'Sanctuary Symbolism', 21.

[23] Callender, *Adam in Myth and History*, 29.

The priestly king of Genesis

This reading of Genesis is confirmed intertextually in the Old Testament and throughout the intertestamental and rabbinic literature.[24] Perhaps the clearest inner-biblical reflection on the nature of the primal human is found in Ezekiel's famous lament over the King of Tyre (Ezek. 28:1–19).

Among numerous echoes of the original Eden account, Ezekiel describes the king as created in Eden, which is depicted as 'the garden of God' and the 'holy mountain of God' – that is, as a symbol of the site of the Temple (vv. 13, 14, 16). He 'walks among (הלך) the stones of fire' or burning coals (v. 14), which elsewhere are associated with the divine presence (Ezek. 1:3; Ps. 18:13). He is stamped with a 'signet' of 'perfection' or 'resemblance' (v. 12) – a symbol elsewhere associated with royal likeness and authority (Gen. 41:42; Hag. 2:23; Jer. 22:24–25).

As the king's creation is described in Adamic and priestly terms, so his sin is characterized as a form of sacrilege and profanation punished by exile and 'deconsecration.' The king's sin, like Adam's, is grasping after divinity – wanting to be 'like a god.' This becomes the refrain of Ezekiel's indictment (compare Gen. 3:5, 22; Ezek. 28:2, 6, 9). Driven by cherubim he is cast from God's presence as a 'profane thing' who has desecrated God's sanctuaries (Ezek. 28:16, 18; compare Gen. 3:23–24).

This passage of Ezekiel suggests that already within the Old Testament there was a traditional understanding of the human person as created in relationship with God and endowed with an identity that is at once royal and priestly, filial and liturgical.[25] The terms of the human relationship with God are ordered by the covenant of the Sabbath established on the seventh day.[26]

---

[24] See Oberholzer, 'What is Man …?'; Louis, *Theology of Psalm 8*. The Psalter, the wisdom literature, and the prophets all give us the picture of creation as a cosmic or heavenly sanctuary and the Temple as a microcosm (Ps. 52:8; 78:69; 92:13–15; Lam. 2:6; Isa. 60:13, 21). The Chronicler understands the task of the Levitical priesthood in terms of the serving, guarding and gatekeeping imagery in Genesis (1 Chr. 9:17–27; 2 Chr. 23:19; Neh. 11:19). 'The garden of Eden was the holy of holies and the dwelling of the Lord,' we read in the intertestamental *Book of Jubilees* (8:9). A midrash on Genesis describes Adam's primordial task as that of offering priestly sacrifices (*Genesis Rabbah* 16:5). In a Targum, Adam is described as having been formed from dust at the precise site where the Temple sanctuary would later be built (*Targum Pseudo-Jonathan Gen.* 2:7). The Qumran community apparently saw itself as the 'Temple of Adam' (4Q174 1:6). For a good review of these themes, see Beale, *Temple*.

[25] Callender, *Adam in Myth and History*, 132.

[26] The term 'covenant', of course, is not used in the creation account. However, that creation is ordered to the covenant is everywhere implied. See Murray, *The Cosmic*

The first of God's mighty works then, the creation of the world, has a liturgical climax – the divine and human 'rest' of the seventh day. This becomes clearer further on in the Pentateuch, as we will see with Moses' building of the tabernacle, and God's giving of the Sabbath ordinances.

The priestly people of the exodus

These creation themes – man as made for worship in a covenant relationship as God's royal and priestly firstborn – are made explicit in the canonical account of the Exodus. As Adam was made in God's image and likeness, God identifies Israel as 'my own people' (Ex. 3:7, 10, 12; 5:1; 6:5, 7) and 'my son, my first-born' (Ex. 4:22–23). And as Adam was made to worship, God's chosen people are liberated expressly for worship.

The early chapters of Exodus involve a play on the word עבד, ('serve' or 'work'), the word that described the primeval vocation given to man (Gen. 2:15). The word is used four times to stress the cruel slavery ('hard service') inflicted upon the Israelites by the new Pharaoh (Ex. 1:13–14; see also 5:18; 14:5, 12). But the same word is also used to describe what God wants of the Israelites (Ex. 3:12; 4:22; 7:16; 9:1, 13; 10:3, 24–26). They are to serve, not as slave laborers but as a people that serves him in prayer.[27] They are to 'offer sacrifice' (זבח; Ex. 3:18; 5:3). Moses and Aaron are instructed to tell Pharaoh that God wants Israel to hold a religious 'feast' or 'festival' (חג; Ex. 5:1; cf. Ex. 12:14; 23:16; 34:25).

Israel's vocation is most clearly stated in the preamble to the covenant at Sinai. There God calls Israel 'a kingdom of priests (ממלכת כהנים) and a holy nation (גוי קדוש)' (Ex. 19:5–6).[28] Israel is to be corporately what Adam was created to be individually – the firstborn of a new humanity, a liturgical people that will dwell with God in a relationship of filial obedience and worship.

The covenant at Sinai is ratified by liturgical actions – the reading of the book of the law, the profession of fidelity sworn by the people, the offering of sacrifices, the sprinkling of 'the blood of the covenant' and the meal eaten in

---

Covenant. The Sabbath was seen as a sign of God's covenant oath with the first man and woman in the rabbinic and intertestamental literature. See, for instance, the midrashic *Sifre Deuteronomy*; the *Book of Jubilees* (36:7), and *1 Enoch* 69:15–27. See also de Vaux: 'Creation is the first action in this history of salvation; once it was over, God stopped work, and he was then able to make a covenant with his creature ... The "sign" of the covenant made at the dawn of creation is the observance of the Sabbath by man (Ezek. 20:12, 20)' (*Ancient Israel*, 481). Recent Catholic magisterial documents have referred to the Sabbath of creation as 'the first covenant.' See John Paul II, *Dies Domini*; cf. *Catechism of the Catholic Church*, no. 288.

[27] Note the use of עבד to describe the priestly liturgical service offered to God in the tabernacle (Num. 3:7–8; 4:23; 7:5; 16:9).

[28] Wells, *God's Holy People*, 34–35.

the presence of God (see Ex. 24:1–9). Much of the Law, in fact, consists of regulations regarding how God is to be rightly worshipped – the design of the tabernacle and furniture, the priestly vestments, the liturgical calendar of festivals and ceremonial rubrics of the sacrificial system. In their worship, the Israelites celebrated their birth as a people of God and rededicated themselves to their royal and priestly vocation (Deut. 6:4–5).[29]

As creation was ordered to the Sabbath, the exodus is likewise ordered to a liturgical 'end.' The exodus was begun with a liturgical act – the celebration of the Passover – and it 'concludes' in the canonical text with the construction of the tabernacle. The literary parallels with the creation account suggest a close connection between Sabbath, creation, covenant, and the dwelling that Israel is instructed to build.[30] The plans for the dwelling are given by God immediately after the liturgical ratification of the Sinai covenant in Exodus 24. Moses' time on the mountain can be seen as a kind of 'new creation' – the cloud of divine presence covers the mountain for six days and on the seventh Moses is called to enter the cloud and receive the divine blueprint for the dwelling. God's instructions consist of a series of seven commands that continue for seven chapters and conclude with the ordinances for the seventh day, the Sabbath (Ex. 31:12–17).

The making of the priestly vestments and the building of the tabernacle again recall the creation narrative. In both, the work is also done in seven stages, each punctuated with the words, 'as the Lord commanded Moses.' As God did, Moses beholds his handiwork, and blesses it (Ex. 39:43). As God 'finished his work,' so Moses 'finished the work' (Gen. 2:1–2; Ex. 40:34). And as God rested on the seventh day, blessing and hallowing it, when Moses finished his work, the divine presence filled the tabernacle (Ex. 40:34).

In the Israelites' work to build the tabernacle we glimpse what the royal and priestly service of the human person was meant to be about: God's sons and representatives were to rule in his name, according to his commands. Through their work they were to bring creation to its fulfillment, to complete God's work by making the world a home in which they dwell with him and live as his people.[31]

All of creation is ordered to the covenant, this familial dwelling of God with his people. The Sabbath, as the sign of God's 'perpetual covenant' (Ex. 31:16), is meant to be a living memorial of the original perfection and intention of God's creation – his desire to 'rest' in communion with creation. The Sabbath orders human work to worship, labor to liturgy. The royal calling to subdue

---

[29] Levenson, *Sinai and Zion*, 80–81.

[30] For these parallels, see Balentine, *Torah's Vision of Worship*, 136–41; Anderson, *Genesis of Perfection*, 200–202.

[31] See Anderson, *Genesis of Perfection*, 201–202.

the earth finds its expression in the liturgical consecration of the earth's fruits to God. Through their worship on the Sabbath, God bestows his blessings on his people and makes them holy (Ex. 31:13).[32]

As Israel is given an 'Adamic' vocation, it experiences an Adamic fall from grace. And as the primeval fall results in exile and deconsecration of the royal priestly figure, so too does Israel's worship the golden calf.[33] God calls the people 'corrupted,' using a Hebrew term (שִׁחֵת Ex. 32:7) found elsewhere to describe an animal too blemished to sacrifice or a priest unfit for service.[34] In defiling itself through ritual rebellion, Israel, like Adam, is rendered unfit for its divine vocation. It is interesting that the royal-priestly title of Exodus 19:6 is never again used to describe Israel in the Old Testament.

According to the biblical narrative, the apostasy results in the Levitical priesthood becoming the locus of the holiness that God intended for all Israel.[35] God's presence remains among the people, but access is highly restricted and must be mediated by the Levites. A complex array of cultic laws were introduced for apparently penitential and pedagogical purposes – as mechanisms that will enable Israel to atone for its inevitable sins against the covenant and to teach them the true meaning of worship.[36]

---

[32] Ratzinger: 'The Sabbath is the sign of the covenant between God and man; it sums up the inward essence of the covenant ... [C]reation exists to be a place for the covenant that God wants to make with man. The goal of creation is the covenant, the love story of God and man ... If creation is meant to be a space for the covenant, the place where God and man meet one another, then it must be thought of as a space for worship ... Now if worship, rightly understood, is the soul of the covenant, then it not only saves mankind but is also meant to draw the whole of reality into communion with God' (*Spirit of the Liturgy*, 26–27).

[33] See Hahn, 'Kinship by Covenant', 226–53.

[34] See also Lev. 22:25; Mal. 1:14; 2:8. Rodriguez writes: 'The point to notice here is that the people of Israel as a whole now have a moral defect that separates them from God. They cannot come to the sanctuary for they have rejected God, and thus have become like a defective animal or a disqualified priest, unable to come into God's presence' ('Sanctuary Theology', 139).

[35] Scholer, *Proleptic Priests*, 13–22. Although well beyond what I can do here, it is worth noting that the 'liturgical reading' of Scripture helps us to understand why, by the Second Temple period in general, and in the Qumran material in particular, we have such an explicitly developed Adamic, high priestly theology. In other words, Israel's high priest is portrayed as a kind of 'new Adam' who represents Israel, which in turn is seen as a kind of 'new humanity' that exists for 'liturgical' ends. See, Fletcher-Louis, 'Jesus and the High Priest', and *All the Glory of Adam*.

[36] See the important contributions of Gese on 'The Law' and 'The Atonement' in his *Essays on Biblical Theology*, 60–116.

The priestly kingdom of David

Creation was ordered to the Sabbath worship of the royal and priestly first couple. The exodus was ordered to the establishment of Israel as a priestly people to offer service to God. The exodus began with the Passover liturgy and culminated in the building of the tabernacle, and the liturgical celebration of God's presence filling the sacred space. The conquest of the land was ordered to the establishment of the priestly kingdom of David. Following the pattern of the exodus, the conquest of the land began with the overthrow of Jericho by 'liturgical' means – not by military engagement but by a liturgical procession led by the Ark of the Covenant and Israel's priests. Also, as the exodus culminated in the erection of the tabernacle, so too, the conquest culminates in the construction of the Temple and the liturgical celebration of God's abiding presence.

The Davidic kingdom marks the fullest expression of the Bible's liturgical anthropology and teleology. In the dynasty established by his covenant with David, God restates his divine will for the human person – to be a son of God, a priest and a king.[37] The royal–priestly primogeniture granted to David's seed (2 Sam. 7:14; Ps. 110:4; 89:26–27) is linked to the royal priesthood intended for Israel (Ex. 3:6–17; 4:22; 19:5–6). David is portrayed as a 'new Melchizedek' – a priest and king who serves the most high God from his capital in Salem, that is, Jerusalem (cf. Gen. 14:18; Ps. 76:2; 110). David is shown taking actions that are at once cultic and political, military and liturgical. His first act after establishing Jerusalem as capital of his kingdom, is to restore the Ark of the Covenant – the defining symbol of Israel's election and the site of God's living presence among the people during the wilderness period (Ex. 25:8–22; Josh. 3:8–11).

David's great concern for the Ark is central to the early drama of his reign, and the Ark's installation in the Temple marks the culmination of the Chronicler's account.[38] As the architectural expression of the Sinai covenant was the tabernacle, the architectural expression of the Davidic kingdom was not a royal palace, but the Temple.

The building of the Temple is presented as a new creation. As creation takes seven days, the Temple takes seven years to build (1 Kgs. 6:38; Gen. 2:2). It is dedicated during the seven-day Feast of Tabernacles (1 Kgs. 8:2) by a solemn prayer of Solomon structured around seven petitions (1 Kgs. 8:31–53).

In the Temple worship, the precise sacrificial system of the Mosaic cult continues, but there are new elements and accents. The kingdom's corporate worship takes the form of praise and thanksgiving. Many commentators have

---

[37] See the discussion in Hahn, 'Kinship', 359–60; see also Kruse, 'David's Covenant'; Levenson, 'Davidic Covenant'.

[38] See Begg, 'Ark'.

identified the centrality of songs of praise (תהלה) and songs of thanksgiving (תודה) in the Temple liturgy. Many of the psalms of praise appear to have been written to accompany the offering of sacrifices in the Temple (Ps. 27:6; 54:6, 8; 141:2). This is true also for the 'thanksgiving songs' organized by the Levites (Neh. 11:17; 12:8, 31).

David's own thanksgiving hymn (1 Chr. 16:7–36) is presented as a kind of paradigm for Israel's prayer. It is, in essence, a celebration of God's covenant in liturgical form. This hymn sets the tone and provides the content for the acts of worship and the theology of worship we find in the Psalter. God is praised and thanked in remembrance of his mighty works in creation and for his saving words and deeds in the life of Israel – the defining experience being that of the exodus and the covenant.

The sacrifice of praise

Praise and thanksgiving, accompanied by sacrifice, is understood to be the only appropriate response to the God who has created Israel to be his own and rescued them from death.[39] This is seen most evocatively in the *todah* (תודה) or thanksgiving psalms (for example, Ps. 18; 30; 32; 41; 66; 116; 118; 138). Composed to accompany the offering of a sacrificial meal of bread and meat in the Temple (Lev. 7:1–21), these are some of the highest expressions of the Old Testament's liturgical anthropology.[40]

In the *todah* psalms, the experience of the individual believer is almost typologically compared to that of Israel's captivity and exodus experience. Typically these psalms begin with a confession of faith and a vow of praise and self-offering. There follows a lament concerning some life-threatening distress that had befallen the believer. Then the believer describes how God delivered him from death or Sheol (the netherworld) and brought him to sing God's praises in the Temple.[41] In these psalms, 'life' is equated with worship and sacrifice in the presence of God in his Temple; 'death' is seen as a sort of exile or captivity, to be cut off from God's presence, outside of his Temple.[42]

We see in these psalms and in the prophetic literature a new and deepening understanding of the liturgical vocation of biblical man. In the prophets, this recognition of the inner truth of sacrifice often takes the form of denouncing

---

[39] Kuntz, 'Grounds for Praise', 182–83.

[40] Gese writes: 'It can be said that the thank-offering constituted the cultic basis for the main bulk of the psalms. It not only represents the high point of human life, but in it life itself can be seen as overcoming the basic issue of death by God's deliverance into life' (*Essays on Biblical Theology*, 131). On the spirituality of the *todah* and its influence on Christology, see Ratzinger, 54–57.

[41] See Gunkel, *Introduction to the Psalms*, 199–221.

[42] Anderson, 'Praise of God', 28.

the corruption of Israel's cult and worship (e.g. Is. 1:10–13; 66:2–4; Jer. 7:21–24; Amos 4:4–5, 6b; Mic. 6:6–8; Hos. 6:6; Mal. 1:10, 13–14). Positively, worship comes to be seen as a sacrificial offering in thanksgiving for redemption, for deliverance from death. Praise is revealed as the sacrifice by which men and women are to glorify God (Ps. 50:14, 33; 141:2). God is portrayed as desiring that Israel serve him – not with the blood of animals but with their whole hearts, aligning their will with his, making their whole lives a sacrifice of praise and thanksgiving (Ps. 40:6–8; 51:16–17).

With this profound understanding that they are called to a pure worship of the heart comes the recognition that no amount of ethical striving or moral reform can make them holy enough to serve their God. A new covenant is promised as a new exodus and a new creation in which there will be a forgiveness of sins and a divine transformation of the heart (Jer. 31:31–34; 32:40; Ezek. 36:24–28).

In the vision of the prophets, the new exodus will mark a renewal of Israel's vocation as the firstborn and teacher of the nations. Isaiah sees Israel fulfilling its ancient vocation as 'priests of the Lord' (Isa. 61:6), and the instrument of God's blessings for the nations (Isa. 19:24). Isaiah foresees nations streaming to Zion to worship the Lord (Isa. 2; see also Jer. 3:16–17) – including arch-foes Egypt and Assyria, which serve (עבד) Israel's God and offer sacrifices and burnt offerings.[43]

We see then, on the threshold of the New Testament, the promise that man's primal vocation will be renewed, that Israel will be gathered together with all nations at Zion to offer acceptable sacrifice to the God of Israel.

Reading Scripture Liturgically: The New Covenant Witness

The new Genesis and the new Adam

In the New Testament, Jesus and his church are presented as the fulfillment of the promises and institutions of the old covenant.[44] The story of the incarnation is told as a new creation. In Jesus there is a new beginning for the human race. He is explicitly called the new Adam (Rom. 5:12–20; 1 Cor. 15:45–49). In the early chapters of the letter to the Hebrews – especially in the opening catena of seven Old Testament quotations – Jesus is described in terms of Adam's original royal, filial and priestly vocation.[45] Here and throughout the Pauline

---

[43] Begg, 'Peoples'; Clements, 'A Light to the Nations'.
[44] For extensive bibliographies, see Moyise, *The Old Testament in the New*.
[45] See Lane, *Hebrews 1–8*, 46–50.

corpus, it is understood that the human vocation was frustrated at the outset by Adam's sin.

It is impossible to put forward here a biblical-theological argument concerning the specific nature of Adam's sin.[46] However, I would suggest that Adam's disobedience was understood inner-biblically as having something to do with a failure to offer himself – what we might call a failure of worship. His transgression of God's command betrays a broader abdication of his task of priestly service in the temple of creation.[47] In this sense, the story of the fall is truly the first chapter of the Bible, preparing the reader for Israel's history. That history unfolds according to the pattern of Eden – divine benediction is offered and accepted only to be followed quite immediately by human profanation, resulting in punishment by exile from the land of God's presence.[48]

I do not want to reduce the history of sin in the Bible to a story of cultic failure. But I do want to suggest that a liturgical reading of Scripture enables us to understand better why Christ's 'obedience' is so often cast in cultic, sacrificial and priestly terms. The identification of Christ's redemptive work with cultic sacrifice is especially strong in those passages that most scholars agree represent christological hymns used in early Christian worship.[49]

The hymn in Paul's letter to the Philippians (2:6–11)[50] underscores the dramatic reversal of Adam's sin. Unlike Adam, who was made in the image of God, Christ did not grasp at equality with God, but instead offered his life in humility and obedience to God. In Hebrews, this obedience is compared to the liturgical act of high priestly sacrifice (Heb. 9:11–28). As Israel's high priests would enter the sanctuary once a year to offer animal blood in atonement for the people's sins, Jesus enters the 'true' sanctuary – 'heaven itself' (Heb. 9:24) – to offer his own blood in sacrifice 'to take away the sins of many' (Heb. 9:28).

By this priestly act, this offering of blood, Jesus does even more than atone for sin. He also reveals the true nature of sacrifice as intended by God from the beginning – man's offering of himself in filial obedience to the divine will. Hebrews explains this through a christological reading of Psalm 40,

---

[46] For recent theories, see Barr, *Garden of Eden*, 1–20; Towner, 'Interpretations and Reinterpretations'.

[47] Beale, *Temple*, 69–70.

[48] Anderson notes: '[T]he story of Adam and Eve in the J source shows a striking parallel to Israel's larger national story. We might say that the entire narrative of the Torah is in tersely summarized form … Adam and Eve fall at the first and only command given to them. And like the nation Israel, the consequence of their disobedience is exile from a land of blessing' (*Genesis of Perfection*, 207–208).

[49] For example, see the redemptive 'blood' imagery in Rom. 3:24–25; Eph. 1:3–14; 2:13; Col. 1:15–20; Heb. 1:3; 1 Pet. 1:18–21. On these hymns, see Hengel, 'Hymns and Christology'.

[50] Martin, *Carmen Christi*.

finding in it a prophecy of Christ's offering of his body on the cross (Heb. 10:5–10).

Christ's self-offering is the worship expected originally of Adam and again of Israel as God's firstborn, royal and priestly people. His sacrifice marked the fulfillment of all that Israel's sacrificial system was intended to prepare and instruct Israel for – that through Israel all the nations of the world might learn to make a perfect offering of heart and will to God.[51]

The new exodus

As the New Testament presents it, Jesus' sacrificial death brought about a new exodus – liberating God's people from slavery to sin and subjection to death, ending their exile from God, gathering them and all peoples and leading them into the promised land of the heavenly kingdom and the new Jerusalem.

This 'new exodus' theme is now widely recognized as a decisive and shaping factor in the New Testament.[52] It is now widely accepted that Jesus is presented as a 'new Moses.' His passion and death are described as an 'exodus' (ἔξοδον; Lk. 9:31) in a transfiguration scene filled with allusions to the theophanies of the wilderness period. His death on the cross is described as a paschal sacrifice – that is, in terms of the liturgical sacrifice commanded by God to be offered on the night before Israel's exodus (Jn. 1:29, 33; 19:14, 33, 36; 1 Pet. 1:19; 1 Cor. 5:7; Rev. 5:6, 9; 7:17; 12:1; 15:3).

This typological reading of a new exodus and a new passover is hardly contested. It is also generally accepted that the New Testament writers present the sacraments of baptism and the Eucharist as means by which Christian believers are joined to the new exodus. Baptism is prefigured by the Israelites' passage through the Red Sea, the Eucharist prefigured by the manna and the water from the rock in the desert (1 Cor. 10:1–4; Jn. 6). As the first exodus is preceded by the institution of a liturgical memorial, by which Israelites would annually celebrate their establishment as a people of God, so too Christ institutes a memorial of his exodus sacrifice in the Eucharist inaugurated in the last supper with his disciples.

But a critical aspect of the typology has gone largely unnoticed in the literature – how the New Testament writers appropriate the Old Testament understanding of the *purpose* for the exodus. As we saw, God's liberation of Israel was ordered to a very specific end – namely the establishment of Israel as God's royal and priestly people destined to glorify him among the nations.

Echoes of that exodus purpose are clearly heard in Zechariah's canticle at the outset of Luke's Gospel (1:67–79). In a song resounding with exodus

---

[51] Congar, *Mystery*, 126, 141.
[52] See most recently, Allison, *New Moses*; Watts, *Isaiah's New Exodus*; Pao, *Acts*; Keesmaat, *Paul and His Story*.

imagery,[53] Zechariah sees the 'goal' of Christ's exodus as precisely that of the first exodus – to establish Israel as a holy and righteous people that worships in God's presence. Luke even employs here the specific term for the covenant 'service' (λατρεύω; Lk. 1:74) that God intended for Israel.[54]

In 1 Peter, we encounter a rich passage (1 Pet. 1:13–20; 2:1–10) in which the exodus themes are applied to the newly baptized. They are told to 'gird up the loins,' as the Israelites did on the night of their flight (Ex. 12:11). Peter says they have been 'ransomed' (λυτρόω; 1 Pet. 1:18), using the same word used to describe Israel's deliverance (Ex. 15:13), by the blood of a spotless unblemished lamb (Ex. 12:5). Their lives are described as a sojourning like that of Israel in the wilderness; they too are fed with spiritual food as the Israelites drank living water from the rock in the desert.

Finally, this passage culminates with the explicit declaration that the church is the new Israel – 'a chosen race, a royal priesthood, a holy nation.' This direct quotation from the Septuagint translation of Exodus 19:6 is joined to a quote from an Isaianic new exodus text that foresees the world-missionary dimension of Israel's royal and priestly vocation as 'the people whom I formed for myself, *that they might announce my praise*' (1 Pet. 2:9–10; Isa. 43:21).

The new priestly kingdom

Christ's new exodus is ordered to the establishment of the priestly kingdom that God intended in the first exodus. This understanding is enriched by another type found in the New Testament writings – that of the church as the restored kingdom or house of David. Jesus is portrayed throughout the New Testament as the son of David anticipated in the Old Testament, a priest–king according to the order of Melchizedek.[55] The church, heir of the royal priestly sonship of Israel, is said to participate in the heavenly high priesthood and royal sonship of Christ.

The redemptive work of Christ is both sacrificial and priestly. It brings about 'purification from sins,' Hebrews tells us in language drawn from the Old Testament purification rites (καθαρισμός; Heb. 1:3).[56] Through his priestly work, Christ 'consecrated' believers (ἁγιάζω; Heb. 2:10; 10:10), as previously

---

[53] See the review of 'scriptural metaphors derived from the exodus' in Green, *Luke*, 110–20.

[54] See Deut. 11:13. In the Septuagint, λατρεύω routinely translates עבד, which, as discussed above, means 'to serve or worship [God] cultically, especially by sacrifice.' Mathewson, *New Heaven*, 205–206. See also Fitzmyer, *Luke*, 1:385; Green, *Luke*, 117.

[55] See Hahn, 'Kingdom and Church'; idem, 'Kinship', 592–93; Strauss, *Davidic Messiah*.

[56] Cf. Ex. 29:37; 30:10; Lev. 16:19; 2 Pet. 1:9. Lane, *Hebrews 1–8*, 15.

God consecrated the Israelites (Ex. 31:13; Lev. 20:8; 21:15; Ezek. 20:12; 37:28). The Christian life is depicted as a living out of this priestly consecration. The believer, Hebrews says, has been consecrated and purified 'in order to serve (λατρεύειν) the living God' (Heb. 9:14; 12:28).

The 'holy priesthood' of all the faithful is to render liturgical service, offering 'spiritual sacrifices acceptable to God through Jesus Christ' (1 Pet. 2:5; Rom. 12:1).[57] Speaking in the sacrificial vocabulary of the Temple, Paul urges the Philippians to live as 'without blemish' (ἄμωμα; Phil. 2:15) and exhorts them in the 'sacrifice and liturgy of [their] faith' (τῇ θυσίᾳ καί λειτουργίᾳ τῆς πίστεως ὑμῶν; Phil. 2:17). Life itself is here seen as liturgy (λειτουργίᾳ), with Paul adopting the Septuagint word for the ritual worship of God – λατρεύειν – to define the Christian way of life.[58]

The highest expression of this liturgy of life is seen in believers' participation in the cosmic liturgy, the worship in heaven mediated by the high priest Christ. Hebrews describes the Eucharist as a 'festal gathering' celebrated by the 'church of the firstborn' (ἐκκλεσίᾳ πρωτοτόκων) with the angels on 'Mount Zion … the city of the living God, the heavenly Jerusalem.'[59] The liturgy of the new covenant, the Eucharist, forms the pattern of life for the firstborn of the new family of God. Like the liberated Israelites, they no longer serve as slaves but as sons. By joining themselves sacramentally to the sacrifice of Christ, the sons and daughters were to offer themselves 'through him' as a continual 'sacrifice of praise' (Heb. 13:15).[60]

The liturgical consummation of the canon

The New Testament also depicts the church fulfilling the mission of Israel – to gather all nations to Zion to offer spiritual sacrifices of praise to God.[61] This is the vision we see in the Bible's last book. John's Apocalypse is a liturgical book. The literary evidence clearly indicates that the book was intended to be read in the liturgy, most likely in the celebration of the Eucharist 'on the Lord's day,' (Rev. 1:10).[62] The Apocalypse is also a book 'about' liturgy. What is unveiled is nothing less than the liturgical consummation of human history in Christ. The vision John sees is that of a Eucharistic kingdom, in which angels and holy men and women worship ceaselessly around the altar and throne of God. The vision

---

[57] Corriveau, *Liturgy of Life*.

[58] See, for example, Acts 24:14; 27:23; Rom. 1:9; 2 Tim. 1:3. See Corriveau, *Liturgy of Life*, 141–42.

[59] Of course, many recent commentators reject the earliest interpreters of Hebrews and deny that there are Eucharistic references either here or elsewhere in the letter. I am persuaded otherwise. See Hahn, 'Kinship', 624–29.

[60] Lane, *Hebrews 9–13*, 549.

[61] Wells, *God's Holy People*, 243.

[62] Vanni, 'Liturgical Dialogue'; Aune, 'Apocalypse of John'.

even unfolds in liturgical fashion, in a series of hymns, exhortations, antiphons and other cultic forms.[63]

Jesus, described throughout the book as 'the Lamb,' with obvious reference to the lamb of the Passover, brings about a new exodus.[64] In this final book of the canon, we see the fulfillment of the canon's first book: In the new heaven and new earth, the new Jerusalem of Revelation, the children of the new Adam worship as priests and rule as kings, and the entire universe is revealed to have become a vast divine temple.[65]

Gathered together into this new paradise, those redeemed by the blood of the Lamb make up a priestly kingdom, as John sees it, quoting God's commission to Israel in Exodus 19:6 (Rev. 1:6; 5:10). But in this new kingdom, the children of Abraham reign with people from every tribe, tongue, and nation (Rev. 5:9; 7:9). Jesus is the 'firstborn' of this new family of God, the prophesied root and offspring of David (Rev. 22:16; 3:7) in whom all are made divine sons and daughters of God (Rev. 21:7) – royal sons and priests who will rule with him until the end of ages (Rev. 20:6).

Before the throne of God and the Lamb, the royal sons of God are shown worshipping him, gazing upon his face, with his name written upon their foreheads and reigning forever (Rev. 22:1–5). John chooses his words carefully here to evoke the Old Testament promises of God's intimate presence to those who serve him. The word rendered 'worship' in most translations of Revelation 22:3 is λατρεύσουσιν. This, as we have seen, is the word used in the Septuagint to translate עבד – the Hebrew word that describes Adam's original vocation as well as the purpose of the exodus and conquest.[66]

At the conclusion of our liturgical reading of the canon, we hear the purpose and meaning of the entire Bible summed up in the refrain of the Apocalypse: 'Worship God!' (Rev. 14:7; 19:10; 22:9). The human person has been shown from the first pages of Genesis to the last of Revelation to be liturgical by nature, created and destined to live in the spiritual house of creation, as children of a royal and priestly family that offers sacrifices of praise to their Father-Creator with whom they dwell in a covenant of peace and love.[67]

Towards a Liturgical Hermeneutic

Our liturgical reading of the canonical text reveals a clear liturgical *trajectory* and *teleology*. The story of the Bible is the story of humankind's journey to true

---

[63] Gloer, 'Worship God', 38–40.
[64] Mathews, *New Heaven*, 62–64.
[65] Dumbrell, *End of the Beginning*.
[66] Mathews, *New Heaven*, 205–206.
[67] Congar, *Mystery*, 192, 245–48.

worship in spirit and truth in the presence of God. That is the trajectory, the direction toward which narrative leads. This true worship is revealed to be the very purpose of God's creation in the beginning. That is the *teleology* revealed in the canonical text.

The formal unity of Scripture and liturgy, and the recovery of the canonical text's liturgical teleology and trajectory have important methodological implications for biblical scholarship. Indeed, I would argue that three interpretive imperatives arise from our liturgical reading. These imperatives, which I will consider under the headings *economy*, *typology*, and *mystagogy*, undergird the assumptions of the biblical authors and present themselves as crucial dimensions that must be understood for any authentic interpretation of the text.

The unity of Scripture: The divine economy

Our liturgical reading highlights the importance of what ancient church writers called 'the divine economy' – that is, the divine order of history as presented in the canonical text. Throughout the canonical narrative, the divine economy is presented as the motive for God's words and deeds.[68] The biblical writers understood the economy as part of 'the mystery of his will, according to his purpose ... a plan (οἰκονομίαν) for the fullness of time' (Eph. 1:9–10). In this the apostolic witness is faithful to the teaching of Christ, who is shown teaching them to see biblical history fulfilled in his life, death and resurrection (Lk. 24:26–27, 44–47).

As we have seen, the liturgy of both the old and new covenants is founded on remembrance and celebration of God's saving words and deeds. Liturgy, then, as presented in the Scripture, is an expression of faith in the divine economy and a means by which believers gain participation in that economy.[69] The Scriptures themselves are regarded by the biblical authors as the divinely inspired testament to the divine economy as it has unfolded throughout history, culminating in the saving event of the cross.

It follows that if our interpretations are to be true to the integrity of the texts, we must pay close attention to this notion of God's economy. The economy gives the Bible its content and unity.

---

[68] For explanations of God's words and deeds in light of a divine covenant plan, see Ex. 2:24; 6:5; 33:1; Num. 32:11; Deut. 1:8; 9:5; 30:20; 2 Sam. 7:8, 10, 11, 22–25; 1 Chr. 16:14–18; Jer. 31:31–37; 33:14–26; Lk. 1:46–55, 68–79; Acts 2:14–36; 3:12–26; 7:1–51; 11:34–43; 13:16–41.

[69] The purpose of Christian liturgy, says Dalmais, is 'to express man's *faith* in the divine economy and perpetuate the living effects of the incarnation' (*Introduction to the Liturgy*, 27). See also Danielou: 'The object of faith is the existence of a divine plan' ('Sacraments', 29).

The typological pattern

The divine economy is comprehended and explained in Scripture through a distinct way of reading and writing that originates in the canonical text and is carried over into the living tradition of the faith community that gives us these texts. We characterize this way of reading and writing broadly as *typology*.[70]

In our liturgical reading, we observed the pervasiveness of typological patterns of exegesis in both the Old and New Testaments.[71] To recall but a few examples: the world's creation was portrayed in light of the later building of the tabernacle. The tabernacle in turn was described as a 'new creation.' Jesus' death and resurrection are seen as a new Passover and a new exodus. The Christian sacramental life is illuminated by the exodus event.

The extensive use of typology in the Scriptures reflects a profound biblical 'worldview.' If the economy gives narrative unity to the canonical Scriptures, fashioning them into a single story, typology helps us to understand the full meaning of that story. Recognition of this biblical worldview has important hermeneutical implications. The interpreter of the Bible enters into a dialogue with a book that is itself an exegetical dialogue – a complex and highly cohesive interpretive web in which the meaning of earlier texts is discerned in the later texts, and in which later texts can only be understood in relation to ones that came earlier.

In order to read the texts as they are written, the exegete needs to acknowledge the authors' of the Bible deep-seated belief in both the divine economy and in the typological expression of that economy. From our liturgical reading, we see that three moments in the economy of salvation stand out as having decisive typological significance for the entire canonical text – creation, the exodus, and the Davidic kingdom. These in turn should have special significance for the exegete.

We must remain mindful that the foundation of all authentic biblical typology is the historical and literary sense of the text. Typology is not an arbitrary eisegesis. For the biblical authors, God uses historical events, persons, and places as material and temporal symbols or signs of future events and divine realities. The prophets can speak of a 'new exodus' only because they presuppose the historical importance of the original exodus. The exegete likewise must see the literal and historical sense as fundamental to his or her approach to Scripture.

Mystagogy: Living the Scripture's mysteries

The final hermeneutical imperative that emerges from our liturgical reading is *mystagogy*. Mystagogy recognizes that the same typological patterns by which

---

[70] See most recently, Dawson, *Figural Reading*; Seitz, *Figured Out*.
[71] Fishbane, *Biblical Interpretation*; Daniélou, *The Bible and the Liturgy*, 5.

the divine economy is comprehended in Scripture continue in the church's sacramental liturgy. As we noted at the start of this paper, the canon was a liturgical enactment – the Scriptures come to us as the authoritative texts to be used in Christian teaching and worship. But as it was written and passed on to us, Scripture has more than an instructional or exhortative function. When proclaimed in the church's liturgy, Scripture is intended to 'actualize' what is proclaimed – to bring the believer into living contact with the *mirabilia Dei*, the mighty saving works of God in the Old and New Testament.[72]

Mystagogy focuses our attention on the deep connection between the written 'Word of God' – the Scripture itself – and the creative Word of God described in the pages of the Old and New Testaments. From the first pages to the last, we see expressed the biblical authors' faith that God's Word is living and active and possesses the power to bring into being what it commands. The church's traditional understanding of the sacramental liturgy is built on this belief in the performative power of the Word of God as a 'divine speech act.'[73]

Proclaimed sacramentally and accompanied by the ritual washing of water, the Word brings the Spirit upon people, making them sons and daughters of God through a real sharing in his life, death and resurrection (Rom. 6:3; Gal. 4:6; 1 Pet. 1:23). Proclaimed as commanded in the Eucharistic liturgy, the word brings about true participation in the one body and blood of Christ (1 Cor. 10:16–17). The Word in the sacramental liturgy continues the work of the Word in Scripture. This pattern, too, is shown originating in the pages of Scripture. The interpretation of Scripture is ordered to the celebration of baptism (Acts 8:29–38) and the Eucharist (Lk. 24:27–31). The New Testament also gives us numerous passages in which the sacraments are explained 'typologically', that is, according to events and figures in the Old Testament (1 Cor. 10; 1 Pet. 3:20–21). This paschal catechesis is at the heart of what early church writers called *mystagogy*.[74]

At a minimum, then, our interpretations of Scripture must respect the mystagogic content of the New Testament. In this exegetes will do well to recall that the sacramental liturgy afforded the first interpretive framework for the Scriptures. But on a deeper level, the exegete must appreciate the *mystagogic intent* of the Bible. The exegete must always be conscious that the Word he or

---

[72] Pontifical Biblical Commission: 'In principle, the liturgy, and especially the sacramental liturgy, the high point of which is the eucharistic celebration, brings about the most perfect actualization of the biblical texts, for the liturgy places the proclamation in the midst of the community of believers, gathered around Christ so as to draw near to God ... *Written text thus becomes living word*' (*Interpretation of the Bible in the Church*, IV, c, 1. Emphasis supplied).

[73] Ward, *Word and Supplement*; Vanhoozer, 'Speech Acts'.

[74] Mazza, *Mystagogy*.

she interprets is written and preserved for the purpose of leading believers to the sacramental liturgy where they are brought into a covenant relationship with God.[75]

Towards a liturgical hermeneutic

I believe that, as a natural outgrowth of the past century's rediscovery of Scripture's liturgical sense, we are prepared for the development of a new, *liturgical hermeneutic*. As I have tried to sketch in this paper, this new hermeneutic is at once literary and historical, liturgical and sacramental. It will be capable of integrating the contributions of historical and literary research while at the same time respecting the traditional meanings given to the Bible by the believing community in which the Bible continues to serve as the source and wellspring of faith and worship. A liturgical hermeneutic will recognize the liturgical content and 'mission' of the Bible – its mystagogic purpose in bringing about, through the sacramental liturgy, the communion of believers with the God who has chosen to reveal himself in Scripture. It is, then, a hermeneutic that grasps the profound union of the divine Word incarnate in Christ, inspired in Scripture, and proclaimed in the church's sacramental liturgy.

Much work remains to be done. But, I believe this understanding of Scripture has great potential to renew the study of the Bible from the heart of the church. Reading Scripture liturgically, we will find no tension between letter and spirit, between the literary and historical analysis of Scripture and the faithful contemplation of its religious and spiritual meaning.

---

[75] Daniélou, 'Sacraments', 28, 31. See also DiNoia and Mulcahy, 'Authority'.

Bibliography

Allison, D.C., Jr., *The New Moses: A Matthean Typology* (Minneapolis: Augsburg Fortress Press, 1993)

Anderson, G.A., 'The Praise of God as a Cultic Event', in *Priesthood and Cult in Ancient Israel* (JSOTSup 125; ed. G.A. Anderson and S.M. Olyan; Sheffield: Sheffield Academic Press, 1991), 15–33

—, *The Genesis of Perfection: Adam and Eve in Jewish and Christian Imagination* (Louisville: Westminster John Knox Press, 2001)

Aune, D., 'The Apocalypse of John and the Problem of Genre', *Semeia* 36 (1986), 65–96

Balentine, S., *The Torah's Vision of Worship* (Minneapolis: Fortress Press, 1999)

Barr, J., *The Garden of Eden and the Hope of Immortality* (Minneapolis: Augusburg Fortress Press, 1992)

Bartholomew, C.G., and M.W. Goheen, *The Drama of Scripture: Finding Our Place in the Biblical Story* (Grand Rapids: Baker Academic, 2004)

Beale, G.K., *The Temple and the Church's Mission: A Biblical Theology of the Dwelling Place of God* (Downers Grove: InterVarsity Press, 2004)

Begg, C., 'The Peoples and the Worship of Yahweh in the Book of Isaiah', *Worship and the Hebrew Bible: Essays in Honour of John T. Willis* (JSOTSup 284; ed. M.P. Graham, R.R. Marrs, and S.L. McKenzie; Sheffield: Sheffield Academic Press, 1999), 35–55

—, 'The Ark in Chronicles', in *The Chronicler as Theologian: Essays in Honor of Ralph W. Klein* (JSOTSup 371; ed. M.P. Graham, S.L. McKenzie and G.N. Knoppers; London: T&T Clark, 2003), 133–45

Brown, R.E., 'The Johannine Sacramentary', in *New Testament Essays* (Ramsey, NJ: Paulist Press, 1965), 51–76

Bruce, F.F., *The Canon of Scripture* (Downers Grove: InterVarsity Press, 1988)

Callender, D.E., Jr., *Adam in Myth and History: Ancient Israelite Perspectives on the Primal Human* (Harvard Semitic Studies 48; Winona Lake: Eisenbrauns, 2000)

Childs, B.S., 'The Canon in Recent Biblical Studies: Reflections on an Era', *ProEccl* 14 (2005), 26–45; reproduced in this volume

Clements, R.E., 'A Light to the Nations: A Central Theme of the Book of Isaiah', in *Forming Prophetic Literature: Essays on Isaiah and the Twelve in Honor of John D.W. Watts* (JSOTSup 235; ed. J.W. Watts and P.R. House; Sheffield: Sheffield Academic Press, 1996), 58–69

Congar, Y., *The Mystery of the Temple: The Manner of God's Presence to His Creatures from Genesis to the Apocalypse* (Westminster, MD: Newman Press, 1962)

—, *The Meaning of Tradition* (New York: Hawthorn Books, 1964)

—, *Tradition and Traditions: An Historical and a Theological Essay* (London: Burns and Oats, 1966)

Corbon, J., *The Wellspring of Worship* (trans. M.J. O'Connell; Mahwah, NJ: Paulist Press, 1988)

Corriveau, R., *The Liturgy of Life: A Study in the Thought of St. Paul in His Letters to the Early Christian Communities* (Studia Travaux de Recherche 25; Brusells: Desclée De Brouwer, 1970)

Cross, F.M., 'Kinship and Covenant in Ancient Israel', in *From Epic to Canon: History and Literature in Ancient Israel* (Baltimore: Johns Hopkins University Press, 1998), 3–21

Cullmann, O., *Early Christian Worship* (trans. A.S. Todd and J.B. Torrance; London: SCM Press, 1953)

Daniélou, J., *The Bible and the Liturgy* (Notre Dame, IN: University of Notre Dame Press, 1956)

—, 'The Sacraments and the History of Salvation', in *Liturgy and the Word of God* (papers given at the Third National Congress of the Centre de Pastorale Liturgique; Collegeville: Liturgical Press, 1959), 21–32

Dalmais, I.H., *Introduction to the Liturgy* (trans. R. Capel; Baltimore: Helicon, 1961)

Daube, D., 'The Earliest Structure of the Gospels', *NTS* 5 (1958), 174–87

Dawson, J.D., *Christian Figural Reading and the Fashioning of Identity* (Berkeley: University of California Press, 2002)

De Lubac, H., *Medieval Exegesis* (2 vols.; trans. E.M. Macierowski; Grand Rapids: Eerdmans, 2000)

DiNoia, J.A., and B. Mulcahy, 'The Authority of Scripture in Sacramental Theology: Some Methodological Observations', *ProEccl* 10 (2001), 329–45

Dumbrell, W.J., *The End of the Beginning: Revelation 21–22 and the Old Testament* (Grand Rapids: Baker, 1985)

Faley, R.J., *Bonding with God: A Reflective Study of Biblical Covenant* (New York: Paulist Press, 1997)

Ferguson, E., 'Factors Leading to the Selection and Closure of the New Testament Canon', in *The Canon Debate* (ed. L.M. McDonald and J.A. Sanders; Peabody, MA: Hendrickson, 2002)

Fishbane, M., *Biblical Interpretation in Ancient Israel* (Oxford: Oxford University Press, 1985)

Fitzmyer, J.A., *The Gospel According to Luke*, Vol. 1 (AB; 2 vols.; New York: Doubleday, 1981)

Fletcher-Louis, C.H.T., *All the Glory of Adam: Liturgical Anthropology in the Dead Sea Scrolls* (Studies on the Texts of the Desert of Judah 42; Leiden: Brill, 2002)

—, 'Jesus and the High Priest', paper delivered to British New Testament Society Conference (2003); published at: http://www.marquette.edu/maqom/jesus

Gese, H., *Essays on Biblical Theology* (Minneapolis: Augsburg, 1981)

Gloer, W.H., 'Worship God! Liturgical Elements in the Apocalypse', *RevExp* 98 (Winter 2001), 35–57

Goulder, M.D., *The Evangelists' Calendar: A Lectionary Explanation of the Development of Scripture* (London: SPCK, 1978)

Green, J.B., *The Gospel of Luke* (Grand Rapids: Eerdmans, 1997)

Gunkel, H., *An Introduction to the Psalms* (Macon, GA: Mercer University Press, 1988)

Hahn, S.W., 'Kinship by Covenant: A Biblical Theological Study of Covenant Types and Texts in the Old and New Testaments' (Ph.D. diss., Marquette University, 1995)

—, 'Covenant in the Old and New Testaments: Some Current Research (1994–2004)', *CBR* 3 (2005), 263–92

—, 'Kingdom and Church: From Davidic Christology to Kingdom Ecclesiology in Luke-Acts', in *Reading Luke* (SHS 6; ed. C. Bartholomew et al.; Milton Keynes: Paternoster; and Grand Rapids: Zondervan, 2005), 294–321

—, *Letter and Spirit: From Written Text to Living Word in the Liturgy* (New York: Doubleday, 2005)

Haran, M., 'The *Berît* "Covenant": Its Nature and Ceremonial Background', in *Tehillah le-Moshe: Biblical and Judaic Studies in Honor of Moshe Greenberg* (ed. M. Gogan, B.L. Eichler and J.H. Tigay; Winona Lake: Eisenbrauns, 1997), 203–19

Hengel, M., 'Hymns and Christology', in *Studia Biblica 1978* (JSOTSup 3; ed. E.A. Livingstone; Sheffield: Sheffield Academic Press, 1980), 173–97

Pope John Paul II, *Dies Domini*, Apostolic Letter on Keeping the Lord's Day Holy (July 5, 1998)

Keesmaat, S.C., *Paul and His Story: (Re)-interpreting the Exodus Tradition* (JSNTSup 181; Sheffield: Sheffield Academic Press, 1999)

Kline, M.G., *By Oath Consigned: A Reinterpretation of the Covenant Signs of Circumcision and Baptism* (Grand Rapids: Eerdmans, 1968)

—, 'The Correlation of the Concepts of Canon and Covenant', in *New Perspectives on the Old Testament* (ed. J. Barton Payne; Waco, TX: Word, 1970), 265–79

Kruse, H., 'David's Covenant', *VT* 35(1985), 139–64

Kuntz, J.K., 'Grounds for Praise: The Nature and Function of the Motive Clause in the Hymns of the Hebrew Psalter', in *Worship and the Hebrew Bible: Essays in Honour of John T. Willis* (JSOTSup 284; ed. M.P. Graham, R.R. Marrs and S.L. McKenzie; Sheffield: Sheffield Academic Press, 1999), 149–83

Lane, W.L., *Hebrews 1–8* (WBC 47a; Nashville: Thomas Nelson, 1991)

Leonard, R.C., 'The Origin of Canonicity in the Old Testament' (Ph.D. diss., Boston University, 1972)

Levenson, J.D., 'The Davidic Covenant and its Modern Interpreters', *CBQ* 41 (1979), 205–19

—, *Sinai and Zion: An Entry into the Jewish Bible* (Minneapolis: Winston Press, 1985)

—, 'The Temple and the World', *JR* 64 (1984), 275–98

Louis, C.J., *The Theology of Psalm 8: A Study of the Traditions of the Text and the Theological Import* (Washington, DC: Catholic University of America Press, 1946)

Maly, E.H., 'Israel – God's Liturgical People', in *Liturgy for the People: Essays in Honor of Gerhard Ellard, S.J., 1894–1963* (Milwaukee: Bruce Publishing, 1963), 10–20

McCarthy, D.J., *Institution and Narrative: Collected Essays* (Analectica Biblica 108; Rome: Biblical Institute Press, 1985)

McDonald, L.M., *The Formation of the Christian Biblical Canon* (rev. edn.; Peabody, MA: Hendrickson, 1995)

—, and J.A. Sanders (eds.), *The Canon Debate* (Peabody, MA: Hendrickson, 2002)

McGowan, A.B., '"Is There a Liturgical Text in This Gospel?" The Institution Narratives and their Early Interpretive Communities', *JBL* 118 (1999), 73–87

Martin, R.P., *Carmen Christi: Philippians 2:5–11 in Recent Interpretations and in the Setting of Early Christian Worship* (SBLMS 4; Cambridge: Cambridge University Press, 1967; reprint Grand Rapids: Eerdmans, 1983)

Mathewson, D., *A New Heaven and a New Earth: The Meaning and Function of the Old Testament in Revelation 21:1–22:5* (JSNTSup 238; Sheffield: Sheffield Academic Press, 2003)

Mazza, E., *Mystagogy: A Theology of Liturgy in the Patristic Age* (New York: Pueblo, 1989)

Moule, C.F.D., *The Birth of the New Testament* (3rd edn.; San Francisco, Harper & Row, 1981)

Moyise, S., *The Old Testament in the New* (New York: Continuum, 2001)

Murray, R., *The Cosmic Covenant* (London: Sheed & Ward, 1992), 2–13

Oberholzer, J., 'What is Man …?', in *De Fructu Oris Sui: Essays in Honour of Adrianus van Selms* (ed. I.H. Eybers, F.C. Fensham and C.J. Labuschagne; Leiden: Brill, 1971), 141–51

Old, H.O., *The Reading and Preaching of the Scriptures in the Christian Church* (5 vols.; Grand Rapids: Eerdmans, 1997)

Östborn, G., *Cult and Canon: A Study in the Canonization of the Old Testament* (Uppsala Universitets Årsskrift 1950:10; Uppsala: A.-B. Lundequistska Bokhandeln, 1950)

Pao, D.W., *Acts and the Isaianic New Exodus* (Grand Rapids: Baker Academic, 2000)

Pagolu, Augustine, *The Religion of the Patriarchs* (JSOTSup 277; Sheffield: Sheffield Academic Press, 1998)

Pontifical Biblical Commission, *Interpretation of the Bible in the Church* (Vatican City: Libreria Editrice Vaticana, 1993)

Ratzinger, J., *Behold the Pierced One: An Approach to Spiritual Christology* (San Francisco: Ignatius, 1986)

—, *The Feast of Faith: Approaches to a Theology of Liturgy* (trans. G. Harrison; San Francisco: Ignatius, 1986)

—, 'The New Covenant: On the Theology of the Covenant in the New Testament', in *Many Religions – One Covenant* (San Francisco: Ignatius Press, 1999), 47–77

—, *The Spirit of the Liturgy* (trans. J. Saward; San Francisco: Ignatius Press, 2000)

Rendtorff, R., 'Canonical Interpretation: A New Approach to Biblical Texts', *ProEccl* 3 (1994), 141–51

Rodriguez, A.M., 'Sanctuary Theology in Exodus', *AUSS* 24 (1986), 127–45

Sanders, J.A., *From Sacred Story to Sacred Text* (Philadelphia: Fortress, 1987)

Scholer, J.M., *Proleptic Priests: Priesthood in the Epistle to the Hebrews* (JSNTSup 49; Sheffield: Sheffield Academic Press, 1991)

Segal, A., *Rebecca's Children: Judaism and Christianity in the Roman World* (Cambridge, MA: Harvard University Press, 1986)

Seitz, C.R., *Figured Out: Typology and Providence in Christian Scripture* (Louisville: Westminster John Knox Press, 2001)

Strauss, M.L., *The Davidic Messiah in Luke-Acts: The Promise and its Fulfillment in Lukan Christology* (JSNTSup 110; Sheffield: Sheffield Academic Press, 1995)

Swartley, W.M., *Israel's Scripture Traditions and the Synoptic Gospels: Story Shaping Story* (Peabody, MA: Hendrickson, 1994)

Towner, S., 'Interpretations and Reinterpretations of the Fall', in *Modern Biblical Scholarship: Its Impact on Theology and Proclamation* (ed. F. Eigo; Villanova, PA: Villanova University, 1984), 53–85

Vagaggini, C., *Theological Dimensions of the Liturgy: A General Treatise on the Theology of the Liturgy* (trans. L.J. Doyle and W.A. Jurgens; Collegeville, MN: Liturgical Press, 1976)

Vanhoozer, K.J., *First Theology: God, Scripture and Hermeneutics* (Downers Grove, IL: InterVarsity Press, 2002)

—, 'From Speech Acts to Scripture Acts: The Covenant of Discourse and the Discourse of the Covenant', in *After Pentecost: Language and Biblical Interpretation* (SHS 2; ed. Craig Bartholomew et. al.; Carlisle: Paternoster; and Grand Rapids, MI: Zondervan, 2001), 1–49

Vanhoye, A., *Old Testament Priests and the New Priest According to the New Testament* (Petersham, MA: St. Bede's Publications, 1986)

Vanni, U., 'Liturgical Dialogue as a Literary Form in the Book of Revelation', *NTS* 37 (1991), 348–72

Van Olst, E.H., *The Bible and Liturgy* (Grand Rapids: Eerdmans, 1991)

de Vaux, R., *Ancient Israel: Its Life and Institutions* (2 vols.; New York: McGraw-Hill Co., 1961)

Ward, T., *Word and Supplement: Speech Acts, Biblical Texts and the Sufficiency of Scripture* (New York: Oxford University Press, 2002)

Watts, R.E., *Isaiah's New Exodus in Mark* (Grand Rapids: Baker, 2000)

Weiser, A., *The Old Testament: Its Formation and Development* (Göttingen: Vandenhoeck & Ruprecht, 1957)

Wells, J.B., *God's Holy People: A Theme in Biblical Theology* (JSOTSup 305; Sheffield: Sheffield Academic Press, 2000)

Wright, N.T., *The New Testament and the People of God* (Christian Origins and the Question of God, Vol. 1; Minneapolis: Fortress Press, 1992)

8

Towards Transformational Reading of Scripture

Jean Vanier and Frances Young

To love people as Jesus loves them
    is to wash their feet, to serve them in humility;
    it is to help·them rise up in truth and love.
Here Jesus is revealing something more:
    to love is to lay down one's life for others,
    to place their interests before our own.
It is to give them life.
That can mean accepting difficulties, danger and even death
    so that they may live and grow in love.
To love is to live in communion with others,
    to transmit to them the life and love of Jesus.
It is to reveal to them that they are loved,
    loved by Jesus.
In this way we become their friend
    because we are a friend of Jesus.

So writes Jean Vanier in his book, *Drawn into the Mystery of Jesus through the Gospel of John*.[1] The extract alerts us to the difference between this and those commentaries which are generally recognised as scholarly. Interpretation is not an end in itself but its aim is to draw us closer to Jesus. So we have a meditation that fits no ordinary categories, written in a kind of poetic prose that draws us into the text. As the Gospel of John becomes transparent, we look through it to Jesus, and are invited to let Jesus transform us. We may not learn anything specifically new about John's Gospel (as one reviewer commented[2]); rather we are called into a process of growth in relationship with Jesus, from discipleship to friendship. It is a way of reading which is not shy of allowing the context and circumstances of the reader to illuminate the text, while expecting to be

---

[1] Vanier, *Drawn into the Mystery*, 274–75.
[2] Review in the *Methodist Recorder*.

transformed personally within those circumstances by listening to the Gospel. Some would call it *lectio divina.*[3]

The problem with this kind of interpretation is that the traditions of scholarship have left many with no means of engaging with it. It is easily dismissed as 'subjective', or as harking back to pre-critical devotional practices. But is this to pre-judge? What is offered in this chapter is Jean Vanier's own brief overview of his approach to John's Gospel (Part A), followed by a methodological reflection by Frances Young, which teases out what is happening in the process, and shows how this kind of interpretative depth relates to the work of scholars. The overview scarcely does justice to what Jean Vanier is able to offer in the book, and the reader is urged to ponder the book as a whole, not only in order to pursue the methodological questions further, but also to experience the transformation made possible by allowing the heart[4] to be touched.

The Gospel of John and Life in the Community of l'Arche
Jean Vanier

L'Arche

Before explaining how I approach the Gospel of John, I need to say something about what we are living in the communities of l'Arche, which now number 130 around the world.

We are communities where people with disabilities and people who have chosen to be with them, share our lives together in a spirit of communion and friendship.

At the heart of our communities there is pain, weakness and vulnerable bodies, hurt through sickness or some form of malformation but also through all the forms of rejection and even contempt that people with disabilities are so often subjected to.

Our communities seek to be places of healing and growth for all. Wounded hearts, which bring anguish, loneliness and feelings of guilt or shame ('if I am not wanted or appreciated it is because I am no good'), are gradually brought to healing through relationships. People with disabilities discover meaning to their lives and can develop their human and spiritual potential as they discover that they are loved, seen as unique and valuable.

Eric was born blind, deaf and with severe autism. When we first met him he was in the local psychiatric hospital where he had been placed at the age of four.

---

[3] See further below.

[4] Biblical scholars will remember that in the ancient world the heart was the seat of the mind, not just the feelings!

He was unable to walk or eat by himself. I do not think I had ever met anyone so filled with anguish and a desire to die. Living in l'Arche he discovered he was loved and thus he was someone. He became more peaceful and learned to eat by himself and gradually to walk. His life was transformed little by little.

Our communities are places of transformation also for those who come to share their lives with them.

Ethel came to our community when she was thirty. She had decided as an adolescent to put all her energies into succeeding in school and at work; her parents had always lived in conflict and so she saw relationships as something painful and dangerous. She built solid barriers around her heart and wore a mask to protect herself. These masks gradually caused a certain feeling of discomfort and dis-ease. It was really by chance that she 'fell' into a community of l'Arche and discovered a love that was liberating and healing, that allowed her to grow and be herself.

A community is not just a group of people who come together through and for a common goal. People in community are bonded to one another in mutual respect, trust and affection. Our communities are like 'schools of transformation' where we learn to forgive, to accept each other as we are and to free each other in order to be more truly ourselves. Assistants – as we call them – do not come just to be generous and competent and to do good things *for* people with disabilities; they come to live and grow in communion with them. In l'Arche generosity is called to lead to an encounter in friendship. We are all called to meet the other in his or her person which is often hidden behind a very visible handicap or one's incapacity to accept others as they are, or behind other forms of handicap which may be less visible such as one's need for power.

Some assistants come for a short period of time – a few months. During that time, many live an experience of transformation as they begin to meet people as persons and discover their own inner person. But l'Arche can only continue to exist if some assistants stay and make their home in the community and create covenant relationships with people with disabilities.

It is clear that l'Arche is counter-cultural. For many people in our rich societies, where one has to compete and be successful, to live with people who are weak and limited is foolish, even absurd. They are unable to accept the person behind the weakness. Yet the gospel message reveals that it is the so-called foolish and weak that God has chosen (1 Cor.). It is those that society excludes who come to the wedding feast (Mt. 22; Lk. 14). They have a special place in the heart of God. In all their weakness they can lead us to Jesus.

The Gospel of John

The Gospel of John has helped me to give meaning to the 'foolishness' of our lives. We need a spirituality, a spirit, priorities, a motivation and nourishment in order to live every day what appears to many as meaningless. We need also an anthropology and a theology which put words on what we are living. It is never easy to be constantly close to people who are weak and in pain, whose limits and handicaps are irremediable and to be with them as friends. Assistants in l'Arche soon discover their own limits, vulnerability and weaknesses, the places of violence, of fear and of anguish within themselves. The Word of God in John allows them and helps them to enter the places of darkness and anguish within themselves so that they may enter into transformation. Maybe it is not possible to really enter into the full meaning of the Word of God without living anguish and yearning for transformation through the Spirit of God.

What does John tell us in his Gospel?

He tells us about the Word of God, who is God, who became flesh, became one of us; he pitched his tent amongst us, to enter into a relationship of trust with people. He came to seek people out, to meet them personally, to enter into a dialogue of communion with them and to liberate them from fear. It is through these personal encounters that people began to open their hearts and minds to Jesus and were transformed. Some people, however, refused to trust Jesus and rejected him in spite of the signs he accomplished. Many in our societies today reject people with disabilities, unable to see the person and his or her value underneath the handicap.

Let us go through the Gospel and see how Jesus meets and transforms people.

The first significant meeting in this Gospel is with two disciples of John the Baptist who leave him in order to follow Jesus whom John had announced as the 'Lamb of God, who takes away the sin of the world' (Jn. 1). Jesus turns around and asks them: 'What are you looking for?' They answer: 'Teacher, where do you live?' to which Jesus responds: 'Come and see.' So they went and saw and stayed with Jesus. After this first meeting with Jesus, Andrew, one of the two disciples goes to find his brother Simon and tells him: 'We have found the Messiah.' The two disciples no longer see Jesus as a teacher but as the Christ, the Anointed One. They then want to remain with him, follow him, learn from him and be transformed by him.

Their journey in trust and faith begins. Jesus leads the two men, and the three others who have also begun to follow him, to a wedding feast in Cana. The wedding feast is a sign of the wedding feast of love that Jesus is leading all of his disciples to – a union of love with God. We human beings are made for love, a love that flows from God, a love that transforms us and liberates us from all forms of violence and self-centredness.

Jesus' first mission is in Samaria. Tired, he sits down near the well of Jacob, meets a Samaritan woman who has come to draw water. She is a woman who must be in a lot of inner pain for she has lived five broken relationships. It is never easy to feel rejected, not loved, pushed aside. Her heart is probably filled with guilt and a feeling of worthlessness. Jesus enters into conversation with her humbly asking her for some water to drink. He needs her. She is astonished, perplexed: how can a Jew speak to a Samaritan woman and ask for some water? Jews never spoke to Samaritans, let alone a Jewish *man* to a Samaritan *woman*! Jesus enters into a dialogue with her. She asks questions. Jesus answers, revealing little by little who he is. She begins to trust him and to realise that he must be a prophet. Then Jesus reveals to her that he is the Messiah, the one who reveals all things. She is deeply moved and runs off to tell people in the village that she has met a man who may be the Messiah. The love, humility and goodness of Jesus have opened her heart.

In John 9, we see a blind beggar who is healed by Jesus. That is all he knows for certain: he was blind and now he can see. So for him Jesus must be a man sent by God. The religious authorities on the other hand are living in an ideology; they are unable to see and accept reality. They excommunicate the healed beggar. He meets Jesus again and kneels down and worships him and proclaims his trust and faith in Jesus.

The eleventh chapter reveals for the first time Jesus not only teaching people but loving three people who form a little family in Bethany: Lazarus, Martha and Mary. There is clearly a deep intimacy between Jesus and this little family. Who is Lazarus? A man who never speaks. Luke's Gospel refers to the house in which they were living as 'Martha's house': two unmarried sisters – strange for the Jewish society. Could Lazarus, called by his sisters 'The one you love', be a man with severe disabilities? It seems quite possible.

'*Menein*', translated as 'remain' or 'dwell' or 'abide', is an important word in John's Gospel. It is used thirty-five times, not just to designate remaining in a particular place, but above all to designate friendship. Jesus tells his disciples: 'I no longer call you servants but I call you friends.' To be a friend is to dwell in the heart of another. 'Remain in my love' is to remain in Jesus. If we remain in Jesus, we will bear much fruit and give glory to God. The temple is God's dwelling place or home on this earth; we, his disciples, are called to become the dwelling place or home of God: 'The person who loves me, will keep my words and my Father will love this person and we will come and dwell in this person.' So it is that when we eat his body and drink his blood, Jesus dwells in us and we in him (Jn. 6).

L'Arche is a place of friendship and of a communion of hearts, where we live covenant relationships together. It is not just about doing things *for* people with disabilities but to be with them, to create a home with them. As we do this, we give meaning to their lives; we transform them but they also transform us.

A business man I know, who was used to doing 'important' things, wrote to me recently. His wife had developed Alzheimer's disease. He decided not to put her in an institution but to continue to live with her, to 'remain' with her.

He now bathes her and cares for her tenderly. He told me that his life had been completely changed. 'I have become more human.' As we care for people who are weak or in need, as we look after their bodily needs, we too in l'Arche discover that we are becoming more human. The Gospel of John gives us a spirituality that helps us to become more human.

Transformation from being a success in a society of competition to covenant and interpersonal relationships takes time. John's Gospel is a Gospel of transformation over time. It does not just reveal moments and events in the life of Jesus, but the journey that disciples of Jesus must make in order to become themselves as they grow in friendship with him. We need to move from seeing Jesus as a charismatic leader who does great things (signs), not only to becoming his disciples but his friends. This growth in friendship implies a growth in trust and in faith. We must gradually live as Jesus lived, love as he loved and accept to become little and humble as Jesus was. This will imply many inner deaths. We have to let go of our psychological compulsions for success and power, even spiritual success and power, in order to live the very life of God which John calls 'eternal life' (Jn. 12). This life is his union with the Father. We are called to gradually become one with Jesus as he is one with the Father. The Gospel of John leads us to become men and women of contemplation – to be in communion with Jesus, to dwell in his love in order to dwell in the presence of the Father. 'I have made known your name to them, and I make it known to them so that the love with which you love me, may be in them and I in them' (Jn. 17:26).

John's Gospel reveals to us how our God of power came to reveal the foolishness and littleness of God as he seeks to live a communion of hearts with each one of us. We may admire and even fear people who have power, but we love those who show their littleness and even their need of us. At the end of this Gospel we see Jesus kneeling down humbly at the feet of each one of his disciples, to wash their feet, in order to help them find trust in themselves, to raise them up and discover their mission which is to continue the mission of the love of Jesus. We, too, in l'Arche are called to lower ourselves and wash the feet of people with disabilities, to help them to rise up in greater self-confidence and thus discover their mission in life. We are called to follow a path of littleness and vulnerability, and so discover our real self. Power frequently leads to loneliness whereas a humble life of service brings us to togetherness and unity. Our experience in l'Arche of the transformation of assistants and of people with disabilities helps us to understand the transformation Jesus offers us, just as the Word of God in John's Gospel sheds light on our own experience of transformation. Experience and the Word of God come together to enlighten each other and to enlighten our shared life in community.

Our experience with people who have been rejected and have a broken self-image helps us to understand this Samaritan woman. In order to rise up and find trust in themselves, people who suffer rejection need to meet someone who sees them as valuable.

At the beginning of this Gospel (Jn. 3), Jesus reveals to Nicodemus that in order to enter into the kingdom of God we must be born from on high, we need to be reborn of water and the Spirit. At the end (Jn. 14 – 15), Jesus reveals that he and the Father will send us the 'Paraclete', the Spirit of truth, who will be with us and transform us and lead us into the fullness of truth. To live our lives in l'Arche, to live this friendship with people with disabilities, we need to be reborn from on high, to receive the Paraclete, the Spirit of truth. L'Arche is a school of love, sometimes painful, where our own inner poverty and brokenness is revealed. In this school we also discover our own beauty, our capacity to love and give life to others and receive life from them. Our communities are called to be a little sign of the presence of God in our broken world today.

Methodological Reflection on Jean on John
Frances Young

The l'Arche communities have been paralleled with early Christian monasticism, when people went into the desert, not just to face their own demons, but to meet God.[5] Jean Vanier's approach to the Gospel of John provides evidence of another possible parallel: the monastic tradition produced *lectio divina*, a reading of Scripture oriented towards the growth of the person towards Christlikeness.[6] Two questions arise: (1) how does Jean Vanier's treatment relate to other commentaries? And (2) how is such a reading of Scripture to be given hermeneutical underpinning in the contemporary context?

Jean Vanier's work within the spectrum of biblical commentary

It is not as easy as one might imagine to define the commentary *genre*. Its origin lies in the marginal notes and reminders (*scholia*) of the Graeco-Roman world, and these simply reflect the oral activity of reading and commenting on the classics in the rhetorical schools.[7] In other words, commentary by its very

---

[5] Moubarac, 'Alongside L'Arche', 89–93.

[6] The recovery of *lectio divina* for all believers is the aim of the Catholic Biblical Federation; it involves the kind of contemplation that enables insight into the human situation which is being experienced, as well as the sacred text – the so-called 'base-communities' known through Latin-American liberation theology demonstrate a socio-political variant of this tradition.

[7] See further my articles, 'The Rhetorical Schools' and 'Interpretative Genres'; also my discussion in *Biblical Exegesis*.

nature is piecemeal and problem-oriented, except that paraphrase and summary was also encouraged in schools, in order to identify the subject-matter
(*heuresis* or *inventio*) and observe the way an appropriate style was adopted to
express it. These elements are evident in patristic and modern commentary
alike.

In an article entitled 'What did the term *Commentarius* mean to sixteenth-
century theologians?' Kenneth Hagan[8] concludes that it is a difficult question:
there was no clear understanding of what constituted a commentary over
against annotations, expositions, paraphrases and so forth, and 'a variety of
commentary forms existed from the beginning of Christianity to today.' Some
light may be thrown by exploring medieval, and indeed earlier, work: Hagan
notes that Theodore of Mopsuestia distinguished between the task of the exegete and that of the preacher, the former being to explain words that most
people find difficult, and the latter to reflect on words that are perfectly clear
and speak about them; while Jerome thought commentary involved discussion
of the interpretation of other exegetes and the clarification of difficult texts.
Hagan's finding is, however, that this term and others are used for a variety of
different kinds of exegetical enterprises which, whether in the form of notes
and comments or paraphrases, he designates: *sacra pagina*, *sacra doctrina* and *sacra
littera*.

Roughly speaking *sacra pagina* and *lectio divina* overlap, and it is in this category that Jean Vanier's work must surely belong: Scripture is seen as 'directly
from God, about God, and for the pilgrim's journey to God' – in other words,
the aim of commentary is to serve the divine purpose of bringing home the lost.
Scholasticism, however, focussed on *sacra doctrina*, on faith seeking understanding, posing dialectical questions concerning doctrine as Scripture was perused;
while the rise of humanistic approaches, with Erasmus, led to preoccupation
with the Scripture as literature (*sacra littera*) educating human beings for piety,
morality and justice. In one way or another all three had precursors in the
patristic period.[9]

The legacy of the last is found in the modern 'historico-critical' commentary, concerned with philological and historical problems raised by the text, but
also with paraphrastic summaries which clarify the sequence of thought or the
logic of the argument. Embracing analysis of a text's integrity and reconstructing original intention and meaning, the commentary now endeavours to
bridge the perceived 'gap' between the world of the text and that of the reader
through explications of various kinds. So,

> the commentary embraces a multitude of tasks and works at a multitude of levels,
> from straight bits of useful fact, such as identifying a quotation, to vast hypothetical

---

[8] In Irena Backus and Francis Higman, *Théorie et pratique de l'exégèse*, 16.
[9] Young, *Biblical Exegesis*.

constructions purporting to provide background context, religious ideas, authorial intentions or structural patterns that explain the text. This variety of tasks and levels explains the oddity of the genre.[10]

Some of the philological and historical material found in such a commentary has influenced and informed Jean Vanier's interpretation, but it does not dwell on problems presented by the text as a scholarly commentary would. Rather it ponders the significance of the text for the believer's pilgrimage towards God, responding to the friendship of Jesus so as to discern the divine presence in human relationships. Thus it treats Scripture as *sacra pagina*, in a way largely ignored in the modern scholarly commentary.

Jean Vanier's work in relation to contemporary hermeneutical theory

In the latter part of the twentieth century scholarly interpretation of Scripture largely remained in its historico-critical phase, but some of the fundamentals of this method were also challenged.[11] In the 'modern' period it was assumed that you could distinguish between 'exegesis' and 'eisegesis', the latter being 'subjective' and importing meanings into the text, the former 'objective' and extracting meaning from the text. Now the possibility of such objectivity[12] began to be questioned, given the impossibility of divesting the investigator of all presuppositions,[13] and so was the value of an exclusively 'archaeological' approach to meaning, distancing the reader from the text.

Meanwhile, across the whole field of literary studies, critical theory changed the approach to texts, and this began to affect biblical interpretation in some quarters. Structuralism shifted the focus away from the original 'authorial intention' – from the 'romantic' idea that ideally a reader 'thinks the author's thoughts after him';[14] Roland Barthes wrote a famous essay entitled, 'The Death of the Author'.[15] Attention was given instead to analysis of the text itself: for texts could carry meaning, actually or potentially, that the author never intended, and over which, as Ricoeur had noted,[16] he or she had no control

---

[10] Young, 'Interpretative Genres', 101.

[11] I have discussed the question of interpretation in the light of late twentieth-century developments previously, often drawing on patristic exegesis to provide perspective, in *Meaning and Truth* and *The Art of Performance*; current trends are in the background of my more formally historical study, *Biblical Exegesis*.

[12] Davies, 'Subjectivity and Objectivity'.

[13] Stanton, 'Presuppositions'.

[14] Jowett, 'On the Interpretation of Scripture'.

[15] This, and many other seminal pieces of work, can be found reproduced, with introduction and comment, in Lodge, *Modern Criticism*.

[16] Ricoeur, *Interpretation Theory*; see also Thompson, *Paul Ricoeur*.

once the text was published. Structuralism, however, soon gave way to interest in the reader: for texts have no reality until 're-played' through reading, through someone making sense of the black and white patterns on the paper.[17] So the reader's contribution became paramount.[18] It was then noticed that traditions of reading are formed in 'reading communities',[19] that texts can acquire authority and 'create worlds' – so, for example, the Bible had reinforced social orders which included slavery and patriarchy. The future of the text, its potential to generate new meaning, became important for interpretation, not just its past, or its background.[20] Meanwhile, hermeneutics had been attending to questions concerning the gap between the world of ancient texts and the world of the reader.[21]

One way and another, therefore, the question how texts, particularly sacred texts, are to be read is more open now than it was 100 years ago.[22] Then it was generally assumed that arguments, especially between liberals and conservatives, were about the 'facts behind' the text, such as questions about miracles; while that has not exactly disappeared, now arguments are often about the 'future in front of' the texts, issues such as the position of women or the acceptance of persons who are gay. At one level the climate is more open to a plurality of readings,[23] or different 'reading genres'.[24] Yet this greater openness creates confusion, and also anxiety about the possibility of meaning and communication: 'Is there anything in what we say?' – the question posed by George Steiner in response to the relativism of postmodern literary theory.[25] Can we make texts mean anything we like, or are there ethical standards of reading?[26]

---

[17] Note the methods of 'deconstruction' developed by Jacques Derrida. See also 'Structure, Sign and Play'.

[18] See McKnight, *Postmodern Use of the Bible*.

[19] Notably Stanley Fish. See e.g. 'Interpreting the *Variorum*'.

[20] Notably through the influence of Paul Ricoeur, for whom a considerable bibliography might be compiled; additional to those in note, the following are recommended: Ricoeur, *Time and Narrative*; Valdes, *A Ricoeur Reader*.

[21] Thiselton, *Two Horizons*; and subsequent writings, including contributions to this Scripture and Hermeneutics Series. The relationship between hermeneutics and literary theory is addressed by Weinsheimer in *Philosophical Hermeneutics*.

[22] See Watson, *Open Text*.

[23] The development of liberationist, feminist, Asian, black and other readings is well known. See also my article, 'Interpretative genres'.

[24] A term used by Jeanrond, *Text and Interpretation*.

[25] Steiner, *Real Presences*.

[26] In addition to George Steiner, the question was raised by Booth, *The Company We Keep*. It has been taken up in Jeanrond, *Text and Interpretation*; and by myself in 'Pastoral Epistles'.

What I want to suggest is a model[27] of what goes on in the process of reading and interpreting which allows room for both scholarly research and *lectio divina*, taking seriously the dynamics of objectivity and subjectivity implicit in each. It derives from ancient rhetorical theory, but has some resemblance, I understand, to modern communication theory. It is superbly exemplified, I suggest, in the work of Jean Vanier on John's Gospel. We might call it a dynamic model of interpretation.

The object of rhetoric in the ancient world was to achieve persuasion or conviction (= πίστις (faith), usually translated 'faith' in a New Testament context!) Three things were required for this:

The ἔθος of the author/speaker. The author's character and lifestyle had to be such as to inspire trust in his integrity and authority – in other words, should carry conviction.

The λόγος. The argument, narrative, discourse of the speech/text had to be logical, reasonable, convincing.

The πάθος of the audience. If the readers/hearers were not swayed by the author and the argument – if there was no response, then the whole thing was ineffective and unconvincing.

The orator needed to make three different kinds of appeals, the ethical, the 'pathetic' and the logical, or, we could say, conviction depended on the dynamic interplay of author/orator, text/speech and reader/audience. Three elements were interacting, and as it happens they are the three which modern and postmodern criticism have successively prioritised. In other words, there is some truth in all three positions, but it is not the whole truth. We approximate to the reality of the interpretative reading process only when we take account of all three, as in Figure 1.

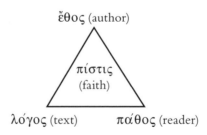

But in the case of Scripture, we can see a series of different dynamic triangles. The author may be identified, say, as Paul, writing a letter to his converts in Corinth (Figure 2);

---

[27] The model was partly derived from, partly inspired by reading Kinneavy, *Greek Rhetorical Origins*: see particularly 46. I have previously used a similar model in 'Pastoral Epistles'.

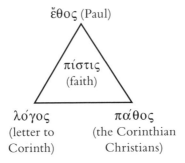

ἔθος (Paul)

πίστις
(faith)

λόγος   πάθος
(letter to   (the Corinthian
Corinth)   Christians)

But if that is the case, 'we' are not the intended readers, and there is no way in which exactly that original situation can be recreated. We may try to reconstruct it; we may try to exercise empathy and enter into the impact of the letter on the original readers, though the historico-critical method was more interested in trying to enter into Paul's intentions and the situation he was addressing. But whatever we do the original dynamic is elusive. Alternatively, we may identify the author as the Holy Spirit, ourselves as believers in the context of liturgy – part of the church universal over time and space, and the material as an extract from the timeless, canonical 'Word of God' (Figure 3).

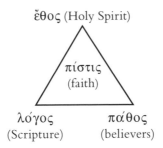

ἔθος (Holy Spirit)

πίστις
(faith)

λόγος   πάθος
(Scripture)   (believers)

This is a different 'reading genre' with a very different dynamic, and it never exists in a 'pure' sense; for we carry over the previous dynamic triangle, knowing that the text was shaped by human history and by particular circumstances, and that we are too – we do not read Holy Scripture in the same way as believers in the Middle Ages. Scripture is the divine Word in human words – it is incarnational, and the point of Scripture is transformation: it is meant to carry conviction and change people's lives. In every generation and in different cultures particularities somehow carry the eternal Word of God. This truth is fundamental to the nature of Scripture itself, as well as to the way we read it. Somehow we need to keep both dynamic triangles in play, and the concern of the 'modern' scholar, to be 'objective', and the concern of the believer, 'subjectively' to hear the Word of God, are both valid and true to the nature of Scripture. In practice it means that doing justice to the original dynamic, insofar as we can, may illuminate the text and its meaning in a different context. But that other context where the text is now read also has to be taken into account. The interest of the present reader is inevitably involved. So Jean Vanier clearly reads John's Gospel from the perspective of the l'Arche experience, but it is John's Gospel that he reads, imaginatively entering into another world and into relationship with Jesus through reading the text, while allowing it to engage with the life he lives in relationship with others.

The reader's interest cannot be excluded, and yet this does not undermine the ethics of reading. Indeed, this dynamic in fact reflects the stance towards literature which Wayne Booth seeks in his discussion of the ethics of fiction. He contrasts 'analyzing texts' with 'reading stories', reclaiming the traditional notion that actually we read for the sake of personal improvement – we expect to be changed by what we read, as people always have, at least until literary theory encouraged critics to keep their distance. Interestingly, given Jean Vanier's stress on friendship with Jesus, Booth treats the notion of friendship as the principal metaphor of reading. 'To begin with doubt,' he says, 'is to destroy the datum.'[28] We commonly experience being 'taken over' by what we read: when I consider my avid teenage reading of Jane Austen, I realise that in various ways my world was shaped by her world, and she was my 'friend', subtly subverting the romantic novel with independent women, even as she wrote within that genre. Similarly, the reading of the Bible shapes the world of the believer, the way that world is configured, the expectations the believer lives with, the interpretations the believer brings to relationships and events.

Yet for Wayne Booth responsible reading also involves criticism. After all, we discriminate between our friends!

> I serve myself best, as reader, when I both honor an author's offering for what it is, in its 'otherness' from me, and take an active critical stance against what seem to me its errors or excesses.[29]

Respect for the 'other' involves articulation of difference. 'Courtesy' towards the text does not require capitulation. It is not simply by identifying ourselves with characters in the story, or with the implied author, but by differentiation, whether by sympathetic listening across differences of culture and time, or by critical distancing, that we properly engage with what we read. Wayne Booth's ambiguous response to Huckleberry Finn, once the issue of racism has been made overt, is not unlike the potentially ambiguous response of Christians to those texts of early Christianity which have fostered anti-semitism or patriarchy. The actual reader, especially of a text from the past, is not identical to the

---

[28] Booth, *The Company We Keep*, 32.
[29] Booth, *The Company We Keep*, 135.

reader implied by the text, and an ethical reading has to take account of that gap. Yet critical assessment cannot neutralize the challenge of a classic text to reshape the reader's world, or the believer's sense that Scripture carries authority. A communication is to be received with respect and attention. So to take the ethics of reading seriously would appear to reduce the extent to which readers can treat texts arbitrarily, yet necessitates a kind of 'allegory' whereby we read ourselves into the literature.[30]

So our model necessitates the recognised involvement of the reader when it comes to the interpretation of Scripture. The reader's interests and response are not to be bracketed out; but they are to be in a dynamic relationship with author and text. The reader cannot simply make the text mean anything he or she likes – he or she must respect the 'otherness' of the text. So while the scholar may still wish to be as 'objective' as possible, trying to release the text from its accumulated meanings, its multi-levelled resonances, and all the traditions of the interpretative communities which have overlaid it, at the same time the scholar will inevitably have his or her own interests, explicit or implicit, and might even admit an interest which derives from not leaving his or her faith at the door, but rather from a search for meaning that is potentially enhanced, despite the enormous cultural gap between the ancient and modern worlds, through the empathy of considerable shared perspectives, such as belief in God. On the other hand, we can discern a legitimate place for the believer approaching the texts for insight and spiritual transformation, despite the fact that his/her interests have been liable to be dismissed, as merely 'subjective' and as making the texts mean what they like; for it is new insight that the believer seeks from the texts – a mirror reflecting back his or her own prejudices is a danger, but not necessarily the outcome: rather the text itself aims at transformation and stands over against the reader, challenging and calling into a new future. The different reading genres may be analytically distinguishable, but in the end they interact. 'Objective' and 'subjective' readings shade into one another. But always the reader interacts with author and text, and ideally is changed by the process – for the point of Scripture is transformation. It is surely that kind of dynamic reading that Jean Vanier achieves in his reading of John's Gospel.

Transformational reading: L'Arche and Pauline material

To illustrate this dynamic, I offer another example of transformational reading – a piece inspired by Jean Vanier and written especially for l'Arche. It is an interpretation of a biblical metaphor, which draws on historical research to bring the metaphor alive in a different culture, and also ponders the context

---

[30] See further my 'Allegory and the Ethics of Reading'.

and argument of Paul, insofar as we can reconstruct it – in other words, exploits the scholar's interests. But metaphors work through processes of association, cross-reference, allusion and layers of meaning.[31] They have potential to reach beyond the immediate context and shape a new world of understanding. So this exegesis also finds new insight arising from the l'Arche experience. As a result, the metaphor is enabled to bring hope into the midst of fragility. Here then is a reading of 2 Corinthians 4.7: 'we have this treasure in clay pots'.

Clay pots were used for all sorts of storage in the ancient world. They were part of everyday life, not just for ordinary things like grain and oil but for precious things like books – the Nag Hammadi codices were found in earthenware jars. Of course, there was an implied contrast with gold or silver containers but that just reinforces the everyday ordinariness at the heart of the metaphor. Treasure is secreted in ordinariness. Treasure is not at the inaccessible end of the proverbial rainbow; nor is it the object of a long quest, as legend would have it. We have this treasure in ordinary clay pots.

But the context and the clay are suggestive of a specific application. The treasure is secreted in human bodies. It was a commonplace in the ancient world to think of the body as a container of the mind or soul, and the picture of God creating human beings in Genesis 2 provides a potential inter-textual resonance. God took dust, turned it into clay, moulded something very like the clay figurines found by archaeologists all over the Middle East, then breathed life into it. The breath or spirit of God was contained in the clay vessel. Treasure is secreted in ordinariness, the image of God in ordinary human being. Paul's reference in the previous verse to God's creative word, 'Let light shine out of darkness' reinforces the cross-reference to the creation narrative. The treasure is the divine light, which has shone in our hearts to give us the knowledge of the glory of God in the face of Jesus Christ. When the Greek word, *thesauros* ('treasure'), appears in the LXX, it refers to God's wisdom (Wisdom 7.14; Sirach 1.25); the only other place the word appears in the Pauline Epistles is Colossians 2.3, referring to Christ in whom are hidden 'all the treasures of wisdom and knowledge'. Such clues identify the treasure secreted in our vulnerable and fragile bodies.

The metaphor is used to reinforce the contrast between God's power and human weakness: the next few verses affirm the experience of being afflicted, persecuted, struck down, but not crushed or destroyed, spelling out the sense that the treasure secreted within provides divine resources that can safeguard life even as the body bears the death of Jesus. Clay pots are expendable – cheap

---

[31] Metaphor has been much discussed: e.g. Ricoeur, *The Rule of Metaphor*; Soskice, *Metaphor and Religious Language*. For a previous attempt at hermeneutical use of a metaphor, see 'The Economy of God: exploring a metaphor', in Young and Ford, *Meaning and Truth in 2 Corinthians*, ch. 6.

they may be, but they are also not reparable, easily fractured, easily shattered; bodies, too, are fragile and vulnerable. But the treasure, the light and life of God, is exposed in the process, rather than damaged. Paul emphasises the incongruity and the paradox – the vehicle containing the all-surpassing treasure is of no enduring value. This may both obscure and reveal the extraordinary value of the contents.

Paul was, of course, defending his claim to be an apostle, despite his apparent defeats, his weakness and his incompetence, at least in the eyes of the Corinthians. But the metaphor need not be confined to the author's context-specific intent. Grounded as it is in the notion of *imitatio Christi* it is possible to see this aspect of the metaphor transcending that context. It is clear from the sequel that Paul does not simply treat the body as the temporary container for the immortal soul. Rather he focuses on the inherent creatureliness of human beings, on the divine spirit secreted within, and on the creative power of God which is capable of transforming bodies so that the mortal is taken up into the eternal. There is a long-standing tradition within Catholicism of discerning the image of God within those who are not rich, powerful or capable in this world, and seeing this as a prime motive for charitable works. But the l'Arche communities go further, and their perspective may enhance the reading of this metaphor.

The l'Arche communities challenge the assumptions of modernity. In a world where competence and success are highly valued, where the success of science has fostered the perception that all ills can be overcome, death endlessly postponed and suffering alleviated, where the cult of sport has exposed perfect bodies and encouraged their nurture through physical discipline, where there's been a reaction against bodily inhibitions and sexual repression, l'Arche has perceived beauty in damaged bodies, treasure in vulnerable and fragile persons. In the everydayness of attending to bodily functions, feeding and defecating, washing and dressing, the sanctity of bodies has been acknowledged, but in a context in which their transformation is not through miracles, but through the recognition of God's love and power in mutual need. The 'gift of the unlikely givers' is 'the capacity to ask for help'. It's not simply that the strong help the weak; rather the weak reveal our common essential vulnerability as human creatures. It is no accident that washing one another's feet has been developed as a paraliturgy in the l'Arche communities, for here in community bodily dependence on one another is sanctified. In the ordinary everyday business of living together, the divine image is discerned, secreted in the ordinariness of clay pots that are breakable, but in their brokenness expose the treasure within.

In the LXX the Greek words here rendered as 'clay pots' are used with reference to the 'vessel in which the temple priest offers certain kinds of sacrifice' (Lev. 6:28; 14:50).[32] Paul has used sacrificial language in describing his own

---

[32] Furnish, *II Corinthians*, 253.

apostolate (e.g. 2 Cor. 2:14–16). His ministry is a kind of incense, 'Christ's aroma to God among those being saved and those perishing, to some a stench from death to death, to others a scent from life to life.' The broken bodies of Christ's followers carry his sacrificial death, and to some this is abhorrent. The majority of people, if honest, would prefer that people with mental and physical disabilities were not around. They do not wish to be reminded of vulnerability, disfigurement, incapability. But to those who can discern it, here is the incense of worship.

Like the Corinthians, we find it difficult to discern power in weakness, treasure in clay pots. We look for the signs of success not defeat. But what we get is a crucified Christ, and an apostle whose catalogue of hardships belies any idea that God is with him. Maybe the sign we need to appreciate the light of the knowledge of God's glory in the face of Jesus Christ is the experience of the l'Arche communities.

Conclusion: Jean on John

When Jean reads John in the light of his experience in l'Arche, as well as modern psychological and anthropological insights, he is not simply distorting what may have been in the mind of the original author, but rather unlocking potential meaning, only discernible in a new context, and finding it rings true to a new human situation, illuminates it and points to the possibility of transformation. John's Gospel itself seeks to convince people, to bring them into a relationship, which is described as friendship, with the person who is the subject of the text, Jesus Christ, the Son of God. Jean facilitates a transformational reading. 'Our experience in l'Arche of the transformation of assistants and of people with learning disabilities helps us to understand the transformation Jesus offers us, just as the Word of God in John's Gospel sheds light on our own experience of transformation.'

Bibliography

Backus, I., and F. Higman (eds.), *Théorie et pratique de l'exégèse. Actes du troisiême colloque international sur l'histoire de l'exégèse biblique du XVIe siècle (Genève, 31 aout – 2 septembre 1988)* (Genève: Librairie Droz S.A., 1990)

Booth, W., *The Company We Keep: An Ethics of Fiction* (Berkeley, Los Angeles, London: University of California Press, 1988)

Derrida, J., 'Structure, Sign and Play in the Discourse of the Human Sciences', in *Modern Criticism and Theory: A Reader* (ed. D. Lodge; London and New York: Longman, 1988), 107–23

Fish, S., 'Interpreting the *Variorum*', in *Modern Criticism and Theory: A Reader* (ed. D. Lodge; London and New York: Longman, 1988), 310–29

Furnish, V.P., *II Corinthians* (AB; New York: Doubleday, 1984)

Jeanrond, W., *Text and Interpretation as Categories of Theological Thinking* (Eng. trans.; Dublin: Gill and Macmillan, 1988)

Jowett, B., 'On the Interpretation of Scripture', in *Essays and Reviews* (London: Longman, Green, Longman and Roberts, 1861), 330–433

Kinneavy, J.L., *Greek Rhetorical Origins of Christian Faith: An Inquiry* (New York and Oxford: Oxford University Press, 1987)

McKnight, E.V., *Postmodern Use of the Bible: The Emergence of Reader-Oriented Criticism* (Nashville: Abingdon, 1988)

Ricoeur, P., *Interpretation Theory: Discourse and the Surplus of Meaning* (Fort Worth: Texas Christian University Press, 1976)

—, *The Rule of Metaphor: Multi-disciplinary Studies of the Creation of Meaning in Language* (trans. R. Czerny, with K. McLaughlin and J. Costello; Toronto: University of Toronto Press, 1977)

—, *Time and Narrative* (3 vols.; trans. K. McLaughlin and D. Pellauer; Chicago: University of Chicago Press, 1984–88)

Soskice, J.M., *Metaphor and Religious Language* (Oxford: Clarendon, 1985)

Stanton, G., 'Presuppositions in New Testament Criticism', in *New Testament Interpretation: Essays in Principles and Methods* (ed. I.H. Marshall; Exeter: Paternoster, 1977)

Steiner, G., *Real Presences: Is There Anything in What We Say?* (London: Faber and Faber, 1989)

Thiselton, A.C., *The Two Horizons: New Testament Hermeneutics and Philosophical Description with Special Reference to Heidegger, Bultmann, Gadamer, and Wittgenstein* (Exeter: Paternoster, 1980)

Thompson, J.B. (ed.), *Paul Ricoeur, Hermeneutics and the Human Sciences* (Cambridge: Cambridge University Press, 1981)

Valdes, M.J. (ed.), *A Ricoeur Reader: Reflection and Imagination* (New York/London: Harvester Wheatsheaf, 1991)

Vanier, J., *Drawn into the Mystery of Jesus through the Gospel of John* (Ottawa: Novalis; London: Darton, Longman & Todd, 2004)

Watson, F. (ed.), *The Open Text: New Directions in Biblical Studies?* (London: SCM, 1993)

Weinsheimer, J., *Philosophical Hermeneutics and Literary Theory* (New Haven and London: Yale University Press, 1991)

Young, Francis, 'The Rhetorical Schools and their Influence on Patristic Exegesis', in *The Making of Orthodoxy: Essays in Honour of Henry Chadwick* (ed. R. Williams; Cambridge: Cambridge University Press, 1989), 182–99

—, *The Art of Performance: Towards a Theology of Holy Scripture* (London: Darton, Longman & Todd, 1990); published in the USA as *Virtuoso Theology*

—, 'The Pastoral Epistles and the Ethics of Reading', *JSNT* 45 (1992), 105–20

—, 'Allegory and the Ethics of Reading', in *The Open Text: New Directions in Biblical Studies?* (ed. F. Watson; London: SCM Press, 1993), 103–20

—, 'Interpretative Genres and the Inevitability of Pluralism', *JSNT* 59 (1995), 93–110

—, *Biblical Exegesis and the Formation of Christian Culture* (Cambridge: Cambridge University Press, 1997)

— (ed.), *Encounter with Mystery. Reflections on L'Arche and Living with Disability* (London: Darton, Longman & Todd, 1997)

—, and D. Ford, *Meaning and Truth in 2 Corinthians* (London: SPCK, 1997)

Part 2
Reading the Old Testament
Canonically

Torah

9

Old Testament Laws and Canonical Intentionality
Gordon McConville

Among the most obvious implications of a canonical approach to the Bible is the idea that all of the Bible plays a part in its use for theology. The Old Testament laws are perhaps a good place from which to explore this postulate, not only because they imply the question to 'gospel' that has always been put by 'law', but also because of their strangeness in the modern world, and finally because of the variety and disharmony among the law codes themselves. In what follows I will first illustrate the diversity and strangeness of the laws. I will go on to consider whether the concept of canonical unity is intrinsic to the biblical texts, or whether it is based on the fact of the canon as a previously determined entity. In that connection I will respond to the criticism that canon serves the vested interests of a particular group both in conception and in usage. Finally, I will apply the semiotic category of *intentio operis* to the canon, as a means of freeing it from subservience to such interests.

Diversity in Pentateuchal Laws

If diversity in the biblical literature is a problem for reading it canonically, the Pentateuchal law codes offer a particular challenge. In the progress from Egypt to the verge of the promised land on the plains of Moab, Moses sets at least three distinct law codes before the Israelites (the Book of the Covenant (BC), the Holiness Code (H), and the Deuteronomic Code (D)). This plurality is remarkable in itself in an apparently connected narrative of the formative events in Israel's life. Here is the story of Israel's exodus, wilderness wanderings, covenant-making with Yahweh at Sinai incorporating Decalogue and other laws, and march on the land, all within a forty-year time-span under the leadership of one man, Moses. The story in itself scarcely demands the plurality that we find. A reader might be content with a single telling of the Sinai event, together with a single, streamlined set of laws.

Yet the plurality of the law codes is no half-hidden secret, discoverable only by the wily reader. On the contrary, it is trumpeted, most obviously by Deuteronomy (whose 'deutero' is in one sense a misnomer,[1] but which in another illuminates the point). Deuteronomy has its own individual account of wilderness wandering, apostasy and lawgiving, and boldly renames Sinai Horeb. And here we even have a reprise of the Decalogue (Deut. 5:6–21) with alterations from the 'first' version in Exodus 20:1–17. The plurality of the law-codes cannot be accounted for as merely complementary, one simply supplying the deficiencies of another. In Deuteronomy's alternative version, there is more than a hint of the gauntlet being thrown down.

These first pointers to serious difference are confirmed by closer consideration of the laws themselves. For the codes sometimes address similar topics in quite different ways, sometimes amounting to head-on collision. The laws of worship afford examples of sharp difference, including the law of the altar itself, and the laws of offerings. The deuteronomic law of the tithe, for example (Deut. 14:22–29), presents this offering as a feast, in contrast to its character as a perquisite of the Levites in Numbers 20:21–24.[2] In what follows I want to focus on the laws governing slavery (Ex. 21:1–11, 20–21, 26–27; Lev. 25:39–55; Deut. 15:12–18).

The nature of the problem may be seen clearly from a comparison of BC and D. In common is the obligation to release the Hebrew slave after six years of service, together with the provision that the slave might opt for permanent servitude. Apart from this core everything else is different. Some of the differences might seem to be simple extensions of BC. D provides a rationale for the release, grounding it in Yahweh's deliverance of Israel from slavery in Egypt: Israelites should not be slaves because Yahweh's decisive act on Israel's behalf was precisely a freeing from slavery (Deut.15:15). It also goes beyond BC's declaration that the slave must go out debt-free to a more generous requirement that the owner supply him with the means for an independent life (Ex. 21:2; Deut. 15:13–14). But in fact the differences go deeper, to the position of the slave as such. In BC the relationship between master and slave is based on a commercial transaction in which the master 'buys' or 'acquires' (*qānâ*) the slave, whereas in Deuteronomy this impression of the transaction is carefully avoided.[3] In the most important single development in D,

---

[1] The name Deuteronomy is apparently based on a LXX misreading of Deut. 17:18, where 'a copy of this law' has been taken as 'this second law'.

[2] This was the topic of my first research over twenty years ago, published as *Law and Theology in Deuteronomy*. Deuteronomy's altar-law (Deut. 12) is widely held to support centralization of the cult in contrast to Ex. 20:24–25.

[3] The niphal phrase in Deut. 15:12 might be taken either as a passive 'is sold to you' (NRSV), or a reflexive ('sells himself to you', NRSV mgn). The latter possibility permits the reading that the impoverished person acts voluntarily in entering service.

that person's full citizenship is asserted at the outset by the use of the term 'brother' (applied to both male and female, Deut. 15:12), and correspondingly the term *'ebed* and its concomitant *'āmâ*, used throughout the law in BC, are withheld in D until the point at which the impoverished person opts for life-long servitude (Deut. 15:17). The impression that BC operates with a concept of the slave as property is supported by the law governing the death of a slave following violence by the master (Ex. 21:20–21), in which both male and female slaves are said to be the master's 'money' (*kaspô*).[4] There is no reason to think that this law pertains to non-Israelite slaves, or to a particular class within Israel.[5] D in contrast insists on the impoverished person's full citizenship, that he or she is in control of the decision to enter service.

As is already clear, the codes diverge sharply on the position of women. In BC the first part of the law concerns the male slave only, and the position of his wife is dealt with in secondary clauses. A wife given him by his master after the servitude has begun may not leave with him, but remains in the master's household. The difference in status between male and female slaves is then the subject of a separate paragraph (Ex. 21:7–11), where the slave-woman (*'āmâ*) is apparently also regarded as a concubine, either for the master himself or for his son. D's express and repeated provision that the female slave has the status of 'brother' in Israel and is subject to the same conditions as the male (Deut. 15:12, 17b) seems deliberately to counter this distinction between male and female found in BC (Ex. 21:7).

My point is that the differences between BC and D are not simply matters of detail. Rather they appear to diverge on matters of principle, taking different views about the status of slaves and the nature of slavery, and perhaps of the nature of Israel. It may even be that D responds critically to BC.[6]

---

[4] Ex. 21:21 is unlikely to permit routine violence against slaves or to constitute an exception to Ex. 21:12. The act of violence against the slave is regarded as reprehensible (hence 21:20). The exclusion in 21:21 may be explained by the doubt as to whether the slave's death was caused by the beating. In that case the note that 'the slave is his money' is adduced as evidence that the master is unlikely to have wished to kill him; Houtman, *Exodus*, Vol. 3, 156–57; cf. Wright, *God's People*, 241.

[5] The term *'ibrî* ('Hebrew', Ex. 21:2; Deut. 15:12), being cognate with the term *'apiru* in the Nuzi texts, has sometimes been taken to designate a social group which by definition lacked the status of full citizen in Israel; see Durham, *Exodus*, 320–21 (though he is cautious about the evidence). However, the term is used generally in Exodus as a name for Israelites as such (e.g. Ex. 2:11; 3:18; 5:3), and this appears to be its sense in the laws of Ex. 21 and Deut. 15 also; so Tigay, *Deuteronomy*, 148; Christensen, *Deuteronomy 1:1–21:9*, 320.

[6] It might be argued that the laws in Exodus and Deuteronomy are addressing different kinds of situation, that the former deals with the special case of the status of a wife granted by the master to the slave, and children born of the marriage, as well as the

The picture may be filled out further by noticing the law in Leviticus 25:39–55 (H), which introduces a dimension that is not present in either BC or D, namely the distinction between Israelites and foreigners. H is close to D in the sense that it affirms that Israelites should not be slaves, on the grounds that Yahweh delivered them from slavery in Egypt.[7] The affinity is greatest at Leviticus 25:39–43, which could be followed directly by verse 55. Here, the slave-master is addressed, and obliged to release slaves (together with their children, v. 41) for this theological reason. However, the point is reinforced by the distinction made between Israelites and people from the other 'nations' (*gôyîm*), including 'aliens' in their midst (*tôšābîm*). (This sits oddly, incidentally, with another refrain in H, that 'there shall be one law for the native and the *gēr*, e.g. Leviticus 19:34; 24:22, notwithstanding the difference between the terms used.) These foreigners may become slaves in perpetuity, the property of Israelites (vv. 44–46). And verses 47–53 serve to show that this state of affairs may not be reversed: Israelites may not become permanently enslaved to 'aliens'. This requirement is not addressed to the 'aliens', but still to the 'you' of verses 39–46, that is, it is a piece of theoretical reflection, which again places a distinction between Israelites and others. Leviticus thus inculcates the principle of no-slavery in an exclusive way, a way that gives unequivocal support to chattel-slavery as such, and which therefore falls short of affirming, on the basis of the divine nature, that slavery should have no place whatever in human society.

This law, then (ironically situated in the context of the celebrated 'jubilee' provisions, which have acquired a certain standing in contemporary ethical discourse), introduces a jarring note when placed alongside the 'egalitarian' deuteronomic law. Strictly, it is not directly at odds with D, since D addresses only the position of Israelite slaves and does not deal with the holding of foreigners as such (though it comes close in Deut. 21:10–14). Indeed the restriction in Deuteronomy 15:12 *might* permit some such practice as is provided for in Leviticus 25:44–46 – the silence may perhaps be read either way.[8]

---

case of the woman sold as a slave-wife, whereas Deuteronomy deals with independent women. Christensen appears to take this view: 'The equal treatment of the sexes, "whether a Hebrew male or a Hebrew female," does not indicate that the law here supersedes that of Ex. 21:7–11, which refers only to sale for the purpose of marriage' (*Deuteronomy 1:1–21:9*, 320). But this scarcely meets the point that Deuteronomy moves away from forced sale, and chooses to stress the equality of women in respect of slavery.

[7] I am not convinced by the view that differences between Leviticus on one hand and Exodus and Deuteronomy on the other are explained by supposing that the former deals only with landed Israelites while the latter two deal with the landless (e.g. Wright, *God's People*, 253), as it depends on the view that *'ibrî* refers to a disadvantaged class (on which see n. 5).

[8] So also Houtman, *Exodus*, Vol. 3, 121.

D elsewhere distinguishes between the treatment of Israelites and foreigners, and in one place suggests that a foreigner might be commercially sold (Deut. 21:10–14; note v. 14 where the protection of the captive foreign woman from being sold as a slave appears to be a dispensation). The cross-reading of D and H reminds us that none of the codes quite corresponds to modern expectations.

In stressing the differences between the laws for the purposes of the present argument, I do not mean to underestimate their positive force. Wright has argued persuasively that in Exodus, which I have portrayed as the most troublesome in its provisions on slavery, the slave appeared to have legal right of redress against the owner (Ex. 21:20–21, 26–27), implying that his status as slave did not negate certain fundamental rights under the law, unique among the ancient law codes.[9] The biblical laws in general had considerable subversive tendencies in their time, which have even been called democratic.[10] Even so, from the above comparison of the Pentateuchal laws on slave release at least two things follow. First, they cannot be simply reconciled with each other, since they appear to take significantly different views about important issues. Second, they enshrine attitudes which belong firmly within their own world and which are alien to most modern readers. The latter point is a salutary reminder that even in those places where biblical law codes tend towards modern attitudes, as in the social egalitarianism of D, they are often underpinned by assumptions which cannot be so readily accepted by modern Christian readers. The ideological distinctions between the texts, and between the texts and modern Christian readers, mean that canonical reception of the texts is complex. It cannot consist, for example, in discerning (among divergent texts) that text which seems most suitable to the reader's current situation.[11]

Critical Responses

For biblical criticism, the diversity of the texts is stock-in-trade, and the discovery of it needs no further justification. Classical source-criticism was based partly on the kinds of divergences noticed above. Differences among texts, indeed, were not accidental or incidental, but marked deeper rifts, caused by religious development or ideological conflict. The texts that we have examined illustrate the point. Deuteronomy is widely held to emphasize the transcendence of God and to take a more spiritual and ethical view of religion than other views found alongside it in the Pentateuch, especially J and P. This is one

---

[9] Wright, *God's People*, 240–44.
[10] Ska, 'Biblical Law', 146–58.
[11] This is no doubt partly true, and a point advocated by Sanders in relation to such divergences as between texts of judgment and salvation (*Sacred Story*, 84). But it does not cover all kinds of discrepancy.

aspect of the reform of King Josiah, which not only centralizes religion, but changes its character. Israel shows its true identity, not by the maintenance of certain rituals but by living up to certain humanitarian standards, expressed for example in its attitude towards marginalized persons in a number of its laws (e.g. Deut. 14:28–29; 16:14).[12] This approach sets texts at odds with each other by definition. In a recent work, Bernard Levinson has argued that the deuteronomic laws, as part of Josiah's religious reform, set out to replace BC by a sophisticated reuse of its terms that was calculated to render it null and void.[13] Criticism, therefore, often makes texts uncomfortable canonical bedfellows.

And this can be seen as its great virtue. For John Barton, the discovery of diversity, sometimes entailing incompatibility with Christian beliefs, is one result of the careful and unbiased work of historical criticism, which refuses to be shaped by prior religious commitment. His recent appraisals of canonical interpretation accept that they give a scholarly basis to the religious believer's natural inclination to find cohesion in the Scriptures. Indeed, many historical critics, he argues, have been favourably disposed to finding such compatibility, in spite of a contrary impression given by many 'canonical' interpreters.[14] However, Barton maintains the independence of historical-critical readings over against religious ones. Biblical critics must sometimes 'interfere in the activities of doctrinal and systematic theologians' to show that certain interpretations cannot stand.[15] He believes that the canonical approach is in principle at odds with such independent interpretation, and 'ultimately tells the student of the Bible what to think the text says on doctrinal grounds, rather than on the basis of the philological and textual criteria which historical criticism has developed'.[16] For this reason, he goes on: 'Biblical criticism has always been, and rightly so, of its essence anti-canonical in the sense that it refuses to allow for the framework within which the Church has placed the Bible when asking about the Bible's meaning.'[17]

This distinction in principle between historical and canonical readings seems to me to be less clear-cut than Barton believes, for two reasons. First, canonical interpretation is fully cognizant of diversity, and not always as committed to rescuing texts for orthodoxy as Barton implies. For example, Childs, in his

---

[12] Weinfeld, *Deuteronomy and the Deuteronomic School*, 210–24.

[13] Levinson, *Deuteronomy and the Hermeneutics of Legal Innovation*; see, for example, 53–97 on the deuteronomic law of Passover. (I have argued in contrast that the differences between Deuteronomy and Exodus need not have aimed at replacement, but rather represented a growth and development in the legal tradition: 'Deuteronomy's Unification of Passover and Massot', 47–58.)

[14] Barton, 'Canon', 37–52, here 39–43.

[15] Barton, 'Canon', 50.

[16] Barton, 'Canon', 50.

[17] Barton, 'Canon', 51.

commentary on Exodus, says of the slave law in BC: 'The sense of cruel incon-sistency between this stipulation and the concept of marriage found in Gen. 2.24 – not to speak of Matt. 19.6 – would finally destroy this law within Israel, but only after considerable passage of time.'[18] This rejection of a canonical text by appeal to other canonical texts looks somewhat similar to the constraints on theological reading that Barton advocates.[19] Second and conversely, Barton's account of the separate activities of biblical criticism and theology allows theol-ogy little space to engage with the diversity of Scripture as part of its task.

Canonical Dimensions

The conflictual model of canonical approach and historical criticism poses the question what kind of claim is really made by the former about diverse or oth-erwise awkward texts. To take an example of Barton's, when it is said in Psalm 97:7 that 'all gods bow down to Yahweh', does a canonical approach depend on the text not having originally borne a polytheistic sense? Barton thinks the historical critic will be open to the possibility of such a meaning, while a canon-ical reader is bound to see the reference to the 'gods' as at best metaphorical.[20] But it seems to me that the rationale for a 'monotheistic' reading of the text (granted an original polytheistic one) is not afforded by an essentially harmonistic 'metaphorical' reading, but by the fact of the canon itself.

At this point we need to be clear about the sense in which the canon may be said to have a unity. Such unity might be approached in either of two ways, internally or externally. One might assert the unity of the canon from within, by recognizing within it a unified or unifying logic. That is, the canon in fact testifies to a unified theology. In this category might be placed all those attempts to discern a 'centre' in Old Testament theology, and also perhaps James Sanders' belief in the canon's 'monotheizing tendency'. Alternatively, one might hold that the unity of the canon is not intrinsic in this sense, indeed that the canon contains highly disparate material and came to its present form more by accident than theological judgment. In this case the unity of the canon is imposed from outside, and depends on the decision of the church, *post factum*, to regard it as a unified witness to Jesus Christ.

Both these points of view have their force. In favour of the first (as regards the Old Testament) is the likelihood that much of the Old Testament's

---

[18] Childs, *Exodus*, 468.

[19] He also notes a *Tosephta* comment which blames the slave for not choosing freedom – this as an example of a later view which 'opposed slavery as degrading the image of God'; Childs, *Exodus*, 469. Childs thus adduces judgments against a canonical text, from both inside and outside the canon.

[20] Barton, 'Canon', 50.

theology is fashioned in critical dialogue with the religions of the nations that dominated its environment. In the context of confrontation with Canaan, Assyria, Babylon and Persia, its belief in the oneness of Yahweh was asserted. Eckhardt Otto finds the beginning of the formation of the Hebrew Bible in the conflict with Assyria.[21] And Horst Seebass takes this point in a specifically canonical direction, when he sees the concept of *tora* as a programmatic sketch (*programmatischer Entwurf* [italics original]), arising in reaction to Assyrian claims to absolute loyalty to its kings. Thus Deuteronomy is 'a historical-political transposition of the specifically Israelite understanding of God into the international world of its day'.[22] The most characteristic Old Testament tenet, the oneness of God, belongs in this matrix of critical dialogue with polytheistic religion. James Sanders too has seen this concept of the oneness of God as the key to understanding the Old Testament's unity that cuts across diversity.[23] Its cogency may be seen in relation to certain parts of the Old Testament: Genesis 1 – 11 over against Canaan and Babylon; Deuteronomy and Isaiah 40 – 55 vis-à-vis Assyria and Babylon. Internal unifying tendencies have also been recognized by Old Testament criticism in their postulates of grand movements, especially the deuteronomic, which on some accounts has subjected most of the Old Testament to rigorous editing in terms of its theological emphases. However, it is doubtful whether the type of unity required by the canonical approach can be quite secured by this discovery of unity from within. Proposed 'centres' tend not to command large followings, the various books of the Old Testament are likely to conform in different degrees to overarching concepts, and whether they do so at all may be subject to exegetical judgment, which may not be constant.

   The 'external' concept of canonical unity also has force. Michael Wolter gives a preliminary account of this, which is important because it is rooted in a strong statement of the diversity of the New Testament canon. Wolter describes the earliest Christian theological self-definition as taking place aside from the formation of the canon.[24] The balance of unity and diversity in

---

[21] 'Die literarische Formulierung der hebräischen Bibel setzt mit einem Paukenschlag während der assyrischen Krise des 8. und 7. Jh. v. Chr. ein'; Otto, *Krieg und Frieden*, 76. He explains this by saying that Torah and prophecy originate in this time, and the loyalty-oath contained in Deut. 13:28 expressly aims to counter Assyrian claims to hegemony.

[22] Seebass: 'eine historisch-politische Umsetzung des spezifisch israelitischen Gottesverstehens in die damalige Völkerwelt' ('Erstes oder Altes Testament', 27–43, here 38).

[23] For him the oneness of God corresponds to the 'Integrity of Reality – God's onto-logical and ethical oneness', *Sacred Story*, 4.

[24] Wolter, 'Vielfalt', 45–68, here 51–53. Among those who take a similar view is Young, *Art of Performance*, on which see further below.

Christianity was an issue prior to canon. Yet the search for a theological centre in early Christianity was not congruent with canonical formation. The canon in its diversity reflects the struggle of the early church to articulate what lay at the heart of the gospel, and so it betrays evidence of the disagreement over central issues such as the relation of the gospel to Jewish practice (in Acts 15 on the one hand and Galatians on the other).[25]

It follows that in the canonizing process itself theological coherence played no part. It arose, in contrast, not only out of a need for continuity, but also out of a *crisis* of coherence, in the sense that it sought to put limits on a tendency of early Christianity to become ever more differentiated.[26] Diversity in the canon is not a problem because it mirrors diversity in the formation process, and the canon even has an *intention* of compromise (its diversity 'entspricht der Intentionalität seines Kompromisscharakters'), by which disparate writings are gathered together without respect to their relative importance ('ungewichtet'), though at the same time excluding works that were important only to marginal groups.[27] The plurality of the canon even has a positive significance, because it maintains that Christian identity can and must take different forms in different social contexts, without, however, becoming subsumed by any such context.[28]

The story of the canon's formation, however, does not determine its interpretation. This is because it has become 'part of the cultural identity of the churches'.[29] That is, through usage, it has become in itself an integral part of the church's identity. Its authority, therefore, is *a posteriori*. In Jan Assmann's words, the canon has become 'Kennzeichen einer textual community'.[30] There are, moreover, strictly *hermeneutical* consequences of this. The specific point about canonicity is that no text has canonical status in itself, but only in conjunction with others.[31] Canon thus takes on a *hermeneutical* quality, since texts must always be read with alertness to other texts. And the effect of this

---

[25] Wolter, 'Vielfalt', 54–60.

[26] Wolter: 'insofern nämlich die Fixierung des Kanons der zunehmenden Ausdifferenzierung des Christentums in eine Vielzahl von miteinander konkurrierenden Christentümern entgegentreten wollte' ('Vielfalt', 61).

[27] George Aichele has his own take on this with regard to Mark's Gospel, namely that its dangerous unorthodoxy was tamed by its inclusion in the canon, and conversely that nothing would be lost from the canonical message if Mark were not in it. 'Mark contributes nothing to the orthodox Christian message of the canon', Aichele, *Control*, 196–97.

[28] Wolter, 'Vielfalt', 61–62.

[29] Wolter: 'zu einem Teil der kulturellen Identität der Kirchen geworden' ('Vielfalt', 64).

[30] Wolter, 'Vielfalt', 64. Wolter cites Assmann, *Fünf Stufen auf dem Wege zum Kanon*, 26.

[31] Wolter, 'Vielfalt', 65.

canonical hermeneutic is to stress that which unites Christianity rather than divides it.[32]

Wolter, having spoken of the canon's intention of compromise, now takes the idea of intentionality further, by applying Eco's concept of the 'intention of a work' (*intentio operis*) to the canon.[33] Since the *intentio operis* is distinct at once from the *intentio auctoris* and the *intentio lectoris*, it liberates the interpretation of the canon from the control of those who determined its contents, as well as from that of the reader. He then brings this to bear on another postulate found in Eco, the distinction between the *use* and *interpretation* of a work. In this distinction 'interpretation' is the critical attention to the nature of a text, while 'use' means 'to start from [the text] in order to get something else'.[34] In theological exegesis of the canon, claims Wolter, this distinction may be expressed in a particular way, namely as the decision to put aside the intentions of both author and reader, and 'understand the *intention* of the canon as a manner of its *use*'.[35] Eco, too, thought that there were cases when the 'convenient' distinction between use and interpretation was difficult to maintain.[36]

Canonical Intentionality

Wolter's proposal seems helpful to me in calling into question any dichotomy between a postulated real or detached interpretation of the constituents of the canon and a 'canonical' reading which is characterized in contrast by *parti pris*. We may pursue the point by asking further in what way the semiotic notion of the *intentio operis* might bear upon that of 'canonical intentionality', a phrase used by Childs in his *Introduction to the Old Testament as Scripture*.[37] The connection between the two is made by Barton, who thinks the concept of *intentio operis* may help to meet James Barr's objection to Childs's phrase, which he called 'a mystic phrase'.[38] However, Barton actually uses the idea of *intentio*

---

[32] Wolter, 'Vielfalt', 65–66.

[33] He cites two essays of Eco: 'Overinterpreting Texts', and 'Between Author and Text', in *Interpretation and Overinterpretation*, 45–66, 67–88. Wolter refers to the German collection, *Zwischen Autor und Text: Interpretation und Überinterpretation*, 52–74, 75–98.

[34] Eco, '*Intentio Lectoris*: the State of the Art', in *Limits of Interpretation*, 44–63, here 57. He attributes the use/interpretation distinction to Rorty.

[35] Wolter, 'wenn sie [die Exegese] nämlich diese doppelte Unterscheidung für sich ausser Kraft setzt und die *Interpretation* des Kanons als eine Weise seines *Gebrauchs* versteht' ('Vielfalt', 68).

[36] Eco, '*Intentio Lectoris*: the State of the Art', 62.

[37] Childs, *Introduction*, 78.

[38] Barton, 'Unity and Diversity', 11–26, here 21, n. 21, citing Barr, 'Childs' Introduction to the Old Testament as Scripture', 12–23, especially 13.

operis in such a way as to distinguish it from what is involved in the canonical approach. He aligns it rather with the kind of coherence which I have described above as 'internal'. He exemplifies such coherence by reference to O. Kaiser's belief that the 'Torah' is the centre of the biblical canon. This is offered by Kaiser as a historical claim about the text, namely (as Barton puts it):

> that the Pentateuch emerged as central in Judaism precisely because it really was the focal point around which other biblical material had gathered. In treating Torah as the fundamental unifying principle of the Old Testament we are doing justice to something inherent in the texts themselves, recognizing what is really there.[39]

Canonical interpretation, in contrast, 'is not a matter of empirical observation, on a par with the equally empirical observation of its diversity, but a theologumenon deriving from a doctrine of Scripture'.[40] This theologumenon is prescriptive for Christian readers, so that they are not at liberty to interpret the diversity of Scripture as evidence of basic disunity. Observations of disunity have their place within historical study, but 'do not have the power to overrule the Church's perception of the unity of Scripture once we move on to the level of a *theological* appropriation of the text'.[41]

It is immediately noticeable how much Barton differs from Wolter on the locus of the canonical text's intentionality, since for the latter the New Testament canon was precisely not coherent at the level of its formation. Wolter's understanding of *intentio operis* is, in the terms I have used, external rather than internal. And in Eco's understanding of *intentio operis* it is closely bound up with what might be made of it by a reader. Far from being a function of empirical observation, it is a device of the text intended to create a model reader.[42] Textual intention, model reader and model author relate to each other within a form of the 'hermeneutic circle':

> Since the intention of the text is basically to produce a model reader able to make conjectures about it, the initiative of the model reader consists in figuring out a model author that is not the empirical one and that, in the end, coincides with the intention of the text. Thus, more than a parameter to use in order to validate the interpretation, the text is an object that the interpretation builds up in the course of the circular effort of validating itself on the basis of what it makes up as its result.[43]

Striking here are the function of the model reader's conjectures, the construction of the text itself in the process of these conjectures, and of course the clear

---

[39] Barton, 'Unity and Diversity', 21; Kaiser, *Der Gott des Alten Testaments*.

[40] Barton, 'Unity and Diversity', 21.

[41] Barton, 'Unity and Diversity', 22. He cites in support of this position Moberly, *Bible, Theology, and Faith*.

[42] Eco, 'Overinterpreting Texts', 64.

[43] Eco, 'Overinterpreting Texts', 64.

distinction between the model author and the empirical one. (For Eco, the idea of the intention of the empirical author is 'radically useless'.)[44]

Does this mean that the semiotic notion of *intentio operis* may after all be ranged on the side of the canonical approach? The point depends initially on the assumption that the canon can be considered 'a work', and that the church or Christian readers may be capable of performing the role of model reader. It also needs to find a way of incorporating Eco's notion of the model reader's conjecture as to the meaning of a text, a part of which is the capacity of the text to prove the conjecture false.

As a first observation on these questions, we may note that Eco's formulation offers a different way of framing the problem from one in which the canonical view may be contradicted by the discovery of empirical facts. A canonical approach does not fix interpretation so much in advance that certain facts discovered about the canonical material might simply be found contradictory to its proposed meaning. Rather, the canonical approach, while it operates with the basic assumption that the unity of the canon is grounded in the death and resurrection of Jesus Christ, also has the character of a hypothesis, or a whole series of hypotheses, which need testing, rather like Eco's conjectures.

The canon as a set of texts taken to be meaningful in their mutual relations creates a host of intertextual possibilities: 'The texts in the intertextual mechanism resonate, interfere with, or otherwise contact each other in various and complex ways'.[45] Aichele thus highlights an important implication of the canonical approach for interpretation, which in my view introduces a host of possibilities into the act of canonical reading.

However, before proceeding, we must note that Aichele has actually taken a quite different view, and in doing so touches on a key issue. For him, the potentially unlimited possibilities entailed in the juxtaposition of many texts in a canon is constrained by the nature of the canon itself, a kind of constraint that can be understood as a strict ideological control.[46] Aichele thinks: 'the canon completes the inherent incompleteness of the story. The canon arises from the desire to end the ceaseless demand for a meaningful written text by completing the uncompletable story.'[47]

The concept of canon as control may be compared with that view (in Old Testament interpretation) according to which the Pentateuch and Historical Books were read after the exile as part of an effort of an élite group within the

---

[44] Eco, 'Overinterpreting Texts', 66.

[45] Aichele, *Control*, 19. There is an interesting point of contact with rabbinical method here, in the idea that 'there is no before and after in the canon', cited in Barton, 'Canon', 44.

[46] Noting that intertextuality is always ideological, he goes on, 'and canon is a very explicit, aggressive sort of intertextuality'; Aichele, *Control*, 19.

[47] Aichele, *Control*, 24.

post-exilic community to understand its identity in terms of its past (and even to construct a past from traditions and memories with a view to forming an identity in the present). This approach, associated with Morton Smith,[48] P.R. Davies, Joseph Blenkinsopp and E.T. Mullen among others, echoes one version of 'canonical' interpretation.[49] The concept of canon as an implement of an élite has also been adopted from a liberation theology perspective by Itumeleng Mosala. Mosala thinks that the canon (Old Testament and New Testament) is the product of the narrow interests of a particular group, and thus tainted with oppressive ideology. He argues that black theology has exposed not only the ideological bias of white theology but also the ideological character of the Bible, and therefore that the Bible as such cannot be appropriated by black theology. The idea that the Bible as a whole is the word of God is an ideological manoeuvre that allows certain biblical ideologies of power to be appropriated by ascendancy groups for their own interests:

> as products, records and sites of social, historical, cultural, gender, racial, and ideological struggles, they radically and indelibly bear the marks of their origins and history. The ideological aura of the Bible as the word of God conceals this reality.[50]

In another place, he reads the book of Micah in support of liberation hermeneutics, and addresses his enquiry not to the 'surface' of the biblical text, but to the constituent parts that lie behind it. He does so on the grounds that those texts reflect a diversity of political and religious interests, while the canonical final form represents a re-appropriation of texts that once exposed the oppression of the poor, by an élite that now casts itself in the role of victim.[51] Mosala thus makes the move from the thesis that the canon was formed as an ideological measure to secure the interests of a class, to the postulate that it is intrinsically likely to have a similar force today. It is a directly anti-canonical move, re-instating the authority of pre-canonical texts which the canonical approach disputed. One response to Mosala came from Christopher Rowland, who argued in contrast that it is the final form that preserves the variety of readings. Readily conceding that liberative readings jostle with more accommodating ones (he refers especially to the Gospel of Luke), he argued that this at least

---

[48] Smith, *Palestinian Parties*. Sanders, while counting Smith among the originators of the canonical approach, regarded his method as one of 'political determinism'; *Sacred Story*, 82. See also Mullen, *Ethnic Myths*; Blenkinsopp, *Prophecy and Canon*; Davies, *In Search of Ancient Israel*.

[49] Childs has categorized this trend as a type of history-of-religions approach, and questioned its capacity to lead to theological interpretation: 'The Canon in Recent Biblical Studies: Reflections on an Era'.

[50] Mosala, 'Biblical Theology', 51–73, here 56.

[51] Mosala, *Biblical Hermeneutics*, cited in Rowland, 'In This Place', 169–82, here 177.

ensures the survival of the liberative voices, and that readers of Luke have had no difficulty in hearing them.[52] Rowland does not deny that Luke may have been produced by an élite, but he shows that the text could nevertheless not be reduced to an instrument of their ideology.[53]

Rowland's response supposes that the reader is able to hear the canonical text in ways that are free from any kind of control that the canon may seek to impose. And indeed, the reader's capacity to hear and make sense is demonstrated by the diversity of Christian interpretation on major issues. Rowland thus resists the idea that the canon exerts rigid control, of the sort proposed by Aichele.[54] Eco's 'hermeneutical circle', which allows the texts to re-educate the reader's conjectures about what is implied by the canon, also implies a more flexible understanding of the way in which the canon may be said to have an 'intention'.

Before returning to the laws with which we began our enquiry, the idea of canonical 'intention' may be approached from another, more strictly theological, viewpoint. Frances Young, arguing that the canon is not capable in itself of conveying its own determinative meaning,[55] finds the idea of the 'mind' of Scripture in Christian writings from Irenaeus to Athanasius. The canon cannot provide the criterion for interpreting its parts, but needs an overarching story which, though based in the texts, is supplied by the Christian tradition.[56] In the work of Irenaeus, this story is the 'Rule of Truth',[57] which functions as a

---

[52] Rowland, 'In This Place', 178–82.

[53] Rowland, 'In This Place', 182. Similarly, Wolter refutes the dictum of Wrede that whoever accepts the authority of the canon accepts the authority of the Christian bishops who decided upon the contents of the canon; on the contrary, their 'intention', as 'authors', is irrelevant: Wolter, 'Vielfalt', 45–68, here 67. Wrede stated: 'Wer also den Begriff des Kanons als feststehend betrachtet, unterwirft sich damit der Autorität der Bischöfe und Theologen jener Jahrhunderte. Wer diese Autorität in anderen Dingen nicht anerkennt – und kein evangelischer Theologe erkennt sie an –, handelt folgerichtig, wenn er sie auch hier in Frage stellt' (Wrede, *Aufgabe*, cited in the reprint in Strecker (ed.), *Das Problem der Theologie des Neuen Testaments*, 81–154, here 85).

[54] Aichele illustrates what he sees as the power of the canon to govern interpretation by reference to Mark's Gospel, his example of a major text that does not readily fit: 'In effect the New Testament "quotes" the entire story of Mark, making it part of a much larger story, and thus it reduces or even eliminates the referential ambiguity that characterizes that text' (*Control*, 24).

[55] Referring to the significance of the placement of an individual work within the canon she writes: '[such placement] is not determinative of interpretation and the canon cannot itself provide a unitive framework'; Young, *Art of Performance*, 45.

[56] Young, *Art of Performance*, 46–53.

[57] Young, *Art of Performance*, 49. The Rule of Truth is also the 'Rule of Faith', as in writers such as Tertullian and Origen; ibid.

'hypothesis' for reading, that is, a basic understanding of the whole which allows the reader to read the parts correctly.[58] She goes on to draw attention to the terms *skopos* and *dianoia*, used respectively by Origen and Athanasius to refer to the 'mind' of Scripture. Origen, in distinction from the Antiochenes' idea of the *skopos* of individual biblical books, looked for the *skopos* of Scripture as a whole. In his *De principiis*, for example, discussing inspiration, he uses the term several times, to mean the Spirit's intention 'to enlighten the prophets and apostles so that they become partakers in all the doctrines of the Spirit's counsel'.[59] For Athanasius 'discerning the unitive "mind" (*dianoia*) of Scripture was seen as essential to reaching a proper interpretation'.[60] On this basis he was both to oppose Arius on passages which on the surface seemed to favour the latter, and to deploy key concepts not found in Scripture, such as *homoousios*.[61] Athanasius' *dianoia* is thus close to Irenaeus' *hypothesis*, both referring to the plot or story of Scripture, 'the overarching narrative from creation through incarnation to the eschaton'.[62]

The point of contact between Eco and patristic interpretation in relation to canonical intentionality is intriguing. I suggested above that the canonical approach to biblical interpretation had the character of a hypothesis, rather like Eco's reader's conjectures. The Irenaean *hypothesis* is less redolent of scientific model, but it knows, like Eco, that the meaning of the part is affected fundamentally by the way in which it relates to other parts in a larger entity. It knows too that sense can only be made of part and whole from an initial standpoint outside the text. The Fathers' reading of the Scripture is a case-study in Eco's hermeneutical category of *intentio operis*. Like Eco, the Fathers knew that there might be other readings of that intention, and of individual texts, and they faced such readings in their formative controversies over Christian doctrine. For them, however, the *intentio operis* was not merely a concept arising in the encounter between text and reader, but rather it originated in the purpose of God. Canonical interpretation is theological by definition, and cannot be explained in the categories of general hermeneutics alone.

---

[58] Young, *Biblical Exegesis*, 19–20. Irenaeus thus opposes the Rule of Faith to other false *hypotheseis*, espoused by opponents such as Valentinus; Young cites *Adversus haereses* I.viii–ix, in *ANCL* I, 32, 40–41.

[59] Young, *Biblical Exegesis*, 23–24.

[60] Young, *Biblical Exegesis*, 29.

[61] Young, *Biblical Exegesis*, 34. She refers here to the 'sonship' of Christ and the interpretation of Prov. 8:22, 15; also Phil. 2:9–10; Ps. 45:7–8 (ibid., 42–43).

[62] Young, *Biblical Exegesis*, 43, 45. See also her remarks on the meanings of *skopos* and *dianoia* in a comment on Pollard, 'The Exegesis of Scripture in the Arian Controversy', 414–29; ibid., 29–30, n. 2. She entertains elements in them both of the storyline of Scripture and of a 'canon of truth'.

The Fathers' overriding doctrinal impetus did not mean that they paid scant attention to the diversity of Scripture; as we have seen, they also contended for the meaning of individual texts in ways that are not reducible to convenient categories.[63] However, it is in terms of the diversity of Scripture and its intrinsic difficulties (our own starting point) that modern approaches have furnished kinds of questions that the Fathers did not know. If the Fathers insist that the unity of Scripture is in the mind of God, may this yet be squared with the internal differences revealed by historical criticism? It is in facing such questions, I think, that theology and hermeneutics may engage fruitfully with each other. It must be admitted that the concept of intentionality is quite differently constructed in the two cases. For Eco it hardly exists apart from the reader's initiative, whereas for the theologian it is more akin to an article of faith. We run the risk of a kind of 'dual description', therefore, when we try to bring the two together. Even so, the nuanced response of hermeneutics to historical criticism's microscopic exposure of scriptural diversity may be called in aid of theology.

The Laws in the Canon

We have observed the raw differences between the several laws of slave release in the Pentateuch, and the difficulties of a reconciliation of them on a surface reading. Does the application of *intentio operis* to the canon as a whole help to a coherent reading of these laws that does not simply select among them?

The canonical context of the laws may be defined in various ways, as broad as the whole Bible, as narrow as close co-texts, and in intermediate ways, with the proviso that these are held ultimately to cohere. The laws' immediate canonical neighbourhood is the Pentateuch, or better, Genesis–Kings. The situation of the laws in an extended narrative is itself the subject of canonical 'signals' (the leadership of Moses throughout the story of exodus to land; the explicit 'editorial' linkages between the books that make up Genesis–Kings;[64] thematic echoes such as right worship, leadership, the gaining and losing of land). The application of narrative criteria to the reading of Genesis–Kings, therefore, is at the same time a function of canonical reading. (This does not

---

[63] Young shows that the method of Athanasius could not be explained simply by categories such as literal, allegorical or typological, but rather was 'deductive': 'The deductive process involves attention to the meaning of words, their particular biblical sense, the syntax and the context of the text in question – the basic techniques of the *grammaticus* attending to the verbal configuration of a passage' (Young, *Biblical Exegesis*, 40).

[64] With or without Ruth.

mean that canonical reading of Genesis-Kings is limited to reading it as a narrative. And conversely, non-narrative texts may have their own specific criteria for canonical reading.)

If '[a] text is a device conceived in order to produce its model reader' (who is entitled to make conjectures about its meaning), the differences among the laws of slave release are intrinsically part of the text and offered to the model reader for sense to be made of them. For reasons we have seen, it is not open to the model reader to try to understand the differences by means of harmonistic devices. The meaning cannot be composed out of some aggregate of the laws. To go this way leads only to perplexity. As Eco points out, the meaning of the text is unlikely to be found in a simple way at the surface level.[65] The alternative, then, is to ask what function the laws might have in the context of this ostensibly coherent narrative. They themselves offer initial pointers. First, the slave release laws have in common with the laws in general their function to explicate the obligation of Israel to work out in practice the meaning of their status as covenant partner of Yahweh. Second, in particular they convey the message that the status of slavery is incompatible with the nature of Israel, the explicit rationale in both H and D (Lev. 25:38, 55; Deut. 15:15). In addition, as we have seen, they agree in subordinating master and slave alike to the process of law.

Yet these pointers to the laws' interpretation stop short of explaining the diversity we have observed. They even sharpen the problem, because the issue now is not mere incompatibility at the surface level, but rather the existential questions that the laws leave unanswered. What kind of institution is slavery in Israel? Are people liable to become the property of others by monetary transaction, as assumed in BC? The question is unavoidable because both H and D appear to respond to BC by declining this possibility. In the process, D uniquely declares the equal rights of women. A certain tension remains between H and D, however, because while H's jubilee restores the enslaved without exception, D grants that the impoverished person may choose permanent servitude. But a new question is posed to the model reader by the conjunction of H and D, namely the relative position of Israelites and foreigners in regard to slavery. H, as we saw, asserts the freedom of Israelites from slavery in principle precisely by contrasting their situation with that of foreigners. D's concentration on the status of 'brothers' in Israel brings no special contribution on that point in the law of slave release itself (though as we have seen, it leaves a

---

[65] Eco: 'The text's intention is not displayed by the textual surface. Or, if it is displayed, it is so in the sense of the purloined letter. One has to decide to "see" it. Thus it is possible to speak of the text's intention only as the result of a conjecture on the part of the reader. The initiative of the reader basically consists in making a conjecture about the text's intention' ('Overinterpreting Texts', 64).

door ajar to it elsewhere, and D makes other distinctions between appropriate attitudes to Israelites and foreigners, as in the case of interest-taking). It is possible to imagine clashes of various interests behind these laws, or indeed a dialogue between such interests and the voices that want to subordinate them to higher ones. The model reader, however, has other reasons to think further about the status of the foreigner. Did not this narrative begin with an affirmation that all human beings were created 'as the image and likeness of God'? Was not Abram promised that in his blessing all the families of the earth would be blessed? How do the distinctions proposed or assumed in the laws relate to the narrative's creational perspective, and further to those texts which suggest that Israel's special status has as its purpose to reveal the nature of God to the world (such as Deut. 4:6–8)? Such questions are opened by the laws of slave release, and are not closed within the limits of the laws themselves.

In perceiving and pondering these questions, however, the model reader is doing what the text leads him or her to do. The model reader is called to participate in making judgments. If the laws in themselves will not lead him or her infallibly to conclusions on the unity of humanity as the 'image' of God, how then is he or she to think of it in relation to the weightier matters placed before him or her by the narrative? The function of the narrative, with its pointed discrepancies, is to draw the reader into this role.

The call to the reader to act as critical judge is implicit in the compound character of the narrative of Sinai covenant and law-giving, that is, where Deuteronomy reprises the Sinai-Horeb event in considered re-orientation to it. This self-understanding of Deuteronomy is manifest in its structure, which reflects on the relationship between the covenants at Sinai/Horeb and Moab. More than a covenant-renewal, the Moab event is a way in which the Moab generation places itself once more at Horeb, as if it were 'today'. Yet the trajectory from Horeb to Moab exists in a tension between the old and the new, the same and the different. While nothing may be added to or taken away from what Moses commands (Deut. 4:2), his words loudly proclaim both addition to and subtraction from what went before. The subtle interplay of identity and non-identity between the 'book of the law' as an entity that Deuteronomy can refer to and a sobriquet for Deuteronomy itself is a further instance of this orientation to the past while ushering in a new and different future.[66] Nor is the Moab horizon the only 'future'; rather, the appointed seven-yearly readings of 'this law' point into an indefinite future of new 'todays', and thus an infinite regression (or *progression*) of old in tension with new. The Horeb–Moab trajectory becomes a metaphor for all reappropriation of the decisive moment of encounter. And so the story contains a pointer for all re-reading, which may include canonical re-reading.

---

[66] This is persuasively expounded by Sonnet, *Book Within the Book*.

The model reader stands with Israel as it is called to perpetual renewal, with all the hermeneutical implications of this. The reader is thus invited to interpret the text, specifically the differences between the laws, in his or her capacity as both receiver of authoritative tradition and arbiter of the shape of it in a new 'today'. This means that all the laws are posed as questions for interpretation. The reader's work of interpretation is not done when it is observed that one code succeeds another. The interrelationships between the codes are too convoluted to admit of an evolutionary schema in which one code becomes definitive and the others redundant. In fact, as we have seen, all the codes are questioned by important theological signals embedded in the narrative. In particular, the reader has done less than justice to the text if she merely extracts from it aspects which are somewhat congenial to approved opinions, whether her own or those of her contemporary society, since all the laws will ultimately fail by those standards.

The proposal thus made for a reading of the laws coheres well with the idea of the text as 'open', in the sense of being available for engagement with a myriad of conjectures about its meaning. The narrative of Genesis–Kings has built into it (via Deuteronomy) a temporal depth-dimension which makes it available for re-reading in multiple horizons. At this point, the logic of reading makes contact again with that of canon. For the possibility of multiple model readers corresponds to the possibility of multiple 'canonical' horizons. For canonical reading is also open, in the sense that the literature may be read canonically at different times and in different situations. A canonical reader located soon after the exile may have read the slave release laws in a context in which the nature of Israel was being re-imagined, and in which slavery and slave release were potential real-life issues. Nehemiah's action against slave-making shows outrage at the enslavement of 'brother'-Israelites, yet sees no implication that slavery as such is unjust (Neh. 5). A modern canonical reading knows stronger reasons against slavery in the gospel's vision of a wholly inclusive society, and is informed in addition by the legacy of a culture that has seen it bear fruit in inhumanity.

The Laws in Themselves

Our outline so far of a canonical approach to the interpretation of the slave-release laws has pointed away from the discrete laws to a wider context with which they partly cohere but also questions aspects of them. We now ask finally if there is a sense in which the individual laws still have their own voice. The question first invites the commonplace but necessary response that it is impossible to avoid the historical otherness of the Bible in all its parts. If some parts seem particularly alien, one must be aware of supposing that others are not. All biblical interpretation, therefore, involves an element of distance between text and reader, and good interpretation needs to recognize this. The usefulness of the laws, indeed, may even lie in their very alienness, because they confront us from the perspective of a culture quite distinct from our own and so have the capacity to make us question ourselves. A reading of BC's law that finds forms of oppression in it can move beyond mere rejection to reflection on forms of oppression prevalent in the reader's society, together with pointers to limiting or dismantling them, in compassion, integrity and the refusal to exploit. A law that seemed to connive with the interests of the wealthy and powerful can turn out to have a prophetic edge. A pattern for such appropriation is found in the Old Testament in a narrative about the time of Jeremiah and King Zedekiah, when the landed classes were almost persuaded to release their slaves, but stumbled over the essential issue, failing to accept the crucial point that no Israelite should be a slave (Jer. 34:8–22). The moral impact of the law of release (in that case the deuteronomic law is expressly in view) is unmistakable. If and when, in our world, systems of oppression are disclosed for what they are and a believing response is made, the mismatch between that world and this, and that particular case and this (as indeed between the various twenty-first century worlds that the laws might confront) becomes unimportant beside the forceful impact of the word of God.

The specifically canonical aspect of this hermeneutical point is that the canon's inclusion of texts that seem awkward or alien to central themes compels us to reckon with them rather than neglect them on those grounds. As Rowland puts it: 'Even what appear to some of us to be the Bible's more difficult passages may help us understand something of our own prejudices as we glimpse something of the compromises in the texts of the past;' and indeed 'what appear to us to be the most reactionary texts may surprise us by offering what [Frederic Jameson] calls a "utopian impulse"'.[67] It is the diversity of the canon that illustrates the nature of biblical interpretation in practice: not the imagined abstraction of permanently valid principles, but in many and diverse encounters with the word of God illuminating our own world and lives in unexpected ways.

---

[67] Rowland, 'In This Place', 177. His reference is to Jameson, *Political Unconscious*. A similar point is made by Fiddes, 'The Canon as Space and Place', 127–49.

Bibliography

Aichele, G., *The Control of Biblical Meaning* (Harrisburg: Trinity Press International, 2001)

Assmann, J., *Fünf Stufen auf dem Wege zum Kanon: Tradition und Schriftkultur im frühen Judentum und in seiner Umwelt* (Münster: LIT Verlag, 1999)

Barr, J., 'Childs' Introduction to the Old Testament as Scripture', *JSOT* 16 (1980), 12–23

Barton, J., 'Canon and Old Testament Interpretation', in *In Search of True Wisdom: Essays in Old Testament Interpretation in Honour of Ronald E. Clements* (JSOTSup 300; ed. E. Ball; Sheffield: Sheffield Academic Press, 1999), 37–52

—, 'Unity and Diversity in the Biblical Canon', in *Die Einheit der Schrift und die Vielfalt des Kanons* (BZNW 118; ed. J. Barton and M. Wolter; Berlin: de Gruytes, 2003), 11–26

Blenkinsopp, J., *Prophecy and Canon: A Contribution to the Study of Jewish Origins* (London: Notre Dame University Press, 1977)

Childs, B.S., *Exodus* (OTL; London: SCM, 1974)

—, *Introduction to the Old Testament as Scripture* (London: SCM, 1979)

—, 'The Canon in Recent Biblical Studies: Reflections on an Era', *ProEccl* 14 (2005), 26–45; reproduced in this volume

Christensen, D.L., *Deuteronomy 1:1–21:9* (WBC; Nashville: Thomas Nelson, 2001)

Davies, P.R., *In Search of Ancient Israel* (Sheffield: Sheffield Academic Press, 1995)

Durham, J.I., *Exodus* (WBC; Waco, TX: Word, 1987)

Eco, U., '*Intento Lectoris*: The State of the Art', in *The Limits of Interpretation* (Bloomington, IN: Indiana University Press, 1990), 44–63

—, *The Limits of Interpretation* (Advances in Semiotics; Bloomington, IN: Indiana University Press, 1990)

—, 'Between Author and Text', in *Interpretation and Overinterpretation* (Cambridge: Cambridge University Press, 1992), 67–88

—, 'Overinterpreting Texts', in *Interpretation and Overinterpretation* (Cambridge: Cambridge University Press, 1992), 45–66

—, *Zwischen Autor und Text: Interpretation und Überinterpretation. Mit Einwürfen von Richard Rorty, Jonathan Culler, Christine Brooke-Rose und Stefan Collini* (trans. H.G. Holl; Munich: Hanser, 1994)

—, et al., *Interpretation and Overinterpretation* (ed. Stefan Collini; Cambridge: Cambridge University Press, 1992)

Fiddes, P., 'The Canon as Space and Place', in *Die Einheit der Schrift und die Vielfalt des Kanons* (BZNW 118; ed. J. Barton and M. Wolter; Berlin: de Gruyter, 2003), 127–49

Houtman, C., *Exodus*, Vol. 3 (4 vols.; HCOT; Peeters: Leuven, 2000)

Jameson, F., *The Political Unconscious: Narrative as a Socially Symbolic Act* (Ithaca, NY: Cornell University Press, 1981)

Kaiser, O., *Der Gott des Alten Testaments: Theologie des Alten Testaments*, Vol. 1: *Grundlegung* (Göttingen: Vandenhoeck & Ruprecht, 1993)

Levinson, B., *Deuteronomy and the Hermeneutics of Legal Innovation* (New York: Oxford University Press, 1997)

McConville, J.G., *Law and Theology in Deuteronomy* (JSOTSup 33; Sheffield: JSOT Press, 1984)

—, 'Deuteronomy's Unification of Passover and Massot – A Response to B. M. Levinson', *JBL* 119 (2000), 47–58

Moberly, R.W.L., *The Bible, Theology, and Faith: A Study of Abraham and Jesus* (Cambridge: Cambridge University Press, 2000)

Mosala, I., *Biblical Hermeneutics and Black Theology in South Africa* (Grand Rapids: Eerdmans, 1989)

—, 'Biblical Theology and Black Hermeneutics in South Africa: The Use of the Bible', in *The Bible and Liberation: Political and Social Hermeneutics* (2nd edn.; ed. N.K. Gottwald and R.A. Horsley; Maryknoll, NY: Orbis, 1993), 51–73

Mullen, E.T., *Ethnic Myths and Pentateuchal Foundations* (Atlanta: Scholars Press, 1997)

Otto, E., *Krieg und Frieden in der Hebräischen Bibel und im Alten Orient* (Stuttgart: Kohlhammer, 1999)

Pollard, T.E., 'The Exegesis of Scripture in the Arian Controversy', *BJRL* 41 (1958–59), 414–29

Rowland, C., 'In This Place: The Center and the Margins in Theology', in *Reading from this Place: Social Location and Biblical Interpretation in Global Perspective* (ed. F.F. Segovia and M.A. Tolbert; Minneapolis: Augsburg Fortress, 1995), 169–82

Sanders, J.A., *From Sacred Story to Sacred Text: Canon as Paradigm* (Philadelphia: Augsburg Fortress, 1987; repr. Eugene, OR: Wipf and Stock)

Seebass, H., 'Erstes oder Altes Testament', in *Die Einheit der Schrift und die Vielfalt des Kanons* (BZNW 118; ed. J. Barton and M. Wolter; Berlin: de Gruyter, 2003), 27–43

Ska, J.-L., 'Biblical Law and the Origins of Democracy', in *The Ten Commandments: The Reciprocity of Faithfulness* (ed. W.P. Brown; Louisville: Westminster John Knox Press, 2004), 146–58

Smith, M., *Palestinian Parties and Politics That Shaped the Old Testament* (New York: Columbia University Press, 1971)

Sonnet, J.-P., *The Book Within the Book: Writing in Deuteronomy* (BIS 14; Leiden: Brill, 1997)

Strecker, G. (ed.), *Das Problem der Theologie des Neuen Testaments* (Wege der Forschung 367; Darmstadt: Wissenschaftliche Buchgesellschaft, 1975)

Tigay, J.H., *Deuteronomy = Devarim* (Jewish Publication Society Torah Commentary; Philadelphia and Jerusalem: Jewish Publication Society, 1996)

Weinfeld, M., *Deuteronomy and the Deuteronomic School* (Oxford: Clarendon Press, 1972)

Wolter, M., 'Die Vielfalt der Schrift und die Einheit des Kanons', in *Die Einheit der Schrift und die Vielfalt des Kanons* (BZNW 118; ed. J. Barton and M. Wolter; Berlin: de Gruyter, 2003), 45–68

Wrede, W., *Über Aufgabe und Methode der sogenannten neutestamentlichen Theologie* (Göttingen: Vandenhoeck & Ruprecht, 1897)

Wright, C.J.H., *God's People in God's Land: Family, Land and Property in the Old Testament* (Carlisle: Paternoster; and Grand Rapids: Eerdmans, 1990)

Young, F., *The Art of Performance: Towards a Theology of Holy Scripture* (London: Darton, Longman and Todd, 1990)

—, *Biblical Exegesis and the Formation of Christian Culture* (Cambridge: Cambridge University Press, 1997)

10

Response to Gordon McConville
Christopher J.H. Wright

One of the major contributions that Gordon McConville has made to Deuteronomy studies has been his insistence that we take full account of the book's
theological depth and creativity, and that where we find differences between it
and other Pentateuchal texts, we should seek to discern its distinctive theological reasoning rather than resort to the source-critical knife or to speculative
explanations derived from hypothetical reconstructions of its historical prove-
nance and religio-political agenda. In this paper he demonstrates the same
instincts, this time relating textual discrepancies not only to the theological
intentions of distinct texts, but also to the wider phenomenon of their having
been consigned to permanent cohabitation within the canon. I find the intention behind this reflection to be entirely valid, and part of the process by which
those who are confessionally committed to the whole canon of Scripture as a
comprehensive revelation of the living God seek to understand and interpret its
internal diversity.

The choice of the slave laws, as an illustration for his argument, is an apt one,
since McConville is certainly right to point out the variances that exist between
the three main groups of laws regarding slaves, and especially the release of
slaves, in Exodus, Leviticus and Deuteronomy. It is unquestionable that there
are significant differences in the laws in Exodus 21, Deuteronomy 15 and
Leviticus 25 especially, and attempts to 'harmonise' them (in the sense of trying
to show that they are all saying virtually the same thing) are certainly futile. On
the other hand, it seems to me that McConville somewhat overplays the
divergences when he speaks of 'a gauntlet thrown down [by Deuteronomy]',
'diverge sharply', 'responds critically', 'a jarring note', 'raw differences' and
'insurmountable difficulties of reconciliation'. Perhaps he is seeing a difference
at the level of 'fundamental outlook', where we might better speak of a developing and living legal tradition that modifies and refines itself along the path of

---

[1] Beginning with his published dissertation, *Law and Theology in Deuteronomy*, and
culminating in his fine commentary, *Deuteronomy*.

a constant fundamental outlook. That outlook comprises several elements: the historical fact of the exodus, giving release to the Israelites from slavery and thereby making slavery within Israel something of an anomaly (so that the very first law about slaves in the Book of the Covenant significantly has to do with their *release*); the inclusion of slaves within the community, religiously as well as socially (e.g. in their presence, if circumcised, at Passover, their inclusion in the annual feasts, and in the prescribed rest of the Sabbath day); the unique nature of some Old Testament laws on the treatment of slaves and their legal rights (including those found in Exodus, not just in Deuteronomy); and the fundamental assumption of the slave's humanity and created equality before God, whatever his or her economic status, as articulated in Job 31.

McConville says that it is not open to the 'model reader' to 'understand the difference by means of harmonistic devices.' While agreeing with this, if 'harmonistic devices' mean strained and implausible attempts to dissolve all elements of variety within the texts, I do think it is reasonable for the reader (whether model or empirical) to work with the texts that have been deliberately kept together within a single intentional framework (whether by that is meant the Torah itself, or the wider biblical canon), on the assumption that the compilers themselves did not regard them as hopelessly incompatible and conflicting in fundamental outlook. After all, whatever divergences between the different laws on the same subject are apparent to us cannot have been invisible to those who kept these texts together. And if we go back to the pre-canonical phase of the emergence of the texts themselves, it would presumably have been possible for whoever produced the wording of the slave release regulations that we now call Deuteronomy 15 to expunge the earlier Exodus form of the wording from the record altogether, if they felt the new wording was a radically irreconcilable change. But they did not. Nor did the final editors of the Pentateuch do so, which suggests to me that they perceived Deuteronomy to be modifying, extending, and to some extent reforming earlier laws, with additional explicit theological rationale and motivation, but not throwing down a 'gauntlet' of alternative and conflicting legislation.

On some of the specific details, McConville rightly points out how Deuteronomy changes the Exodus regulations in favour of women (by including them in the sabbatical release, regardless of the distinction that Exodus had made between wives who came with the Hebrew slave, or wives given by the owner); and how it adds the requirement of a generous redundancy package for the Hebrew slave who chooses to go free. But I'm not so convinced of the material significance of some of the other differences he mentions. The status of the slave as owned property is probably common to both texts, not confined to Exodus. The use of *qana* in Exodus can mean buy or simply acquire; and the niphal of *makar* in Deuteronomy most probably means 'sells himself '. The fact that the word 'brother' is used in Deuteronomy may not signify any *elevation* of the status of the slave to full citizenship beyond what is implied in Exodus (where, as we have noted, slaves could participate in definitive religious ceremonies). *'Ah* is a term of wide scope. Of course it normally designates kinship, but it can be used beyond that, e.g. in political alliance with foreigners (1 Kgs. 9:13), or to express humane obligations (Amos 1:9). So its use in Deuteronomy 15:1 may simply clarify what was always presupposed in Exodus, namely that the Hebrew slave was to be regarded as a brother, whatever his or her precise legal, social or economic status. This is actually stated in Leviticus in relation to the resident alien (Lev. 19:34), and so it is not inconceivable that such an ethos was implied in Israel's slave laws, even if the economic reality was still that the slave was legally the property of the owner. It would fit with the other counter-cultural aspects of Israel's slave laws when compared with surrounding cultures, which McConville rightly observes. There is more than a hint that slavery was always seen as something that did not accord with Israel's self-understanding as the liberated and covenant people of the God Yahweh, even if it was tolerated but with mitigating and subverting legislation.

The major difference is undoubtedly between Exodus and Deuteronomy on the one hand, with their seventh-year release, and Leviticus, with its complex chapter 25 combining redemption procedures for land and people with the jubilee regulations for the fiftieth year. McConville remains unconvinced by my own attempt to account for the difference in terms of different social and economic realities to which the respective laws refer. So we must cheerfully agree to disagree. I have argued that 'Hebrew' slavery in Exodus and Deuteronomy refers to a form of partially voluntary self-sale by persons who for one reason or another did not have a share in the ownership of the land, whereas Leviticus is referring to impoverished Israelites mortgaging their family land and eventually being forced to put themselves and their families into a form of debt-bondedness until the jubilee would restore them to their original family land. The first was a kind of contract with a landless labourer that was limited to six years, unless the Hebrew wanted to make it permanent. The second was a mechanism to limit the effect of economic collapse within an Israelite land-owning family to a maximum of two generations.

Now my argument depended on earlier scholarship concerning the identity of the *'ibri* and its connection with *'apiru*, and I am well aware that there is still a lot of uncertainty around that subject, and I am no longer *au fait* with current scholarship on the matter. I agree of course that 'Hebrew' becomes the ethnic designation for the Israelites. However, several thoughts lead me still to wonder if the word had a socio-economic undertone related to roots in a category of people throughout the ancient Near East, who were generally a despised underclass. It would not be at all impossible for the same word to have both socio-economic and ethnic reference and for either to be more appropriate in specific contexts. After all our English word 'slave' (and its equivalent in several European languages) is derived from the Slav nation, which by the ninth century had become so dominated and exploited that the ethnic term came to have the socio-economic meaning. The reverse process is not inconceivable (i.e. a generic social term becoming a specific ethnic descriptor).

The word Hebrew is used predominantly in two contexts in the Old Testament: as a descriptor for the Israelites in slavery in Egypt, and during the years of Philistine domination (and then often in the mouths of Philistines themselves about the Israelites). Previous use of the term in Genesis includes: 'Abram the Hebrew' (and his non-landowning status is a key point in the biblical tradition; Gen. 14:13); Joseph (also referred to disparagingly as 'this Hebrew', 'that Hebrew slave'; Gen. 39:14, 17; 40:15; 41:12); and significantly to the social snobbery that prevented Egyptians eating with Hebrews (the term seems to be generic, not merely referring to the sons of Jacob/Israel only; Gen. 43:32). After the frequent use for the Israelites in slavery in Egypt and in the laws of Exodus and Deuteronomy, it is not used again until the Philistines subjected Israel to degrading oppression. Then it becomes a term of contempt (1 Sam. 4:9; 13:19; 14:11). In one verse a distinction is made between at least some Hebrews and Israelites, since Hebrews who had taken the Philistine side now went over to the Israelite camp (1 Sam. 14:21) – a memory that later made the Philistine generals understandably suspicious of David and 'these Hebrews' who were with him in their army (1 Sam. 29:3). In other words, it is not unreasonable to suppose that although Israelites could be described as Hebrews, the reason was not purely ethnic, but included an element of social denigration. Nor is it unreasonable to suppose that not all 'Hebrews' in the region were ethnically Israelite. That is, there may have been 'Hebrews' around who did not belong within the Israelite kinship and land-owning network. The terms may have overlapped, and eventually the ethnic significance became primary and finally exclusive. But at the time of the formation of Israel's earlier legal traditions, 'Hebrews' may have been a broader category, and 'the Hebrew slave' may not be simply synonymous with an Israelite one. This may be why the word order of the text of Deuteronomy 15:1 defines the 'brother' as a Hebrew (male or female), not the other way round. That is, it is not elevating the slave to citizenship (as we saw, slaves were already included in the covenant community); it is qualifying the status of the member of the community ('brother') to whom the following law applies: 'one who is a Hebrew', on the assumption that not all 'brothers' could be so described.

At any rate, it seems to me significant that the word Hebrew is completely absent from Leviticus 25. And likewise, the word that is used for the Hebrew slave of Exodus and Deuteronomy on his or her release, *hopsi* (a class of freed but still landless persons), is also completely absent in Leviticus. The person restored in jubilee does not become a *hopsi*, but returns to full ownership of land and family. There are other differences that I assembled when I first argued this case, but they need not be listed here.[2]

Of greater significance, and here I agree with McConville, is the way Leviticus 25 explicitly says that *Israelites*, even when they have been reduced to irrecoverable debt and have no option but to sell themselves to their creditor, must not be made to 'slave the slavery of a slave' (lit. 25:39), whereas *foreigners* could be bought and sold as slaves 'on the open market' as it were (Lev. 25:44–46). I do not see this as a discrepancy with Exodus and Deuteronomy (on the grounds outlined above, that I believe those laws relate to a distinct social phenomenon from what Leviticus 25 is dealing with). But it certainly does create tensions within the wider framework of the Old Testament canon.

So we come to McConville's discussion of how we are to relate the divergences within the laws to the discernable intentions of the canonical process.

In this section of his paper, I found much that was helpful, in terms of reflection on how the sheer fact of canonical collection of these documents, with all their variation, forces the observant reader to engage in some act of discernment between them. Set within its own immediate context, we can read the Exodus 21 passage and appreciate some aspects of its humaneness towards slaves, while wondering about the institution itself in the light of the rest of our knowledge of Scripture. But when we then read Deuteronomy 15, we should note that even for the ancient Israelite the new law was in tension with the old. At the very least one can say that an Israelite owner of a Hebrew slave who withheld freedom from the slave's wife in the sabbatical year (in obedience to Exodus) would have thereby been infringing the requirement of Deuteronomy. To obey Deuteronomy necessarily meant no longer complying with Exodus. I see this as an example of the living, historical and contextual nature of the growth of Scripture, and not in itself a huge problem – at least not any more than other cases where later revelation or commandment relativises previous levels of knowledge or patterns of behaviour. On a larger scale, for example, Walter Moberly points out the way the post-Sinai arrangements in Israel made the patriarchal forms of worship not only obsolete, but in some cases forbidden to Israelites.[3] Some Old Testament exclusion laws seem to be repealed (in eschatological vision, if not in political programme) within the Old Testament itself (e.g. the contrast between Isa. 56:1–8 and Deut. 23:1–8). And so one could go on.

The point then is that we cannot fully interpret any single text with confidence that we have 'heard the mind of God' on the matter, until it is set in the wider light of canonical teaching. So I am struck by McConville's pointing out that even the Torah itself provides a 'relativising' framework for the laws on

---

[2] See *God's People*, 249–59; and earlier in full in, 'What Happened Every Seven Years in Israel?', 129–38, 193–201.

[3] In Moberly, *Old Testament*.

slavery. For we read these laws in the light of a narrative that began its first book with the creation of all human beings without distinction in the image of God, and began its second book precisely with God's dissatisfaction (to put it mildly) with people suffering in political, economic and social slavery, and accomplishing their liberation in no uncertain manner. So 'the problem of slavery' in the Old Testament is not merely something that occurs to us from some elevated position of modern moral superiority. It is implicit in the canonical narrative, acknowledged (I think) in Job 31, and given a remarkably subversive response in the unparalleled law of asylum in Deuteronomy 23:15–16.

If Jesus had ever been faced with a similar testing question regarding slavery as he was over divorce, I wonder if his answer might have been comparable. I do not know (to my shame) if first-century Jewish society included slaves, but let's imagine it did and that some legal experts asked Jesus on what grounds it was permissible to take somebody into slavery, or on what conditions they should be released. One can imagine exactly the same dialogue as happened over divorce: a dispute over the meaning of particular Pentateuchal legislation, leading to Jesus saying something like: 'Moses allowed slavery because of your hardness of heart, but from the beginning it was not so', and then using texts from Genesis to point to the original intentions of God for human life – just as he did in relation to marriage. One might even argue that the divorce controversy is there in the Gospels with, in part, precisely that function, to show us how we are to handle those aspects of the Mosaic law that seem less than ethically ideal within the wider context of biblical ethics. We are to balance ideals from the creation and redemption narratives with the social realities that emerge from human hardness and need legislative control, and to exercise appropriate discrimination over which context shows us the ultimate will of God, while acknowledging the divine source of both dimensions of the text. Why? Because the canon itself does so. And Jesus (as a model reader?) gives us a case study in just such discerning reading.

Even within the Old Testament we are aware of other parts of the canon, other than divergent legal texts, where it is essential to suspend judgement on what we finally deem to be the message of particular smaller text units until we have listened to their wider context. We could be in danger of exaggerating the optimistic assumption that life will be successful, prosperous and long if only we live by the exhortations of Proverbs, until we hear Wisdom's balancing dose of realism in Ecclesiastes. Conversely, we could become unduly cynical if we accepted some of Qoheleth's reflections without the stronger ambient faith and conviction of the Wisdom tradition as a whole. Certainly, the reader of the book of Job knows that he cannot take the face value meaning of the friends' speeches without setting them in the framework of critique that the book as a whole places on them. We cannot read Psalm 72, 'for or about Solomon', without thinking of the tragic negation of most of what it affirms by the real

Solomon in the narratives, or even read the early splendour of his reign without the balance of what the narrator reveals later. And canonical approaches to the Book of the Twelve are urging us to recognise that while each prophetic book has its own integrity, their combination in the canon as single 'book' affects many issues of interpretation when we read them all in the light of each other.

Taking up the example of Jesus again, we note that he interprets the particular text in the Mosaic legislation in the light of the prior teaching of Genesis, and affirms the latter as the original intention of God the creator. In other words, he not only discerns where canonical priority lies in matters of ethical judgement, he also affirms the divine 'authorship' behind the canon itself. He is not contradicting 'what Moses said' by 'what God said', for of course Jesus treated all Scripture as the word of God ultimately. Rather, he distinguishes *within the canon itself* between the higher intention of God and the provisional engagement of God with the world of sinful human beings. The 'intention of the canon', then, would, for Jesus, be equivalent to the intention of God in and behind the human processes that were involved in its formation.

This, in my view, would be where a confessional approach to canonical interpretation, pursued by those who accept these Scriptures as God's normative revelation within the community of faith (in both testaments), would want to ground the approach that McConville grapples with here. For I have to say that I found the discussion of the *intentio operis*, and especially McConville's use of Eco's approach, very hard going. As I recall, questions were also raised about this in the course of the seminar in Rome. 'Intention' is something we associate with persons. Texts by themselves, and even a canon of texts by itself, are objects. If we speak of them having 'intention', we surely can only mean that there were people somewhere in the process of them coming into existence who had 'intentions' – intentions now carried, successfully or otherwise, and, of course, with all kinds of indeterminacy, within the texts and their arrangement. So if I speak of the intention of the canon (speaking personally), I can only make sense of that phrase by thinking of intelligent people somewhere who had a reason why they put this text with that one and left this body of literature in the shape it now is. I cannot make sense of a 'self-organising canon' with intrinsic intention, any more than I can think of my computer that way (however much it seems to have a mind of its own at times).

I have the same difficulty with the concepts of model reader and model author. At one level, I do understand it, for, of course, as an author myself, I know that in my writing I am hoping that the text I produce will persuade my reader into certain ways of thinking and acting in response. I am hoping to move the empirical reader to be the kind of model reader that I would wish for, not one who will misunderstand me, or distort my meanings, or mockingly dismiss what I have to say – even though I am fully aware that any empirical reader may do such things or worse. Similarly, I am aware that when somebody reads my text, they may well have a picture of me as a model author, and make assumptions about my intentions in writing the text they are reading – which may or may not be the case. But what I struggle with is the way the language of model author and reader then *dispenses with* the empirical author and any concern for his or her actual intention. For Eco to say that the idea of the intention of the empirical author is 'radically useless', ends up being vacuous. Presumably Eco is an empirical author who intended to say that and meant it, but (according to his view), his own intention in the matter is 'radically useless'. Or at least for me, radically incomprehensible. I'm sure the problem is mine, but I'm afraid I have read the paragraph that McConville quotes from him in the section 'Canonical Intentionality' concerning the intention of a text and a model reader, again and again, but I still fail to construe what it means – especially the second sentence.

> Thus, more than a parameter to use in order to validate the interpretation, the text is an object that the interpretation builds up in the course of the circular effort of validating itself on the basis of what it makes up as its result.

It is either circular itself, or just the grammatical equivalent of 'a bridge too far'. But if it means that a text itself is merely the construction of the conjectures of the model reader, then I cannot somehow fit that into any reality that I can make sense of. As I say, I can understand what model readers and model authors are in the process of reading texts. But for a text to exist in the real world at all requires the existence of an empirical author who at some time or other had some intention in producing it. And for a vast collection of texts such as the canon of Scripture to exist in the real world requires empirical collectors, editors and compilers, who likewise had intentions as they did their work.

As McConville rightly and helpfully points out, they did not see it as any part of their intention to smooth over the rough textures and awkward cross-grains of the texts they inherited – either by excluding some and leaving only later 'final revisions', nor by attempting to harmonise everything. They do indeed, therefore, invite the reader to read widely and as a whole, and to engage in warranted discernment within and between all that they pass on to us as Scripture (which is how I would prefer to phrase the matter, rather than the reader acting as 'critical judge' – though I think McConville may be using the term 'critical' in its more neutral sense of 'discerning and discriminating'). If, then, we come to these texts with the confessional commitment that the canon actually has both theological and conceptual coherence as well as a revelatory and didactic intention, it seems to me that we are certainly committed both to wrestle with the kind of diversity that McConville well illustrates, and to search for the mind of the canonical constructors in preserving it in all its puzzling inner conflicts, and thereby, through both processes, to discern the voice of God both in the particular and in the whole.

Bibliography

McConville, J.G., *Law and Theology in Deuteronomy* (JSOT Press, Sheffield: 1984)
—, *Deuteronomy* (Apollos, Leicester: 2002)
Moberly, R.W.L. *The Old Testament of the Old Testament: Patriarchal Narratives and Mosaic Yahwism* (Minneapolis: Fortress, 1992)
Wright, C.J.H., 'What Happened Every Seven Years in Israel? Old Testament Sabbatical Institutions for Debt, Land and Slaves', *EvQ* 56 (1984), 129–38, 193–201
—, *God's People in God's Land: Family, Land and Property in the Old Testament* (Grand Rapids: Eerdmans; and Carlisle: Paternoster, 1990; reprinted as digital edition, Paternoster, 2006)

Prophets

11

The Prophets, the Canon and a Canonical Approach[1]

No Empty Word

Stephen G. Dempster

The Prophets are part of the canon of Scripture because their words were not empty words; they were replete with power originating from the Ultimate Authority. It has been Brevard Childs who has emphasized this point more than most in the last few decades of biblical scholarship. The purpose of this essay is to describe the place and significance of the Prophets in the Bible and the contribution Childs has made to their study with his canonical approach. This will be discussed in five sections: (1) The Prophets and the Canons of Judaism and Christianity; (2) The Prophetic Message: A Canonical Message – No Empty Word; (3) The Relationship Between the Torah and the Prophets: Continuity and Overflow; (4) The Prophets and the New Testament: Continuity and Rupture; and (5) The Impact of a Canonical Approach in Studying the Prophets: No Empty Word.

The Prophets and the Canons of Judaism and Christianity

The Hebrew Bible and the Christian Old Testament[2] arrange the same content differently. The name for the Hebrew Bible is the *TaNaK*, an acronym

---

[1] Deut. 32:39. I am indebted to Gerhard von Rad's insight on this text and I have used it to structure this essay. See *Old Testament Theology*, Vol. 1, 339. I have also profited a great deal from his observation that the Old Testament is a book of ever increasing anticipation. See the second volume of his *Old Testament Theology*.

[2] The Protestant Old Testament. There are some additions in the Roman Catholic and Orthodox Old Testaments.

for three major complexes of books: The *Torah* (law or instruction) consisting of the five books of Moses; the *Nevi'im* (Prophets) comprising eight books (the Former and Latter Prophets);[3] the *Ketuvim* (Writings) containing eleven books. These twenty-four books multiply into thirty-nine books in the Christian Old Testament and are organized differently. In both canons the Prophets follow the Torah, but this sequence has a different significance for each collection.

In the Hebrew Bible, the primacy of the Torah was probably not just chronological but hermeneutical and theological as well. By virtue of its initial position, the Torah has a unique stature in the literary arrangement. Evidence at the junctures of the major canonical divisions implies a hermeneutical centrality for the Torah. A focus on the supreme importance of the Torah is found at its conclusion,[4] the beginning and ending of the Prophets,[5] and at the beginning of the Writings.[6] Ancient synagogue practices lend some support for this hermeneutical dominance of Torah, as tradition indicates that the Torah and Prophets were read regularly but the latter not to the same extent as the former,

---

[3] The designation of Former and Latter Prophets is not attested before the eighth century AD.

[4] Deut. 34:10–12 (cf. 18:15–18). This text concludes the Torah with a statement about the incomparability of Moses as prophet, the medium of revelation to Israel. It suggests the end of an era, while anticipating another one in which prophets patterned in the Mosaic image will arise, but who will not exactly correspond to it. A natural reading of the incomparability formula points to the uniqueness of the Torah and its qualitative difference from other parts of the canon. Chapman has recently argued that this formula only signifies the preeminence of Moses among the prophets, but this would indicate in this context – at the end of the Torah – the preeminence of revelation associated with his name – at least until a new Moses arrives. See Chapman, *Law and Prophets*, 111–31, 240–76. Chapman has done an important service in showing the continuity of the Prophets with the Law; however, that continuity does not imply the absence of hierarchy.

[5] Josh. 1:8–9; Mal. 4:5 (Heb. 3:22).

[6] Ps. 1:2–3; cf. Josh. 1:8–9. For further elaboration of some of these particular texts as contextualizing redactions (the term is mine) which function to orient the reader of the biblical writings see Blenkinsopp, *Prophecy*; Sailhamer, *Introduction*; Dempster, 'Extraordinary Fact'. See also Chapman's (*Law and Prophets*) detailed and insightful study in which he regards the ending of the Torah and Prophets as 'hermeneutical guides' but does not view Josh. 1:8–9 and Ps. 1:2–3 as having significance for the larger divisions of the Hebrew Bible (but cf. 288). It is true that there are a variety of orders attested for the Writings, but the oldest external indicators point to a collection with the Psalms at the beginning (Luke 24:44, 4 QMMT, *Against Apion* (Josephus) 1:37–43, *De Vita Contemplativa* (Philo) 25. The fact that Ps. 1:2–3 is a virtual duplication of Josh. 1:8–9 suggests a direct link between the two complexes of books. See Dempster, 'Many Texts'.

while the Writings did not receive liturgical prominence until later.[7] The structure of the Jewish Bible can be described with a diagram of three concentric circles in which the innermost one is the Torah, extending outward to the Prophets and the Writings. This would suggest an ethical hermeneutical focus, with the Prophets reinforcing the ethics of the Torah.[8]

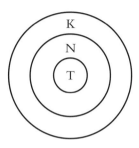

The canonical sequence which Christians later adopted was different.[9] The Torah was followed by each of the historical books in chronological order, beginning with Joshua and ending with Esther. Together with the Torah, these books stressed Israel's *past*. This section was followed by the poetical books of Job, Psalms, Proverbs, Ecclesiastes and Song of Songs, which emphasized Israel's *present*. Finally the prophetic writings rounded out the canon with a focus on Israel's *future*. Daniel was also included in this latter group by being placed with the major prophets and thus with its apocalyptic imagery, reinforced the future orientation of this collection. The diagram of an arrow with its base indicating the past (Torah and historical books), its shaft the present (poetic writings) and its tip the future (the Prophets)[10] could be used to convey

---

[7] See Lk. 4:16–20 for the oldest explicit evidence for the reading of Scripture in the synagogue. One could assume that a reading from the Law had preceded Jesus' reading from the Prophets here, since James at the Jerusalem council indicates that 'from the earliest times' Moses has been preached and read in the synagogues every Sabbath (Acts 15:21; cf. 2. Cor. 3:15). Another passage in Acts (13:15) reflects the custom of reading the law and the prophets after which an individual would be invited to speak. This coheres with the later practice in Judaism. See Beckwith, *Old Testament Canon*, 144; cf. Chapman (*Law and Prophets*, 268–71) who is more cautious here, arguing that one should not read into earlier periods later conceptions.

[8] See e.g. Barton, *Oracles*, 16–23.

[9] It is important to note that only one major Greek codex has this order and the question remains as to whether this was a sequence that was *adopted* from a Jewish group or one that was *produced* by Christians. For possible evidence suggesting the adoption of a Jewish order see Sirach 39:1 (Lebram, 'Aspekte').

[10] The Latter Prophets in the Hebrew Bible with the addition of Daniel and Lamentations.

the more eschatological focus of this particular hermeneutical arrangement of the canon.[11]

Thus the Old Testament ends with the prophets looking forward to the coming kingdom of God, while the New Testament begins with John the Baptist and Jesus proclaiming this kingdom. The Old Testament closes with the prediction of Elijah's advent to herald the Day of the Lord;[12] the New Testament opens with Elijah announcing this ominous Day.[13] In this arrangement of the canon the prophets are not so much enforcers of the covenant and interpreters of the Torah as heralds of the future. Although some would suggest that this order would make the prophets more like radical reformers and has encouraged a latent anti-Semitism, this surely stretches the evidence too far.[14]

The Prophetic Message: A Canonical Message – No Empty Word

There is no question that the prophetic message was a crucial part of Israel's and the Christian church's canon. One of the most common designations for the scriptures of Israel and the early church was 'the Law and the Prophets.'[15] Ancient liturgical practice in the synagogue included readings from both canonical divisions and as early as the second century AD there is evidence that in Christian services readings from the apostles and prophets were combined.[16] In ancient Israel, biblical texts themselves allude to the different media of divine revelation in ancient Israel, which reflect the name later given to the sacred writings. Jeremiah's enemies believed that it would be no great loss to eliminate him since the stream of revelation would not be impaired: 'Torah will not perish from the priest, or advice from the wise, or a word from the prophet' (Jer. 18:18). A similar passage stems from a judgement speech in the

---

[11] For the elaboration of this idea and its antiquity see Lebram, 'Aspekte'. See also Barton, *Oracles*, 16–23.

[12] Mal. 4:5–6 (Heb. 3:23–24).

[13] Mt. 3:1–3, cf. 11:13–14.

[14] See Rendtorff, 'Jews and Christians'.

[15] E.g. see 2 Macc. 15:9; *CD* 7:15–17; 1 *QS* 1:1ff.; *4 QMMT*; Mt. 5:17; 7:12; 22:40; Lk. 16:16; Acts 3:15; 24:14; Rom. 3:21.

[16] Justin Martyr, *First Apology* LXVII.

book of Ezekiel in which the people in desperation 'will seek a vision from a prophet, and torah will perish from a priest and advice from the elders' (Ezek. 7:26).[17]

Certainly by this time and earlier, prophecy was viewed as a means through which God communicated directly with humanity; thus along with torah and wisdom, this mode of revelation had an extremely significant place. 'Torah' referred to the teachings of the priesthood in which rulings were made on diverse subject matter based on a previous deposit of revelation;[18] a 'word' referred to the immediate revelation granted an individual, designated a prophet, through a dream or vision for the community or an individual; 'advice' indicated the considered judgement of someone with an enhanced ability of observation and insight. Although sometimes the various groups responsible for these modes of revelation were at odds with each other,[19] this was not an epistemological problem in which authoritative tradition was incompatible with spontaneous revelation, or faith with reason. The media were meant to be complementary not competitive, but human interests and ambitions could collide. When conflict appeared between the groups, these all too human interests were frequently the cause, with one group accusing the other of having 'sold out' and betrayed its calling. More often the conflict occurred within members of the same prophetic group. Prophets who simply supported the status quo were often regarded as false.[20]

The main term for prophet (נָבִיא) is a word that either means 'called out', i.e. a called out one (by the deity) or 'one who calls out', i.e. one who calls out (the words of the deity).[21] Although the evidence suggests a passive meaning, there is no doubt as to the function of the prophet. The prophet is clearly one who receives a message from the divine world and relays it to the human one.[22] The main formula which the prophet uses derives from the 'secular' sphere and is an expression that a messenger utilizes to preface the contents of a speech

---

[17] Margolis (*Hebrew Scriptures*) argued that this threefold designation of revelation reflected an early structure of a collection of Israel's authoritative writings, which he used to postulate a theory of canonical origins. See Brueggemann (*Creative Word*) for an heuristic use of this tripartite formulation for educational purposes.

[18] It later came to stand for the five books of Moses as the supreme instruction from which rulings could be made.

[19] See e.g. Amos: 5:21–27; Isa. 1:10–17; Jer. 7:21–26; 8:8–10.

[20] Jer. 23; Ezek. 13. See Overholt, *Threat*.

[21] Jeremias, 'Prophet, Prophecy', 697–710. There is clearly a history associated with this term since it gradually supplanted an older term for a person who had the same function (רֹאֶה). See 1 Sam. 9:9.

[22] See e.g. 1 Kgs. 22:19–24; Amos 3:7. The prophets hear a decision made in the divine council (סוֹד).

[23] Lindblom, *Prophecy*.

issued to a third party: 'Thus says X.'[23] In the prophets' case the 'X' is the Lord. This formula, along with variations, is a characteristic trademark of prophecy, indicating the divine source of the message, and hence ultimate authority. In the biographical accounts about the prophets in which they receive revelations, God is clearly the source of their messages.[24] The focus on the lips or mouth of the prophet emphasizes the importance of human speech, consecrated to communicate the divine will.[25]

According to the biblical evidence, Moses, the one whose name is largely associated with the first canonical division – Torah, was the supreme prophet. Torah is regarded as originating in Prophecy – the direct communication of the divine will. Sinai, the ultimate expression of the Torah, is regarded as the cause of prophecy. The people were unable to hear the actual voice of God because they were paralyzed with fear before the holy, divine presence. Consequently a mediator or *human* channel for the divine words was necessary.[26] Moses became that mediator and thus the pre-eminent prophet. His call to become the deliverer of Israel becomes the prototypical pattern for the later call of prophets.[27] Similarly he uses prophetic language when he delivers the announcement of the plagues to Pharaoh.[28] In contrast to all Israelite prophets, Moses is regarded as unique since he alone communed with God directly, 'face to face.'[29] It is clear that Moses' last words – Deuteronomy – are also prophetic as they sketch out two possible futures for the nation: obedience leading to life or disobedience leading to death.[30] The divine word is not empty but is a life and death matter.[31] At the same time, Moses predicts death for the people but they will be able to obtain renewed life if they repent when God's judgement comes to them in the last days.[32]

---

[24] This is not the case for the false prophets as they speak words 'from their own heart.' (cf. Num. 16:28; Jer. 23:16).

[25] Jer. 1:9; Ezek. 3:1–3; Isa. 6:5–7.

[26] Ex. 20:18–20; Deut. 18:16.

[27] Ex. 3:1–12. See Habel, 'Form'. The call usually consists of a divine confrontation, an introductory word, a commission, an objection, a reassurance, and a sign.

[28] Ex. 4:22; 5:1; 7:17; 8:1, 20; 9:1, 13; 10:3; 11:4.

[29] Num. 12:6–8. The actual expression in the Hebrew is 'mouth to mouth.' Cf. Ex. 33:7–11. See also Deut. 34:11 where the expression 'face to face' actually occurs. While it is true that God *spoke* to Israel 'face to face' at Sinai (Deut. 5:4) that was precisely the problem. Israel could not bear to hear the words of God and thus needed Moses in the capacity of a prophet. Cf. Deut. 5:23ff. and see Chapman (*Law and Prophets*, 120–23), who understates the meaning of this phrase in my judgment. It is because Moses has intimate knowledge of Yahweh that he can be a covenant mediator.

[30] Deut. 28.

[31] Deut. 32:47.

[32] Deut. 4:30; 30:1; 31:29.

The Former Prophets contain a history of the people and their response to the exhortations of Moses. It extends from the conquest and settlement of the land of promise to the exile. It is largely a history of disobedience to the Torah and it eventually leads to the death of the exile, confirming the Torah. The people learn that the Torah was not an 'empty word.'[33] The narrative breaks off in exile with the imprisoned king of Judah, Jehoiachin, being released and elevated to a position of dignity by the Babylonian monarch.[34] The Latter Prophets follow, four anthologies of the speeches of prophets who largely addressed Israel and Judah during the period described in the book of Kings.

The four books of history – the Former Prophets – complement the ensuing four anthologies since a similar editing process suggests that they were meant to be read together. Significant narrative sections from the history books are also repeated within the Latter Prophets.[35] The silence of the Former Prophets about the Latter Prophets was probably intentional since their editors were aware of the related four-volume companion.[36]

The Former Prophets contain many *stories* about prophets and the Latter Prophets are mainly collections of prophetic *speeches*. In the Former Prophets there are many examples of the fulfillment of prophetic predictions.[37] These accounts are intermingled in the historical narrative, stressing the importance of the prophetic word for shaping history. It is not an 'empty word.' At the end of this section there is a large segment of text that is devoted to the prophets Elijah and Elisha.[38] The importance of all the divine messengers noted in the Former Prophets is indicated by the reason given for the destruction of both kingdoms, Israel and Judah: the words of the prophets enjoining the people to follow the Torah were largely ignored.[39] Thus it is clear that this section of the canon, which consists of historical narrative, is a prophetic history shaped by the Word of God *in continuity with* the Torah.

The continuity of the Prophets and the Torah is most perspicuous at the end of the Former Prophets. When the book of the Torah is found in the temple during Josiah's reign, he rips his garments while it is read to him; this is no empty word – mere information. A *prophet* interprets the significance of the *Torah* for him.[40]

One of the central themes of this literature is repentance, which further links the Former and Latter Prophets. This is indicated by the Hebrew root שׁוּב

---

[33] Deut. 32:47. See von Rad, *Old Testament Theology*, 1:339.

[34] 2 Kgs. 25:27–30.

[35] 2 Kgs. 18:13 – 19:37 and Isa. 36–37; 2 Kgs. 24:18 – 25:21 and Jer. 52.

[36] Clements, *Prophecy*, 487.

[37] Von Rad, *Old Testament Theology*, 1:339–46.

[38] 1 Kgs. 17 – 2 Kgs. 13.

[39] 2 Kgs. 17:13ff.; 22:14–20.

[40] 2 Kgs. 22:14–20.

which is virtually a leading idea in both collections. Wolff has shown that this is an important theme in the first collection.[41] Deuteronomy holds out the importance of repentance as a means of receiving again God's blessing after apostasy.[42] When Israel repents, a setback at the conquest is averted and at the end of the book of Joshua there is a call for national repentance.[43] Repentance is the key for restoration in the book of Judges.[44] Samuel calls Israel to repentance in a key speech in the book that bears his name.[45] And in Kings even a repentant Ahab can stave off divine judgment,[46] while the king without equal is one who turned to the Lord with all his heart, soul and mind and led his nation in reform and renewal.[47] Finally it is the people's failure to repent and turn to the Torah at the preaching of the prophets that leads to exile.[48]

As for the complementary collection of the Latter Prophets, the repetition of the word שוב is striking throughout.[49] The call to repent is a distinguishing mark of a prophet and its omission the trademark of false prophecy.[50] Consequently, the message of these prophets was a message of repentance that largely fell on deaf ears. Their speeches provide the reason for the fall of the two kingdoms. The people were told by these prophets to repent or die, and they chose death. If they had repented, they would have been spared the disaster.[51]

But the message of these prophets also looked beyond the judgment to a new day for Israel and the world. A particular prophetic theme that is adumbrated in the narrative history and largely plays a minor role there is taken up in the Latter Prophets to play a major role. This is the prophecy of a dynasty for the house of David.[52] It is the one hope that runs like a thread through the book of Kings as the nation plummets into the depths of exile.[53] This dim light becomes a scintillating star in the Latter Prophets, whose rays would illuminate the way for a judged and refined people. They were able to see in the prophetic vision a new future in which Israel would be

---

[41] Wolff, 'Kerygma'.
[42] Deut. 4:30–31; 30:1–5.
[43] Josh. 7:16–20; 24:14–25.
[44] Judg. 2:11–23.
[45] 1 Sam. 7:3–5; 12:6–25.
[46] 1 Kgs. 21:27–29.
[47] 2 Kgs. 23:25.
[48] 2 Kgs. 17:13ff.
[49] See Holladay, *The Root SHUBH*.
[50] Jer. 23:14, 22; Ezek. 13:22.
[51] Amos 5:13–15; Jer. 18; Ezek. 18; Jonah 3–4. Note the consequence of a failure to repent: Amos 4:6, 8, 9, 10, 11.
[52] 2 Sam. 7.
[53] 1 Kgs. 11:13, 32, 34, 36; 2 Kgs. 8:19; 19:34; 20:6.

led by a new David into a new world.[54] There had been hints of this future in the Torah.[55]

It is not certain why speeches were collected and preserved for the Latter Prophets and not for the prophets who appeared sporadically in the prophetic history. What few clues there are can be found in the writings themselves. Isaiah tells his disciples to seal up his prophetic words – likened to torah and testimony – while he and his disciples 'wait for Yahweh who hides his face from the house of Jacob' (Isa. 8:16–17). The people were told to reject any revelation other than the prophetic word (Isa. 8:19–20). Prophetic words were regarded as a transcendent authority that the passage of time would prove; thus they had to be written down – textualized – to function as a witness to a later generation. Meanwhile, Isaiah and his disciples would be 'signs and portents' to the people, but afterwards the written words would perform a similar function (Isa. 8:18). They have a transcendent quality about them.

A similar factor is present in a detailed description of the production of a prophetic scroll. Jeremiah is told to have his speeches recorded from the time when he began to prophesy, roughly a period of twenty years.[56] The document is to be taken and read in its entirety to the people in the temple precincts when they are observing a holy day. The intent is that the collective impact of the oracles with their message of divine judgement would possibly induce repentance and thus avert an ominous destiny. Jeremiah's scribe, Baruch, faithfully records the prophecies and then reads the scroll at the temple. The scroll is later taken to the king. After segments of the scroll are read to him, he cuts them into pieces and throws them into a fire. It is noted that the king and his attendants do not tremble or rip their garments in an attitude of repentance (Jer. 36:24). Of course, the prophetic word is not so easily terminated. It is no empty word. Another scroll is produced to which are added many more oracles (Jer. 36:32). Consequently, this prophetic anthology of speeches was not only intended to evoke repentance but also serve as a witness to the truth of the divine word when the events predicted actually came to pass.[57]

That this textual form of the prophet's oracles was significant is shown by the obvious parallel that is drawn between a father's reaction (Josiah) to the

---

[54] Isa. 9:5–6; 11:1; 16:5; Jer. 23:5; 30:9; 33:17–22; Ezek. 34:23, 24; 37:24, 25; Hos. 3:5; Amos 9:11–13.

[55] Gen. 12:1–3; 49:1ff.; Num. 24:14ff.; Deut. 4:30; 30:1–10.

[56] Jer. 36.

[57] 'There can be little doubt that the motive which led Jeremiah to dictate the oracles of his life's ministry was to demonstrate how old predictions were on the point of fulfillment' (Jones, 'Traditio', 229). See also Barr, *Holy Scripture*, 6. The completed scroll in Jeremiah 36 represents an early stage in the formation of the book of Jeremiah.

reading of a Torah scroll in the Former Prophets and a son's response to the reading of a prophet's scroll in the Latter Prophets. The son should have had the same response as his father to the divine word.[58] But instead he ripped the scroll in defiance rather than his garments in repentance.

An important witness to the authority of the prophetic speeches is found in the superscriptions attached to the beginning of the prophetic collections in the Latter Prophets. They usually identify the human author, often providing information about his historical setting. Technical terminology often defines the speeches as divine revelation.[59] In fact in the earliest prophetic text, Amos, the superscription reads, 'The words of Amos … which he saw against Israel … happened two years before the earthquake.'[60] This specific time reference helps the reader locate the text – probably in recent memory since such a time only needs specification by the use of the definite article (*the* earthquake). The importance of this superscription testifies to the truth of the content of the book, which contains predictions of a seismic catastrophe, whose announcement fell upon deaf ears.[61] These were no empty words; they fractured the earth.

Accordingly the superscriptions testify to an evolution of understanding and betray an early canon consciousness on the part of the tradents responsible for transmitting the prophetic books. Very human words are identified with divine words:

> The specific intentions of the prophetic superscriptions are reflected above all in the particular vocabulary used to classify the books. The basic concern behind this language is the theological problem of authority and revelation. Thus the fundamental intention of the superscriptions is to identify the prophetic books as the word of God.[62]

These superscriptions testify to collections of literature viewed as divine revelation and therefore of ultimate significance. Tradents preserved this literature because it witnessed to the truth of the judgement contained in its words. But this was done not only to verify the judgement but so that the literature could speak to future generations and encourage them to hope in restoration which had also been announced by these same prophets. This was no empty word.

---

[58] See the careful study by Dearman ('My Servants'), who demonstrates the intentional nature of these parallels.

[59] Tucker, 'Prophetic Superscriptions', 65.

[60] Amos 1:1.

[61] Amos 2:13ff.; 9:1ff.

[62] Tucker, 'Prophetic Superscriptions', 68.

The Relationship Between the Torah and the Prophets: Continuity and Overflow

As indicated above, the different arrangements of the canons in Judaism and Christianity suggest different hermeneutical understandings of the Law and the Prophets and their relationship to each other. The Jewish canonical structure emphasizes the prophets as guardians and interpreters of the covenant, and the canon therefore has an ethical orientation while the Christian organization with the Latter Prophets at the end indicates an eschatological focus. In both cases the prophets assume the priority of the law.

In the history of scholarship this understanding has not always been the case. During the nineteenth century this relationship was reversed as critics argued that the prophets were the real pioneers and innovators of the Israelite faith, with their message of ethical monotheism coming from the unsullied springs of religious devotion. The prophets were radical individuals, endued with charismatic power. Unfortunately the Law came later and with its strictures dried up the springs of fervor.[63] When many features of this analysis were rightly called into question, the priority of the Torah and that of the canonical picture were generally reestablished. But at the same time there were different understandings.

Some scholars contend that the Prophets were clearly subordinated to the Torah, providing a type of commentary on the foundation of law. Gerald Sheppard explicitly makes this point when he argues that Joshua 1:8, which stands at the beginning of the Prophetic Division and urges meditation on the Torah, was added by a redactor who wished to subordinate the Prophets to the Torah and 'in effect serve as a commentary on it.'[64] Rolf Rendtorff argues even more forcefully for this subordination stating that 'the other parts of the canon are related to the Torah ... the Torah concludes with a look towards prophecy, but all the prophets who follow are subordinate to the one Prophet through whom God gave his Torah.'[65]

This subordination stresses the continuity between the two canonical divisions. Some would suggest that competing interests produced this relationship in which the Prophets have been 'domesticated' by the Torah. Blenkinsopp has argued that these two canonical divisions reveal the fundamental constituent element of Judaism, i.e. a basic tension between normative order (law) and charisma (prophecy).[66] First the Torah was canonized and concludes with a statement about the incomparability of Moses as a prophet; this was a move by a theocratic, priestly party that wished to proscribe any additional canonical

---

[63] Wellhausen, *Prolegomena*, 406.

[64] Sheppard, 'Theology', 153.

[65] Rendtorff, *Canonical Hebrew Bible*, 6.

[66] Blenkinsopp, *Prophecy*.

material. Only later was a prophetic division, the work of a more charismatic party, uneasily accommodated to the Pentateuch in a subordinate position.

While others agree that the Torah has a priority and the prophets are in fundamental continuity with this canonical division, they maintain the essential parity of these canonical divisions. The Prophets have a more dialectical relationship with the Torah. Walter Brueggemann, John Goldingay, and Brevard Childs stress the parity of the Torah and Prophets.[67] Brueggemann remarks that the Torah presents a more legal, normative order and the prophets a more disruptive order, ensuring that a new word can keep the old order from being domesticated.[68] Goldingay states that the prophets add the dimension of freedom to the order of the Torah and prevent it from being fossilized, while the Torah preserves boundaries for the freedom of the prophets.[69] Childs emphasizes the priority of the Torah but states that the prophetic division has it own independence and radical freedom that can never be subordinated to Law as 'mere commentary.'[70] Chapman extends the argument in a detailed analysis that provides a strong textual foundation for this point of view. For him the Torah has only literary priority and nothing else.[71]

Finally other commentators claim that the Torah is subordinated to the Prophets, providing as it were background for the prophetic message with its radical newness. These Christian commentators detect a strong Law/Gospel tension between these different parts of the canon. The Torah provides the background that is necessary to understand the importance of the promise – a note on which the Old Testament concludes and the New Testament begins.[72]

If these views sketch the main positions of scholarship, what about the texts themselves? There is no question that the prophets were concerned with the fundamental themes that dominated the Torah, namely righteousness and justice.[73] As

---

[67] For further views which can be categorized with these scholars see also Zimmerli, *Law and Prophets*; Tucker, 'Law', 201–16. Zimmerli sees the prophets as bringing to light the problem contained in the Torah, i.e. curse for disobedience as well as blessing for obedience. Thus there is a fundamental 'tension which lies behind these two entities' (92).

[68] Brueggemann, *Creative Word*.

[69] Goldingay, *Models*, 134.

[70] Childs, *Biblical Theology of the Old and New Testaments*, 175. Here Childs's views are similar to von Rad's. The latter stressed the radical newness of the prophetic message in his second volume of *Old Testament Theology*.

[71] Chapman, *Law and Prophets*, 275–76. By literary priority Chapman does not mean chronological priority but simply the fact that by being placed first in the canon the Torah has the priority of *story*. It thus has a type of literary privilege, but this does not mean it has superior status as revelation.

[72] Gunneweg, *Understanding the Old Testament*, 178; see also Bultmann, 'Prophecy'.

[73] Gen. 18:19; Amos 5:24; Isa. 5:7.

mentioned before, the prophets are anticipated in the Torah with the fountain-head of prophecy being regarded also as the mediator of the Torah, namely Moses. He is regarded as the prophet *par excellence*, the one on whom the divine Spirit rests in abundant manner,[74] the one distinguished from all the prophets because of unique communion with God.[75] The book of Deuteronomy emphasizes that God will establish the institution of prophecy in order to continue the revelation of Sinai, i.e. the communication of the divine will. A prophet like Moses will be raised up who will speak the words of Yahweh to the people, and criteria for the genuineness of prophecies will be established. Moses is the prototype of all later prophets.[76] Unmistakably, there is no tension, then, between Sinai and the prophetic institution. They are complements not competitors.[77]

At the end of Deuteronomy, two statements distinguish Moses from all others. It is stated that he is the 'servant of Yahweh' when he dies outside of the land.[78] The people will enter in but he remains outside.[79] This is the first time that such a title is used, and it suggests an honorific title, functioning as a most appropriate epitaph. But secondly, there is a statement about Moses' incomparability since there has been no prophet who has been his equal, who has experienced such direct communion with God, and brought about such a great salvation as in the Exodus.[80] This text directly echoes Deuteronomy 18:15 and gives the institutionalization of prophecy established there an individualistic twist. The latter text prepared the way for the canonical prophets – 'my servants the prophets,'[81] showing that they are to be seen in continuity with Moses – the Torah; the former text indicates that a fully Mosaic prophet has not yet appeared. At the end of the Torah, then, there is literarily an anticipation of further prophecy – the next canonical division – but also the expectation of a unique prophet who has not yet emerged. Consequently those who would see Deuteronomy 34:10–12 as a prohibition of prophecy are mistaken.[82] By

---

[74] Num. 11:17.

[75] Num. 12:6–8. Only Moses sees the 'form of Yahweh.' This implies direct, immediate access to God whereas all other prophets experienced divine revelation through dreams and visions.

[76] Childs, *Biblical Theology of the Old and New Testaments*, 169.

[77] Clearly, however, all prophecy must be tested by the claims of Torah (Deut.13).

[78] Deut. 34:5.

[79] Von Rad sees the parallels clearly between the servant of Yahweh here and the Isaianic servant of Yahweh: *Old Testament Theology*, Vol. 1, 295, cf. Vol. 2, 261–62. Both die so that their people might live. Miller develops the parallels more fully: 'My Servant Moses'. Cf. also Clements, 'Isaiah 53'.

[80] Deut. 34:10–12.

[81] 2 Kgs. 17:13; Jer. 7:25; Ezek. 38:17; Zech. 1:6.

[82] Cf. Blenkinsopp, *Prophecy*, 85ff. Chapman (*Law and Prophets*, 113–31) has an excellent discussion of this point. But when he relativizes the notion of the

virtue of its strategic placement this text validates the next prophetic corpus by showing that the figures who will be found there will be in fundamental continuity with Moses, yet not his equals. That person – that new Moses who will be a servant of Yahweh – is yet to come. This text is thus both retrospective and prospective, foundational and eschatological.

Consequently, the Prophetic division of the canon is linked to the Torah by the encouragement of the Israelite leader Joshua, to whom the prophetic spirit of Moses has been transferred, to meditate upon the Torah day and night and experience success in the land of promise.[83] At certain key points within the Former Prophets, the individual admonitions of prophetic figures are viewed collectively as a comprehensive warning for Israel to keep the Torah, or experience judgment. When the Northern Kingdom is judged, the correlation of Torah and Prophecy appears in the summary statement:

> Yet the Lord warned Israel and Judah by every prophet and every seer, saying, 'Turn from your evil ways and keep my commandments and my statutes in accordance with all the law which I commanded your fathers, and which I sent to you by my servants the prophets.'[84]

Not only could 'prophecy be viewed as possessing some kind of uniform message';[85] it was also in harmony with the Torah.

Similarly, two prophets emerge in this corpus who are most like Moses, echoing Deuteronomy 34:10 and 18:15. The first is the great Elijah who appears on the top of a mountain to see a divine vision, much like his distinguished predecessor. However, he only hears the divine voice in a whisper and is told twice that he has no business being there.[86] In fact, unlike Moses, he does not even get a glimpse of God.[87] The second prophet is Jeremiah; in an echo of Deuteronomy 18:18, he is told that he will have the divine words placed in his mouth.[88] He even demurs at being called to be a prophet, much like Moses. But Jeremiah is no new Moses.[89] He presides over the destruction of his people

---

incomparability of Moses, he does not take sufficiently into consideration the context of such a statement (Deut. 34:10) at the *conclusion* of the Torah.

[83] Josh. 1:8–9.

[84] 2 Kgs. 17:13–15.

[85] Clements, 'Prophecy', 44.

[86] 1 Kgs. 19:9, 13.

[87] Note that he is wearing a covering over his head when the divine theophany passes (1 Kgs. 19:13; cf. Ex. 33:23). It is true, as Chapman (*Law and Prophets*, 195–198) astutely observes, that there are significant parallels between Moses and Elijah. But these highlight the differences more sharply.

[88] Jer. 1:9.

[89] For the similarities and major differences between these two prophets see Alonso Schökel, 'Jeremiah', 27–38.

and goes back with them to Egypt. At the same time, however, he prophesies of a new covenant in which the Sinai Torah will be able to be obeyed because it will be written on the people's hearts.[90] The message of the prophets and the Torah could not be more complementary here. A new humanity is envisaged complete with a Torah heart![91]

If these prophets fail to equal Moses, a figure emerges in the corpus who is a candidate. In Isaiah 40 – 55, this figure surfaces in a new Exodus context,[92] who will lead his people out of captivity. This individual is none other than the pre-eminent servant of Yahweh, who proclaims a new Torah,[93] not just for Israel but for the world, and who has the responsibility of restoring the tribes of Jacob.[94] Like Moses, this person is willing to suffer for his people – even die for 'the many.'[95] He has uninterrupted access to God.[96] Although identified with Israel, he will bring salvation to Israel.[97] Somehow his mission will coincide with the whole complex of events recorded in Isaiah 40 – 66: the return of Israel to Zion, Yahweh's return to Zion in kingship, forgiveness and healing for Israel as well as the nations, and the exaltation of Zion as a light for the entire world.[98]

At the end of the Prophetic Division, as at the beginning (cf. Josh. 1:8–9), there are seams that stitch the Torah together with the Prophets. There is an explicit reference to both canonical sections. The people are encouraged to remember the Torah of Moses and prepare for the coming of the prophet Elijah whose presence will immediately precede the awesome day of Yahweh, when the prophet like Moses will come bringing Exodus-like salvation and judgment.[99] There is the retrospective look back at the foundation of the Torah and a prospective look ahead, just as there was at the end of the Torah. These texts appended to the end of the Prophetic Division ensure that 'the law and

---

[90]   Jer. 31:31–33.

[91]   Cf. Ezek. 36:26–27; Isa. 54:13–14. This develops the idea found in Deut. 30:1–10 of a new heart that will desire to practise the Torah.

[92]   The interpretive problems of course with this section of Scripture are legion. But see now the fine study by Hugenberger (*Servant*) who argues that the servant songs *in their context* suggest that a new Moses is envisioned as the servant of Yahweh. See his comprehensive survey of the evidence for the various interpretations. See also North, *Suffering Servant*.

[93]   Isa. 42:1–4.

[94]   Isa. 49:1–6.

[95]   Ex. 32:32; Isa. 50:6; 53:1–12.

[96]   Isa. 50:4–5.

[97]   Isa. 49:3, 5–6.

[98]   See the excellent survey of prophetic themes which will coincide with Yahweh's kingship: Hooker, *Jesus*, 30–40.

[99]   Mal. 4:4–6 (Heb. 3:22–24).

prophets are not rivals but complements' and balance 'the memory of the past with the anticipation of the future.'[100] Or as Rendtorff more forcefully puts it, 'The canon-consciousness which appears in the last paragraphs of the Torah and the Prophets shows the strong canonical link between the two.'[101] The reference to Elijah coming to bring about national reconciliation (turning the hearts of fathers to sons and vice-versa) surely contributes to the anticipation of the prophet like Moses. Blenkinsopp observes that already this passage may have apocalyptic overtones.[102] Sirach cites it in such a way as to suggest it refers to the coming mission of the Isaianic servant of Yahweh.[103]

But it is not only the case that there has been an integration of the Prophets with the Torah; the opposite has also occurred. In a number of key places there has been a profound prophetic influence on the Torah. The motif of promise unites all the patriarchal narratives of Genesis and becomes the engine which drives the Pentateuchal narrative forward, a promise which goes back to the pivotal call of Abram in which he is promised a seed which will be a blessing to all the nations of the world.[104] Coming as it does on the heels of a world under curse, this promise about the people of Israel means that they are not just any people – they have eschatological significance! Somehow they carry in their identity the secret of universal blessing. At hermeneutically strategic places in the Pentateuch, prophecies describe events that will take place in the last days.[105] These prophecies suggest that an Israelite king will lead a restored Israel over its enemies and establish an age of blessing. Thus not only have the Prophets been 'Torahized,' the Torah has been 'Eschatologized.' The two divisions present the one divine word.

Nevertheless, the Mosaic revelation has by virtue of its uniqueness a hermeneutical authority. The Prophets develop the implications of that authority and they remain the authoritative interpreters of this revelation. A notable example of this feature is the prophet Huldah, who interprets the

---

[100] Childs, 'Canonical Shape', 46. Childs sees this appendix as applying primarily to Malachi.

[101] Rendtorff, *Canon*, 64.

[102] Blenkinsopp, *Prophecy*, 122.

[103] Sirach 48:10b: 'to turn the heart of the father to the son, and to restore the tribes of Jacob.'

[104] Gen. 12:1–3.

[105] Gen. 49:1; Num. 24:14; Deut. 4:30; 31:29; cf. 30:1. The relevant Hebrew expression is בְּאַחֲרִית הַיָּמִים. For the significance of these examples see Sailhamer, 'Canonical Approach', 307ff.; *Introduction*, 207ff; 'Creation.' In an unpublished paper read at the National Association of Professors of Hebrew at Stanford University (June, 2005), I have also presented similar conclusions about the use of the Hebrew expression for the latter days (בְּאַחֲרִית הַיָּמִים.) in the entire Hebrew Bible. It is an eschatological technical term.

significance of a reading from the Torah during Josiah's time.[106] Prophets attempted to prevent a distortion of the cult by keeping in focus heartfelt repentance[107] and the importance of justice and righteousness;[108] they sought to prevent an interpretation of election which emphasized privilege and not responsibility;[109] they 'unpacked' the meaning of the divine attributes revealed to Moses,[110] whether to stress mercy to repentant Israelites[111] or hated Assyrians;[112] they invoked the divine judgment for covenant disobedience of the Torah.[113] A recent study stresses that the Prophets are necessary for the canon to demonstrate to Israel 'that election is *for* the nations, not against them; and that Israel was not chosen on the basis of merit but of grace; that its presence in the land depends on the quality of its justice, especially for the stranger (e.g., Ezek. 20, Amos 9:7–8; Zech. 7:9–10).'[114] But the prophets are not adding to the revelation of the Torah here; they are correcting distorted interpretations of the Torah, stressing the 'weightier matters of the Law.'[115] The prophets are authoritative hermeneutical guides for the Torah.

Yet, the prophets were also innovators. Like the Torah, their words were not empty but they overflowed the container of Torah! They kept alive the promises made to Israel and the house of David that some day there would be *universal* blessing, and they developed them in a way that seemed completely new – they exceeded the Torah's expectations.[116] God would make a way through the desert instead of the sea for the people in Babylon.[117] He would not only create streams of water in the desert; he would transform the desert into a garden.[118] He would give a new heart and spirit to keep the Torah;[119] he would create a new humanity by resurrecting a mass graveyard of corpses, breathing his life-giving spirit into them as he once did to Adam.[120] Death would be

---

[106] 2 Kgs. 22:14–20. This Torah may represent some form of the book of Deuteronomy.

[107] Hos. 6:1–6; Joel 2:12–14; Isa. 58.

[108] Isa. 1:10–18; 5:1–7; Jer. 7; 26; Amos 5:21–24.

[109] Amos 3:2; Jer. 37:17–21.

[110] Ex. 34:6–7.

[111] Joel 2:13.

[112] Jon. 4:2.

[113] Amos 2:6ff.; Hos. 4:1–3; cf. 2 Sam. 12 and 1 Kgs. 21 where kings are confronted with the Decalogue's prohibition of murder by prophets. See Zimmerli, *Law and Prophets*, 63ff.

[114] Chapman, *Law and Prophets*, 291.

[115] Mt. 23:23.

[116] Isa. 2:1–4; 9:5–6; 11:1–9; 19:24–25; Amos 9:11–12; Zeph. 3:9–11; Zech. 8:23.

[117] Isa. 40:3

[118] Isa. 35:1, 6; 41:18–19; 43:19–20.

[119] Isa. 54:13; Jer. 31:33; 32:39–40; Ezek. 36:25–27.

[120] Ezek. 37; cf. Gen. 2:7.

obliterated forever.[121] The year of Jubilee would be expanded not only to proclaim good news for the poor but for the blind, the crushed and all who
mourn.[122] The ark would become obsolete since the Divine King would actually reside in Zion;[123] and Zion would become Everest, a beacon to the nations,
from whose life-giving waters the whole world would experience shalom.[124]
No longer would an animal die for an individual's sins but now a servant would
bring about a great salvation for the nations. Who could have ever believed
this?[125] In that day the *Shema* would become a reality for the whole world as
Yahweh would alone be king and his name the only one![126] The prophetic
word was no empty word for certain but it was also one which overflowed the
container of Torah.

The Prophets and the New Testament: Continuity and Rupture

While stressing the fundamental fact that the promises made in the prophets are
fulfilled in the person of Jesus Christ and the community associated with him,
the New Testament writers see the prophetic message as not a break with the
Torah but as in fundamental continuity with it. There is a unity to this message
of the Law and the Prophets. Both the Torah and Prophets looked forward to a
prophet like Moses who would be announced by Elijah, who would come
before that new day of revelation. Matthew's Gospel portrays Jesus as saying
that the kingdom of God was dawning and that John the Baptist was the prophetic Elijah ushering in that day in which the tribes of Jacob would be
restored, climaxing in the ultimate prophetic word.[127] Jesus stated about John:

> This was written about him: 'I will send my messenger ahead of you, who will pre-
> pare the way for you.' I tell you the truth, John the Baptist is greater than any other
> person ever born, but even the least important person in the kingdom of heaven is
> greater than John. Since the time John the Baptist came until now, the kingdom of
> heaven has been going forward in strength, and people have been trying to take it by
> force. All the prophets and the law of Moses told about what would happen until the
> time John came. And if you will believe what they said, you will believe that John is
> Elijah, whom they said would come.[128]

---

[121] Isa. 25:1–8.
[122] Isa. 61:1–3.
[123] Jer. 3:15–17.
[124] Isa. 2:1–5; Mic. 4:1–4; Ezek. 47:1–12; Zech. 14:10–11.
[125] Isa. 53.
[126] Zech. 14:9.
[127] Heb. 1:1.
[128] Mt. 11:10–14 (*New Century Version*).

If John is Elijah bringing about national repentance, this must mean that a turning point in history has happened and that the prophet like Moses has appeared. Consequently the Gospels, particularly Matthew, are virtually repertoires of fulfilled prophecies. Jesus is the new Moses promulgating a new Torah, which brings out the implications of the old Torah – yet transcends it.[129] Jesus' ministry points to the fulfillment of the Torah and Prophets.

A number of key texts in particular suggest this. On the Mount of Transfiguration the disciples have a vision of Jesus conversing with Moses and Elijah,[130] the classic representatives of the Law and the Prophets and the ones united at the end of the prophetic canonical division. They are gazing at Jesus whose face shines like the sun with a greater glory than that of Moses.[131] At Sinai Moses saw only the 'back parts' of God,[132] while Elijah on the same mountain did not get even a glimpse. Here they get a full frontal view of the *face* of God! While the disciples watch, a cloud descends on them and they cower in fear before the divine presence. When they look up, Moses and Elijah have vanished and only Jesus remains; a divine voice interprets the event: 'This is my beloved Son in whom I am delighted. Hear Him.' These words echo a number of Old Testament texts. Two of them are Deuteronomy 18:15 and 34:10 – the promise of a prophet like Moses. Another text describes the suffering Mosaic servant of Isaiah (42:1), who was going to promulgate a new Torah to the nations and also suffer for them. It would seem that now this prophet is here – the goal of the Torah, the goal of the Prophets – the goal of the Canon! Then, Jesus discusses his suffering and death with his disciples and mentions that most of the people did not recognize Elijah when he came, i.e. John the Baptist![133]

Therefore it is no accident that the Gospels are no ordinary biographies since they focus largely on the last few weeks of Jesus' life. In fact one of the most cited passages in the New Testament is the passage about the servant of Isaiah.[134] The ultimate revelation of Torah and Prophecy is being focused in a human life.

In the early days of the first Christian community, Peter interprets Christ's life and death as the fulfillment of all the prophetic hopes:

---

[129] Mt. 5–7.

[130] Mt. 17:1–11.

[131] Ex. 34:29–35.

[132] Ex. 33:23.

[133] Mt. 17:10–13.

[134] What should give pause to those who question the prominence of this servant theme in the New Testament is the fact that the New Testament contains 48 references (allusions or quotations) to the fourth servant song of Isaiah! This is only surpassed by Daniel 7 to which 59 references are made: Aland, *Novum Testamentum*. I owe this observation to Block, 'My Servant David', 44.

God said through the prophets that his Christ would suffer and die. And now God has made these things come true in this way. So you must change your hearts and lives! Come back to God, and he will forgive your sins. Then the Lord will send the time of rest. And he will send Jesus, the One he chose to be the Christ. But Jesus must stay in heaven until the time comes when all things will be made right again. God told about this time long ago when he spoke through his holy prophets. Moses said, 'The Lord your God will give you a prophet like me, who is one of your own people. You must listen to everything he tells you. Anyone who does not listen to that prophet will die, cut off from God's people.' Samuel and all the other prophets who spoke for God after Samuel, told about this time now. You are descendants of the prophets. You have received the agreement God made with your ancestors. He said to your father Abraham, 'Through your descendants all the nations on the earth will be blessed.' God has raised up his servant Jesus and sent him to you first to bless you by turning each of you away from doing evil.[135]

Peter's argument is based on a unity of the prophetic message, a unity which is often not visible to an atomistic, historical analysis. But when the entire range of the literature is seen, patterns of judgment and restoration emerge clearly. There is a development from the suffering of Christ to the renewal of the cosmos, which was predicted by the prophets. Then there is a movement from the prediction of a prophet like Moses, to a succession of prophets with one fundamental message, a message that was rooted in Genesis 12:1–3 and which reached a climax in the sending of the holy servant (cf. Isa. 53). This is not proof-texting but represents an understanding of prophecy that surveys the Law and the Prophets panoramically. Clements concludes his study of this phenomenon:

> There are therefore good reasons for recognizing that the basic features of the interpretation of the OT prophecy which are evident by NT times do not represent a hermeneutic imposed upon the prophetic writings entirely from outside, but rather must be seen as an extension of patterns of interpretation which are woven into the literary structure of the prophetic corpus.[136]

But if the Prophets spill over the container of Torah, the New Testament ruptures the wineskins of the Prophets. Jesus not only heals the sick and the lame; he cleanses lepers and raises the dead;[137] he is not just the son of David but a greater than he;[138] he is not just a prophet – he is the Eternal Word, the final and full declaration of the heart of God;[139] if Moses was the supreme servant, Jesus is

---

[135] Acts 3:17–25 (*New Century Version*).
[136] Clements, *Patterns*, 45.
[137] Mt. 11:4–5; cf. Isa. 35:5–6; 61:1–3.
[138] Mt. 22:41–46.
[139] Jn. 1:1–3, 14, 18.

God's son.[140] The ramifications are astonishing. Now the least person in the kingdom of God is greater than Moses or Elijah;[141] each individual can have a shining face;[142] all can have shining faces as they turn to the Lord.[143]

In the early church the choosing of an existing sequence among various canonical options,[144] with the prophets (including Daniel) at the end, to precede the New Testament, clearly had the effect of increasing the prophetic temperature in the scriptures of Israel by linking explicitly the prophetic promise with its fulfillment in Jesus of Nazareth. The choice of the book of Revelation to conclude the Christian Bible makes the New Testament a mirror image of the revised Old Testament canon with history (Gospels and Acts) followed by the present (Pauline and General Epistles) concluded with a look to the future (Apocalypse). The ending vision of the prophetic Revelation resonates with the beginning of the Torah, but it explodes those constraints. Now heaven has finally united with earth and there is a city with an innumerable host of people, not just a garden with two individuals.[145] There is not just one tree of life but two;[146] there is no more sea,[147] no more night,[148] no more sun,[149] no more temple.[150] For the Lord and his Servant are there – with their people forevermore. The city will be a perfect cube – one gigantic holy of holies![151] All things have been made new![152] The prophets spoke their words in faith and although they knew their words were not empty, they probably had no idea of their explosive power![153]

The Impact of a Canonical Approach in Studying the Prophets: No Empty Word

The study of the Prophets has evoked an abundance of books, monographs, and articles from scholars in the last century. Biblical interpretation of the

---

[140] Heb. 3:5–6.

[141] Mt. 11:11.

[142] Mt. 11:11.

[143] 2 Cor. 3.

[144] Or the intentional transformation of one.

[145] Rev. 21–22. For the development of these themes in a canonical approach see Dumbrell, *End*.

[146] Rev. 22:2.

[147] Rev. 21:1.

[148] Rev. 22:5.

[149] Rev. 22:5.

[150] Rev. 21:22.

[151] Rev. 21:10ff.

[152] Rev. 21:5.

[153] Mt. 13:17.

prophets has moved through a number of phases which have characterized the discipline of biblical studies in general and which have mirrored to some degree the developments in the wider field of literary criticism. If one can conceive of an author communicating a message, i.e. a text, to an audience, there has been a shift in which the focus of interpretation has shifted first from the author, then to the text (the word), and finally to the audience. The following diagram illustrates this development:

$$\text{Author} \longrightarrow \text{Text (Word)} \longrightarrow \text{Audience}$$

Thus the locus of authority has likewise shifted from that which was behind the text (the author), to the text itself, to that which is in front of the text (the audience).[154] The author-centered methodology had a long and venerable history. It was mainly the viewpoint of pre-critical exegesis in which the words of the prophets were taken for granted to be their words as well as the words of God. But the problem with this approach was that it was often insufficiently aware of its own assumptions and consequently would read out of the Bible the standard church doctrine of its time.[155] But with the rise of historical criticism in which the words of the prophet were viewed against the background of historical scrutiny, the historical distance between the text and the interpreter became more of a reality. At the same time the growing elevation of reason resulted in the decline of the authority of the church and scripture. Consequently, the identification of the prophetic words with the historical prophet was no longer assumed. Historical critics began to drive a sharp wedge between the original prophets and the messages collected in their names as more and more of their message was viewed as additions and supplements to their original words.

The real goal of the program was historical. Decisions were made on the basis of historical criticism in order to construct a history of ancient Israel. A wide variety of methods was used to attain this goal whether they were source criticism, textual criticism, archaeology, tradition history or form criticism, etc.[156] Thus an analysis of the book of Amos would conclude that the optimistic oracles of hope at the end of the book (Amos 9:11–15) could not belong to the original prophet, who was a predictor of doom. Hence Wellhausen's famous conclusion about the incongruity of 'roses and lavender' with 'blood and iron.'

---

[154] The latter focus, i.e. the postmodern approach, will not be discussed. There are a number of studies of the prophets that are utilizing this approach. See e.g. Conrad, *Reading*.

[155] See the comments by Wright, *New Testament*, 3–28.

[156] See e.g. Perdue, *Collapse of History*, 19.

'Roses and lavender' had to appear in a more congenial age.[157] Of course, it was not so neat and tidy as this, for when the historical-critical method was applied consistently there was no limit to the individual scholar's ability to detect more and more sources; the original author under whose name the prophetic material was assigned became more and more of a phantom. Thus a recent study on Isaiah can claim:

> While there is no reason to doubt that a prophet or man of God called Isaiah was known to have existed, and did in fact exist, and while prophetic books are not self-referential, attribution of the pronouncements of Isaiah must be considered weak on any showing. He is named as their author three times (Isa. 1:1, 2:1, 13:1) but all three titles are acknowledged to be late and one (13:1), introducing a pronouncement against Babylon, cannot be from Isaiah .... It is beginning to look as if the book named for him can be assigned to Isaiah only in somewhat the same way that Psalms are assigned to David and sapiential compositions to Solomon.[158]

The same is true of other prophetic books. The result in general in prophetic studies was a trend toward atomization and fragmentation and lost in it all was the concept that the prophet had a word from God – a word that was not empty!

Increasing skepticism about the results of historical criticism led to a shift from the author to the text as the new locus of meaning. Some have seen in this shift 'the collapse of history.'[159] This is not to say that historical criticism was no longer practiced. The quote above indicates the opposite. The historical critical method exerts a powerful influence even today; however, its hermeneutical hegemony has been largely broken.

To connect the text rigidly to the author was due to the intentional fallacy, for scholars had become aware that texts were not just dependent on authors for their meaning. Texts had their own autonomy – they took on a life of their own – once reduced to writing. Consequently interpreters came to be concerned with the final literary product, and not what its chronological layers revealed. Fragmentation gave way to coherence. Rhetorical devices, literary structures, poetic arrangements were now appreciated and the final form of the text was emphasized. In biblical studies rhetorical criticism, redaction criticism and the concern for the Bible as literature began to flourish. Thus, for example, James Muilenburg's commentary on Deutero-Isaiah focused on the text as a literary unity, which was signaled by an inventory of literary devices that the

---

[157] Sweeney writes: 'The fallen booth of David ... speaks to the aspirations of the Jewish community in Jerusalem during the early Persian period that sought to restore Zerubbabel to the Davidic throne' (*Isaiah*, 12).

[158] Blenkinsopp, 'Formation', 61.

[159] Perdue, *Collapse of History*.

author had at his disposal.[160] There were many gains here but often it seemed that the words that were studied were examples of great literature. But were the prophets interested in eloquence? Surely their speech was poetic and imaginative[161] but was that why it was preserved?

One particular influential methodology arising within this text-centred milieu was the canonical approach developed by Brevard Childs. It profoundly shaped biblical interpretation of the prophets as well as other areas of biblical studies. Childs himself was something of a prophet for he put his finger on what was wrong in the study of Scripture – it was not *Scripture* that was being studied! His approach – for he eschewed the term 'method' as if he was offering one more method of biblical study – has both a literary/historical and theological dimension: literary/historical for after all the prophets spoke in a particular period of time; theological since after all they were *prophets* who claimed to speak a transcendent Word – no empty word – and whose words were preserved by a community *for precisely this reason.*

Frustrated with the growing separation of the church from the academy and the fact that the text of Scripture was being studied simply as an ancient near eastern artifact, Childs felt that the solution was to be found in wrestling with the final form of the text as *Scripture.* In his program he was first concerned with the fact that the text was understood to be a word from God which addressed ancient communities of faith and which continues to address believing communities today. This led him to show the hermeneutical impasse which had been reached by using the methods of historical criticism alone, in which the text (as witness) as Holy Scripture is not nearly as important as the text (as source) as part of an ancient near-eastern culture. In fact the hold historical-critical methodology had on biblical scholarship at the time in which Childs was developing his methodology is shown by the excessive attention he gives to describing its problematic nature.[162]

Childs essentially argues that historical criticism de-canonizes sacred Scripture – empties it – by taking it out of its canonical context and placing it in its historical context. After this procedure it becomes virtually impossible to re-canonize this meaning for contemporary believers. Lessing's ugly ditch becomes impassable. A

---

[160] Muilenburg, 'Isaiah 40–66'.

[161] Brueggemann, *Finally Comes the Poet*; and *Hopeful Imagination*.

[162] Scalise writes: 'A reader of Childs's Old and New Testament introductions cannot help but notice how preoccupied Childs seems with the detailed rehearsal and evaluation of the historical-critical state of the question against which the canonical proposal is set. At times the focus upon the historical-critical reconstruction of tradition is so great as to outweigh Childs's efforts to specify both the canonical shape of a biblical book and its larger theological and hermeneutical implications' (*Hermeneutics*, 67).

'secular' word – an empty one – is given to a community in need of a sacred one. Consequently, 'to assume that the prophets can be understood only if each oracle is related to a specific event or located in its original cultural milieu is to introduce major hermeneutical confusion into the discipline and to render an understanding of the canonical Scripture virtually impossible.'[163]

This leads Childs to de-canonize history and accept the canonical claims of the text. Therefore the historical context of a prophetic passage would be minimized and its canonical context maximized – the opposite of the critical approach. For example, in an important prophetic narrative in the Former Prophets, Childs observes how a typical historical approach listens for all the background noises (lions, trees) while being 'tone deaf' to the foreground ones (the divine word, truth).[164] In a study of the Elijah narratives Childs notes how typical historical-critical methods can distort the essential message:

> Is it possible that something significant happens in the retelling of the biblical story when elements which are in the background suddenly are raised to the foreground, or when everything is represented in the same sharp focus?[165]

Although it is probably not coincidental that Childs's concern for the text coincided with literary criticism's concern for 'textual autonomy,' it would be a mistake to equate the two.[166] The canonical approach uses historical criticism to provide a 'depth dimension' to the text and theological exegesis to communicate a word from God. The text is more than a literary vehicle. 'Its function as scripture is to point to the substance (*res*) of its witness, to the content of its message, namely to the ways of God in the world.'[167] And although historical criticism can recover various stages in the development of the text, none of these is authoritative except the final one. 'In the end, it is the canonical text that is authoritative, not the process, nor the self-understanding of the interpreter.'[168]

Childs's influence on the interpretation of the prophets has been revolutionary. Not that all scholars who now study the prophets have accepted his canonical approach, but they now have to reckon with it. Even staunch critics of the canonical approach reluctantly admit that Childs has 'shifted the goal-posts' of the interpretive game. [169] In an illuminating study Childs himself

---

[163] Childs, 'Canonical Shape', 48.

[164] The passage is the story of the man of God from Judah and his condemnation of the altar at Bethel (1 Kgs. 13). Childs, *Biblical Theology*, 142.

[165] Childs, 'Elijah Narratives', 128.

[166] See e.g. Barton, *Reading the Old Testament*, 90ff.

[167] Childs, *Isaiah*, 4.

[168] Childs, *Isaiah*, 4.

[169] Barton uses this metaphor. Note also his further comments: 'We should not measure Childs's importance simply in terms of adding up his disciples, who are

provides an overview of the ways in which a canonical approach can help elucidate the texts of the Latter Prophets: (1) In Amos an original message of judgment is reshaped by being placed in a larger theological context. This is the effect of the addition of the concluding oracle of hope in 9:11–15. Consequently 'from God's perspective there is hope beyond the destruction seen by Amos.'[170] (2) In Hosea the opposite occurs when chapters 1 – 3 are added to the beginning of the prophecy, thus providing a new lens through which chapters 4 – 14 are viewed. Israel's unfaithfulness is now understood metaphorically under the image of a failed marriage. (3) Sometimes historical details are effaced and an original context subordinated to a new theological context. Thus Deutero-Isaiah has been wrested from its historical context, dehistoricized and added to First Isaiah, to make it relevant as 'a purely eschatological word.'[171] (4) In the case of Jeremiah, the prose sermons have been reworked by the Deuteronomic school in order to pattern the prophet in the Mosaic tradition.[172] (5) Nahum's prophecy of doom against Nineveh which brims with historical detail is eschatologized by prefacing it with an acrostic hymn celebrating the ultimate triumph of God.[173] (6) An interpretive guideline is added to the prophetic material in order to ensure that the literature is not misunderstood. This explains the so-called prophetic appendices to the book of Malachi, one which points out that the law and prophets are not rivals but complements and the second which 'balances the memory of the past with the anticipation of the future.'[174] (7) The literature has been rearranged so that a new typological sequence subordinates an original historical sequence. Thus throughout many prophetic books judgement and salvations oracles complement one another.[175] (8) Finally, original prophetic symbols are given new meaning by being placed in a new context. Thus the plague of locusts in Joel (chs.1 – 2) becomes a pointer to the final eschatological day of Yahweh (ch. 3).

A concrete example of Childs's work can be seen in his study of Isaiah. Historical criticism had divided the book into three separate documents that are

---

admittedly few, but should credit to him at least part of the great sea-change which has come over Old Testament study in our day, as a result of which the exegesis of whole books and even the Old Testament as a whole is now on the agenda in a way unthinkable in, say, the 1950s or 1960s' ('Canon', 36). See also Tate's observations about the many recent 'one book' approaches to Isaiah. They 'constitute a paradigm shift in Isaiah studies … [and] an important anchor point is found in B.S. Childs's treatment of Isaiah' (Tate, 'Book', 43).

[170] Childs, 'Canonical Shape', 44.
[171] Childs, 'Canonical Shape', 45.
[172] Childs, 'Canonical Shape', 45.
[173] Childs, 'Canonical Shape', 45.
[174] Childs, 'Canonical Shape', 46.
[175] Childs, 'Canonical Shape', 46.

the writings of at least three different authors. This was one of the assured results of modern scholarship. Original unity had given way to fragmentation and as Childs has noted, although historical problems may have been 'solved,' a host of other problems multiplied. For example in so-called First Isaiah it could not be determined whether the prophet's original message contained promise as well as judgment and whether the prophet's message concerning Assyria and Jerusalem remained constant in his ministry.[176] As for the latter half of the book, major issues also remain unresolved, as to whether it was a literary composition or simply a collection of oracles.[177] But the larger problem overshadowing everything was that 'critical scholarship has atomized the book of Isaiah into a myriad of fragments, sources and redactions which were written by different authors at a variety of historical moments. To speak of the message of the book as a whole has been seriously called into question.'[178] Moreover the multiplication of speculative historical reconstructions for the settings in the latter half of the book did not promise to solve the problem. Consequently, a new hermeneutic was needed, one that took seriously the form which the canon had given the book of Isaiah.

This shape differed radically from the setting that historical-critical scholarship provided, i.e. that these oracles were originally addressed to the Hebrew exiles in Babylon by an anonymous prophet (Deutero-Isaiah). In the canon 'they are now understood as a prophetic word of promise offered to Israel by the eighth-century prophet, Isaiah of Jerusalem.'[179] This new 'non-historical context' is highly reflective and theological. This explains the lack of historical detail in these chapters since the new context has swallowed up the historical, universalizing 'God's redemptive plan for all history.'[180]

This canonical understanding of the text helps the reader perceive the integral relationship that exists between the various parts of Isaiah:

> The message of Second Isaiah is not an interpretation of history as such. Its meaning does not derive from a referential reading based on events recorded in the sixth century; rather its message turned on the fulfillment of the divine word in history … What the exilic prophet announced as fulfilling itself is the plan which First Isaiah had previously proclaimed and had been adumbrated in the events of 36–39.[181]

Numerous other correspondences between the two halves of the book are noted. The glory of God appears only to the prophet in first Isaiah but to all

---

[176] Childs, *Introduction*, 320.
[177] Childs, *Introduction*, 321–22.
[178] Childs, *Introduction*, 324.
[179] Childs, *Introduction*, 325.
[180] Childs, *Introduction*, 326.
[181] Childs, *Introduction*, 328.

peoples in Second Isaiah. 'The first prophet testifies to God as king (ch. 6), but his coming to Zion is only announced by the second messenger (Isa. 56:7).'[182] Thus an important thrust of the theological editing of First Isaiah was to connect it to Second Isaiah and vice versa, to ensure that they mutually interpreted one another.[183]

The book of Amos offers another instructive example of Childs's approach. As far as historical critical research is concerned, Childs accepts the conclusions of Hans Walter Wolff that the book of Amos has passed through a lengthy process of oral literary transmission.[184] Wolff distinguishes at least six different stages: oracles original to Amos (the five words and five visions [Amos 3:1 – 9:4]; earliest level of redaction by Amos' disciples (Amos 1:1b; 7:10–17); the three stanzas of a hymn; the Deuteronomic redaction (Amos 1:1, 9–11; 2:4f.; 3:1f.; 3:7; 5:25f.) and the post-exilic addition of promise (Amos 9:11–15).[185] For Childs this method is flawed since it assumes a specific historical cause that produced each stage in the text. Accordingly,

> speculation is constitutive to the method since the very information needed for such literary and historical judgment is largely missing from the biblical text and must be supplied. By the linking of exegesis directly to historical reconstruction the integrity of the biblical text and the theological enterprise is seriously jeopardized.[186]

This of course leads to reading the material counter to the direction of the text itself. Thus 9:11ff. is viewed as a commentary on the exile whereas from the book's perspective this is an event lying in the distant future.[187]

The important consideration for Childs is not to seek to recover the original message of the prophet through literary critical analysis, but rather 'the goal of canonical interpretation is to discern in the final composition how the message of Amos was appropriated and formed to serve as authoritative Scripture within the community of faith.'[188] When viewed in terms of the final canonical shape, the message was transformed into a word for all future generations.

How does one evaluate Childs's approach? First, it is clear that the approach of Childs is rather prophetic, i.e. it is concerned that the word of the living God is to be heard in the voices of the prophets. He reminds everyone that the literature to be examined is not just a collection of documents from ancient near eastern history but it is part of the canon of Holy Scripture. While there are

---

[182] Childs, *Introduction*, 330.
[183] Childs, *Introduction*, 333.
[184] Wolff, *Joel and Amos*.
[185] Childs, *Introduction*, 399.
[186] Childs, *Introduction*, 408.
[187] Childs, *Introduction*, 408.
[188] Childs, *Introduction*, 408.

similarities with other literature, one must approach this material differently since it is *sui generis*, and as a result needs its own exegetical method. But the important issue is that Childs is trying to let the canon speak, not the contingency of a word dependent on historical reconstruction. 'Canon serves as a guarantee that the biblical material has not been collected for antiquarian reasons, but as an eternal Word of God laying claim to each new generation.'[189]

Consequently, Childs has sought to build a hermeneutical bridge for Lessing's deep ditch. It is now easier to move to the contemporary world from the ancient text. This is because the reconstruction of historically contingent facts can never become the sure basis for religious faith; instead a canonical fact addresses the religious community with a divine word. The canonical Isaiah and Amos (and not necessarily the historical prophets) are bearers of the divine word. Their texts are able to speak to every generation and have been shaped by canonical tradents in such a way as to do this very thing. 'The grass and flower of historical contingency fade away but the word of the canon shall stand forever!'

Secondly, Childs deserves much praise for his courage and boldness in challenging the historical critical paradigm with its axiom that the prophetic word can never be disassociated from the time at which it was uttered. Childs has provided a viable alternative to the various exegetical options with their poverty of application; more and more interpreters can cross the bridge from history to faith. In the heyday of historical criticism the gulf between exegesis and application was shown clearly by the line on the pages of the *Interpreter's Bible* that separated exegesis from application. Although the line was thin, it amounted to a theological iron curtain.[190] Or to change the metaphor, Lessing's ugly ditch was impassable.

Thirdly, with Childs's approach there is a refreshing stress on the text itself, a practice that yields rich exegetical insights. It is not just a window into history as if history is the canon. Childs's comments on the elements that unify Isaiah demonstrate a careful concern for the text. But he also shows that the witness of Isaiah has a unique voice to sing with the other members of the canonical choir. One of the real strengths of Childs's exegetical work is the concern for the text before him, not the text as he would like it to be.

---

[189] Childs, 'Canonical Shape', 48.

[190] Note Childs's comments regarding his commentary on Exodus: 'The author does not share the hermeneutical position of those who suggest that biblical exegesis is an objective, descriptive enterprise, controlled solely by scientific criticism, to which the Christian theologian can at best add a few homiletical reflections for piety's sake. In my judgment, the rigid separation between the descriptive and constructive elements of exegesis strikes at the roots of the theological task of understanding the Bible' (Scalise, *Hermeneutics*, 59).

At the same time, the program of Childs leaves certain lingering questions. Childs is clearly a post-critical scholar. While he attacks historical criticism for its deficiencies, he does not wish to turn back the clock and embrace pre-critical methods. Although decrying the results of historical criticism and the wasteland it has made of the canon – the emptying of the Word, Childs accepts in general what he believes to be the major results of the historical method in order to gain a depth dimension to the biblical text. Thus the radical critic of a method still uses its results unquestioningly in a way that differs from his rejection of other methodologies, suggesting its greater scientific objectivity and neutrality.[191] Therefore there must be two or three authors for the work of Isaiah, and there are various stages in the book of Amos, culminating with an exilic phase. But canonical tradents removed most of the historical concreteness of the exile in Isaiah in order to make the book relevant to every age. Thus the complete book was envisaged as the word of Isaiah of Jerusalem (eighth century BC) – even though it was not historically. Childs emphasizes that this is not pious historical fiction. He accepts the results of historical criticism, but clearly believes they are insufficient to explain the canonical role the material now plays. Similarly for Amos, while the concrete nature of the original oracles of Amos have been preserved in their historical particularity, they have been provided with 'a powerful theological framework which transcended the perspective of the historical Amos.'[192]

Examples like these frustrate Childs's critics. Although he valiantly attempts to allay their concerns,[193] one wonders whether he himself has emptied the word of its radicality, by seeking a word free from the contingencies of history. For within the Israelite and Christian faiths there is the scandal of particularity and thus the problem of history. The divine word may transcend history but it is an incarnated word just as well, embodied in space and time. The word becomes flesh in a particular historical context and it has to do first of all with its historical referents, who lived in a particular place and time. If the word did not have a particular historical reference, it would not have been important. Consequently the acid test of a prophet was the truthfulness of the word, i.e. whether it would prove to be true in history (Deut. 18:15–22). Micaiah's

---

[191] See e.g. his copious criticisms of Brueggemann and Gottwald for their acceptance of postmodern and social scientific models of criticism. This incisive point is made by McConville, 'History', 78. The question needs to be asked, 'Why is historical criticism immune from such similar strictures?' Barr points out that Childs's ambivalence to the historical critic method – antipathy for but utilization of – 'constitutes a contradiction within his entire operation' (*Holy Scripture*, 133).

[192] Childs, *Introduction*, 409–10.

[193] Childs is extremely sensitive to this point but surely this is telling. See Childs, *Biblical Theology of the Old and New Testaments*, 104–106.

prediction of the death of Ahab on the battlefield stood in stark contrast to the prognostications of the false prophets (1 Kgs. 22). It would have been easy to have been vague like the Oracle of Delphi, but Micaiah is certain of the divine word. Only divine certainty can explain his conviction about the outcome of an imminent historical event. Throughout the Former Prophets the fulfillment of the divine word within history is noted repeatedly, and finally a prophet predicts the doom of the nation. The reason why the oracles of the Latter Prophets were preserved was because of the truthfulness of their words. Thus an editor adds to the book of Amos, 'These are the words of Amos … which he saw, two years before the earthquake.'[194] In many of the superscriptions there is a concern for historical specificity. Prophecy happened at a particular place and time and that is why it can be addressed to later generations. Its authority had been proven. Childs thinks that linking exegesis with historical reconstruction jeopardizes the integrity of the biblical text and the theological enterprise, but it would seem that prophecy is crucially related to history; the transcendent word has to be immanent to prove its transcendence. That is what the generation in exile putting the final form on the Former Prophets realized – the word of the prophets was not empty! They were in exile precisely because they ignored them.

As for Isaiah, a question to the first audience which heard the complete *book* read might be put as follows: How do you hear the Word of God? Is Cyrus a 'theological construct'? Was the word of the prophet a prophecy after the fact? Or was it the powerful word – unusual to be sure – of a true prophet who wished to speak across the generations with some specificity, so much so that this predictive capacity becomes an apologetic for the divine word that knows the beginning from the end?[195]

Scholars on the left and right often criticize Childs at this point.[196] He wishes to accept the results of historical criticism and then, it seems, ignore them when it comes to understanding the text. Thus ostensive references in the biblical material to historical reality which are patently untrue from a historical critical perspective become somehow true canonically. It is for this reason that conservative scholars believe Childs gives up too much with his uncritical acceptance

---

[194] Amos 1:1.

[195] Note McEvenue's observation about Cyrus and the historical specificity of Deutero-Isaiah: 'the mention of Cyrus (no matter how theological) has been left there [in Deutero-Isaiah] to smash any attempt to float in abstract timelessness' ('Old Testament', 234).

[196] *JSOT* 16 (1980) was devoted to evaluations of Childs's *Introduction* and his response. For conservative criticisms of his approach see the contributions by Oswalt ('Canonical Criticism'), Henry ('Canonical Theology'), and Brueggemann ('Brevard Childs' Canon Criticism').

of a particular version of the historical method and liberal scholars cannot accept his canonical readings. It seems that Childs has not overcome the classical faith-reason dichotomy. On the one hand he uses what he believes is a 'value-free' rationality to discern the historical 'truth' behind the shaping of the biblical text; on the other he accepts the biblical text's canonical claims. Thus we can read of a canonical personage and an historical personage who may not have much in common except the same name. This lays Childs open to the charge by James Barr that Christians need not a canonical Christ but a historical one.[197]

It is clear that historical reference is absolutely essential to prophecy. The canon does not contain the prophetic literature simply because it is timeless, nor because it provides fodder for historical reconstruction but because it has to do with events that happened and without these events the literature is just that – literature. This is not to say that the purpose of exegesis becomes all about events – the failure of the biblical theology movement – but that exegesis reckons with how these events were understood and interpreted by the Word. Like it or not, Word and Event are inextricably linked. If Word is empty of Event, bibliolatry is the result. Event empty of Word results in idolatry of event. Thus the importance of the Cross and Resurrection in the New Testament *and* their interpretations; thus the importance of the Exodus and Sinai events in the Old Testament *and* their interpretations.

It may be true, as Hans Frei has argued, that conservative scholars have bought into enlightenment epistemology unwittingly in their understanding of Scripture, trying to fit the biblical events into a narrative constructed by modernity, as opposed to earlier interpreters of the Bible who read the Bible as a narrative into which they fitted the facts of history.[198] But one common denominator of both pre-enlightenment scholars and conservative, post-enlightenment scholars was the belief in the link between the text and the external world. If the proper contemporary methodology is to read the Bible as history-like narrative, this does not mean that it is to be read with the emphasis on *like* only.

What is needed is an approach that actually is more canonical if that is possible, an approach that moves beyond the faith-reason dichotomy in which both the canons of Scripture and history are yoked in an uneasy union. A more wholistic canonical approach would be to start with faith and the canon and develop a critical approach from an explicit canonical perspective. Thus one

---

[197] Note Barr's criticisms regarding the prophets: '[Canonical criticism] does not attempt to wrestle with the question of truth. It does not tell us whether the view of God as presented by, let us say a prophetic book like Amos or Nahum, taken as a whole, is true or adequate or not' (*Canon*, 102).

[198] Frei, *Eclipse*.

does not drive a wedge between a historical and canonical prophet that can never be equated in reality. Historical study will accept the claims of the canon and seek to understand the historical context in ways that can elucidate these claims. Albert Wolters and Alvin Plantinga are seeking to develop an approach in this direction that seeks to develop a more wholistic canonical epistemology.[199]

While scholars of the left and right can debate the merits of Childs's approach, he has worked tirelessly 'in the trenches' to restore the prophetic word to a central place. As mentioned before, in some ways he himself has taken on the mantle of a prophet and proclaimed the way forward: It is by going back to the Scripture, which is not an empty Word, but a Word essential for human life![200] For this, Professor Childs deserves much thanks.

---

[199] Plantinga, 'Two Types'; Wolters: 'No Longer Queen'; 'Reading the Gospels'; 'Nature and Grace'.

[200] Deut. 32:47: 'For it is not an empty word for you but your very life.' Cf. Deut. 8:3 and Mt. 4:4.

Bibliography

Aland, B. et al. (eds.), *Novum Testamentum Graece* (27th edn.; Stuttgart: Deutsche Bibelgesellschaft, 1993)

Alonso Schökel, L., 'Jeremiah as an anti-Moses', in *The Literary Language of the Bible: The Collected Essays of Luis Alonso Schökel* (BIBAL Collected Essays 3; North Richland Hills, TX: BIBAL Press, 2000), 27–38

Barr, J., *Holy Scripture: Canon, Authority, Criticism* (Philadelphia: Westminster Press, 1983)

Barton, J., *Reading the Old Testament: Method in Biblical Study* (2nd edn.; Louisville: Westminster John Knox Press, 1996)

—, *Oracles of God: Perceptions of Ancient Prophecy in Israel after the Exile* (London: Darton, Longman and Todd, 1986)

—, 'Canon and Old Testament Interpretation', in *In Search of True Wisdom: Essays in Honour of Ronald E. Clements* (ed. E. Ball; Sheffield: Sheffield Academic Press, 1999), 37–52

Beckwith, J., *The Old Testament Canon of the New Testament Church* (Grand Rapids: Eerdmans, 1985)

Blenkinsopp, J., *Prophecy and Canon: A Contribution to the Study of Jewish Origins* (Notre Dame: University of Notre Dame Press, 1977)

—, 'The Formation of the Hebrew Bible Canon: Isaiah as a Test Case', in *The Canon Debate* (ed. L.M. McDonald and J.A. Sanders; Peabody: Hendrickson, 2002), 53-67

Block, D., 'My Servant David', in *Israel's Messiah in the Bible and the Dead Sea Scrolls* (ed. R. Hess and M. Daniel Carroll; Grand Rapids: Baker Academic, 2003), 17–56

Brueggemann, D.A., 'Brevard Childs' Canon Criticism: An Example of Post-critical Naiveté', *JETS* 32 (1989), 311–26

Brueggemann, W., *The Creative Word: Canon as a Model for Biblical Education* (Philadelphia: Fortress Press, 1982)

—, *Hopeful Imagination: Prophetic Voices in Exile* (Minneapolis: Augsburg/Fortress, 1986)

—, *Finally Comes the Poet* (Minneapolis: Augsburg/Fortress, 1989)

Bultmann, R., 'Prophecy and Fulfillment', in *Essays in Old Testament Hermeneutics* (ed. C. Westermann; Atlanta: John Knox Press, 1963), 50–75

Chapman, S.B., *The Law and the Prophets* (FAT 27; Tübingen: Mohr Siebeck, 2000)

Childs, B.S., *Biblical Theology in Crisis* (Philadelphia: Westminster Press, 1970)

—, *Introduction to the Old Testament as Scripture* (Philadelphia: Fortress Press, 1979)

—, 'On Reading the Elijah Narratives', *Int* 34 (1980), 128–37

—, 'The Canonical Shape of the Prophetic Literature', in *Interpreting the Prophets* (ed. J.L. Mays and P.J. Achtemeier; Philadelphia: Fortress Press, 1987), 41–49

—, *Biblical Theology of the Old and New Testaments: Theological Reflection on the Christian Bible* (Minneapolis: Fortress Press, 1992)

—, *Isaiah* (OTL; Louisville: Westminster John Knox Press, 2001)

Clements, R.E., *Prophecy and Tradition* (Atlanta: John Knox Press, 1975)

—, 'Patterns in the Prophetic Canon', in *Canon and Authority: Essays in Old Testament Religion and Theology* (ed. G.W. Coates and B.O. Long; Philadelphia: Fortress, 1977), 42–55

—, 'Isaiah 53 and the Restoration of Israel', in *Jesus and the Suffering Servant: Isaiah 53 and Christian Origins* (ed. W. Bellinger and W.R. Farmer; Harrisburg: Trinity Press International, 1998), 39–54

Conrad, E., *Reading the Latter Prophets: Towards a New Canonical Criticism* (JSOTSup 376; London: T&T Clark, 2003)

Dearman, A., 'My Servants the Scribes: Composition and Context in Jeremiah 36', *JBL* 109 (1990), 403–21

Dempster, S.G., 'An Extraordinary Fact: *Torah* and Temple and the Contours of the Hebrew Canon', *TynBul* 48 (1998), 23–53, 191–218

—, 'From Many Texts to One: The Formation of the Hebrew Bible', in *The World of the Arameans: Studies in Honour of Paul-Eugène Dion* (JSOTSup 324; ed. M. Daviau, J.W. Wevers and M. Weigl; Sheffield: Sheffield Academic Press, 2001), 19–56

Dumbrell, W.J., *The End of the Beginning: Revelation 21–22 and the Old Testament* (Grand Rapids: Baker, 1985)

Frei, H., *The Eclipse of Biblical Narrative* (New Haven: Yale University Press, 1974)

Goldingay, J., *Models for Interpretation of Scripture* (Grand Rapids: Eerdmans, 1995)

Gunneweg, A.H.J., *Understanding the Old Testament* (Philadelphia: Westminster Press, 1978)

Habel, N.C., 'The Form and Significance of the Call Narratives', *ZAW* 77 (1965), 297–323

Henry, C.F.H., 'Canonical Theology: An Evangelical Appraisal', *Scottish Bulletin of Evangelical Theology* 8 (1990), 76–108

Holladay, W.L., *The Root SHUBH in the Old Testament: with Particular Reference to its Usages in Covenantal Contexts* (Leiden: E.J. Brill, 1958)

Hooker, M., *Jesus and the Servant* (Cambridge: SPCK, 1958)

Hugenberger, G.P., 'The Servant of the Lord in the "Servant Songs" of Isaiah: A Second Moses Figure', in *The Lord's Anointed: Interpretation of Old Testament Messianic Texts* (ed. P.E. Satterthwaite, R.S. Hess and G.J. Wenham; Grand Rapids: Baker, 1995), 105–40

Jeremias, J., 'Prophet, Prophecy', *TLOT* 2, 697–710

Jones, D., 'The Traditio of the Oracles of Isaiah of Jerusalem', *ZAW* 67 (1955), 226–46

Lebram, J.C.H., 'Aspekte der alttestamentlichen Kanonbildung', *VT* 18 (1968), 173–89

Lindblom, J., *Prophecy in Ancient Israel* (Oxford: Basil Blackwell, 1962)

Margolis, M., *The Hebrew Scriptures in the Making* (Philadelphia: Jewish Publication Society, 1922)

McConville, J.G., 'History, Criticism and Biblical Theology', in *Issues in Faith and History* (ed. N.M. de S. Cameron; Edinburgh: Rutherford House, 1989), 68–86

McEvenue, S., 'The Old Testament, Scripture and Theology', *Int* 35 (1981), 229–42

Miller, P., 'My Servant Moses: The Deuteronomic Portrait of Moses', *Int* 41 (1987), 245–55

Muilenburg, J., 'Isaiah 40–66', *Interpreter's Bible*, Vol. 5 (Nashville: Abingdon, 1956), 381–773

North, C.R., *The Suffering Servant in Deutero-Isaiah: An Historical and Critical Study* (Oxford: Oxford University Press, 1948)

Oswalt, J., 'Canonical Criticism: A Review from a Conservative Viewpoint', *JETS* 30 (1987), 317–25

Overholt, T., *The Threat of Falsehood: A Study in the Theology of the Book of Jeremiah* (Naperville: A.R. Allenson, 1971)

Perdue, L., *The Collapse of History: Reconstructing Old Testament Theology* (Overtures to Biblical Theology; Minneapolis: Augsburg Fortress, 1994)

Plantinga, A., 'Two (or More) Kinds of Scripture Scholarship', *Modern Theology* 14 (1998), 243–78

Rendtorff, R., *Canon and Theology* (Minneapolis: Fortress Press, 1993)

—, 'Jews and Christians: Seeing the Prophets Differently', *BRev* 19 (2003) 24–31, 54

—, *The Canonical Hebrew Bible: A Theology of the Old Testament* (Leiden: Deo, 2005)

Sailhamer, J.H., 'The Canonical Approach to the OT: Its Effect on Understanding Prophecy', *JETS* (1987), 307–15

—, *Introduction to Old Testament Theology: A Canonical Approach* (Grand Rapids: Zondervan, 1995)

—, 'Creation, Genesis 1–11 and the Canon', *BBR* 10 (2000), 89–106

Scalise, C.J., *Hermeneutics as Theological Prolegomena* (Studies in American Biblical Hermeneutics 8; Macon: Mercer University Press, 1993)

Sheppard, G., 'Theology and the Book of Psalms', *Int* 46 (1992), 143–55

Sweeney, M., *Isaiah 1–39: With an Introduction to Prophetic Literature* (Grand Rapids: Eerdmans, 1996)

Tate, M.E., 'The Book of Isaiah in Recent Study', in *Forming Prophetic Literature: Essays on Isaiah and the Twelve in Honor of John D. W. Watts* (JSOTSup 235; ed. J.W. Watts and P.R. House; Sheffield: Sheffield Academic Press, 1995), 43–50

Tucker, G.M., 'Prophetic Superscriptions and the Growth of the Canon', in *Canon and Authority: Essays in Old Testament Religion and Theology* (ed. G.W. Coates and B.O. Long; Philadelphia: Fortress, 1977), 56–70

—, 'The Law in the Eighth Century Prophets', in *Canon and Authority: Essays in Old Testament Religion and Theology* (ed. G.W. Coates and B.O. Long; Philadelphia: Fortress, 1977), 201–16

von Rad, G., *Old Testament Theology* (2 vols.; New York: Harper & Row, 1962, 1965)

Wellhausen, J., *A Prolegomena to the History of Israel* (Gloucester: Peter Smith, 1973)

Wolff, H.W., 'Das Kerygma des deuteronomistischen Geschichteswerkes', *ZAW* 73 (1961), 171–86

—, *Joel and Amos: A Commentary on the Books of the Prophets Joel and Amos* (Hermeneia; Philadelphia: Fortress, 1977)

Wolters, A., 'Nature and Grace in the Interpretation of Proverbs 30:10–31', *CTJ* 19 (1984), 153–66

—, 'No Longer Queen: The Theological Disciplines and Their Sisters' (unpublished Paper: Wheaton College, 2004)

—, 'Reading the Gospels Canonically: A Methodological Dialogue with Brevard Childs', in *Reading the Gospels Today* (ed. S. Porter; Grand Rapids: Eerdmans, 2004), 179–92

Wright, N.T., *The New Testament and the People of God* (Christian Origins and the Question of God, Vol. 1; Minneapolis: Fortress, 1992)

Zimmerli, W., *The Law and The Prophets: A Study of the Meaning of the Old Testament* (New York: Harper & Row, 1965)

Writings

12

Towards a Canonical Reading of the Psalms

Gordon Wenham

Introduction

The twentieth century saw two revolutions in approaches to reading the Psalms. At the beginning of the century scholarship generally regarded the psalms as poems of personal devotion that were taken over for use in meditation or worship. Though many of the psalms had titles implying they had been written by David or other luminaries such as Asaph, most scholars around 1900 placed little store by these ascriptions but supposed most of the psalms had been composed much later, some time between the exile and the Maccabean era.

The first revolution in twentieth-century Psalm study was introduced by H. Gunkel, *Die Psalmen* (1926) and carried through by S. Mowinckel.[1] Their method of form criticism is well known and set out in the standard textbooks. It involves classifying the psalms into different types, hymns, laments, wisdom psalms and so on, and then suggesting possible *Sitze im Leben* for the different categories. These settings usually turned out to involve worship in the pre-exilic temple, though it was recognised that some psalms were composed in later times.

Both form critics and their immediate predecessors tended to view the psalms as historical artefacts which shed light on their authors or the circumstances of their composition or their subsequent use. According to earlier critics[2] Psalm 46 may have reflected the lifting of a siege on Jerusalem in 701, while form critics appealed to Psalms 2 and 110 to illuminate royal coronation ceremonies or Psalms 93 – 100 to demonstrate that the autumn festival was the

---

[1] Mowinckel, *Psalms in Israel's Worship.*

[2] Kirkpatrick writes: 'The miraculous deliverance of Jerusalem from the army of Sennacherib (BC 701) may be assigned as the occasion of these Psalms, with a probability which approaches certainty' (*Book of Psalms,* 253; cf. Alexander, *Psalms Translated,* 209).

occasion of Yahweh's enthronement.[3] Commentaries on the Psalms thus tended to have a history-of-religions perspective rather than a theological focus.

It was also characteristic of these earlier approaches to read the psalms as individual poems or worship songs, and to pay little attention to the collection as a whole and to its arrangement. Certain obvious groupings were noted, such as the Songs of Ascents or the Psalms of the Sons of Korah. It was often noted that Psalm 1 is an appropriate introduction to the Psalter as a whole, but the implications of its message for the whole were rarely touched on. Form criticism encouraged readers to compare psalms of the same genre, but seldom were the relationships between adjacent psalms in the Psalter explored.

All this began to change with the publication of Gerald Wilson's *The Editing of the Hebrew Psalter* (1985). This heralded the second revolution in twentieth-century Psalm study, which is the topic of the paper. In the following I want first to explain Wilson's work and the way his method and insights have been developed especially by American scholarship. Then second, I want to discuss the commentary of Hossfeld and Zenger on Psalms 51 – 100: this is a great work in Herder's Theologischer Kommentar zum Alten Testament series. Two more volumes are projected to cover the rest of the Psalter, which I hope will appear in due course. It well illustrates the methods of canonical reading, so I will use their interpretation of one psalm to illustrate their approach to canonical reading of the Psalms. Then I shall conclude by reflecting on some of the problems that canonical readings raise: what is the historical context in which the Psalter was compiled? What difference do the Psalm titles make to canonical interpretation? How does the total canonical context affect our understanding and appropriation of the Psalms? Are we talking simply of the Old Testament and New Testament canon of Scripture, or are we thinking of the church's use of the Psalms down the ages?

Gerald Wilson, *The Editing of the Hebrew Psalter* (1985)

Gerald Wilson, *The Editing of the Hebrew Psalter* (1985) began life as a dissertation at Yale and, among others, it is dedicated to Brevard Childs 'who taught me to respect the canon'. This book has blazed a trail, which many others have since followed and indeed tried to improve on. Though initially this was largely an American and Protestant project, it has been enthusiastically taken up by Catholic scholars in Europe such as Lohfink, Hossfeld, Zenger and Auwers.

However though the arrangement of the Psalter has been discussed intensively only in the last two decades, earlier writers did make occasional

---

[3] E.g. Mowinckel, *Psalms*, 61.

observations on the topic. For example, Rabbi Abbahu and Eusebius noted that it was association of ideas that linked the psalms not chronology. Basil and Jerome noted that Psalm 1 seemed to serve as a title or introduction to the whole Psalter.[4] In his nineteenth-century commentary on the Psalms, Delitzsch noted how consecutive psalms were linked together by key words. At the end of the century Jacob in an article on 'Die Reihenfolge der Psalmen'[5] noted some structural features of the Psalter, such as blessings at the beginning and end of books,[6] the placing of acrostic psalms,[7] and the gathering of prayers of the individual at the end of books.[8] But Delitzsch and Jacob were voices crying in the wilderness. For most of the nineteenth and twentieth centuries scholarly interest was focused on the earliest form of the text, its genesis and meaning, not on the final or canonical form. But when Wilson published his book on the editing of the Psalter final-form readings of Old Testament narrative were very much in vogue.[9] So far from being ignored, Wilson's work initiated a new wave of interest in final-form and canonical readings of the Psalms.

The Editing of the Hebrew Psalter begins by reviewing evidence from Mesopotamia that collections of temple songs were arranged according to a variety of criteria, such as genre, deity addressed, similar phrases.[10] The next two chapters review the evidence of the Qumran Psalm manuscripts to see if there are discernible patterns in the arrangement of the psalms. Among these manuscripts there seems considerable fluidity in the order of the last book of the Psalter, leading Wilson to agree with those who think that this section of the Psalter may not have been canonised till very late.[11]

The last two chapters of *The Editing of the Hebrew Psalter* are the most original. In the first of these Wilson asks whether the psalm titles give any insight into the principles of arrangement. He does not think this is the case, as a title describes the particular psalm it heads, not a group of psalms. Nevertheless, psalms with similar titles do seem to be grouped together, e.g. psalms of David (e.g. 3 – 41; 51 – 65; 68 – 70; 138 – 145), but common authorship is not obviously an overriding factor in the arrangement, or else all the psalms of David would have been grouped together; similarly one might have expected all the psalms of Asaph or the sons of Korah to have been grouped together.[12] Only in

---

[4] Auwers, *Composition*, 12–14.

[5] *ZAW* 18 (1898), 99–119.

[6] Ps. 1:1; 2:12; 41:1; 72:17; 89:(15)16; 106:3; 144:15; אשרי.

[7] Ps. 111 – 112 after three Davidic psalms; Ps. 119 after the Passover Hallel; Ps. 145 at the end of the third and last Davidic collection, Ps. 138 – 145.

[8] Ps. 38 – 41; 69 – 71; 86; 88; 102; 140 – 143

[9] E.g. Alter, *Art*; Sternberg, *Poetics*.

[10] Wilson, *Editing*, 13–61.

[11] Wilson, *Editing*, 93–121.

[12] Wilson, *Editing*, 155–73.

the case of the Songs of Ascents (Ps. 120 – 134) does a common generic title seem to have led to them all being put together.

More revealing of editorial purpose Wilson suggests are the conclusions to each of the five books of the Psalms. Each book ends with a benediction, e.g. 'Blessed be the LORD, the God of Israel, from everlasting to everlasting. Amen and Amen.'(41:13 [14]), or 'Blessed be the LORD for ever! Amen and Amen.' (89:52 [53]; cf. 72:18–19; 106:48). The Psalter concludes with a group of psalms that amount to an extended doxology to the whole work (Ps. 146 – 150).[13] Wilson notes that the first psalm appears to be an introduction to the whole collection, while Psalm 2 introduces the first book of the Psalms (Ps. 2 – 41).[14] The Davidic titles by identifying David as the speaker allow the reader praying or meditating on the psalms to put himself in David's shoes.[15]

In his final chapter Wilson begins to explore the theological implications of recognising an editorial purpose in the arrangement of the Psalter:

> The effect of the editorial fixation of the first psalm as an introduction to the whole Psalter is subtly to alter how the reader views and appropriates the psalms collected there. The emphasis is now on meditation rather than cultic performance; private, individual use over public, communal participation. In a strange transformation, Israel's words of response to her God have now become the Word of God to Israel.[16]

The division of the Psalter is also significant according to Wilson. He notes that at the seams of the first three books (Ps. 1 – 41; 42 – 72; 73 – 89) are psalms about the Davidic covenant, recalling God's promise to David that he would be the founder of an eternal dynasty (see Ps. 2:7–9; 41:11–12 [12–13]; 72:17; 89:19–37 [20–38]). But whereas the references to the Davidic covenant are quite positive in the first two books, Psalm 89 laments the fact that God does not appear to be keeping his promises.

'You have renounced the covenant with your servant;
you have defiled his crown in the dust.'

(Ps. 89:39 [40])

And the psalm ends with an appeal to God to remember his promises.

'Lord, where is your steadfast love of old,
which by your faithfulness you swore to David?'

(Ps. 89:49 [50])

---

[13] Wilson, *Editing*, 182–86.

[14] Wilson, *Editing*, 173.

[15] Wilson, *Editing*, 173: 'The final effect within the Psalter has been to provide a hermeneutical approach to the use of the psalms by the *individual*. As David, so every man!'

[16] Wilson, *Editing*, 206.

This dismal close to book 3 of the Psalter is responded to by book 4 (Ps. 90 – 106), which Wilson declares to be 'the editorial "center" of the final form of the Hebrew Psalter.'[17] The answer to the non-fulfilment of the Davidic promises is that 'the LORD reigns' (Ps. 93:1; 96:10; 97:1; 99:1). Back in the time of Moses (Ps. 90:1) the LORD was Israel's refuge. He still is, and Israel must continue to trust in him. Two groups of Davidic psalms are found in book 5 (Ps. 108 – 110; 138 – 145). Among the Songs of Ascents (Ps. 120 – 134) is one (Ps. 132) which celebrates the Davidic covenant, but Wilson is not sure that this is a reaffirmation of the Davidic promises. He seems to think that though this might have been the conviction of those who compiled the Songs of Ascents, this is not the view of the final editor, who wanted readers to put their trust in Yahweh the eternal king, not in a temporal earthly one.[18]

Wilson's work opened a new era in Psalm study and the validity of many of his observations has been widely acknowledged. The importance of Psalms 1 and 2 for the theology of the Psalter is now accepted: the first gives a wisdom slant to the collection and the second draws attention to the role of the king. Whether the promises to the house of David were understood messianically by the Psalter's editor is still a matter of contention. Wilson utilised the titles of the psalms as a means of classifying and grouping them, but he did little to exploit their exegetical potential as a route into the mind of the canonical editor.

Wilson's work prompted a wave of new Psalm studies. McCann's collection of essays *The Shape and Shaping of the Psalter* (1993) gives a glimpse of the enthusiasm of eminent American Alttestamentler for this new approach. It opens with an essay by J.L. Mays and responses from R.E. Murphy and W. Brueggemann. The last suggests the Psalms should be seen 'as a dramatic struggle from obedience (Psalm 1) through dismay (Psalm 73 after 72) to praise (Psalm 150).'[19] Wilson contributes two essays to the collection. In the second of these he argues that the Psalter is bound together by two frameworks: the inner framework relates to the Davidic covenant (Ps. 2; 72; 89, 144), whereas the outer is a final wisdom frame (Ps. 1; 73; 90; 107; 145).

Perhaps the most stimulating article in this collection is Patrick Miller's 'The Beginning of the Psalter',[20] which puts the structural insights of Wilson and others into the service of exegetical theology. Psalms 1 and 2 are often held to come from different redactional layers, though some have argued that the two were originally a single psalm that has been split in two (cf. Ps. 42 – 43). But whichever diachronic explanation is right, in the present Psalter the two

---

[17] Wilson, *Editing*, 215.
[18] Wilson, *Editing*, 225, 228.
[19] McCann, *Shape*, 41.
[20] Miller, 'The Beginning of the Psalter', 83–92.

psalms are distinct but closely related verbally and this needs to be borne in mind as we interpret them.

Psalm 1 sets the agenda for the Psalter by dividing mankind into two categories: the righteous who keep the law and inherit God's blessing and the wicked who suffer destruction. These two groups of people keep on reappearing in the subsequent psalms. In the laments the righteous repeatedly cry out to God for deliverance from their oppressors, the wicked:

> [In] Psalm 37, we have the most extensive discourse on the relation of the wicked and the righteous and their two ways outside of Psalm 1. In general, the plight of the victim, the *saddiq*, in the face of the wicked is very much to the fore at the beginning of the Psalter and throughout much of Book 1.[21]

Also prominent in Psalm 1 is the joy of studying the Torah, and its positive benefits for those who do. This emphasis on obeying the law reappears elsewhere in book 1 of the Psalter. Psalms 15 and 24 are entrance liturgies setting out the moral requirements for those who would worship in the temple, while Psalm 19 compares the life-giving power of the Torah to that of the sun. The penultimate psalm of book 1 echoes the sentiments of Psalm 1:

> I *desire* to do your will, O God;
> your *law* is within my heart.

(Ps. 40: 8 [9])

After Psalm 1 comes Psalm 2, which sounds another note. It is all about the king and the nations and their rulers who plan to attack him. This theme of the king under attack is explicit in the next three royal psalms 18, 20, 21. But the juxtaposition of Psalms 1 and 2 suggests that the righteous of Psalm 1 could be identified with the king of Psalm 2, while the wicked of Psalm 1 could be the king's enemies. This seems to be confirmed by comparing Psalm 1:6, 'the way of the wicked will perish', with the warning to the king's enemies in Psalm 2:12, 'Kiss the Son, lest he be angry and you perish in the way.'

This linkage between the two psalms leads to two insights into how the subsequent psalms in book 1 should be read. First, 'that we are to hear in the psalms the voice of the king, however subtly it may be present.'[22] This suggestion is reinforced by the psalm titles of book 1, which all include an ascription to David. Thus Psalm 3 'is understood easily, if not preferably, as the voice of the king surrounded by his foes and praying for God's deliverance and blessing on the people or nation.'[23]

---

[21] Miller, 'The Beginning of the Psalter', 85–86.

[22] McCann, *Shape*, 88.

[23] McCann, *Shape*, 88.

On first sight Psalm 8 does not fit this observation, though it does mention foes in verse 3. It is though thoroughly integrated into the sequence of psalms: it focuses on the majesty of God's name (vv. 1, 9 [2, 10]), which is how Psalm 7 closes and Psalm 9 begins (Ps. 7:17 [18]; 9:2 [3]). Furthermore, echoing Genesis 1:26–28, it teaches that every human being is a king:

> What is man that you are mindful of him
> and the son of man that you care for him?
> Yet you have ... crowned him with glory and honour.
> You have given him dominion over the works of your hands,
> you have put all things under his feet.
>
> (Ps. 8:4–6 [5–7])

This allows us to see the righteous sufferer as not only a just king who upholds the law, but any righteous person who does this:

> While Psalm 2 invites the reader to hear the voice of the Lord's anointed in the following psalms, Psalm 1 says that what we hear is the voice of *anyone* who lives by the Torah, which may and should include the king. But as such, the anointed one is simply a true Israelite, even as he is a true king.[24]

Whybray, *Reading the Psalms as a Book* (1996)

The first British contribution to this debate came from R.N. Whybray, well known for his studies of the Wisdom literature. In *Reading the Psalms as a Book* he examines the claims that the Psalter has been systematically arranged to bring out the two main themes of obedience to the law and the promises to David. He is somewhat sceptical about the first, but more positive towards the second. He acknowledges that there are a number of wisdom psalms which stress that obedience to the law will be rewarded, and that several of them open different books of the Psalter (Ps. 1 book 1; Ps. 73 book 3; Ps. 90 book 4; and Ps. 107 book 5). He also allows that quite a few psalms seem to have been tweaked editorially to give them a Wisdom thrust (e.g. Ps. 18:20–24 [21–25];[25] 92:5–9 [6–10], 12–14 [13–15].[26] He suggests that Psalm 19 originally consisted only of verses 1–6 [2–7] (about the sun) and that the rest of the psalm (vv. 7–14 [8–15], about the law) was added later by a wisdom editor.[27]

But this, according to Whybray, does not add up to proof that the book of Psalms has undergone a systematic Wisdom redaction. He is very dubious

---

[24] McCann, *Shape*, 91–92.
[25] Whybray, *Reading*, 51.
[26] Whybray, *Reading*, 55.
[27] Whybray, *Reading*, 46.

about the claim of Howard and others that there are verbal linkages between consecutive psalms: he suspects these apparent links may be in the mind of the reader rather than the editor of the Psalter.[28] He does not dismiss those who see some loose progression in the Psalter (e.g. from obedience to praise) but his main concern is not to read too much into the development. He finds 'no tangible evidence of a consistent and systematic attempt to link the whole collection together by editorial means'.[29]

Whybray is more impressed by the positioning of the royal psalms 2, 72 and 89 at the seams of the books. He is favourably inclined to seeing the position of these psalms as pointing to an eschatological or messianic reading, though he does not find much evidence of redactional modification to the psalms in question to make this clearer. Psalm 2, for example, envisages a universal rule for the Davidic king, something neither he nor any of his successors achieved. In the post-exilic era when there was no Israelite king at all, it could have been understood to express a hope for a new David. In such a situation 'a messianic interpretation would be a natural one'.[30] Whybray thinks the last verses of Psalm 18 might also point in this direction, and especially verses 7–15 [8–16], which picture God appearing in a Sinai-style theophany to help the king. It is natural to take them as 'speaking of a "new David" greater than the historical David.'[31] He thinks that Psalm 72 envisages not simply the Davidic dynasty lasting for ever as 2 Samuel 7 promises, but of the particular king reigning for ever (Ps. 72:5): 'The hyperbolic language' points 'beyond the present to a future saviour-figure'.[32]

While Wilson and McCann argue that Psalm 89 suggests that the failure of the promises to David prepares the way for book 4 of the Psalter, which celebrates the reign of Yahweh substituting for the rule of David's son, Whybray disagrees. He reads verse 46 [47] 'How long, O LORD? Will you hide yourself forever?' and verse 49 [50] 'LORD, where is your steadfast love of old?' not as cries of despair but of faith:

> It is important to bear in mind that laments in the Psalter … are not expressions of despair. However much the psalmists may accuse God of breaking his word and becoming an enemy, hope always remains that intercession will be effective: hence the characteristic 'How long?' … Even in apparently hopeless circumstances … the psalmists continued to hope. So here in Psalm 89 the psalmist urges God not to forget the promises that he has made that the Davidic dynasty would be forever (vv. 5, 22, 29, 30) and stresses his faithfulness in passages to which he gives such

---

[28] Whybray, *Reading*, 81–83.
[29] Whybray, *Reading*, 84.
[30] Whybray, *Reading*, 90.
[31] Whybray, *Reading*, 91.
[32] Whybray, *Reading*, 92.

prominence that they cannot have been intended merely as foils for the account which follows of disillusion and consequent loss of faith.[33]

Whybray argues that the very positive remarks about the Davidic king in book 5, especially Psalms 110 and 132, also make it hard to believe that the compilers of the Psalter had lost hope in the revival of the Davidic dynasty.[34]

Auwers also holds that the editors of the Psalter believed that the promises to David were still valid, but he is unsure whether this involves a restoration of the Davidic monarchy, a personal messiah, or a collective messianism. 'So, when Israel recites the psalms, it does it *in persona David*, and YHWH recognises the voice of the son of Jesse through that of the faithful. The sap of the Jesse tree still flows in their veins.'[35]

— Christ in the Psalter

The Titles

Final-form and canonical readings of the Psalter have to take seriously the Psalm titles. Traditional critics disregarded these titles holding that they were nearly all later accretions that despite their claim tell us very little about authorship or the contexts in which the psalms originated. Most canonical critics would not dispute that the titles do not give historical information about the psalms' origins, but it is clear that these titles were important for the Psalter's editors, who either knew the psalms with their titles or added the titles themselves. Either way the titles give an important glimpse into the way the psalms were interpreted. The grouping of psalms by author (David, Asaph, etc.) or type (Songs of Ascents) probably reflects the contents of earlier psalm collections from which the present Psalter was compiled. But in the present setting in the canonical Psalter that is not the function of the titles: they encourage the reader to understand the psalm with a particular heading in a particular way.

The Psalter contains several groups of psalms with the title 'A Psalm of David'. The first of these, the first Davidic psalter, consists of Psalms 3 – 41. Psalm 3 is headed 'A Psalm of David, when he fled from Absalom his son.' But this is not the first time David's voice is heard in the Psalter: he is clearly the main speaker in Psalm 2, where he introduces himself as the LORD'S anointed. But the key-word linkages between each psalm and the next, as well as the Davidic titles, create the impression that the prayer continues through the psalms without interruption, putting the whole collection under the patronage of David.[36]

---

[33] Whybray, *Reading*, 93–94.
[34] Whybray, *Reading*, 94–98.
[35] Auwers, *Composition*, 122.
[36] Auwers, *Composition*, 136.

Furthermore, when the titles with biographical elements as in Psalms 3; 7; 18; 34; 51; 52; 54; 56; 57; 59; 60; 63; 142 are analysed, it appears that most of them relate to the period before David became king. They describe his persecution by Saul, and of the three that are placed in his reign (Ps. 3, 51, 60) the first two describe unhappy episodes, his flight from Absalom (Ps. 3) and his adultery with Bathsheba (Ps. 51):

> Les titres 'historiques' du Psautier présentent donc … un David non encore installé, dont les larmes et les 'pas errants' sont comptés au grand livre divin (Ps 56: 9). Ce David est configuré à l'image de son peuple de pauvres et devient ainsi un modèle pour Israël dans son abaissement et son errance. Les titres historiques donnent ainsi au lecteur des psaumes, comme type et modèle, un certain David, plein d'humilité, de confiance en YHWH et de componction.
>
> Paradoxalement, l'attribution du Psautier à David a eu pour effet de faciliter l'appropriation des psaumes par tout israélite pieux, dans la mesure où le fils de Jessé a été présenté comme le modèle auquel chacun devait chercher à s'identifier.[37]

The theological significance of the Davidic titles has been more fully explored by Martin Kleer in *Der liebliche Sänger der Psalmen Israels* (1996). Kleer holds that the phrase *leDawid* originally meant 'about David' and that at a later stage in transmission, when the biographical elements were being included, it came to be understood as indicating authorship 'by David'.[38] This makes book 1 of the Psalter a spiritual diary of the praying David:

> Mit Hilfe seiner Psalmen geht David seinen Weg von der Not zur Rettung, von der Tiefe zur Höhe, aber nicht ohne viele Zwischenhöhen und -tiefen, bis er letztlich abschliessend bekennen kann: 'Gepriesen sei JHWH, der Gott Israels, von Ewigkeit zu Ewigkeit! Amen, ja amen!' (Ps 41:14). Diesen geistlichen Weg mit- und nachzugehen, lädt der 1. Davidpsalter die Beter, besonders die Armen und Elenden, ein; mit und wie David: Durch das Beten seiner Psalmen.[39]

Most of the biographical headings are found in the second Davidic collection, which runs from Psalm 51 to 72. Kleer notes that these biographical snippets draw not on the portrait of David found in Chronicles, where he is portrayed as the founder of the temple and the organiser of its worship, but on the difficult periods in his life mentioned in the books of Samuel, but not in Chronicles. 'The biographical headings portray David predominantly as the persecuted, betrayed and captured, as the mourning and guilty one.'[40] These psalms exemplify problems that the pious may experience and they invite him 'like David to

---

[37] Auwers, *Composition*, 151.
[38] Kleer, *Sänger*, 78–85.
[39] Kleer, *Sänger*, 93.
[40] Kleer, *Sänger*, 116.

overcome ... particularly life's crises with the help of his psalms and with God.'[41]

Book 2 concludes with Psalm 72, whose title 'to' or 'by Solomon' leads Kleer to take this Psalm as a prayer by David for Solomon. Thus the first two Davidic collections cover episodes from David's life, though not in chronological order. But the great hopes for David's descendants expressed in Psalm 72 were apparently shattered by the fall of Jerusalem and the monarchy, events alluded to in many psalms of book 3, and most explicitly in the final Psalm 89.

However, books 4 and 5 respond to Psalm 89's lament with the call to trust in the LORD's rule not in human rulers, 'without giving up the hope in the eternity of the Davidic covenant'.[42] Kleer holds that in the fourth and fifth books of the Psalter, the Davidic psalms must be understood as the psalms of a future David. For example, Psalms 101 – 104 do not look backwards but forwards. Psalm 101 envisages a new Davidic king, whose prayer (Ps. 102) will lead to the universal recognition of Yahweh (Ps. 102 – 103).

In the fifth book of the Psalms are two Davidic collections (Ps. 108 – 110) and (Ps. 138 – 145), placed at both ends of the book. In Psalm 110 Yahweh is given victory over those who were afflicting the new David in Psalms 108 – 109. Despite oppression this David maintains his faith in the LORD and praises him before the nations, so the LORD 'installs the new David as royal-priestly Messiah and intervenes himself against the enemies.'[43] The second Davidic collection (Ps. 138 – 145) is the new David's response to the questions and doubts of the exiles (Ps. 137:4). For Psalm 138 this is an opportunity to make the praise of the LORD clear to all the kings of the earth (Ps. 138:4), while the last verse of Psalm 145 announces the theme of the concluding Hallel (Ps. 146 – 150), 'let all flesh bless his holy name forever and ever' (Ps. 145:21).

Hossfeld and Zenger's Commentary

Kleer's study is one of a number[44] that give an overview of how the Psalms may be read canonically. There is an inevitable tendency in such works to focus on the points that can be easily connected together and to ignore psalms or parts of psalms that do not fit into the pattern. But a commentator cannot do this: he must exegete every verse and this poses challenges for canonical reading. But these challenges are tackled head on by Hossfeld and Zenger in their

---

[41] Kleer, *Sänger*, 118.

[42] Kleer, *Sänger*, 120.

[43] Kleer, *Sänger*, 123.

[44] E.g. Howard, *Structure of Psalms 93 – 100*; Mitchell, *Message of the Psalter*; Cole, *Shape and Message of Book III*.

contribution to Herders Theologischer Kommentar zum Alten Testament. It therefore seems fitting to summarise their treatment of a particular psalm to illustrate canonical exegesis in practice. Their volume only deals with a third of the Psalter, so there is much work to be done yet.

Zenger summed up his principles of canonical exegesis of the psalms in an article published in 1991:[45]

1. Canonical exegesis pays attention to the connections between one psalm and its neighbours.
2. Canonical exegesis pays attention to the position of a psalm within its redactional unit.
3. Canonical exegesis sees the titles of the Psalms as an interpretative horizon.
4. Canonical exegesis takes into consideration the connections and repetitions of Psalms within the collection.

Before examining how these principles operate in the interpretation of a particular psalm, we should say something about Hossfeld and Zenger's diachronic assumptions. For they are not content with a final-form synchronic exegesis, but frequently use the presumed origin of a psalm, or its place in an earlier collection to illuminate the meaning of the text.

The earliest (pre-exilic) collection of psalms is found in Psalms 3 – 41. In the exile various sub-collections were assembled, which were brought together in a final redaction of the Psalter between 200 and 150 BC.

Within these later collections Psalms 52 – 68, which are full of war imagery, were probably brought together first. In the fifth century this exilic collection was expanded and given a Davidic colouring to produce the second Davidic psalter, Psalms 51 – 72. Also in the fifth century this Davidic Psalter was expanded by encircling it with the psalms of Asaph (Ps. 50; 73 – 83), and prefacing it with the psalms of the sons of Korah (Ps. 42 – 49). Still in the Persian period, further psalms were added at the beginning (Ps. 2) and end of the collection (Ps. 89) to create a messianic psalter. It was in this phase that the first three books were distinguished by ending each with a doxology (Ps. 41:13 [14]; 72:18–19; 89:52 [53]).

Psalms 90 – 92, a tightly integrated group of psalms, are the first response to the issues raised by the messianic psalter. Psalms 93 – 100, 'the LORD is king' psalms which form another clear group, concluded a fourth-century version of the whole Psalter, which then consisted of Psalms 2 – 100.[46]

For an example of Hossfeld and Zenger's canonical interpretation I shall look at Psalm 51, the greatest of the penitential psalms, *Miserere mei*. After a

---

[45] Zenger, 'Was wird anders bei kanonischer Psalmenauslegung?', 397–413.
[46] Hossfeld and Zenger, *Psalmen 51 – 100*, 26–35.

bibliography and translation the commentary begins with detailed notes on the text and translation. These emphasise syntactical issues and show an aversion to emending the MT. Under *Analysis* there follows a fairly conventional discussion of the genre of the Psalm (penitential), a discussion of its sections, and the case for seeing verses 18–19 [20–21] as an addition to the original psalm (vv. 1–17 [3–19]), which was composed in the post-exilic era.

It is under *Auslegung* (Exegesis) that some of the characteristics of canonical exegesis start to be apparent. It begins with a long discussion of the title, which ascribes the psalm to David and connects it with his affair with Bathsheba. Zenger notes that this is the first of a series of biographical notes connecting psalms with episodes in David's life, mostly from the time of his conflict with Saul. These make a theological point that David suffered as a result of his affair, and his prayer for forgiveness (51:1–12 [3–14]) is not really answered until Psalm 65:2 [3]: 'O you who hear prayer, to you shall all flesh come.' Despite the praise that follows (Ps. 65 – 68), David still suffers for God's sake (Ps. 69). David does not see true *Shalom* himself, but Solomon his son does (Ps. 72:3, 7). 'What began with David's sin with Bathsheba eventually ended with Solomon's reign of peace, the son of David and Bathsheba. David's sin was turned into the salvation that Solomon could experience.'[47]

Then follows a full and thorough discussion of the theology of verses 1–17 [3–19] with much cross-referencing to the Pentateuch and other psalms. Notably absent though is discussion of 2 Samuel 11–12 and its possible relationship to this psalm. In other words, the exegesis is on the original psalm in its posited post-exilic original setting. Verses 18–19 [20–21] with its prayer that God will build up the walls of Jerusalem is not speaking about a literal rebuilding of Jerusalem such as Nehemiah carried out, for according to Zenger these verses post-date Nehemiah, but it is praying about the eschatological renewal of Jerusalem. The post-exilic theology, especially the Isaianic school, used to dream of this.[48] In this revived city, whose inhabitants have been saved by God from their guilt and have experienced recreation, their sacrifices will be acceptable to God. Though these last two verses were added later to the psalm, Zenger thinks they make a very fitting conclusion:

> The people who have been newly created through the forgiveness of their sin are in reality the ideal inhabitants of the new Jerusalem. Conversely the renewal of Zion as the centre of creation begins with the recreation of its inhabitants. Indeed where sinners allow themselves to be recreated by YHWH, the people of God will be renewed. And when this occurs on Zion … Jerusalem will be the city of righteousness.[49]

---

[47] Hossfeld and Zenger, *Psalmen 51 – 100*, 49, quoting Kleer, *Sänger*, 112.
[48] Hossfeld and Zenger, *Psalmen 51 – 100*, 55.
[49] Hossfeld and Zenger, *Psalmen 51 – 100*, 56.

Under 'Context, Reception, Meaning' Zenger explores subsequent settings and interpretations of the psalm. First is the stage of its incorporation into the second Davidic psalter (Ps. 51 – 72). At this stage the title was added and the psalm became seen as David's confession. Zenger notes many verbal affinities within the psalm with the accounts in 2 Samuel 11 – 12. The deliberate positioning of the psalm as the first in this collection gives it a programmatic quality, making David a model for Israel, even a messianic figure. 'From David Israel should learn that whoever stands can fall, but also whoever has fallen can by the mercy of God … be raised up again, even be recreated.'[50]

But Psalm 51 does not just serve as a programmatic opening to the second Davidic psalter, but also as a summary of the end of the first Davidic psalter, i.e. Psalms 35 – 41. Even closer connections may be seen between Psalms 50 and 51. Both criticise empty sacrificial ritual and demand worship that springs from an acknowledgement of one's helplessness and from a righteous lifestyle (Ps. 50:8–15, cf. 51:14–19 [16–21]). They are also linked by the theme of God's judging and saving righteousness (50:6; cf. 51:4 [6], 14 [16]; 50:23; cf. 51:12 [14], 14 [16]).[51] This link between Psalms 50 and 51 ties together the second Davidic psalter (Ps. 5 – 72) with the Asaph collection (Ps. 50, 73 – 83). The Asaph collection engages with the theological crisis engendered by the destruction of the temple. Both psalms present a critique of worthless sacrifice and a vision of sacrificial worship that is acceptable to God. At the same time, the promise of a rebuilding of Jerusalem by Yahweh (Ps. 51:18 [20]) gives the laments in the Asaph collection about the destruction of the temple and the city a special piquancy.

Zenger does not explicitly discuss the meaning of the psalm within the context of the complete Psalter, though obviously his comments on the Davidic theme of the Psalter give some pointers in that direction. He then makes a few comments on the way the Septuagint and Targum translate the psalm, before offering some reflections on the New Testament use of Psalm 51. In Jesus' parables of the prodigal son and the Pharisee and the publican both penitents quote Psalm 51:1 [3], 4 [6] (cf. Lk. 18:13; 15:18, 21). More importantly, Luke 15 gives a vivid illustration of the whole structure of Psalm 51: acknowledgement of sin – confession to a merciful God – recreation – festive meal.

Though Paul quotes Psalm 51 only in Romans 3:4, Zenger holds that it forms the background to the whole of his discussion in Romans 1:18 – 3:31, which concerns the revelation of God's wrath on those who reject the knowledge of God and the eschatological revealing of God's saving righteousness.[52]

This discussion of the New Testament use of Psalm 51 paves the way for Zenger's final section, 'Bedeutung' (meaning), where he reflects on the

---

[50] Hossfeld and Zenger, *Psalmen 51 – 100*, 56.
[51] Hossfeld and Zenger, *Psalmen 51 – 100*, 57.
[52] Hossfeld and Zenger, *Psalmen 51 – 100*, 58.

subsequent use of the psalm. It is important in the Jewish Day of Atonement liturgy and is the Christian penitential psalm *par excellence*. It paved the way for Luther's doctrine of grace. Though some have misapplied Psalm 51:5 [7] to prove the doctrine of original sin, the psalm does bear witness to the environment of guilt into which everyone is born and perpetuates by his own sin: 'But simultaneously the psalm maintains that the destructiveness of this sinful environment is counteracted by the renewing reviving gift of the merciful God.'[53]

Summary

This paper has sought to trace the development of canonical readings of the psalms: from Childs, via Wilson, Whybray, and Kleer, to Hossfeld and Zenger. There are many others who have contributed to the discussion, but time does not permit further discussion. I hope my selection gives a glimpse of the best of canonical readings of the psalms.

There is, I think, no doubt that this approach has led to a deeper and richer theological approach to reading the psalms, an approach that is especially congenial to the Christian interpreter. The earlier historically orientated and formcritical readings seem threadbare by comparison. But this is not to say that any of the studies included here are the last word on the subject. There are a number of issues that need further discussion.

The most fundamental issue is: what is the canonical context in which we read each psalm? Hossfeld and Zenger see a variety of contexts for reading each psalm. They look at the meaning of Psalm 51 in its original form (i.e. minus title and last two verses), its meaning as part of the second Davidic psalter, its setting when linked with the psalms of Asaph, its use in the New Testament, and in Christian and Jewish devotion. McCann,[54] by contrast, focuses on the meaning of Psalm 51 in the present book of the Psalms with some reference to the New Testament.

Which of these contexts is most appropriate for a canonical reading, or are all equally valid? I tend to think three canonical contexts are more important than others.

First, there is the canonical context of the whole Psalter. If, as I think has been demonstrated, the psalms have been arranged thematically, by title, and by keywords to form a deliberate sequence, it is imperative to read one psalm in the context of the whole collection and in particular in relationship to its near neighbours.

---

[53] Hossfeld and Zenger, *Psalmen 51 – 100*, 59.

[54] McCann, 'The Book of the Psalms', 884–89.

Second, there is reading the psalms in the context of the Jewish canon, the Hebrew Bible. The psalms themselves invite this by their frequent reference to historical figures and episodes from the past. Some (e.g. Ps. 104; 105; 106) seem to retell the Pentateuch in poetic fashion. Psalm 1 invites the reader to meditate on the law day and night. The titles of the psalms, as well as some of the texts, point to David's connection with the psalms. Furthermore, in writing Old Testament theology it is surely appropriate to compare the message of the psalms with other works, such as Chronicles, that originated in the post-exilic era.

Third, of course, the psalms need to be read in the context of the Christian canon of Old and New Testaments. The Psalms are the book of the Old Testament most quoted in the New Testament: it appears that the early Christians inhabited the thought world of the psalms, so that any biblical theology that would be Christian must read the psalms in this context.[55]

The second major issue facing the canonical reader is not simply knowing which literary context to read the text in, but which historical setting. Should we see the Psalter as compiled during the exile, after the exile, or even later? It could make a difference to the way we read it. Wilson[56] appears to favour the final arrangement of the Psalter in the first century AD, Hossfeld and Zenger[57] early in the second century BC, while Auwers[58] thinks somewhere between 350 BC and 200 BC is possible. McCann,[59] on the other hand, does not think it really matters, since we do not know very much about the post-exilic era and throughout it the Jews enjoyed neither independence nor monarchical rule nor real ownership of the land. These were grave drawbacks especially when contrasted with the hopes and aspirations expressed in the psalms. We could therefore read the psalms as reassertions of these historic beliefs in the face of present experience.

A similar uncertainty surrounds the place of the Psalms within the Hebrew canon, for we cannot be sure when that was closed. At least that problem does not arise with the Christian canon, for from the beginning of the Christian era the psalms formed part of Christian devotion. But should a Christian canonical reading be based in the first century AD or are other later settings just as valid as canonical readings?

Finally, we must admit the tentativeness of canonical readings offered to date. There are plenty of divergent interpretations offered by those who

---

[55] Moyise and Menken, *Psalms in the New Testament*.

[56] Wilson, *Editing*, 92. This is much too late because the Septuagint translation of the Psalter dates from about 200 BC. Auwers, *Composition*, 168.

[57] Hossfeld and Zenger, *Psalmen 51 – 100*, 27.

[58] Auwers, *Composition*, 170.

[59] McCann, 'The Book of the Psalms', 661.

believe in reading the Psalter in its final form. There are many issues that require further discussion. And there are still those who hold that there is no method underlying the arrangement of the Psalter: that it is all eisegesis. This paper presupposes that such scepticism is unwarranted, but it has also drawn attention to unanswered questions that canonical approaches raise. How does the wisdom theme cohere with the royal theme? Is a messianic reading of books 4 and 5 of the Psalter justified? How far can one go with the early church in reading the Psalms as prophecy? The voice of the righteous royal figure, who suffers persecution, is often heard in the Psalms and clearly invites christological interpretation. But we must ask if this is warranted.[60] Much attention has been paid to the Davidic titles and their significance in interpretation, but what about the titles ascribing psalms to Asaph or the sons of Korah? Should we see them as more than just telling us about their source? Diachronic issues must also not be forgotten (e.g. the dating of individual psalms). Are any of the titles authentic?[61] And if they were, would it make a difference to interpretation? These are just some of the issues that need further discussion in years to come. But they are relatively minor. They should not obscure the great gains canonical reading of the Psalms has brought us. To quote Brevard Childs:

> The canonical shape of the Psalter assured the future generations of Israelites that this book spoke a word of God to each of them in their need. It was not only a record of the past, but a living voice speaking to the present human suffering. By taking seriously the canonical shape the reader is given an invaluable resource for the care of souls, as the synagogue and church have always understood the Psalter to be.[62]

---

[60] For an argument in favour see Braulik, 'Psalter and Messiah', 15–40.
[61] Goulder, *Prayers of David*, 24, argues that these psalms do originate in the Davidic era, perhaps written by a son of David 'for David'.
[62] Childs, *Introduction*, 523.

Bibliography

Alexander, J.A., *The Psalms Translated and Explained* (Edinburgh, 1873; reprinted Grand Rapids: Baker, 1975)

Alter, R., *The Art of Biblical Narrative* (New York: Basic Books, 1981)

Auwers, J.-M., *La Composition littéraire du psautier: un état de la question* (Paris: Gabalda, 2000)

Braulik, G., 'Psalter and Messiah: Towards a Christological Understanding of the Psalms in the OT and the Church Fathers', in *Psalms and Liturgy* (ed. D.J. Human and C.J.A. Vos; JSOTSup 410; London: T&T Clark International, 2004), 15–40

Childs, B.S., *Introduction to the Old Testament as Scripture* (London: SCM Press, 1979)

Cole, R.L., *The Shape and Message of Book III (Psalms 73 – 89)* (JSOTSup 307; Sheffield: Sheffield Academic Press, 2000)

Delitzsch, F., *Biblical Commentary on the Psalms* (trans. F. Bolton; Grand Rapids: Eerdmans, n.d.)

Erbele-Küster, D., *Lesen als Akt des Betens: Eine Rezeptionsästhetik der Psalmen* (WMANT 87; Neukirchen: Neukirchener Verlag, 2001)

Goulder, M., *The Prayers of David (Psalms 51 – 72)* (JSOTSup 102; Sheffield: JSOT Press, 1990)

Gunkel, H., *Die Psalmen* (Göttingen: Vandenhoeck & Ruprecht, 1926)

Hossfeld, F.-L., and E. Zenger, *Psalmen 51 – 100* (Herders Theologischer Kommentar zum Alten Testament; Freiburg: Herder, 2000)

Howard, D.M., *The Structure of Psalms 93 – 100* (Winona Lake: Eisenbrauns, 1997)

Jacob, B., 'Die Reihenfolge der Psalmen', *ZAW* 18 (1898), 99–119

Kirkpatrick, A.F., *The Book of Psalms* (Cambridge: Cambridge University Press, 1902)

Kleer, M., *Der liebliche Sänger der Psalmen Israels* (Bodenheim: Philo, 1996)

McCann, J.C., *The Shape and Shaping of the Psalter* (JSOTSup 159; Sheffield: JSOT Press, 1993)

—, *A Theological Introduction to the Book of Psalms* (Nashville: Abingdon, 1993)

—, 'The Book of the Psalms', in *The New Interpreter's Bible*, vol. IV (Nashville: Abingdon, 1996), 641–1280

Miller, P.D., 'The Beginning of the Psalter', in *The Shape and Shaping of the Psalter* (ed. J.C. McCann; JSOTSup 159; Sheffield: JSOT Press, 1993), 83–92

Mitchell, D.C., *The Message of the Psalter: An Eschatological Programme in the Book of Psalms* (JSOTSup 252; Sheffield: Sheffield Academic Press, 1997)

Mowinckel, S., *The Psalms in Israel's Worship* (trans. D.R. Ap-Thomas; Oxford: Blackwell, 1962)

Moyise, S., and M.J.J. Menken, *The Psalms in the New Testament* (London: T&T Clark, 2004)

Sternberg, M., *The Poetics of Biblical Narrative* (Bloomington: Indiana University Press, 1985)

Whybray, R.N., *Reading the Psalms as a Book* (JSOTSup 222; Sheffield: Sheffield Academic Press, 1996)

Wilson, G.H., *The Editing of the Hebrew Psalter* (Chico: Scholars Press, 1985)

Zenger, E., 'Was wird anders bei kanonischer Psalmenauslegung?', in *Ein Gott, eine Offenbarung: Beiträge zur biblischen Exegese, Theologie und Spiritualität* (ed. F.V. Reiterer; Würzburg: Echter, 1991), 397–413

13

Reading Wisdom Canonically
Tremper Longman III

The purpose of this chapter is to explore a canonical interpretation of wisdom literature in the Old Testament. While there is a place for studying these books in isolation from each other, it is important to ultimately read each wisdom book in the context of the others, and also to read them in the light of the broader canon including the New Testament.

Defined narrowly as Proverbs, Ecclesiastes, and Job, the wisdom texts of the Old Testament fit strangely with one another and with the rest of the canon, at least on a first reading. Proverbs' optimistic view that wisdom leads to reward ('the LORD will not let the righteous go hungry' [10:3] seems in tension with Ecclesiastes' skepticism about appropriate retribution ('nor bread to the wise, nor riches to the intelligent, nor favor to the skillful' [9:11]) as well as with a righteous, but suffering Job.

In addition, Christian interpreters are further concerned with the question of wisdom literatures' relationship to the New Testament. Or perhaps I should say, ought to be concerned. Conservative scholars as well as others today are loath to read the Old Testament in the light of the New Testament for fear of distorting the original message of the book. While I agree that there is a danger of such distortion, this should lead us to be careful rather than to avoid a canonical reading. Indeed, I would suggest that to read the Old Testament without reference to the New Testament is not a Christian reading of the Old Testament at all.

The Book of Proverbs

We begin with an analysis of the book of Proverbs in isolation from the rest of the canon. In this way, we will recognize the apparent tension of the book with the other two main exemplars of biblical wisdom, Job and Ecclesiastes. Note that we will examine the finished form of the book of Proverbs and not discuss the pre-history of the book in any detail.[1] In spite of the opening superscription that appears to assign the whole book to Solomon, there are multiple indications that the book as we have it now is a collection of wisdom sayings and proverbs that came from diverse historical periods.[2] I will address the issue of the coherence or lack thereof in the final form of the book as I describe it, but if there is coherence, it is a redactional and not an authorial coherence.

As is well known, Proverbs has two major components, themselves amenable to subdivision. Chapters 1 – 9 are largely extended discourses of two types. The predominant type is a father's speech to his son; the less frequent type is the speech of a woman named Wisdom addressed to all the young men who pass her by (Prov. 1:20–33; 8; 9:1–6). In one place, very significant as we will discover, another woman, named Folly, addresses the exact same audience (Prov. 9:13–18). Fox has correctly described the typical components of the discourse as consisting of an exordium, a lesson, and a conclusion, though there is considerable variety in the amount of space devoted to these three elements. The exordium includes a call for the recipient to pay attention, which is accompanied by motivation to do so. The lesson is the object of teaching and the conclusion, which brings the teaching to a close sometimes by describing the consequences of listening or not listening to the lesson.[3]

Proverbs 2 is an example of a discourse that has a major emphasis on the exordium, which essentially takes up the first half of the chapter. It invokes the son ('my son', v. 1), calling on him to pay attention. Motivations are given, notably the fact that if the son seeks wisdom God will grant it to him. The lesson includes avoiding evil women and men (vv. 12–19) and the conclusion is stated in the last three verses (vv. 20–23).

On the other hand, the second main component of Proverbs is chapters 10 – 31, where the predominant genre is the proverb *per se*. We will describe the proverb in the light of a specific example, namely Proverbs 10:4:

> A slack hand makes poverty;
> a determined hand makes rich.

This proverb is not chosen because it is a particularly impressive proverb, rather because it is fairly typical. The proverb is a brief, pointed statement. Proverbs express ideas that are commonly accepted as true. They do not argue for the truth of the statement or nuance it. Proverbs can state an insight, make an observation, or offer advice in the form of an admonition or prohibition. This

---

[1] I give consideration to these matters in Longman, *Proverbs*.

[2] For instance, the reference to 'the wise' in 22:17 and 24:13, 'the men of Hezekiah' (25:1), Agur (30:1), and Lemuel (31:1).

[3] Fox, *Proverbs 1–9*, 45–46.

particular proverb is an observation. Even an observation, however, can imply advice. The fact that it is hard work and not laziness that makes a person rich is intended to motivate a person to get to work.

Though formally different, the two sections of Proverbs are similar in their lack of obvious theological language. Indeed, the theology of the book of Proverbs has often been approached more as a problem than anything else. The book's teaching majors in practical advice and observations and seems distant from the theological concerns of the bulk of the Old Testament. We look in vain, for instance, for any connection with the events of redemptive history. Nothing is said of the patriarchs, the exodus, the establishment of the monarchy and so on. In addition, while the term covenant (*berit*) is not absent from the book (Prov. 2:17) and associated words like 'covenant love' (*hesed*)[4] – occur even more often (Prov. 3:3; 14:22; 16:6; 19:22; 20:6, 28), the concept of covenant cannot be said to be a major theme of the book. Finally, it may also be pointed out that reference to God, though frequently made by using God's covenant name Yahweh, occurs sporadically in the text. In particular, many of the proverbs in 10 – 31 have no reference to God and at first glance appear relatively isolated from a broader context. No wonder the book has been described as containing secular advice.[5] Some scholars have even gone so far as to say that when Yahweh's name is found in a proverb that it is a sign of a late addition to a consistently secular book.[6]

However, such a view can only be sustained if Proverbs is read in a piecemeal fashion. That is, if proverbs, such as Proverbs 10:4, cited above, are isolated from the book as a whole, it is possible to think of it as simply a book of good advice, helpful to navigating life. However, the context of the book as a whole does not allow this reading. We begin by recognizing that the second half of the book must be read through the prism of the first half.

But first I would like to address the question of the coherence of Proverbs 10 – 31. As mentioned above, the second part of the book is made up of proverbs. On first reading, the proverbs seem more or less random. In another paper,[7] I have disputed recent attempts to understand these proverbs as having some kind of deep structure. As illustrative of this trend I will review the recent book by K.M. Heim, *Like Grapes of Gold Set in Silver: An Interpretation of*

---

[4] Contra Sakenfeld, *Faithfulness in Action*.

[5] Eissfeldt, says, 'The basis for the commendation of wisdom and piety is on the one hand purely secular and rational' (*Old Testament*, 47).

[6] The view that earlier secular wisdom has been Yahwized by later theologically minded redactors may be associated with Whybray, *Wisdom in Proverbs*, 72; McKane, *Proverbs*, 1–22. It is properly disputed by Boström, *The God of the Sages*, 36–39.

[7] Longman, 'Narrative Impulses'.

Proverbial Clusters in Proverbs 10:1–22:16. Heim incorporates a number of other studies in his own understanding of the arrangement. This includes earlier studies by Hermisson, Perry, Krispenz, Whybray, Meinhold, Murphy, Hildebrandt, Scoralik, and others. But we should not get the impression from this long list of names that there is any consensus here beyond the basic premise that there is some arrangement of proverbs hidden from casual reading. There are as many different nuances in the schemes suggested to unravel the mystery as there are scholars. Heim is aware of this fact, but he is not rattled or dissuaded from the search. Rather, he quotes approvingly Whybray's response to McKane's conclusion that individual proverbs have no broader context as follows: 'McKane's assumption that individual proverbs have no context but occur in random order "amounts to no more than an admission that modern scholars have so far not been able satisfactorily to discover what such a context, whether literary or theological, might be".'[8] Heim gains further encouragement from the fact that seven out of nine of the most recent commentaries affirm some form of structure of the proverbs in the latter part of the book that is relevant to interpretation.

Surveying these previous attempts, he sees that there are 'multiple strategies employed together to find editorial groupings: chapter divisions, educational sayings, paronomasia and catchwords, theological reinterpretations, proverbial pairs, and variant repetitions.'[9] Heim says that none of these will quite do. For instance, he shows how educational sayings appear only sporadically at the beginning of sections. The use of repeated words as catchwords to form a unit is done, in his opinion, without controls. There is after all a rather basic wisdom vocabulary in Proverbs.

Heim ultimately argues for coherence between sayings through phonological, semantic, syntactic and thematic repetition.[10] He believes that scholars make a huge mistake by looking for thematic or logical development within these short units. He says that once a unit is determined it is equally possible to read it from the beginning to the end, the end to the beginning or from the middle outwards. Nonetheless, the units do provide a context in which the proverbs should be read. The analogy that he provides in terms of the association of proverbs within a unit is from the title of the book which is taken from Proverbs 25:11: 'The right word at the right time is [like] grapes of gold set in silver.' In his own words:

> The cluster forms an organic whole linked by means of small 'twiglets,' yet each
> grape can be consumed individually. Although the grapes contain juice from the

---

[8] Whybray, *Composition*, 65.
[9] Heim, *Like Grapes of Gold*, 64.
[10] Heim, *Like Grapes of Gold*, 106.

same vine, each tastes slightly different. It doesn't matter in which sequence the grapes are consumed, but eating them together undoubtedly enhances the flavour and enriches the culinary experience.[11]

However, let me immediately register my concern about the criteria that he uses to divide these units. Unlike some before him, he gives up on the possibility of finding 'boundary markers' that delineate clear units but rather looks for repetitions of a variety of sorts, both sound and meaning, to associate a group of proverbs and then he reads them in the light of each other. My problem is that the criteria of association are so broad and varied that different scholars will continue to come up with different units. Also there is by his own admission no correlation between the various criteria of association or even any coherence of criteria within a proverbial unit. And once the unit is determined in this rather ad hoc way, there is of course no problem with doing a contextual reading. Our minds can associate the most disparate facts.

Thus, I conclude that the proverbs in chapters 10 – 31 are relatively randomly structured. Of course, I recognize that there are some groupings such as the Yahweh-proverbs in chapter 16, but they are the exception rather than the rule and in my mind are probably the result of a long-term redactional process where occasionally similarly themed proverbs were placed next to each other.

A proverb is meant to be read independently from the proverbs that immediately follow it, and it takes a wise person to know when the right time is to activate the proverbs. Let's take Proverbs 10:1 as an example:

> Wise children bring joy to their father,
> but foolish children bring grief to their mother.

This is an observation that seems at first self-evident in meaning. It also does not seem particularly theological at first glance. However, while this proverb is not illumined by reading it in the light of the proverbs that follow, we must read it in the light of the dynamic of the book as a whole. That is, as Childs observed briefly, chapters 10 – 31 must be read in the light of chapters 1 – 9. Citing Zimmerli's naming these later chapters a 'hermeneutical guide,' Childs points out that these initial chapters are the framework for the rest of the book.[12]

Childs points to the foundational teaching in 1:7, 'The fear of Yahweh is the beginning of knowledge,' to indicate that the very nature of wisdom is rooted in theology. This theological nature of wisdom is even more extensively taught through the personification of wisdom found in Proverbs 1:20–33 and 8:1 – 9:6. Much debate surrounds the details of interpretation of this

---

[11] Heim, *Like Grapes of Gold*, 107.
[12] Childs, *Introduction to the Old Testament as Scripture*, 552–54, citing Zimmerli, 'Zur Struktur der alttestamentlichen Weisheit', 189.

mysterious woman, and here I will present my own understanding. I am not so interested in the question of the possible ancient near-eastern background of the picture of Wisdom encountered here, but rather in the use of the image in the interpretation of the book.[13]

Woman Wisdom is first encountered in the second discourse, following the preamble (Prov. 1:1–7), in Proverbs 1:20–33, where she calls out to the simple-minded from her place in the public square. In chapters 8 and 9 she is again calling out from a public place, speaking to all the men who are passing by.

The men are on a path, a well-known metaphor used throughout these opening chapters. The path stands for one's actions in life. It implies a current point of origin, a destination, and key transitional moments. In fact, two paths are open to the son. The father warns the son of a path that is variously termed 'crooked' (Prov. 2:15) and 'dark' (Prov. 2:13).

While there is not a systematic coherent narrative shape to the discourses, I do think it is fair to say that the theme of the path and Woman Wisdom culminates in chapter 9, at the transitional moment in the book, the climax of the discourses immediately preceding the proverbs. It is the climax because in this chapter Woman Wisdom is contrasted with her rival Woman Folly who is mentioned here for the first time in a manner that calls on the addressees, the young men, to make a choice between the two as is made obvious when comparing the two relevant descriptions:

> Wisdom has built her house;
> she has set up its seven pillars.
> She has prepared her meat and mixed her wine;
> she has also set her table.
> She has sent out her servants, and she calls
> from the highest point of the city.
> 'Let all who are simple come to my house!'
> To those who have no sense she says,
> 'Come, eat my food
> and drink the wine I have mixed.
> Leave your simple ways and you will live;
> walk in the way of insight.'
>
> (Prov. 9:1–6)

> Folly is an unruly woman;
> she is simple and knows nothing.
> She sits at the door of her house,
> on a seat at the highest point of the city,
> Calling out to those who pass by,
> who go straight on their way,

---

[13] See the discussion in Day, 'Foreign Semitic Influence', 68–70.

'Let all who are simple come to my house!'
To those who have no sense she says,
'Stolen water is sweet;
food eaten in secret is delicious!'
But little do they know that the dead are there,
that her guests are deep in the realm of the dead.

(Prov. 9:13–18)

Who are these women? The key to their identity is the location of their houses.
They both call from the 'highest point of the city.' Since temples are found on
high places in the ancient Near East and in Israel, they both represent deities. In
the case of Woman Wisdom, she is unarguably a personification of Yahweh's
wisdom, and I would hazard to go further and say that she stands for Yahweh
himself. Woman Folly represents the 'wisdom' of idolatry and ultimately false
gods. As I say this, it is important to press the point that the text does not identify Woman Wisdom as Yahweh and Woman Folly as a false god. This is
poetry, not prophecy (the error of Arianism), and so the details of the image
may not be simply attributed to its reference.[14]

The young men are thus forced into a decision as to which woman, which
G/god, they will be intimate with. Thus, the very concepts of wisdom and
folly have theological significance and this should be kept in mind when the
following proverbs are read.

Returning to Proverbs 10:1 then, we can say that the son who brings joy to
his parents is wise, meaning he is acting like a good follower of Yahweh, while
the one who brings grief to his parents, is acting like an idolater.

So far we have established that reading Proverbs as a whole reveals the book
of Proverbs' profound theological nature. Wisdom is not just a practical skill of
life; wisdom is at bottom relational, that is it begins with a relationship with
Yahweh.

As we read Proverbs, the father encourages the son to develop a relationship
with Yahweh/Wisdom and to avoid a relationship with Folly/idols. He often
does so by pointing to rewards and punishments. The rewards for embracing
W/wisdom are described in terms of material wealth, health, a happy and long
life:

---

[14] Specifically, the fact that Woman Wisdom was created before the foundation of
the world and observes how creation is put together serves to make the point
that if one wants to know how the world works it is good to know this woman
(Yahweh). It does not intend to say that Yahweh created Yahweh, nor even that
Yahweh created his own wisdom. Arianism errs by not treating the poem as a
poem. Thus, when the New Testament uses the language of Proverbs 8 in
reference to Jesus (see below), it should not be treated as literal fact in all of its
details.

Don't be impressed with your own wisdom.
Instead, fear the LORD and turn away from evil.
Then you will have healing for your body
and strength for your bones.

(Prov. 3:7–8)

I love all those who love me.
Those who search will surely find me.
I have riches and honor,
as well as wealth and justice.
My gifts are better than gold, even the purest gold,
my wages are better than sterling silver!
I walk in righteousness,
in paths of justice.
Those who love me inherit wealth.
I will fill their treasuries.

(Prov. 8:17–21)

On the other hand, the cost of following F/folly is just the opposite as is made clear by the following antithetical proverbs:

The LORD will not let the godly go hungry,
but he refuses to satisfy the craving of the wicked.

(Prov. 10:3)

The fears of the wicked will be fulfilled;
so will the hopes of the godly.

(Prov. 10:24)

No harm comes to the godly,
but the wicked have their fill of trouble.

(Prov. 12:21)

Godliness guards the path of the blameless,
but the evil are misled by sin.

(Prov. 13:6)

The house of the wicked will be destroyed,
but the tent of the godly will flourish.

(Prov. 14:11)

While such language serves the obvious purpose of motivating the readers of the book to pursue wisdom, the question immediately arises as to its truth. Is it really the case that the godly wise prosper and the ungodly wicked diminish?

Before going on to Ecclesiastes and Job, books that I believe offer a canonical corrective to such an over-reading of Proverbs, let me just quickly point out that Proverbs is certainly not the only book in the Old Testament that might lend credence to such a prosperity theology. Think of the whole structure of Deuteronomic theology. The covenantal structure instructs that obedience to the law brings reward and disobedience brings curse (Deut. 27 – 28). Then the historical books, particularly those often described as Deuteronomic, illustrate that from Israel's past. Why is Israel in exile? According to Samuel–Kings, it is because they broke the law of centralization (Deut. 12), did not listen to the prophets (Deut. 13 and 18), and their kings departed from Yahweh (Deut. 17). And when they did break the law, prophets like Jeremiah came and confronted them with their disobedience and pointed to the covenantal curses. Indeed, there is much in the Old Testament that would fuel the thought that sin brings punishment.

But then there are Ecclesiastes and Job.

Qohelet's Questioning

It is not hard to demonstrate diverse interpretations of the book of Ecclesiastes.[15] However, it is hard to miss the fact that Qohelet questions the connection between good and bad actions and their respective rewards and punishments. One of the most remarkable statements in the book is found in Ecclesiastes 7:15–18:

> In this meaningless life of mine I have seen both of these:
> The righteous perishing in their righteousness,
> and the wicked living long in their wickedness.
> Do not be overrighteous,
> neither be overwise –
> why destroy yourself?
> Do not be overwicked,
> and do not be a fool –
> why die before your time?
> It is good to grasp the one
> and not let go of the other.
> Whoever fears God will avoid all extremes.

In this passage we hear about Qohelet's observations in the real world. What he 'sees' bothers him greatly; the world does not work in an expected way. If one

---

[15] For a helpful, but not exhaustive survey that summarizes recent approaches to the book of Ecclesiastes, see Fox, *A Time to Tear Down*, ix–xii.

reads Proverbs, one would expect that the righteous would live long and the wicked die young. On the basis of this observation, Qohelet issues the following startling advice: pursue a middle way between wisdom and folly. No matter how this is interpreted, one cannot imagine finding anything like this in Proverbs!

Occasionally, what Qohelet 'sees' comes into conflict with what he believes (signaled by 'knows') as in Ecclesiastes 8:9–15:

> All this I saw, as I applied my mind to everything done under the sun. There is a time when a man lords it over others to his own hurt. Then too, *I saw* the wicked buried – those who used to come and go from the holy place and receive praise in the city where they did this. This too is meaningless.

> When the sentence for a crime is not quickly carried out, people's hearts are filled with schemes to do wrong. Although a wicked person who commits a hundred crimes may live a long time, *I know* that it will go better with those who fear God, who are reverent before him. Yet because the wicked do not fear God, it will not go well with them, and their days will not lengthen like a shadow.

> There is something else meaningless that occurs on earth: the righteous who get what the wicked deserve, and the wicked who get what the righteous deserve. This too, I say, is meaningless. So I commend the enjoyment of life, because there is nothing better for people under the sun than to eat and drink and be glad. The joy will accompany them in their toil all the days of the life God has given them under the sun.

This passage begins with an observation similar to that of 7:15–18. The wicked do not get what they deserve; rather they are blessed in life and they are properly buried. Qohelet then moralizes on this fact by saying that since punishment does not follow evil, evil multiplies. But then Qohelet shifts his whole tone with a statement of what he knows. What he knows is that the wicked will not prosper. But then he cannot maintain that line of thought too long before reality again forces him to the conclusion that 'the righteous get what the wicked deserve' and vice versa. He concludes the section with a carpe diem statement that can only properly be read as resignation.

My point is this: Qohelet expects the world to work in a way where the righteous prosper and the wicked languish, and it frustrates him that it does not. Indeed, it is a major factor that leads him to the conclusion 'Meaningless, meaningless, all is meaningless.'

How, though, are we to understand Qohelet's statements in the context of the whole book?[16] Again, interpreters differ on this question so I will explain

---

[16] For a more detailed exposition and defense of this approach to Ecclesiastes, see Longman, *Ecclesiastes*.

my view. Along with Fox,[17] I recognize two voices in the book. There is Qohelet's voice (first person) and then there is a voice that speaks about Qohelet (third person). The most natural reading of this is that these are two different people. Once recognized, the following dynamic of the book is clear. Qohelet's presence in the book is explained by the fact that his words are a lengthy quotation of a second wise man who is speaking to his son (Eccles. 12:12). After all, Qohelet's words are framed by the second voice who only emerges in the body of the book at Ecclesiastes 7:27 where we have a reminder of the nature of Qohelet's speech as a quotation ('says Qohelet').

    I.   Prologue (1:1–11)
    II.   Qohelet's Speech (1:12 – 12:7)
   III.   Epilogue (12:8–14)

The gist of Qohelet's speech is that 'life is hard, and then you die.' Indeed, better stated, 'life is hard because you die.' In the light of death, every pleasure, status, achievement, and accumulation is rendered meaningless. In addition, as we have seen, this present life is not fair either. As for the afterlife, he is either agnostic (Eccles. 3:16–22) or a complete skeptic (Eccles. 12:1–7).

    The unnamed second wise man exposes his son to this thought for two reasons. In the first place, it is a true observation (Eccles. 12:10). Life 'under the sun' is meaningless, out of control, unfair. Considering all the intertextual connections with Genesis 3,[18] it is not misleading to say that Qohelet well understands the nature of a fallen world. The question that can't be answered is why Qohelet remains 'under the sun' in his thinking, not availing himself of a heavenly perspective that might be provided by other Scripture. However, what can be seen is that in the final two verses of the epilogue, the frame narrator turns his son away from Qohelet's obsession with the meaninglessness of the world under the sun and toward something better:

    Now all has been heard;
    here is the conclusion of the matter:
    Fear God and keep his commandments,
    for this is the duty of every human being.
    For God will bring every deed into judgment,
    including every hidden thing,
    whether it is good or evil.

                            (Eccles. 12:13–14)[19]

---

[17] First articulated in Fox, 'Frame-Narrative and Composition'.
[18] Clemens, 'The Law of Sin and Death'.
[19] I am quoting the TNIV, which like the NIV, has a tendency to overpoeticize the book.

It is interesting to note among other things that here the second wisdom teacher does not try to say that retribution works in the present but does point to a future judgment where God will work things out properly.

The Book of Job

In my opinion, Job too serves as a canonical corrective to a possible overreading of the book of Proverbs. I am not claiming that such a function exhausts the purpose of the book of Job in the canon, far from it, but it is one such function.

The book accomplishes this by presenting us with a main character who is unarguably 'blameless and upright' (*tam weyasar*). Both *tam* (Job 1:12; 2:7, 21; 11:3, 4, 20; 13:6; 19:1; 20:7; 28:6, 10, 18; 29:10) and *yasar* (Job 1:3; 2:7, 13, 21; 4:25; 8:6, 9; 9:15; 11:3, 4, 6; 12:6, 15; 13:23*; 14:11; 15:8; 16:13; 17:25; 20:11; 21:2, 8; 23:16; 29:10) are frequently used in Proverbs to refer to the godly, righteous, wise person. Not only is Job described as 'blameless and upright' in 1:1, but God himself describes him as such adding that he is a man who fears God and shuns evil, of course reminiscent of Proverbs 1:7. In a word, Job is the model wisdom figure. One would expect him to be the recipient of great material blessing and indeed he is at the beginning of the book. However, the accuser (the Satan) challenges God by suggesting that Job's righteousness is contingent on his blessed life. It is for this reason that Job is now subjected to a series of well-known tribulations.

The prose prologue of Job thus gives us as readers information that none of the book's characters know for sure. We know that Job is blameless and God-fearing, but he suffers in spite of that fact.

The three friends come along to console him. They do so for seven days until Job's lament (chapter 3) energizes them to combat. In my opinion, the three friends take the same position. It is a position that incarnates what I have been calling an overreading of the book of Proverbs. They say the following: Sin leads to suffering; thus suffering is a symptom of sin. If Job suffers, he must be a sinner in need of repentance (Job 4:7–11; 11:13–20).

The three friends and Job debate for what seems to be an interminable period of time. Three rounds of back and forth. None of them give ground. Job may admit that he is not perfect (Job 9:2), but he believes that his suffering is way out of proportion with his sin. His growing complaints against God and his desire for an audience with him so he can set him straight indicates that actually Job himself buys into this retribution theology. 'I am innocent and suffering. This is unfair.'

Of course after a while the three friends' arguments peter out. But then Elihu picks up the torch. How Elihu figures into the book is a matter of debate.[20] Some take him as a precursor to the Yahweh speech and it cannot be denied that some aspects of his speech in chapter 37 anticipate the Yahweh speeches at the end. However, I understand Elihu as simply mouthing the same truisms as the three friends. He comes in with great energy. He has restrained himself out of respect for the wisdom of the aged, but now that the three friends have disappointed him he insists that it is not advanced years, but rather 'the spirit' or the 'breath of the Almighty' in a person that gives them insight (Job 32:8). Even so, when he starts to speak, he repeats the view that it is one's sin that leads to suffering (Job 34:11, 25–27, 37). He claims to have something new to say (Job 32:14), but he really does not. That is why I think Job does not respond to him and also why he is totally ignored in the epilogue. He says nothing worthy of comment.

Thus, an overreading of the retribution principle in a wisdom book like Proverbs is incarnated in all of the human characters of the book (Job, three friends, Elihu), and at the end of the book they are all put in their proper place. All the characters, with the exception of God, have affirmed the doctrine of retribution and all of them have been shown to be wrong. Elihu is ignored; the three friends are told that they have not spoken what is right (Job 42:7). Job is subjected to four chapters of divine chastisement. The attitude God takes with Job does raise the question of what Job has said that is right as expressed in 42:7. I believe this can only be taken as a reference to his repentance. It is not repentance for sin that led to his suffering but repentance of his challenge to God as a result of his suffering.[21]

Returning to Proverbs

While a superficial reading of Proverbs has led many to believe that the rewards attendant to wise behavior are guaranteed, Ecclesiastes and Job both resist that notion. Ecclesiastes does so by relating Qohelet's honest examination of life under the sun that does not allow him to rest comfortably with what he 'knows.' Job resists that notion by incarnating retribution thinking in all its major human characters and revealing the inadequacy of their thinking.

We now return to Proverbs and reread the book tempered by our readings of Ecclesiastes and Job. What does Proverbs really teach in regard to the relationship between proper behavior and consequences? Answering this question will take us away from the superficial reading of the book of Proverbs that has concerned us above.

In the first place van Leeuwen has noted a minor key in the book that recognizes the fact that there is not an absolute connection between wisdom and

---

[20] See the discussion in Barr, 'Job'.

[21] The best treatment of Job at present is Zerafa, *Wisdom of God*.

reward.[22] He observes this especially in the so-called 'better-than proverbs.' While, on the one hand, Proverbs 3:15–16 claims:

> She [Wisdom] is more precious than rubies;
> nothing you desire can compare with her.
> Long life is in her right hand;
> in her left hand are riches and honor.

Proverbs 16:8, on the other hand, states:

> Better a little with righteousness
> than much gain with injustice.

While Proverbs 3:15–16 could be read in a way that would guarantee wealth to those who embrace wisdom, Proverbs 16:8 recognizes that actually at times one must make a decision between the two, the way of wisdom and wealth.

As Waltke has reminded us, Proverbs is not in the business of giving guarantees.[23] The rewards are not promises. The sages do tell their readers the optimum path to reach a desired consequence and avoid trouble. And, indeed, all things being equal the way of wisdom is the best path toward desired consequences. Going back to Proverbs 10:4, one can insist that it is generally true that lazy hands make for poverty but diligent hands bring wealth, even though we can cite some incredibly lazy people who have inherited large sums of money or those who have worked hard and are still poor due to an injustice or some other catastrophe. Again, Job is our example. He was wise, but suffered.

Even so, one must wonder whether it was this struggle concerning proper retribution that contributed to a developing idea of an afterlife. I think of a wisdom poem like Psalm 73 where the psalmist-sage struggles with his troubles in the light of the seeming care-less prosperity of the evil people around him. His experience made him stumble in his relationship with God (v. 2) until he 'entered the Sanctuary of God' and came to understand the 'final destiny' of the wicked. He goes on to affirm God's presence with him in the present and then he states, according to the TNIV translation, 'and afterward you will take me into glory.' I am fully aware of the ambiguity of this statement particularly in the light of the fact that the teaching on the afterlife is questionable in the Psalms and in the rest of the Old Testament. On the other hand, when exactly in this life does the negative 'final destiny' of the wicked come to fruition (remember Eccles. 8:9–15)? And what basis would the psalmist have for thinking that 'glory' or 'honor' (*kabod*) would come later in life? Even if the original

---

[22] Van Leeuwen, 'Wealth and Poverty'.
[23] Waltke, 'Does Proverbs Promise Too Much?', 319–36.

psalmist did not have in mind the afterlife, one cannot now read the Psalm in the light of fuller revelation without giving it that deeper sense.[24]

Reading the Wisdom Books in the Light of the New Testament

The relationship between the Old and the New Testaments is of course an enduring issue among scholars. Disagreements abound even among evangelical Protestant scholars on this issue. Waltke has described three major schools of thought on this issue, namely dispensationalist (with strong discontinuity), theonomic (with strong continuity), and covenantal (recognizing discontinuity and discontinuity). He advocates rightly for the latter position.[25]

However, these three categories are a bit too black and white when it comes to the work of individual scholars. I think, for instance, of Walton and Kaiser, who are not doctrinaire dispensationalists, but who resist reading the Old Testament in the light of the New Testament. The work of John Goldingay is perhaps an even better illustration of an evangelical scholar who is not a dispensationalist but who steadfastly refuses to read the Old Testament in the light of the New Testament.[26] On the other hand, even a theonomist has to recognize some measure of discontinuity, though the recently deceased Rousas Rushdoony did argue that Christians should keep kosher and that not only should the death penalty be applied to those who break the laws requiring (in his mind) capital punishment, but that the penalty had to be applied by stoning.[27]

I refer here only to evangelical scholars because non-evangelical Protestant scholars are much less likely to allow for this type of canonical coherence. Brueggemann, for instance, argues against reading the Old Testament from a New Testament perspective, though he does affirm that the New Testament rightfully appropriates the Old Testament. The reason why the latter can be true, though not the former, is because the New Testament picks up on one, though only one, of the many possible readings of the Old Testament. The meaning of the Old Testament is 'polymorphic' and 'elusive,' and the New Testament uses imaginative power to connect the Old Testament to the ministry of Christ. In this way, Brueggemann can affirm the New Testament without invalidating Judaism.[28] Childs is an exception to this rule. Though he

---

[24] See the helpful discussion in Johnston, *Shades of Sheol*, 202–204.

[25] Waltke, 'Theonomy ', 59–88.

[26] Kaiser, *Exegetical Theology*; Goldingay, *Old Testament Theology*. For J. Walton, see how he handles (or does not) New Testament allusions to Genesis in his *Genesis*.

[27] Rushdoney, *Institutes of Biblical Law*.

[28] See the discussion in his *Theology of the Old Testament*, 729–33. One might also refer to Barr, *Concept of Biblical Theology*, where he questions attempts to 'Christianize the Old Testament' (253–65).

rightly insists that the Old Testament be read in its own terms ('The aim of biblical theology is not to christianize the Old Testament and thus to drown out its own voice'[29]), he also affirms the Old Testament bears witness to Jesus Christ.[30]

I believe a canonical interpretation insists on reading the Old Testament, in the present case the wisdom books, in the light of the New Testament. Indeed, as the Pontifical Commission document entitled 'The Interpretation of the Bible in the Church' puts it:

> Each individual book only becomes biblical in the light of the Canon as a whole.' It thereby advises that the canonical approach 'interprets each biblical text in the light of the Canon of Scriptures, that is to say, of the Bible as received as the norm of faith by a community of believers.[31]

Indeed, according to the post-resurrection account of Luke, Jesus spent considerable time giving his disciples a lesson in canonical interpretation, a canonical interpretation that focuses on himself. I am thinking of the two meetings recorded in Luke 24. In the first, Jesus walks with two of his disciples who are utterly confused and dismayed at his recent crucifixion. They do not recognize him,[32] and as they express their consternation, they reveal their previous expectation when they say, 'we had hoped that he was the one to redeem Israel' (Lk. 24:21). Jesus replies: 'Oh, how foolish you are, and how slow of heart to believe all that the prophets have declared! Was it not necessary that the Messiah should suffer these things and then enter into his glory?' These words are backed by his appeal to Scripture when the narrator reports that 'beginning with Moses and all the prophets, he interpreted to them the things about himself in all the scriptures' (Lk. 24:25–26). Soon thereafter, in the second meeting, he appears to a broader group of disciples and Luke reports the event as follows:

> Then he said to them, 'These are my words that I spoke to you while I was still with you – that everything written about me in the law of Moses, the prophets and the psalms must be fulfilled.' Then he opened their minds to understand the scriptures, and he said to them, 'Thus it is written, that the Messiah is to suffer and to rise from the dead on the third day, and that repentance and forgiveness of sins is to be proclaimed in his name to all nations, beginning from Jerusalem. You are witnesses of these things. And see, I am sending upon you what my Father promised; so stay here in the city until you have been clothed with power from on high.'
>
> (Lk. 24:44–49)

---

[29] Childs, *Biblical Theology*, 616.
[30] Childs, *Biblical Theology*, 78.
[31] *Interpretation*, 51 and 50 respectively.
[32] 'Their eyes were kept from recognizing him' (Lk. 24:16).

There is much about this passage that we can debate; however, there are certain things that are clearly delineated here. First, the disciples had an expectation though it was apparently not clearly formed or accurate. The imperfection of their expectation is implied by their confusion at the time of the crucifixion and also about reports of the empty tomb. Second, Jesus is angry or at least disappointed that they did not know what to expect. After all, he taught them during his earthly ministry. I hope this is not disrespectful, but he sounds like a peeved professor who has labored to teach his students something that they just have not understood. Third, he gives him another lesson, a lesson in hermeneutics, that we are to assume registered with them this time in the light of the resurrection. From this point on, the disciples cannot read the Old Testament except in the light of the resurrected Jesus.

Reading Wisdom in the Light of Christ

For the reasons cited above, I would like to suggest a reading of wisdom literature, in particular Proverbs, in the light of Christ.[33] However, as we have observed above, the book of Proverbs presents a striking metaphor of God's wisdom and arguably God himself in the form of Woman Wisdom. Readers of the New Testament cannot help but notice the description of Jesus as, in the first place, the very epitome of God's wisdom, and secondly in association with Woman Wisdom herself.

We begin by an exploration of those New Testament passages that characterize Jesus as the apex of God's wisdom. The infancy narratives are brief but they pay special attention to the growth in Jesus' extraordinary wisdom. Of the two Gospels that report his birth and youth, Luke shows a special interest in Jesus' wisdom. For instance, after Jesus is born, we learn twice that this young man grew physically but also 'with wisdom beyond his years' (Lk. 2:40, cf. also 2:52). These two notices surround a story that gives us Christ's wisdom, and it too comments on one of the few events related to us from Jesus' youth.

Like good Jewish parents, Mary and Joseph took their son every year to Jerusalem for Passover. When Jesus was twelve, they made the trip as usual, but this time, as they returned to Nazareth, they panicked when they realized that Jesus was not with them. With fear in their hearts, they rushed back to Jerusalem and spent three days frantically searching for him. They finally discovered him in the Temple 'sitting among the religious teachers, discussing deep

---

[33] See also the helpful study, Witherington, *Jesus the Sage*. One could also suggest a Christocentric biblical theological reading of Ecclesiastes (Longman, *Ecclesiastes*, 39–40) and Job (Dillard and Longman, *Introduction to the Old Testament*, 209–10).

questions with them' (Lk. 2:46). People were watching with amazement 'at his understanding and his answers' (Lk. 2:47). After all, he was not speaking with just anyone, he was in a discussion with the leading theologians of his day, and they were paying attention to what he was saying. Here is a child who reflects God's wisdom.

When Jesus began his ministry, people recognized him as a wise teacher. In Mark's first report of his teaching, we hear the people's reaction: 'Jesus and his companions went to the town of Capernaum. When the Sabbath day came, he went into the synagogue and began to teach. The people were amazed at his teaching, for he taught with real authority – quite unlike the teachers of religious law' (Mk. 1:21–22). Later, in Nazareth, those who knew him while he was growing up also acknowledge his gifts: 'Where did he get all his wisdom and the power to perform such miracles?' (Mk. 6:2).

The most characteristic form of Jesus' teaching, the parable, was part of the repertoire of the wisdom teacher. Indeed, the Hebrew word (*masal*) was translated into the Greek word 'parable' (*parabole*). Accordingly, it is not a stretch to say that Jesus was a first-century wisdom teacher.

Jesus recognized himself as wise and condemned those who rejected his wisdom. In Luke 11:31, he tells the crowd: 'The queen of Sheba will rise up against this generation on judgment day and condemn it, because she came from a distant land to hear the wisdom of Solomon. And now someone greater than Solomon is here – and you refuse to listen to him.'

While the Gospels demonstrate that Jesus was wise – indeed, wiser than Solomon – Paul asserts that Jesus is not simply wise; he is the very incarnation of God's wisdom. Twice Paul identifies him with God's wisdom. First in 1 Corinthians, a passage that will occupy our attention later, he says, 'God made Christ to be wisdom itself' (1 Cor. 1:30). Second, in Colossians 2:3 Paul proclaims that in Christ 'lie hidden all the treasures of wisdom and knowledge.' With this as background, it is not surprising that the New Testament subtly associates Jesus with Woman Wisdom, particularly as presented in Proverbs 8.

Gospels and epistles both attest to Jesus' wisdom being the most profound expression of God's wisdom. Moreover, the link with Woman Wisdom is explicit in several other passages that we will now explore.

We begin with Matthew 11. In this passage, Jesus addresses opponents who argued that John the Baptist was an ascetic in his lifestyle, while Jesus was too celebratory. Notice the final assertion in his reply:

> For John came neither eating nor drinking, and they say, 'He has a demon.' The Son of Man came eating and drinking, and they say, 'Here is a glutton and a drunkard, a friend of tax collectors and 'sinners.' But wisdom is proved right by her actions.
>
> (Mt. 11:18–19 NIV)

In that last sentence, Jesus claims that his behavior represents the behavior of Woman Wisdom herself. Elsewhere in the New Testament Jesus is described in language that is reminiscent of Proverbs 8. We turn first to Colossians 1:15–17:

> Christ is the visible image of the invisible God.
> He existed before anything was created and is supreme over all creation,
> for through him God created everything on earth.
> He made the things we can see
> and the things we can't see –
> Such as thrones, kingdoms,
> rulers, and authorities in the unseen world.
> Everything was created through him and for him.
> He existed before anything else,
> and he holds all creation together.

Though clearly not a quotation from Proverbs, this text would be recognized by someone as well versed in the Old Testament as Paul was, as saying that Jesus occupies the place of Wisdom. Indeed, the literal rendition of the Greek of the sentence that ends 'is supreme over creation' is 'He is the firstborn of creation.' Paul is inviting a comparison: Wisdom was firstborn in Proverbs 8; Jesus is firstborn in Colossians.[34] Wisdom is the agent of divine creation in Proverbs; Christ is the agent in Colossians. In Proverbs 8 we read:

> By me kings reign,
> and nobles issue just decrees.
> By me rulers rule,
> and princes, all righteous judgments.
>
> (Prov. 8:15–16)

And in Colossians 1:16, Christ made 'kings, kingdoms, rulers, and authorities.' The message is clear: Jesus is Wisdom herself.

The author of Revelation is a further witness to the connection between Wisdom and Jesus. In the introduction to the letter to the church at Laodicea, we read 'This is the message from the one who is the Amen – the faithful and true witness, the ruler of God's new creation' (Rev. 3:14). The last phrase (*he arxe tes ktiseos tou theou*) resonates with the ideas behind Proverbs 8:22–30. In particular, the phrase may represent the meaning of that difficult word in

---

[34] Of course, this raises the whole issue of the fourth century AD Arian debates. Is Jesus a created being? The orthodox church responded negatively to this question and rightly understood the language to be poetic. In other words, Jesus is not identified here with Woman Wisdom; he is associated with Woman Wisdom. The vehicle and the tenor of a metaphor are not alike in every way, but only in certain ways.

Proverbs 8:30, the 'architect' ('*amon*) of creation. The allusion is subtle but clear: Jesus stands in the place of Woman Wisdom.

Even more subtly, we might note that the great preface to the Gospel of John echoes with language reminiscent of the poem about Woman Wisdom in Proverbs 8. The Word of God (the Logos), who is God himself (Jn. 1:1), was 'in the beginning with God.' He created everything there is. Indeed, the 'world was made through him.' Jesus, of course, is the Word, and the association is with language reminiscent of Woman Wisdom.[35]

Seeing the connection between Jesus and Woman Wisdom has important implications for how Christians read the book of Proverbs. We have already established the fact that the ancient Israelite reader would read the metaphors of Woman Wisdom and Woman Folly as a choice between Yahweh and the false gods of the nations. This decision would have little relevance to modern readers who are not trying to make a choice between God and Baal, the latter is not a live option and the New Testament claims to reveal the nature of the Godhead more carefully. That is, the New Testament presents Jesus as the mediator of our relationship with God. The gospel choice is a decision whether or not to follow Jesus. Thus, to understand the invitation of Woman Wisdom as the invitation of Christ to relationship with God makes the book contemporary to Christian readers.

As for Woman Folly, she may be taken as anything or anyone who seeks to divert our primary attention away from our relationship with Jesus. Idols today are typically more subtle than in ancient times. Rather than deities and their images, we are lured by more abstract and conceptual idols: power, wealth, relationship, status, and so forth.[36]

---

[35] There is a debate over whether Wisdom is the agent through whom God created creation or simply a witness to it. Of course, if the latter is the correct view, then the connection is weaker with John 1.

[36] For an examination of modern idols in the light of the book of Ecclesiastes, see Allender and Longman, *Bold Purpose*.

Bibliography

Allender, D., and T. Longman III, *Bold Purpose* (Wheaton, IL: Tyndale House, 1998)

Barr, J., *The Concept of Biblical Theology* (Minneapolis: Fortress, 1999)

—, 'The Book of Job and Its Modern Interpreters', *BJRL* 54 (1971–72), 28–46

Boström, L., *The God of the Sages: The Portrayal of God in the Book of Proverbs* (Stockholm: Almqvist & Wiksell International, 1990)

Brueggemann, W., *Theology of the Old Testament: Testimony, Dispute, Advocacy* (Minneapolis: Fortress, 1997)

Childs, B.S., *Biblical Theology of the Old and New Testaments* (London: SCM Press, 1992)

Clemens, D.M., 'The Law of Sin and Death: Ecclesiastes and Genesis 1–3', *Themelios* 19 (1994), 5–8

Cook, J., *'isha zara* (Proverbs 1–9 Septuagint): A Metaphor for Foreign Wisdom?', *ZAW* 106 (1994), 548–76

Day, J., 'Foreign Semitic Influence on the Wisdom of Israel and Its Appropriation in the Book of Proverbs', in *Wisdom in Ancient Israel: Essays in Honour of J.A. Emerton* (ed. J. Day et. al.; Cambridge: Cambridge University Press, 1995), 55–70

Dillard, R., and T. Longman III, *An Introduction to the Old Testament* (Grand Rapids: Zondervan, 1994)

Eissfeldt, O., *The Old Testament: An Introduction* (New York: Harper and Row, 1965)

Fox, M.V., 'Frame-Narrative and Composition in the Book of Qohelet', *HUCA* 48 (1977), 83–106

—, *A Time to Tear Down and a Time to Build Up: A Rereading of Ecclesiastes* (Grand Rapids: Eerdmans, 1999)

—, *Proverbs 1–9* (AB; Garden City, NY: Doubleday, 2000)

Gemser, B., 'The Spiritual Structure of Biblical Aphoristic Literature', in *Adhuc Loquitor* (ed. A. Van Selms and A.S. Van der Woude; Leiden: Brill, 1968), 138–49

Goldingay, J., *Old Testament Theology: Israel's Gospel* (Downers Grove: InterVarsity Press, 2003)

Heim, K.M., *Like Grapes of Gold Set in Silver: An Interpretation of Proverbial Clusters in Proverbs 10:1–22:16* (Berlin/New York: de Gruyter, 2001)

Johnston, P., *Shades of Sheol: Death and the Afterlife in the Old Testament* (Downers Grove: InterVarsity Press, 2002)

Kaiser, W., *Toward an Exegetical Theology* (Grand Rapids: Baker, 1998)

Leeuwen, R. van, 'Wealth and Poverty: System and Contradiction in the Book of Proverbs', *HS* 33 (1992), 599–610

Longman III, T., *Ecclesiastes* (NICOT; Grand Rapids: Eerdmans, 1998)

—, 'Narrative Impulses in the Interpretation of Psalms, Proverbs, and Song of Songs: A Reappraisal', the 2002 Brownlee lecture, sponsored by the Institute for Antiquity and Christianity (Claremont College, April 18, 2002)

—, *Proverbs* (BCOTWP; Grand Rapids: Baker Academic, 2006)

McKane, W., *Proverbs: A New Approach* (Philadelphia: Westminster, 1975)

Rushdoony, R.J., *The Institutes of Biblical Law* (Vallecito, CA: Ross House, 1982)

Sakenfeld, K.D., *Faithfulness in Action: Loyalty in Biblical Perspective* (Philadelphia: Fortress, 1985)

Waltke, B., 'Theonomy in Relation to Dispensational and Covenant Theologies', in *Theonomy: A Reformed Response* (Grand Rapids: Zondervan, 1990), 59–88

—, 'Does Proverbs Promise Too Much?', *AUSS* 34 (1996), 319–36

Walton, J., *Genesis* (NIVAC; Grand Rapids: Zondervan, 2002)

Whybray, R.N., *Wisdom in Proverbs: The Concept of Wisdom in Proverbs 1–9* (London: SCM, 1965)

—, *The Composition of the Book of Proverbs* (Sheffield: JSOT Press, 1994)

Witherington, B., *Jesus the Sage: The Pilgrimage of Wisdom* (Fortress, 1994)

Zerafa, P.P., *The Wisdom of God in the Book of Job* (Rome: Herder, 1978)

Zimmerli, W., 'Zur Struktur der alttestamentlichen Weisheit', *ZAW* 51 (1933), 177–204; English translation 'Concerning the Structure of Old Testament Wisdom', in *Studies in Ancient Israelite Wisdom* (ed. J.L. Crenshaw; New York: Ktav, 1976), 175–207

14

Wisdom as Canonical Imagination

Pleasant Words for Tremper Longman

Ryan P. O'Dowd

Introduction

Longman's chapter very helpfully demonstrates both thematic and theological unity within the Old Testament wisdom books. In doing so, he repudiates many careless readings of the wisdom literature which oppose the wisdom in Proverbs to that in Job and Ecclesiastes. He also provides an insightful summary of Old Testament wisdom as it unfolds through Jesus the Messiah in the New Testament. In this regard, I am grateful for the high quality of his scholarship in Old Testament and wisdom studies over the last two decades. At the same time, I will argue here that by attending to the *hermeneutical nature of wisdom itself* we can rise freely and imaginatively above Longman's insights in search of a canonical interpretation of wisdom. This argument will proceed in three stages. First, with an eye towards the hermeneutical nature of Old Testament wisdom, I will propose an 'imaginative' hermeneutic in contrast to Longman's more Christological and topical methodology, suggesting that wisdom is a hermeneutical enterprise which 'opens up' the task of canonical interpretation. Second, using this imaginative approach, I will attempt to expand upon his reading of wisdom in Proverbs and Ecclesiastes. Finally, building on the previous two stages, I will demonstrate how the wisdom of the Old Testament unfolds into an eschatological picture of creation Christology in the New Testament.

Wisdom as Hermeneutical Imagination

My response to Longman is rooted in the pivotal relationship which exists between *hermeneutics as interpretation* and *wisdom as a hermeneutical concept*. Although Longman does not address this relationship specifically, his use of the terms 'reading' and 'overreading' to classify various interpretations of the wisdom books points to an important set of interpretive issues in the wisdom literature. That is, I find it interesting and helpful that he chooses the more forgiving label of 'overreading' rather than misreading or misinterpretation to describe those who find ironclad causality or a rigid theory of retribution in the book of Proverbs (the righteous always prosper and the wicked always perish). In this way, he indicates that there is a window of acceptable interpretations in Proverbs, rather than wisdom in a strict right or wrong paradigm, such that the ironclad causality we find in Proverbs is only part of a larger and multifaceted literary picture. In so doing, he helps us appreciate how the wisdom literature consists of what Eco calls 'open' texts.[1] I will use the rest of this section to move from Longman's reading of Proverbs to a more imaginative one which corresponds more closely to the quality of 'openness' inherent in the wisdom literature.

To begin, I question whether 'overreading' really captures the techniques which have produced these more rigid interpretations of the book's theory of retribution. Following Sternberg, I take overreading to be an act of finding too much, often personal or psychologistic meaning in the text, a practice common in postmodern or reader-response interpretation that involves following trails of meaning where the reader wants to go, despite the direction of the text.[2] Eco, too, credits the overemphasis on reader-response motivations to 'overinterpretation.'[3] But the methods which Longman rightfully critiques[4] are not cases of seeing too much in the text, but rather of seeing too little. They are interpretations driven primarily by historical concerns or social theories, which, focusing on the world behind the text, fail to describe accurately the world which the text unfolds to the reader. Sternberg cites this very example –

---

[1] Eco, *Interpretation*, 140, says that creative texts are 'open works' which require a different mode of interpretation than 'closed' texts which are not written to provoke a wide spectrum of possible readings. Cf. also Lash, *Theology*, 38.

[2] Sternberg, *Poetics*, 50, 235–38; and 'Biblical Poetics', 469–71.

[3] Overinterpretation, according to Eco, results from neglecting the 'similarities' which are 'significant' and 'relevant' in favor of those which are 'fortuitous' or 'illusory'. *Interpretation*, 46–48.

[4] In addition to Longman's argument on this subject which appeals to the work of Van Leeuwen and Whybray, it is helpful to mention Gladson's work, *Paradoxes*, which identifies more than 100 'retributive paradoxes' in Proverbs that serve to balance what seems to be naïve optimism throughout the rest of Proverbs.

of being overly distracted by historical plausibilities – as a symptom of underreading and even misreading the biblical texts.[5] In this case, underreading occurs when an 'imagination of historical reconstruction' usurps the imagination of textual unfolding. In both cases, the imagination serves the interpreter's task of getting behind the *otherness* of these ancient, literary and poetic texts.

Hermeneutics is just such an imaginative process of filling the gaps and reconstructing the unknowns that arise in reading. The gaps and holes are the result both of historical distance – for which archaeology and social theory provide a basis for reconstruction – but also of genre-specific literary phenomena like repetition, chrononology, gaps, metalepsis, prolepsis, parallelisms and intertextuality, all of which force the reader to reconstruct the world or worlds to which the text points. Like the process of building a puzzle, interpretation requires the imagination to test probabilities and postulate solutions on the way to the most defensible solutions. Interpretation thus avoids misreading while navigating between under- and overreading.

Of course, for many the very idea of imaginative interpretation engenders guarded apprehension, and I am grateful for the way in which Chapman's helpful summary of the subject serves to allay our natural fears.[6] Good interpretive 'imagination,' according to Chapman, does not imply an unconditional 'what if' or endorse 'liberation *from* the text,' but rather fosters a movement '*toward* Scripture.'[7] This imagination is not reserved only for the 'genius', nor is it a secret/Gnostic or stucturalist search for the Freudian unconscious, but an imagination which nevertheless gathers the full range and depth and the human faculties as it opens, reconstructs, and hypothesizes about the meaning of a text. In fact, like his colleague at Duke, Richard Hays,[8] Chapman wants to encourage an imagination corresponding to the Bible as creative and religious literature that requires a transformation of the reader's epistemological framework in the process of understanding and appropriating the text.[9] Vanhoozer, too, puts this in his own words:

---

[5] *Poetics*, 236–37. On this tendency as a hermeneutical distraction, see Ricoeur, *Hermeneutics*, 143–44.

[6] See Chapman, 'Readings'.

[7] Chapman, 'Readings', 412–13. (emphasis his).

[8] See Hays, who, keenly aware of the subtlety and creativity in biblical echoes and intertextual allusions, wants to eliminate mathematical exegesis as a foolproof method of identifying an intertextual link. Instead, he offers seven guiding criteria to accompany the converted imagination as it discerns these links: 'availability' of original sources, 'volume' of the echo, 'recurrence or clustering', 'thematic coherence', 'historical plausibility', 'history of interpretation', and 'satisfaction' (*Conversion*, 34–45).

[9] Chapman, 'Readings', 423, 433–34. and Hays, 'Reading Scripture', 235. Cf. also Lash, *Theology*, 40, who likens biblical interpretation to musical performance – something that requires imagination and yet also 'fidelity' and 'truthfulness' to the original score.

> By imagination I mean the power of synoptic vision – the ability to synthesize heterogeneous elements into a unity. The imagination is a cognitive faculty by which we see as whole what those without imagination see only as unrelated parts ... Where reason analyzes, breaking things (and texts) up into their constituent parts, imagination synthesizes, making connections between things that appear unrelated.[10]

While I suspect that Longman would agree with much, if not most, of what I have said here, his tendency is to divide and conquer rather than synthesize and imagine. Thus, following the unfortunate oversights of Chapman and Hays, he overlooks the most obvious connection in this regard: the wisdom literature is the biblical genre of imagination *par excellence*; its concern is primarily to shape the epistemological and ontological orientation of the reader, rather than to point to historical settings or doctrinal formulations.

In other words, my aim here is to flesh out the remarkable parallels between the imagination involved in interpretation (creating, filling, and reconstructing) and biblical wisdom as an imaginative and creative engagement of life in the world. These parallels, in turn, will explicate wisdom's hermeneutical ability to guide us through the linguistic, literary, and theological artistry of the wisdom literature towards the manifold world which these texts (and the canon) open to us. Longman, like most wisdom scholars, neglects this interpretative aspect of wisdom and is thereby prone to underread its prominent role in the canon.

It is neither possible nor necessary here to demonstrate these connections in overwhelmingly persuasive fashion. Rather, unpacking the creation-theological nature of wisdom in the Old Testament will allow us to appreciate the philosophical distinctiveness of the biblical wisdom literature[11] and thereby convey the fuller hermeneutical potential of wisdom.

(1) First, there are a few important theological motifs in Proverbs 1 – 9 and 31 where we encounter a significant union between hermeneutical themes and creational theology. Proverbs 3:18ff. and 8:22–36 are passages commonly associate with wisdom within the created order, but also the more specific 'boundaries' or the 'carved' nature God placed into the creation.[12] Likewise, Psalm 104 attributes 'wisdom' (v. 24) to the fact that God has made a niche for everything from stars, birds, grass and water to beasts, food and humanity (cf. Job 26:5–14). Furthermore, in Proverbs 8, wisdom, personified as a woman, offers herself as the key to understanding the boundaries God has made for creation

---

[10] 'Lost in Interpretation', 121.

[11] I will also make slight reference to the wisdom material in the Psalter and Sirach and the Wisdom of Solomon. Unfortunately, while I am aware of the important contributions of these deuterocanonical wisdom books, I am regrettably unable to incorporate them here with any degree of expertise.

[12] On this point, see especially Van Leeuwen, 'Liminality'. Cf. Fox, *Proverbs*, 284–85.

and for living an upright life in the created world. Thus, contrary to Longman who finds the (absence of) theology in Proverbs 1 – 9 to be a 'problem,'[13] I find a strong theological and literary unity in a theology of creation,[14] which, via wisdom, is communicated to humanity as an interpretative tool.

This interpretative aspect of wisdom is even clearer in Proverbs 26:1–12. While there is some disagreement as to whether this is a single Proverb poem, I am persuaded by what I think is convincing evidence that the passage fits very well together.[15] As such, the introductory verse in 26:1 sets the theme for the next twelve verses:

> Like snow in summer, or like rain in harvest
> So honor is not fitting (*nāʾweh*) for a fool.

With little exception, the rest of the passage (vv. 2–12) builds upon the themes of fittingness and foolishness. The most salient test of 'fittingness' comes in the paradoxical challenge in Proverbs 26:4–5:

> Do not answer a fool according to his folly,
> Lest you be like him yourself.
> Answer a fool according to his folly,
> Lest he become wise in his own eyes.

The basic point of this passage is that answering a fool is a situational exercise that requires a creative and careful response, or, borrowing from Chapman's terminology, 'imaginative practices of critical attentiveness'.[16] Danger exists both in speaking and remaining silent. It is quite obvious that wisdom provides the essential means to confront this almost impossible task. Fittingness and foolishness thus come together to make a larger point about wisdom. Referring to the extended context in 26:1–12, Van Leeuwen appropriately calls this a '"treatise" on the "hermeneutics" of wisdom'. He continues, '(w)isdom, to a very large extent, is a matter of interpreting people, events, situations, actions in relation to norms for existence.'[17]

---

[13] Longmann, 'Reading Wisdom Canonically', above.

[14] According to Van Leeuwen, the creation order is the framework or worldview which contextualizes the web of metaphors in Prov. 1–9 ('Liminality', 111–14). On the predominant theology of creation, see also von Rad, *Wisdom in Israel* (74–95, 144–76), Perdue, *Wisdom*; Schmid, 'Creation', 114; and Witherington, *Sage*, 10–11.

[15] Cf. van Leeuwen, *Context*, 87–110; Murphy, *Proverbs*, 198–203; and Whybray, *Composition*, 123–24.

[16] 'Readings', 425.

[17] *Context*, 99, 101.

As such it is quite reasonable to follow scholars like von Rad and Van Leeuwen who see a two-fold nature to wisdom in Proverbs: first establishing a theology of the created order (Prov. 1 – 9), and then guiding humanity into the hermeneutical exercise of interpreting and responding to the world around us in light of that order (Prov. 10 – 29).[18] Proverbs invites us to think imaginatively (i.e. hermeneutically) about the created world that it unfolds before us, tying together a creation theology with life in the real world – apparent disorder with theological order.[19]

Put another way, the literary relationship between Proverbs 1 – 9 and 10 – 29 points to a larger set of theological implications as it juxtaposes two of the most basic aspects of being human: *life before God and life in the world*.[20] Wisdom, with its exclusive access to the created order, bridges the felt gap between our relationship with God and our often troubling existential experience on earth. O'Donovan says, 'Wisdom is the perception that every novelty, in its own way, manifests the permanence and stability of the created order, so that, however astonishing and undreamt of it may be, it is not utterly incommensurable with what has gone on before.'[21] O'Donovan's description of wisdom resists the common reduction of wisdom to a mere pedagogical or pragmatic guide to moral behavior (cf. Col. 2:20 – 3:4),[22] upholding it instead as the hermeneutical key to the created order which provides the interpretive framework necessary to navigate the often diverse and ambiguous paths through life in God's world. Biblical wisdom is quintessentially a theological hermeneutic.

(2) Given this theological description of wisdom, we can now turn to the field of philosophical hermeneutics[23] to speak more specifically about wisdom's

---

[18] Van Leeuwen, 'Liminality', 117; von Rad, *Wisdom in Israel*, 105.

[19] Alter puts it in terms of a 'double dialectic between design and disorder, providence and freedom' (*Narrative*, 33, cf. also 115).

[20] O'Donovan, *Resurrection*, 189–90, makes this point in aligning wisdom with torah as they function within the created order. On the emergence of wisdom's theological manifestation in the Old Testament, see also footnote 21 below.

[21] O'Donovan, *Resurrection*, 189. On the dual or bipolar nature of living before God and in the world, see also von Rad, *Wisdom in Israel*, 105–106; and Van Leeuwen, 'Liminality', 117.

[22] Here I am speaking particularly about the wisdom in Proverbs and the rest of the wisdom literature. As Fox rightly notes, not all uses of wisdom (*ḥokmah*) in the Old Testament have this holistic theological connotation, yet the Old Testament also produces its own critiques of simple and pragmatic wisdom in places like Job, Ecclesiastes, and 1 Kings 1–11 (*Proverbs*, 32–36). See Fox, 'Indeterminacy', 188–89; and Parker, 'Solomon'. Thus it does seem reasonable to see 'true' wisdom emerging in the Old Testament rooted in the theological wisdom presented in Proverbs.

[23] That is, a continental approach to hermeneutics which encompasses the more confined exegetical hermeneutics of the Anglo-American tradition.

hermeneutical potential. In other words, hermeneutics seeks to bring together disparate horizons of understanding. It is the search for meaning between the ancient horizon of the text and the contemporary horizon of the reader. One gains understanding by *merging* horizons[24] or *translating* the distant and foreign realities from the past into new realities which are recognizable in the present. As we will see, merging horizons is an imaginative process of (re)construction akin to the activities in biblical wisdom.

The hermeneutical tradition I am working with is driven largely by the philosophical and epistemological ethos of the post-Enlightenment era. While the Enlightenment (*Aufklärung*) relied upon reason, science, and autonomy as sources of truth, the emerging opposition of the *Sturm* und *Drang* sought to preserve places for history, theology (faith), social theory, and aesthetics in the search for knowledge and understanding.[25] A resulting set of oppositions or dialectics emerged between the natural or physical sciences of *explanation* and the social sciences of *understanding*.[26] The intense polemical character of this post-Kantian era has been described in the following ways: epistemology against ontology, engagement against distanciation, faith against reason, and science against aesthetics.[27] The new world in many ways seemed to be on the verge of unavoidable fragmentation.

While these tensions are not identical to the theological tensions described above, there are still conspicuous and important parallels between them. For Gadamer, Ricoeur, and others in the hermeneutical tradition, these tensions or poles, rather than being isolated and opposed, are brought together in the hermeneutical circle where the act of reading moves constantly between them.[28] Explanation and understanding are complementary parts of a hermeneutical task, a task which is *simultaneously* ontological, historical, religious, and aesthetic. Furthermore, for Ricoeur, the very cross-disciplinary ambition of hermeneutics to retain the polarity between explanation and understanding within a healthy tension, naturally appeals to 'creativity' and the 'imagination' in order to reconstruct the unknowns of the hermeneutical progress of understanding which led to the unnecessary opposition of the

---

[24] Or what Gadamer called the 'fusion' of horizons.

[25] See Beiser, *Fate of Reason*.

[26] Here, 'explanation' and 'understanding' are used in their formal sense as they emerged in hermeneutical theory between Kant and Gadamer. See Apel, *Understanding and Explanation*, 1–3, 29–30; and von Wright, *Explanation and Understanding*, 4.

[27] See especially Beiser, *Fate of Reason*, 16–108. Critchley, too, describes a 'gap' which emerges in the seventeenth and eighteenth centuries between philosophy as knowledge and philosophy as wisdom. *Continental Philosophy*, 6–9.

[28] Ricoeur, *Hermeneutics*, 176–81, speaking in the context of metaphor and interpretation.

Aufkärung.[29] Creativity, in this sense, is *thinking productively about a picture of the whole* such that different ways of understanding remain true in their own right. Hermeneutics thus resists a total opposition between explanation and understanding in order to wrestle with what it views as a fuller and truer picture of the whole. It embraces the full historical, epistemological, spiritual, and ontological world as it serves the reader's search for meaning.

Again, without trying to equate hermeneutics and wisdom, the parallels between them are conspicuous and expose to us the full potential built into biblical wisdom. Philosophical hermeneutics thus helps us appreciate the *bipolarity* which endows Job, Agur (Prov. 30) and Ecclesiastes with their unique and often troubling contributions to Old Testament wisdom. Each, in its own way, carries us through the processes and outcomes of various existential experiences and epistemological perspectives.[30] In fact, this aspect of wisdom, which is given to retribution theory, wonder, irony, complaint, and pessimism, accompanies the tensions of historical progress in the Old Testament as Israel moves from victory in conquest to despair in exile.[31] By the time of Ecclesiastes and Proverbs 31, Hebrew wisdom seems to be aware even of the pitfalls of Hellenistic philosophy.[32] Biblical wisdom, then, testifies to the fact that sages faced the constant need to accommodate the mundane with the mysteries of human life and the assurance of divine order with the transcendence of an all powerful Creator.[33] Israel was able to use the full range of the wisdom genre to gain a theological-historical-existential *picture of the whole* and thereby understand the uniqueness of her particular identity in each era. Witherington provides a helpful spectrum which allows us to see how the breadth and interdependencies of Old Testament wisdom accomplished this for Israel:

Conventional Wisdom		**Wisdom of a Counter-Order**[34]
Proverbs	*Job*	*Ecclesiastes*
Sirach	*Wisdom of Solomon*	

---

[29] Ricoeur, *Hermeneutics*, 35–39.

[30] Cf. Fox, 'Qohelet's Epistemology'; Seow, *Ecclesiastes*; and Bartholomew, *Reading Ecclesiastes*.

[31] Bockmuehl, *Reason*, 58.

[32] Fox, 'Qohelet's Epistemology'; and Wolters, *Song*.

[33] See footnote 21 above. Cf. also the insightful union of wisdom in Israel's deuteronomic theology which wrestles with immanence and transcendence. Geller, 'Fiery Wisdom', 45–59.

[34] Adapted from Witherington *Sage*, 295. A fuller version of the table is reproduced in the section on New Testament wisdom below.

As we will see below, this spectrum can be described in terms of a polyphonic harmony of wisdom voices.[35] Each of these books contains facets of the others, yet each also has its own role in communicating a particular perspective on reality which can then be used to understand the world in light of God's created order.

So, while I am not claiming that wisdom has a theoretical approach to post-Enlightenment hermeneutics, it does have very significant parallels with the creative activity in the hermeneutical circle. And, while I do not want to equate wisdom and hermeneutics on every level, the wisdom which we find in the Bible can still very well be described as one of hermeneutical imagination. The wisdom sage, rather than reducing the world to naturalist or rationalist polar oppositions, seeks to acknowledge the extraordinary complexity of the world as it is grounded in one much larger theological and orderly reality. It is on the basis of this reality that life in this world is understood in its relationship (and service) to life before God.

In sum, I find the imaginative and creative work that is characteristic of the theological hermeneutic described above endorsed by wisdom itself. Ironically this seems to put Longman in the position of writing about the interpretation of wisdom without realizing the imaginative and creative hermeneutical nature within it. His approach, funded by Christological and ethical hermeneutics, yields wisdom in Christological and ethical terms, and misses the more foundational and *primary* function of wisdom in the canon: to provide humanity with an interpretative framework shaped by a theology of creation – a theology of the world as a whole. It is in this creation theology that ethics and history are grounded and out of which Christology arises. Longman's interpretation lacks the more foundational structure of a theology of creation[36] and, with this primary function displaced, his interpretation tends to underread the canon in several places. The rest of this response will attempt to show how Longman's underreading can be given an imaginative correction.

Challenges to Longman's Old Testament Wisdom Interpretation

Proverbs

First, I would like to challenge Longman's concession, following a virtual consensus, that the 'lack of obvious theological language' in Proverbs is a 'problem.' If he means that the book lacks explicit reference to redemptive, historical, and/or covenantal theology, this is surely true. Yet, the nature of

---

[35] On polyphonic voices in the wisdom literature, see Thiselton, 'Action', 172–82.

[36] For a helpful discussion and argument for a theology of creation, see Rae, 'Creation', 283ff.

wisdom as an imaginative literary genre, along with the explicit repetition in the book, give us good reason to appreciate the important underlying theological assumptions behind it. I have already noted above the material in Proverbs 3:18ff. and 8:22ff. as the foundation for a theology of creation – what I have called a picture of the whole. The resonances between these chapters and passages like Genesis 1 – 3, Job 26, 28, and Psalm 104 point consistently to Israel's theology of the created order.[37]

In addition to this, Proverbs begins with the explicit demand, 'The fear of Yahweh is the beginning of wisdom.'[38] In fact, 'the fear of Yahweh' is repeated some fourteen times in the book. While I am certainly keen to avoid overreading these references, I am equally compelled to account for the emphatic identification of the fear of Yahweh as the *beginning* of wisdom, and also the wise woman's chief characteristic (Prov. 31:30) in the book's conclusion.[39] These prompt us to ask, hermeneutically, what Proverbs intends for us to reconstruct by the explicit and carefully placed repetition of this phrase. Longman is right to see this signifying the need for a 'relationship with Yahweh.'[40] Yet, given the rich use of this phrase in Deuteronomy and the deuteronomistic literature, there is a strong likelihood that it alludes to a more extensive theological context.[41] In fact, without resorting to Weinfeld's wisdom source theory for Deuteronomy,[42] there is still good reason to see

---

[37] This makes sense, given the parallel correspondence of wisdom and order in other ancient Near Eastern cultures – especially *ma'at* in Egypt.

[38] Prov. 1:7a obviously makes fear the beginning of 'knowledge' (*da'at*), not wisdom. Yet 'wisdom' (*ḥokmah*) in 1:7b sits in synonomous parallel, implying that wisdom is also meant; see Fox, *Proverbs*, 31–32. Furthermore, the repetition of the phrase with 'wisdom' in 9:10 (cf. 2:6; 15:33) confirms that wisdom is included (if not truly intended) by this qualification.

[39] Obviously not all Proverbs scholars accept the inclusion formed by women and fear in Prov. 1–9 with the valiant woman who fears Yahweh in Prov. 31. In their informative reviews of interpretation in the twentieth century Wolters, *Song*, 134–54, and Whybray, *Proverbs*, 153–56, both support this reading.

[40] Longmann, 'Reading Wisdom Canonically', above.

[41] Though there are many variations to this phrase, the literal rendition 'fear of Yahweh' appears more in Proverbs and the deuteronomic/deuteronomistic literature than anywhere else. In addition to this, the language of teaching and instruction paralleled in Deuteronomy makes it likely that Proverbs echoes the use of 'fear' there, intending to make covenant love, trust, and commitment a precondition to the path of wisdom. This is also strengthened by the familiar warning in Prov. 3:5–7 to trust in Yahweh with the whole 'heart' (*leb*) which also echoes Deut. 6:4–9 and 10:12–13. See Waltke, 'Fear of the Lord', 17–18. and Weinfeld, *Deuteronomy*, 274–81.

[42] Cf. Weinfeld, *Deuteronomy*, 244–81. Weinfeld's observations, while overstated, still point to a valid connection between wisdom and torah as Fox, 'Indeterminacy', 189, and many others also recognize.

something like narrative 'metalepsis'[43] occurring here, by which 'the fear of
Yahweh' in Proverbs persuades us to exercise a critical intertextual imagination
and conclude that covenant commitment to Yahweh – with all of its redemptive history and theology – is the entrance to the path of true wisdom.[44]
Wisdom in Proverbs thus unites a theology of creation with a theology of
redemption such that wisdom, besides being theological, is conscious of the
history of Israel's redemption. Its hermeneutics work out of a theological/
redemptive/historical picture of the whole. If this is true, as we will see below,
then the New Testament writers have all the more reason to appeal to wisdom
in their understanding and explanation of the Messiah.

Ecclesiastes

Given wisdom's historical consciousness, or, more specifically, its awareness of
the history of Israel's story of creation, fall, promise and redemption, then it is
crucial to place the wisdom in Ecclesiastes correctly within the lines of this historical progress. In this sense, there seems to be little doubt that even if Solomon originally wrote Ecclesiastes, its most suitable historical context is in post-
exilic Israel, where the likelihood of Israel's faithfulness and hope in God's
promises are at an all-time low.[45]

For these and other reasons, Longman chooses to interpret the voice of
Qohelet in the book as a highly pessimistic sage who has rejected the
original wisdom tradition. Qohelet is then corrected by the frame narrator
(12:13–14.) who puts wisdom back onto a theologically optimistic plane.
Where I want to challenge Longman is in his rather brusque statement regarding Qohelet and the frame narrator: 'The most natural reading of this is that
these are two different people.'[46]

In saying this, I think Longman begins to diverge from two of the major
cues in the book which would hold Qohelet and the frame together in a way
that produces a more unified message in the book, and a more cohesive reading
of the Old Testament wisdom literature. First, his chapter (and commentary)
gives little attention to the empirical epistemology which dominates the introduction in Ecclesiastes 1 – 2. Second, and related, his treatment of the language
in the book focuses so much on the autobiographical material and the sense of

---

[43] Cf. Hays, *Imagination*, 2–3.

[44] Weinfeld, *Deuteronomy*, 274ff., gives several further examples where 'the fear of
Yahweh' in Deuteronomy parallels the sense used in Proverbs.

[45] Ecclesiastes' post-exilic dating can be argued on the basis of language, genre (and
possibly Greek philosophical parallels) which indicate heavy Persian and Aramaic
influences. Cf. Seow, 'Evidence', 643–66, and Longman, *Ecclesiastes*, 9–15.

[46] Longmann, 'Reading Wisdom Canonically', above.

predominant skepticism that he misses the rhetorical irony that is central to their purpose. I will discuss each of these briefly.

First, Longman tells us a great deal about *what* Qohelet knows, but very little about the implications of *how* he knows – his epistemology. As Fox observes, however, epistemology is one of the 'main' if the not the 'central' concerns of the book.[47] Furthermore, Fox points out that Qohelet's epistemological method – which Qohelet often calls 'wisdom' – is in fact a nuanced use of wisdom which applies a unique epistemology: 'Qohelet's epistemology, is, as far as I can tell, foreign to the ancient Near East,'[48] yet, significantly, common to rationalist or empiricist approaches to knowledge found in early Greek philosophies. In other words, Qohelet is using wisdom uniquely, and the effect is to draw the reader's attention to the knower and his process of knowing.

My second contention flows immediately from this: Qohelet's way of knowing is necessarily related to his rhetoric, or his way of expressing his epistemological journey to his readers. Again, quoting Fox on this point: 'Qohelet's new epistemology engenders a new rhetoric … Qohelet bares his soul, not only his ideas, because he seeks to persuade by empathy.'[49] This is where Longman stops short of linking the autobiographical rhetoric to his empirical epistemology. Qohelet is in fact luring the reader into a way of thinking about the world, but perhaps not so naively as Longman imagines. Might his rhetorical method, rather than being skeptical, be ironic such that Qohelet is aware of his method and seeks rhetorically to deconstruct certain ways of thinking about the world? While I cannot argue the point here, Longman gives no attention to this possibility nor the many strong arguments which have been made in its favor.[50]

Returning to the issues of a canonical imagination, I think Longman overlooks Qohelet's rhetoric and therefore underestimates his imaginative use of wisdom as it depicts a view of the world through a *misuse* of wisdom. Longman thus sides with pre-reformation *contemptus mundi* readings of Qohelet's dialogue which fail to see that his rhetoric in fact invites us to embrace the goodness and wholeness of the created order to which his epistemology will not submit. Qohelet's use of wisdom is wisdom of the counter-order as it demonstrates the dangerous and corrupted uses of wisdom from the inside out. If this is true, one could argue that our epistemology, by contrast, should be one that faithfully and imaginatively embraces God's purpose for humanity (life before

---

[47] Fox, *Time*, 71.

[48] Fox, *Time*, 81.

[49] Fox, *Time*, 79.

[50] See e.g. Fisch, 'Qohelet', 158–95; Bartholomew, *Reading Ecclesiastes*, 229–37; and Seow, *Ecclesiastes*, 42–43. Cf. also Ogden, *Ecclesiastes*, 20–22.

God) in light of the ambiguities we face (life in the world). The absence of Qohelet's bipolar epistemology, imaginatively and ironically, begs for ours.

Finally, we might ask, if this is true, how does it change our reading of the Old Testament wisdom literature? Generalizing greatly, I think we can at least begin to see that Qohelet, instead of refusing to be wise, might be using his imagination to take wisdom in a new direction – a direction which contemplates the utter ambiguity which often meets us in this world. In this way, Qohelet contributes one extreme voice to those of Job, Solomon, Hezekiah, Agur, and King Lemuel as they together constitute the polyphonic harmony of Old Testament wisdom. The world as it really is can only be described and understood in the company and harmony of several discreet voices which speak imaginatively from the full spectrum of life in the created order.

Wisdom in the New Testament

Turning at last to the New Testament and to the Synoptic Gospels in particular, we are immediately struck with the conspicuous absence of the major proverbial themes in Jesus' sayings, such as creation theology and the fear of Yahweh.[51] While this is somewhat troubling at first, it must be understood in light of the very important spectrum of wisdom material which we find in the New Testament, including: Jesus' heavy use of parables and aphorisms in the Gospels, Matthew's particular depiction of wisdom, Paul's multifaceted Christological wisdom hermeneutic which he variously appropriates throughout his letters, the more traditional material in James' wisdom, and the Christological wisdom material in John and Hebrews 1. The secondary literature on these subjects is massive as would be any responsible discussion of all their implications. In keeping with the summary nature of this response, I will draw our attention to three salient aspects of New Testament wisdom related to my hypothesis about the hermeneutical character of wisdom in the canon. These are (1) Christ's in-breaking wisdom in his sayings, (2) Paul's creation theology in Ephesians and Colossians, and finally (3) Paul's wisdom of counter-order in 1 Corinthians 1 – 4.

I will touch on the first point only briefly as it relates to the anomalous aspects of Jesus' own sayings. Although they lack explicit references to traditional wisdom theology, they are nevertheless deeply embedded in the language and themes of post-exilic wisdom such as Ben Sira and Pseudo-Solomon.[52] What distinguishes his wisdom from this context and from traditional Hebrew wisdom is, ironically, what also keeps him in line

---

[49] See Witherington, *Sage*, 161.

[50] Witherington, *Sage*, 158–59.

with the full scope and trajectory of wisdom's voice in the Old Testament. That is, Jesus gives limited attention to the heady theological musings of cultural upper-class wisdom in the first century and instead channels most of his wisdom through the context and language of the masses.[53] In this way, Jesus' wisdom is different in its originality but in line with Old Testament wisdom for its appeal to the theme of cultural counter-order (like Job and Ecclesiastes). The importance of this fact becomes clearer when understood in the light of the next two points.

Secondly, Paul's understanding of wisdom is Christological and this Christological wisdom is a central part of Paul's letters, having at least two distinct roles: creation theology and counter-order.[54] The first is treated here and the second below.

On the one hand, Paul develops a creation theology and creation order – founded on Christ – which corresponds to the creation theology and order in the Old Testament. This is particularly significant if, as I have argued, Old Testament wisdom used creation theology in the form of a hermeneutical response to the world. With creation as an interpretative grid, wisdom provided a picture of the whole, with origins, history and purpose, in order for new developments and new experiences of life in the world to be understood and navigated obediently.

With his theology grounded in a theology of creation, Paul looks to wisdom in order to understand his present day. Wisdom thus provides the grid for his historical, redemptive (soteriological), and teleological understanding of the world, in which Christ could then be interpreted as the climax of God's intentions in Israel and the sign of God's eschatological purposes. In fact, wisdom in the Old Testament, personified as a woman with pre-creation origins and historical proximity to God's work, has unprecedented expertise on God's purposes and plans (Prov. 8:22–36). For Paul, the arrival of the personified God in Christ eclipses this perspective and reveals all that woman wisdom could not – God in the flesh – redeeming, revealing and re-creating. Thus Paul's prison epistles major in their emphasis on what Schnabel calls a 'creation theology' which is recontextualized as a 'creation Christology'.[55]

Paul's prison epistles share their personified 'creation Christology' with John 1 and Hebrews 1. The overwhelming result is that creation theology of the Old Testament is Christologically focused in the New Testament.[56] What we are witnessing, then, is a transformation of the hermeneutical imagination.

---

[53] Witherington, *Sage*, 165.
[54] Taking some liberties, I am assigning all thirteen New Testament letters to Paul or a 'Pauline' source consistent with Paul's theology.
[55] *Law and Wisdom*, 318–19.
[56] See Bockmuehl, 'Reason', 57–58.

Christ becomes the foundation for a new grid, the center of a new picture of the whole through, upon and around which all else will be understood.[57] So, while Paul prays for hermeneutical wisdom in his epistolary prayers in Ephesians, Colossians, Philippians and Philemon,[58] John writes poetically of a new created order in Christ and the writer of Hebrews unveils Christ as the fulfillment of God's purposes in creation and with Israel. Witherington rightly observes that '[d]ifferent authors used the sapiential material in different ways'[59] and the reason is that wisdom, now focused on a creation-Christology, has refreshed the hermeneutical and eschatological imagination of God's people to give way to a new (mimetic) statement of wisdom based on the new emerging realities of the present (2 Cor. 5:17).

Third, and finally, we turn to the counter-order form of wisdom in the New Testament. I have already mentioned Jesus' sayings, and in what follows now, I want to show how Paul's discourse in 1 Corinthians 1 – 4 establishes a similar counter-order that flows from the Christological wisdom of creation order found primarily in his prison epistles.

The polemical wisdom in 1 Corinthians is noticeable from the beginning as Paul contrasts the wisdom of this world, or human wisdom (1 Cor. 1:17, 21, 25), with God's wisdom (1 Cor. 1:21, 24, 30). The eloquence, loftiness, and essential superficiality of Greek wisdom are set against the ultimate power of the foolishness of God's wisdom. Remembering Paul's hymns to Christological wisdom in the prison epistles, it is significant that this true wisdom, while being of a counter-order, is nevertheless still the wisdom of Christ. Yet here, as in Philippians 2, the supremacy of God's wisdom is explicitly associated with the cross. Wisdom's glory is in divine suffering, humility, meekness, and self-judgment unto death. While worldly wisdom repels and devalues this lowly form of wisdom, it nevertheless emerges as that *central theological and hermeneutical key* to understanding the structure and purpose of the creator and the new created order.

Thus, being in Christ, the Corinthians are given the mind of Christ and know the very thoughts or spirit of God (1 Cor. 2:16). As a consequence, they are in a position to see God's wisdom as a cosmic *power* grounded not in human strength, but in divinely sanctioned weakness, fear, and trembling (1 Cor. 2:3). Morally, the Corinthians are exhorted to follow the ways of Paul and his companions whose knowledge of the wisdom and character of God leads them to become 'fools for Christ'. God's wisdom shines forth as they are hungry,

---

[57] Bockmuehl, 'Reason', 63–66. Consider also how Col. 2:22ff. does not present wisdom in abstract rules of prohibition, but rather as beginning by setting our minds upon the things above, i.e. the new created order in Christ.

[58] Schnabel, *Law and Wisdom*, 331; O'Brien, *Ephesians*, 109–37.

[59] *Sage*, 247.

thirsty, in rags, brutally treated, and homeless (1 Cor. 4:11). Similarly, in Philippians Paul unites his own knowledge of the power of Christ's resurrection with the fellowship of his sufferings (1 Cor. 3:10). Thus, wisdom is hermeneutically equipped both to understand the cruciform nature of our moral imperatives, and also to encounter God the Father through the sufferings, death and resurrection of Jesus Christ. It is in the cross that we understand our purpose and role in this world; because God himself is a God of amazing goodness, justice, faithfulness and accommodation, we can and should bring accommodation, justice, faithfulness, goodness, suffering and mercy to his creation. The Christological renewal of wisdom brings new meaning to the bipolar relationship between life in the world and life before God: we are meek, lowly, patient servants in this world *because* that is what God is like.

Coming full circle, then, wisdom in the Old Testament has manifold hermeneutical potential because it is expressed in a polyphony of harmonic voices. Similarly, wisdom in the New Testament, owing to a new redemptive and eschatological created order, has a polyphonic nature whose harmony is quintessentially Christological. Looking again to Witherington's model, we can express wisdom canonically this way:

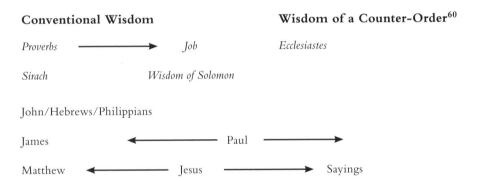

Conventional Wisdom   **Wisdom of a Counter-Order**[60]

Proverbs ⟶ *Job*   *Ecclesiastes*

Sirach   *Wisdom of Solomon*

John/Hebrews/Philippians

James ⟵ Paul ⟶

Matthew ⟵ Jesus ⟶ Sayings

Just as this view of wisdom militates against underreadings which are overly simplistic or given to internal and inter-canonical oppositions, it also exemplifies the multifaceted hermeneutical sophistication of wisdom. Wisdom, grounded in creation and Christological re-creative orders, reveals a view of the whole through an aesthetically creative variety of voices. Wisdom can, with internal consistency, answer the question: 'What is the world really like?' with the hermeneutical (not relativistic) answer, 'it depends on your point of view', thus affirming the use of a constructive imagination to make sense of the whole. As Vanhoozer says, 'By learning imaginatively to follow and indwell

---

[60] Witherington, *Sage*, 295. I have made some changes to reflect what I think sustains the flexibility in these books.

the biblical texts, we see through them to reality as it really is "in Christ",[61] which is for us to embody the wisdom and power of God (1 Cor. 2:16).

Conclusion

My objective in this response has been to demonstrate the way in which wisdom's hermeneutical nature begs for an imaginative approach to its canonical interpretation. Thus, while staying within the trajectory of Longman's interpretation, I have tried to show that we can and should add whole new theological dimensions to our understanding of wisdom. While I follow Longman's progression from Woman Wisdom to Christ, I have situated both Christ and Wisdom within a larger theology of creation. This theology encourages the learner to interpret the whole spectrum of life's experiences in relationship to the boundaries and purposes set down by God in creation. Canonically, we must be able to see that wisdom does not disappear into Christ, but matures to reveal Christ at its center. Wisdom in the New Testament, then, is not so much Christological, but a creation Christology with a view of creation whose centre, author, redeemer and restorer is God the crucified and risen Christ. It then beckons our imagination to work out our obedience in a cruciform manner, participating in the redemption of creation through weakness, suffering and the apparent 'foolishness' of the world.

---

[61] Vanhoozer, 'Lost in Interpretation', 122.

Bibliography

Alter, R., *The Art of Biblical Narrative* (New York: Basic Books, 1981)

Apel, K.O., *Understanding and Explanation: A Transcendental-Pragmatic Perspective* (trans. Georgia Warnke; London: MIT Press, 1984)

Bartholomew, C.G., *Reading Ecclesiastes: Old Testament Exegesis and Hermeneutical Theory* (Analecta biblica 139; Rome: Pontifical Biblical Institute, 1998)

Beiser, F.C., *The Fate of Reason: German Philosophy from Kant to Fichte* (Boston: Harvard University Press, 1987)

Bockmuehl, M., 'Reason, Wisdom and the Implied Disciple of Scripture', in *Reading Texts, Seeking Wisdom* (ed. D. Ford and G. Stanton; London: SCM Press, 2003), 53–68

Chapman, S., 'Imaginative Readings of Scripture and Theological Interpretation', in *Out of Egypt: Biblical Theology and Biblical Interpretation* (ed. C. Bartholomew, M. Healy, K. Möller and R. Parry; SHS 5; Carlisle: Paternoster; and Grand Rapids: Zondervan), 409–47

Crithley, S., *Continental Philosophy: A Very Short Introduction* (Oxford: Oxford University Press, 2001)

Eco, U., R. Rorty, J. Culler, and C. Brooke-Rose, *Interpretation and Overinterpretation* (ed. S. Collini; Cambridge: Cambridge University Press, 1992)

Fisch, H., 'Qohelet: A Hebrew Ironist', in *Poetry with a Purpose: Biblical Poetics and Interpretation* (Bloomington: Indiana University Press, 1990), 158–78

Fox, M., 'Qohelet's Epistemology', *HUCA* 58 (1987), 137–55

—, 'The Uses of Indeterminacy', *Semeia* 71 (1995), 173–92

—, *A Time to Tear Down and a Time to Build Up: A Rereading of Ecclesiastes* (Grand Rapids: Eerdmans, 1999)

—, *Proverbs 1–9: A New Translation with Introduction and Commentary* (AB; New York: Doubleday, 2000)

Geller, S., 'Fiery Wisdom: The Deuteronomic Tradition', in *Sacred Enigmas* (ed. S. Geller; London: Routledge, 1996), 30–61

Gladson, J.A., *Retributive Paradoxes in Proverbs 10–29* (Ann Arbor: University Microfilms International, 1979)

Hays, R.B., *The Conversion of the Imagination: Paul as Interpreter of Israel's Scripture* (Grand Rapids: Eerdmans, 2003)

—, 'Reading Scripture in the Light of the Resurrection', in *The Art of Reading Scripture* (ed. E.F. Davis and R.B. Hays; Grand Rapids: Eerdmans, 2003)

Lash, N., *Theology on the Way to Emmaus* (London: SCM Press, 1986)

Longman, T., *The Book of Ecclesiastes* (Grand Rapids: Eerdmans, 1998)

O'Donovan, O., *The Ways of Judgment* (Grand Rapids: Eisenbrauns, 2005)

—, *Resurrection and Moral Order: An Outline for Evangelical Ethics* (Leicester: Inter-Varsity Press, 1986)

Parker, K.I., 'Solomon as Philosopher King: The Nexus of Law and Wisdom in 1 Kings 1–11', *JSOT* 53 (1992), 75–91

Perdue, L., *Wisdom and Creation: The Theology of the Wisdom Literature* (Nashville, TN: Abingdon Press, 1994)

Rae, M., 'Creation and Promise', in *Behind the Text: History and Biblical Interpretation* (ed. C. Bartholomew, C.S. Evans, M. Healy and M. Rae; SHS 4; Carlisle: Paternoster; Grand Rapids: Zondervan, 2003), 267–99

Rad, G. von, *Wisdom in Israel* (London: SCM Press, 1970)

Ricoeur, P., *Hermeneutics and the Human Sciences* (Cambridge: Cambridge University Press, 1981)

Schmid, H.H., 'Creation, Righteousness, and Salvation: "Creation Theology" as the Broad Horizon of Biblical Theology', in *Creation in the Old Testament* (ed. B.W. Anderson; London: SPCK, 1984), 102–17

Schnabel, E., *Law and Wisdom from Ben Sira to Paul: A Tradition Historical Inquiry into the Relation of Law, Wisdom and Ethics* (Tübingen: J.C.B. Mohr [Paul Siebeck], 1985)

Seow, C.L., 'Linguistic Evidence and the Dating of Qohelet', *JBL* 115 (1996), 643–66

—, *Ecclesiastes* (New York: Doubleday, 1997)

Sternberg, M., *The Poetics of Biblical Narrative* (Bloomington, IN: Indiana University Press, 1987)

—, 'Biblical Poetics and Sexual Politics: From Reading to Counterreading', *JBL* 111 (1992), 463–88

Thiselton, A.C., 'Communicative Action and Promise in Hermeneutics' in *The Promise of Hermeneutics* (ed. R. Lundin, C. Walhout and A.C. Thiselton; Grand Rapids: Eerdmans; and Carlisle: Paternoster, 1999)

Vanhoozer, K.J., 'Lost in Interpretation: Truth, Scripture, and Hermeneutics', in *Whatever Happened to Truth?* (ed. A. Köstenberger; Wheaton: Crossway, 2005), 93–136

Van Leeuwen, R., 'Liminality and Worldview in Proverbs 1–9', *Semeia* 50 (1990), 111–44

—, *Context and Meaning in Proverbs 25–27* (SBLDS 96; Atlanta, GA: Scholars Press, 1988)

Von Wright, G.H., *Explanation and Understanding* (Cornell: Cornell University Press, 1971)

Waltke, B.K., 'The Fear of the Lord: The Foundation for a Relationship with God', in *Alive to God: Studies in Spirituality* (ed. J.I. Packer and L. Wilkinson; Downers Grove: InterVarsity Press, 1992), 17–33

Weinfeld, M., *Deuteronomy and the Deuteronomic School* (Winona Lake: Eisenbrauns, 1992; Oxford: Clarendon, 1972)

Whybray, R.N., *The Composition of the Book of Proverbs* (Sheffield: Sheffield Academic Press, 1994)

Witherington, B., *Jesus the Sage: The Pilgrimage of Wisdom* (Minneapolis: Fortress, 1994)

Wolters, A., *The Song of the Valiant Woman: Studies in the Interpretation of Proverbs 31:10–31* (Carlisle: Paternoster, 2001)

15

Prolegomena to Christian Theological Interpretations of Lamentations
Robin Parry

Lamentations, like the personified Lady Jerusalem within its pages, often sits alone within the landscape of the Christian Bible calling out to those readers who pass by to take notice but, as with Lady Jerusalem, there is no one to comfort. Lamentations is one of those Old Testament books that has never really attained a place of prominence in Christian spirituality and reflection. This means that when attempting to think theologically about the book one does not have the rich heritage of theological interpretation to draw on that one finds with books such as Genesis, Exodus, Psalms or Isaiah. Perhaps this is to be expected because Lamentations is neither quoted nor even alluded to in the New Testament while a book such as Isaiah seems omnipresent. So when one comes to read Lamentations theologically as a Christian one has to start with a comparatively slender thread of prior reflection as a guide.

Contemporary academic commentaries tend to avoid any Christian theological interpretation of the texts in question (although often Christian theological drives are at work beneath the surface). Their agenda is a different one concerned mostly with seeking to establish the pre-history of the text, or what light it may shed on the history of Israel, or how the text would have been received by its original audiences, and so on. To seek to read the text in the light of, and as a source for, Christian theology is often regarded as a 'devotional', non-academic and anachronistic reading back of later meanings into ancient texts.

Where one does find contemporary Christian theological interaction with Lamentations it tends not to be distinctively *Christian*. So one can find modern texts which use Lamentations as the basis for reflections on the importance of giving space for lament, grief, protest against God in the face of suffering and so on.[1] Whilst such discussions are helpful and very worthwhile they fail, in my view, to really explore the tremendous potential offered by a *distinctively Christian* engagement with this text. In this essay I want to suggest one way in which Christians can theologically wrestle with the Lamentations.

---

[1] For instance, O'Connor, *Lamentations*.

Lamentations Within its Own Horizons

The academy typically seeks to read Lamentations within the horizons of its original contexts. So the scholar aims to set the text (or a hypothetical reconstruction of its sources) against its historical, socio-cultural, linguistic and literary background and to understand it (or its postulated sources), as far as is possible, in ways its original hearers/readers would have done. Historical-critical study often seeks to get 'behind' the text to peek, if at all possible, at its evolution in oral and written tradition, the life of the ancient culture it manifests, the history of Israel, the social settings in which it (or a hypothetical earlier edition or a hypothetical reconstructed source) was used, and so on. Newer literary critical approaches set aside the attempt to get 'behind' the text and focus on the text in its final form. Whilst such interpretation is not the only helpful way of reading the Bible it is an essential one for Christian readers for whom the final form is the 'authorised' scriptural text. So while a reader who wishes to read theologically may want to draw on insights from historical-critical methods *the text that they are seeking to theologically interpret will be the final form that made it into the Christian Bible.* With this in mind I suggest that certain of the newer literary critical approaches have an especially useful place in thinking through a Christian theological reading. It will become clear, however, that a literary critical reading is *not* to be mistaken for a Christian theological reading.

I want to make use of Mark Allan Powell's account of narrative criticism in my explication of the kind of literary criticism I am keen to adopt.[2] Powell helpfully distinguishes 'expected responses' to a text from 'unexpected responses'. Expected responses are the responses that might be attributed to the text's implied readers. The implied readers are not flesh and blood readers who ever existed in the real world. They are *not* the original readers/hearers of the text living back in the ruins of Jerusalem. Rather they are 'an imaginary set of people who may be assumed to read a given text in a way that they are expected to read it, bringing to their reading experience the knowledge, competence, beliefs, and values that appear to be presupposed by the text in question'.[3] When Powell talks of an 'expected response' he does not mean 'expected by the author' but rather 'expected by the text'. Obviously this requires us to personify the text (texts do not literally have intentions and expectations) but such personification, perhaps expressed in terms of an implied author, is helpful.

So what might be the competence, knowledge, beliefs and values of the implied readers of Lamentations? Clearly there would be a linguistic competence in the Hebrew of the period and also a literary competence that would enable an appreciation of the genre of the various poems. There would also be a

---

[2] Powell, *Chasing the Eastern Star.*
[3] Powell, *Chasing the Eastern Star*, 64.

basic reading competency. That is to say that the implied readers/hearers are expected to read the *whole book* of Lamentations and not just one poem. Attempting to interpret each poem without seeing its connections with the other poems is not to read in the way the *book of Lamentations* 'expects'. Such ideal readers are also expected to read the book of Lamentations *starting at the beginning* and moving sequentially through to the end. This means that the reader will be expected to bring previous material from the book to bear on the interpretation of a specific part but *not*, in the first instance at least, subsequent material. This reading competency is actually more of a super-competency because implied readers are expected to be attentive to all the subtle nuances and details of the text. Real readers often fail to notice or remember some aspect or feature of a text but our implied readers/hearers do not for they are the text's *ideal* readers/hearers.

Implied readers are not expected to know everything that people living at the time and place the text was written might know but they are expected to know what is revealed within the text. The 'danger' is of over-competence on the part of the scholarly real reader that leads to their attributing unexpected interpretations to the implied readers/hearers. Powell suggests that the implied readers of a text can be 'assumed to possess *whatever knowledge concerning the spatial, temporal, and social setting of the* [text] *would have been regarded as common knowledge in the world that formed the discourse setting for the* [text]'.[4] In the case of Lamentations it seems highly plausible that the gap between the situation in Jerusalem to which the book refers and its implied readers is minimal. That is to say, the text originates in the ruins of Jerusalem reflecting on a *current* situation (the struggles of life within the shattered city of Jerusalem) and a not-too-distant past (the decimation of the city by the enemy). So the implied readers would be expected to have some understanding of the geography of Palestine and, more particularly, of Jerusalem and Judah. They would be expected to know something of the history of the people of Israel and of the city of Jerusalem. They would be expected to know about the social and cultural realities of life in sixth-century Jerusalem and its environs. They would be expected to appreciate symbolic actions such as the public stripping and shaming of a faithless wife. They would be expected to know *and share* the religious worldview of the implied author. They would be expected to be familiar with the religious traditions and practices of Israel: Traditions such as the inviolability of Jerusalem (Ps. 46; 48; 76; cf. Lam. 2:15; 4:12, 20; 5:19) or the exodus story, and practices like the annual pilgrimages to the Temple. They would be expected to recognise inter-texts – allusions to and quotations of existing religious texts such as parts of the Psalms, Exodus, Deuteronomy or Jeremiah in whatever forms those texts were known at the time of writing.

---

[4] Powell, *Chasing the Eastern Star*, 90.

Several reflections are in order at this point. First, it is important to make clear that an expected reading of a text is not the *only* legitimate reading of a text. Indeed it is probably the case that most of the interpretations of the text by real live readers deviate in various degrees from the expected reading. This is especially the case for the vast majority of interpretations because they are not *trying* to uncover the response expected of the implied readers. We are not the implied readers of Lamentations and never could be. Perhaps the original audiences of the book in various degrees approximated quite closely to the implied readers but no modern readers do. We are not ancient Jews living amid the rubble of Jerusalem nor should we aspire to be. 'We cannot know everything that they would be expected to know, and no matter how good we are at pretending, we cannot really forget everything that they are not expected to know.'[5] Scholarly interpretations such as those of source criticism, tradition criticism or redaction criticism that seek to get 'behind' the text generate unexpected interpretations. In just the same way modern Marxist, psychoanalytic, feminist, or liberationist readings are unexpected. Christian theological interpretation is also unexpected by the implied author. Indeed, *it is essential for a Christian theological reading of Lamentations that the reader is not standing in the shoes of the implied reader.* To anticipate where I am going here: a Christian theological interpretation of Lamentations will reframe the text in the light of the full Christian canon of Old and New Testaments both seen through the lens of the ongoing history of Christian reflections on those texts. More on that later.

Second, whilst Christian theological reading of Lamentations must clearly and unashamedly distinguish itself from an expected reading, the expected reading does have much to contribute to the theological reading. I propose that for a Christian reading of Holy Scripture there should be an *organic relationship* between the expected response of the implied readers/hearers and the unexpected theological interpretation. This bold claim is founded upon traditional Christian beliefs about the inspiration of the texts and their authority for the faith community. Consequently, the clarification of the expected reading will be important for testing the legitimacy of theological responses. Theological readings that ride roughshod over original meanings (as far as we are able to establish them) implicate themselves as possible impostors.[6] I am not suggesting that theological interpretation *must* be preceded by a literary reading to gain

---

[5]   Powell, *Chasing the Eastern Star*, 85

[6]   Inevitably objectors will claim that New Testament interpretations of Old Testament texts often ride roughshod over expected responses to the original texts. Am I saying that New Testament uses of the Old Testament are illegitimate Christian uses? No. The topic is vast and complex but I would simply register the following assertions. (a) Most importantly, I think that the majority of New Testament uses of the Old Testament *are* organically related to the expected responses. This claim is controversial but it seems to me that the trajectory in modern New Testament

legitimacy. Most theological readers of Lamentations have done fine without following such a procedure. What I am saying is that the practice of distancing the horizon of the text and that of the reader creates the space for the text to resist some of the ways we might choose to appropriate it. It provides, in other words, a safeguard against disrespectful appropriation of the text.

Third, it is increasingly appreciated by scholars that there is no neutrality even in this realm of 'objective' readings. That is not to suggest for one moment that there is not a legitimate distinction between what a text meant in its original context and what it might mean in different contexts. Readers need not simply see their own reflection in a mirror when they gaze into a text. However, the distinction is a relative one and not an absolute one.[7] Given that implied readers are a construct, it is clear that different actual readers who are seeking to clarify what the expected response to the text is will construct slightly different implied readers.[8] This is especially so with readers as far removed from the original worlds of the texts as we are.

Now seeking to read Lamentations against its original horizon will involve dealing with its use of other biblical texts. Lamentations is widely regarded as reflecting knowledge of several of Israel's holy books. There seems, for instance, to be a knowledge of the theology of Exodus,[9] Deuteronomy,[10] parts of the text of Jeremiah,[11] and especially of the Psalmic traditions in general and

---

scholarship on this issue is towards recognising that New Testament uses of the Old Testament are far more sensitive to the original contexts of the texts than used to be appreciated (see, for instance, the work of N.T. Wright, R. Hays, G.K. Beale, R.E. Watts). (b) Not all New Testament uses of the Old Testament are theological interpretations and are thus not invalidated by ignoring original expected responses. (c) I do wish to allow for the possibility that legitimate theological interpretation can run *counter* to the expected response. For instance, some of Paul's use of the Old Testament in Romans 9 – 11 runs counter to any expected response to those texts (see Chae, *Paul as Apostle to the Gentiles*) but Paul is quite conscious of what he is doing and it is precisely his radical reading that is so theologically powerful. But running *counter* to the expected response is not the same as *ignoring* it.

[7] Stiver, *Theology After Ricoeur*.

[8] Powell, *Chasing the Eastern Star*, 71.

[9] Dobbs-Allsop (*Lamentations*, 59) sees about a dozen allusions to the Exodus narrative in Lamentations 1.

[10] Gottwald (*Studies in the Book of Lamentations*) argues that Deuteronomic theology is a major strand in the theology of Lamentations. Albrektson (*Studies in the Text and Theology of the Book of Lamentations*, 234) sees the covenant curses of Deuteronomy 28 as especially relevant to Lamentations.

[11] There are many Jeremiah–Lamentations links at the level of theology (which for both books is essentially that of Deuteronomy), but also at the level of issues addressed, and many connections at the level of vocabulary and imagery (see House, *Lamentations*, 283–303). Whilst the Jewish and Christian traditions saw Jeremiah as

some Psalms in particular.[12] These inter-textual connections come out both at the level of underlying theology and at the level of linguistic parallels. Lamentations could be considered as a carpet that has been woven from numerous threads that include previous texts, religious traditions, and the actual experience of the destruction of Jerusalem. The upshot of this is that seeking to read Lamentations against its original horizon will require reading it alongside certain other biblical texts because the implied readers would be expected to recognise the quotations and allusions as they engage in meaning-making. This is a step towards reading Lamentations canonically *but it is only a step.*

Lamentations Within the Canon of the Church

Canonical shape and context

Some biblical texts have a very complex history which scholars may desire to attempt to unravel but the text that has theological significance for Christians is the text as it is found in the canon of Scripture. This is not to suggest that theological interpreters will have no interest in the pre-history of the text but it does mean that any such interest will be in the service of better understanding the final form. There has been much debate in Lamentations studies about whether the different poems and their parts had varied origins and were compiled and modified by a later redactor.[13] The current trend is towards seeing the five poems as being specifically written to fit together as the book we now have and, if this is so, the poems (or parts of them) never would have existed in any other context than that in which we now have them.[14] Either way, the object of interpretation for the theological reader is the full, final form of

---

the author of Lamentations, the tide began to turn when, in 1712, Hermann von der Hardt challenged this view. The mainstream of Old Testament scholarship is now almost unanimously against the idea that Jeremiah wrote Lamentations but there has been an increasing trend towards arguing that the author(s) of Lamentations knew the book of Jeremiah. Nancy Lee has gone so far as to argue that Jeremiah's is one of the voices that speaks in Lamentations (though Jeremiah's voice is only a literary device) enabling the book of Lamentations to function as something like an extension of the book of Jeremiah (Lee, *Singers of Lamentations*). Others hear not Jeremiah's voice but a Jeremiah-like voice which reflects an awareness of the earlier text (see references in House, *Lamentations*, 405–406).

[12] E.g., the allusions to Ps. 33 in Lam. 3:37.

[13] See Westermann, *Lamentations*, and the Introduction to House, *Lamentations*, for up to date overviews of the discussions.

[14] For instance, Renkema, *Lamentations*; Berlin, *Lamentations*; Dobbs-Allsop, *Lamentations*; House, *Lamentations*.

Lamentations. However, it is not simply the canonical shape of a book that interests theological readers but also its broader canonical context.[15]

The modern biblical scholar reading Lamentations is supposed, at least when they are doing their historical work, to bracket out of their minds the fact that for Christians Lamentations is now relocated within the broader context of the biblical canon of Old Testament and New Testament. It is clear that reading Lamentations in the light of later Jewish literature like Second Isaiah or of Christian literature like 2 Corinthians is not going to help when seeking to read the text against its original horizon. In fact, it will distort *that* project. Fair enough. However, this simply highlights the point that for Christians no 'original horizon interpretation' can count as *a full-blown Christian theological interpretation even if it may function as a step on the way to one.* This is because for Christians Lamentations is part of Holy Scripture and Christian engagement with the book *as Scripture* will be an engagement which seeks to hear God speak afresh into our contexts. Simply understanding how the implied readers would receive the text is only of partial help because, as we have already made clear,

---

[15] Space does not permit a discussion of the implications of the locations Lamentations has occupied in the orders of Israel's canon. The placing of Lamentations within the canon was not unintentional and was intended to guide Jewish readers in their reading of the text. However, Lamentations has occupied various places within the canons of the Jews. The Septuagint (LXX) places Lamentations after the book of Jeremiah (as do extant Hebrew manuscripts antedating the sixth century AD). This is clearly because the editors thought that Lamentations was written by Jeremiah and historically most Jews and Christians read it that way. The Christian Bible has always followed the LXX location of the book. The Hebrew canon reflected in the MT seems to be the ordering of Medieval Jewish communities and places Lamentations in a section of the Writings knows as the *Megilloth* (festive scrolls) right after Psalms and Proverbs. The *Megilloth* are Ruth, Song of Songs, Ecclesiastes, Lamentations, and Esther although different Hebrew manuscripts order the five scrolls differently (see Gerstenberger, *Psalms Part 2 and Lamentations*, 467–69). This is a liturgical placing reflecting its use in Jewish festivals. Neither of these locations for our book are the 'right' one and both can be of profit for theological re-appropriation. For instance, some commentators now argue that Lamentations itself, whilst not actually written by Jeremiah, is consciously Jeremiah-like perhaps even speaking at times in the voice of Jeremiah (so Lee, *Singers of Lamentations*). This would suggest that the LXX location and superscription rightly picks up on intentional textual indicators. The location alerts readers to this and asks for them to read the book as a lament for the destruction Jeremiah predicted would befall Jerusalem at the hands of Babylon. This leads me to resist Brevard Childs's claim that the final canonical form of Lamentations is a reason to reject associations with Jeremiah (Childs, *Introduction to the Old Testament as Scripture*, 596–97). His reasoning is that the man in Lamentations 3 functions to typify Israel's experience and allow its application beyond the particular experiences of the sixth century. Childs fears that a link between the man in Lamentations 3 and Jeremiah would not allow the text to function in this way. I disagree.

no *Christian* reader is, or ever has been, standing in the same shoes (or, perhaps, sandals) as one of the implied readers.

It is crucial to appreciate that for Christians Lamentations must be interpreted within the context of the entire biblical canon, and that includes the New Testament. Biblical books can only be read *as Christian Scripture* when read in their canonical context. Now it is true that one can fruitfully read biblical books in relation to all sorts of inter-texts including modern movies and literature. However, for the community of the church not all inter-textual relationships are equal for Christian interpretation. The other books in the canon form a privileged set of texts for inter-textual relationship.

A Christian reading of Lamentations will recognise that by situating it within the canon the interpretational context for it has changed. Just as the interpretation of a painting will change if the context in which it is displayed – the frame and the gallery – changes so too the meaning of a biblical book will be opened up in new ways when it is set up in relation with new contexts. This is especially so given that biblical texts do not set themselves up as timeless, self-contained units of meaning. Rather they are situated within and arise from the dynamic and ongoing story of God's relationship with his covenant people. There is a strong sense in which these texts do not see their meaning as closed but open to being perceived afresh as the story continues to unfold. So it is that many biblical books lack a sense of closure but look forward to the ongoing story which will unfold. Consistent with this is the inner-biblical reuse of earlier traditions and texts in fresh ways to fit the changing context of the story. This is seen clearly both in the Old Testament reuse of the Old Testament as well as in the New Testament reuse of the Old Testament. The creation of scriptural canons within the Jewish and Christian communities reflected precisely this dynamic of seeing new meanings in old Scriptures. The canon privileges certain texts for the Christian community and invites unexpected readings that go beyond the 'original horizons' of the individual books – old stories are invited to be read against the expanding horizon of the grand story of God's relationship with his people as it moves ever-onward.

Lamentations read through Isaiah 40 – 55

It is time then to reach out beyond Lamentations itself into the beginnings of its afterlife in the reading community of Israel. There is some inner-canonical guidance provided for theological readers of Lamentations in particular – namely the way that Lamentations has found itself being taken up as an element that has been reused in Isaiah 40 – 55. [16] This is especially significant for

---

[16] Apart from the commentaries see especially Willey, *Remember the Former Things*; Sommer, *A Prophet Reads Scripture*; Linafelt, *Surviving Lamentations*, ch. 3. Numerous other scholars have recognised the connections even though they have not

Christian readers because Isaiah 40 – 55 has exerted more influence on the theology of New Testament literature than perhaps any other part of the Old Testament. Isaiah thus becomes a canonical bridge between Christian theology and Lamentations. If we see how the prophet appropriated the book of Lamentations and then how the New Testament writers interpreted the prophet we can begin to imagine canonical ways of connecting Christian reflection with Lamentations in a controlled way.

The prophet of Isaiah 40 – 55 is usually thought to have prophesied towards the end of Israel's exilic period. He clearly anticipates the end of the period of suffering so acutely given voice in Lamentations. As part of his message he seems to have quite consciously taken up the text of Lamentations. Second Isaiah clearly sees himself as announcing Yahweh's response to the pain of Jerusalem expressed in Lamentations. Texts from all five chapters of the lament are taken up and reused in the prophecy and the overall effect is one of *radical reversal* for Jerusalem. Consider the following:

In Lamentations 1 Lady Jerusalem is overwhelmingly cast as one who suffers without anyone to comfort (נחם) her (1:2, 9, 16, 17, 21). The lack of a comforter is the constant refrain of that pitiful opening chapter. Second Isaiah opens with the words, 'Comfort, comfort (נחמו) my people, says your God. Speak tenderly to Jerusalem, and cry to her that her warfare is ended, and that her iniquity is pardoned, that she has received from the LORD'S hand double for all her sins' (Isa. 40:1–2). The comfort theme then recurs as a major motif throughout Isaiah 40 – 55 with Yahweh himself coming to take on the role of the comforter (Isa. 40:1; 49:13; 51:3, 12, 19; 52:9; 54:11).[17]

The fate of those in Jerusalem was bitter. Special attention is given to the children who are not cared for by their parents (Lam. 4:3), who have no water or bread (Lam. 4:4), and who, in the extreme circumstances of famine, are even eaten by their own mothers (Lam. 4:10). Isaiah 40 – 55 is also concerned with the fate of Jerusalem's children. The children of Zion (here a metaphor for the citizens of Jerusalem) who went into captivity (Lam. 1:5) will return (Isa. 49:18, 25). And the children who were slaughtered (Lam. 1:20; 2:21) and who died in the famine (2:11–12, 20, 22) will be alive again and say, 'This place is too crowded for me; make room for me to dwell in' (Isa. 49:20).[18] Clearly this is only a poetic resurrection but it seeks to provide a rhetorical response to the

---

developed them at length. For instance, Gottwald, *Studies in the Book of Lamentations*, 44–46; Porteous, 'Jerusalem-Zion', 238; Turner, *Daughter Zion*; Berlin, *Lamentations*; House, *Lamentations*.

[17] The theological interpreter, so I would argue, will be interested to ask how Paul's use of Isaiah's 'comfort' motif in 2 Corinthians 1 impacts our engagement with Lamentations. But space does not permit such an exploration here.

[18] For a defence of the claim that the poet imagines the dead children as alive again in Isa. 49:20 see Linafelt, *Surviving Lamentations*, 76–77.

rhetoric of Lamentations. Zion will be amazed at all the children she has and will wonder where they came from (Isa. 49:21).

In Lamentations 4:17 the besieged citizens look and look, and wear their eyes out in the hope that another nation would come to their rescue. They looked in vain. But now, says the prophet, the watchmen lift their voices and sing for joy because they see Yahweh himself returning to Zion (Isa. 52:8).

After the defeat of the city Judah was led into exile (Lam. 1:3) and roads mourn for lack of pilgrim travellers (Lam. 1:4) but the prophet foresees a return of the exiles with the roads to Zion filled with celebrating pilgrims (Isa. 51:11; 49:18). Pursuers 'overtook' (נשג in Hiph) Zion and imposed 'suffering' and 'groaning' (אנח in Niph) on her (Lam. 1:3–4), but now gladness 'overtakes' (נשג in Hiph) her and 'suffering' and 'groaning' (אנח in Niph) flee away (Isa. 51:11).

The central pain at the heart of Lamentations is the pain caused by Yahweh's abandonment of Jerusalem. Lamentations draws close to an end with the words: 'Why do you *forget* (שכח) us forever, why do you *forsake* (עזב) us for so many days?' (Lam. 5:20). This concern is picked up in Isaiah 49:14 where the question becomes a statement in the mouth of Zion, 'But Zion says, "The LORD has *forsaken* me (עזבני); my Lord has *forgotten* me (שכחני)."' What does Yahweh say to this complaint? He asks rhetorically, 'Can a woman forget her nursing child, that she would have no compassion on the son of her womb?' Then, perhaps recalling the extreme situations in Lamentations itself when mothers do indeed forsake their children (Lam. 2:20; 4:1–4, 10), Yahweh continues, 'Even these may forget, *yet I will not forget you.*' Linafelt writes, 'the poet chooses here the one metaphor for Yahweh that can bring to answer the rhetoric of Lamentations: Yahweh as a mother who also laments and hopes for the return of her children.'[19] The rest of Isaiah 49 reinforces the theme of Yahweh remembering Zion. So in place of being 'forgotten' (שכח) and 'abandoned' (עזב) (Lam. 5:20) Yahweh says that he did 'abandon' Israel (עזבתיך) *but only for a moment* and now in great pity he will gather them (Isa. 54:7). Zion will now 'forget' (שכח) the shame of her youth and her widowhood (Isa. 54:4). Lamentations complains of divine 'anger' (קצף) and 'rejection' (מאס) (Lam. 5:22). Yahweh says that whilst Zion was indeed 'rejected' (עזובה) and that in a flood of 'anger' (קצף) he did hide his face from her (Isa. 54:6, 8) it was *only for a moment* and now in everlasting love he will have compassion on them (Isa. 54:8).

The prayer in Lamentations is that Yahweh would forgive his people and that the pagan enemies who inflicted such cruelty on Zion would experience the same fate as just retribution: 'Let them be as I am' (Lam. 1:21–22; cf. 3:58–66). Lamentations 4 offers hope that the cup of wrath Jerusalem had drunk would be passed over to Edom who would be stripped bare as Jerusalem had been (Lam. 4:21–22). Isaiah 51:17–23 sees the immanent fulfilment of this as the

---

[19] Linafelt, *Surviving Lamentations*, 75.

cup of wrath passes from Israel to the tormenters. The humiliation experienced by Jerusalem would now be experienced by Babylon (Isa. 47). Babylon would sit on the ground in the dust (Isa. 47:1 – the vocabulary is drawn from Lam. 2:10) as Zion had done. Babylon would be stripped of her clothing (Isa. 47:2–3) leaving her nakedness uncovered and her shame for all to see (Isa. 47:3) as was Jerusalem's (Lam. 1:8). Now she must sit in silence (Isa. 47:5; cf. Lam. 2:10). And worst of all she will become as a widow and lose her children (Isa. 47:8–9) just as Lady Jerusalem had (Lam. 1:1, 16–18). The description of Babylon's fate in Isaiah 47 seems to draw explicitly on the fate of Zion in Lamentations in order to show the fulfilment of Jerusalem's prayer in Lamentations 1:21–22.

And just as the enemies of Zion are punished for their cruelty to God's people so the humiliation of Jerusalem is reversed. Zion had fallen to the ground with her skirts unclean (Lam. 1:9) but now she is told to shake off the dust (cf. Lam. 2:10), rise up from the ground (Isa. 52:2) and to 'put on beautiful garments' (Isa. 52:1). The yoke of sin that was placed upon her neck (Lam. 1:14) must now be loosed (Isa. 52:2). The 'widow' (Lam. 1:1) will be married to Yahweh again (Isa. 54:4–8) and the mother bereft of children will receive her children back. The devastated city of Jerusalem (Lam. 2:5–9) will be rebuilt with precious stones (Isa. 54:11–12). The nations that once entered her sanctuary profaning it (Lam. 1:10) will do so no more (Isa. 52:1). The complaint in Lamentations 5:1–2 that the land of the people had been taken by foreigners so that they even had to buy water from their own wells to drink is also answered – the people possess their land again (Isa. 54:3) and are invited to come and drink from the waters – to buy food and drink without money (Isa. 55:1–2).

So far we have considered the reversal of fate for both Jerusalem and her tormenters which Second Isaiah portrays. What I have not mentioned yet are the connections between the man in Lamentations 3 and the Servant of Yahweh in Isaiah. It is the work of this Servant that is key in the restoration of Zion and the return from exile portrayed in Isaiah 40 – 55. One enters a minefield when discussing the Servant figure in Isaiah 40 – 55 and I can do no more here than to simply state my position. I think that the Servant figure is clearly the nation of Israel in chapters 40 – 48.[20] However, Israel's ongoing sin means that it is unable

---

[20]   The more plausible alternative suggestions include Cyrus (so Watts, *Isaiah 34–66*), Deutero Isaiah (so Whybray, *Isaiah 40–66*), a Davidic Messianic figure (so Eaton, *Festal Drama in Deutero-Isaiah*; Motyer, *Prophesy of Isaiah*), a new Moses figure (so Hugenberger, 'The Servant of the LORD in the Servant Songs of Isaiah') and Israel. The servant is clearly a royal figure (see Williamson, *Variations on a Theme*, 132–35) but contextually Israel is explicitly identified with the servant (Isa. 41:8–9; 42:19; 43:10; 44:1–2, 21, 26; 48:20) and given that Isaiah 55:3–5 confers the David role upon the nation the royal imagery becomes understandable. The Servant is Israel personified as a royal figure. This explains the many parallels between descriptions of the servant and the King as well as those between the servant and Israel.

to fulfil its mission to the nations (Isa. 42:16–25; 43:24; 46:8–13; 48). Thus in chapters 49 – 53 an individual takes on the identity and mission of the nation in order to deliver Israel (Isa. 49:1–13) and free her up to function as the Servant to the nations.[21] So the Servant in chapters 49 – 53 is a Servant who embodies the mission of Servant Israel with the goal of rescuing Israel. It seems that this deliverance is achieved in Isaiah 53 where the servant shares in the exilic sufferings of the exiles even though he does not deserve them. His wounds brought peace and healing for Israel (Isa. 53:5). The servant dies embodying the exilic death of the nation (Isa. 53:9) and is *then* glorified (Isa. 52:12; 53:10b–12). Arguably the salvation of Zion and Israel in chapters 54 – 55 *follows on from* the work of the Servant in Isaiah 52:13 – 53:12. Now there are numerous Zion-Servant parallels in Second Isaiah and the effect of this is to draw their stories into parallel. Patricia Tully Willey sums up: 'In each, the story line moves from abuse, shame, despair, and recrimination to promise, vindication, fulfilment, and exaltation.'[22] Whilst the Servant is not Zion, he participates in her humiliation apparently in order to deliver her from it.

But the portrait of the Servant character in Isaiah 40 – 55 has been deeply influenced by the man in Lamentations 3.[23] To list the most obvious connections let us start with the links between Lamentations 3 and Isaiah 50: the man advises the devout as follows: 'let him give his cheek to the one who strikes, and let him be filled with insults' (Lam. 3:30). The Servant replies, 'I gave my back to those who strike, and my cheeks to those who pull out my beard' (Isa. 50:6).[24] The man goes 'into darkness without any light' (Lam. 3:2) as does the Servant (Isa. 50:10). Both struggle with the issue of faith in the midst of opposition. Willey lists numerous other verbal and thematic links between the man in Lamentations 3 and the Servant in Isaiah 50. In Isaiah 53 the Servant suffers in silence (v. 7, cf. Lam. 3:28), is rejected by others (v. 3, cf. Lam. 3:46, 53, 60–63), is stricken (v. 4, cf. Lam. 3:30), 'afflicted' and 'crushed'[25] (vv. 4–5, cf. Lam. 3:33–34), suffers the perversion of justice (v. 8, cf. Lam. 3:35), is 'cut off' (v. 8, cf. Lam. 3:54) and 'buried' (v. 9, cf. Lam. 3:53, 55).

---

[21] In Isa. 49:3 the Servant is clearly *identified with* Israel but in Isa. 49:5–6 he is clearly *distinguished from* Israel. There are numerous explanations for this but the most plausible is that an individual assumes the role of the nation. He now does for Israel what Israel was to do for the nations: he is a 'covenant for the people' (cf. Isa. 42:6) and releases the prisoners (Isa. 49:9; cf. 42:7).

[22] Willey, *Remember the Former Things*, 222. Numerous Zion-Servant parallels are listed on the same page. See also Sawyer, 'Daughter Zion'; Wilshire, 'Servant City'.

[23] Willey, *Remember the Former Things*, ch. 5.

[24] Willey, *Remember the Former Things*, observes that Isaiah has expanded the one phrase of Lamentations into two parallel ones (216).

[25] A rare combination of words. For other rare combinations shared by Isaiah 40–55 and Lamentations see Willey, *Remember the Former Things*.

It is of considerable interest then to note then that the man in Lamentations 3, like the Servant in Isaiah, parallels Lady Zion in numerous ways. Commentators on Lamentations who have an interest in the final form often note how he seems to be a male equivalent to Zion – a representative sufferer who experiences the same kinds of suffering that she does.[26] Also of interest is that the speakers in both Lamentations and Isaiah 53 look back in time to the destruction of Zion/the *geber*/the Servant and look to the future for the hoped for restoration. This locates all the voices in the exilic present. Now the book of Isaiah develops the *geber* (valiant man) of Lamentations 3 in certain directions but in retrospect one may possibly see clues in Lamentations 3 for those developments. For instance, one can plausibly read the story of the man in Lamentations 3 as follows: here is a man who embodies the suffering of Jerusalem in his own suffering (Lam. 3:1–18). However, the man recalls Yahweh's covenant faithfulness in the midst of his pain and hope is rekindled (Lam. 3:21–26). He calls on the LORD from his pit of 'death' and Yahweh delivers him from immediate danger (Lam. 3:52–58).[27] But the enemies who cast him into the pit are still seeking him so he asks the LORD for salvation from their ongoing persecution (3:59–66) and calls Israel to do likewise (Lam. 3:40–51). The man's suffering parallels Jerusalem's suffering, the beginnings of his salvation provide hope for Israel, and his expectation of complete deliverance parallels Israel's hope for future deliverance in ways Isaiah would develop further.

The New Testament sees the glorious promises of Isaiah 40 – 55 as being fulfilled in the person of Jesus, the Servant of Yahweh, whose death and resurrection fulfils Isaiah 53. The new exodus salvation of return from exile is now experienced in the resurrection and in the church in proleptic ways although its fullness is still future.

So where does all this take us hermeneutically? First, I suggest that it confirms a longstanding Christian instinct that the man in Lamentations 3 is significant for the interpretation of the book as a whole. The man has been seen as a partial type of Christ and the links we have observed from the *geber* to the Servant to Christ provide a non-arbitrary chain that justifies such a reading strategy. Later we shall query the overemphasis on the man to the neglect of Lady Jerusalem in the interpretation of Lamentations. However, the longstanding

---

[26] See House, *Lamentations*, and Renkema, *Lamentations*.

[27] There is a complicated exegetical debate regarding whether the man does look back to a past deliverance. The issue hinges on whether we translate the perfective verbs in 3:52–66 as (a) simple past tenses (e.g. Westermann), (b) prophetic perfects, (c) present tense (e.g. Renkema), (d) precative perfects (e.g. Provan, Hillers, Berlin, Dobbs-Allsop). I would argue that (a) is the most likely interpretation and, in spite of its current popularity, (d) is the least likely. That said, a Christian theological reading could work with any of these even though the end results would be slightly different.

tradition of seeing chapter 3 as central to the book has theological (as well as literary) merit.

Second, a Christian or a Jew should not read Lamentations as if Isaiah 40 – 55 had not been written. When reflecting theologically on particular texts in Lamentations they will be interested in how Isaiah 40 – 55 engages those same texts. I shall argue later that there is a non-negotiable 'moment' in the reading of the text when one does need to hear its voice without the prophetic response but such a hearing cannot be the end of the hermeneutical engagement with the text. The coming of Yahweh to comfort does have implications for how we hear the pain of Lady Jerusalem for we now know what she did not.

Third, New Testament development of the themes in Second Isaiah also opens up fruitful avenues for fresh hearing of the text. In Christ and the Spirit, Yahweh comes to comfort Jerusalem. But now we see God not simply as the one who punishes Jerusalem but also as the one who suffers the pains of Jerusalem alongside Jerusalem. I will develop this insight in the next section. Lamentations starts to sound very different once such connections start to appear.

Finally, it is important to make clear that Second Isaiah uses the text of Lamentations selectively for his own contextual purposes and we must not feel unduly limited in our use of the text by this. So it has to be emphasised that whilst Isaiah should guide and shape Christian reading of Lamentations, it should not be seen to close down other insights.

A biblical-theological framework for reading Lamentations

If we are to read Lamentations in canonical context we need to do so in an informed and controlled way. Seeing how Isaiah 40 – 55 engages with the book suggests a fruitful way of connecting with some broader biblical-theological currents to create an interpretative framework within which Lamentations will open up some of its treasures for Christian theological reflection. It is important to clarify the status of the framework that I am about to sketch out. One of the great dangers of theological systems extracted and abstracted from biblical texts is that the systems themselves become the goal of reading as if once the system has been 'discovered', the Bible can be set aside. That is *not* what I am wanting to do. To my mind the biblical-theological system functions something like a map. Take the magnificent city of Rome. There is something wrong with the person who thinks that reading the map is a *substitute* for going to Rome ('who needs to *visit* Rome when you can read the map?') or that reading the map is the *purpose* of going to Rome. There is no substitute for being in the city of Rome itself and the map functions as an aid to enhance *that* experience. In the same way the biblical-theological 'map' I am working with here is not the goal of reading the Bible but is useful *insofar as* it serves to enhance the engagement with the particulars of texts. Another aspect of maps that is important to highlight is that maps are highly selective in the features that they pick out. Not all the buildings are on the map, not all the roads are on the map – indeed, the vast majority of features of Rome will not be present on the map of Rome. The map may not even be to scale. It may artificially enlarge some features to better enable people to navigate around the selected areas. However, the map must still correspond to certain aspects of the reality of Rome or it would not enhance the visit but seriously mislead its users. In a similar way the framework I am proposing does not include all the roads around Scripture, does not show all the twists and turns on the roads it does include, and may artificially enhance some features to enable them to be better seen. That said, it does matter that the key elements of the 'map' are grounded in the teachings of the Bible or the map will serve not so much to open up texts like Lamentations but to misguide us. Consequently, this framework is not proposed as the only way of mapping the canon (indeed I can think of several others off the top of my head which pick out different routes), but it is offered as a textually grounded and useful one that resonates well with Second Isaiah's use of Lamentations and can stand alongside others with an equal claim to being an enlightening guide to the Bible.

My framework requires us to appreciate the connections between humanity, Israel, Christ and the church. I believe that the connections that I draw out here were made by many of the New Testament writers and were grounded in Old Testament texts. I do not claim that all biblical writers made them nor that any biblical writer sets them out in the way I will do.

In a nutshell, following scholars such as N.T. Wright, I think that the story of humanity is recapitulated in the story of Israel and that the story of Israel is re-enacted in the story of Christ.[28] Let's begin with the basic connections between the story of Israel and the story of humanity. It looks very much like the story of humanity as told in Genesis has been narrated in ways which consciously reflect the story of Israel. Adam's story has been told in the light of Israel's story with the effect that Israel's story is presented as a retelling of Adam's. Adam is created outside the Garden and is placed in it by Yahweh to look after it (Gen. 2:8). He is arguably presented as being in covenant relationship with Yahweh, living in the covenant blessings yet under a divine command and warning (Gen. 2:16–17).[29] The violation of that command leads to curse and expulsion from the Garden (Gen. 3:22–24). That expulsion is taken a step further in the story of Cain (Gen. 4:11–14).[30] In Genesis 1 – 11 the human situation spirals violently

---

[28] See Wright, *Climax*, ch. 2 ('Adam, Israel and the Messiah'). The theme is central to much of Wright's work.

[29] That humanity in Eden was in a covenant relationship with Yahweh is admittedly controversial. The word 'covenant' is not used in Genesis 1 – 3. However, in support of the claim see Dumbrell, *Covenant and Creation*, Ch. 1.

[30] See Gordon, *Holy Land*, ch. 2 ('The Land Theology of Genesis 4').

downward until the flood and beyond. The canonical shaping of the book of Genesis presents the story of the calling of Abram in this context. His calling is Yahweh's strategy for dealing with the human predicament.[31] Abram is presented in Genesis as a new Adam and by implication his descendants are a new humanity.[32] The Adam-Israel associations are found in various Old Testament traditions. The story of Israel is seen to parallel the story of Adam: Like Adam, Israel was created outside of the Promised Land and then placed within the land by Yahweh. The land of Canaan is presented in some Old Testament books in distinctly Edenic terms (Num. 13:20–27; Deut. 8:7–9; 11:9, 11–15; 26:15; Joel 2:3; Isa. 11:6; 51:3; Ezek. 36:35, etc.) and the links between Eden and the Jerusalem temple are also strong.[33] Israel, like Adam, lives in covenant relation with Yahweh enjoying the divine blessings of the covenant (Gen. 1:28; cf. 12:2; 17:2, 6, 8; 22:16ff.; 26:3ff.; 28:3; etc.),[34] and the call to reproductive fruitfulness[35] yet are also subject to divine commands (Gen. 2:17; cf. Ex. 20ff.). And, just as Adam violated the covenant command and was expelled from Eden (Gen. 3:23–24) so too Israel violated the commands and was sent out of the land in exile. It seems to me that, in some Old Testament traditions at least, there are some clear Israel–Adam, Eden–Canaan and Expulsion–Exile links. The story of humanity in Adam is recapitulated in the new humanity of Israel.

Various streams of eschatological hope arose within Israel in the midst of her oppression. The prophets said that after a time of exile God would restore Israel to the land. He would pour out his Spirit upon all flesh (Joel 2:28–29) and would enable Israel's obedience to the commandments (Deut. 30:6; Jer. 31:31–34; Ezek. 36:25–27). The restoration of Israel would be accompanied by the destruction of their oppressors (e.g. Isa. 34) but subsequently by the salvation of those very same nations (e.g. Isa. 19:18–25; 45:20–25). The nations would stream to Zion to join Israel in the worship of Yahweh and creation would be renewed (Isa. 2:1–4; 11:10–12; 60:1–16; Ps. 138:4–5 etc). So it will be that Israel will fulfil its God-given mandate to be the vehicle through which God would restore the whole of humanity. The return from exile will trigger events that lead to the restoration of the nations. Now these eschatological hopes are configured differently in different Old Testament traditions and in

---

[31] In defence of the claim that Abram's call is directly related to God's plan to deliver humanity from its Gen. 3 – 11 predicament see Clines, *The Theme of the Pentateuch*.

[32] See Wright, *Climax*, ch. 2; and especially Beale, *Temple*, chs. 2–3.

[33] See Wenham, 'Sanctuary Symbolism'; Beale, *Temple*.

[34] The theme of 'blessing' in Genesis 1 – 11 is closely linked to the theme of blessing in Genesis 12 – 50. See Wenham, *Story as Torah*, ch. 3; and it is a major link between Israel and Adam.

[35] Along with the blessing theme the reproductive fruitfulness theme is another strong link between Adam and Eve's original commission and Israel's covenant blessings. See Wenham, *Story as Torah*.

different streams of Second Temple Judaism but the basic plot-line above provides at least a broad summary and synthesis of some of the main elements that one finds.

The actual return from exile under Persian oversight fell short of the glorious visions of prophets such as Deutero-Isaiah and this led to expectations for further and fuller fulfilment. Israel was still under Gentile rule (Persian, Greek, Ptolemaic, Seleucid, and Roman) and some Jews found it hard to believe that the exile had really come to its proper end.[36] The promise of return, of the outpouring of the Spirit and restoration of Israel, of the pilgrimage of the nations – this must await a fuller, future fulfilment. It is in this context that early Christian theology makes sense.

Christ, as the Messiah of Israel, functioned as the representative of the nation. In one sense Jesus *is* Israel. N.T. Wright has argued controversially that the cross of Christ was conceived of as the climax of the curse of the law – namely exile (Gal. 3:13).[37] I think that the logic of at least some important early Christian theology would confirm this. First, I suggest that seeing Christ's cross, as the early Christians did, in terms of the suffering Servant in Isaiah 53[38] would probably have involved seeing it in terms of participating in Israel's exilic sufferings (see our earlier discussion on the Servant's suffering). Second, the exile and return were spoken of in Ezekiel as the death and resurrection of the nation (Ezek. 37) and, according to the prophetic expectations sketched above, the return of Israel would be followed by the outpouring of the Spirit and the pilgrimage of the nations. Those motifs find their counterpart in the day of Pentecost (Acts 2) and the conversion of the Gentiles to faith in Christ (Acts 10ff.). Both of those signs would indicate that the exile of Israel had come to an end, at least that it had done so proleptically in Christ's resurrection. That would lend weight to Wright's claim that the cross of Christ is the exile of Israel at the hands of the pagan nations writ small.[39]

The connections between Christ and Israel would also illuminate the connections between Christ and the whole of humanity also found in the thought of the earliest Christians. Christ is Israel *and is thus* a new humanity and a second

---

[36] That many Jews at the time of Jesus thought of themselves as still in exile in the land is controversial (it is denied by J.D.G. Dunn, M. Casey and A. Segal) though has been defended by Wright, *People of God*; and Evans, 'Jesus and the Continuing Exile of Israel'.

[37] See Wright, *Climax*, ch. 7 ('Curse and Covenant: Galatians 3:10–14').

[38] See, for instance, Acts 8:26–35; 1 Pet. 3:22–25.

[39] It is sometimes objected that the New Testament conceives of salvation in terms of exodus language and not overtly in the language of return from exile. However, we need to appreciate that the exodus language in the New Testament documents is usually exodus language *as filtered through the text of Isaiah 40 – 55* where it is used of the return from exile. Consequently, the new exodus salvation images in the New Testament often *are* return from exile images.

Adam (Rom. 5:12–21; 1 Cor. 15:45–49). Christ's death is Israel's exile writ small *and hence is also* the sufferings of humanity living east of Eden. Christ's resurrection is the return from exile *and so also* corresponds to the resurrection of all humanity and indeed the whole of creation (Rom. 8). A further step would be to appreciate the relationship between the sufferings of Christ and the sufferings of the church. That the Church participates in the apocalyptic sufferings of her Lord is a recurring theme in the New Testament (Mk. 8:34–38; Rom. 8:17; Phil. 3:10; 2 Cor. 1:5; 4:10–12; 1 Pet. 2:21–25).

My contention is that these biblical-theological connections create a framework for some very fruitful, imaginative, Christian *re*-appropriation of Lamentations. Lamentations concerns the devastation of the exilic experience from the perspective of those who have been 'left behind'. It is the Holy Saturday of Israel's life caught between exilic death at the hands of Babylon and the desperate, though fragile, hope for resurrection. The future exile of Israel was seen by Leviticus as an enforced Sabbath rest for the land because Israel had neglected to observe the Sabbaths (Lev. 26:34–35). So it is that Christ's death on Good Friday is followed by the 'exilic', Sabbath rest of Holy Saturday. The framework outlined above allows a Christian reader to connect the suffering of Lamentations with the sufferings of humanity more generally and, in accord with the rule of faith, with the sufferings of Christ in particular and with those of the church. Locating the tears of Lamentations in these inter-canonical flows allows us to read the tears of the world through the tears of Lamentations and vice versa. It also invites us to read Lamentations in the light of the cross and the cross in the light of Lamentations. The connections between Christ's suffering and that of the church would also help us to connect Lamentations to the plight of suffering Christians across the globe. The potential for fresh insight emerging from such imaginative theological engagements with the text is immense and very open-ended. Such engagements would be guided by a biblical theology which emerges from various texts in Scripture but the possibilities for fresh interpretations, even within this Christian framework, are immense.

This approach to Lamentations allows us to connect its words to suffering in all sorts of contexts. The sufferings of the Jews not simply at the time of the Babylonian exile but later at the hands of Rome and on through a history of sorrow and suffering. Lamentations can speak to the Jew but, perhaps ironically, also to the Palestinian suffering at the hands of the policies of the state of Israel. It can address the sufferings of persecuted churches like those in Sudan as well as the survivors of the Hiroshima bomb or any number of other sufferings. It also allows us to connect all of these sufferings to those of Christ and consequently to invest all such situations with the hope that springs from his resurrection.

This approach helps address a concern raised by the Jewish scholar Tod Linafelt in his excellent study *Surviving Lamentations*. Linafelt protests against the privileging of the suffering man in Lamentations 3 to the relative neglect of Lady Jerusalem in chapters 1 and 2. He argues with some justification that this bias in part reflects the influence of Christian theology. The suffering man in Chapter 3 seems a candidate for being a type of Christ whilst Lady Jerusalem does not. However, my suggested approach to Christian theological engagement with Lamentations does not require the marginalisation of Lady Jerusalem even if it does affirm the centrality of Lamentations 3. It invites the Christian reader to connect Christ's suffering not simply with the man in Chapter 3, *but also* with the sufferings of Lady Jerusalem – the desolate, God-forsaken, naked and publicly shamed rape victim whose husband is gone and whose children have been taken away by her attacker. Indeed such avenues of exploration may be more creative for Christian theological reflection because they have been neglected in the past. The inter-canonical case for connecting the sufferings of Jesus with those of Jerusalem can be strengthened from the Gospels where Jesus himself saw his death as embodying in microcosm the coming death of the city at the hand of Rome.[40] So this linking of Jesus' sufferings with Jerusalem's is not an arbitrary move on my part but motivated by currents within parts of the Bible. The canon itself is what invites us to join the dots and make the connections.

Lamentations then is to the exile and restoration of Israel what Holy Saturday is to the cross and resurrection of Christ. 'Under the immediate impact of the catastrophe of 587 BC the collapse of Jerusalem was described [in Lamentations] in such a way that motifs from the [funeral] dirge enriched the communal lament. This was because the collapse of the city was experienced as its death.'[41] Lamentations is the Old Testament equivalent of Paul's claim 'that [Christ] was buried' (1 Cor. 15:4) and the statement in the Apostles Creed that Christ 'descended into hell'. This connection between Christ and Lady Jerusalem displays the kind of organic link with the original horizon of the text that I think a theological reading requires.

The rule of faith

So a crucial move towards a Christian theological interpretation is to use some of the canonical interconnections which will open up the text to re-readings. But theological interpretation is more than simply a biblical theological interpretation. The canon *is* privileged in theological interpretation and serves as a plumb line against which Christian readings are measured. However, the story of Christian theological reflection did not end with the formation of the canon. In the early church various groups arose who were reading the same sacred

---

[40] Wright, *Victory of God*, ch. 12.
[41] Westermann, *Lamentations*, 11.

books but were reading them in radically diverse ways. The matter became a serious concern in the second century when Gnostic groups were interpreting the Scriptures in very different ways from the proto-orthodox. In this context the proto-orthodox appealed to 'the rule of faith' as a guide to legitimate biblical interpretation. The 'rule of faith' was a summary of the key Christian beliefs passed on in the churches set up by the apostles. It is not enough, they said, simply to have all the correct sacred texts but also to understand them in the right way.

The 'rule of faith' is expressed in many different ways in early Christian literature but its basic content is straightforward and organised Trinitarianly around the one God and Father; the one Lord, the crucified and risen Jesus Christ; and the one Holy Spirit. As with the later creeds the story of Jesus is the focus of the rule of faith and, as theological reading was guided by the rule, Christian readers were led to maintain a tradition of reading, rooted in the New Testament, which saw all of the Scriptures as related to Christ in some way. What came to be called the Old Testament, no less than what became the New, speaks of Christ.

So a robust *Christian theological* hermeneutic operates with a full-blown Trinitarian vision of God. Such an engagement with the text requires readers at least to ask how the Father, the Son and the Spirit are revealed through that text. Lamentations speaks only of Yahweh and mainstream Old Testament scholars, given the goal that they usually set themselves of understanding the text within its original horizons, would not seek to read Trinitarianly. However, Christian theological interpretation must do so. I have indicated how one may begin to connect *Christ* to the interpretation of Lamentations, but how is the *Spirit* connected with the sufferings in Lamentations? Nothing in the book of Lamentations will answer that question and no other biblical text directly addresses it either. However, there is a Pauline text that allows us to begin to see how we can imagine an answer to it. In Romans 8 Paul connects the sufferings and groans of the church awaiting its full salvation with the sufferings and groans of creation awaiting its full redemption. The logic of the rest of the chapter would also suggest that Paul connected the church's suffering with Christ's (8:17). What is of special interest for us is the way Paul weaves the Spirit into this web. The Spirit, he says, is also groaning with the church and with creation, interceding from the depth of his being for their fullness of salvation. If we take this Pauline insight and connect it with our humanity–Israel–Christ–church links above we create the space to see the Spirit in the sufferings of Lamentations. Paul gives us a way to see the Spirit as groaning with the sufferers in Lamentations, interceding and looking for the redemption of Jerusalem.

I have argued that some of the theological connections made in canonical texts between the sufferings of Israel and those of humanity in general, of

Christ in particular, and even of the Spirit, have the potential to put Lamentations in quite a new light. But not only do these 'insights' put Lamentations in a new light, Lamentations can shed light upon the sufferings of humanity, of Christ, of the church and of the Spirit. Lamentations may allow us to see the crucifixion stories from a new angle; we may also be equipped to understand the sufferings of Christians and of human beings in general in new ways.

History of reception and modern contexts

More than reading by the light of the 'rule of faith' Christian theological interpretation will need to engage with the reception history of the texts in question, with the story of the church, both past and present, with the experience of God and of his world, and with the broader currents of theology. All of this means that there will never be such a thing as *the* Christian interpretation of Lamentations. This is because the meanings to which it gives birth are not so much 'in the text' as born out of the interaction of the text and the Spirit-led activity of its readers. Christian readers will be mixing the genes of Lamentations with the genes of other biblical texts, Christian theological reflections through the ages, the experiences of various readers and so on. The book is simply so pregnant with potential meaning that the meanings to which it gives birth will be diverse even within the constraints imposed by reading in canonical context, the rule of faith and the history of Christian interpretation.[42]

Does this theological hermeneutic rob the text of its power?

A possible criticism of the kind of Christian interpretation I am advocating is that it robs Lamentations of its power. Lamentations is hard-hitting because it arises from the experience of suffering, and yet within its pages deliverance seems as far off at the end as it does at the beginning. There are multiple voices in the book but the one that is conspicuous by its absence is that of Yahweh. Once Lamentations is read through Christian theological lenses, we insert Yahweh's voice back into the text. We see that God actually stands in solidarity with Jerusalem in its sufferings through Christ and by his Spirit. We see that Yahweh himself eventually provides the comfort so longed for by Jerusalem. But, the critic may argue, this domesticates the book and emasculates its ability to address the bleakest of human situations.

Several things need to be said here. First, crucial to an adequate response is the need for Christian readers to appreciate *both* the canonical form of the text

---

[42] Sadly space does not permit us to see how Christian theological interpretation will also seek to engage with a whole host of other resources. For instance, the history of Jewish interpretation of the book, historical-critical readings, contemporary 'unexpected' readings such as feminist, Marxist, psychological and so on.

and the canonical context. It is the canonical context which allows us to read the book in the light of the cross and resurrection of Christ but it is the canonical form which *preserves the voices of the sufferers as uttered on their Holy Saturday.* The canonisation of the book in this form requires that we find a way to respect the integrity of that pain without allowing it to be lost in the canonical context. On the other hand, it needs to be acknowledged that respecting only the canonical form but not the canonical context fails to read the text as Scripture. It needs to be recognised then that Christians cannot read Lamentations with the same hopelessness felt by Lady Jerusalem because they know that Christ has been raised. The resurrection generates a hermeneutic of hope that can transform the darkness of Lamentations and infuse it with a light not found in the book itself. But, and this is important, it does *not* make the pain of Lamentations less dreadful and dark. It does not explain why the pain was as it was. It is not a theodicy that seeks to justify God. It does not trivialise the suffering any more than the resurrection trivialises the cross. So, while a canonical interpretation of Lamentations will not allow destruction and death to have the last word, it can allow them a penultimate word. The book of Lamentations speaks during its Holy Saturday experience and is then silent *and the Bible preserves it in that form.* We have to wait for Isaiah 40 – 55 to hear the build up to the Easter Sunday deliverance. The canon allows a pause between these two and does not seek to prematurely collapse them. Similarly, the disciples experienced the desolation and despair of Saturday before experiencing the joy of Sunday. A Christian theological reading of the book can bracket out for a moment the resurrection hope and allow the shock of the pain to have its full force. Often even Christians feel the depths of the darkness in their pain as resurrection hope fades. However, this bracketing out of resurrection hope can only be temporary to allow the pain time to breathe. The Christian simply cannot forget the resurrection and, once it is factored in, hope will enter the equation again. The world cannot be the same after Easter and sufferings cannot be seen as our final destiny.

I would like to seek guidance for handling this dilemma in Alan E. Lewis' book *Between Cross and Resurrection: A Theology of Holy Saturday.* Lewis was concerned that Christians move too quickly from Good Friday to Easter Sunday and pass over the 'brief, inert void' of Easter Saturday. Lewis proposed that we need to stand imaginatively again on Holy Saturday and consider the view both ways, looking back to the Friday and forward to the Sunday. We start, he suggested, by trying to hear the crucifixion story again as first time hearers would – not knowing that the resurrection is coming. 'Far from being the first day, the day of the cross is, in the logic of the narrative itself, actually the last day, the end of the story of Jesus. And the day that follows it is … an empty void, a nothing, shapeless, meaningless, and anticlimactic: simply the day after the end.'[43] On Holy Saturday 'Death is given time and space to be itself, in all its coldness and helplessness.'[44] The resurrection must be heard first of all as an unexpected and shocking event. Clearly, then, the Christian reader must look again at the cross event in the light of the resurrection and see it in new light but this new understanding does not mean that we can leave behind the first hearing. 'This is a story which must be told and heard, believed and interpreted, *two different ways at once* – as a story whose ending is *known*, and as one whose ending is discovered only as it *happens* … the separate sound in each ear creating, as it were, a stereophonic unity.'[45] Holy Saturday serves to keep the crucifixion and resurrection apart and to hold them together.

For Lewis, God himself is convicted by Jesus' death because of the identity of the crucified one. Jesus was one who had known an intimacy of relation with his 'Father in heaven' unknown by any other human. For *him* to die a God-forsaken death is to imply that *God* has failed him. It is important to ponder the implications of this for reading Lamentations. Lewis' respect for the integrity of Jesus' cry of dereliction and God's non-response is instructive for us as we seek to do justice to Lady Jerusalem analogous cries of dereliction and Yahweh's failure to reply to her.

The resurrection is the vindication not only of Christ (he really is the Son of God) but also of God (he really is the loving Father of Christ) and it offers hope not merely for Christ but for Israel, for humanity, for the cosmos. But the resurrection must not be seen to put the cross out of sight – resurrection is only reached through the cross and 'the only flower of victory is one which germinates and grows in the darkness of the tomb'.[46]

---

[43] Lewis, *Between Cross and Resurrection*, 31.
[44] Lewis, *Between Cross and Resurrection*, 37.
[45] Lewis, *Between Cross and Resurrection*, 33.
[46] Lewis, *Between Cross and Resurrection*, 77.

Bibliography

Albrektson, B., *Studies in the Text and Theology of the Book of Lamentations* (Lund: Gleerup, 1963)

Beale, G.K., *The Temple and the Church's Mission: A Biblical Theology of the Dwelling Place of God* (Leicester: Inter-Varsity Press, 2004)

Bergant, D., *Lamentations* (Abingdon Old Testament Commentaries; Nashville: Abingdon, 2003)

Berlin, A., *Lamentations* (OTL; Louisville: Westminster John Knox Press, 2002)

Chae, D.J.S., *Paul as Apostle to the Gentiles* (Carlisle: Paternoster, 1997)

Childs, B.S., *Introduction to the Old Testament as Scripture* (London: SCM, 1979)

Clines, D.J.A., *The Theme of the Pentateuch* (2nd edn.; Sheffield: Sheffield Academic Press, 1997)

Dobbs-Allsop, F.W., *Lamentations* (Interpretation; Louisville: Westminster John Knox Press, 2002)

Dumbrell, W.J., *Covenant and Creation: An Old Testament Covenant Theology* (Exeter: Paternoster, 1984)

Eaton, J.H., *Festal Drama in Deutero Isaiah* (London: SPCK, 1979)

Evans, C.A., 'Jesus and the Continuing Exile of Israel', in *Jesus and the Restoration of Israel: A Critical Assessment of N.T. Wright's Jesus and the Victory of God* (ed. C.C. Newman; Downers Grove: InterVarsity Press, 1999), 77–100

Gerstenberger, E.S., *Psalms Part 2 and Lamentations* (Grand Rapids: Eerdmans, 2001)

Gordon, R.P., *Holy Land, Holy City: Sacred Geography and the Interpretation of the Bible* (Carlisle: Paternoster, 2004)

Gottwald, N.K., *Studies in the Book of Lamentations* (London: SCM, 1954)

Gous, I.G.P., 'Exiles and the Dynamics of Experience of Loss: The Reaction of Lamentations 2 on the Loss of Land', *Old Testament Essays* 6 (1993), 351–63

Hillers, D.R., *Lamentations* (rev edn.; AB; New York: Doubleday, 1992)

Houk, C., 'Multiple Poets in Lamentations', *JSOT* 30 (2005), 111–25

House, P.R., *Lamentations* (WBC; Nashville: Thomas Nelson, 2004)

Hugenberger, G.P., The Servant of the LORD in the Servant Songs of Isaiah', in *The Lord's Anointed: Interpretation of Old Testament Messianic Texts* (ed. P.E. Satterthwaite et al.; Grand Rapids: Baker; and Carlisle: Paternoster, 1995), 105–40

Joyce, P., 'Lamentations and the Grief Process: A Psychological Reading', *BibInt* 1 (1993), 304–20

Lee, N., *The Singers of Lamentations: Cities Under Siege from Ur to Jerusalem to Sarajevo* (Leiden: Brill, 2002)

Lewis, A.E., *Between Cross and Resurrection: A Theology of Holy Saturday* (Grand Rapids: Eerdmans, 2001)

Linafelt, T., *Surviving Lamentations: Catastrophe, Lament, and Protest in the Afterlife of a Biblical Book* (Chicago: Chicago University Press, 2000)

Motyer, A., *The Prophecy of Isaiah* (Leicester: Inter-Varsity Press, 1993)

O'Connor, K.M., *Lamentations* (NIB; Nashville, Abingdon, 2001)

—, *Lamentations and the Tears of the World* (New York: Orbis, 2002)

Piper, H., 'Reading Lamentations', *JSOT* 95 (2001), 55–69

Porteous, N., 'Jerusalem-Zion: The Growth of a Symbol', in *Verbannung und Heimker* (ed. A. Kuschke; Tübingen: J.C.B. Mohr, 1961)

Powel, M.A., *Chasing the Eastern Star: Adventures in Biblical Reader-Response Criticism* (Louisville: Westminster John Knox Press, 2001)

Provan, I., 'Past, Present and Future in Lamentations III 52–66: The Case for the Precative Perfect Re-examined', *VT* 41 (1991), 164–75

—, *Lamentations* (The New Century Bible Commentary; Grand Rapids: Eerdmans, 1991)

Reimar, D., 'Good Grief: A Psychological Reading of Lamentations', *ZAW* 114 (2002), 542–59

Renkema, J., *Lamentations* (Historical Commentary on the Old Testament; Leuven: Peeters, 1998)

Sawyer, J., 'Daughter Zion and the Servant of the LORD in Isaiah: a Comparison', *JSOT* 44 (1989), 89–107

Sommer, B.D., *A Prophet Reads Scripture: Allusions in Isaiah 40–66* (Stanford: Stanford University Press, 1998)

Stiver, D., *Theology After Ricoeur: New Directions in Hermeneutical Theology* (Louisville: Westminster John Knox Press, 2001)

Turner, M.D., 'Daughter Zion: Lament and Restoration' (Ph.D., Emory University, 1992)

Watts, J.D.W., *Isaiah 34–66* (WBC; Waco: Word, 1987)

Wenham, G.J., 'Sanctuary Symbolism in the Garden of Eden Story', *Proceedings of the World Congress of Jewish Studies* 9 (1986), 19–25

—, *Story as Torah: Reading the Old Testament Ethically* (Edinburgh: T&T Clark, 2000)

Westermann, C., *Lamentations: Issues and Interpretation* (Minneapolis: Augsburg Fortress, 1994)

Whybray, R.N., *Isaiah 40–66* (Grand Rapids: Eerdmans, 1975)

Willey, P.T., *Remember the Former Things: The Recollection of Previous Texts in Second Isaiah* (SBLDS 161; Atlanta: Scholars Press, 1997)

Williamson, H.G.M., *Variations on a Theme: King, Messiah and Servant in the Book of Isaiah* (Carlisle: Paternoster, 1998)

Wilshire, L.G., 'Servant City: A New Interpretation of the Servant of the LORD in the Servant Songs of Deutero Isaiah', *JBL* 94 (1975), 356–67

Wright, N.T., *The Climax of the Covenant: Christ and the Law in Pauline Theology* (Edinburgh: T&T Clark, 1991)

—, *The New Testament and the People of God* (Christian Origins and the Question of God, Vol. 1; London: SPCK, 1992)

—, *Jesus and the Victory of God* (Christian Origins and the Question of God, Vol. 2; London: SPCK, 1996)

University of Gloucestershire

We are delighted to see the publication of this latest volume in the Scripture and Hermeneutics Series, following the eighth Consultation in the Project, which took place in June 2005 at the Pontifical Biblical Institute in Rome. Among participants from the University of Gloucestershire in Rome were Dr. Fred Hughes and Prof. Gordon Wenham. As both have since moved to other things, it is appropriate here to express our thanks and good wishes to them. Fred Hughes' tireless representation of the university in the Project over a number of years has been exceptional and should be particularly acknowledged. And we have benefited from Gordon Wenham's meticulous scholarship, not only in several of the Consultations (and the present volume), but in general because of his enormous contribution to Old Testament studies.

The meeting in Rome was an auspicious moment in the history of the Project. Not only does it reflect its ambition to be uncompromising in its scholarly rigour, but it betokens its ecumenical reach, which has grown over the years. The strength of the Catholic representation at the Consultation, and in this volume, is most welcome. We are grateful to Prof. Nuria Calduch-Benages for facilitating our meeting in the Pontifical Biblical Institute.

The topic of the Consultation on this occasion was the canon of Scripture. Canonical interpretation has been one of the most productive developments in biblical scholarship in the last quarter of a century, and points up issues which go to the heart of the understanding and use of Scripture. Besides the strictly hermeneutical issues it raises, one of its central characteristics is attention to the use of Scripture by the church, and for this reason the ecumenical nature and location of the Consultation has been especially appropriate and encouraging. We are grateful to have been able to approach the topic along with a range of outstanding scholars from all parts of the academic and theological spectrums in an atmosphere that was unfailingly constructive and irenic. We believe the present volume amply testifies to this.

As a complex topic, the canon took its place properly in the latter stages of the Project, and leads naturally to its finale in Baylor, at which we shall consider the task of interpreting Scripture in the contexts of both church and academy. We look forward to bringing the Project (at least in its present form) to a culmination at Baylor, and are grateful to our colleagues there for their invitation to host it.

Gordon McConville
Professor of Old Testament Theology
University of Gloucestershire, Francis Close Hall
Swindon Road, Cheltenham
Gloucestershire GL50 4AZ, UK

The British and Foreign Bible Society

The 2005 consultation which prefigured this volume in the Scripture and Hermeneutics Series was a landmark event. We enjoyed the hospitality of the Pontifical Biblical Institute in Rome, even if the heat did threaten our stamina. More seriously, the fellowship and the scholarship were mightily enhanced by the almost equal numbers of Catholic and Protestant scholars gathered to present papers and discuss this very important topic of the Canon of Scripture. Every consultation is unique and the presence of Jean Vanier of the l'Arche Community brought a special contribution to this one.

It is always a pity that a volume cannot capture adequately the richness of the discussion, although the papers represented here have benefited from the insights shared so generously in the consultation. For eight years BFBS has been proud to be the main sponsor of this robust process alongside our partners, Redeemer University College, Baylor University and the University of Gloucestershire. It is a first rate example of international cooperation that works. Friendships and associations have been formed that will far outlast the project.

This phase of the project is due to come to an end in 2007 with the final volume following a consultation hosted by Baylor University in 2006, when we shall look at the most contemporary of subjects, 'The Bible and the Academy'. Such a consultation will not only address the question of what the Bible is but also what it does in and for our postmodern world.

The whole series will far outlast the ten years of the project. One scholar has commented that its real impact will be in the studies of those doing theology and the work of preachers in the years to come. We are grateful to Professor Craig Bartholomew whose genius this project was, and to Rosemary Hales without whom it could not have happened.

Ann Holt OBE
Director of Programme
British and Foreign Bible Society
Stonehill Green
Westlea
Swindon
SN5 7DG
UK

Baylor University

Baylor University is honored to be able to join once again with the British and Foreign Bible Society, Redeemer University College and the University of Gloucestershire in supporting the Seminar on Scripture and Hermeneutics as a North American partner. As a university with more than 160 years of continuous commitment to Christian higher education, and the largest Baptist university in the world, we are deeply interested in the kinds of issues to which the Seminar has directed its attention. This present volume, and the rich consultation at the Pontifical Biblical Institute in Rome which it represents, offers in our view an exemplary opportunity to register our support and appreciation for the work of the Seminar.

Where scholarship on the Bible is concerned, canonicity has long been a topic of critical as well as theological and apologetic interest. Unfortunately, in the past this topic has often tended to divide Christian communities. Those issues, we may be thankful, are no longer as divisive as once they were among orthodox proponents of the authority of Scripture across the Christian intellectual world. In several ways canon criticism has recently worked to bring various constituencies in the Christian world together. In this consultation notably, with significant participation by Roman Catholics and scholars from various Protestant traditions, there has been a welcome experience of the strength of Christian scholarship in the service of vital faith. Because the participants share confidence in the Scriptures as a reliable witness to the resurrected Christ, moreover, scholarly considerations of apostolicity, usage, *lectio divina*, recognition by the churches and a Christocentric view of canon were seen by them not as of merely academic interest, but as the lifeblood in the heart of our common calling.

We congratulate the editors and contributors to this volume on the vigor and quality of their exchange of views and findings. Once again this volume makes evident that biblical interpretation is neither a sterile nor a static discipline, but an intellectual work prefaced by prayer, imbued itself with the spirit of *lectio divina,* and ultimately undertaken in a spirit of service to the worship life of our churches. This wider sense of our accountability, we believe, has been and should always be central to the intellectual life of Christian scholars.

David Lyle Jeffrey
Distinguished Professor of Literature and the Humanities
Baylor University
One Bear Place
Waco, TX 76798-7404

Redeemer University College

Redeemer University College has been honored in the past year to continue giving a 'home' to the Scripture and Hermeneutics Project as the seventh volume in its series on Scripture and Hermeneutics, *Canon and Biblical Interpretation,* has been prepared for publication. We have been glad to work together with our older partners – the British and Foreign Bible Society, the University of Gloucestershire, and Baylor University – who have given support to this important international project.

It has given us a sense of gratitude to see the development of this volume. One of the defining features of this project is its ecumenical character. Especially noteworthy has been the cooperation between Catholic and Protestant scholars. The address for the consultation at which the papers which make up this volume were first given, the Pontifical Biblical Institute, indicates something of the character of this work. The essays which make up this volume reflect careful scholarship of academics not afraid to admit to basic faith commitment. One of the things that ties together the disparate topics and confessional backgrounds of the contributors, Protestant and Catholic, is commitment to what St. Vincent of Lerins called 'that which has been believed everywhere, always, by all.'

Redeemer University College is proud to identify with, and to do its modest share to push forward, this project. Redeemer University College is a confessional university rooted firmly in the catholic creeds of the Christian church and the distinctive features of the Reformed theological tradition. Open and confident about its moorings, Redeemer is committed to engaging the intellectual currents in our culture. This is what this volume, and the entire Scripture and Hermeneutics Series, is committed to doing.

Jacob P. Ellens PhD
Vice-President (Academic)
Redeemer University College
Ancaster
Ontario
Canada

Scripture Index

Names Index

Abbahu, Rabbi   335
Abraham, W.J.   156, 189, 196
Achtemeier, P.J.   170–72
Adler, A.P.   146–48, 162
Aichele, G.   267, 270, 272
Albertz, R.   11, 38, 45
Albrektson, B.   397
Allender, D.   371
Allison, D.C.   222
Alonso Schökel, L.   193–94
Alter, R.   335, 379
Anderson, G.A.   216, 219, 221
Anicet, Pope   119
Apel, K.O.   380
Aquinas, Thomas   102–103
Assel, H.   100
Auwers, J.-M.   335, 341–42, 348
Avis, P.   187

Backus, I.   243
Bacote, V.   171, 181
Bakhtin, M.   25
Balentine, S.   216
Barr, J.   2, 20, 40, 60, 68–71, 75–76,
    84–85, 95, 103, 177, 187, 192, 195,
    221, 268, 301, 322, 324, 364, 366
Barrera, T.   75
Barth, K.   15, 64, 69–70, 85, 100, 199
Barth, M.   192
Barthes, R.   244
Bartholomew, C.G.   6, 10, 165, 184,
    212, 381, 385
Barton, J.   15–16, 36, 65–67, 75, 83–
    86, 88, 90–91, 95, 97, 169–70, 186,
    264–65, 268–70, 295–96, 317

Basil   335
Bauckham, R.   42, 67, 93, 158
Bauer, W.   43
Beale, G.K.   214, 221, 397, 408
Beckwith, J.   295
Beckwith, R.T.   37, 96, 169
Beegle, D.M.   177–78, 189
Begg, C.   218, 220
Beiser, F.C.   380
Benson, B.E.   183
Berlin, A.   398, 401, 405
Best, E.   13
Blauw, J.   194
Blenkinsopp, J.   38, 271, 294, 303,
    305, 308, 315
Block, D.I.   181, 311
Bloesch, D.   181, 191, 199
Blue, S.A.   183
Bockmuehl, M.   93, 381, 388
Booth, W.   245, 248
Boström, L.   354
Bovon, F.   42
Bowker, J.   26, 132
Braulik, G.   349
Brett, M.G.   61, 97
Brogan, J.J.   177, 181
Brown, R.E.   40, 212
Brueggemann, D.A.   179, 297, 323
Brueggemann, W.   15–16, 41, 62, 70,
    72, 77–78, 80, 85–88, 103, 304, 316,
    322, 337, 366
Buber, M.   16
Bultmann, R.   33, 44, 128, 304
Burkett, D.   131

Subject Index